Believers Church
Bible Commentary

Elmer A. Martens and Willard M. Swartley, Editors

BELIEVERS CHURCH BIBLE COMMENTARY

Old Testament
Genesis, by Eugene F. Roop, 1987
Exodus, by Waldemar Janzen, 2000
Judges, by Terry L. Brensinger, 1999
Ruth, Jonah, Esther, by Eugene F. Roop, 2002
Jeremiah, by Elmer A. Martens, 1986
Ezekiel, by Millard C. Lind, 1996
Daniel, by Paul M. Lederach, 1994
Hosea, Amos, by Allen R. Guenther, 1998

New Testament
Matthew, by Richard B. Gardner, 1991
Mark, by Timothy J. Geddert, 2001
Acts, by Chalmer E. Faw, 1993
2 Corinthians, by V. George Shillington, 1998
Ephesians, by Thomas R. Yoder Neufeld, 2002
Colossians, Philemon, by Ernest D. Martin, 1993
1-2 Thessalonians, by Jacob W. Elias, 1995
1-2 Peter, Jude, by Erland Waltner and J. Daryl Charles, 1999
Revelation, by John R. Yeatts, 2003

Old Testament Editors
Elmer A. Martens and Allen R. Guenther (for *Jeremiah*), Mennonite
   Brethren Biblical Seminary, Fresno, California

New Testament Editors
Willard M. Swartley and Howard H. Charles (for *Matthew*),
   Associated Mennonite Biblical Seminary, Elkhart, Indiana

Editorial Council
David Baker, Brethren Church
Lydia Harder, Mennonite Church Canada
Estella B. Horning, Church of the Brethren
Robert B. Ives, Brethren in Christ Church
Gordon H. Matties, Mennonite Brethren Church
Paul M. Zehr (chair), Mennonite Church USA

**Believers Church
Bible Commentary**

Revelation

John R. Yeatts

HERALD PRESS
Scottdale, Pennsylvania
Waterloo, Ontario

Library of Congress Cataloging-in-Publication Data
Yeatts, John R., 1946-
   Revelation / John R. Yeatts.
     p. cm. — (Believers church Bible commentary)
  Includes bibliographical references and index.
   ISBN 0-8361-9208-7 (pbk. : alk. paper)
   1. Bible. N.T. Revelation—Commentaries. I. Title. II. Series.
   BS2825.53 .Y43 2003
   228'.07—dc21   2002015024

Bible text is mostly from *New Revised Standard Version Bible*, copyright 1989 by the Division of Christian Education of the National Council of the Churches of Christ in the USA, and used by permission. Abbreviations listed on page 6 identify other versions briefly compared.

BELIEVERS CHURCH BIBLE COMMENTARY: REVELATION
  Copyright © 2003 by Herald Press, Scottdale, Pa. 15683
  Released simultaneously in Canada by Herald Press,
  Waterloo, Ont. N2L 6H7. All rights reserved
Library of Congress Control Number: 2002015024
International Standard Book Number: 0-8361-9208-7
Printed in the United States of America
Cover and charts by Merrill R. Miller

12 11 10 09 08 07 06 05 04 03 10 9 8 7 6 5 4 3 2 1

To order or request information,
please call 1-800-759-4447 (individuals); 1-800-245-7894 (trade).
Website: www.mph.org

To my family

Amy, Marcus, Emily, Patrick, and Helena

Abbreviations/Symbols

For additional abbreviations and symbols, see the Bibliography (pp. 489-490).

*	The Text in Biblical Context (as starred in Contents)
+	The Text in the Life of the Church (as in Contents)
BCBC	*Believers Church Bible Commentary*
//	equal, parallel to
cf.	compare
ch/s.	chapter/s
e.g.	for example(s)
et al.	and other(s)
LXX	Septuagint
n	note
note/s	Explanatory notes in sequence of chapters/verses
NRSV	New Revised Standard Version
TDNT	*Theological Dictionary of the New Testament*
TBC	The Text in Biblical Context
TLC	The Text in the Life of the Church
v./vv.	verse/verses

Contents

Series Foreword

The Believers Church Bible Commentary Series makes available a new tool for basic Bible study. It is published for all who seek more fully to understand the original message of Scripture and its meaning for today—Sunday school teachers, members of Bible study groups, students, pastors, and others. The series is based on the conviction that God is still speaking to all who will listen, and that the Holy Spirit makes the Word a living and authoritative guide for all who want to know and do God's will.

The desire to help as wide a range of readers as possible has determined the approach of the writers. Since no blocks of biblical text are provided, readers may continue to use the translation with which they are most familiar. The writers of the series use the *New Revised Standard Version*, the *Revised Standard Version*, the *New International Version*, and the *New American Standard Bible* on a comparative basis. They indicate which text they follow most closely, and where they make their own translations. The writers have not worked alone, but in consultation with select counselors, the series' editors, and the Editorial Council.

Every volume illuminates the Scriptures; provides necessary theological, sociological, and ethical meanings; and, in general, makes "the rough places plain." Critical issues are not avoided, but neither are they moved into the foreground as debates among scholars. Each section offers explanatory notes, followed by focused articles, "The Text in Biblical Context" and "The Text in the Life of the Church."

The writers have done the basic work for each commentary, but not operating alone, since "no . . . scripture is a matter of one's own interpretation" (2 Pet. 1:20; cf. 1 Cor. 14:29). They have consulted with select counselors during the writing process, worked with the editors for the series, and received feedback from another biblical scholar. In addition, the Editorial Council, representing six believers church denominations, reads the manuscripts carefully, gives churchly responses, and makes suggestions for changes. The writer considers all this counsel and processes it into the manuscript, which the Editorial Council finally approves for publication. Thus these commentaries combine the individual writers' own good work and the church's voice. As such, they represent a hermeneutical community's efforts in interpreting the biblical text, as led by the Spirit.

The term *believers church* has often been used in the history of the church. Since the sixteenth century, it has frequently been applied to the Anabaptists and later the Mennonites, as well as to the Church of the Brethren and similar groups. As a descriptive term, it includes more than Mennonites and Brethren. *Believers church* now represents specific theological understandings, such as believers baptism, commitment to the Rule of Christ in Matthew 18:15-20 as crucial for church membership, belief in the power of love in all relationships, and willingness to follow Christ in the way of the cross. The writers chosen for the series stand in this tradition.

Believers church people have always been known for their emphasis on obedience to the simple meaning of Scripture. Because of this, they do not have a long history of deep historical-critical biblical scholarship. This series attempts to be faithful to the Scriptures while also taking archaeology and current biblical studies seriously. Doing this means that at many points the writers will not differ greatly from interpretations that can be found in many other good commentaries. Yet these writers share basic convictions about Christ, the church and its mission, God and history, human nature, the Christian life, and other doctrines. These presuppositions do shape a writer's interpretation of Scripture. Thus this series, like all other commentaries, stands within a specific historical church tradition.

Many in this stream of the church have expressed a need for help in Bible study. This is justification enough for the Believers Church Bible Commentary. Nevertheless, the Holy Spirit is not bound to any tradition. May this series be an instrument in breaking down walls between Christians in North America and around the world, bringing new joy in obedience through a fuller understanding of the Word.

—The Editorial Council

Author's Preface

My love for the Book of Revelation goes back many years, at least to when I began teaching the book at Messiah College exactly thirty years ago. Revelation is a wonderful book speaking to the victory of Christ over the powers of Satan and evil in preparation for the inauguration of the kingdom of God. The focus of Revelation is not only upon the judgment of the evil ones and the tribulation of the faithful, but also upon the peaceable kingdom that results when evil has been destroyed through the word of God and the testimony of Jesus Christ. Anabaptists will be particularly attracted to familiar themes of Revelation: martyrdom, suffering, hope, the triumph of Christ, and the role of the church in bearing witness to the triumphant Christ. The focus of this commentary is thoroughly Anabaptist, but it has broader appeal because these themes are also familiar to other church traditions.

The Book of Revelation has evoked strong and contrasting responses. Some people love it, revel in its apparent predictions of the future, and seem to think it is the most important book in the Bible and the key to a vast puzzle that predicts the future with remarkable accuracy. Revelation instead is much more like an art gallery that speaks in images rather than predictions. Its symbols are not confined to one interpretation but contain many levels of meaning. Like a painting, a chapter in Revelation opens the reader, not to one answer, but to many possibilities. The Book of Revelation is ultimately and universally relevant as it prepares all Christians for the battle they must wage every day with the powers of evil, as they suffer with Christ to establish the peaceable kingdom. In that sense, there is no more relevant book in the Bible. However, it is not immediately relevant in the sense of predicting an immediate future leading to the imminent end of the world.

The writing of this commentary has in many ways been a community effort. Many people have contributed to its making, but are not responsible for its shortcomings. Bruce Metzger at Princeton Seminary deserves thanks for drawing my attention to the beauty of Revelation. Editor Willard Swartley gave encouragement, invaluable aid with sources, and keen attention to detail in the manuscript. The editorial council also gave helpful advice. The copy editing work of Elizabeth Yoder certainly makes the final product more consistent and polished. Readers have been very helpful: Lamar Nisly made copious comments regarding how to improve the manuscript stylistically; Wilma Ann Bailey rendered the assistance of a most competent biblical scholar; and David Bestwick-Saterlee gave advice regarding how the manuscript might address a contemporary audience. Work study students, Michael Sullivan, Suzanne Miller, and Andrea Blatt, contributed many hours attending to details in the text. Indeed, three of my Apocalyptic Literature classes read rough manuscripts of the commentary and gave valuable help in revision for clarity.

Messiah College granted a sabbatical for work on the commentary. My wife Anna also spent many hours editing, encouraging, and supporting. Perhaps my finishing the commentary is most due to the patience and encouragement of my family. Therefore, I dedicate this book to them.

—*John R. Yeatts*
 Messiah College
 Grantham, Pennsylvania

Entering the World of Revelation

Getting Our Bearings

Like other biblical books, Revelation was written in a specific historical context. The content reflects the reality that it was written when Jewish Christians were under Rome's imperial power. As will be evident, many of the symbols refer either to Rome or to some characteristic of the Roman Empire. Therefore, to make sense of the teachings of Revelation, the reader must understand what was happening in the contemporary world.

By the time the book of Revelation was written, the *Pax Romana* (peace of Rome) was in place. The Roman government had brought relative tranquility to the empire. That does not mean that there were not uprisings, but these were usually local and quickly squelched by those who ruled on behalf of Rome. In short, the Romans had brought law and order to Asia. Goodspeed writes: "This was *pax Romana*. The provincial, under Roman sway found himself in a position to conduct his business, provide for his family, send his letters, and make his journeys in security, thanks to the strong hand of Rome" (1937:240). As a result of the Pax Romana, the provinces were grateful. They expressed this gratitude by desire to worship and give divine status to the empire. Temples to the goddess Roma and to various Roman emperors sprang up throughout the empire, including the province of Asia. As this sentiment grew, emperor worship became more com-

19

mon *[Essay: The Emperors and Emperor Worship].*

Several characteristics of emperor worship are especially relevant to an understanding of Revelation (see Barclay, 1960:1.19-24 for a more complete discussion of caesar worship). First, it originated with the people, not the emperors themselves. For the most part, it was not imposed by the Roman government but instead grew out of the gratitude of the people for the peace that Rome had brought to the world. Therefore, the pressure on Christians was imposed, not by the heavy hand of the government in Rome, but by the patriotism of the population in Asia. Second, emperor worship was not exclusive. Persons could worship other gods as long as they said, "Caesar is Lord!" There was no attempt to obliterate other religions; instead, they were incorporated into the culture of Rome. The situation was more analogous to civil religion in North America than to the threat to religious belief and evangelism from repressive governments around the world. Third, failure to worship the emperor was viewed, not as apostasy, but as political revolt. Not to worship the emperor—and thus not to recognize all the Roman government had done for the empire—was perceived to be a lack of gratitude. The person who refused to give honor to the emperor was considered unpatriotic.

Christians and Jews both adhered to exclusive religions; they could not say, "Caesar is Lord," because such worship could only be given to God. Therefore, they were considered to be political subversives who undermined the stability of the Roman social order. Thompson, who has argued against widespread persecution of Christians at the time Revelation was written, admits that Christians did not conform to the Roman government's expectations for citizens:

> Christians did not ... take part in civic and provincial celebrations of the emperor. Followers of Christ did not offer sacrifices as imperial processions went by their homes. They did not even offer sacrifices to local, established dieties—Artemis, Zeus, Cybele, Asclepius—that supported public, imperial life. Christian households contained no statues or images of any of the Caesars or of any other god. In short, Christians gave the appearance of not supporting the public order. (Thompson, 1998:28)

At times it was recognized in the empire that, because Jews were monotheists, they could not worship Caesar and therefore were to be given exemption. When the Christians sought similar treatment, Jews became fearful that they would lose their exclusion if others wanted it also. Therefore, Christians were a threat to both Jewish and other Roman subjects. In any case, because Christians could not worship the emperor, they believed persecution to be imminent.

In this context, the political message of Revelation is clear: do not compromise with the world; do not give to the state honor that should be reserved for God (see Barr, 1998:165 for the extent of nonconformity demanded of Christians in John's community). Turner says it well: "Be faithful, even to the point of death. Don't let the world around you squeeze you into its mold of values by forcing a civil religion—any civil religion—upon you" (2000:30). This message seems to be at odds with the teachings of Paul (Rom. 13:1-7) and Peter (1 Pet. 2:13-17). This apparent conflict may be explained by the different contexts in which the books were written. Assuming Revelation was written at the end of the first century [Essay: Dating of Revelation], the deification of the state would probably have progressed further by that time than it had when Peter and Paul wrote in the middle of the century. Nero's earlier persecution of Christians, including Peter and Paul, was probably to find a scapegoat for the fire of Rome or to deal with potential religious instability rather than to judge their lack of political commitment to the empire [Essay: Persecution during Nero's Reign]. In any case, Revelation teaches that worship belongs to God alone, not to the emperor and the empire. Pilgrim asserts that Revelation proclaims "one mighty NO to imperial Caesar." The assumption here is that evil is in the political and systemic abuse of power and wealth (1999:161, 179). For Christians at the end of the first century, following this affirmation to resist the Roman state brought the threat of persecution and perhaps even death [Essay: Persecution in Revelation].

The Immediate Context of Revelation

It seems likely that Revelation was written when the conflict between the empire and the church had reached a crisis. The reigns of two emperors are the most likely possibilities for this crisis point—Nero in the early sixties, and Domitian in the mid-nineties [Essay: The Authorship of Revelation]. Although the exact date of Revelation is not crucial to its message, it seems most likely from both the content of Revelation itself and the witness of various writers that the expected persecution of Domitian is the probable context for the book. Recent scholarship has raised questions about the extent of the persecution under Emperor Domitian [Essay: Persecution During Domitian's Reign]. Yet Yarbro Collins has argued that the expectation of persecution was present and even dominated the thinking of Christians at the end of the first century:

> Revelation does not seem to have been written in response to an obvious, massive social crisis recognized as such by all Christians, not even a

regional one. But the social status of Christians in Asia Minor was threatened in several ways. Christians were·being ostracized and sometimes accused before the authorities by their Jewish neighbors. Local Gentiles despised and were suspicious of them and were also inclined to accuse them before the magistrates.... Roman magistrates ... increasingly looked with disfavor upon Christians and condemned their endurance as stubborn disobedience. It is likely that John the prophet was affected deeply by these elements of crisis and that they had an impact on the shape of his book. (1984:98-99)

The apparent lack of persecution at the end of the first century has led some scholars to suspect that the crisis evident in Revelation is internal, between factions of the churches in Asia, rather than external persecution from Rome. Royalty and Duff both believe that the conflict was tied into social position and economic mobility—between the higher-status nobility, who inherited money, and the lower-status working class, who gained wealth through labor of manufacture and commerce. The wealth of the merchants is associated with Babylon, while that gained by inheritance is associated with the New Jerusalem. John identifies his followers with the nobility and his opponents, the Nicolaitans and Jezebel, who tolerate idolatry and fornication, with the merchants (Royalty, 1988:24, 71, 102, 111, 123-24, 207-10, 222-33, 238-39, 241-46; Duff, 2001:14-15, 18-21, 48-59, 126).

Although the extent of persecution when Revelation was written may have been exaggerated in the past, Sordi is no doubt correct to insist that actual persecution was present: "I still maintain that the mere fact of there being so many individual reports of the persecutions having taken place, makes it unreasonable to harbor any serious doubts on the subject" (1986:45). Wengst documents this persecution from the book of Revelation itself: the mention of the martyrdom of Antipas in Pergamum (2:13); the souls under the altar, slaughtered for the word of God and their testimony (6:9); those beheaded for their testimony (20:4). Moreover, Revelation declares that the beastly Rome wages war on those who obey God's commands and give testimony to Jesus (12:17); is drunk with the blood of saints and martyrs (17:6); and bears responsibility for the blood of the slain prophets and saints (18:24). Although Wengst recognizes that there was no widespread persecuting of Christians when Revelation was written, he affirms that it was "the aim of John that his readers should understand what has already happened as a sign of the times indicating the fundamental opposition between the community and Rome, and between Christ and the emperor, and that they should accept and demonstrate this opposition in a consistent Christian existence" (1986:118-19).

The history of Anabaptists has links to the persecution faced by first-century Christians because Anabaptists have not been strangers to social crisis. Yet how should Christians react when faced with persecution? Boring identifies six possibilities. The first option is to quit or to give up the faith, and Revelation was written to keep persons from accepting this option. The second possibility is to lie, a morally untenable option. A third alternative is to fight, which has been consistently rejected by nonresistant Anabaptists. A fourth option is to change the law, but the separatism of Anabaptists has caused them to reject this alternative. A fifth option is to adjust; nevertheless, the Anabaptists have always hesitated to accommodate to the world. Boring says that Revelation advocates a final alternative, to die; and this is the alternative that Anabaptists have often taken (1989:21-23).

Christians throughout history who have chosen this final option find support and consolation in the affirmation of Revelation: the Christian must be ready to die at the hands of persecutors. Yarbro Collins says that John accepts the Zealot practice of refusing to pay taxes and to buy and sell using the Roman coins, while rejecting the Zealot propensity for violent resistance in favor of a passive acceptance of suffering. John's readers "are not to take up arms in active resistance, not even in the final battle. Rather they are to endure persecution including death and to hope for ultimate salvation" (1977:251-53).

The Setting of Revelation

Although the immediate context of Revelation is the first-century Roman Empire, the visions of Revelation have both earthly and heavenly settings. In chapter 1, John is transported from Patmos to heaven to observe the vision of Christ. Yet he is back on earth in chapters 2-3, addressing the churches in the province of Asia. At the beginning of chapter 4, John is ushered through a door into heaven to receive the visions of God and Christ in chapters 4 and 5. In chapter 6, he is back on earth where the seal judgments are poured out, with the 144,000 sealed and protected in the first half of chapter 7. John is then transported into heaven in the latter part of chapter 7 to see the great victorious multitude, who conquered the persecution of the seals. John stays in heaven for the seventh bowl (8:1-5) but then returns to earth for the trumpet judgments and its interludes (8:6–11:19). The setting is heaven in chapter 12, where a battle between Michael and Satan is fought; then earth in chapter 13 for the vision of the two beasts; and heaven again in chapter 14 for the 144,000 on Mt. Zion. The setting of chapters 15-18 is earth, where the bowls of God's wrath are poured out and Babylon is destroyed.

The rest of the book (chs. 19-22) is set in heaven, where the bliss of the conquerors is elucidated. This alternating pattern between heaven and earth seems to indicate that earth and heaven are related and the salvation that has been won in heaven parallels the victory of the faithful on earth.

The Message of Revelation

The message of Revelation to Christians in the first century as well as today is straightforward: persevere, because the forces of evil will be defeated and the overcomers will be rewarded with a new heaven and new earth where they will dwell with God. This message of eschatological salvation gives readers the courage to overcome political persecution. Johns communicates clearly Revelation's emphasis on overcoming rather than enduring persecution: "[Revelation] is a vision designed to empower the community, to enter the fray with a courageous nonviolent resistance that may well lead to martyrdom. This sort of resistance is as active as any physical warfare" (1998:239). Bauckham insists that the faithful overcome through their witness and martyrdom rather than by violence: "While rejecting the apocalyptic militancy that called for literal holy war against Rome, John's message is not, 'Do not resist!' It is, 'Resist!—but by witness and martyrdom, not by violence'" (1993b:92).

The violent symbolic language of Revelation should be interpreted as calling the wicked to repent and the faithful to resist through suffering and death. Regarding the celebration of the Lamb's victory in Revelation 15:2-3, Caird says: "because that triumph has been won by no other weapons than the cross of Christ and the martyr testimony of his followers, this song is also the song of the Lamb." Commenting on the warrior on the white horse armed with a sharp sword, Caird affirms: "The only weapon the Rider needs, if he is to break the opposition of his enemies, and establish God's reign of justice and peace, is the proclamation of the gospel" (1966:245). Bauckham says that the followers of the Lamb enter into this conflict with the military, political, and economic power of the beastly Babylon as a strategy for bringing God's kingdom into effect, thus giving meaning to their suffering and martyrdom (1993b:150, 160). In this struggle, Swartley insightfully suggests that the central question of Revelation is: "Who is the true Lord of this world?" The answer is that God rather than the emperor Domitian is the Lord and worthy of worship: "Worship God" (19:10; 22:9). Hence, the role of the Christian is passive resistance—courageous worship and witness but ultimately trusting God for the victory (1996:2373-74).

This message of Revelation was given to Christians, a group set over against the dominant Greek-Roman culture. It is this message that has spoken to the Anabaptists throughout their history. Anabaptists in many parts of the world today are also at opposition to the worldview of the time. Revelation gives strength to those who are oppressed to resist the dominant culture of the world.

Interpreting Revelation

Although the message of Revelation is powerful and relevant, it is often obscured because the language used to communicate it is symbolic. In interpreting the symbols of Revelation, scholars are divided according to where they look for the referents to the symbols: in the time when the document was written, in the history of God's people, in the future, or in the realm of ideas.

The *preterist* searches for referents in the time in which Revelation was written, the first-century Roman Empire. In arguing for this interpretive scheme, Weaver appeals to the view that the seven seals correspond to seven Roman emperors between Tiberius and Domitian (1994a:280). According to preterists, Revelation was written to confirm the believer's faith during the expectation of persecution at the hands of Emperor Domitian, but it has permanent value as it strengthens the faith of persons who read its words at any time. Thus, Revelation is to be read like the Pauline letters. For example, Paul wrote the letter to the Galatians to counter the arguments of the Judaizers. Although there are no Judaizers in the church today, Galatians teaches how to deal with those who would place restrictions on persons who wish to become Christians. Similarly, although Revelation is written in symbols that relate directly to the church of the first century, Christians understand the message to relate to any situation of persecution that they encounter. The shortcoming of this position is that it locks the direct message of Revelation in the distant past.

The *historicist* looks for the referents to the symbols in the history of the church. For historicists, Revelation is a symbolic prophecy of the history of Christianity. The symbols designate historical movements and events. The major criticism of this position is its radical subjectivity. The historicist method leads to confusion because there are no fixed guidelines regarding what events are in mind. For example, the beast from the sea in Revelation 13 has been identified with Mohammed, Luther, Napoleon, Hitler, and Kissinger. Another limitation of this approach is that historicists tend to focus on the church in the West to the neglect of the rest of the world (Beale, 1999:46).

The *futurist* seeks the referents for the symbols of Revelation in the near future. These interpreters see Revelation as a prediction of events in their present context that mark the imminent end of the world. Today, futurists usually find fulfillment for these predictions in situations related to the founding of the state of Israel. This method has the same problem as the preceding one. In the twentieth century, the ten horns of the beast were interpreted as the League of Nations, the Common Market, and the states of what was the Soviet Union. Another shortcoming in the futurist position is that it makes the message of Revelation irrelevant to the Asian churches to which it was addressed (for a biblically based refutation of the futurist approach, see Eller, 1974:12-24).

Idealists believe that the referents for the symbols in Revelation are to be found, not in specific events in any time period, but in the realm of ideas. Revelation is thus a symbolic portrayal of the spiritual conflict between the forces of God and Satan. What is important is not the referents of the symbols but the spiritual truths that these symbols evoke. The shortcoming of this position is that it rejects the more literal view that many Christians have insisted is appropriate for interpreting the Bible.

Of course, categories such as these are never clear-cut, and combinations are possible, even likely. Preterists may admit that the first-century application can be the basis for the timeless truths of the idealists; historicists may see their referent in the history of the church to be a secondary meaning in addition to the first-century preterist one; futurists may allow that the end might not be as imminent as they seem to imply, and that the text has relevance for the reader anyway; and idealists may feel more comfortable if their meaning has roots in the first-century setting. Yet categorizations permit distinctions to be made so that the various interpretations of Revelation are more understandable.

Overview of Revelation

The message of Revelation is developed around the primary symbol of Christ the Lamb, who overcame persecution, not by military force and political violence, but by suffering love and exemplary martyrdom. Thus, the vision of the Lamb in chapter 5 is the fulcrum of Revelation.

Yet the focus on Christ begins in the first chapter. Revelation is given by God to Christ, who is described symbolically in a manner that brings comfort to those facing persecution. Christ is portrayed as the King of Kings, who possesses wisdom, insight, stability, strength, and glory. For this reason, there is no need for Christ's followers to fear the persecution that is imminent if they separate from the evil world in which they find themselves.

Chapters 2-3 give a picture of what that evil world looks like. By describing real churches that struggled to be faithful to God in difficult times of oppression, they place Revelation squarely in the context of the first-century Roman Empire. Although the messages of the letters are specific to the first-century churches in the province of Asia with their unique strengths and weaknesses, the church throughout history can see itself in the pictures presented. Thus, Christians of all times can identify struggles of their world with persecutions that were faced by the churches at the end of the first century in the Roman province of Asia.

Following the presentation of realities that Christians face in this world, chapters 4-5 carry the reader into the heavenly realm, which is the spiritual context for the earthly struggles. Here the visions of God and Christ give comfort and strength. The vision of God reminds the Christian that the one who created the world is the one who is able to make sense of the situation of persecution in which humanity finds itself. Chapter 5 suggests that God did this by sending Jesus Christ into the world to overcome Satan and the forces of evil. Yet Christ conquers, not by violent force, but by suffering. This is the truth on which Revelation is built: God's plan of salvation comes through the suffering and death of Christ, which serves as a model for the suffering and death of the followers of Christ. The rest of the book describes this central theme: overcoming through suffering.

The root causes of the suffering are focused in chapter 6, which presents a series of six seal judgments portraying the inevitable progression in a world that trusts in military solutions to problems. The point is that war leads to civil strife, which in turn leads to material deprivation and finally to death. The chapter centers on the martyrs in heaven, who ask how long it will be before God will judge this preoccupation with violence.

The answer comes in chapter 7, where the 144,000 saints, who are standing on the brink of tribulation, are contrasted with the great throng who have overcome tribulation and received their reward in heaven. Although the duration of tribulation is not specified, the message is that those who overcome persecution will find their place with God and the one who was their example in persecution, Christ the Lamb that was slain.

In chapters 8-16, this progress from tribulation to glory is compared to the Exodus of Israel from Egypt. In chapters 8-9, the seventh seal introduces a series of seven trumpet judgments that parallel the ten plagues of the Exodus. They remind the followers of Christ that their suffering is the means by which God is delivering them from the sinful world. Using the image of eating a scroll, chapter 10 tells Christ's followers that, although the deliverance is sweet, it involves suffering and maybe even death. In chapter 11, the images of the measuring of the temple and the suffering and ascension of the two witnesses remind the followers of Christ that in persecution and martyrdom they will be protected by God and ultimately taken to heaven. Chapter 12 instills confidence in the spiritual reality of this deliverance, which is rooted in the victory in heaven of the forces of God over those of Satan. Yet this deliverance is contingent on the choice to identify with the suffering and martyrdom of Christ rather than with the violent reign of Antichrist. Chapters 13-14 present a contrast between those who identify with Satan and his two beastly representatives by wearing the mark of the beast and those who identify with the followers of the Lamb on Mount Zion by being imprinted with the seal of the redeemed. Chapters 15-16, along with chapters 8-9, form an *inclusio* (bookends) for this section, reiterating the tribulations, again using imagery from the plagues and the Exodus.

Chapters 17-22 communicate eschatological truths related to the outcome of the historical struggle. The final fates of the beast and the Lamb and their followers are contrasted. The destruction of the great whore tells the fate of the beast, and the fall of Babylon describes that of his followers and those who benefit materially by their alliance with Babylon and its beastly leader. By contrast, the marriage of the Lamb celebrates the exaltation of Christ, while the new heaven and new earth disclose the destiny of the overcomers who follow the Lamb.

Thus, Christians under persecution are exhorted to identify with Christ the Lamb rather than with the beastly antichrist. While the faithful forfeit the material gains in this world that would come through following the beast, they gain spiritual rewards in heaven that await those who overcome tribulation and even death through suffering love. The historical struggle of Christians is won, not by forceful violence, but by suffering love. By overcoming through suffering, Christians are winning on this earth the victory that Christ has already achieved in the spiritual realm by his suffering and death on the cross.

Diagram of Revelation

The previous section discusses the trajectory of the content of Revelation. As the following diagram portrays, the thematic content of Revelation moves from a vision of Christ the overcomer (ch. 1) to a description of the suffering church (chs. 2-3). God's solution for the struggle of the church is overcoming through suffering (chs. 4-5). The cause of the suffering is rooted in war, which leads to strife, famine, and death (ch. 6). Yet in this struggle, hope is promised for those who overcome with the 144,000 and become part of the great heavenly throng (ch. 7). Indeed, suffering is portrayed as the means for overcoming the tribulations of the trumpets and the bowls (chs. 8-9 and 15-16). Moreover, those who overcome suffering will be protected ultimately from these tribulations (chs. 10-11). This protection comes through the heavenly victory that Christ has won over the powers of evil (ch. 12). Yet a choice is presented to all persons: follow either the Lamb or the beast (chs. 13-14). Disincentive for following the beast is focused in the destruction of the beast (ch. 17) and its followers (ch. 18). Motivation for following the Lamb is found in the triumph of the Lamb (ch. 19) and the faithful (chs. 20-22).

This outline of the content of Revelation can be diagramed as follows:

Diagram

Vision of Christ (ch. 1)	Seven Letters (chs. 2-3)	God and Christ (chs. 4-5)	Seal Judgments (ch. 6)	Two Multitudes (ch. 7)	Trumpets and Bowls (ch. 8-9, 15, 16)	Scroll and Witnesses (ch. 10-11)
Christ the Overcomer	Struggling Church	Solution for Creation: Overcoming by Suffering	Causes of Suffering: War-Strife Famine-Death	Hope for Suffering Saints	Suffering as the Means for Overcoming	Ultimate Protection in Persecution
Mother of Messiah (ch. 12)	Beasts and Lamb (chs. 13-14)	The Great Whore (ch. 17)	Fall of Babylon (ch. 18)	Marriage Supper of Lamb (ch. 19)	Millennium and New Heaven and Earth (chs. 20-22)	
Victory Won by Christ in Heaven	Choice: Follow Lamb or Beasts	Doom of Beast	Doom of Beast's Followers	Triumph of Lamb	Triumph of Lamb's Followers	

Revelation 1:1-20

The Vision of Christ

PREVIEW

The full title of the book given in its text is the *Revelation of Jesus Christ*. Since *revelation* translates the Greek word *apokalypsis,* the title establishes the apocalyptic nature of the book. Indeed, *apokalypsis* designates the name of both the book and the genre. Given that this is the first time the word was used to describe a document, its occurrence initiates the designation of the genre of apocalyptic, although Revelation certainly is not the first text that one would describe as apocalyptic *[Essay: Apocalyptic Literature].*

Although the title calls Revelation apocalyptic, in verse 3 the author designates the work as a prophecy and himself as a prophet in the line of the Hebrew prophets (see 22:7, 10, 18, 19). While he does not use the prophetic formula "thus says the LORD," it is clear that John sees himself as the one who proclaims God's message to the churches in Asia. So the opening lines of Revelation establish it as a prophetic work.

Yet the form of Revelation is a letter *[Essay: Genre of Revelation].* Verses 4-8 designate the sender (John) and the recipients (the seven churches in Asia) and issue a greeting ("Grace and peace"). Later, chapters 2 and 3 include seven messages to churches written in the epistolary form. In them, John includes practical, situation-specific information to fellow Christians in churches that he knows intimately. After more than eighteen chapters of apocalyptic visions, John returns to the epistolary form to provide a conclusion with admonitions, warnings, and a benediction (22:6-21).

Despite its characteristics of prophecy and epistle, Revelation is primarily an apocalyptic book of visions described with symbolic language. Verses 9-20 of chapter 1 present the first vision, which includes the use of symbols to describe Christ. Although the visionary technique is not used in the letters of chapters 2-3, they are bound to chapter 1 by the repetition of the symbols describing Christ, whose words to the seven churches are the content of each of the seven letters. Thus, the opening words of Revelation establish the kind of literature it is: *Through the format of letters to beloved Christians in the churches of Asia, the Book of Revelation speaks the prophetic words of God using visions described in symbolic, apocalyptic language.*

Besides articulating the genre, the introductory verses clarify the divine source of Revelation. The originator of the book is identified as God, who communicates through the mediation of Jesus Christ to an angel, then through the angel to God's servant John, and finally through John to the churches. This resembles the Jewish Mishnah, where the Law is given from God to Moses, to Joshua, to the elders, to the prophets, to the men of the great synagogue (*Pirke Aboth* 1:1). This pattern probably grew out of the Hellenistic belief that God was so far removed from the evil world that intermediaries were necessary to bridge the gap. Yet the point is that Revelation is of divine, not human origin. John is the interpreter of the divine vision much like Daniel interpreted the visions of King Nebuchadnezzar (Dan. 2:25-45).

OUTLINE

An Apocalyptic Title, 1:1-3
An Epistolary Address, 1:4-8
The Context of the Vision, 1:9-11
The Vision of Christ, 1:12-16
The Response to the Vision, 1:17-20

EXPLANATORY NOTES

An Apocalyptic Title 1:1-3

The word *revelation* translates the Greek word *apokalypsis*. This is a compound word composed of *apo,* meaning "away from," and *kalypsis,* meaning "hiding" or "covering." Therefore, *revelation* means to "show" or "uncover." It is used for the revealing of previously hidden spiritual truth (Rom. 16:25; 1 Cor. 14:6; Gal. 1:12; 2:2; Eph. 3:3;

1 Pet. 1:7; 4:13). Rowland suggests that here "for the first time ... a Christian text ... comes close to portraying itself as sacred scripture on a par with the writings of the old covenant" (1998:568). Moreover, the truth revealed in Revelation is the same as throughout the New Testament—God's redemption in Christ (Rom. 8:18; 1 Cor. 1:7; 2 Thess. 2:8; 1 Pet. 1:13; 5:10).

The expression *revelation of Jesus Christ* may include either a subjective or objective genitive. It may be that Jesus Christ is the object of the revelation, "the revelation *about* Jesus Christ," or the subject of the revelation, "the revelation *given by* Jesus Christ." The context, which includes revelation's passage from one entity to another (see Preview), favors the latter, that the revelation of God is communicated by Jesus Christ. This establishes that the authority of Revelation is in Jesus Christ, not in the author as was the case with other apocalypses of the time *[Essay: Pseudonymity].*

That Revelation is given by God to *Jesus Christ* makes it clear that Christ is dependent on God, especially for what he says—a theme Revelation shares with the Gospel of John (John 5:19-23; 8:26-30; 12:49; 14:10; 17:8). Yet it is interesting that Christ is mentioned first here. It is clear that God and Christ are intimately related.

Although the subject of *made it known* may be either Christ or God (Aune, 1997:6), the manner of communicating Revelation is *by sending his angel*, a common means of communication in Revelation (11:15; 19:9; 21:9; 22:16). The use of angels as messengers is rooted in the Old Testament "angel of the LORD" and probably results from the effort to bridge the perceived distance between the transcendent and the human (Zech. 1:7-17; Acts 7:53; Gal. 3:19).

The angel was sent by God *to his servant John*. This link in the revelatory chain indicates that humans have a role in divine revelation. Although the source is divine, the communication is through human channels, thus making Revelation both divine and human. John has an important position in the chain of revelation; he stands in the presence of God and is the agent communicating the divine word to the churches. Surprisingly, Revelation is about *what must soon take place*. Depending on one's approach to interpreting Revelation (see Entering the World of Revelation: Interpreting Revelation), the word *soon* is interpreted differently. The futurist, who looks for the meaning of Revelation in the present-day reader's immediate future, encounters difficulty in the first verse of Revelation. Indeed, the idea that what is recorded will happen soon after John received his visions is quite common in Revelation (2:16; 3:11; 6:11; 10:6; 12:12; 17:10; 22:6, 7, 10, 12, 20). John has replaced Daniel's "at the end of days" with *soon*. Some futurists substitute the phrase, "must soon begin to take place," but that is not what the passage says. Others substitute the word "suddenly" for soon, which is a more acceptable translation of the word; however, the context, especially the clause, *the time is near*, in verse 3, clearly favors *soon*. Some preterists, who relate the content of Revelation to the context of its writer, believe that John is speaking, not of a future event, but of what will happen immediately—the persecution of the first-century church. Idealists, who relate the content of Revelation to ideas rather than to specific events, either personalize the coming, saying that Christ will soon come for the individual, or generalize it, making it apply to a permanent spirit of expectancy. The precise specification in chapters 2-3 of the nature of persecution in the churches in Asia makes it clear that the primary reference is to the persecution of the first century. Yet the passage has implications for the persecution of the church in any age, including the present.

The revelation to which John witnessed is called *the word of God and the testimony of Jesus Christ*. Revelation here and elsewhere puts God and Jesus on the same plane (1:9; 19:10; 20:4). The word of God is the active purpose of God (Ps. 33:9; Isa. 55:10-11), confirmed by the testimony (*martyria*) of Jesus Christ (John 1:14; 7:16; 8:28; 12:49). Eller notes that this phrase is used in two senses by John: "the testimony Christians make *to* Jesus, the testimony that he is Lord"; or "a testimony he himself made (or makes) ... [to] the coming of the kingdom of God." Therefore, "one way we witness *to* him is by joining him in *his* witness" (1974:44). Slater affirms that Christ provides the model for the witness of Christians: "Just as Christ suffered, they will suffer; just as he remained faithful, they must remain faithful" (1999:93).

In verse 3, the first of seven beatitudes occurs (1:3; 14:13; 16:15; 19:9; 20:6; 22:7, 14), each beginning with the word *blessed*, which refers to God's approval regardless of outward circumstances. "Happy" is an unfortunate modern translation that connotes fortune or luck. Instead, true blessedness comes from God and is independent of happenstance. Revelation pronounces a blessing on the congregations where the book is received.

The blessedness is attributed to *the one who reads aloud the words of the prophecy*. The primary point here is that John intended his book to be read in public worship. Jews commonly read aloud in the synagogues, and the practice seems to have been carried over into the worship of the Christian church (Exod. 24:7; Neh. 8:2-3; Luke 4:16; Acts 13:15; 1 Cor. 14:26-33; 2 Cor. 3:15; Col. 4:16;

1 Thess. 5:27; 1 Tim. 4:13). According to Schüssler Fiorenza, "Revelation is conceived as a rhetorical work to be recited in the assembly of the community.... [I]t comes to life only when read aloud to an audience" (1991:40). Barr contends that Revelation should be read aloud whenever possible and that interpreters should hear it as well as read it (1998:6; see also Gloer, 2001:38-39). The blessing is pronounced on *those who hear and who keep* what is written in Revelation (see Luke 11:27-28). The Hebrew *shema* means both hear and act, thus implying obedience. John uses two words in Greek to capture the Hebrew meaning. The verb *hear* also indicates again that Revelation was intended for use in public worship.

After the beatitude, Revelation is called *the prophecy*. John considers his book to be a prophecy and himself to be a prophet (see Preview). Revelation begins very much like several of the books of the Hebrew prophets (Isa. 1:1; Hos. 1:1; Amos 1:1; see Fekkes, 1994). In that tradition, the prophet was not so much a foreseer of the future as an interpreter of God's will. The popular conception now considers a prophet to be one who foretells the future. Futurist interpreters emphasize this aspect of prophecy. The function of prediction, however, is only a small part of the prophet's role. A more adequate conception is that the prophet, under the influence of the Holy Spirit, proclaimed the will of God, promoting obedience and faithfulness (Koester, 2001:44-47).

At the end of this paragraph, John reminds the reader that *the time is near*. The word *time* here is *kairos*, which refers, not to chronological time, but to the "fitting season" or "decisive moment" (Matt. 8:29; 16:3-4; 26:18; Mark 1:15; Luke 12:56; 19:44; 1 Cor. 4:5; 2 Thess. 2:6; 1 Pet. 4:17; Rev. 11:18). Again, it is clear that John believes the fulfillment of Revelation's visions is close at hand.

An Epistolary Address 1:4-8

Although the title identifies it as apocalyptic and the author clearly considers it to be prophesy, Revelation is written in the form of a letter. It includes the elements typical of New Testament epistles (Rom. 1:1-7; 1 Cor. 1:1-9; 2 Cor. 1:1-11). In verse 4, the sender is identified as *John,* and the recipients as *the seven churches that are in Asia.*

The word for church is *ekklēsia*, which means "assembly" or "congregation." The local, visible church is clearly in mind here *[Glossary: Church]*. There were more than *seven churches* in the Roman province of Asia. In addition to the seven mentioned in chapters 2 and 3, churches had been established in Colossae (Col. 1:2),

Hierapolis (Col. 4:13-15), Troas (Acts 20:5-12; 2 Cor. 2:12), Magnesia (Ignatius, *Magn.*), and Tralles (Ignatius, *Trall.*). The number seven represents the complete church both temporally and geographically (Beale, 1999:204), since in the Hebrew tradition the seventh day, or Sabbath, completed the week; the seventh year completed the sabbatical year sequence; and the year of Jubilee completed seven sabbatical years (see also 1 Enoch 21:3). Besides their symbolic importance, the seven churches focused in Revelation may have been chosen for their location along a common circular trade route around Asia, the route that the Book of Revelation would probably have taken as it was communicated to the churches there (Ramsay, 1904:185-196; cf. Aune, 1997:131).

The greetings, *grace* and *peace*, were quite common in the early Christian church (Rom. 1:7; 1 Cor. 1:3; 2 Cor. 1:2; Gal. 1:3; Eph. 1:2; Phil. 1:2; Col. 1:2; 1 Thess. 1:1; 2 Thess. 1:2; 1 Tim. 1:2; 2 Tim. 1:2; Tit. 1:4; 1 Pet. 1:2; 2 Pet. 1:2; 2 John 3). Grace was a common Greek greeting, and the Hebrew *shalom* (peace) is still commonly used. So the New Testament writers combine Greek and Hebrew words to form a solemn, rather than a casual, greeting. Mauser argues that *peace* used as a greeting carries the theological import connected with the conditions of those who live in Christ—health, salvation, and righteousness (1992:31-33).

The greeting is from *who is and who was and who is to come, the seven spirits,* and *Jesus Christ.* Wall argues that this section is a confession of core beliefs about God and Christ that the early Christians in Asia Minor shared (1991:56). Although that may be true, one must be careful not to read too much theology into the passage. While the Trinity may be implied, the formulation is primitive and undeveloped (see TBC, Beginnings of Trinitarianism). The traditional order of the Trinity is altered, putting Christ last to provide a transition into the vision of Christ to follow.

The one *who is and who was and who is to come* clearly refers to God. There is here an unmistaken allusion to the divine name Yahweh, variously defined as "I am," "the One who is," or "the One who causes to be" (Anderson, 1962:410; see Exod. 3:14; Deut. 32:39; Isa. 43:3-5; Jer. 1:6; 14:13). Here the designation for God is in the nominative case (subject) where the accusative (object) would be grammatically correct. Although this may be the result of quoting exactly a Hebrew source (R. Charles, 1920:1.10) or creating an Old Testament biblical context (Beale, 1999:189), it is more likely an indication that the name of God was too holy to be declined by changing the form to adapt to the grammar of the sentence. In addition, the

order of the tenses is odd; placing the present first probably emphasizes the present aspect of God's work. Although substitution of "is to
come" for "will be" is due to the lack of a future participle of "to be"
in Greek, the phrase certainly echoes the Messianic "one who is coming" (Mowinckel, 1954; the book's title, *He That Cometh* gives
prominence to the phrase). Caird says that the passage "sets the
church's coming ordeal against a background of God's eternity, but it
also brings God down into the arena of history" (1966:16).

The greeting also comes *from the seven spirits who are before
his throne* (see Heb. 2:4; Rev. 3:1; 4:5; 5:6; 22:6). Isaiah enumer-
ates the seven-fold gifts of the God's Spirit (11:2). Some believe that
the seven spirits are the messengers who deliver the letters, and others that the reference is to angelic beings like the seven archangels of
apocalyptic literature (1 Kings 22:21-23; Heb. 1:7, 14; Tob. 12:15;
1 Enoch 20:1-7; 90:21). Because the number seven connotes the
completeness of the Spirit's gifts *[Gematria]*, it is most likely that the
seven spirits represent the complete Spirit of God, or the Holy Spirit,
who is with the Christian in times of persecution (cf. Murphy,
1998:67-70).

The third source of the greeting is *Jesus Christ, the faithful witness, the firstborn of the dead, and the ruler of the kings of the
earth* (see Ps. 89:27-37). This passage answers the question: Who is
Jesus Christ? First, he is *the faithful witness*. The words "witness"
and "martyr," translate the same Greek word, *martys*. It is common
in Johannine literature, used ten times in Revelation (1:2; 1:5; 2:13;
3:14; 11:3; 17:6; 20:4; 22:16, 18, 20), thirty-three times in the
Gospel of John, and ten times in the Johannine epistles. The forensic sense of a witness in a court of law is the dominant meaning. Jesus
Christ is a reliable witness because he has firsthand experience with
God. Certainly, though, the connotation of martyrdom is also present
(see 2:13). Second, Jesus Christ is *the firstborn of the dead*. The primary reference here is to Christ's resurrection (see also Col. 1:15,
18). Because he was the first to return from death, Christ makes it
possible to overcome persecution and conquer death. Even if martyred for the faith, Christians shall rise with Christ, the first martyr.
Third, Jesus Christ is *the ruler of the kings of the earth*. If the first
two attributes of Christ refer to his martyrdom and resurrection, the
third speaks of his exaltation with God (see Phil. 2:9-11; Eph. 1:19-
23). Although Rome seems now to be in control of the world, in actu-
ality Christ is the ruler even of kings like Caesar. Christians appear to
be a helpless bunch, but they are true royalty. Christ has made them
rulers with him over all the powers of this earth.

After revealing who Jesus Christ is, this passage answers the question: What does Jesus do? Again three responses are made. First, he *loves us.* The present tense here denotes continuous action: Christ keeps on loving or loves continually. Emphasis is on the permanent, abiding love of Christ—the love that his followers are, in turn, to have for others (Gal. 2:20; Eph. 2:4-7; 5:25-27; 2 Thess. 2:16-17; Rev. 2:4, 19; 3:9).

Christ's second action is that he *freed us from our sins by his blood.* The King James Version reads "washed" instead of "freed." The difference grows out of the distinction between *lusanti,* "freed," and *lousanti,* "washed," two words pronounced identically in Greek. The rendering could easily have been changed when read aloud for the purpose of copying. Walvoord argues for *washed* on the basis that it would have been easier for the copier to drop than to add a letter (1966:38). Yet the earliest manuscripts have *freed,* which is most likely the better reading. The tense here is aorist, which denotes a one-time event. In his death on the cross, Christ has, once and for all, freed us from our sins and the power of the evil one (see Gal. 3:13; 4:4-5). The work of redemption is finished, and its cost is the blood of Jesus Christ.

Third, Christ *made us to be a kingdom, priests serving his God and Father.* Ancient Israel was considered to be a priestly kingdom (Exod. 19:5-6; Isa. 61:6). Indeed, every member of the Northern Kingdom could be made a priest, not just the Levites (1 Kings 12:31; 13:33). As followers of Jesus, Christians are a kingdom of priests (1 Pet. 2:5, 9; Rev. 5:9-10). That means the congregation of believers has direct access to God (Rom. 12:1; Heb. 4:16; 10:19-22; 13:15). In this passage the priesthood of believers applies, not to individuals, but to the corporate, visible church, an idea that Anabaptists have emphasized.

The extended section on the nature and work of Jesus Christ ends with a doxology. Usually reserved for God, *dominion* was given to Jesus Christ. The phrase *his God and Father* clarifies the parental relationship between God and Jesus. Because dominion refers to political power, Jesus Christ is contrasted with the Roman emperor who is apparently in control.

The word *Look!* always marks divine intervention in Revelation and may signal oracular speech (Aune, 1983:279). Verse 8 implies that God is the speaker. Here, God announces a major theme of the Book of Revelation: *Christ is coming with the clouds.* In scriptures, clouds are common accompaniments of the manifestation of God (Exod. 13:21; 16:10; 19:16; Dan. 7:13; Matt. 17:5). Here, their association with the coming of Christ indicates another major emphasis of Revelation, placing Christ on the same level as God.

When Christ comes, *every eye will see him* (Zech. 12:10; Matt. 24:30; 26:64; Mark 13:26; 14:62; Luke 21:27; Acts 1:9; Did. 16:6-8). Here the return of Christ is presented as a public, visible event. The point is that, although Christ's power is debated now, then everyone will recognize it. Yet as a result of seeing Christ, *the tribes of the earth will wail.* It is not clear here whether their wailing is due to judgment or repentance. Perhaps the former is the best option because, elsewhere in Revelation, people of the earth refuse repentance (9:20; 16:8-11). The ones who do not repent are characterized as *those who pierced* Jesus (Zech. 12:10; John 19:34-37). Of course, there is here an allusion to the events of the crucifixion. The piercing probably refers, though, not only to those who actually crucified Christ, but to all who reject him. The doxology ends with: *So it is to be. Amen—* a solemn affirmation of what has been said about Christ.

The passage concludes with God giving several words of self-description. At the end of the description of Christ, God speaks and thus verifies the validity of what is said about Christ's character and actions. The first self-description is *alpha and omega,* the first and last letters of the Greek alphabet. This formulation means that God is the complete, all-inclusive one and that God is eternal, the source and finality of all things (see also Isa. 44:6). Another of God's self-descriptions is *the Almighty,* a favorite title for God in Revelation (4:8; 11:17; 15:3; 16:7,14; 19:6, 15; 21:22), which occurs only once elsewhere in the New Testament (2 Cor. 6:18). The Septuagint uses it to translate the Hebrew *Yahweh Sabaoth,* "The LORD of Hosts" (2 Sam. 7:26-27; Ps. 24:10; see also Isa. 1:9). It indicates that God has sovereignty over all things. There is a word play here that sets God in contrast to the power of Rome: the emperor was commonly called *autocrator,* self-ruler; God here is called *pantocrator,* ruler of all.

The Context of the Vision 1:9-11

This section answers the major questions regarding the vision that John is to receive (Boring, 1989:80-85): Who? John. Where? Patmos. Why? Banishment. When? The Lord's Day. How? In the spirit. What? A vision. The first question has already been answered in verse 1; the recipient of the vision is John. Rather than making apostolic claims, John merely calls himself a *brother* or equal partner (Thompson, 1998:54, 57), who shares *the persecution and the kingdom and the patient endurance.* The central message of Revelation is suggested here: those who endure persecution with

Christ will rule with Christ. The word *persecution* means "pressure" or "tribulation" (John 16:33; Acts 14:22). John expected immediate persecution for the church of his day (see also Matt. 11:12; 2 Tim. 3:12) because of the imposition of emperor worship (see Entering the World of Revelation: Getting Our Bearings). Exemption from worshiping Caesar was given to Jews, and Christians were also exempt as long as they were considered a sect of Judaism. John probably saw his own exile as an indication that Christians would soon face persecution for their faith in Christ. Some commentators believe that this is a reference to the great tribulation of the end of time, but the text here refers only to John's being exiled to the island of Patmos.

The empire of Rome is implied in the word *kingdom*. Kingdom and tribulation are two sides of the same coin (Sweet, 1990:67). Participation in the kingdom is the positive side of following Christ; tribulation is the negative side. Ewert combines the words in this passage quite effectively: "'Kingdom' is the divine alchemy that transforms tribulation into triumph, and so it can be endured with patience" (1980:49).

A key word in Revelation is *patient endurance* (2:2-3, 19; 3:10; 13:10; 14:12). This is not weakness, but it calls for active courage that does not strike back. Johns says it envisions, not "passive acceptance of suffering," but "nonviolent resistance to evil" (1998:215). The word connotes a strength that acts without vengeance. Johns elaborates on the active nature of the words used here:

> The "endurance" the author calls for is no hands-wringing, pietistic hypomonē (transliteration of Greek). Rather, he calls for a courageous and active "resistance" (hypomonē) to the evils of Graeco-Roman culture and religion. It is a clear "No" to the possibility of humanity's bringing in the fullness of God's reign, and a joyful and confident "Yes" to the way of Christ, demonstrated most poignantly in his faithful witness—a witness that led to his death on the cross. (1998:234)

Such courage is needed to overcome tribulation and translate its suffering into the expectancy of the glory of the kingdom (see Matt. 24:13; Acts 14:22; 2 Tim. 2:11-13). It should be emphasized that the resistance to evil relies, not on violent revolution against the oppressors, but on suffering love (Pilgrim, 1999:174-75).

John continues: *I ... share with you in Jesus the persecution.* Paul and Peter make similar claims (Rom. 5:3; 2 Tim. 2:12; 1 Pet. 5:1). Stories indicate that John refused to sacrifice to the emperor's image in Ephesus and was subsequently tried in the imperial court in Rome and condemned by Domitian to be boiled in oil or to drink poison (R. Smith, 2000:10-11). Nevertheless, it is John's present exile to Patmos that is the basis for this claim to have suffered tribulation in following Jesus.

The *island called Patmos,* a Sporades island in the Aegean Sea (see Map), was a stopping point about seventy-five miles from Ephesus, west of Miletus on the journey to Rome (Acts 20:15-17). Patmos is a barren, rocky, and hilly island—thirty miles in circumference, ten miles north to south, six miles wide, and sixteen square miles in area. Its crescent shape made it a good natural harbor. Sparsely populated, it was located away from civilization. Evidence indicates that the islands of the Aegean were used for the banishment of prisoners (Tacitus, *Annals* 3.68, 4.30, 15.71; Juvenal, *Satires* 1.73, 6.563-64, 10.170). Since Christians were likely a political threat to the empire (Acts 17:6-7), John may have been a political prisoner. That he *was* on the island called Patmos may indicate he wrote Revelation after returning to Ephesus, but such an interpretation is probably making too much of the verb tense.

Although some believe that John was on a mission to Patmos for the purpose of preaching the *word of God and the testimony of Jesus Christ,* the preposition *dia* denotes cause, not purpose. Despite the suggestions that Patmos may have been a typical Greek city with a gymnasium and a shrine devoted to Artemis (Vinson, 2001:17), the island would certainly not have been "a prime spot for mission" (Murphy, 1998:15, 86; Worth, 1999:95-96). So John was mostly likely on Patmos as a result of his passion for God's word and Jesus' testimony.

John's vision came because he was *in the spirit,* likely referring to the psychological mindset of a visionary state often in connection with prayer or praise (Fekkes, 1994:46). Such ecstatic visions were a common biblical way of receiving divine insight (Isa. 6:1; Ezek. 3:12; Acts 9:1-9; 11:5; 22:17; 2 Cor. 12:1-6). The senses of the physical world faded, and spiritual sensitivities opened John to deeper realities.

The time of the vision was *the Lord's day.* There are two possible interpretations of this phrase. It may refer to the Day of the Lord, a time when judgment comes upon all who undermine God's justice and righteousness (Amos 5:18, 24). The judgment theme of Revelation lends support to this interpretation. Nevertheless, it is not the most natural meaning of the words. The more likely interpretation of the Lord's day is that it refers to Sunday, the Christian Sabbath, a view that most commentators accept. Although this is the only occurrence of the phrase in the Bible, there is some biblical evidence supporting the idea of a Sunday Sabbath. Acts speaks of Christians meeting to break bread on the first day of the week (20:7), and Paul tells the Corinthians to put aside money on the first day of the week (1 Cor. 16:2). These practices are clearly based on the fact that the resurrection of Christ occurred on the first day of the week (Matt. 28:1; Mark 16:2, 9; Luke 24:1; John 20:1, 19), and they lend credence to understanding John's phrase to refer to Sunday. Its use here emphasizes the gathered worshiping community in the heavenly sanctuary (Fekkes, 1994:42).

As John entered the visionary state, he *heard a loud voice like a trumpet* (see TLC on ch. 8, The Trumpets). The word translated "like" *(hōs)* is used fifty-six times in Revelation. What John has seen is beyond the description of normal speech, so he has to use similes. This further supports the contention that Revelation contains symbolic material that cannot be described directly but only by simile and analogy.

The Vision of Christ 1:12-16

At the beginning of Revelation's first vision, John *saw seven golden lampstands*. There were no candlesticks in antiquity; these were earthenware bowls holding oil that was ignited. The bowls were placed on decorated golden lampstands connoting splendor (see comments on 1:20, where John interprets this symbol).

In this vision, Christ was called *one like the Son of Man*. This designation has its source in Daniel (7:13), where it may be the equivalent of the Ancient One (Aune, 1997:91-92). It is used frequently in the Gospels as Jesus' self-designation, but it appears elsewhere only twice in addition to this passage (Acts 7:56; see Note on 14:14). Peterson says that it is a title focusing both on the divine glory of Christ's dominion and power, and on the one who is comfortable in ordinary, human experience. Like the Son of Man, his followers both believe that their actions are "part of the victorious rule of God's kingdom" and "immerse themselves in cross-bearing, self-denial, suffering, and death" (1988:30-31).

The symbolic significance of the Son of Man's attire aids our understanding of his role and identity. The *robe* was the garment of the Hebrew priest (Exod. 28:4, 31; 29:5; 39:27-28; Lev. 16:4; Ezek. 9:2; see also Jos., *Ant.* 3.154). Since the description of the robe as *long* indicates the high status of the person who wore it, the long robe might well refer to the dress of the high priest (cf. Aune, 1997:94; Murphy, 1998:90). This priestly image emphasizes Christ's direct access to God. Yet the long robe was also worn by kings (1 Sam. 24:4-5; Ezek. 26:16; Wis. Sol. 18:24). If royalty is implied (cf. Isa. 6:1), the meaning is identical to the next symbol.

The *golden sash across his chest* probably alludes to the golden belt worn by ancient royalty (1 Macc. 10:89). Workmen tucked their robes around their belts to labor more easily (Jos., *Ant.* 3.156), but Christ has finished his work and can allow his robe to flow long without its being an encumbrance. This symbol attributes to Christ the dignity of a king. Later he will be given the title "King of Kings" (19:16).

Christ's *head and his hair were white as white wool, white as snow*. This was also part of the description of the Ancient One, a phrase Daniel used to designate God (Dan. 7:9; see also 1 Enoch 46:1). Among the Hebrews—and, indeed, among many cultures—the white-haired, elderly person was honored as one having "respect, honor, wisdom, and high social status" gained from experience (Aune, 1997:94; Lev. 19:32; Prov. 16:31; see also Isa. 1:18). Therefore, the symbol most likely connotes wisdom.

The vision also indicated that *his eyes were like a flame of fire*. In the Greek tradition, the eyes of the gods are characterized as "bright and shining" (Aune, 1997:95). In the Bible, eyes are associated with judgment, whether in anger or in love (Isa. 11:3; Mark 3:5; 10:21-23; Luke 22:61; 2 Enoch 1:5). Yet the symbol likely refers to the all-seeing nature of Christ—his omniscience. The image of fire alludes to purification. The omniscient nature of Christ is for the purpose of judging and making pure (19:2).

That *his feet were like burnished bronze* is reminiscent of the cherubim of Ezekiel (Ezek. 1:4-7, 26-28; 8:2). In contrast, the image in Daniel's vision crumbled because its feet were made of iron and clay (Dan. 2:31-35). Thus, bronze feet may connote Christ's stability and immovable strength (see also Isa. 60:17). That the bronze was *refined as in a furnace* may indicate that Christ is morally pure (Beale, 1999:209-210).

As the vision continues, *his voice was like the sound of many waters*. This description most likely refers to the strength of his word (see Ezek. 1:25; 43:2). Ford says, "All else is drowned out and his judgment alone prevails" (1975:383).

John's next observation about Christ is that *in his right hand he held seven stars*. Later, the referents for the seven stars are explicitly identified as the angels of the seven churches (v. 20). In ancient astrology, stars were thought to control the universe and to commend emperor worship; Domitian's son was pictured on coins "as an infant Zeus playing with the stars" (Caird, 1966:15). The seven stars in this passage clearly allude to the complete astrological system. That Christ holds them in his hand means that he, not the emperor, controls the powers that govern the universe (Gen. 37:9; Deut. 4:19; Ps. 8:3; 147:4; 148:3; Isa. 14:13; Amos 5:8). The stars in Christ's hand also indicate his protection and care of his churches (see John 10:28).

The clause, *from his mouth came a sharp, two-edged sword,* contains imagery that is quite common in the biblical and apocryphal writings (Isa. 11:4; 49:2; Eph. 6:17; 2 Thess. 2:8; Heb. 4:12; Wis. Sol. 18:15; 1 Enoch 62:2; 2 Esd.13:9-11) and probably means that Christ's words penetrate and thus are authoritative. This is analogous to the creation story, where "God spoke, and it was done" (Ladd, 1972:33). In Revelation, Christ's word judges the evil powers, and his only weapon in his final battle against Satan and his followers is the word of God. Peterson summarizes an important truth: "Gradually, and in Jesus finally, military force becomes a metaphor for the word of God. Christ does not come with the sword (he ordered Peter to put his sword away for good), but with the word, which is like a sword" (1988:37).

The final element of the symbolic description of Christ is *his face was like the sun shining with full force.* The Hebrew scriptures speak of God's face shining (Num. 6:25), and Moses is described similarly when he comes down from Mount Sinai where he has seen God (Exod. 34:29). When Jesus was transfigured on the mountain, "his face shone like the sun" (Matt. 17:2). God's followers are also given faces that shine (Judg. 5:31; Matt. 13:43). This symbolic description reveals the glory of the divine Christ.

The Response to the Vision 1:17-20

After observing the tremendous vision of Christ, John *fell at his feet as though dead.* When confronting God, Moses covered his face (Exod. 3:5-6), Jeremiah exclaimed that he was "only a boy" (Jer. 1:6), and Ezekiel and Daniel fell prostrate on their faces (Ezek. 1:28; 3:23; 43:3; Dan. 8:17; 10:7-9). Upon seeing the miraculous power of Christ, Peter said, "Go away from me, Lord, for I am a sinful man" (Luke 5:8). Paul was struck down by God in order to receive a divine message (Acts 9:1-9; 26:12-18; see also Josh. 5:14; Isa. 6:5; 1 Enoch 14:24). A vision of God, or in this case, of the divine Christ, causes fear and awe; it is truly an awesome experience.

In response, Jesus says: *Do not be afraid; I am the first and the last.* Although we have seen that the appearance of the divine inspires respect and fear, here we are told that Jesus alleviates fear and brings comfort to his followers (Matt. 14:27; 17:7; Mark 6:50; John 6:20). *I am* alludes to the name of God (Exod. 3:14). The phrase, *the first and the last*, used in the Bible to refer to God (Isa. 41:4; 44:6;

48:12), is identical in meaning to "alpha and omega" (see comments on 1:8). Bauckham argues that both phrases are used interchangeably for God and Christ (1:8, 17; 21:6; 22:13; cf. 2:8; Isa. 44:6; 48:12), witnessing to the "unique divine identity" of Jesus (1998:53-54). Like God, Christ comprehends everything and, according to Beasley-Murray, is "the initiator of all things and the finisher of God's purpose for ... creation" (1974:67). Thus, the reason there is no need for fear is that Christ is the Lord of all things.

Christ also calls himself *the living one. I was dead, and see, I am alive forever and ever.* In the scriptures, the adjective *living* is often attributed to God (Josh. 3:10; Ps. 42:2; 84:2; Jer. 10:10-16; Hos. 1:10; Matt. 16:16; Acts 14:15; Rom. 9:26). God is referred to in Revelation as the one "who lives forever and ever" (4:9; 10:6; 15:7). John's Gospel tells us that this life of God is given to Christ and his followers (John 5:26; 11:25-26; 14:6, 19; see also 2 Tim. 1:10; 1 Pet. 3:18-20). Earlier in this chapter, the epithet attributed to Christ, "the firstborn of the dead," indicates that it is through Christ that the faithful are resurrected from death to life (see comments on 1:5).

Christ reiterates the previous point when he says, *I have the keys of Death and of Hades.* In Jewish thought, the key was the symbol of authority. Commenting on Deuteronomy 28:12, the Jerusalem Targum says: "Four keys are delivered into the hand of the Lord of the world which he has given to no ruler: the key of life, the key of the graves, the key of food, the key of rain" (quoted in Beasley-Murray, 1974:68). In the Hebrew and Christian scriptures, death and Sheol, or Hades, are described as having gates (Ps. 9:13; 107:18; Isa. 38:10), and this passage says Christ has the key to those gates. The meaning is that even if Christians die for their faith, Christ's resurrection has given him authority over death.

John is then told: *Now write what you have seen, what is, and what is to take place after this.* The dispensationalist interpretative approach places great emphasis on this verse, seeing it as an outline for Revelation (Scofield, 1945:1330) *[Essay: Dispensationalism].* The wording of the Greek seems to favor a two-fold division. The text is best punctuated as follows: *write what you have seen: what is and what is to take place after this.* Wall captures this two-fold distinction quite well: *what is* refers to the christological—what has already been realized in Christ—and *what is to take place after this* refers to the eschatological—what is expected yet to be accomplished (1991:64).

Finally, *the mystery of the seven stars that you saw in my right hand, and the seven golden lampstands* is explained. A mystery is not something hidden. On the contrary, it is the symbolic significance of a physical sign revealed only to special people, in this case, followers of Christ (Barr, 1998:40).

The first part of the mystery is that *the seven stars are the angels of the seven churches.* Some commentators think the angels are the bishops of the churches; but in the Bible, angels are never church leaders, and bishops of churches are not mentioned elsewhere in Revelation. Others believe that the messengers who delivered the letters are in focus (1:20; 2:1, 8, 12, 18; 3:1, 7, 14; see also Mal. 2:7). Although the word *angel* does literally mean "messenger," this interpretation would require that the letters to the churches be addressed to the messengers delivering the letters, an odd formulation. Still others believe the referent is to the guardian angels of the churches. Indeed, the scriptures do speak of angels guarding individuals (Matt. 18:10; Acts 12:15), and the archangel Michael is presented as protecting God's people from other nations (Dan. 10:13, 20-21; Herm. Sim. 8. 3. 3.; cf. Heb. 1:14; Rev. 12:7-9; Asc. Isa. 3:15).

A related interpretation is that the angels are spiritual counterparts to the churches, representing the supernatural nature of the churches (see Eph. 2:6-7). Sweet summarizes this idea well: "The churches spiritually replace the planetary powers, commonly held to control human destiny" (1990:73). Wink sharpens this idea considerably, contending that the angel is "the actual spirituality of the congregation as a single entity.... Angel and people are the inner and outer aspects of one and the same reality." He notes that almost all the second person pronouns in the letters to the churches are singular, referring to the angel of the specific church. This angel incorporates "every aspect of a church's current reality, good and bad alike.... The angel of the church is the coincidence of what church is—its personality—and what it is called to become—its vocation" (1986:70-73). Hence, the *angels of the seven churches* are best understood as the heavenly, spiritual identities of the earthly, physical churches in the province of Asia, which in turn represent the complete church in this world. Communicating messages from Jesus to angels, John is able "to maintain his position as 'brother' and still offer the most authoritative praise and blame" (Barr, 1998:36).

The second part of the mystery is that *the seven lampstands are the seven churches.* If the seven stars are the heavenly counterparts of the complete church, then the seven lampstands are the complete earthly church (see Zech. 4). The image of the lampstands emphasizes that the churches are to give light or to bear witness to Jesus Christ. The churches are to transmit the light from Christ, who holds them in his hand and is the "light of the world" (John 8:12; Walhout,

2000:30). The lampstand symbol is linked to the menorah, the seven-pronged candelabra that represented the Jewish people to the other cultures of the time. For example, what appears to be a menorah is the central feature in the arch of Titus, built in Rome to commemorate her military victory in Palestine in A.D. 66-70 (Efird, 1989:50). This symbol is here applied to the church, the symbolic Israel, suggesting that the heavenly and earthly churches are unified in Christ, who holds the seven stars and seven lampstands. That the suffering Christ holds his persecuted followers in his hands means that he cares for and protects them.

THE TEXT IN BIBLICAL CONTEXT

The Background for the Vision in Daniel and the Hebrew Scriptures

The vision recorded in Daniel, chapter ten, bears striking resemblance to the one in the passage under discussion. Daniel prepared himself for his vision by "mourning for three weeks"; eating "no rich food, no meat or wine"; and refraining from anointing himself with oil (vv. 2-3). While the location of John's vision was the island of Patmos, Daniel's was on the bank of the great Tigris River (v. 4). The subject of Daniel's vision was "clothed in linen, with a belt of gold from Uphaz around his waist. His body was like beryl, his face like lightning, his eyes like flaming torches, his arms and legs like the gleam of burnished bronze, and the sound of his words like the roar of a multitude" (vv. 5-6). Although the people around him did not see Daniel's vision, they trembled, "fled and hid themselves" (v. 7). At the end of the visions, both Daniel and John fell to the ground. In each vision, the subject then touched Daniel or John and told him not to be afraid. The similarity of the two visions makes it highly likely that John was dependent on his knowledge of the passage in Daniel in recounting his own vision. Indeed, his imagery seems dependent on numerous texts from the Hebrew scriptures:

> *clothed with a long robe* (Exod. 28:4, 31; 29:25; 39:27-28; Lev. 16:4; 1 Sam. 24:4-5; Ezek. 9:2; 26:16; Wis. Sol. 18:24)
> *with a golden sash across his chest* (Exod. 28:27; 1 Macc. 10:89)
> *head and hair ... white as white wool* (Lev. 19:32; Prov. 16:31; Dan. 7:9; 1 Enoch 46:1)
> *eyes ... like a flame of fire* (Isa. 11:3; 2 Enoch 1:5)
> *feet ... like burnished bronze* (Ezek. 1:7, 27; 8:2)
> *voice ... like the sound of many waters* (Ezek. 1:22-25; 43:2)
> *held seven stars* (Gen. 37:9; Deut. 4:19; Ps. 8:3; 147:4; 148:3; Isa. 14:13; Amos 5:8)

> *sharp, two-edged sword (from his mouth)* (Isa. 11:4; 49:2; 2 Esd. 13:10; 1 Enoch 62:2)
> *face ... like the sun shining with full force* (Exod. 34:29; Num. 6:25)

Clearly, the imagery John used to describe the vision he received of Christ was rooted in the Hebrew scriptures, which provided symbols understandable to those listening to the words of Revelation.

The Exaltation of Christ

The Book of Revelation has the most exalted Christology in the New Testament *[Essay: Christology of Revelation].* The present passage includes only the first of seven visions of Christ (5:6-7; 12:1-6; 14:1-5; 19:11-16; 22:12-17). In an artistic manner, John expresses the complete exaltation of Christ by including seven visions.

John's respect and worship for Christ are overwhelming. In the present chapter we have seen this in his use of Hebrew parallelism: the word of God and the testimony of Jesus Christ (vv. 2, 9). In synonymous parallelism, a feature of Hebrew poetry, the parallel items are to be seen as identical. We see this usage elsewhere in Revelation: "the kingdom of our Lord and of his Messiah" (11:15), "for their testimony to Jesus and for the word of God" (20:4), and "the throne of God and of the Lamb" (22:3). Thus, Revelation places Jesus Christ on par with God, which is particularly unusual for a Jewish writer steeped in the monotheism of the Hebrew tradition (but cf. Ford, 1975:12-18, who finds little Christology in the visionary sections of Revelation).

The overpowering Christology is also seen in the plethora of titles given to Christ in this first chapter of Revelation: "the faithful witness, the firstborn of the dead, and the ruler of the kings of the earth" (v. 5), "the Son of Man" (v. 13), "the first and the last" (v. 17), and "the living one" (v. 18). Moreover, the accolades for Jesus Christ continue throughout Revelation: "the holy one, the true one, who has the key of David" (3:7), "the Amen, the faithful and true witness, the origin of God's creation" (3:14), "the Lion of the tribe of Judah, the Root of David," the "Lamb" (5:5-6), the "Word of God" (19:13), the "King of kings and Lord of lords" (19:16); "the Alpha and the Omega" (22:13). Note that some of the designations for Christ are elsewhere attributed to God: "the living God" (Josh. 3:10; Ps. 42:2; 84:2; Hos. 1:10), "the first and the last" (Isa. 44:6; 48:12), the "voice like the sound of mighty waters" (Ezek. 43:2), the "face like the sun" (Num. 6:25), and "the alpha and the omega" (1:8). Taken together, these titles present the most exalted picture of Christ found in the Bible. Moreover, Beasley-Murray says that in Revelation "Christ is presented as the mediator of creation (3:14), as he is of redemption (ch. 5) and of the final kingdom (19:11-16)" (1974:24). Thus, Christ is central to the major activity of God in the world.

It is interesting to note that John speaks of "those who have been slaughtered for the word of God and for the testimony they had given" (6:9). Substituting "the testimony they had given" for "the testimony of Jesus Christ" (1:2, 9) indicates that the testimony of Christians who witness to their faith even to the point of death are part of the witness that Jesus Christ gave and that the witness of Christians is the continuation of the incarnation of Jesus Christ.

Beginnings of Trinitarianism

The trinitarianism of the church is based on passages like the one under study here. The combination of Hebrew monotheism and the identity of Jesus and God caused the doctrine to develop (John 5:19-24). Bauckham has argued persuasively that early Christian belief joined Jesus' identity with God's; thus they retained their commitment to monotheism (1998). The Jewish Christian writer of Revelation would have been fully committed to the monotheism of his heritage—God is one. An analysis of Revelation indicates that God and Jesus share the same identity as the Alpha and Omega, the first and the last (1:8, 17; 2:8; 21:6; 22:13). Early Christology was thus high Christology (Bauckham, 1998:53-54). In 19:10 Jesus and the Spirit are linked (cf. 22:17). The trinitarian doctrine is implicit and begins to become evident (see Ladd, 1972:94).

The relationship between God and Christ is further elaborated in the Fourth Gospel. Jesus is said to be with God in the beginning (1:1), to be the firstborn and only son of God (1:14; see also Heb. 1:5-6), to be the one who makes God known (1:18), to be sent by the Father (5:36-37; 6:44, 57), to speak only what the Father has told him (8:28; 12:49-50), and to be one with the Father (14:8-14; see also Col. 2:9; Tit. 2:13).

Although the Spirit or "wind" of God is present from the time of creation (Gen. 1:2; Isa. 40:13; 48:16), the Fourth Gospel unites the Holy Spirit with the Father and the Son (20:21-22) and comments on the relationship among the three. The Holy Spirit is sent by God and witnesses to what Christ taught (14:26; 15:26; 16:7-15). Furthermore, Jesus says the Holy Spirit instructs Christians what to say when they are brought before authorities to witness to their faith (Luke 12:11-12).

Although the Father, Jesus Christ, and the Holy Spirit are certainly recognized in the scriptures, it is more difficult to formulate a clear doctrine regarding their relationship. The earliest suggestions of something like the doctrine of the Trinity, viewed in retrospect, are found in plural references to God in the story of the creation and fall (Gen. 1:1, 26; 3:22), the story of the three visitors that appear to Abraham (Gen. 18:1-22), and the three-fold repetition of the word *Holy* in speaking of God (Isa. 6:3). In the New Testament, the three-fold designation of God is more explicit (Matt. 28:19; 1 Cor. 12:3-6). The relationship of God as the Father of Jesus Christ is stated by Paul and Peter (Rom. 15:6; 1 Cor. 1:3; Eph. 1:3; 1 Pet. 1:3). Christians are told that they share in that relationship through belief in Jesus Christ (John 17:20-23). These passages serve as a background for the symbolic way that the three-fold God is presented in the passage under study: *from him who is and who was and who is to come* (God the Father), *and from the seven spirits who are before his throne* (the Holy Spirit), *and from Jesus Christ, the faithful witness, the firstborn of the dead, and the ruler of the kings of the earth* (1:4).

THE TEXT IN THE LIFE OF THE CHURCH

A Spiritual Description of Christ

Although medieval artists interpreted the description of Christ in Revelation 1 literally, picturing Jesus with white hair, bronze feet, a sword protruding from his mouth, and so forth, most Christians believe that this picture of Christ is symbolic. To treat the passage literally would do damage to its communicative power. The description portrays symbolically some aspects of Christ's character, rather than literalistically some features of his appearance. These symbols tell us far more than descriptive words could communicate in a similar number of written lines. Hence, the vision of Christ is to be understood symbolically, not literally.

The artistic and symbolic nature of the text contributes significantly to the overall structure of this portion of Revelation. Elements in the symbolic description of the Christ in chapter 1 occur again in the introductions to each of the letters to the churches in chapters 2-3. The literary artistry of Revelation is evident as each letter begins with a description of Christ, many of them taken from the vision of chapter 1.

Virtually all scholars agree that some of Revelation is to be interpreted symbolically. The task is to decide what is symbolic and what is to be taken literally. In general, it seems best to let the passage itself communicate the meaning intended. Sometimes this is obvious. In contrast to the vision of Christ in chapter 1, it seems evident that the letters to the churches should be taken in the literal sense—although, ironically, some interpreters, who are otherwise quite literalistic, interpret the letters to the churches to refer to periods of church history. It seems better, though, to see the letters as what they plainly appear to be, letters written by John to seven churches in Asia. On the other hand, a great red dragon with seven heads and ten horns, a beast rising from the sea with two horns and a voice like a dragon, and a woman sitting on a scarlet beast with blasphemous names all seem to be symbolic entities despite some commentators' insistence that these refer to actual persons. Although in these several examples the literal or symbolic nature of the entities is fairly obvious, in many instances it is less clear. Therefore, one must constantly decide whether to take passages of Revelation literally or symbolically.

The Anabaptist View of Christ

For the most part, Anabaptists accepted and promoted a conception of the nature of Christ consistent with that of the orthodox Christian teaching reflected in the historic creeds of the Church (Klaassen, 1981:23-40). Indeed, Anabaptist writers quoted heavily from the first chapter of Revelation, assuming that the symbols used reflect a proper view of Christ—his divinity, his eternality, the authority of his word, and so forth.

Yet certain themes regarding Christ are emphasized among Anabaptists. First, Christ is seen as a support in persecution. Revelation describes the great tribulation that the church has endured and must endure again. Menno Simons uses the imagery found in this passage to strengthen the oppressed:

> Thus it is powerfully manifest that our faithful brothers and sisters in Christ Jesus, those dear companions in tribulation and in the kingdom and patience of Christ ..., love and fear the Lord their God so fervently that they would rather surrender, as a prey to the bloodthirsty, their good name and fame, money, property, flesh and blood, and all things that might appeal to human nature, than knowingly and willfully to speak a falsehood or act the hypocrite over against God's Word. (1956:527)

A second point from Revelation 1 that has been stressed by Anabaptists is the judgment of Christ. The reason that God gives strength to face tribulation is that God will judge those who do not stand strong. The symbol that has been used to portray this is that Christ's "eyes were like a flame of fire." In the Explanatory Notes, this symbol was interpreted as Christ's seeing all things for the purpose of judging and purifying. The Anabaptist martyrs repeatedly appealed to this image as motivation for keeping the faith in face of a suffering death (van Braght, 1950:527, 587, 850, 953).

Third, the emphasis on the second coming found in this passage was attractive to early Anabaptists. This hope undergirded their faith in times of persecution and was part of several early Anabaptist confessions of faith (van Braght, 1950:406, 808, 1108). One might think that the emphasis on judgment and persecution would mean that the Anabaptists viewed Revelation with an attitude of fear and dread. That does not seem to be the case. Instead, the emotion is more comfort and compassion, captured well in the following quotation from Dirk Philips, which appeals repeatedly to imagery from Revelation.

> But you, my dear brothers and fellow companions in the faith, in the kingdom and patience of Jesus Christ, Rev. 1:9, be of good courage, and do not turn aside or vacillate, for your deliverance is near, that you who now in manifold ways are tempted and must suffer much ... have whitened your clothes and have washed your robes in the blood of the Lamb, Rev. 7:14. Yes, you are marked on your forehead with the sign of the living God and therefore may not worship that ugly beast, nor receive his sign, that you, I say, will be delivered out of all sorrow and come to eternal gladness, where you will neither hunger nor thirst, and the Lamb which is in the middle of the throne will feed you and lead you to the living fountain of water, and God will dry every tear from your eyes. (1992:424)

The Lord's Day

A rather minor element of this passage focuses an issue that has been a major concern of the Christian church. Christians have usually worshiped on Sunday rather than on the Jewish Sabbath. The designation of Sunday as the Lord's day first came into use in Asia, based on the concept of the Emperor's day. Deissmann indicates that "the lord's" was used to describe what was the property of the Caesar—"the lord's treasury," "the lord's service," and "the lord's finances" (1901:217-18).

By the end of the first century, Christians called Sunday the Lord's day. The *Didache*, a handbook of church government dating from perhaps as early as the first century, tells Christians to "come together, break bread and hold eucharist on the Lord's day" (14.1). Pliny the Younger says that Christians "met regularly before dawn on a fixed day to chant verses alternately amongst themselves in honor of Christ as if to a god" (*Letter* 10.96). In the early second century, Ignatius affirmed that Christians were "no longer living for the Sabbath, but for the Lord's Day" (*Magn.* 9). Mileto, who lived in Sardis, wrote a treatise entitled *Concerning the Lord's Day*. The practice of Christians observing the first day of the week became so widespread that, in modern Greek, Sunday is called "the Lord's." Thus, the designation of Sunday as the Christian Sabbath was a gradual process that began in the first century and was later widely accepted.

There has been considerable debate on how the Lord's day should be celebrated. Should the Hebrew Sabbath laws be applied to the Christian Sabbath? At times, rather rigid restrictions have been placed on Sunday activity. The Bible does not give clear guidance regarding what activity is appropriate for Sunday or, indeed, whether or not it is appropriate to transfer the Sabbath laws to Sunday. At a most basic level, it has often been argued that the concept of Sabbath is healthy psychologically; rest is something that humans need. Furthermore, the New Testament does indicate that Christians gathered on Sunday (Acts 20:7; 1 Cor. 16:2). Therefore, the practice of Sunday worship seems appropriate. Beyond that, unless one incorporates Sabbath guidelines, the biblical record is silent regarding how Sunday should be observed.

Revelation 2:1–3:22

The Seven Letters

PREVIEW

Chapters 2–3 are clearly in epistle form—a series of seven letters to seven churches in the province of Asia (cf. Murphy, 1998:98). Yet there is no evidence that the seven letters were independently composed or circulated separately. Instead, they were constructed as a part of the overall literary structure of Revelation.

The characteristics of Christ in chapter 1 are repeated in the references to Christ as the source of the letters in chapters 2–3. Thus, this section relates the vision of chapter 1 to those of chapters 4–22. The exhortation to overcome, common in the letters, is repeated in chapters 19–22. Moreover, there may be a chiastic ordering of the letters: the first and last address the most apathetic of the churches; the second and sixth letters address the most excellent of the churches; and the middle three letters address those less extreme churches (Wall, 1991:69; see also Morris, 1969:57-58).

Each of the seven letters shares a similar internal structure. First, there is the opening command to write to the angel of the particular church. Although the meaning of the word *angel* is, of course, "messenger" (Matt. 11:10; Luke 9:52), and although the letter form might lead us to believe that reference is to the human messenger who delivers the letters, the word is only used of supernatural beings in Revelation (cf. Rowland, 1998:571). Second, Christ, the origin of the letter, is identified by a title, introduced by *the words of,* an unmistakable parallel to the prophetic "Thus says the LORD." Each title is uniquely applicable to the church addressed; most are taken from the description of Christ in chapter 1. The titles indicate an intimate relationship between Christ and the churches addressed. Third, several features about the life of the church are introduced by *I know* (cf. Exod. 3:7; Jer. 48:30; Hos. 5:3; Amos 5:12). These statements of the conditions of the church are detailed enough that the author must have been intimately acquainted with the churches addressed. Included may be either a commendation or a rebuke: there is unqualified praise for the poorest churches, Smyrna and Philadelphia, and unqualified censure for the wealthy churches in Sardis and Laodicea, while the other three receive a mixture of both (Pilgrim, 1999:164). Fourth, a promise to the conquerors includes threat or hope, depending on the conditions of the church. This promise is to prepare them for immediate persecution. The virtues of patience and endurance are advocated for Christians who win the victory over persecution at the possible cost of their lives. Moreover, the concept of conqueror is turned on its ear. Johns says it well: "What may *seem* to be victory through violent aggression and forceful subjugation, may actually be defeat. What may *seem* to be defeat ... may actually be victory" (1998:223). Fifth, each of the letters includes the words: *Let anyone who has an ear listen to what the Spirit is saying to the churches.* God's word in this era comes through the Holy Spirit (cf. John 16:7-13). This call to listen attentively is functionally equivalent to the prophetic "Hear the word of the LORD" (Isa. 1:10; 7:13; 28:14, 23; 48:1, 14; Jer. 2:4; 5:21; 6:18; 7:2; 10:1; 13:15; Hos. 4:1; 5:1; Amos 3:1, 13; 4:1; 5:1; 7:16; 8:4; Matt. 11:15; 13:9, 43; Mark 4:9, 23; Luke 8:8; 14:35).

These structural considerations make it clear that in chapters 2-3 the apocalyptic genre recedes in favor of the epistolary and the prophetic. The presence of the former is obvious from observing the letter format. Aune argues that the structure is also consistent with the prophetic oracle tradition, which includes praise, censure, demand for repentance, threat of judgment, and promise of salvation (1983:275-79). Johns emphasizes that, as prophetic oracles, the exhortations to the churches "goad the comfortable, to call for renewed commitment to the gospel, to call for resistance—a costly resistance that the author was convinced would cost them their lives" (1998:220).

In a quite different treatment of structure, Scofield argues that each of the churches represents one of seven dispensations in the history of the church (1945:1332). This scheme suffers from several fundamental problems. First, it is arbitrary to assign certain churches to specific ages, because every age has demonstrated the characteristics of each church. Any preacher who has delivered sermons on the letters to the churches has seen that each of the churches has a message to the contemporary world because in any age the characteristics of all of the churches are in evidence. Second, the historical facts in the letters make it clear that the primary reference is to the churches in Asia Minor in the first century (2:2, 10, 13, 19-20; 3:4, 8-9, 17). Why did John mention the churches by name and with such detail if he did not primarily mean the message to apply to them?

Hence, the evidence is against taking the churches to refer symbolically to ages of church history. There is no compelling reason to seek a meaning other than the literal one. The message is directed to the first-century churches in the province of Asia. Nevertheless, they also have more general application to the church in the time of the reader of Revelation in the same way that other epistles are commonly interpreted (see Entering the World of Revelation: Interpreting Revelation). Paul's first epistle to the Corinthians was written to the problems of schisms, incest, and improper practices at the Lord's Supper that were experienced in that church. Yet it also has universal application as readers experience similar problems in the church of their day. Thus, John's letters should be interpreted like other New Testament epistles rather than by seeking a symbolic meaning beyond their plain sense.

Finally, something should be said about the meaning of the word *church* (*ekklēsia*). In Revelation, the local church predominates over the universal [Glossary: Church]. The former refers to congregations or groups of congregations that met in homes in the province of Asia at the end of the first century rather than to all believers across the world. It may have roots in the ancient legal assembly (Ford, 1975:387). The message in chapters 2-3, addressed to these gathered Christians, is to patiently endure the imminent tribulation that is described in the remainder of Revelation.

OUTLINE

The Letter to Ephesus: Testing False Teaching 2:1-7
The Letter to Smyrna: Faithful in Tribulation, 2:8-11
The Letter to Pergamum: The Cost of Compromise, 2:12-17
The Letter to Thyatira: Toleration of Evil, 2:18-29
The Letter to Sardis: The Spiritually Dead, 3:1-6
The Letter to Philadelphia: An Open Door of Opportunity, 3:7-13
The Letter to Laodicea: The Poverty of Riches, 3:14-21

EXPLANATORY NOTES

The Letter to Ephesus: Testing False Teaching 2:1-7

Because it was the port of access for Asia, Ephesus was the largest commercial center in the province (Strabo, *Geog.* 14.1.24). A great center of religion, Ephesus' temple to the goddess Diana (Acts 19:35) was one of the seven wonders of the ancient world: at 425 feet long, 200 feet wide, and 60 feet high, it was four times the size of the Parthenon (Mounce, 1977:86). It had 127 pillars, 36 of which had relief carvings (Pliny, *Nat. Hist.* 36.21). Moreover, Ephesus was a center of emperor worship, devoting a precinct of Diana's temple to the worship of the goddess of Rome and the emperor Julius (*Dio's Roman History* 59.28.1). Temples to honor emperors Claudius and Nero and later Hadrian and Severus were constructed there, and a gigantic statue of Domitian is preserved today in the museum of Ephesus (Murphy, 1998:112). The local officials of the imperial government and religion in Ephesus were called Asiarchs (Acts 19:31). In addition, Ephesus was a center of pagan magic (Acts 19:13-19; for a complete discussion of power and magic in Ephesus, see Arnold, 1989). Finally, a large Jewish population practiced its religion in Ephesus. According to Josephus, Jews had been granted citizenship and freedom to observe traditional Jewish Sabbath practices (*Ant.* 12.125-128; 16.160, 162-173; *Against Apion* 2.39; see also Philo, *The Embassy to Gaius,* 315). Such protection was also desired by the Christian church.

So it is perhaps not surprising that Ephesus was the location of the most important Christian church in Asia, founded by Paul (Irenaeus, *Adv. Haer.* 3.3.4) along with Aquila and Priscilla in about A.D. 50 (Acts 18:18-22). Paul spent approximately three years there, more time than he was engaged evangelizing anywhere else (Acts 19:8-10; 20:31; cf. Aune, 1997:140). While in Ephesus, he was persecuted for converting persons from the worship of Diana (Acts 19). Later, Timothy was a minister—and perhaps the first bishop—in Ephesus (1 Tim. 1:3; Titus 1:5; Eusebius, *Eccl. Hist.* 3.4), and the Baptist, Apollos, and certain elders had connections with the city (Acts 18:18, 24, 26; 19:1-7; 20:17-38). Onesimus, possibly the runaway slave who became Paul's associate, was also bishop in Ephesus (Philem. 10; Col. 4:7; Ignatius, *Eph.* 1, 6). According to tradition, John the apostle was bishop of the church in Ephesus for many years; brought Mary, the mother of Jesus, to live and die in this city; wrote his gospel, Revelation, and his letters from here; and died and was buried in the city (Irenaeus, *Adv. Haer.* 3.3.4; Eusebius, *Eccl. Hist.* 3.1, 4, 39; 5.8,

24; Aune, 1997:140-41). Yet false teachings had gained a foothold in this church (Acts 20:17-38; Eph. 4:17-32; 5:10-20).

Title of Christ: Christ is designated as *the one who holds the seven stars in his right hand*. The accusative case indicates that he holds all the stars: he has a firm grip on them. Christ is aware of his churches and holds them in his care (see John 10:28). In spite of their tribulations, Christ strongly supports his people and helps them to be faithful.

Christ is also *the one who walks among the seven golden lamp-stands*. There is certainly an allusion here to God walking in Eden with the first couple after their disobedience (Gen. 3:8). Walking is most likely a euphemism for living (Ford, 1975:387): Christ lives among his earthly churches (Lev. 26:12; Dan. 3:25; John 8:12; 12:35; 1 John 2:11).

Conditions in the Church: The clause *I know your works* is repeated three times in the letters (3:1, 8, 15), and the idea of judging on the basis of works is developed in 20:12 (see TBC, Faith and Works). John commends the Ephesians for several activities and then condemns them for one.

First, the Ephesians are commended for their *toil*. The word used here (*kopos*) is related to the one in verse 3 translated "grown weary" (*kopiaō*). The root means "labor to the point of exhaustion" (1 Cor. 15:10; Gal. 4:11) and describes missionary activity (1 Cor. 15:58; 1 Thess. 2:9). The Ephesians are praised for their unrelenting labor even in the face of persecution (Acts 19:8-40). They are not "burned out" in their service of Christ (Walhout, 2000:39).

Second, the *patient endurance* of the Ephesians is commended. A dominant theme of the letters (1:9; 2:2, 3, 19; 3:10), *patient endurance* refers to the courage that accepts suffering and transforms it into glorious victory (2:13). It probably specifically refers to endurance in the face of persecution at the hands of the Nicolaitans (v. 6).

Third, the Ephesians are praised because they *tested those who claim to be apostles but are not, and have found them to be false*. Apostles, literally the "sent ones," were "messengers," "delegates," or "emissaries." There were both true and false apostles in the early church (see TBC, True and False Apostles), and the Ephesians were outstanding in their ability to tell the difference (Acts 20:28-31; 1 Cor. 14:29; 1 Tim. 1:3-7; 1 John 4:1). Ignatius commends the Ephesians because no false teaching could gain a hearing among them (*Eph.* 6.2; 9.1). This characteristic produced a church outstanding for doctrinal purity.

Nevertheless, John says to the Ephesians, *you have abandoned the love you had at first.* This statement may mean that their original enthusiasm for the faith is gone (Jer. 2:20). Ellul explains: "Perhaps, she has fallen from the spontaneity of the relationship with God, from the attempt to please this Lord in everything, from an attachment, always new, radiant, and renewed, from the power of novelty in work that characterizes love, and from the glow of passion" (1977:128). Glasson says they lack "fervent devotion" (1975:44), and Beale indicates that it is the zeal of the Ephesian church for witness in the world that has been lost (1999:230-31). Mulholland affirms: "It had lost the offensive of love and adopted the defensive of orthodoxy" (1990:95). The context, however, makes a second meaning possible: Christian fellowship and brotherly love are gone. Richard says they lack "the solidarity that holds the community together" (1995:56), a theme also found in the letter to Thyatira (2:19). Verse 2 of the Ephesian letter seems to be speaking of a conflict in the church. Dissension may have killed their mutual love (2 Thess. 3:14-15; 2 Tim. 2:24-26).

Whatever the sin, it requires repentance. Indeed, all of the churches except Smyrna and Philadelphia are called to repentance. Verse 5 outlines three steps for followers who have fallen away and wish to repent. First, they are to *remember.* The present tense carries the sense that they should keep on remembering. The penitent is to realize that things are not as they once were (Luke 15:17). The second step is to *repent,* or change one's mind, with the Greek aorist tense denoting a decisive event (1 Sam. 26:21; Luke 15:18). The third step is to *do the works you did at first.* In this case, the works refer to the restoration of love and fellowship.

After this condemnation, John commends the Ephesians for one thing: they *hate the works of the Nicolaitans.* This heresy, identical to the followers of Balaam and Jezebel, tolerated immorality *[Essay: Nicolaitans].* Here the Ephesians are commended for refusing to compromise. Hating evil is seen as an admirable trait. The message of Revelation is: No compromise with the world, regardless of persecution.

Promise to the Conqueror: Christ promises *I will come to you and remove your lampstand from its place, unless you repent.* Actually, the tense is present, making it very unlikely that the statement refers to the judgment of Christ at his second coming. Moreover, to make the second coming conditioned on the Ephesians' repentance would be strange. Therefore, it is more likely that the judgment is historical and indicates that Christ will remove the church (lampstand) at Ephesus or at least remove its witness.

More encouraging words are given to *the one who conquers,* or who remains faithful to God and perseveres to the end. Following Christ involves a struggle that is likened to warfare. Special reference may be intended to those who are martyred. In any case, the one who perseveres to the end will *eat from the tree of life that is in the paradise of God.* Eating from the tree of life is contrasted with consuming food offered to idols. Here the tree is used to represent eternal life (22:14) and refers to the restoration of the paradise that was lost in the beginning of time. Perhaps the tree of life also alludes to the "tree" on which Christ died, the cross of Calvary (Hemer, 1986:42-44).

The word *paradise* is from the Persian word meaning "park." In the Septuagint, it designates the Garden of Eden (Gen. 2:8, 15; 3:23-24) or more generally, a beautiful, stately garden (Eccl. 2:5; Isa. 1:30; Jer. 29:5; see also Xenephon, *Oeconomicus* 4.13). The early Christians saw paradise as an intermediate state between earth and heaven (Tertullian, *A Treatise on the Soul* 55; Origen, *On First Principles* 2.11.6). Later, it became equivalent to heaven—paradise regained. Revelation promises to the conqueror the restoration of the condition that was created in the beginning (21:10-22:4; see also Luke 23:43; 2 Cor. 12:2-4). Part of the paradise of the Garden of Eden was the tree of knowledge of good and evil (Gen. 2:9, 16, 17). Subsequently, the obedient were promised the tree of life (Prov. 3:18; 11:30; cf. 13:12; 15:4; 1 Enoch 24:3-5; 25:4-5). Paradise and the tree of life are used in Revelation to symbolize eternal life, which is promised to the one who conquers (Gen. 3:22).

The present participle indicates that eating of the tree of life in paradise is something that happens continuously. Through suffering persecution, the Christian wins the victory and is rewarded in paradise with God. Victory through suffering is a common theme in John's writings (12:11; John 16:33; 18:36-37) and is contrasted with Satan's conquering through violence (11:7; 13:7). The forces of Satan overcome through warfare and bloodshed, but the followers of Christ the Lamb conquer through suffering persecution and overcoming it.

The Letter to Smyrna: Faithful in Tribulation 2:8-11

Because of its land-locked harbor that stood at the end of a vital trade route, the commerce of Smyrna rivaled and later surpassed Ephesus. Smyrna was one of the few planned cities in the ancient world. Founded in 1200 B.C., it was destroyed by the Lydians in 600 B.C. and did not exist for 300-400 years. In the third century, Lysimachus rebuilt it, consolidating a number of smaller towns and following the plans of Alexander the Great. Therefore, Smyrna was a particularly beautiful city with an acropolis, the Pagos, which rose 500 feet high, was covered with temples and other buildings, and was called the crown of Smyrna.

Smyrna was a center of caesar worship and boasted of being the most loyal to Rome of all the Asian cities. Cicero called Smyrna "the most faithful of our allies" (Ramsay, 1904:276). The city had supported Rome in battles with the Mithridates, Carthaginians, and Seleucids (Ford, 1975:394). In 195 B.C., Smyrna was the first city to erect a temple to the goddess of Rome; and in the third decade of the first century, Smyrna competed for and won the privilege to build a temple to Tiberius, Livia, and the Senate because of her sustained loyalty to Rome (Tacitus, *Annals* 4.55-56). Each person was required to worship the emperor regularly, and certificates were at times issued for such worship.

As a result, great pressure, which at times broke out in persecution, was exerted on both Jews and Christians to show loyalty to Rome. Yet the Jewish population in Smyrna was largely exempt from caesar worship and hesitant to share this privilege with Christians; therefore, fights broke out between Christians and Jews. In A.D. 155, Polycarp was martyred here, with Jews participating in his persecution even though it took place on the Sabbath (*Mart.* 8–18; Eusebius, *Eccl. Hist.* 4.15). Christians seem to have been excluded from the Jewish synagogue and from Roman protection (Schüssler Fiorenza, 1991:55). Certainly, life for Christians in Smyrna was dangerous (see TLC, Faithful in Tribulation).

Little is known about the church in Smyrna. Perhaps it was founded during Paul's first visit to Ephesus (Acts 19:26). By the early second century, the church was organized under Bishop Polycarp with elders and deacons (Ignatius, *Eph.* 2, 5; Irenaeus, *Adv. Haer.* 3.3.4). Irenaeus implies that John was one of the apostles who consecrated Polycarp bishop of Smyrna (*Adv. Haer.* 3.3.4). Ignatius wrote four letters from here, and from Troas he wrote one letter to the church at Smyrna and one to Bishop Polycarp. Although this correspondence indicates that the church was divided by a docetic heresy (*Smyrn.* 2-5), John gives the church nothing but praise.

Title of Christ: The ascription *the first and the last* alludes to the words of the prophet Isaiah (44:6; 48:12) and to Smyrna's claim to be first in Asia. Calling Christ *the one who was dead and came to life* parallels the situation of the city of Smyrna, which was destroyed and did not exist for more than three hundred years before coming to life again in the third century B.C. (Ramsay, 1904:269-70; Hemer, 1986:61-64). The title for Christ reminds the Christians of Smyrna, in their times of persecution and possible martyrdom, that Christ went before them by suffering death on the cross and being resurrected to new life.

Conditions in the Church: Among the things that John knows about the church in Smyrna is that they suffered *affliction* and *poverty*. The word *affliction* (*thlipsis*) means "pressure" or "crushing weight." It resembles the persecution of God's people in Egyptian slavery (Exod. 3:9; 4:31) and their exile in Babylon (Deut. 4:25-31; 28:47-68). The word is also commonly used in the Septuagint for persecution (2 Kings 19:3-4; Obad. 13; Nah. 1:7; Zeph. 1:15). As a result of affliction, the Christians were reduced to poverty (*ptōkos*), a word denoting absolute destitution (Matt. 5:3; Luke 6:20; 2 Cor. 6:10; Jas. 2:5). It was difficult for Christians to earn a living in the hostile environment of Smyrna (1:9; 2:13; Heb. 10:34). Etymological connections between the name Smyrna and the word *myrrh,* a perfume used for embalming and symbolically connected with mourning, adds to the image of persecution (Hemer, 1986:58-59).

Persecution in this passage is called *slander* (*blasphēmia*), a word meaning defamation or abuse. Jews slandered Christians because they were rivals for exclusion from emperor worship (see TBC, The Jews). Yet John says the slander is from *those who say that they are Jews and are not, but are a synagogue of Satan.* This is a word play on the term that the Jews used to identify themselves—"the assembly of the Lord." Perhaps these are ethnic Jews who denounced or persecuted Christians to preserve exclusive Jewish identity as the people of God (Hemer, 1986:66-67). Perhaps the Jews of Asia also forfeited their identity through worshiping Zeus (Ford, 1975:393) or participating in pagan or imperial worship (Beale, 1999:287). If this was the case, they had turned from the worship of one God, the cardinal tenet of Judaism. Yet these may not be ethnic Jews but Jewish Christians or Christians who considered themselves to be Jews or practiced the Jewish law (Rowland, 1998:577). A specific historical situation may explain the conflict. Beginning under Vespasian, Jews were allowed to pay a specific Jewish tax (used to help build the Roman Capitoline temple, as reported by Dio Cassius 100 years later). This tax exempted them from imperial cult activities (Suet., *Domitian* 12.2). During Domitian's reign pressure mounted to require the tax from Jews who might be concealing their identity as well as nonethnic Jews who embraced Judaism (Bredin: 61). In this context the *slander* from non-Christian Jews against Jewish Christians would be, "they say they are Jews but are not." Apparently Jewish Christians in Smyrna had not paid the tax; thus the accusation is slander. John retorts by identifying the blasphemers as a "synagogue of Satan." For John, any collusion with Rome, the 'beast,' puts believers under Satan's sway (cf. Kraybill, 1996:170). Hemer says that there were two temptations for the churches in Asia: one from the pagan society that demanded sacrifice to the emperor and participation in religious aspects of the guilds; the other from Judaism, which probably expected "at least an implicit denial of the Lord" (1986:10). The latter was the temptation in Smyrna and Philadelphia.

John goes on to say that more suffering is in store for the Smyrnians at the hands of *the devil*. The word *devil* (*diabolos*) means "slanderer," "accuser," or "adversary." In the Old Testament, the devil is like a public prosecutor (Job 1–2; Zech. 3). In the New Testament, he is the source of all falsehood and deception. John warns that this devil will *throw some of you into prison*. In the ancient world, prisons were not primarily for punishment but were places where the prisoners were held until trial and sentencing. Yet it is clear that beatings did occur there (Acts 16:23; 2 Cor. 11:23). John says that this persecution is *that you be tested*. God is allowing Satan to test the faith of the Christians, providing the opportunity for them to show their commitment to suffer for Christ. Their affliction is to last only *for ten days*, a period of time common to scripture (Gen. 24:55; Jer. 42:7; Dan. 1:12-14; Acts 25:6). Time is often used symbolically in Revelation; here the reference is probably to the short duration of the persecution.

John has no criticism for the church in Smyrna.

Promise to the Conqueror: The one who is *faithful unto death* is promised a *crown of life*. The Smyrnians, who thought of themselves as the most faithful to Rome, are now called to be faithful to Christ. The reference here is particularly to those who die a martyr's death, like Bishop Polycarp, who later gave his life in the city of Smyrna (see TLC, Faithful in Tribulation). Yet those who are faithful to the point of being willing to die for the cause of Christ may also be in view. The crown of life image is likely from the athletic events held in the stadium of Smyrna. The winner was given a crown consisting of a wreath of leaves (1 Cor. 9:24-25; 2 Tim. 4:7-8; see also 1 Thess. 2:19; 2 Tim. 4:8; Jas. 1:12; 1 Pet. 5:4). Similarly, the conqueror is given a crown consisting of life—eternal life.

In addition to receiving a crown of life, the conqueror *will not be harmed by the second death*. In rabbinic literature, the first death refers to natural, physical death, and the second death to judgment by God. Although the phrase *second death,* which refers to punishment or annihilation, is used only in Revelation (20:6, 14; 21:8), the idea is found in the words of Jesus (Matt. 10:28; Luke 12:4-5). All persons must go through the first death, but the one who overcomes persecution will escape the second death.

The Letter to Pergamum: The Cost of Compromise 2:12-17

Pergamum, historically the most famous city in Asia (Pliny, *Nat. Hist.* 5.33), came into prominence as the capital of the Seleucid dynasty in 283 B.C. At the death of Attalus III in 133 B.C., it was given to Rome and became the capital of the province of Asia. Built on a high rocky hill covered with temples, Pergamum had the appearance of a royal city (Ramsay, 1904:281-84).

Indeed, Pergamum was a greater religious center than Ephesus or Smyrna. The sick from all over Asia came to sleep at a shrine to Aesclepius, the god of healing, hoping that the deity would appear in a dream or that one of the sacred snakes would touch and heal them. The serpent, symbol of the cult of Aesclepius, became associated with medical practice. Moreover, a college of medical priests was located here. Galen, the proverbial father of medicine and "the dominant authority in medicine throughout Europe during the Middle Ages and Renaissance" hailed from Pergamum, where he claimed to receive direct communication in dreams from Asclepios regarding medical matters (Worth 1999:30-31). It is no wonder that R. H. Charles called the city the "Lourdes of the Province of Asia" (1920:1.60). Pergamum was also a stronghold of emperor worship. Dedicated to Emperor Augustus and the goddess of Rome, the first temple to the imperial cult was built here (Tacitus, *Annals* 4.37), and Pergamum became the center of emperor worship for Asia. Finally, in 240 B.C., to commemorate Rome's victory over the Galatians, an altar to Zeus was constructed (Barclay, 1960:1.108).

Title of Christ: In this letter, Christ is called *the one who has the sharp two-edged sword* (see 1:16). This word for *sword* (*romphaia*) is consistently used by John in the figurative sense (see TBC, The Sword). It designates the sword coming from the mouth, the word of God (2:16; 19:15, 21). When John wishes to use *sword* literally, he employs the word *machaira* (6:4; 13:10, 14). In this passage *sword* alludes to the symbol of the power of Rome, which was invested in the governor of Asia (Rom. 13:3-4). Pergamum was the seat of the imperial power symbolized by the sword. The message is that Christ, not the Roman magistrate, has the sword of judgment and justice. The Christian who comes under persecution remembers that true power lies with Christ, not with the persecuting emperor. The sword will later be used in judgment against the Nicolaitans, who have compromised with the imperial cult (v. 16).

Conditions in the Church: The first characteristic that John knows about the church at Pergamum is that its members live *where Satan's throne is.* Among other things, sacrifice to the local pagan gods prevalent in Asia may be in mind here. Also, because the Roman judge's bench was located in Pergamum (Aune, 1997:182-83) and divine titles for the emperors like "Lord" and "Savior" have been found there (Hemer, 1986:86), the city would merit the name *Satan's throne.* Moreover, because the symbol of both Satan and the cult of Aesclepius, the Roman god of healing, is the serpent, *Satan's throne* would be an apt phrase to apply to Aesclepius's shrine. Finally, the altar to Zeus, which protruded from the hillside like a huge seat with a frieze interpreted in the first century to exalt Zeus and Domitian, would give the impression of being *Satan's throne* (Yarbro Collins, 1997:184). Perhaps all of these allusions were in the author's mind, so that the symbol connotes the worship of pagan gods.

John then addresses the Christians at Pergamum with words of commendation: *you did not deny your faith in me.* The aorist tense indicates that John probably had a specific situation in mind, perhaps *the days of Antipas my witness, my faithful one, who was killed among you.* Although we know very little about Antipas, Mounce documents the legend that he was "roasted in a brazen bull" (1977:97). The word *witness* (*martys*) may be used here for the first time with the sense of "martyr," which it later came to assume (*Mart.* 14). Although the text states that Antipas was killed in Pergamum for his faith, that he was singled out may indicate that he was the only one who lost his life at this time. Moreover, Vinson argues that the words *in the days of Antipas* suggest that his death was in the past. Indeed, he concludes that John remembers Christians who have died for their faith in the past, and he expects that more will soon die but is not clear that he believes persons are dying in his day (2001:12, 15-16). Yet in discussing the death of Polycarp in Smyrna in A.D. 155, Eusebius identifies Carpus, Papylus, and a woman, Agathonice, as martyrs in Pergamum (*Eccl. Hist.* 4.15). In any case, Antipas is an example for others tempted to deny the faith in the face of persecution. Those who, like Antipas, overcome this temptation will be given the titles *faithful* and *witness,* designators also used of both Antipas and Christ, and will participate with the latter in his reign. Indeed, the indication is that most of the saints in Pergamum are *holding fast.*

Nevertheless, John condemns the Christians of Pergamum because they *hold to the teaching of Balaam.* This calls to mind the one who for financial reward promised to bless Balak of Moab and curse Israel (Num. 22-24). Moreover, on the advice of Balaam, the women of Moab enticed the Israelites to have sexual relations with them and to worship their gods (Num. 25:1-5; 31:16). Caird says that Balaam became "a typical example of the mercenary spirit" and "the father of religious syncretism" (1966:39). Thus, tradition made Balaam a transgressor and a traitor (2 Pet. 2:15-16; Jude 11; *Pirke Aboth* 5.21-22; Josephus, *Ant.* 4.102-30). Sweet says that Balak and Balaam "prefigure the beasts, false king and false prophet" of Revelation 13 (1990:89).

John also speaks of *some who hold to the teaching of the Nicolaitans*. Hemer notes etymological connections between Balaam and Nicolaus (1986:89). Indeed, the followers of Balaam, Nicolaus, and Jezebel (vv. 20-23) probably represent the same gnostic heresy that perverted Paul's doctrine of Christian liberty to mean that one did not need to keep separate from pagan cultures (Sweet, 1990:32-33; Schüssler Fiorenza, 1991:56-57). Because pagan gods had no real existence, the Nicolaitans argued they could be recognized without harm. The presence of this heresy of tolerating evil indicates that the situation in Pergamum was the opposite of the one in Ephesus, where there was intolerance of all false teaching *[Essay: Nicolaitans]*.

The beliefs of this group *put a stumbling block before the people of Israel*. The word translated *stumbling block* includes the image of "baiting a trap." As Balaam set a trap for the men of Israel using the women of Moab, so the followers of Nicolaus and Jezebel caused the Christians of Pergamum and Thyatira to sin (vv. 20-23). Their first sin was to *eat food sacrificed to idols* (see TBC, Food Sacrificed to Idols). In Pergamum, meat previously dedicated to idols was sold in the marketplace. It may be, however, that what is referred to here is actually participating in the idolatrous cult by eating at feasts held in pagan temples. The second sin of the heretics in Pergamum was the *practice of fornication*. Just as Israelites were seduced into intercourse with Moabite women (Num. 25:1), sexual immorality was a concern in the early church (Matt. 5:32; Acts 15:20; 1 Cor. 5:1; 6:9-20; 1 Pet. 4:3-4; see also 2 Macc. 6:3-4) exacerbated by the availability of temple prostitutes. Yet the context of idolatry may favor a symbolic interpretation of fornication. The two metaphors used here are equivalent to "eating forbidden fruit" and "being in bed with the enemy" and thus refer to conforming to the dominant culture by worshiping false gods (R. H. Smith, 2000:18). The use of sexual immorality as a symbol of idolatry is certainly common in the Bible (Isa. 1:21; Ezek. 23:37-39). Indeed, the sins of idolatry and fornication are considered together in the New Testament (Acts 15:28-29; 1 Cor. 6-10). In Revelation, the idolatry is associated with the imperial cult (Pilgrim 1999:163). On behalf of those who have sinned, the Christians of

Pergamum are told: *Repent then,* or Christ will judge *with the sword of [his] mouth,* the word of God (Eph. 6:17; Heb. 4:12).

Promise to the Conqueror: John promises *hidden manna* to the one who does not compromise. This alludes to the manna given by God to the Israelites during their wilderness wandering (Exod. 16; *see also* Ps. 78:24-25). Aaron put some manna in a golden pot and placed it in the ark (Exod. 16:33-34; Heb. 9:4; *see* TBC on chs. 11, The Ark of the Covenant). It was thought that the manna would be miraculously preserved for the time of the Messiah when the gift of manna would be repeated (2 Bar. 29:8; 3 Bar. 6:11; Sib. Or. 7:149). Thus, to eat of the hidden manna was to enjoy the blessings of the Messianic age. John uses the symbol of manna to indicate admission to the messianic feast, the marriage supper of the Lamb (19:9). The food of this banquet is promised to those who have not eaten the food offered to idols.

The conqueror is also promised *a white stone.* A rabbinic tradition indicates that in the wilderness "precious stones and pearls" fell from heaven with the manna (Yoma 75a). The meaning of the image in Revelation is uncertain. First, it may allude to the law court, where jurors would pass a white stone for acquittal and a black one for condemnation. If so, then the meaning is that overcomers are acquitted before God. This symbol is consistent with the judgment theme of Revelation. Second, the image may be taken from the ancient theater, where a flat stone was used as ticket. The context of the messianic feast, which might require such a ticket, favors this interpretation. Third, the symbol may allude to the stones in Aaron's priestly robe (Exod. 28:30). Finding the context for both manna and stone in the story of Aaron favors this interpretation. If it is correct, the resultant meaning is that the conqueror, like the priest, has direct access to God. Fourth, stones were used as charms with magical power. That names like the one on the stone were also thought to have such power makes this view probable. The meaning, then, is that the one who overcomes persecution is given the power of the name of God. Fifth, colored stones were used to make calculations in the ancient world. If this is the correct allusion, the connotation is that the overcomer will be counted with the people of God. Sixth, stones were tickets given to the poor for use in exchange for food (Suetonius, *Augustus* 40, 42). This idea indicates that the conqueror will have all needs met by God. Seventh, a good day was noted with a white stone (Pliny, *Nat. Hist.* 7.40). This would signify that the overcomers are blessed on the Day of the Lord. As is obvious from this plethora of possible allusions, the symbol demonstrates very well the fluidity of the images in Revelation.

The meaning of the *new name* on the stone depends on the interpretation of the stone. Because one's name in the ancient world demonstrated character, the overcomer is given a name that matches the character of one who follows Christ. Indeed, name changes were quite common in the ancient world (Gen. 17:5; 32:28; Isa. 44:5; 62:2; 65:15). Emperor Octavian changed his name to Augustus, the name of a god. The new name here may be "Christ" (19:2). The idea would be that no one knows the name without experiencing the suffering that Christ endured. Alternatively, the name may refer to the holder of the stone, who has a new character as one who has refused to compromise with evil.

The Letter to Thyatira: Toleration of Evil 2:18-29

It is ironic that John wrote his longest letter to the most insignificant of the seven cities addressed. Thyatira owed its importance entirely to trade. Metzger says that archaeological inscriptions in the city "mention guilds of woolworkers, linen workers, makers of outer garments, dyers, leatherworkers, tanners, potters, bakers, slave dealers, and bronzesmiths" (1993:36; also Ramsay, 1904:324-26; cf. Aune, 1997:186). Specifically, there was a purple cloth factory, where Lydia, a native of Thyatira, most likely worked at her trade (Acts 16:14). In the town were many trade guilds that held common meals dedicated to pagan gods and to the imperial cult. Refusal to participate in the functions of the guilds made it difficult to find employment. The problem in Thyatira was whether or not the Christians could participate in such activities.

Thyatira was not a religious or political center. A local god Tyrimnus was identified with the Greek Apollo and pictured on coins holding the emperor's hand, and a fortune-telling shrine commemorated the Oriental prophetess Sanbethe. Yet there was no temple to the emperor, and very few temples at all. Indeed, there was no acropolis in the city (Ford, 1975:404).

Title of Christ: The title *the Son of God* occurs only here in Revelation, and yet God is designated the Father of Christ several times (1:6; 2:28; 3:5, 21; 14:1). The title here probably alludes to the quotation in verse 27 from a Psalm that also includes the words, "You are my son; today I have begotten you" (Ps. 2:7). John is reflecting a high view of Christ as one who has a unique relationship to God.

The other two titles are taken from 1:14. The *eyes like a flame of fire* indicate Christ's anger at what he knows about the Christians in Thyatira. The *feet ... like burnished bronze* may be a technical term from Thyatira's bronze-melting industry (see Hemer, 1986:111-

17). The referent is probably to God's just judgment. The stern impact of these titles sets the stage for verses 26-27.

Conditions in the Church: John begins with a word of commendation for the Christians of Thyatira because of their *love, faith, service, and patient endurance.* The majority have patiently endured and kept the faith by serving God in the pagan environment of Thyatira. Indeed, their *last works are greater than the first;* that is, the virtues of *love, faith, service, and patient endurance* have grown steadily. The situation is in contrast with Ephesus, whose zeal had waned or whose Christian love had grown cold.

Yet John does condemn the Christians in Thyatira because they *tolerate that woman Jezebel*, a reference to the wife of Ahab who led Israel into idolatry and apostasy (see TBC, The Prophetess Jezebel and Sexual Immorality). She became a symbol of all false prophetesses and here prefigures the great whore (Rev. 17-18). Some have argued that she was the wife of the bishop of Thyatira because a few manuscripts read, "your wife, Jezebel." Others think she was the fortune-teller, Sanbethe. There may be a connection between Jezebel and Montanism, a prophetic movement prominent in Asia Minor in the latter second century, which gave a major role to female prophets (Rowland, 1998:573). If Jezebel is an actual person here, it is best to assume her identity is unknown. Perhaps she was a prophetess in the gnostic group called the Nicolaitans (2:6, 15) *[Essay: The Nicolaitans]*. If so, she advocated accommodation with pagan practices by participating in trade guild meals. The situation seems to be worse than at Pergamum. There only a few were following her teachings; here a majority seems to be involved. The situation in Pergamum and Thyatira contrasts with Ephesus, where Christians consistently rejected false teachings.

After giving her *time to repent*, this Jezebel will be judged by *throwing her on a bed*. The prophetess, who seduced the Christians on a bed of fornication, is being thrown on a sickbed (see Exod. 21:18). Indeed, sickness was considered appropriate punishment for sin (1 Cor. 11:29-30). Rowland suggests that *those who commit adultery with her* are pagan comrades, and *her children* are church members who follow her (1998:581); Slater argues that the former are her sympathizers, and the latter are her disciples (1999:135). Her adulterers are punished with *great distress;* her children are threatened with death. This is in line with the Hebrew concept that children suffer for the sins of their parents (Exod. 34:7; Josh. 7; Dan. 6:24). The situation may anticipate the judgment in chapters 17-18 of the whore Babylon and her followers (Beale, 1999:262-63).

The false teachings are called *the deep things of Satan*. This phrase echoes the talk of the gnostics, whose name is from the Greek word for knowledge (*gnōsis*). The gnostics loved to speak of deep underlying meanings (cf. Aune, 1997:207-8). To them, to know the deep things of Satan would be to triumph over the evil one *[Gnosticism]*. Likely, the followers of Jezebel said that they could gain knowledge of the satanic world without harm if they did not sincerely believe in the false gods (Beale, 1999:265). Here the phrase is used sarcastically. Although they claim to know the deep meaning of reality, their knowledge is really satanic; true knowledge is found in Christ (Rom. 11:33; Col. 2:2-3; Eph. 3:18-19). Indeed, such esoteric knowledge is useless unless matched with consistent behavior (Rowland, 1998:581).

Promise to the Conqueror: To *everyone who conquers and continues to do [Christ's] works to the end* will be given *authority over the nations*. The Bible repeatedly promises that those who suffer with Christ will also rule with him (cf. Matt. 19:28; Luke 22:30; 1 Cor. 6:2; 2 Tim. 2:3, 11-13; Rev. 1:6). It is ironic that perhaps the weakest of seven churches is given authority. Premillennialists see this authority as promise of a temporal kingdom in this world; others see it as a spiritual kingdom that comes through Christ's suffering and death.

The conqueror will also *rule them with an iron rod, as when clay pots are shattered* (Num. 24:17; Ps. 2:9; Jer. 51:20; Rev. 12:5; 19:15-16). Although the image appears violent, the devastation is softened when it is realized that *rule* translates the verb "shepherd" (Matt. 2:6; John 21:16; Rev. 7:17). Thus, the nations are shattered, not by violence and destruction, but by the rod of Christ the shepherd.

Finally, the overcomer is given *the morning star* (22:16). There is likely an allusion here to Venus, the herald of the dawn, to whom the emperors of John's day built temples. Yet in Revelation the morning star is Christ, who on behalf of God breaks through the darkness of an evil, idolatrous world to bring the dawn of the eternal day (21:23; 22:5; see also Luke 1:78; John 1:4, 5, 9; 8:12; Test. Levi 18:3-14; Test. Judah 24:1-6; 1 QM 11.6-7). For participating in the triumph over the powers of evil, the Christian will shine forever like Christ, the morning star (Dan. 12:3; Rom. 13:12; 2 Pet. 1:19; 2 Esd. 7:97; CD 7.18).

The Letter to Sardis: The Spiritually Dead 3:1-6

Founded about 1200 B.C., Sardis was one of the oldest cities in Asia Minor. Seven hundred years before John wrote to Sardis, it was the capital of Lydia and one of the greatest cities in the world. Later, in the Persian period under Croesus, the wealth of Sardis was legendary. Mounce points out that "gold and silver coins were first struck" in Sardis (1977:109). It has been proverbial even to the present to say that a very wealthy person is "as rich as Croesus."

Originally located on a hill 1,500 feet high, Sardis was thought to be impregnable to attack. Yet the city was overcome twice when the troops of the Persian Cyrus and the Seleucid Antiochus, on separate occasions, crept up through the openings in the rock for surprise attacks. The city vanished for a time under the rule of Persia, later surrendered to Alexander, and still later was conquered by the Romans. Yet during the first century the city was wealthy and was known for luxurious but degenerate living.

Sardis was also a center of religion. Tiberius rebuilt the city after its destruction by an earthquake in A.D. 17 (Tacitus, *Annals* 2.47); and out of gratitude, Sardis built an unauthorized temple to Tiberius (Ford, 1975:410). The worship of Cybele, the nature goddess of Asian mystery religions, became identified in Sardis with the Greek Artemis; and this cult was syncretized with emperor worship. The Sardians also worshiped the Lydian version of the Greek god Zeus. Furthermore, Sardis had a large community of wealthy and influential but religiously compromising Jews (Jos., *Ant.* 16.171; see Ford, 1975:411-12).

Finally, the city of Sardis had a church composed of nominal, self-satisfied Christians. There was no evidence of persecution. The difficulty was spiritual apathy, which is often present when there is no persecution. The Christians of Sardis present a contrast with those in Smyrna, where physical death was all around, but they were spiritually alive. In Sardis, Christians gave the appearance of being alive, but they were spiritually dead.

Title of Christ: Christ is described in this letter as *him who has the seven spirits of God and the seven stars* (see comments on 1:4, 16). The former symbol alludes to the seven-fold operations of the spirit of God (Zech. 4:2,10; see also LXX on Isa. 11:2) and designates the Holy Spirit. The Sardians, who were spiritually dead, needed the Spirit to bring life. It was noted in chapter 1 that *seven stars* connote the spiritual counterparts of the seven churches. The presence of the symbol here emphasizes Christ's concern for his churches, even the ones that have fallen into complacency.

Conditions in the Church: John says to the church at Sardis: *you have a name of being alive, but you are dead.* Usually the name connotes character, but here it is used ironically. The Sardians have a reputation for life and vitality (see 2 Tim. 3:5), but their lack of Christian works bears witness that they are spiritually dead (Jas. 2:17, 26). The New Testament relates sin to death and ungodliness (Luke 15:24,32; Rom. 6:13; Eph. 2:1, 5; Col. 2:13; 1 Tim. 5:6). Beasley-Murray compares the church at Sardis to a corpse—beautiful, but dead (1974:95). Nothing good is said about this church.

John's exhortation to the church of Sardis is: *Wake up*. This command is particularly appropriate for a city that was supposedly impregnable to attack but had twice been overcome by trickery. The emphasis here is on avoiding evil and being prepared for the coming of Christ (Matt. 24:42-51; 25:13; 26:38, 41; Mark 13:33-37; 14:34, 37, 38; Luke 12:35-48; Acts 20:31; Rom. 13:11; 1 Cor. 16:13; 1 Thess. 5:2, 4, 6; 1 Pet. 5:8; 2 Pet. 3:10). The danger is that they are *on the point of death* and the little life they exhibit will be extinguished. Life can be rekindled through remembering, repenting, and obeying, but short of these, spiritual death is imminent. John employs understatement when he says: *I have not found your works perfect*. Since perfection means fullness or completion, their superficial faith cannot bring their works to fruition.

If the Sardians do not wake up, Christ *will come like a thief*. In the New Testament, the motif of Christ as thief emphasizes the unexpectedness of his coming (Matt. 24:42-44; Luke 12:39-40; 1 Thess. 5:2; 2 Pet. 3:10; see also Mark 13:35). The image is used elsewhere of the second coming of Christ. Yet since the coming here is conditional, based on whether or not the Christians wake up, it probably refers to temporal judgment that will come soon upon the church at Sardis.

John recognizes that there are *still a few persons in Sardis who have not soiled their clothes*. Clothes are used to refer to reputation or personality (Zech. 3:3-5). Soiled clothes are thus symbolic of the stain of compromising through participating in the materialistic commerce life of Sardis (Jas. 1:27; Thompson, 1998:80). Sardis seems worse off than the other churches where there are only a few who have fallen away. In Sardis there remains only a loyal remnant in a larger situation of degradation (Gen. 18:25; 1 Kings 14:13).

The reward of that remnant is that *they will walk with me, dressed in white*. This is reminiscent of Enoch who "walked with God; then he was no more, because God took him" (Gen. 5:22-24). The image of white clothing may allude to the custom of the emperor to wear white in military triumph (2 Macc. 11:8) or to the garb of guests celebrating at a banquet (Eccl. 9:8). In Revelation, white is worn by the conquerors who faithfully avoid the stain of idolatry and are with God in their resurrection bodies (6:11; 7:9, 13-14; 19:8; see also Ps. 104:2; Matt. 13:43; 2 Cor. 5:1-5; 1 Enoch 62:15-16; 2 Enoch 22:8; *Asc. Isa.* 4:16; *Herm. Sim.* 8:2-3; *Odes Sol.* 25:8; *Apoc. Peter* 5). The reason *they are worthy* to wear white robes is that, like their model Christ, they have suffered for their faithful testimony (Beale, 1999:276-77).

Promise to the Conqueror: Moreover, to the conquerors, John says: *I will not blot your name out of the book of life.* The book of life probably refers here to the register of the citizens of heaven (see TBC on ch. 20, The Books). Ancient cities kept registers of the names of their citizens, and names were erased due to death or acts of treason (Metzger, 1993:40). The statement means the spiritually dead may not be eternally dead. Christ will allow those who wake up from their spiritual lethargy to participate in his kingdom. Contrary to the popular present-day position of eternal security, the clear indication is that a name, once entered, can indeed be stricken from the book of life.

More positively, Christ tells the conquerors: *I will confess your name before my Father and before his angels.* This alludes to Jesus' words: "Everyone who acknowledges me before others, the Son of Man also will acknowledge before the angels of God" (Luke 12:8; see also Matt. 10:32-33; Mark 8:38; Luke 9:26). Christ seems to be saying that if we bear faithful witness for him in times of tribulation, he will witness to our faithfulness before God and the angels of heaven. In short, if we are true to Christ, he will be true to us.

The Letter to Philadelphia: An Open Door of Opportunity 3:7-13

Philadelphia was named for its founder Attalus Philadelphus, the King of Pergamum, who died in 138 B.C., and who was named Philadelphus because of his love for his brother. Located at the junction of roads to Mysia, Lydia, and Phrygia and at the borders of these provinces, the city was called the "gateway to the East" and was founded to serve as a missionary center for the spread of the Greek language and culture (Mounce, 1977:114-15). The success of its missionary endeavor is evidenced in Ramsay's indication that in Lydia the local language was completely replaced by Greek (1904:392). Later, Philadelphia became a great city—so much so that, by the fifth century A.D., Philadelphia was called "little Athens" (Mounce, 1977:115).

Philadelphia was the newest of the seven cities addressed. An area of frequent earthquakes (Strabo, *Geog.* 12.8.18; 13.4.10; Tacitus,

Annals 2.47; Pliny, *Nat. Hist.* 2.86), almost its entire population along with the city of Sardis was destroyed in 17 B.C. Emperor Tiberius was especially generous in the rebuilding the city, so it was renamed Neocaesarea. It was again renamed Philadelphia during the reign of Nero, only to be changed during Vespasian's reign to Flavia, the family name of the current emperors (Ramsay, 1904:397-98, 409-12). Evidently, the city was intensely loyal to Rome (Mounce, 1977:115).

There was also a weak but faithful Christian church in Philadelphia. Of all the churches, the one in Philadelphia receives the most praise and no criticism. To the mid-twentieth century there were about a thousand Christians in the city of Philadelphia (Barclay, 1960:1.160). Indeed, it remained Christian in a surrounding Muslim context until the fourteenth century.

Title of Christ: The titles given to Christ in this letter are not taken from the vision of Christ in chapter 1. Using *the holy one* to designate Christ indicates that he is different or separate from all else. Because God is commonly referred to in this way (Isa. 1:4; 5:19, 24; 12:6; 17:7; 29:19; 30:11, 12, 15; 37:23; 40:25; 43:15; Hab. 3:3; Rev. 4:8; 6:10), New Testament writers reveal their exalted Christology by using this divine title to speak of Christ (Mark 1:24; John 6:69). Indeed, "saints," the common designator of the faithful in Revelation, translates the same adjective *hagios* and the "holy" city is portrayed as the abode of those who are obedient to the end (Fekkes, 1994:147-48).

The phrase *the true one* can be understood in both a Greek and a Hebrew sense. The Greeks used *true* to mean real or genuine. Understood that way, the point is that Christ is no imitation but the real Messiah, the true revelation of God. The Hebrews understood *true* in the sense of faithfulness (Exod. 34:6; Ps. 146:6; Isa. 65:16). This adds the idea that Christ is faithful to God's covenant.

That Christ *has the key of David* symbolizes his authority. The source of this imagery is the story of Eliakim, who received the key of the steward of Hezekiah's household and with it exercised the authority of the king (Isa. 22:20-25; see also Job 12:14). Furthermore, the Levites and chief priests had custody of the temple key (1 Chron. 9:27). Similarly, Jews claimed, as the true people of God, to hold the key to David's house. Yet John says that this key and its authority belong to Jesus, the king of David, the divine Messiah (5:5; 22:16; cf. 9:1; 20:1). By adding that Christ is the one *who opens and no one will shut, who shuts and no one opens,* John communicates that it is Christ who controls entrance to the kingdom of God (Isa. 22:22;

26:2; 55:5; Matt. 16:19; 23:13; Acts 10).

Conditions in the Church: In this letter John says, *I know your works*, but does not enumerate them. It is likely that he has only praise because of the tone of the letter. Instead of listing the conditions of the church, he says, *Look, I have set before you an open door.* The imagery here points to a door of opportunity (John 10:7, 9; Acts 14:27; 1 Cor. 16:9; 2 Cor. 2:12; Col. 4:3). The allusion is to Philadelphia's mission to serve as a center for the spread of Greek culture; John calls the church, instead, to be a missionary center for the spread of Christianity (see Acts 14:27; 1 Cor. 16:9; 2 Cor. 2:12). Taken together with the imagery of the key of David, the door may particularly refer to a mission to Jews in Philadelphia (cf. Fekkes, 1994:132).

To carry out this missionary endeavor, John knows that the Philadelphians *have but little power*. The translation of the King James Version, "you have a little strength," is probably not the best rendering. The emphasis is on the fact that the church at Philadelphia is small and poor. Yet they have remained faithful. John says they *have kept my word and have not denied my name.* Their faithful testimony is evidence that they belong to Christ.

John again calls the Jews a *synagogue of Satan* (see Notes on 2:9 and TBC, The Jews). While John's words seem at times to border on anti-Semitism, it must be remembered that John and, indeed, most of the earliest Christians were of Jewish descent. Perhaps John is entitled to be more critical of persons from his own ethnicity than readers from other ethnic groups should be. Yet these may have been Jewish Christians who continued to worship in synagogues, to avail themselves of the exemption from persecution granted to Jews (Rowland, 1998:588; see Notes on 2:9). John goes on to say that Christ will make these Jews *come and bow down before your feet.* This has its roots in the Old Testament idea that the nations will come and fall down before Israel (see TBC, The Jews). If these are Jewish Christians, there is irony: the Christians who want to become Jews to escape persecution will fall down before the persecuted Christians. If these are ethnic Jews, John may be anticipating a time when the Jews will accept Christ as a group (Rom. 11:17-20, 23, 26).

John says that if the Philadelphians have *patient endurance,* Christ will keep them *from the hour of trial that is coming on the whole world.* The *hour of trial* is a common theme in the New Testament (Matt. 6:13; 24:21; Mark 13:5-14; 2 Thess. 2:1-12; Rev. 7:14). The phrase *the whole earth* would lead one to believe that eschatological tribulation is in mind. Yet its context here in a letter to a specific first-century church indicates that the reference is to immediate and local danger that faced churches like the one in Philadelphia. In either case, Christ says that they will be kept from trial. This may mean either that they will escape tribulation or that they will be kept faithful in it. The latter meaning seems more consistent with the dominant theme of patient endurance and faithfulness in trial (John 17:15; cf. 2 Pet. 2:9). Beale's words are helpful here: "Both saints and unbelievers experience the same trials, but for the former trials refine faith, whereas for the latter trials only harden" (1999:291).

Hence, there is a word here for both the unbelievers and the Christians. Unbelievers are reminded that the purpose of this hour of trial is *to test the inhabitants of the earth,* indicating that they will be tested rather than simply condemned *[Glossary: Inhabitants of the Earth].* Alternatively, Christians are cautioned to *hold fast to what you have, so that no one may seize your crown.* This is the victor's crown (*stephanos*) awarded to the athlete who won the race in the arena. Here, the image is of the competitor who is disqualified from the contest (Aune, 1997a:241). One forfeits the crown by not persevering to the end of the race or by failing to run the race according to the rules (1 Cor. 9:25; 2 Tim. 2:5).

Promise to the Conqueror: Christ promises that the conqueror will be *a pillar in the temple of my God.* This image speaks of humans comprising a living temple of God (Jer. 1:18; Gal. 2:9). An allusion to the pillar apostles—Peter, James, and John—may be intended (Gal. 2:9; Barker, 2000:108). In Revelation, the heavenly temple is the place where God resides (7:15; 11:19; 14:15; 15:5-8; 16:1). So the point is that the conqueror is assured a place with God; that the one who conquers *will never go out of it* indicates the security of this place in God's presence.

Three names that represent the conquerors are written on these pillars. First, there is *the name of my God.* The high priest wore on his head the words, "Holy to the LORD" (Exod. 28:36-38). To have God's name inscribed is to be the possession of God (Num. 6:27; 2 Cor. 3:3). Just as the followers of the beast wear his name on their foreheads (13:17), the followers of God bear the name of God (7:3; 14:1; 22:4). Second, there is *the name of the city of my God, the new Jerusalem.* In the Old Testament, Jerusalem is portrayed as the city of God (Isa. 2:1-4; Zech. 8:22; 14:16-17; see also Rev. 21:3). Yet just as Philadelphia received the name Neocaesarea, so the city of God receives the name, the New Jerusalem. To bear the name of the city means that the person is a citizen of the New Jerusalem (Gal. 4:26; Phil. 3:20; Heb. 11:10; 12:22; 13:14; see also Isa. 60:14).

The clause, *that comes down from my God out of heaven*, in Greek, denotes a permanent characteristic of the city rather than an act that occurs at the end of time. The new Jerusalem is continuously coming down from God. Third, there is *my own new name*. Here, Christ is given a new name, much like the city of Philadelphia received a new name twice in its history. That Christ's new name is written on the conquerors symbolically designates that the victory of Christ is shared by his followers as they are victorious in their lives.

The Letter to Laodicea: The Poverty of Riches 3:14-21

Because Laodicea was located on the great road to the East at a point where three roads met, it was a crossroads trade center. Laodicea was especially noted for three things. First, it was a banking and financial center (Cicero, *Letter to His Friends* 3.5.4; *Letter to Atticus* 5.15.2). The city was so wealthy that, after being destroyed by an earthquake in A.D. 60-61, it refused help from Rome and financed its own rebuilding (Tacitus, *Annals* 14.27; the wealth of Laodicea is documented in Hemer, 1986:192-96). Second, Laodicea was a center of textile manufacture. It was particularly famous for a black woolen cloth used in making clothing and carpets (Strabo, *Geog.* 12.8.16). Moreover, cheap outer garments were mass produced here. Third, Laodicea was a medical center and the location of a medical school (Strabo, *Geog.* 12.8.20). The region of Phrygia was particularly famous for an eye powder, called *tefra frigia* (Galen, *Hygiene* 6.12; Horace, *Satire* 1.30) although it is questionable whether Laodicea was located within that region (Aune, 1997a:260).

The church in Laodicea, along with those in Hierapolis and Colossae, may have been founded by the Colossian Epaphras (Col. 1:7; 2:1; 4:12-16) during Paul's ministry in Ephesus (Acts 19:10). Epaphras's name has been found on a marble block in Laodicea, and an inscription by a freed slave to owner Marcus Sestius Philemon has led some to believe that Philemon was from Laodicea (Ford, 1975:420). Paul may have visited Laodicea and written a letter from there that was lost, unless it is the epistle to the Ephesians (Col. 4:16). The *Apostolic Constitutions* say that Archippus was the first bishop of Laodicea (8.46; see also Col. 4:17). The church in Laodicea was prosperous and outwardly in excellent condition. It experienced no persecution. Yet its affluence masked its lack of true spirituality.

Title of Christ: The ascriptions to Christ do not come from chapter 1. First, Christ is called *the amen,* which in Hebrew denotes strong agreement but has connotations also of conclusion or fulfillment (2 Cor. 1:20-22). In Jesus Christ, salvation history is concluded, and the promises of God are fulfilled. The word *amen* can also bear the sense of reliable or trustworthy (John 1:51; 3:3, 5, 11). What follows makes the latter meaning more likely and actually defines it more clearly (see Aune, 1997:246 for the meaning "Master Workman," based on a Hebrew mistranslation). Second, Christ is *the faithful and true witness*. The parallelism of terms here requires that *true* be understood, not as the opposite of false, but in the sense of reliable or trustworthy (Isa. 65:16). This characteristic of Christ is particularly relevant for a letter to the unfaithful Laodiceans. Finally, Christ is *the origin of God's creation*. The word *origin (archē)* means not merely the temporal beginning, but the origin or source (Prov. 8:22-31; John 1:1-18; Col. 1:15-20). Caird elaborates John's message clearly when he says: "When God set in motion the creative process, what he intended to produce was Christ and [people] like Christ who would respond to him with utter faith and obedience. Wherever he is present, God's creative and recreative power is at work" (1966:57). Beale argues that John is speaking, not of the original creation, but of the new creation that Christ has inaugurated (1999:301).

Conditions in the Church: Christ knows that the Laodiceans *are neither cold nor hot*. The word *cold* is used of freezing water (Sir. 43:20; see also Matt. 10:42) and *hot* of boiling water (Acts 18:25). The Laodiceans probably thought that they could strike a middle road between worshiping God and the Roman emperor. Christ says he wishes that they *were either cold or hot*. Violent opposition would have been better than a lukewarm middle ground (2 Pet. 2:21-22). They can be contrasted with the Ephesians, who are holding to the faith in the face of violent opposition. Hemer points to a contrast of the Laodicean's lukewarmness with "the hot medicinal waters of Heirapolis and the cold pure [life-giving] waters of Colossae," concluding that the emphasis is on ineffectiveness instead of halfheartedness (1986:187-88). Perhaps both are in mind.

In any case, because the Laodiceans are lukewarm, Christ says: *I am about to spit you out of my mouth*. The idea that Christ will judge by vomiting them requires a rejection that goes beyond the meaning implied by the word *lukewarm*. Although lukewarm water may not be pleasant, it is not nauseating in and of itself. John probably derived this image from the mineral springs in Heirapolis. Laodicea's water supply came from the hot springs of Hierapolis six miles away through an aqueduct whose remains are still observable. Moreover, the water was *lukewarm* by the time it reached Laodicea and left a lime deposit, which adds to the nauseating image (see Scobie, 1993:623).

In addition to being lukewarm, the Laodiceans say, *I am rich,* not knowing that they *are wretched.* This criticism accords with other New Testament warnings against wealth (Luke 6:24; 12:16-21; Jas. 5:1-6). In contrast to the poor Christians in Smyrna (2:9), the Laodiceans were wealthy enough to rebuild their city without Rome's help (Tacitus, *Annals* 14.27). The Laodiceans were prosperous materially but their self-satisfied prosperity probably inhibited spiritual growth (1 Cor. 4:7-13). The image of material wealth anticipates the vision of the great whore.

Christ challenges the Laodiceans: *Buy from me gold refined by fire so that you may be rich; and white robes to clothe you and to keep the shame of your nakedness from being seen; and salve to anoint your eyes so that you may see.* There is much irony in this passage, which may have its roots in Ezekiel (16:8-13). First, the rich Laodiceans must come to God for true gold (Isa. 55:1; 1 Pet. 1:7). The spiritual wealth, symbolized in the gold of the New Jerusalem, is the answer to the Laodicean's poverty (21:18-21; see also Matt. 6:19-21). Second, the city famous for its garment production must come to God for spiritual clothing. In the ancient Hebrew world, nakedness was associated with shame (2 Sam. 10:4; Isa. 20:4; Ezek. 16:37-39; 23:26-29; Hos. 2:3, 9; Mic. 1:8, 11; Nah. 3:5; 2 Cor. 5:2-3), and clothing was a sign of honor (Gen. 41:42; Esther 6:6-11; Dan. 5:29). The *white robes* probably derive their meaning from the heavenly clothing found in apocalyptic literature (2 Esd. 2:39, 40, 45; 1 Enoch 62:15-16; 2 Enoch 22:8; 1 QS 4.6-8; see also Ps. 104:2; Eccl. 9:8) and are a common symbol in Revelation (4:4; 6:11; 7:9, 13, 14; see also 19:8, 14). Third, the city that produced the world-famous eye powder must come to Christ for eye salve (Ps. 146:8; Isa. 29:18; 35:5; 42:7, 16, 18-20; John 9:39). Medicine may heal physical eye infirmities, but Christ heals the spiritual blindness that inhibits perception of the holiness of God and the reality of sin.

Due to the shortcomings of the Laodiceans, Christ says: *I reprove and discipline those whom I love* (Job 5:17; Ps. 94:12; Prov. 3:11-12; 5:12-13; 23:13-14; 27:6; 29:15, 17; Sir. 30:1). The discipline here is most likely the tribulation that will be described later. Even such harsh persecution is not punitive but corrective (1 Cor. 11:32). Walhout says it well: "Severe discipline from the Lord is precisely the evidence that he loves us" (2000:55). The motivation of discipline is love; the purpose repentance.

Indeed, repentance is even open to a group like the Laodiceans. Christ says to them: *Listen! I am standing at the door knocking.* The verb emphasizes the permanent nature of Christ's offer of repentance. Whoever answers the knock will eat with Christ (Isa. 25:6;

Matt. 8:11; 22:1-14; 26:29; Luke 12:35-38; 22:28-30). The word *eat (deipnon)* refers to the main meal of the day, which in the ancient Jewish culture included fellowship among relatives and loved ones (1 Enoch 62:14-16). The imagery here may reflect the eucharistic meal that Jesus shared with his followers in the upper room (John 13:2-20; 1 Cor. 11:20-26). It seems much better in this context, however, to find the symbolism in the marriage supper of the Lamb, the intimate eschatological meal that Christ will share with those who overcome tribulation (Rev. 19:9).

Promise to the Conqueror: To the person who repents and overcomes persecution, Christ promises *a place with me on my throne, just as I myself conquered and sat down with my Father on his throne* (Matt. 19:28; Luke 22:28-30; John 16:33; 1 Cor. 6:2; 2 Tim. 2:11-12). The conqueror follows Christ in his victory over evil (1 Pet. 3:18-22). Indeed, Caird says, "The conqueror is one in whom Christ wins afresh his own victory, which is also God's victory" (1966:58). As Christians face persecution and even death, the cross of Christ is proclaimed again and again. It should be noted that Christ is already enthroned (Acts 2:34; Rom. 8:34; Eph. 1:20; Col. 3:1; Heb. 1:3; 8:1; 12:2; 1 Pet. 3:18-22; Rev. 22:1-3); his kingdom is already in progress but awaits its consummation at his second coming (1 Cor. 15:25; Heb. 10:12-13). This promise should instill confidence in those facing tribulation.

THE TEXT IN BIBLICAL CONTEXT

True and False Apostles

It is clear from the New Testament that the gift of apostleship was given to many in the church. Originally, the term was limited to the twelve who followed Jesus (Matt. 10:2; Mark 6:30; Luke 6:13; 9:10; 17:5; 22:14; 24:10; Acts 1:2, 25, 26; 1 Pet. 1:1; 2 Pet. 1:1). Then it was expanded to include others who had seen Jesus in the flesh, like his brother James (1 Cor. 9:5; 15:7; Gal. 1:19). Finally, *apostle* was expanded to include all who had not seen Christ in the flesh but had encountered him spiritually, like Paul, and had been transformed by that experience of the risen Christ (Luke 11:49; Acts 14:14; Rom. 1:1, 5; 11:13; 16:7; 1 Cor. 1:1; 4:9; 9:1-2; 15:9; 2 Cor. 1:1; 8:23; 11:5; 12:11; Gal. 1:1, 17; 2:8; Eph. 1:1; Phil. 2:25; Col. 1:1; 1 Thess. 2:7; 1 Tim. 1:1; 2:7; 2 Tim. 1:1, 11; Tit. 1:1). It is likely that John uses the term in the latter sense, although it only occurs three times in Revelation (2:2; 18:20; 21:14) and nowhere else in writings attributed to him.

In addition to these genuine apostles, there were also false apostles in the church who are likened to wolves among the flock of God (Matt. 7:15-20; Acts 20:29-30; 2 Cor. 11:13-15; see also Did. 11). To determine which apostles are true and which false, Christians are to test their fruits (Matt. 7:16), the goodness of their words (1 Cor. 14:29; 2 Thess. 5:21), and their "signs and wonders and mighty works" (2 Cor. 12:12). The Ephesians have effectively rooted out the false apostles from their midst (Acts 20:28; 1 John 4:1), but in the process they have abandoned their first affections. For this, they are called to repent.

The Road to Repentance

Martens includes an excellent discussion of repentance, *shub,* which in Hebrew means simply to "turn" or to "turn around." In the convenantal sense, it refers to turning affections from one partner or turning to a stronger relationship with another. Martens says that the Old Testament uses repentance to speak of returning to one from whom one had once turned away, which he then illustrates in the relation between God and Israel (*BCBC,* 1986, on Jer. 3:21-4:2).

Jesus' parable of the prodigal son (Luke 15:11-32) provides an excellent illustration of the pattern for repentance outlined in Revelation—remember, repent, and do (2:5). The son received his inheritance from his father and squandered it in sinful living. When his resources ran out and he found himself tending pigs to avoid starvation, "he came to himself." First, he *remembered* "how many of my father's hired hands have bread enough and to spare." Second, he *returned* to his father and repented: "Father, I have sinned against heaven and before you; I am no longer worthy to be called your son." Finally, he *did* what was required of him: "he set off and went to his father." As a result, he was restored to relationship with the father. The father testifies to this restoration: "This son of mine was dead and is alive again; he was lost and is found!" The story illustrates a pattern for all persons who are estranged from their heavenly father.

The Jews

Many Christians today see a special place for the Jewish people, viewing the founding of the state of Israel as a fulfillment of prophecy. Specifically, many dispensationalists find in the modern Jewish state a fulfillment of the prophecy that Israel would triumph over her enemies (Isa. 49:24-26) and be restored to her land (Ezek. 36:22-38) [*Essay: Dispensationalism*]. Wagner captures this mindset well: "Each modern war won by Israel (1948, 1956, 1967, 1973, 1982)

provided sufficient evidence to me that Israel was becoming a significant military power and might play the predicted role in the prelude
to Armageddon" (1995:25).

Other Christians see no place for the Jews as part of the New
Covenant. They argue that the promise to Abraham was contingent
on obedience and that breaking a covenant through disobedience
causes one to be cut off from the people of God (Gen. 17:9-14; Ezek.
33:23-29). Because Abraham's descendants broke the covenant, they
were exiled from the land God had promised them. Their ultimate disobedience was rejection of the Messiah that God sent in the person of
Jesus Christ. As a result of the disobedience of Israel, the promise
made originally to Abraham was given to Christians, who are obedient to the covenant (Wagner, 1995:63-64). This supersessionalist
interpretation sees little reason to believe Jews have priority over
other nations in God's plan for the world in the present age (see TBC
on ch. 7, The Symbolic Israel). They believe that the promise that the
nations would acknowledge Israel (Isa. 2:3; 45:14; 49:23; 55:5;
60:14; Ezek. 37:27-28; Zech. 8:22-23) is ironically fulfilled in Israel
acknowledging the followers of Christ (3:9).

Perhaps a medial position should be struck between the dispensationalists, who privilege the Jews with an idealistic future focusing on
their restoration, and the supersessionalists, who believe that the
promises made to Abraham are now fulfilled in the Christian church.
Van Buren questions the radical discontinuity between Jews and
Christians assumed by both of the two extreme positions, affirming
that "Second Temple Judaism gave birth to twins: Christianity and
Rabbinic Judaism" (1998:105). He recognizes that the first Christians
were all Jews and that their identity as Christians and their understanding of the death and resurrection of their Lord was rooted in
their reading of the Old Testament (Luke 24:13-35; 1 Cor. 15:3-5),
especially the story of the binding of Isaac (Gen. 22:1-19). Therefore,
the Old Testament is the Bible of both Jews and Christians; the story
of Abraham is not finished for either the Jews or the church. Jews lay
claim to Abraham through physical descent from Jacob/Israel; the
church, through spiritual union with Christ. Although van Buren
believes that the church is the product of how the earliest Christians
read the Old Testament, the Old Testament is not preliminary to New
Testament's "definitive fulfillment," but the two are continuous
(1998:129).

The Old Testament is the church's story too: it can be read both
messianically and christologically. Nevertheless, as the church developed and became more Gentile, it tended to read itself into the

Scriptures and the Jews out—a supersessionalist anti-Jewish tendency. Van Buren supports the movement to return the Jews to their rightful place: "The church that was against the people Israel for nineteen centuries is in fact giving way to a church that is for the people Israel" (1998:104). Any interpretation that makes a radical distinction between the Jews and the church, whether to privilege the Jewish state as a fulfillment of the eschatological Israel or to give priority to the church as the ultimate fulfillment of promises made to Israel, is probably a distortion. Both Jews and Christians are God's people. Jones reminds his readers that Revelation is set in the context of the "Jewish Bible" with repeated reference to the Old Testament "to show that we can be Christian only in the context of the Jewish tradition" (1998:xiv). Therefore, while it is difficult to see why the founding of the secular Jewish state of Israel is of central importance to God's plan for ultimate redemption of the world, it must also be remembered that God did not forget Israel when the church was included as heir to the promises through Christ.

Further, the modern state of Israel is not to be equated either with the Israel of Romans 9-11 or Judaism. Judaism-in-diaspora has existed for more centuries than has a national entity—the first and second temple periods and the modern state of Israel. In speaking of God's continuing relation with Israel, Romans 9-11 does not mention *land or nation per se.*

The Sword

In the letter to Pergamum, Christ is said to be the one who has the sharp two-edged sword. John distinguishes between the military and metaphorical meaning of the sword by consistently using two different words. On the one hand, John uses the normal word, *machaira,* only in the literal sense. The rider on the red horse is given a *machaira* to take peace from the earth (6:4). John says that the person who kills with the *machaira* will be killed by it (13:10). The beast from the earth, the Roman Empire, is said to have been wounded by a *machaira* (13:14). On the other hand, John uses *romphaia*, the word occurring in this passage, consistently in the metaphorical sense of the sword coming from the mouth of Christ, the word of God. Christ will make war against them with the *romphaia* of his mouth (2:16), and with this *romphaia* from his mouth that he will "strike down the nations" (19:15). We are told that "the kings of the earth with their armies" are killed with the *romphaia* that comes from the mouth of Christ (19:19-21).

Elsewhere in the New Testament, *romphaia* is used in a similar metaphorical sense. Luke indicates that a *romphaia* "will pierce your own soul," referring to the revealing of inner thoughts (2:35). Although the word is not used, Paul speaks of Jesus annihilating the "lawless one … with the breath of his mouth" (2 Thess. 2:8).

As would be expected, in the New Testament, *machaira* occurs in a literal sense; yet it is always used by the enemies of God's people (Luke 21:24; Acts 12:2; 16:27; Heb. 11:34-37), except when the literal usage is to communicate the message of peace. An example of the latter is when Peter or one of Jesus' followers uses his *machaira* to cut off the ear of the high priest's slave; in that case, Jesus rebukes him and says, "all who take the sword will perish by the sword" (Matt. 26:51-52; Mark 14:47; Luke 22:49-51; John 18:10-11). Moreover, *machaira* is also used metaphorically (Eph. 6:17; Heb. 4:12), similar to *romphia* in Revelation; and in other occurrences, it is not certain whether the literal or metaphorical meaning is in mind (Matt. 10:34; Luke 22:36; Rom. 8:35; 13:4).

In the Septuagint *romphaia* first occurs as the sword that the angel is given to guard the Garden of Eden after humankind is driven out (Gen. 3:24). Although *romphaia* is used with violent connotations (Ps. 22:20; Amos 9:4), it sometimes occurs to make the point that the enemies of God use the sword, but Israel wins by the power of God (1 Sam. 17:45, 47; 21:8-9). Furthermore, Isaiah uses *machaira* in a metaphorical sense (Isa. 49:2) and mentions that the weapon used against enemies is God's word (Isa. 11:4).

Although the sword is used in a military sense in the Old Testament, the New Testament uses it only metaphorically or to describe the actions of unbelievers or the forces of evil. John makes this distinction clear by employing a different word to distinguish the literal and military use of the sword from its metaphorical and spiritual one. In short, there is no evidence in the New Testament to indicate that Christians should ever use the sword in a literal act of violence.

Food Sacrificed to Idols

The group in the Asian churches called the Nicolaitans, the followers of Balaam, and the followers of Jezebel were accused of eating food offered to idols, which may refer either to meat sold in the marketplace that had been previously sacrificed to idols or to eating meat at feasts held in pagan temples. The former was nearly impossible to avoid, short of vegetarianism; the latter was avoidable, but the temptation was great in a pagan culture. Eating food sacrificed to idols is rooted in the Balaam story, where Moabite women enticed Israelites to consume such meat (Num. 25:1-5), and was practiced in the New

Testament church (Acts 15:20; 1 Cor. 8-10). It probably grew out of the gnostic idea that the body was of no significance and that therefore the use of the body in this way did not defile the soul and was certainly not worth dying for (Schüssler Fiorenza, 1991:56-57). The gnostics even argued that moderate participation involved greater discipline than total abstinence [Essay: Gnosticism].

The message of the New Testament regarding eating food sacrificed to idols is somewhat ambiguous. Paul is clear that there is nothing wrong with the practice unless it is offensive to the conscience of others (Rom. 14:13-23; 1 Cor. 8:4-13; 9:22; 10:19-33), but the Council of Jerusalem advocated avoidance of such meat (Acts 15:20, 29) and John unequivocally condemns the practice (Rev. 2:14, 20). It may be that Paul was speaking of the simple practice of eating food that had been sacrificed, that the Council of Jerusalem was emphasizing unity in the church through the avoidance of anything Gentile Christians might do to offend their Jewish brothers and sisters, but that John saw the practice in Asia as an act of communion with the idol.

In any case, the issue of food sacrificed to idols exemplifies the complexity of participating in worldly practices (see Thompson, 1998:87-88 on compromise and separatism). Although Christians today do not eat food sacrificed to idols, there are many practices that have the potential for compromise. The New Testament counsels Christians to live a holy life. There are some practices that defile and others that do not compromise Christian character. Even in the case of the latter, the Christian must be careful not to destroy the unity of the church by offending the conscience of one who finds the practices objectionable.

The Prophetess Jezebel and Sexual Immorality

The major criticism John has for the church in Thyatira is that they tolerate Jezebel. This image has its roots in the story of King Ahab, whose wife Jezebel led Israel into apostasy (1 Kings 16:31; 18:4, 13; 19:1-2; 21:5-26; 2 Kings 9:4-10, 30-37). There is some evidence of female prophets in the biblical record: Miriam (Exod. 15:20), Deborah (Judg. 4:4), Huldah (2 Kings 22:14), Anna (Luke 2:36), and the daughters of Philip (Acts 21:9). Yet Jezebel is a false prophet who advocated pagan practices like participating in the guild meals in Thyatira, which included eating food sacrificed to idols and sexual immorality (2 Kings 9:22). These trade guild banquets probably turned into sex orgies. The New Testament clearly teaches against such accommodation (Matt 6:24; Rom. 12:2).

Sexual immorality appears to be used metaphorically here; prostitution is used symbolically for apostasy (Exod. 34:15-16; Deut. 31:16; Jer. 3:6, 20; Ezek. 16:15-63; Hos. 2:1-15; 4:12; 9:1; Matt. 16:4; Mark 8:38). The only occurrence of the word *adultery* in Revelation is in 2:22, where the followers of the prophetess Jezebel are called to repent of spiritual whoredom. Thus, Revelation uses the image of sexual immorality to speak of accommodation with the idolatrous materialism of Rome.

Faith and Works

In modern popular Christianity, the emphasis is on the grace of God, on faith rather than works as the basis for our salvation. Yet Revelation emphasizes that the ones who receive God's salvation are those who overcome through patient endurance (1:9; 2:2-3, 19; 3:10; 13:10; 14:12). Indeed, in Revelation, repentance and obedience are highlighted over belief and faith. The verb *believe* does not occur in Revelation; the noun *faith* always means faithfulness (2:13, 19) or the content of belief (14:12); the adjective *faithful* means loyalty or endurance, not belief (1:5; 3:14; 19:11); and the word *grace* occurs only as a greeting and benediction (1:4; 22:21). Indeed, repentance is central to the message of Revelation, which is an appropriate corrective to the modern de-emphasis on good works. According to Beasley-Murray, "works are the criterion of the genuineness of faith" (1974:73).

How do we harmonize John's emphasis on salvation through overcoming and patient endurance in persecution with Paul's emphasis on faith alone as the basis for salvation? Several sound New Testament principles need to be kept in mind. Good works and righteousness are evidences of repentance and guarantees of eternal life (Luke 3:7-14; 10:25-28; 1 John 3:9-12). Therefore, salvation, while not achieved by works, is demonstrated and maintained in what is done (Jas. 2:24; Rev. 2:5). Indeed, the New Testament teaches that Christians conquer and receive God's salvation through following Christ's example of being steadfast in trial (2 Thess. 3:1-5; Heb. 2:18; 5:7-10; 12:1-2; see TBC on ch. 12, Conqueror and Conquerors). Perhaps the Bible's teaching on faith and works can be summed up in this way: although salvation comes initially from God through faith, Christians validate and preserve their faith through enduring persecution as Christ did.

THE TEXT IN THE LIFE OF THE CHURCH

The Cost of Conformity

In the mid-nineteenth century, there was division among the Brethren in Christ, or the River Brethren as they were then known. Matthias Brinser had joined the River Brethren at an early age and became a bishop much in demand for his enthusiastic preaching. Brinser and his followers decided to build a small meetinghouse near Middletown, Pennsylvania. The quite unpretentious building was probably constructed to accommodate the zealous attenders at worship, whose number had outgrown the capacities of the members' houses. Yet the meetinghouse stirred up opposition from other River Brethren communities in Lancaster County.

On a day of torrential rain, a council meeting was convened to address the issue. The debate continued until two o'clock in the morning, when Brinser left, stating that he wanted to avoid being cut off by swollen streams. His opposition interpreted his leaving to be an act of defiance. So a statement was formulated and unanimously accepted asking Brinser and his followers to cease construction of the meetinghouse. They refused, and the Brethren proceeded to excommunicate Brinser. In response, Brinser's followers formed the group known as the United Zion's Children and later as the United Zion Church.

During the course of the debate, it seems that another bishop of the River Brethren had counseled Brinser that if he would be patient, he would get his meetinghouse. A more conservative group heard about or sensed this liberal sentiment in the leadership, and they too severed their relationship to the parent body, forming the group called the Yorkers. The delay in taking action against Brinser and his followers had also probably contributed to this conservative schism.

The irony of the schisms is that by this time union meetinghouses had already been erected by the Brethren in Christ in Hummelstown, Pennsylvania, and in two locations in Ohio. Yet the two schisms that resulted from the controversy have remained to the present. There have been attempts to reunite the groups by the River Brethren in 1876 and by the United Zion's Children in 1917 and some cooperation between them in the early twentieth century. A request for forgiveness was formulated in 1955 by the Brethren in Christ and finally ratified in 1967. The forgiveness was formally accepted the next year by the United Zion Church; yet only informal fellowship has existed between the two groups (Wittlinger, 1978:133-40).

John tells the church in Ephesus, which had rooted out false teachers to the point that they had either lost their original enthusiasm for the faith or lost the original love that they had for each other, that they needed to repent and restore the spirit of fellowship. It is certainly important for a church to resist false teachings and practices. Indeed, John was quite critical of the spirit of compromise in Pergamum and the toleration of evil at Thyatira. Ironically, the greatest sin of the Ephesians grew out of their greatest strength. The ability to identify and eradicate false doctrine and practice is a great asset for a church, but when that strength turns into a spirit that quenches enthusiasm or drives out brotherly love, repentance is in order.

Faithful in Tribulation

Eusebius (*Eccl. Hist.* 4.14-15) describes the tradition that grew up around the martyrdom of Polycarp, a bishop in the church in Smyrna. Polycarp had been taught by apostles who had actually seen Christ and instructed others carefully in the true doctrine that he had learned from them. His witness to the truth in both Asia and Rome served as an important counterweight to heretical teachings that grew up in these early years of the church.

Polycarp set forth his personal faith and understanding of the truth in his epistle to the Philippians (Irenaeus, *Adv. Haer.* 3.3.4), and this instruction led others to stand firm in the face of persecution and martyrdom. An epistle was written from Polycarp's churches to the churches in Pontus that spoke of other martyrs and their strength in the face of death. It included descriptions of grotesque lacerations that revealed inner body organs and exposure to wild beasts.

Because of these persecutions, Polycarp was encouraged to go to his farm not far from the city. As he prayed constantly, he received a vision from God predicting that he would die in flames. Although he was convinced to go away to another part of the country, his persecutors found him by torturing two boys to force them to reveal his whereabouts. He met his persecutors "with a bright and gentle countenance," prepared a table for them, and begged them that he might pray undisturbed for one hour. Some of those who heard him pray repented.

After he finished praying, Polycarp was conducted on the Sabbath to the city, where he met Herod and Herod's father, Nicetes. They took him into their vehicle and asked him: "But what harm is it to say, 'Lord Caesar,' and to offer sacrifice, and to be saved?" After a time of silence, Polycarp responded, "I am not going to do what you counsel me." They threw him from the vehicle with such violence that he sprained his thigh.

He was taken to the stadium where he and many believers present heard a voice from heaven say: "Be strong, Polycarp, and play the man." Then the proconsul encouraged him: "Swear by the genius of Caesar, repent, say: 'Away with the Atheists.'" Nevertheless, Polycarp beckoned to the crowd, looked up to heaven, and said, "Away with the Atheists," but refused to "[s]wear by the genius of Caesar." When the proconsul threatened to throw him to the wild beasts, Polycarp replied, "Call for them." When the proconsul threatened him with fire, Polycarp said: "You threaten with the fire that burns for a time, and is quickly quenched, for you do not know the fire which awaits the wicked in the judgment to come and in everlasting punishment. But why are you waiting? Come, do what you will." When the multitude in the stadium were told, "Polycarp has confessed that he is a Christian," the residents of Smyrna cried out that a lion should be loosed upon him. When they were told that the animal games in the stadium had been completed, they yelled together that he should be burned alive. The crowd then gathered wood and straw for this purpose. Finally, Polycarp asked that he not be secured with spikes so that he could bear the fire without restraint.

After the fire was kindled, a miracle occurred. The flames surrounded Polycarp like an oven so that they did not so much consume but purified him like gold or silver in a furnace. Moreover, a fragrant odor like incense was given off. When it was realized that the fire would not consume him, the executioner plunged a sword into him, and so much blood gushed out that the fire was extinguished. The death of Polycarp inspired others in Smyrna to undergo death for the cause of Christ.

The message of Christ to the church at Smyrna has been a comfort to all who undergo persecution at all times in history. Christ says: "Be faithful unto death, and I will give you the crown of life." This promise was a source of strength to Christians of early centuries who experienced persecution for refusing to give the emperor and the Roman government worship that should only be given to God, to Anabaptists of the sixteenth century who experienced persecution for carrying the tenets of the Reformation to their logical conclusion, and to those today who experience oppression for the stand they take for the cause of Christ.

The Toleration of Evil

My father liked to tell me how hard it was to get a job during the Great Depression of the 1930s. He was a machinist, and there were several applicants for every factory job. He was able to find employment in a small factory as an automatic screw machine operator, but even when he got the job, the situation was not secure. There were always unemployed persons waiting to take his job. Since it was not a union shop, if he did not perform, he would be fired and someone else would take his place.

Converted to Christ in his late twenties by a Brethren in Christ bishop, my father came to believe that war was against the teachings of Christ. As a new Christian, he was probably more zealous than others for his new beliefs. Although he was too old to be drafted during World War II, my father took a verbal stand against war, which made him unpopular with the other workers and with his boss. One day the situation came to a climax when he was presented with the blueprint to make a piece on his machine that he knew would be part of a warhead. Should he compromise and do the job? After all, he was not pulling the trigger. Could he not do this job without damaging his personal nonresistant position? Because of his faith and his commitment to resist war, he refused to run the job, even though he knew that meant he might lose the employment that was so important to him. His refusal angered his fellow workers and the factory management, who were deeply committed to the popular war effort. For a few days my parents were not sure whether or not he would be fired. Finally, the management decided, because the labor supply was so short by this time, that he could remain on the job. Yet for the duration of the war, he received no increase in salary when others in the factory benefited from raises.

In Thyatira, to work at a trade, one needed to join the guilds that were known for their immorality. To refuse meant to risk losing one's means of making a living. Nevertheless, when the choice is between making a living and being faithful to Christ, the message of Revelation is that we choose the latter. For my father's refusal to compromise, he suffered only ridicule and modest financial loss. Many persons have risked their lives by refusing to compromise. The message of the letter to Thyatira is that the one who overcomes through suffering is given authority over the nations.

The Spiritually Dead

North America at the beginning of the twenty-first century is nominally Christian. The overwhelming majority believe in God and accept that Jesus Christ is the son of God, and a sizable minority attend church every week. Yet very few are influenced by these beliefs in the way they live their lives. The time is characterized by persons who designate themselves to be Christians but seem to be such in name only. Christ tells the dead Christians in Sardis to repent and obey. If they do, they will be rewarded with resurrection bodies, because Christ will confess their names before God. The antidote for nominal Christianity, repentance and obedience, are themes that have dominated Anabaptist teaching. They should be restated in each generation.

Just this week, an announcement appeared regarding the divorce of a prominent Baptist minister of a church with more than 13,000 members from his wife of forty-four years. About five years before, the minister had said that if the divorce became final, he would resign as pastor. Yet after the divorce, he resolved to remain pastor at First Baptist. Surprisingly, he affirmed that the failure of his marriage made him a better pastor and that its pain gave validity to his ministry. What is glaringly absent from this account is any mention of repentance. Divorce is seen, not as something to be turned away from in sorrow and resolve, but as a benefit and basis for growth. The example of the church at Sardis is that religious practice without repentance and obedience marks the spiritually dead church.

A Door of Opportunity

Rhoda Lee, a new convert, became committed to foreign missions under the preaching of the World's Gospel Union. As a result, she prepared a paper on the subject, which she read on the last day of the 1894 General Conference of the Brethren in Christ Church (see Wittlinger, 1978:179-84 for a summary of the beginnings of foreign missions in the Brethren in Christ Church). The paper stressed "the needs of the heathen, the gospel call to evangelize, and some of the responses which Christians had made to that call" (179). The conclusion of the paper gave the following appeal:

> O may I dare to hope that a missionary fund may be started and a systematic method of foreign work be organized, and that each of us will practice economy and self-denial to swell the fund? "The King's business requires haste," and may God speed the time when I "hear a rumor from the Lord that an ambassador is sent among the heathen." (179)

The conference took no action, tabling the matter indefinitely, but later the same day, Jacob Stauffer placed five dollars for foreign missions on the table in front of the conference. Lee then passed a hat to take an offering for foreign missions, and Jacob Eshleman put another five dollar bill into the hat. The result was an offering of thirty-five dollars and the following action: "On motion it was decided to organize a Foreign Mission Fund and appoint a treasurer. Brother Jacob E. Stauffer, of Newton, Harvey County, Kansas, was duly appointed" (180).

A few months later, Lee's article in the denominational paper spoke out fervently:

> We hear a great deal of talk about obedience now, but most of us simmer it down to obeying a few church rules and keeping the ordinances, with an occasional testimony in meeting, and expect a blessing; while the greater commands, to "go into all the world and preach the Gospel," to be self-denying and to "give freely," pass, for the most part, unheeded. (quoted in Wittlinger 1978)

Lee continued to call for commitment to missions in a subsequent article in the church paper and another paper prepared for the General Conference the next year.

The result was that a foreign missions board was appointed. By 1896 the fund had increased to $419.60 and an appeal for workers was issued. At the Conference of 1897, Samuel Zook chided the members because no one had applied for missionary service. Frances Davidson, who had heard the appeal of Lee, asked for release from her teaching position to be available for missions. Jesse Engle and his wife subsequently applied for service. Finally, on December 26, 1897, a team of five missionaries arrived in Capetown, South Africa. In August 1899, in a stream in what is now Zimbabwe, Jesse Engle baptized the first converts of Brethren in Christ missions.

The church in Philadelphia had little power but a great opportunity for mission to the people of Asia Minor. If they seized the opportunity, Christ promised that they would be "a pillar in the temple of my God." Rhoda Lee was a person with little power in the days when women's voices in the church usually went unheard. Yet what she did stands as a memorial to her faithfulness.

The Poverty of Riches

The church of Laodicea has been compared more often with the church today in North America than any of the other seven churches. This may be due to the dispensational contention that the present is the Laodicean age. Although characteristics of each of the seven churches are evident in the church of today, it must be noted that trust in wealth is certainly a problem in the church in our day.

Nevertheless, wealth has been recognized as a problem in other ages as well. In the sixteenth century, Dirk Philips spoke these words to the people of his day:

Oh! to what have these poor miserable people come, that they want to place themselves above God the Lord? What will they do? Where will they abide when the Lord visits them?...

They are just as the congregation at Laodicea which spoke, "I am rich, and I have prospered, and I need nothing; and did not know that she was wretched, pitiable, poor, blind, and naked," Rev. 3:17. Therefore she was counseled of the Lord that she should buy gold from him that had been refined through fire so that she might become rich, and that she should put on white garments so that the shame of her nakedness would not be revealed and she should anoint her eyes with salve so that she might see, Rev. 3:[18]. (1992:302-3)

Certainly, the church of our age in North America is no less guilty of self-sufficiency. To a society that controls most of the world's wealth, Christ says *buy from me gold refined by fire so that you may be rich*. To a people that spends millions on the fashion industry, Christ offers *white robes to clothe you and to keep the shame of your nakedness from being seen*. To a culture that prolongs life through the remarkable achievements of modern medicine, Christ offers *salve to anoint your eyes that you may see*.

So the messages of the letters to the seven churches are each relevant to Christians of all ages. Christ warns the Ephesians to beware of false teachers but not to permit their zeal against heresy to allow them to lose their original enthusiasm or compassion. Christ prepares the Smyrnians to face the persecutions that will come upon them from the forces of Satan if they remain faithful to Christ. Christ admonishes the Christians in Pergamum to avoid the worldliness of participating in practices that compromise their faith and involve them in immorality. Christ tells his followers in Thyatira that, although they are to have compassion on sinners, they should not participate in their sins and should keep themselves separate from activities that would lead them into evil and immorality. Christ exhorts the Sardians to awake from their spiritual lethargy and claim the power of the Holy Spirit in the life of their church. Christ encourages the Philadelphians to seize the opportunity they have to spread his gospel to the pagans around them. Christ rebukes the Laodiceans for their trust in wealth and self-sufficiency and for failing to allow him to transform them and make them pure and holy.

All of these messages are relevant for the church today. Faithfulness to God in a materialistic and violent culture might require the follower of Christ to give a graduated tithe to the Lord's work (Sider, 1997:193-96), to place a ceiling on personal income so that income tax would not be used for military hardware, to live in community to demonstrate peace and simplicity in a worldly environment, or to volunteer time to the peaceful and altruistic ministries of the Mennonite Central Committee.

Revelation 4:1-11

The Vision of God

PREVIEW

After three introductory chapters in the epistolary format, the apocalyptic visions themselves begin in chapter 4. Chapters 4 and 5 record two closely related visions of heaven: chapter 4 deals with God and creation, and chapter 5 with Christ and redemption. Bauckham appeals to this juxtaposition as evidence for his thesis on the identity of Christ and God (1998:62).

The sources for these visions are Ezekiel 1, Isaiah 6, and Daniel 7. The two visions are related to chapters 1-3 in the sense that the struggles of individual churches are vitally related to the heavenly events of creation and redemption. Eller ties the themes of Revelation 1-3 together with those of chapters 4-5: the individual churches' struggles are linked with the spiritual struggle against evil directed by the throne of God and accomplished by the death of Christ (1974:71). Moreover, the visions of chapters 4 and 5 are connected to what follows because they present the scroll whose seals will be broken to introduce the visions of chapter 6, and they include many allusions and ideas that will be picked up in chapters 12-13 and 21-22.

The overall purpose of chapters 4 and 5 is to begin the visions of Revelation with a strong statement that God is in control even through all the defiant warfare and chaos. Christ is carrying out God's salvation in the cosmos. It can be said without exaggeration that this statement is the theological center of the book of Revelation, affirmed again and again by outbursts of praise and worship. This central focus should not be lost in the concern to interpret the fantastic symbols of the visions.

A word about the nature of the symbolic visions portrayed in this and succeeding chapters might be helpful. The descriptions of God are indirect; no detail is given about what God looks like (Ezek. 1:4-28; 1 Enoch 14:8-25). Instead, God is spoken of in terms of light (Ps. 104:2; 1 Tim. 6:16). Boring says that the theological meaning, which is more important than the actual description, is: "The universe is not a chaos nor is it ruled by blind fate. Someone is in charge" (1989:103).

It has become popular to interpret chapter 4 as a vision of the raptured church. This dispensational argument is that the church will not experience the tribulations of Revelation because she will be raptured out of the world before they begin. Since tribulations begin in chapter 6, the rapture is said to occur in verse 1, "Come up here," before the visions of assurance in chapters 4-5. Commentators in favor of this view note that the word *church* occurs twenty times in chapters 1-3 and not again until 22:16. But it would be expected that the word would be used in letters to the churches. Moreover, although *church* does not occur in 4:1–22:15, the word *saints* does (see Notes on 5:9). Dispensationalists further assert that the twenty-four elders may refer to the raptured church in heaven. Nevertheless, as will be shown later, it is best not to limit the twenty-four elders in this way. Even premillenialist Ladd admits that there is no reference to the rapture of the church at this point in Revelation (1972:72).

In addition to Ladd's observation, there are several compelling arguments against the idea that the church will be raptured before the tribulation. First, because Revelation is addressed to churches or to the complete church, it is unlikely that the church will escape the tribulation spoken of in the book. That would make Revelation irrelevant to the persons addressed. Second, God's people are pictured as on earth during the tribulation (2:22-25; 6:9-11; 7:1-8, 14; 8:3-4; 12:17; 14:12-13; 16:15; 17:6; 18:4). Hence, there is little reason in this passage to believe that the saints will be raptured before the tribulation described in Revelation [Essay: Dispensationalism].

OUTLINE

The Throne, 4:1-2
The One Seated on the Throne, 4:3-6a
A Response of Praise, 4:6b-11

EXPLANATORY NOTES

The Throne 4:1-2

The visionary section is introduced with the formula *after this I looked,* which seems to be used in Revelation to give importance to what follows (7:1, 9; 15:5; 18:1; 19:1). In each occurrence, the phrase no doubt indicates the order of events in the vision, not in chronological history (Beale, 1999:316-17). Here it also refers back to the opening vision of 1:12-20, alerting the reader that John is again entering a visionary state.

What John first observed was *there in heaven a door stood open!* This is not the door of the kingdom (3:8) nor the door of the heart (3:20) but the door of revelation (Acts 7:56; 2 Cor. 12:2; 1 Enoch 14:15; Test. Levi 5:1). The allusion is to a door in the firmament between heaven and earth (Gen. 1:7-8). John is admitted through this door into heaven, a place considered to be above the physical world. In Revelation, heaven is described as God's dwelling place (3:12), a setting of conflict (12:7), and a place destined for destruction (21:1). Here the meaning is that the dwelling place of God is revealed to John.

John was then addressed by *the first voice,* most likely the same one that introduced the vision in 1:10-12 and will again introduce the next vision in 5:2. The identity of the voice is uncertain and unimportant, merely serving stylistically to link the various visions together. In any case, the voice is said to be *like a trumpet.* The image of the trumpet is commonly used to set the stage for a divine message (1 Cor. 14:8; 1 Thess. 4:16; Heb. 12:19) and has its roots in the Sinai story (Exod. 19:16,19; 20:18).

The voice said, *Come up here, and I will show you what must take place after this.* John was summoned into heaven to receive a divine message. The Sinai motif continues as John's summons to heaven parallels Moses' invitation to go up the mountain to receive the Law from God (Exod. 19:24). John was told that he would receive a message of something that must take place; most likely, the event is inevitable because it is the will of God.

John then says, *I was in the spirit.* Despite the rendering of the NRSV, the definite article does not occur, and it is therefore unlikely that the Holy Spirit is in mind. As in 1:10, the phrase is probably used to indicate that John is going into a visionary trance. Chapters 2 and 3 have formed an interlude between these two visions. The repetition of the clause reminds the reader again that the visionary state is reentered.

This vision is primarily about *one seated on the throne*. The throne is a dominant image occurring in seventeen of the twenty-two chapters of Revelation (see TBC, The Throne) and symbolizing divine authority (Ford, 1975:70-71). The emperor often appeared publicly on a throne (Koester, 2001:75). The image raises a question that is central to Revelation: Who really rules? The answer is: God and the Lamb (Murphy, 1998:171-72). An important message of Revelation is that the authority of this world rests, not in its rulers, but in God who sits on the throne and in those who conquer persecution and thus share God's throne (3:21). Yet neither the throne nor the one on the throne is described in detail; instead, the latter is portrayed in the brilliance of precious stones.

The One Seated on the Throne 4:3-6a

The first of the stones used in connection with God and the throne is the *jasper,* a word used for a variety of quartz found in various colors, but rarely white (Ford, 1975:335). Here it is a transparent, crystal-like stone—a reflector of bright light, perhaps the equivalent of a diamond (see also 21:11; Ezek. 1:22). Thus, it symbolizes the brightness of God's purity.

The second stone used to describe the divine presence is the *carnelian,* a fiery red stone. This color probably connotes the wrath of God, since red is frequently tied to God's anger (Exod. 24:17; Ezek. 1:27). The third stone in the description is mentioned in the words *around the throne is a rainbow that looks like an emerald.* Instead of the normal prism of colors, the rainbow is emerald green. Metzger says: "Green is soothing, like meadows and distant forests" (1993:49). The imagery seems to be that the light of the jasper and carnelian is refracted into a rainbow that has a green cast. This symbol has its roots in the story of Noah, who saw a rainbow after the flood indicating that God would never again destroy the world with water (Gen. 9:8-17). Thus, this symbol refers to the mercy of God, with the rainbow of God's mercy encircling the wrath and purity of God. This states in symbolic language the truth that God's pure essence includes both wrath and mercy; to eliminate either in the interests of consistency distorts God's nature. Paradoxically, they coexist in the divine character.

Around the throne of God, John sees *twenty-four thrones, and seated on the thrones are twenty-four elders.* Unlike the modern Western world where youth is valued, the Jewish and Christian communities had an exalted place for elders. Indeed, seventy elders accompanied Moses, Aaron, and Aaron's priest-sons up the mountain to receive the ten commandments (Murphy, 1998:182). Although the symbolic number twenty-four is found in no other apocalyptic literature, the twenty-four elders occur frequently in Revelation (4:4, 10; 5:8, 14; 7:11, 13; 11:16; 14:3; 19:4). The symbol is likely related to the council of elders that ruled social organizations in the ancient world (Yarbro Collins, 1991:35). In the vision, the twenty-four elders sing praises to God *[Glossary: Twenty-four Elders]*.

There is much speculation regarding the identity of the twenty-four elders. Some have argued that the symbolism focuses on the heavenly council or order of angels that surround God (1 Kings 22:19; Job 1:6; 2:1; Ps. 89:7; Isa. 6:1-2; 24:21-23). Under this conception, their function would be to serve in the heavenly court scene by representing those faithful in persecution before God. Others have found the roots of the imagery in the twenty-four star gods of the Babylonian pantheon, twelve to the north and twelve to the south of the zodiac (Diodorus of Sicily 2.31.4). The meaning, then, is that forces of the cosmos are worshiping the true God (Job 9:7; 38:7). A related idea is that there is an allusion to the twenty-four officers surrounding emperor Domitian (Boring, 1989:103), imparting the meaning that God is really to be worshiped rather than the emperor. Still others locate the imagery in the twenty-four courses of priests that led worship in the temple (1 Chron. 24:1-19). The symbol would then allude to heavenly worship.

While each of these possibilities has its own persuasiveness, the most likely referents for the twenty-four elders are the twelve patriarchs (or the twelve sons of Jacob who gave their names to the twelve tribes of Israel) and the twelve apostles of Jesus. The Bible uses the designator *elder* for both Jewish (Luke 7:3; 9:22) and Christian (Acts 14:23; Tit. 1:5; Jas. 5:14; 1 Pet. 5:1-2; 3 John 1) leaders (Koester, 2001:74). The names of these twenty-four persons are inscribed on the gates and foundations of the holy city, Jerusalem (21:12-14). Together they represent the entire people of God—from the old and new covenants. They are the spiritual counterparts in heaven of the total people of God on earth.

Dispensationalist Christians believe that the twenty-four elders are the raptured church, who are now in the presence of God, thus avoiding the tribulations to be poured out on the earth. The King James Version rendering of Revelation 5:9 implies this when the twenty-four elders say that Christ "redeemed us." This would mean that the twenty-four elders are the redeemed of the earth. Yet the correct reading of the original, preserved by the modern versions, is that God "ransomed humans," clearly setting the twenty-four elders apart from the redeemed. Indeed, the twenty-four elders are contrasted with the redeemed elsewhere in Revelation (7:9-11; 14:3; 19:1-4). As the angels are the spiritual counterparts of the churches in Asia, the twenty-four elders are heavenly counterparts of God's people from the old and new covenants.

Three characteristics of the twenty-four elders are mentioned. First, they are *seated on the thrones* and hence participate with God in ruling and serving (1:6; 3:21; 5:10; 20:6; 22:5). Second, they are *dressed in white robes*, designating their glorified state. This glorification has already begun with the resurrection of Christ but will only be consummated when Christ returns in the future. Third, they have *golden crowns on their heads,* the victor's crown (*stephanos*) rather than the royal crown. That *they cast their crowns before the throne* (v. 10) indicates that their victory over persecution is part of the victory God has won in Christ.

Then from the throne of God come *flashes of lightning, and rumblings and peals of thunder*. These images are rooted in the ancient concept of the manifestation of God's power in the storms that increased the fertility of the land (Yarbro Collins, 1991:35). The words are included in the descriptions of the seventh seal, trumpet, and bowl judgments (8:1-5; 11:15-19; 16:17-21). Such language is associated with divine power and glory throughout the scriptures, especially in the Sinai episode (Exod. 19:16-25; 1 Sam. 2:10; Job 36:30-32; 37:2-5; Ps. 18:9-15; 77:16-18; Ezek. 1:4-28; Matt. 27:51-54; 28:2-3; Heb. 12:18-24).

In front of the throne, John sees *seven flaming torches, which are the seven spirits of God*. The torches allude to the lampstands in the temple of God (Exod. 25:31-40; Zech. 4:2, 10). The seven spirits connote the complete spirit of God or the Holy Spirit (Acts 1:8; 2:1-4; Rev. 1:4; 3:1; 5:6). Here, the Spirit is with God in heaven. The emphasis in this context is on the Holy Spirit's work in creating and preserving the natural world (Ladd, 1972:76; Gen. 1:2; 2:7; Ps. 104:29-30).

Also in front of the throne is *something like a sea of glass, like crystal*. This is a simile; the sea is not constructed from glass or crystal but has the appearance of both. The background of this symbol is the ancient Hebrew concept of the universe, which pictured a sea between the first and second heaven, above which God's palace was located (Gen. 1:6-10; 7:11; Job 37:18; Ps. 104:3; 148:4; Ezek. 1:22-26; 2 Enoch 3:1-3). There may also be an allusion to Solomon's palace, which is described as having a floor of glass that looked like a sea (1 Kings 7:23-26; see also the *Qur'an*, Sura 27.44). The image of glass adds brightness and splendor to the heavenly scene.

Nevertheless, in ancient Hebrew culture the sea was primarily unpleasant and dangerous—a place where the forces of chaos were at work (Exod. 14:21; 15:1; Ps. 74:12-14; Isa. 51:10; Rev. 13:1; 15:2; 21:1). That the sea before the throne is smooth *like crystal* may indicate that those turbulent forces have been overcome (Beale, 1999:328). Indeed, there will be no sea in the new heaven and earth (21:1). Yet in addition to its splendor, the sea symbolizes separateness or otherness; the dominant theme in the symbol is the holy otherness of God, who now is separated from humanity by a crystal sea.

A Response of Praise 4:6b-11

Around the throne, John saw the *four living creatures*. The image is borrowed from Ezekiel 1 (see also Ezek. 10:20). The background for this symbol is found in the seraphim and cherubim, the latter of which were pictured on the mercy seat on top of the ark, the dwelling place of God (Exod. 25:17-22; 37:7-9; 1 Sam. 4:4; 2 Sam. 6:2; Ps. 18:10; 80:1; 99:1; Isa. 6:1-7).

In the numerology of Revelation, *four* is used of completion in the physical universe (5:6; 7:1; see also Dan. 8:8; Acts 10:11). The description of the four living creatures indicates that they together represent all living beings—God's animate universe *[Glossary: Four Living Creatures]*. The individual meaning of each of the four creatures is debated. The most likely scheme, borrowed from rabbinic literature, has the *lion* representing wild animals, the *ox* representing domesticated animals, the *human face* representing humanity, and the *flying eagle* representing birds of the air (Sweet, 1990:120). Taken together, they represent all of creation in praise to God.

The church fathers identified the four living creatures with the four gospels. The most common identification is the one accepted by Jerome and Augustine: Matthew is the lion because Jesus is depicted there as the lion of the tribe of Judah; Mark is the human because this gospel is closest to a biographical account of Jesus' life; Luke is the ox because there Jesus is portrayed as the sacrifice for all humanity; and John is the eagle because this gospel soars to the highest level of thought (see Irenaeus, *Adv. Haer.* 3.11.8 for an alternate representation, and Barclay, 1960:1.200-202 for a more complete outline of the views of the various fathers). Although characterizing the four living creatures as the four Gospels seems far-fetched, the practice has attracted many commentators, and the identification of Jerome and Augustine is the most compelling of the relatively unconvincing options.

The living creatures were *around the throne and on each side of the throne*. It is difficult to imagine how this appeared to John, perhaps like the arrangement of the Greek theater, which included a twenty-four-member chorus located in the orchestra with an altar in the middle (Brewer, 1952:227-31). The meaning of the symbols is more certain: *on each side of the throne* means that the living creatures are in contact with God, and *around the throne* means that they represent God in the world.

Three descriptions are given of these living creatures. That they had *six wings* emphasizes their swiftness and combines Isaiah's six-winged seraphim with Ezekiel's four-winged creatures (Isa. 6:2; Ezek.1:6-10); that they were *full of eyes all around and inside* indicates their complete comprehension (Ezek. 10:12); and that their praise was *day and night without ceasing* stresses their continual calling for and carrying out the will of God (Ps. 19:2; 103:19-22; 148; Isa. 6:1-7; 1 Enoch 39:12; 2 Enoch 21:1; Test. Levi 3:8).

The hymn of praise that follows the vision of heaven is to God who created all that is and who is for that reason both "holy" (v. 8) and "worthy" (v. 11). Later, praise will be given to Christ the Lamb because his suffering demonstrated that he is worthy of such praise (5:9, 12). The affirmation of the world as the creation of God stands in contrast to the gnostic rejection of the world (Boring, 1989:107-8). Thus, the gnostic beliefs of the Nicolaitans in chapters 2-3 are echoed and refuted in the vision of chapter 4.

The brief hymn begins with the words *holy, holy, holy*. The Masoretic Text uses the word *holy* alone, except in Isaiah 6:3, where the threefold repetition is probably for emphasis (see also 1 Clem. 34:7). There may be an allusion here to the Trinity, as in 1:4-5. The word *Almighty* stresses God's power in contrast to the emperor, who was similarly designated; and the phrase *who was and is and is to come* emphasizes God's transcendence of time and history (Beale, 1999:333). Hence, praise is offered by the creatures of the earth (Rom. 1:19-20) for God's holiness, omnipotence, and eternality.

Then the *twenty-four elders*, representing the people of God, join the natural beings in praise of God. John says that they *fall before the one who is seated on the throne and worship the one who lives forever and ever*. To prostrate oneself symbolized the submission of a defeated person asking for leniency. That they *cast their crowns before the throne* continues the same theme. The reference here is to the victor's crown (*stephanos*). When an ancient king surrendered, he threw his crown at the feet of the victorious king. For example, Tacitus describes the Parthian Tiridates placing his crown before

Nero's image (*Annals* 15.29). The action of the twenty-four elders in this passage indicates the complete submission of the saints to God.

The doxology that follows begins with *you are worthy*, a phrase used to attribute honor to Emperor Domitian. *[O]ur Lord and God*, is the Greek form of the title commonly given to Domitian *[Essay: Persecution During Domitian's Reign]*. The word probably combines "physical strength, moral quality, and legal authority" (Thompson, 1998:94). Instead of Domitian the Emperor, God is the one who is worthy to *receive glory and honor and power*. The reason God is worthy is that God *created all things*. The phrase *by your will* indicates that it was God's purpose that brought the world into being. The ordering of *existed and were created* is unusual; the reverse order would be expected. The meaning may be that creation existed in God's mind before it was created. Beale argues that the verb *existed* refers to the preservation of creation while *created* designates its inception (1999:335). In any case, it is clear that in times of persecution the church can take heart because God the creator is in charge of the universe.

THE TEXT IN BIBLICAL CONTEXT

The Visions of Heaven

The two visions in chapters 4–5 are clearly rooted in the Old Testament. They integrate skillfully elements of a variety of passages from the Hebrew tradition (Exod. 24:9-11; Ps. 47:8-9; Isa. 6:1-2; Ezek. 1:26-28; Dan. 7:9; 1 Enoch 39:3-8; 2 Enoch 20-22). The closest parallel to chapter 4 is the vision of Ezekiel 1.

Surprisingly, this is not the first time in the scriptures for a person to be admitted into the heavenly council. Micaiah ben Imlah sees "the LORD sitting on his throne, with all the host of heaven standing beside him to the right and to the left of him." This heavenly council debates: "Who will entice Ahab, so that he may go up and fall at Ramoth-gilead?" (1 Kings 22:19-23). The book of Job describes the council of heaven, including Satan, debating Job's fate, although Job is not personally present (1:6-12; 2:1-6). While no description is given, the heavens open for Ezekiel to receive visions of God (Ezek. 1:1). In the New Testament, the heavens are torn apart so that the Spirit can descend upon Jesus in the form of a dove (Mark 1:10; see also John 1:51; 2 Bar. 22:1; Test. Levi 5:1 for other occurrences of the opening of the gates of heaven). In a less literal and visual sense, Jeremiah says that the criterion of a true prophet is that the person "has stood in the council of the LORD" (23:18), and Amos speaks of God "revealing his secret to his servants the prophets" (3:7). Yet of all these descriptions, the picture of the throne room of heaven that John provides in chapter 4 is the most graphic.

The Throne

The word *throne* (*thronos*), occurs in seventeen of the twenty-two chapters of Revelation—all except chapters 9, 10, 15, 17, and 18. The most occurrences in any other New Testament book are in Matthew where it is mentioned four times. Indeed, forty-seven of the sixty-two New Testament occurrences of the word are in Revelation (Moulton and Geden, 1926:462-63). Obviously, the symbol of the throne is central to the book, which, according to Barr, makes Revelation a political and religious document (1998:63).

Early in Hebrew tradition, God's presence was associated with the mercy seat (Exod. 25:22). Subsequently, God was pictured as seated on a throne (1 Kings 22:19; Ps. 47:8; Isa. 6:1-2; 66:1; Jer. 17:12; Ezek. 1:26; Dan. 7:9; Matt. 5:34; 23:22; 1 Enoch 14:18-21). The images of the mercy seat and the throne were combined in Ps. 80:1. Ford argues that in Asia "'throne' may well be a synonym for the deity as 'heaven' is in the phrase 'kingdom of heaven'" (1975:70-71).

What is emphasized about God in the throne symbolism is sovereignty. Daniel says: "A thousand thousands served him, and ten thousand times ten thousand stood attending him" (7:10). Moreover, the "Ancient One" seated on the throne gave to the Son of Man

> dominion and glory and kingship, that all peoples, nations, and languages should serve him.
> His dominion is an everlasting dominion that shall not pass away, and his kingship is one that shall never be destroyed. (7:14)

The recurrence of the throne symbol indicates that a central feature of Revelation is the sovereignty of God. God's sovereignty is contrasted with the power of Satan, who is also said to have a throne (2:13). The great white throne of God (20:11) is implicitly contrasted with the throne of Caesar, the apparent sovereign of the world.

So Revelation answers this question: Who has authority in this world? It is not the apparent rulers—Satan and Caesar—but Christians who share God's throne (3:21). The sovereignty of God and the followers of God focused in the image of the throne is a central theme of the book of Revelation.

Precious Stones

If the kingly function of God is focused in the throne image, the priestly function of the divine is the meaning of the symbolism of the precious stones. Jasper, carnelian, and emerald are three of the twelve stones in the high priest's robe that represent the twelve tribes of Israel (Exod. 28:17-21). The carnelian is first, representing Reuben; the jasper is last, representing Benjamin; and the emerald is fourth, representing Judah. These are also three of the stones present in the Garden of Eden (Ezek. 28:13) and in the foundations of the holy city (Rev. 21:19-20). Plato uses them as representative of all precious stones (*Phaedo* 110E). In Revelation, these stones symbolize the precious nature of God's people and the holiness of the priesthood that leads those people into the divine presence.

THE TEXT IN THE LIFE OF THE CHURCH

The One on the Throne

Because the term *throne* occurs so often in Revelation, many have seen the book as a political theology. Although John does not advocate the use of force in the political realm, much of his language is infused with political imagery—authority, power, war, kingdom, conquer, ruler of the kings of the earth, as well as throne. My colleague, John Stanley, speaks of his own personal political journey as it pertains to the Book of Revelation:

> I began studying Revelation in 1974 out of political disappointment and a pastoral concern. As a child of the Cold War, as a sojourner to Selma, as a person whose social conscience was sensitized in the civil rights struggle, as a tired veteran of the War on Poverty in Appalachia, and as a former Vietnam hawk who turned dove in 1966, my involvement in the moral struggles of this world had drained me of the basic liberalism and optimism that used to motivate me. I looked to Revelation to see if John's world was at all similar to mine. I found a pastor in Patmos who sent a book to seven churches in Asia Minor warning these congregations against assimilation into the dominant Roman culture. John sensed that some of his readers were wondering if the heavy foot of the Empire would continue to tramp upon the church. Maybe the Roman Empire would have the last word in the conflict between the church and state. I came to apprehend Revelation as a rhetorical strategy designed to encourage readers to believe that evil is not eternal, that the future can be a New Jerusalem rather than Babylon, and that there is virtue and reward in remaining faithful amid social and moral stress. Revelation became a guide for me in the contemporary church's confrontation with wealth, nationalism, violence, and the misuse of power. (1998:39-40)

Hence, Stanley came to follow the God on the throne in Revelation in the struggle against the evil kingdoms that seem to be enthroned in this world.

The Judgment and Mercy of God

The story is told of a man who was lecturing to a large audience. In his lecture, he made blasphemous statements that denied the justice of God. At the end of the lecture, the speaker took out his watch and said: "I will give God five minutes to strike me dead for the things I have said." The minutes ticked off as he held his watch and waited. After about four and a half minutes, several persons in the audience fainted, but nothing happened to the speaker. When the five minutes were up, the lecturer put the watch back in his pocket and walked off the stage with an air of confident victory.

Several days later, a man who witnessed the lecture told his pastor how this man had defied God's justice and escaped judgment. After hearing the story, the pastor remarked: "Did that man really believe he could exhaust the mercy of God in only five minutes?"

This story focuses an issue that is central to the vision of God in this passage—the relationship between God's mercy and judgment. The symbols of the jasper and carnelian stress the purity and judgment of God. Yet this is surrounded by the emerald rainbow of God's mercy. The passage does not resolve the rational contradiction between the judgment and mercy of God, but it does state that both are part of who God is. It is comforting to see the awful judgment of God enveloped in the rainbow of divine mercy.

God the Creator

In the hymn of Revelation 4, God is praised as the creator. Adoration of God as creator is a constant theme in Christian history, but nowhere is it better stated than in "Confession of Faith according to the Holy Word of God," an affirmation from about the year A.D. 1600. Article VI gives a beautiful description of God's creation of the world and then ends with Revelation 4:11.

> Likewise, God Almighty, in the beginning, from nothing, in a most wonderful manner, and above all human reason and comprehension, created heaven, the earth, and the sea, with all their glorious adornment ... the Blessed, only saying: "Let heaven and earth be made; and his word was a perfect work." He also adorned the heavens with many glorious lights ... which he ordained to the honor of their Creator, and the service of men....

Concerning this wonderful creation, read: "Thou art worthy, O Lord, to receive glory and honor and power; for thou hast created all things, and for thy pleasure they are and were created." Rev. 4:11 (van Braght, 1950:376)

Revelation 5:1-14

The Lamb and the Scroll

PREVIEW

Chapter 5 has roots in visions of the Hebrew scriptures (see TBC on ch. 4, The Visions of Heaven) and in the enthronement ceremonies of the ancient world. Beasley-Murray argues that the three-fold structure of these enthronement ceremonies is represented here. The exaltation is in verse 5, the presentation in verse 6, and the enthronement in verse 7 (1974:110). The point is that Christ is now enthroned with God (Phil. 2:6-11; see also Matt. 28:18-20; 1 Tim. 3:16; Heb. 1:5), and Christ's reign has begun (1 Cor. 15:20-28; Eph. 1:20-23; 1 Pet. 3:22).

The major symbol in this passage is the *scroll,* for which many interpretations have been suggested. One possible meaning is that the scroll is the Lamb's book of life, which contains the names of the redeemed, or the closely related book of deeds. However, this interpretation makes the breaking of the seals meaningless. Caird points out that, when the seals are broken, the result is a description of the judgment that is about to take place, not a revelation of the identity of the redeemed. Moreover, the drama of the passage would be removed because the Lamb would have unquestioned right to open the Lamb's book of life (1966:71).

A second interpretation is that the scroll is the last will and testament of God, which includes the kingdom of God and its blessings received through the death of Jesus Christ, the son of God (Heb. 9:15-17; 1 Pet. 1:3-5). In antiquity, wills were authenticated by seven witnesses, each affixing a seal. This inheritance is implemented when

Christ opens the seals. Nevertheless, this interpretation suffers from a weakness similar to the first: the seals do not have to do with inheritance, but with judgment.

A third, futuristic interpretation is that the scroll contains the events of the end times—the judgments that will occur before the end of the world. This interpretation is more consistent with the contents of the scroll, which are judgments, but these judgments seem not to be limited to the distant future. They include realities that happen repeatedly in human history, such as war, civil strife, famine, and death (6:1-8). Moreover, this interpretation renders the judgments described when the scroll is opened irrelevant to the churches in Asia, to whom the letters were addressed.

It is best to take the scroll to contain the redemptive plan of God, which includes the salvation of God's people and the judgment of the wicked (Rom. 5:11; Heb. 1:1-4; 2:3-10). In this interpretation, the scroll contains God's plan for human history (cf. 1 Enoch 47:3; 81:1-2; 106:19; 107:1), the overthrow of evil and the establishment of the kingdom of God through the death and resurrection of Jesus Christ. The content of the scroll, which describes God's judgment, is certainly consistent with this interpretation. The death of Jesus Christ, the Lamb, is the means through which God implemented the divine plan for the universe—the victory over evil and the establishment of the kingdom of God. The past event, the death and resurrection of Christ, establishes the present reality of Christ's supremacy over Satan and the forces of evil. This victory will in the future be actualized by the exaltation of suffering Christians when Christ returns for them. The Lamb's suffering victory in heaven gives meaning to the saints' suffering and overcoming on earth. Johns says this particularly well:

> The lamb is not simply a symbol of weakness: it is really strong and wise. However, its strength is here being redefined, reconceived. The lamb is strong, but the exhibition of its strength is unconventional: its strength lies in its consistent, nonviolent resistance to evil—a resistance that led to its execution. But the lamb stands triumphant, raised from the dead. Essential to a proper understanding of the book's rhetoric is the recognition that the lamb *has triumphed in* his death and resurrection, not that the lamb *will triumph in the future, subsequent to* his death and resurrection. A close reading of the text supports this important distinction. (1998:199-200)

OUTLINE

The Introduction of the Scroll, 5:1-4
The Lamb's Opening of the Scroll, 5:5-7
Hymns to Christ's Redemption, 5:8-14

EXPLANATORY NOTES

The Introduction of the Scroll 5:1-4

The word translated *scroll* is used in Revelation to denote the book sent to the churches, the sealed scroll, the book of life, and the book of judgment (see TBC on ch. 20, The Books). This sealed scroll was *written on the inside and on the back*. Although the ten commandments were written on both sides (Exod. 32:15), it was customary to write only on the inside smoothed surface of a papyrus scroll. Barker says that the writing on both sides points to a codex rather than a scroll (2000:146-47), and Aune recognizes the possibility that it was double-written (1997:343). While it may symbolize the divine and human sides of God's plan (Walhout, 2000:67), it more likely indicates the document's extensiveness or completeness (Ezek. 2:10). It includes God's complete plan for redeeming the world. That the scroll was *sealed with seven seals* again points to the completeness of the seal. A seal was placed on a document to authenticate it, much like a signature would be used today (1 Kings 21:8; Isa. 8:16; 29:11; Jer. 32:10; Dan. 12:4). The completeness of the seal emphasizes that only the person who can fulfill in its totality God's redemption described in the scroll can open it. That person is Jesus Christ, who died and rose from death to accomplish fully God's redemption. Ladd affirms that "apart from the person and redeeming work of Jesus Christ, history is an enigma" (1972:82). No matter how intense persecution becomes, the Christian can take courage because Christ's redemption has already been accomplished by what Christ has done.

Then John saw *a mighty angel proclaiming with a loud voice, "Who is worthy to open the scroll and break its seals?"* The mighty angel alludes to Gabriel, whose name means "God is my strength" (10:1; 18:21); the angel's loud voice enables all creation to hear the words of the angel. The person who is worthy to open the scroll must be able to fulfill what was written in the scroll, the redemption of God.

The drama of the scene is heightened when *no one in heaven or on earth or under the earth was able to open the scroll*. The words reflect the three-storied universe, which was the cosmological understanding in the ancient world. The meaning is that no one in all of creation was able to open the scroll, a profound statement of the gap between God and created beings.

As a result, John *began to weep bitterly because no one was found worthy to open the scroll*. The weeping is not from sorrow but from dismay (Luke 18:7; cf. 18:9-20). Unless the scroll is opened, no one will give purpose to the suffering and martyrdom of Christians;

their deaths will remain meaningless, and history will have no purpose. If the scroll is not opened, God's plan will not be fulfilled. This passage is a dramatic build-up to demonstrate the importance of the death of Jesus Christ.

The Lamb's Opening of the Scroll 5:5-7

One of the elders said to John, *Do not weep* because there is one who can open the scroll. Then John sees a person to whom is given two titles. First, he is called *the lion of the tribe of Judah*. Lions were quite common in both Palestine and Asia Minor during the first century. Ford calls the lion a symbol of "strength, majesty, courage, and menace" (1975:85). Thus, the lion is a military image designating the all-conquering Messiah (see TBC, The Lion and Lamb). Boring says this image "was understood in the first century to promise a David-like warrior Messiah who will fight God's battles and wreak vengeance on 'God's' (our) enemies" (1989:108). The lion image used of Christ thus connotes a mighty, conquering military hero.

Second, Christ is called *the Root of David* (22:16). This phrase presents the imagery of a tree cut down, leaving a stump from which a young shoot grows. Jesus is the shoot out of the dead stump of Israel, the ideal Davidic king (Isa. 11:1-10; 53:2; Jer. 23:5; 33:15; Zech. 3:8; 6:12). The singular *Root* carries the meaning "descendent" (Matt. 1:1; 9:27; 15:22; 21:9; Mark 11:10; Rom. 1:3; 2 Tim. 2:8; Heb. 7:14). In Revelation, Christ as the King of kings fulfills the Davidic hopes (2:9; 3:7-9; 5:5; 12:5; see also Ezek. 34:23-24; 37:24-25). Indeed, Christ is the one who redeems and brings salvation to his people, and his redemption comes because he *has conquered*. The use of the Greek aorist tense indicates that Christ's redemption is a once-for-all event, which took place when he suffered, died, and rose from the dead. Revelation does not present a new theology of redemption, but rather offers familiar New Testament theology in powerful, symbolic language.

Yet there is a surprise in this dramatic presentation. Instead of the lion, whom the elder had introduced, John saw a *Lamb standing as if it had been slaughtered*. Instead of the military symbol of the lion, the image of the Lamb that was slain appears. This presents a dominant theme of Revelation—overcoming, not through military strength and killing, but through suffering and death. Although the Lamb image is only used in the writings of John, it is the main title for Christ in the Book of Revelation. The perfect tense, *had been slaughtered,* denotes a past act with continuing consequences (1 Pet. 1:18-20; Rev. 13:8). The victory of the Lamb has already been accomplished in Christ's death on the cross. The word *slaughtered* is also used of the deaths of martyrs (6:9; 18:24). Just as Christ conquered through suffering and death (5:9; 17:14), so faithful Christians overcome through their suffering and even martyrdom (12:11; 15:2; Rom. 8:36). Boring states: "For Christians, what it means to 'win' has been redefined by the cross of Jesus" (1989:111). How a person can overcome through suffering is one of the paradoxes of Christian theology and is embodied in Christ's victorious sacrifice on the cross. The Lamb *standing* may allude to Christ's resurrection (Aune, 1997:352-53).

The diminutive form of the word *lamb* (*arnion*) is used as a counter-image of the beast (*thērion*). Eller contrasts the little lambkin with the vicious monster: the tiny Lamb conquers the awesome beast (1974:79). Because of the suffering of Christ, wherever the Hebrew scriptures say lion, we are to read Lamb; wherever the Hebrew scriptures speak of victory over God's enemies, that victory must be seen through the cross of Jesus Christ (see TBC, The Lion and Lamb).

In John's vision, the Lamb was located *between the throne and the four living creatures and among the elders*. The first part of this statement connotes the close connection of the Lamb to God, the one who sits on the throne. The second indicates the intimate relationship of the Lamb and God's people, symbolized by the elders.

The Lamb is then described as *having seven horns and seven eyes*. The seven horns suggest complete power (Deut. 33:17; 1 Kings 22:10-11; Ps. 18:2; 112:8-9; Zech. 1:18; Rev. 12:3; 13:1; 17:3), and the seven eyes communicate complete insight or omniscience (Zech. 4:10). Both the power and the insight of the Lamb are complete and available to God's saints (1 Cor. 1:22-24).

The complete power and insight of the Lamb are embodied in *the seven spirits of God sent out into all the earth*. Because the *seven spirits* symbolically represent the Holy Spirit, the profound truth communicated here is that the power and insight of Christ the Lamb are shown forth in the world through the Holy Spirit. Beale communicates this effectively: "As a result of the death and resurrection [of the Lamb], these spirits also become Christ's agents throughout the world, who figuratively represent the Holy Spirit himself" (1999:355).

Then the Lamb *went and took the scroll from the right hand of the one who was seated on the throne*. The right hand is associated with power and might (Exod. 15:6; Ps. 44:3) and with righteousness and salvation (Ps. 17:7; 48:10; 138:7). In Revelation, an angel raises his right hand toward heaven to swear an oath (10:5-6; see also 1:17), and the beast worshipers are marked on the right hand (13:16; see Hay, 1973, for a complete discussion of the image). Here Christ ascends to the throne to receive the power and insight of God for ful-fillment of the redemptive plan, which only Christ can accomplish through his death.

Hymns to Christ's Redemption 5:8-14

In the section that concludes the chapter, heaven is pictured as a temple where everyone is worshiping God. *The four living creatures* symbolize all created beings in earth and heaven, which join in worship of God *[Glossary: Four Living Creatures]. The twenty-four elders* symbolize the heavenly saints who join the faithful on earth in adoration of Christ the Lamb *[Glossary: Twenty-Four Elders]*. All of creation sings hymns of praise to Christ for his redemptive work. The images here describing the heavenly temple are taken from the earthly temple.

The beings mentioned are *each holding a harp*. The *kithara*, which was much smaller than our harp, was the traditional instrument for accompanying the singing of psalms (Ps. 33:2; 43:4; 71:22; 98:5). Elsewhere, John calls the harp the instrument of heavenly music (14:2; 15:2).

They also hold *golden bowls full of incense*. The basis for this image is the altar of incense, which stood in front of the inner veil of the Temple and where the priests offered incense to God daily (Num. 16:6-7; 2 Chron. 26:16-18). These bowls of incense *are the prayers of the saints*. The psalmist says: "Let my prayer be counted as incense before you" (141:2). Here the saints probably pray that the justice of God will be enacted (6:10).

The word *saints* is the most common term in Revelation for the people who are faithful to God in the face of persecution (8:3-4; 11:18; 13:7, 10; 14:12; 16:6; 17:6; 18:20, 24; 19:8; 20:9) *[Glossary: Saints]*. Because they believe that the church is raptured before the tribulation, dispensationalists assert that the saints in Revelation are not the church but pious Jews and Gentiles, who, at the time of the rapture, recognize that Jesus was the Messiah and convert to become his followers *[Essay: Dispensationalism]*. This limitation on the word *saints* is not a natural use of the term. Indeed, Christians are included when the designation *saints* is used (5:8; 11:18; 18:24; 19:8; see also 8:3-4; 13:7,10; 14:12; 16:6; 17:6; 18:20; 20:9). Thus, there is no compelling reason to believe that Christians are not part of the group described in Revelation by the word *saints*.

The four living creatures and the twenty-four elders then *sing a new song*. Because Christ's redemption begins a new era, the animate universe joins with the people of God in celebrating (see TBC, The New Song). The new song begins with the words, *You are worthy.* That this clause refers to God in 4:11 gives further evidence of Christ's divine nature. Pliny the Younger says that Roman emperors often received this acclamation from their subjects when they returned from battle (*Letter* 10.96). Revelation regards Christ, not the emperor, as the one who is worthy.

You were slaughtered and by your blood you ransomed for God ... Christ is worthy because of the redemption brought about by his death on the cross. This idea is rooted in the paschal lamb that was slaughtered in the deliverance of Israel from Egypt (Exod. 12:6). Christians in Asia have confidence that the death they face for the cause of Christ parallels the slaughter of Christ on the cross (6:9; 18:24). Christ's death is called a ransom (see TBC, A Ransom); it was through his death that Christ purchased and set humanity free from slavery to sin and from imprisonment to the sinful nature. The purchase price of redemption was the blood of Christ, which redeems humans from sin and makes them pure before God. The Lamb that was slaughtered is the symbol of Christ's work to redeem humanity.

This redemption of Christ is for *saints from every tribe and language and people and nation.* This phrase emphasizes the universality of the work of Christ. Whereas the Hebrews were the recipients of God's deliverance in the Exodus, all nations receive the benefits of Christ's redemption on the cross.

Those who serve God are called *a kingdom and priests* (Exod. 19:5-6; Rev. 1:6; 20:6; cf. Isa. 61:6). Because of Christ's work, his followers become both kings and priests. As kings, they share in the reign of Christ; as priests, they have full, direct access to God (Ladd, 1972:92). Thus, Christ's redemptive death allows him to continue his kingdom and priesthood in his church.

Both the present and future tenses of *reign* have good textual evidence. Because the saints do not seem to *reign on earth,* it is likely that a scribe would have changed the present to the future and that the present is probably the original reading. However, Beale suggests that this is a futuristic present, giving assurance of a future kingdom and evidence of the already-but-not-yet nature of Christ's reign (1999:362-63).

Then the four living creatures and twenty-four elders are joined by *myriads of myriads and thousands of thousands.* Beasley-Murray calls this "the highest number known to Greeks" (1974:128). Hence, John is saying that the host that joins in the song of praise is innumerable (Ps. 68:17; Dan. 7:10).

The song begins: *Worthy is the Lamb that was slaughtered.* This hymn of redemption parallels the hymn of creation in 4:11: "You are worthy, our Lord and God." It is also the third "Worthy" hymn in the series (4:11; 5:9, 12). The threefold *worthy* (*axios*) is the liturgical antiphonal response to the threefold *holy* (*hagios*) in 4:8. Christ is affirmed as worthy *to receive power and wealth and wisdom and might and honor and glory and blessing!* These same titles are elsewhere attributed to God (1 Chron. 29:10-12). For John, a monotheistic Palestinian Jew, to assign them to Jesus is quite remarkable. It seems clear that John recognizes the divinity of Christ without an awareness of any danger of idolatry. Barclay gives a somewhat detailed analysis of the attributes of Christ and their usage (1960:1.226-27). It is sufficient to note here that the titles serve to link Christ very explicitly to God.

The context of these titles in Revelation also tells something about the nature of Christ's work. The power Christ is worthy to receive does not come by armed force or exploitation of the world's people or resources but by faithful witness in the face of death (1:5). The wealth of Christ is not illicitly accumulated luxury (18:3, 15-17) but gold refined with the purifying fire of God's justice (3:18). The wisdom of Christ is not that which promotes political success but produces innocent victims of a corrupt political system (18:21-24). Rowland summarizes the subversive nature of Christ's titles: "The Christian gospel exposes the distortions and delusions we tell about ourselves, the violence we use to maintain the status quo, and our ways of disguising from ourselves the oppression of the victim" (1998:606).

Joining to sing praise to Christ is *every creature in heaven and on earth and under the earth and in the sea, and all that is in them.* This proclaims as crescendo that the whole creation glorifies God and the Lamb (Ps. 98; 148). The group added to the picture is the dead, those under the earth and in the sea. This praise responds to Christ's redemption of creation from the curse that it was under since the Fall (Gen. 3:14-19; Rom. 8:19-21).

The acclamation is given to *the one seated on the throne and to the Lamb,* since praise belongs jointly to God and to the Lamb. The inclusion of God and Christ in synonymous parallelism indicates that they together are worthy to receive highest and eternal praise *[Essay: Christology of Revelation].*

John concludes the scene with these words: *And the four living creatures said, "Amen!" And the elders fell down and worshiped.* These two groups begin and end the statements of praise. The representatives of creation join the members of the heavenly church. The entire cosmos sings praise to the universality of Christ's redemption. The word *Amen* might best be translated "Yes!" (2 Cor. 1:20) and is a strong statement of affirmation. All creation affirms God's victory in the redemption of Christ, the slain Lamb.

THE TEXT IN BIBLICAL CONTEXT

The Lion and Lamb

The image of the lion of the tribe of Judah emphasizes the all-powerful Messiah. The lion is the most frequently mentioned animal in the Bible (see Johns, 1998:203-7 for a fine treatment of the image in the context of ancient Israel). Although the phrase *lion of the tribe of Judah* occurs only here in the Bible, the image is certainly present in the Hebrew tradition (Ezek. 19:2-9; 2 Esd. 11:37-46; 12:31-34). In the Old Testament, the lion is an animal of destructive strength (Prov. 22:13; 26:13; 30:30). It is compared to the tribe of Judah (Gen. 49:9) but also to the tribes of Gad (Deut. 33:20) and Dan (Deut. 33:22), to the people of Israel (Num. 23:24), and even to God (Num. 24:9). Two lions are engraved on the arms of the throne of Solomon and twelve on the steps approaching the throne (1 Kings 10:19-20; 2 Chron. 9:18-19). Ezekiel says Pharaoh considered himself a lion (32:2). If Christ is the lion, he is the mighty Davidic military warrior who will conquer the enemies of his people (Isa. 11:10; Rom. 1:3; 15:12; Test. Judah 24:4-6).

Although the phrase "root of David" does not occur in the Hebrew Bible, the imagery of a Messiah coming from the Davidic lineage is certainly present (Isa. 11:1-16; see also Ezek. 19:10-14). It communicates the Old Testament idea that the power of Israel will not be permanently taken away (Gen. 49:10; Test. Judah 24:4-6). In the New Testament, Jesus, the Messiah, is given power over Satan (Matt. 12:28-29; Luke 10:18-19; John 12:31; 16:11; Heb. 2:14-15; Rev. 12:7-12), over rulers (1 Cor. 15:24-26; Col. 2:15), and over death (2 Tim. 1:10; Rev. 1:18).

Instead of the powerful and violent lion, however, John sees a Lamb that was slain. The lamb is the most common symbol for Christ in Revelation. It is used twenty-eight times for Christ and once for the second beast (13:11). By contrast, the title Christ is used only eleven times. Lamb also occurs in the Septuagint (Isa. 53:7) and in other New Testament writings (John 1:29,36; Acts 8:32; 1 Pet. 1:19). Outside Revelation, the diminutive form occurs only once in the Septuagint (Jer. 11:19) and once in the Gospel of John (21:15). The image alludes both to the suffering servant of Isaiah (Isa. 49:3-6; 50:10;

52:13; 53:7) and to the paschal lamb (Exod. 12:1-13; 1 Cor. 5:7; 1 Pet. 1:19; 2:21-25). Although contemporary Jewish literature used the lamb or ram to designate a violent leader (Dan. 8:3; 1 Enoch 89:45-49; 90:9-36; Test. Joseph 19:8-9), there is no clear reason to associate this with the Lamb of Revelation. Johns gives a particularly helpful review of possible roots of the lamb imagery in the sacrificial system, the paschal lamb of Exodus, the suffering servant song of Isaiah 53:7, the vision of the ram and goat of Daniel 8, the sacrifice of Isaac, the lambs of Micah 5:6, the peaceful lambs of Isaiah, and the vulnerable lamb of the Septuagint. Although Johns seems to find the most helpful connections in the last two images, he qualifies them by indicating that in Revelation the peaceful Lamb is a conqueror and the vulnerable Lamb is really victorious. Revelation thus redefines victory and conquest in terms of suffering and death (1998:160-87). This conquering through suffering, demonstrated by Christ (3:21; 17:14; see also Luke 24:26; John 1:29; Acts 8:32; 1 Cor. 1:22-24; 1 Pet. 1:18-19), is exemplary for Christians as they conquer amid persecution (2:3, 11, 17, 26-27; 3:5, 12, 21; 12:11; 15:2; 21:7).

According to Ford, the word *slaughtered* means "to kill a person with violence" (1975:90). It is used this way in both the Septuagint (Jer. 52:10) and Josephus (*Against Apion* 1.76). In the New Testament it occurs only in the Johannine writings and refers in each case to violence. In 1 John it is used of murder (3:12), and in Revelation for the violent death of the martyrs (6:9; 18:24) and for slaughter (Rev. 6:4; 13:3). By this time, such suffering was seen as atonement for sin (2 Macc. 6:28-29). Thus, it is by the suffering and death of Christ and the Christian martyrs that God brings the salvation of humanity.

Johns suggests that "neither the lion nor the lamb was a traditional symbol for the messiah," so that they must be used metaphorically but with allusions to traditional symbols. He concludes: "The author thus chose the lion to represent the powerful aggressive force inherent in one vision of Israel's role in the eschaton and the lamb to represent the vulnerability inherent in another" (2000:206-7).

The New Song

In 5:9-10, the four living creatures and the twenty-four elders sing a new song. In the Psalms, this phrase refers simply to an unusual hymn of praise (33:3; 96:1; 149:1). The particular word used, *kainos,* means new in the sense of quality rather than time; it denotes what has been purged of idolatry and "is the opposite of unjust, oppressive, exploitative, uncaring, demonic" (R. Smith, 2000:23). In Revelation many things are new: the new name for the conqueror (2:17; 3:12), the new heaven and new earth (21:1), and the new universe (21:5). In this case, the new event is Christ's redemption, which inaugurates a new covenant and a new era. Revelation also associates songs with redemption (14:1-3; 15:2-3; see also Ps. 40:3; 98:1-3). The new song is sung because of the new deliverance brought about through the suffering and death of Christ. The whole universe and the people of God celebrate Christ's redemption with a new song.

A Ransom

Revelation 5:9 says Christ is worthy because his violent death was a ransom, an image used throughout the New Testament (Mark 10:45; 1 Cor. 6:19-20; Gal. 3:13; 1 Tim. 2:6; 1 Pet. 1:18). A ransom was a commercial transaction. Indeed, Wall argues that it has its roots in the obligation of subjugated persons to purchase their comrades who had been taken prisoner by the oppressor (1991:103-4). The concept of ransom was used primarily in two contexts. First, slaves could be rescued from bondage for a price. A person would purchase slaves from their masters, and, instead of placing them in bondage, ransom them by giving them freedom. As God freed Israel from slavery to the Egyptians, Christ ransomed humans from their slavery to sin. Second, prisoners could be released from sentences by a price. A person would pay the fine assessed on prisoners and thus ransom them and set them free. In this way Christ ransomed humans from the sentence imposed because of sin.

The cost that Christ paid to ransom humanity was his blood (1 Cor. 7:23; 1 Pet. 1:18-19; 1 John 2:2). This idea has its roots in the violent slaughter of the paschal lamb (Exod. 12:1-13; 1 Cor. 5:7). In Revelation, redemption through the blood of Christ is associated with liberation (1:5), cleansing (7:14), and victory (12:11; Glasson, 1965:45). There is a sense in which the witness of Christians in the face of slaughter allows them to participate with Christ in his redemption (6:9; 18:24). In a more spiritual sense, Paul says that, as the self is crucified, the slavery to sin is broken (Rom. 6:6-7). Through the suffering and death of Christ, humans are freed from their slavery to sin and from imprisonment to the destructiveness of the sinful nature.

This redemption that Christ initiated is open to *saints from every tribe and language and people and nation*. These words occur seven times in Revelation although the word order is different (5:9; 7:9; 10:11; 11:9; 13:7; 14:6; 17:15; see also Dan. 3:4, 7, 29). The emphasis is on the universality of Christ's work. All will one day praise the sovereign Lion-Lamb, whether through choice or judgment (chs. 19-22).

THE TEXT IN THE LIFE OF THE CHURCH

Conquering through Suffering

In popular culture, one conquers through strength. Christian preachers tell us that our country must have a strong military to be in a position to conquer our enemies. The mythos of strength is evident in our naming of sports teams after violent animals like lions and falcons. Even patriotic Christian schools use names like crusaders and eagles. It would be rare for teams to be named the lambs or the suffering servants! Yet Revelation makes it clear that the Christian conquers through the power of suffering.

The story is told of a monk named Telemachus who lived at the end of the fourth century and whose death had a great redemptive effect (Drescher, 1974:48-49; Lehn, 1980:27). Telemachus chose to ensure his salvation by secluding himself in the deserts and mountains where he could live in isolation for meditation and fasting. In time he decided through prayer that his life was really selfish and that to serve God he needed also to serve others. So he left the desert and returned to Rome. To his surprise, he found that Christianity had become the official religion of the empire and that Christians no longer needed to worship in seclusion.

Yet the abhorrent games in the arena had continued. Although spectators were no longer entertained by throwing Christians to the lions, slaves and political prisoners were forced to fight to the death for the amusement of the crowds. Christians opposed the games but to no avail. Telemachus decided to observe the carnage for himself.

He seated himself with the spectators and noted Emperor Honorius in his special seat. The gladiators came out, and the fight began. Telemachus rose from his seat. Carrying the cross of Christ, he jumped over the wall and threw himself between the two gladiators. "In the name of our Master," he cried, "stop fighting!"

The gladiators paused in astonishment. But the crowd shouted, "Let the games go on." Telemachus was pushed aside, but he again forced himself between the two gladiators.

There are different versions of what happened next. Either the crowd stampeded into the center of the arena and beat Telemachus to death, or at the commander's order a gladiator struck Telemachus dead. In any case, the crowd grew silent, startled at the killing of a holy man. The emperor left the arena, followed by the crowds. Honorius issued an edict to discontinue the games. By dying, Telemachus had ended the brutal gladiatorial games.

Revelation says that suffering is God's means of redeeming the world. This is a strange, even paradoxical idea—conquering through suffering. In the words of Boring:

> This equation of love-that-suffers-even-to-dying with the messianic conquest of our enemies is either the most blatant case of semantic *chutzpah/tour de force* in literature—the theological equivalent of the nineteen sixties suggestion that the American military 'just get out of Vietnam and declare a victory'—or it is as profound a 'rebirth of images' and redefinition of the meaning of 'power' as anything in the history of theology."
> (1986:266)

The Power of Song

Revelation has long been the inspiration of songwriters. For example, chapter 5 is the basis for the hymn of Isaac Watts:

> Come let us join our cheerful songs
> With angels around the throne;
> Ten thousand thousand are their tongues,
> But all their joys are one.

one from Charles Wesley:

> The praises of Jesus the angels proclaim.
> Fall down on their faces and worship the Lamb.

and finally George Friedrich Handel's great climactic piece in *The Messiah*:

> Worthy is the Lamb that was slain, and hath redeemed us to God by his
>   blood;
> To receive power, and riches, and wisdom, and strength, and honour, and
>   glory, and blessing.
> Blessing and honour, glory and pow'r be unto him, that sitteth upon the
>   throne, and unto the Lamb, forever and ever. Amen.

This last hymn evokes such a powerful positive response to Christ's redemption "because it *is* worship—as close to singing it in heaven as we can get" (Willard Swartley, private communication).

Allan Boesak recalls that black South Africans made freedom songs central to their struggle. "The struggle is inconceivable without them," he says. They sang as they marched into the face of police and army troops. They sang in prison "songs of defiance and faith and freedom," songs that often made the oppressors nervous and aggressive. Their songs paralleled the hosts of heaven who sang:

> Worthy is the Lamb who was slain, to receive power and wealth and wisdom and might and honour and glory and blessing!

Young black Christians in South Africa danced around a police vehicle and sang:

> It is broken, the power of Satan is broken! We have disappointed Satan, his power is broken. Alleluia!

Boesak concludes:

> Others join us as we march, singing and dancing, back into the church. This is a new song, a freedom song, and the power of it ... [inspires] thousands upon thousands throughout South Africa. For although the seals of the scroll must still be opened, the scroll is not in the hands of Caesar but in the hands of the Lamb. (1987:60-62)

Revelation 6:1-17

The Seals

PREVIEW

Up to this point, the message of Revelation has been quite positive. In chapter 6, however, the judgments begin. Catastrophes are released successively as the seals of the scroll described in chapter 5 are opened. Later, two similar series of judgments will be brought about by the blowing of trumpets and the pouring out of the bowls of God's wrath upon the earth.

The visions of heaven and the Lamb in chapters 4 and 5 serve as an introduction to the seal judgments, just as the vision of Christ in chapter 1 introduced the letters to the churches of chapters 2 and 3. In chapter 5, Christ the Lamb took the scroll from God on the throne; here the same Lamb successively breaks open the seven seals of that scroll to produce the seven seal judgments. Such an interlocking of one chapter with the next and paralleling of one section of the book with others are common to the literary structure of Revelation.

Now God's redemption is two-fold, involving both the deliverance of the righteous from their suffering and the terrible judgment of the wicked. The seals also seem to be warnings for the righteous to resist compromise with the world and for the wicked to repent. The judgments are cosmic catastrophes that probably occur simultaneously rather than sequentially (Beale, 1999:370-71).

This passage and the other judgment passages of Revelation cause at least two interpretive difficulties. There is, first of all, the issue of the nature of God's redemption. The previous two chapters detailed the bliss of heaven and the throne of the Lamb; this chapter describes the terrible punishments poured out on the wicked world. Taken together, these chapters teach us that God's salvation includes both the joy of the righteous in heaven with God and the judgment of the wicked in the world apart from God. These responses are opposite and yet complementary parts of God's plan of redemption (Eller, 1974:91). The tribulation of Revelation is a testing for Christians and punishment for the world.

A second issue raised for the first time in this chapter is how the judgments are to be interpreted. There are basically two options. First, they can be taken literally; that is, the seal judgments describe cosmic catastrophes that will actually take place at the end of the world. In support of this method of interpretation is that the Hebrew prophets picture the end as coming in this manner (Isa. 13:10; 34:4; Jer. 4:23-28; Joel 2:31; 3:15; Hag. 2:6). Jesus also uses similar language (Matt. 24:29; Mark 13:24-25; Luke 21:25). Yet it is difficult to take this passage literally. How can the heavens roll up like a scroll (v. 14)? The sky is no longer considered to be a solid substance like the ancient people thought it was. How can the stars fall to the earth like fruit from a fig tree (v. 13)? The stars are many times the size of the earth. Taken in a literal sense, the passage is difficult for moderns to understand.

These considerations have led some commentators to interpret the judgments symbolically. Instead of a literal description of future events, they represent social and economic upheavals on the Day of the Lord. The catastrophes here represent the shaking of the spiritual grounding of peoples and nations. By heaping one catastrophe upon another, Revelation is showing how evil will be overthrown by the forces of God. Moreover, if the language is to be taken symbolically, the judgments represent catastrophes that happen recurrently. Wilcock says: "God is using, to expose the true character of the wicked, the same method which in the case of Job was used to expose the true character of the righteous" (1975:96).

Some persons think that to interpret the Bible literally is to be more faithful to the text than to interpret it symbolically. However, the biblical writers themselves do not hold that view. In Hebrew parallelism, Haggai (2:6-7) speaks of God's shaking the cosmos as being equivalent to shaking all the nations of the earth. Moreover, in Acts, Peter quotes the prophet Joel, *The sun shall be turned to darkness and the moon to blood* (Joel 2:31; Acts 2:20), clearly assuming that this passage was referring to events that occurred on the day of Pentecost. Few persons would believe literally that the sun was darkened and the moon turned to blood on the day of Pentecost. Peter is using the images symbolically, and perhaps it is better to interpret the judgments of Revelation in a similar way. Earlier, we saw that the vision of Christ in chapter 1 was not a literal description of what Jesus looked like—"his eyes were like a flame of fire" and "his feet were like burnished bronze"—but a symbolic portrayal of his characteristics, his omniscience and stability. So here also, the judgments may be symbolic rather than literal descriptions.

OUTLINE
The Rider on the White Horse, 6:1-2
The Rider on the Red Horse, 6:3-4
The Rider on the Black Horse, 6:5-6
The Rider on the Pale Green Horse, 6:7-8
The Martyrs under the Altar, 6:9-11
The Great Earthquake, 6:12-17

EXPLANATORY NOTES

The Rider on the White Horse 6:1-2

When the first four seals are opened, each of the four living creatures in turn says, *Come!* Although most all versions translate it in this way, the word can mean either "come" or "go." The translation seems to be dependent on the point of view of the speaker. Because the four living creatures are in heaven, *go* would seem to be a better translation; the creatures are telling the riders to go from heaven to earth. The word certainly has eschatological overtones. It echoes the call for Christ to *come* at the end of Revelation (22:17, 20). There the sense is certainly an anticipation of the parousia, Christ's second coming. Yet perhaps the real force of the word lies in another direction altogether. The meaning may not be directional but exclamatory; perhaps the sense is better captured by a cry like "Woe!" After all, it is the wrath of God that is being introduced. The translators maintain some of this sense by punctuating with an exclamation mark. Whatever word is used, the meaning is that creation, symbolized by the four living creatures, is calling for Christ the Lamb to come to work out his redemption on the earth. The judgment of this passage is the negative aspect of that redemption.

After the Lamb opened the first of the seven seals and one of the four living creatures cried, *Come!* John saw a white horse whose *rider had a bow; a crown was given to him, and he came out conquering and to conquer.* The interpretation of this horse and rider has been more controversial than the other three. Historically, this image has usually been interpreted in one of three ways.

The rider on the white horse may represent war. This interpretation is favored by the symbols in the text. The *horse* was the animal that military leaders rode in battle (2 Macc. 3:25; 10:29). The *bow* was a traditional weapon of war (Jer. 51:56; Hos. 1:5). Two words are translated *crown* in Revelation: *stephanos,* for the victors' crown; *diadēma,* the royal crown. Here the former is used. In athletic competition in the ancient world, the winner was given a crown, much as a trophy is awarded today. By extension, the crown came to represent military victory. *White* was also a symbol of victory, perhaps owing to the warlike Parthians, who threatened the first-century Roman Empire and were reputed to have ridden on white horses. Because there are so many military symbols in the passage, it is probably best to interpret the rider on the white horse to refer to war. Nevertheless, two other possible interpretations of this rider have been offered.

A second interpretation is that the rider on the white horse is the antichrist—the Satanic, demonic adversary of Christ. This is the position of some futurists, who believe that such a person will arise on the scene at the end of time. It is associated with Ezekiel's prophecy of the invasion of Gog, who also fights with bow and arrows (Ezek. 39:3). The color *white* fits here as a symbol of counterfeit purity. Indeed, the *crown* symbol is consistent with this position because later crowns are placed on the heads of the dragon (12:1-3). Victory is thus the mark of the antichrist, the counterfeit, as well as of Christ (Eller, 1974:85). The main argument against this interpretation is that it makes this rider inconsistent with the others. The riders on the other horses, it will be seen, are not persons but symbols. Therefore, it is more consistent with the context to take the rider to be war than to be the antichrist.

A third interpretation that has been suggested for the rider on the white horse is in sharp contrast to the first two. Some commentators believe that the rider is *Christ* or *the proclamation of Christ's gospel.* Rowland explains the appearance of Christ in this sequence of judgments by asserting that the gospel is "a proclamation of salvation that inevitably includes judgment on unrepentant persons and institutions" (1998:611). In Revelation the color *white* is always a symbol of Christ or spiritual victory and never the victory of the forces of evil (1:14; 2:17; 3:4, 5, 18; 4:4; 6:11; 7:9, 13; 14:14; 19:11, 14; 20:11; Ladd, 1972:98). Indeed, this rider is not said to cause persecution as the others do. This interpretation is further supported by

Jesus in the Olivet Discourse, where he says, in the midst of his prediction of tribulation, that the gospel must be preached to the nations (Matt. 24:14; Mark 13:10). Revelation itself later speaks of the Word of God riding forth on a white horse to judge and make war (19:11-16). Chapter 19 unquestionably has Christ in mind.

Seeing the rider in chapter 6 as representing Christ, however, is problematic. Such an interpretation would require the Lamb to open the seal and then also be the rider that appears as a result of its opening. A more serious problem is that the other horses are out of character with this interpretation of the white horse; they are all symbols of tribulation. Most serious of all, when this horse is seen in parallel with the next three horses, which all have violent consequences, it immediately threatens the Lamb image of Christ. Moreover, the only similarity between the rider in this chapter and the one in chapter 19 is the color of the horse. The weapons are different: a *bow* in chapter 6 and a *sword* in chapter 19. The crowns worn are different: the crown of victory (*stephanos*) is worn in chapter 6, and the royal crown (*diadēma*) in chapter 19. It should be emphasized that it is not necessary always to interpret a symbol the same way in Revelation. In chapter 5, John has changed the traditional messianic symbol of the lion into Christ the Lamb. Indeed, many of the symbols change meanings in different contexts in Revelation.

Although there is considerable debate about the interpretation of the rider on the white horse, it is best taken to be a symbol of war, to test the saints and to punish the unfaithful (Beale, 1999:379). This is consistent with the remaining three riders, whose interpretations are less divergent.

The Rider on the Red Horse 6:3-4

When the Lamb opened the second seal, the second living creature called out, *Come!* and a rider on a *bright red* (literally, *red as fire*) horse appeared. The color of the dragon, or the devil, in 12:3, red is commonly associated with bloodshed. The *great sword* given to this rider reinforces the idea of bloodshed. Yet it is the sword usually associated, not with war, but with civil strife. The prophets connect a disintegration of society and perhaps the cosmos with the Day of the Lord (Isa. 19:2; Zech. 14:13; 1 Enoch 100:10-12; 2 Esd. 5:9; 6:24; 2 Bar. 48:37; 70:2-8). The image is further reinforced by the words: *its rider was permitted to take peace from the earth, so that people would slaughter one another.* The verb *was permitted* indicates that the action of the rider is tolerated, but not approved, by Christ the Lamb. The killing of *one another* reinforces the idea of civil upheaval, similar to that which took place in the years that followed the death of Nero. Indeed, strife and anarchy usually follow war among nations and states as the participants adjust internally to changes made as a result of the warfare. So the red horse and its rider symbolize the bloody civil strife that follows the conquests of war brought by the rider on the white horse.

An historical note will give some necessary background to this image. Revolutions and rebellions had been common in the period from 70 B.C. to A.D. 70. For example, the Romans had put down uprisings by the Anglians (Queen Boudica) in A.D. 62, the Parthians in A.D. 62, Gaul in A.D. 68, Germania in A.D. 69, and Judea in A.D. 66-70. While it is true that Roman rulers had given the world a period of general tranquility through the Pax Romana, this relative peace was based on the power of Rome. Although the general popular sentiment was gratitude, the Roman crushing of all resistance throughout the empire created some resentment, which had the potential to erupt at any time into violence. Indeed, with the expected imposition of emperor worship, John looked for violent warfare to break out soon *[Essay: Emperors and Emperor Worship]*.

Therefore, the first two riders represent war and its logical accompaniment, civil strife and bloodshed. In a similar manner, the interpretations for the next two riders follow logically from the first two.

The Rider on the Black Horse 6:5-6

When the Lamb opened the third seal, the third living creature said, *Come!* and a rider on a *black horse* appeared. This color is associated with mourning; persons wore black sackcloth for that purpose (1 Kings 21:27; 2 Kings 19:1; Esther 4:1; Ps. 35:13; Isa. 37:1-2; Jon. 3:5-6). Yet it is clear from the other symbols in the passage that this horse brings famine, the natural aftermath of war and civil strife. Walhout applies the passage to today: "The resources of the nation are expended in building up military might to enforce its will upon others, and that in turn creates an economic situation in which the regular needs of a daily living become secondary to building up the war machine" (2000:76).

The symbols taken together present a bleak picture. The *pair of scales* was commonly used for measuring out grain. It is therefore a symbol of scarcity (Lev. 26:26; Ezek. 4:16). The phrase *day's pay* translates the Greek word *denarius,* a silver coin that Jesus considers adequate pay for a day's labor (Matt. 20:2). A *quart* of grain was considered to be a normal daily ration (Herodotus 7.187). *A quart of wheat for a day's pay* means that a worker can only earn daily what is necessary for subsistence. By comparison, Cicero noted that in his time a *denarius* would buy twelve quarts of wheat (*Oration against Verres* 3.81). The situation described in this passage of Revelation was serious, but starvation did not seem imminent. The phrase *three quarts of barley for a day's pay* indicates a way that the poor could subsist. Barley was three times as cheap as wheat and was considered the food of the poor. If persons wanted to purchase wheat, they could buy only enough for themselves; if they chose barley, they could scarcely feed their family.

Yet the rider said, *do not damage the olive oil and the wine!* Because olive trees and vineyards are more deeply rooted than wheat and barley, they can survive famine better. It is more important to the meaning of the passage to note, however, that oil and wine were most likely commodities of the rich in the same way that barley was the grain of the poor. Elsewhere in Revelation, oil and wine only occur among the merchants' cargo of luxury items (Royalty, 1998:182). During the days of Nero, famine left the rich untouched; indeed, there seems to have been an over-production of oil and wine and a scarcity of grain. Therefore, in A.D. 92, Domitian issued an edict to cut back the number of vineyards in Asia so that more grain could be grown. However, there was so much opposition that the edict was revoked and the vineyards were left untouched. Others have argued that grain, oil, and cheap wine were all staples of life in the ancient world (Deut. 7:13; 11:14; 28:51; 2 Chron. 32:28; Neh. 5:11; Hos. 2:8, 22; Joel 2:19; Hag. 1:11) and should not be seen as luxuries. Still others have insisted that the oil and wine were sacrificial elements kept in the temple; therefore, to harm them would have been sacrilege. Indeed, during the siege of Jerusalem in A.D. 70, Emperor Titus ordered that the olive trees and vineyards not be ravaged, presumably so that the rituals of worship could continue (Ford, 1975:107). Nevertheless, the theme of the opulent wealth of Rome, especially as portrayed in chapter 17, seems to imply that the oil and wine *are* luxuries. As is often the case in times of famine, the luxuries of the rich are available, but the necessities of the poor are in short supply. The prosperity of the Roman Empire during the Flavian period brought conflict between the rich merchants and the heavily taxed poor (Thompson, 1990:17; Pilgrim, 1999:158-59). Smith notes: "In every economy and also in our own some people amass obscene fortunes while others can barely eke out a living" (2000:28). The sense of the passage seems to be that, in times of scarcity, the rich get richer and the poor get poorer.

The persons of John's day would have known about famine. Historical sources tell us of famines in Rome, Greece, and Judea during the first century. In those days, as today, famine leads ultimately to the judgment of the fourth seal.

The Rider on the Pale Green Horse 6:7-8

When the Lamb opened the fourth seal, the fourth living creature said, *Come!* and a rider on a *pale green horse* appeared. The word describing the color of this horse has been variously translated, but seems to refer to the color of the rotting flesh of a corpse, and thus it clearly represents death, the epitome of the four plagues.

The symbols associated with the rider confirm this interpretation. The name of the rider is *death*, and *Hades* follows *[Glossary: Hades, Gehenna]*. *Hades* is the kingdom where death presides, the under-world or the grave (Aune, 1998a:401). The other symbols—*sword, famine, pestilence,* and *wild animals*—are all associated with death, which was *given authority over a fourth of the earth.* Fractions occur quite often in the judgments of Revelation and are probably not to be taken literally but as a symbol of God's mercy. The meaning is that the judgments of the riders on the horses, which culminate in death brought by the *pale green horse,* are terrible but are not the end. The fraction communicates that no matter how much war, civil strife, famine, and death are experienced in this world, God's mercy preserves those who overcome.

The Martyrs under the Altar 6:9-11

When the Lamb opened the fifth seal, another horse and rider did not appear as would be expected. Instead, John *saw under the altar the souls of those who had been slaughtered.* Some background on the altar of sacrifice illumines this statement. Revelation refers to two of the altars of the Jerusalem temple—the altar of incense (8:3-5), and the altar of sacrifice (11:1). In verse 9, where the blood of the martyrs is described, the altar of sacrifice seems to be in mind. The altar of incense is in focus when the prayers of the saints are offered in verse 10. On the altar of sacrifice, when the animal was killed, the blood was allowed to run off the foot of the altar and was caught underneath (Exod. 29:12; Lev. 4:7). The blood was thought to contain the life of the animal victim (Lev. 17:11, 14); the life of the sacrifice flowed out of the body and onto the floor underneath the altar. This is a vivid way of picturing the martyrdom of the saints *[Glossary: Martyr]*: the mar-tyred saints have been offered as a sacrifice on the altar in the temple. Just as the animal sacrifices were offered to God in the Jerusalem tem-ple, so the martyrs, who suffer and die for their faith, are offered as sacrifices to God in this heavenly temple. Just as Christ the Lamb was slain on the cross for the sins of the world (5:6), so Christians are persecuted and even die as a result of their testimony for Christ. This passage tells us that there is a sense in which, through suffering and dying for their faith in this world, Christians participate with Christ in the redemption brought through his suffering and death on the cross (Col. 1:24). Revelation was written to prepare Christians to undergo such persecutions.

One of the most difficult passages in Revelation to understand and accept is the response of the martyrs: *Sovereign Lord, holy and true, how long will it be before you judge and avenge our blood on the inhabitants of the earth?* This does parallel the attitude found in extracanonical material (1 Enoch 47:1-2; 97:3-5; 99:3, 16; 104:3); yet this vengeful attitude seems inconsistent with Christian principles of forgiveness and longsuffering toward enemies (Matt. 5:44-45; 6:12; 18:21-22).

To understand the attitude, we must know a bit about the historical context of Revelation. It was a time of great catastrophe. We have already referred to the revolutions in Judea, which culminated in the War of Jerusalem in A.D. 70, when the temple was destroyed. Moreover, the volcano of Mount Vesuvius erupted in A.D. 79, and a great famine devastated Judea in A.D. 80. Indeed, Christians had experienced additional trial, because in the A.D. 60s, Nero persecuted them either to divert blame for the fire of Rome from himself to Christians or to avoid possible religiously based insurrections. Some Christians were tarred and ignited to light Nero's racetrack; others were dressed in animal skins and placed in the arena to be attacked by wild dogs *[Essay: Persecution during Nero's Reign]*. Even some non-Christians criticized Nero's persecution of Christians. The portrayal of the martyrs' cry of revenge here must be seen in this context.

Nevertheless, such a vengeful attitude on the part of Christians begs for explanation. Several considerations should be kept in mind (for a more complete treatment of the vengeance theme, see Boring, 1989:112-19). First, it should be noted that the martyrs' cry for revenge is not on their own behalf, because they have already been killed. Their cry is on behalf of those who might be persecuted in the future; they are asking God to intervene for others. Second, the cry of the martyrs may not be so much for vengeance as for justice. The original meaning of the word *avenge* is "deliver" or "save." God's salvation will not be complete unless injustice is punished. Pilgrim affirms: "Without justice, the universe is at the mercy of the powerful and strong.... [Revelation] speaks for the underside of history, from the vantage-point of the marginalized and dispossessed" (1999:176-77). Indeed, Mounce argues that the reputation of God is at stake here: if God does not intervene to judge the wicked, the justice of God is questionable (1977:158). Third, the martyrs' experience must be remembered. The cry for vengeance is a human response. Perhaps what can be learned from the passage is that, although it is easy to criticize the martyrs standing outside their experience, their attitude under the circumstances is certainly understandable (cf. Ps. 137; Jer. 20:12).

Klassen has provided a treatment of vengeance that helps the reader understand this passage and others in Revelation that seem to portray God and the Lamb as warriors. Their warfare is almost always defensive or a means of judgment (19:11); the saints are portrayed as participating in the Lamb's victory but not the warfare (17:14); and the victory is won, not with armed force, but with the Word of God wielded by the slain Lamb (19:15). Klassen summarizes: "The emphasis ... on the time beyond history is not upon viewing with delight the sufferings of the unrighteous but on the unhindered fellowship between those who follow the Lamb and Him who made their obedience possible" (1966:305-11).

The vengeance was called upon *the inhabitants of the earth*. This is a phrase used consistently in Revelation to refer, not to everyone on the earth, but to the wicked *[Glossary: Inhabitants of the Earth]*. It especially refers to those who are hostile to God and are at home in the present wicked world. Later they will be portrayed as the ones who sell out materially to Satan. They stand in contrast to the martyrs, who have given their lives in defiance of the immorality and wicked greed of the world.

These martyrs *were each given a white robe*. In Jewish literature, robes are a sign of heavenly existence (1 Enoch 62:15-16; 2 Enoch 22:8; 2 Esd. 2:39-44; Asc. Isa. 4:16; 9:9). Paul speaks about a spiritual body that replaces the physical one (1 Cor. 15:35-41; 2 Cor. 5:1-5; Phil. 3:21). The white robes are probably these spiritual bodies that are given to saints at their resurrection. Ladd's argument that this symbol cannot refer to resurrection bodies because these would already have been given to the martyrs at death (1972:106) probably imposes too strict a chronology on Revelation. At least, the white robes symbolize the spiritual blessedness of those who are martyred for their faith. Goldsworthy says: "Those who have died for the faith (and those who will yet die), have not suffered in vain. They are secure because they have the robe of Christ's righteousness" (1984:51).

Another element of the passage that is difficult to understand is that the martyrs were *told to rest a little longer, until the number would be complete both of their fellow servants and of their brothers and sisters, who were soon to be killed as they themselves had been killed.* This seems to be saying that the judgment of the wicked will not come until the number of the elect, determined by God, has been completed (2 Esd. 4:33-37). There are several possible interpretations of this phrase. First, the most literal explanation is that God has a limited number of vacancies in heaven, which must be filled before the final judgment can come. The number is most often 144,000 (cf. 7:1-8; 14:1-5). Yet to limit the saints, and even the martyrs, to 144,000 seems to contradict reality and impose an overly literal interpretation on the text. Indeed, in 7:9, Revelation seems to have no interest in numbering the followers of Christ.

Second, it may be that the phrase is simply Revelation's way of saying much more persecution and martyrdom must occur before the end will come, an interpretation that avoids some of the difficulties of the first. Third, the phrase may be indicating that the suffering of the martyrs is the means by which God is carrying out victory over evil and that the victory will not be completed for a while (Caird, 1966:87). Richard Hays says it this way: "Those who follow [the Lamb] in persecution and death are not filling a randomly determined quota of martyrs; rather, they are enacting the will of God, who has chosen to overcome evil precisely in and through righteous suffering, not in spite of it" (1996:179). This interpretation is consistent with what was said earlier about the relation between the suffering of the martyrs and that of Christ. Yet if it seems too complex to be attributed to the author, the second provides a viable alternative.

The Great Earthquake 6:12-17

When the Lamb opened the sixth seal, a *great earthquake* occurred. It was noted earlier that the churches in Asia had experienced a number of earthquakes in the first century. Yet this is not a local quake like they had endured; it is of cosmic proportions. In the prophetic tradition, such earthquakes were associated with the Day of the Lord (Exod. 19:18; Isa. 2:19; 13:9-10; 34:4; Jer. 4:24; Ezek. 32:7-8; Hos. 10:8; Joel 2:10; Amos 8:8-9; Nah. 1:5; Hag. 2:6; 2 Bar. 70:8). Here earthquakes are described in the same way that the prophets described them: *the sun became black as sackcloth, the full moon became like blood, and the stars of the sky fell to the earth as the fig tree drops its winter fruit when shaken by a gale. The sky vanished like a scroll rolling itself up, and every mountain and island was removed from its place.* The darkening of the sun is compared to *sackcloth*, a dark black fabric made from goat's hair. The stars are represented as attached to the firmament from which they come loose and fall to the earth. That the sky *vanished* is stated in a word that literally means to "split," "separate," or "tear." It is used of the rolling up of a cloak or scroll. Thus, the sky is considered a solid substance that can be rolled up. The image is of a heavy metal scroll snapping shut. This ancient conception of the universe is used to portray catastrophic spiritual truths. The most stable elements of the world are only temporary (Aune, 1998a:416). It should be noted that the order in which the earth is destroyed is approximately the order of the creation—earth, sun, moon, stars, sky, mountains and islands, and humans (Ford, 1975:112). Hence, creation is undone by this catastrophic earthquake.

Verse 15 mentions persons of various walks of life who were affected by the earthquake: *the kings of the earth and the magnates and the generals and the rich and the powerful, and everyone, slave and free.* Comments could be made describing each of these social classes, but that would be to miss the primary meaning. Seven classes are included, and it has been noted that the number seven indicates completion *[Essay: Gematria].* While the list emphasizes persons of wealth and power, these seven classifications of persons symbolize that all of humanity are affected by the earthquake, regardless of their social standing. Indeed, they hide *in the caves and among the rocks of the mountains.* The point is that all humans must recoil in recognition of their sin and its resulting guilt. The text refers to this time of judgment as *the great day,* a clear allusion to the Old Testament Day of the Lord (Joel 2:11; 3:4; Nah. 1:6; Zeph. 1:14-16; 2:3; Mal. 3:2), a concept also evident in the New Testament (see TBC, The Relation to the New Testament). The *wrath of the Lamb,* an apparent oxymoron (Barr, 1998:87), most likely describes God's action "to right every wrong, to overturn every injustice, to call a halt to all oppression" (R. Smith, 2000:35). The obvious answer to the question Who is able to stand? is No one (Aune, 1998a:423).

THE TEXT IN BIBLICAL CONTEXT

The Relation to the Old Testament

The structural background of this passage is in the visions of Zechariah. In Zechariah 1, a man is introduced "riding on a red horse ... and behind him were red, sorrel, and white horses" (v. 8). The purpose of these horses is to patrol the earth in a time of peace (v. 11). In Zechariah 6, four chariots appear: "The first chariot had red horses, the second chariot black horses, the third chariot white horses, and the fourth chariot dappled gray horses" (vv. 2-3). In this passage, the chariots are identified with the four winds, and they patrol the various parts of the earth. The colors do not seem at all significant.

While the horses and chariots of Zechariah do not seem to be associated with destruction, a picture of the ultimate disintegration of the evil world and society is present in Zechariah 14:

> the Mount of Olives shall be split in two from east to west by a very wide valley; so that one half of the Mount shall withdraw northward, and the other half southward.... and you shall flee as you fled from the earthquake in the days of King Uzziah of Judah. (vv. 4-5)

These cosmic judgments are accompanied by social disintegration similar to that portrayed by the four horses and their riders:

> This shall be the plague with which the LORD will strike all the peoples that wage war against Jerusalem: their flesh shall rot while they are still on their feet; their eyes shall rot in their sockets, and their tongues shall rot in their mouths. On that day a great panic from the LORD shall fall on them, so that each will seize the hand of a neighbor, and the hand of the one will be raised against the hand of the other; even Judah will fight at Jerusalem. And the wealth of all the surrounding nations shall be collected—gold, silver, and garments in great abundance. And a plague like this plague shall fall on the horses, the mules, the camels, the donkeys, and whatever animals may be in those camps. (vv. 12-15)

As was noted before, these pictures of cosmic and societal judgment are common in the Old Testament prophetic tradition (cf. Isa. 2:19; 13:9-13; 19:2; 34:4; Jer. 4:24; Ezek. 32:7-9; Hos. 10:8; Joel 2:10; Amos 8:8-9; Nah. 1:5; Hag. 2:6; 1 Enoch 100:10-12; 2 Esd. 5:9-13; 6:24; 2 Bar. 48:37; 70:2-8).

The Relation to the New Testament

Although the structure of the vision of the horses and their riders is from Zechariah, the content of the seal judgments is from the Synoptic Gospels, specifically the Olivet discourse of Jesus. The following chart adapted from Court (1979:51) makes the parallels in content between the seal judgments and the synoptic traditions quite clear.

Six Seals in Revelation	Apocalyptic Traditions of Synoptic Gospels
1. 6:1-2 White Horse	Wars/Rumors/Insurrections (Matt. 24:6; Mark 13:7; Luke 21:9) Many will come in my name (Matt. 24:5; Mark 13:6; Luke 21:8)
2. 6:3-4 Red Horse	Nation against nation (Matt. 24:7; Mark 13:8; Luke 21:10) Sword (Matt. 10:34)
3. 6:5-6 Black Horse	Famines (Matt. 24:7; Mark 13:8; Luke 21:11)
4. 6:7-8 Pale Green Horse	Plagues, Pestilences (Matt. 24:7 [Variant]; Luke 21:11)
5. 6:9-11 Souls under Altar	Persecution/Christian Witness (Matt. 24:9-14; 10:17-22; Mark 13:9-13; Luke 12:11-12; 21:12-19) How Long? (Matt. 24:22; Mark 13:20; Luke 18:7-8)
6. 6:12-17 Great Earthquake	Great Earthquakes (Matt. 24:7; Mark 13:8; Luke 21:11) Sun, Moon, Stars (Matt. 24:29; Mark 13:24-25; Luke 21:25) Fear (Luke 21:26) Fall on us (Luke 23:20)

Although the content of the seal judgments is largely based on the apocalyptic traditions of the Synoptic Gospels, the Day of the Lord is also addressed in a number of other New Testament passages (Rom. 2:5; 1 Cor. 1:8; 2 Cor. 1:14; Eph. 4:30; Phil. 1:10; 2 Thess. 2:2; Jude 6). In spite of the emphasis on judgment, the writers of the New Testament recognize a sense of hope for the Christian in time of catastrophe. Along with the martyrs in Revelation, the faithful are told to rejoice because their suffering is an offering of faith (Phil. 2:17-18; 2 Tim. 4:6-8).

Indeed, it must be remembered that the entire biblical witness indicates that the persecution and martyrdom described in the seal judgments of Revelation are not the final word. It is through witness in times of suffering that the saints participate with Christ in his suffering and death. Persecution and tribulation are the means through which Christ's redemption is obtained. Thus, when Christians suffer and die with Christ, they recognize that they will also participate in the resurrection to new life.

THE TEXT IN THE LIFE OF THE CHURCH

A Variety of Interpretations

The church has basically interpreted passages like the horses and their riders in three ways: preterist, futurist, and idealist. This passage provides an excellent opportunity to see these interpretations at work (see Entering the World of Revelation, Interpreting Revelation).

The *preterist* looks for the symbols in the first century. If a person is in mind, the primary referent for the white horse might be Emperor Domitian, the great threat to the faithful saints who was viewed as Nero reborn *[Essay: Nero Redivivus Myth]*. If not limited to a single person, the preterist might find the referent for the rider on the white horse in the Parthians, the warlike people who lived southeast of the Caspian Sea and were a constant threat to the eastern end of the Roman Empire when Revelation was written. They were reputed to be skilled in the use of the bow and to ride white horses into battle. In A.D. 62 Volgesus led the Parthians on white horses in defeat of the Roman army (Slater, 1999:175). The preterist might see the rider on the red horse as the bloodshed by which Rome squelched any civil strife throughout the empire. Indeed, Christians expected more persecution and bloodshed because of their unwillingness to worship the emperor. To the preterist, the rider on the black horse alludes to times of famine during the first century, especially one during the reign of Nero in the early sixties. With the coming of the reign of Domitian, a ruler similar to Nero, more famine was expected. The preterist would probably see the rider on the pale green horse as referring to persons like those who suffered under Nero *[Essay: Persecution during Nero's Reign]*. It was thought that Domitian's rule would kill an even greater number of Christians.

Futurists look for the referents for the horses and their riders in their contemporary context. The rider on the white horse is seen either as the antichrist marching to eschatological battle or as Christ proclaiming the gospel before the end. Because the rider on the white horse does not represent war, the one on the red horse is usually interpreted as such. Walvoord says that "the hope for peace by means of the United Nations and other human efforts is doomed to failure" because of warfare initiated by the rider on the red horse (1966:129). The black horse brings famine resulting from the wars initiated by the rider on the red horse. Finally, the pale green horse causes the death of many persons, perhaps due to the advanced technology of warfare in the modern world.

Idealists propose symbolic referents for the riders on the horses.

The symbols refer to a permanent reality—that war does indeed lead to civil strife, famine, and death. An idealist interpretation might focus on the evil associated with war. Such an interpretation undercuts the attempt to glorify war in every time period in history; war inevitably leads to civil strife, famine, death, and many other tragedies. This is a truth that peace church members should be eager to proclaim.

The question arises: Which of these methods of interpretation is best? There are difficulties with each. The preterist must deal with the problem of not knowing specifically to what aspect of the first-century world the passage is referring. Is the white horse Nero, Domitian, the Parthians, or all three? The futurists have the even greater difficulty knowing what aspects of the present context fit the symbols. Every time period in history has had its alleged antichrist; in the twentieth century the candidates included Mussolini, Hitler, Kissinger, Gorbachev, and Saddam Hussein. Although many Christians are uncomfortable with the symbolic approach of the idealists because it lacks specificity, it does seem that this position avoids the interpretive difficulties of the others.

The Problem of Evil

A major problem that has troubled people of faith throughout history is how evil is related to God. The persecutions and tribulations of Revelation focus this issue. The text says that the riders of the horses were given the power by the Lamb to cause calamity. In what sense is Christ responsible for the evil in the world?

Revelation assumes that all power, whether good or evil, comes ultimately from God. Yet God has given this power to humans to use according to their free will. When humans misuse the power that God has entrusted to them, disasters come—war, civil strife, famine, and death. Nevertheless, in the process, God turns this misuse of power into righteous judgment for breaking the laws of justice built into the created universe. So although God does not approve of the disasters, they are necessary for God to judge this misuse of the divinely given power. Therefore, the evil described in Revelation is due to the sinful misuse of power by human leaders that must be judged if God is to be regarded as just.

An idealistic interpretation of this passage presents the tragic and inevitable progression that takes place as a result of armed conflict. War leads to civil strife, famine, and death. This permanent reality can be seen in the world around us. Living in Africa several years ago, I saw the effects of war. In many of the nations, revolutions were occurring that removed one leader from power and installed another but that left the political situation basically unchanged. Another tragedy was that war also made the human quality of life much worse. War caused incredible pain. Some of my acquaintances, and several of their family members died in the fighting. Moreover, war led to the destruction of crops and widespread famine. The inevitable result was the death of thousands of persons through battle and starvation. Ironically, Revelation reminds us that some persons are not touched by the catastrophes of war. The wealthy and the powerful continue to enjoy their goods and privileges, while the poor and powerless bear the brunt of the suffering. I personally witnessed the poor earning one dollar per day in a country where the expensive luxury cars of the wealthy were constantly evident on the streets. The message of the rider on the white horse is a permanent reality demonstrated by the present situation in the world.

The Witness of the Martyrs

Clarence Jordan's brother was a state senator and chief justice of the Georgia Supreme Court. When asked to support Clarence's racially integrated Koinonia Farms, he declined, saying: "I follow Jesus up to a point." Clarence asked: "Could that [point] be the cross?" His brother responded: "That's right. I follow him to the cross, but not on the cross. I'm not going to get myself crucified" (Turner, 2000:45).

In Revelation, persons killed for their faith are in heaven with God [Glossary: Martyr]. Martyrdom is something with which persons in the believers church tradition can identify. In the sixteenth century many were killed for their witness (see Waltner, 1999:107-9, 149-50). In subsequent years, they have often been persecuted and ridiculed for their opposition to the evil practices of the world. This is the means through which Christ is carrying out the redemption of the world. Christ's suffering and death on the cross is the model; his witness brought about the redemption of the world. Likewise, martyrs participate in Christ's redemption. It is clear from the passage that it is through the suffering of martyrs that Christ's redemption continues to be activated. Eller says: "We contribute to the coming of the kingdom by making like the Lamb, [by] being willing, in love, to *give* ourselves, even to the slaughter" (1974:93).

Revelation 7:1-17

The Two Multitudes

PREVIEW

The vision of the two multitudes in chapter 7 forms a parenthesis between the first six seals (ch. 6) and seventh seal (8:1-5). Yet the sixth seal actually ends the seal cycle of judgments, and the seventh seal announces the trumpet cycle. Moreover, the seven trumpets appear first in the paragraph on the seventh seal (8:1-5). Thus, the judgment series are interlocked. The last member of the seal judgments introduces the trumpet judgments.

Before the trumpet judgments, the people of God are sealed. The breaking of the seals in chapter 6 is followed by the sealings of chapter 7. God's people who remain faithful are sealed for their protection and ultimate survival. The small group of alienated Christians in Asia are told that, in their suffering, they are part of something bigger (Boring, 1989:128). Likewise, Christians who endure persecution for their faith today are shown that they are part of a great multitude who have suffered before them.

The question, "Who is able to stand?" in Revelation 6:17 is answered in chapter 7—"a great multitude that no one could count" (v. 9). After hearing of the persecutions that are poured out on the earth in the seal judgments, Christians logically ask, What will happen to us? Chapter 7 answers this question with words of consolation. This protection of the righteous is affirmed in a context of terrible tribulation, and this gives comfort to followers of Christ the Lamb. They have nothing to fear from the judgments. Although they will go through tribulation, they will be protected by God (9:4) like the Israelites were protected in the midst of the plagues of Egypt. The protection of God's people is contrasted to the fate of the inhabitants of the earth, the unrighteous, who feel the full force of the tribulation (16:2).

The message of the passage is that the persecutions will be withheld until God's people are sealed for their protection. This parallels, in the Hebrew tradition, a pause before the Flood for the building of the ark (Gen. 6-7; 1 Enoch 66:1–67:3) and before the destruction of the Temple for the promise of its restoration (2 Bar. 6:4–7:1).

Chapter 7 falls into two parts, just like the seal judgments are grouped into the four horsemen and the two succeeding catastrophes. Each of the two crowds mentioned in the chapter is introduced by *after this I looked/saw* (vv. 1, 9). The crowds are the same entity viewed from two different perspectives. The 144,000 represent the people of God on the brink of tribulation in this world—the persecuted church; the great multitude symbolizes the people of God who have come out of tribulation and are enjoying their reward in heaven—the triumphant church.

Moreover, the two crowds communicate two paradoxical truths. On the one hand, the 144,000 saints divided into twelve groups of 12,000 each indicate that no one is left out; all are numbered and thus accounted for. In persecution, there is confidence in knowing that God understands the plight of persecuted Christians and cares about each one of them. On the other hand, the great multitude emphasizes that the redeemed are a vast throng beyond counting. In persecution, there is security in knowing that multitudes of people have endured such travail and overcome it. Peterson says that these contrasting ideas are repeated in the manner of Hebrew parallelism (1988:83-84).

OUTLINE

144,000, 7:1-8
Great Multitude, 7:9-17

EXPLANATORY NOTES

144,000 7:1-8

Initially, John *saw four angels*, paralleling the four horsemen of the seal judgments. In Revelation, specific angels have powers over various elements of the physical universe. One angel received power over fire (14:18; see also 2 Bar. 6:4), and another received dominion over the waters (16:5; see also 1 Enoch 66:1-2). In this case, the four angels are in charge of the destructive winds.

These angels of the winds were *standing at the four corners of the earth.* Some think this means that John thought the earth was a rectangle. Yet in the second century B.C., Alexandrian scientists speculated that the earth was round and even calculated its circumference with some degree of accuracy. Furthermore, Isaiah refers to the earth as a circle (40:22). Thus, it is likely that John uses the four corners to refer to what we would call the cardinal points of the compass and, in this way, to the earth in its entirety (Isa. 11:11-12; Ezek. 7:2; Rev. 20:8).

The angels were *holding back the four winds of the earth.* In Hebrew tradition, God held back the angels of the waters so work on the ark of Noah could be completed (1 Enoch 66:1-2), and an angel restrained other angels with torches from burning Jerusalem until the temple articles were protected (3 Bar. 6:4-5). In ancient cosmological thinking, winds were often described as destructive powers (Matt. 14:30-32; Mark 6:47-52; John 6:18; Acts 27:14), and unfavorable winds were thought to come from the corners of the earth (Jer. 49:36; Dan. 7:2; 1 Enoch 76:1-4; 34:1-3; Apoc. PseudoJohn 15). Likewise, destructive nations attacked from the four corners of the earth (Rev. 20:8). Moreover, the judgment of the Lord is pictured as destruction by wind (Ps. 83:13; Jer. 23:19; 30:23; Hos. 13:15). Indeed, the four winds are the same powers as previously were symbolized by the four horsemen (Zech. 6:1-8; Rev. 6:1-8), the destructive forces of the world that are controlled by God (Deut. 33:26; Ps. 29:10; 68:33-34; 104:3-4; Isa. 19:1; 40:7, 24; 66:15; Jer. 4:11-13; 23:19; Hos. 13:15; Nah. 1:8; Hab. 3:8; Zech. 9:14; Jub. 2:2). The meaning of this image is that the destructive powers of tribulation are in the hands of God and the angelic host.

The reason the winds were held back was *so that no wind could blow on earth or sea or against any tree.* Ford suggests that the change from the genitive case for earth and sea to the accusative for tree indicates that tree is an addition (1975:115). Elsewhere, in similar contexts, the mention is not made of a tree (Dan. 7:2; 1 Enoch 76:4). Because there is no textual basis on which to reject it, it is best to assume that the tree is included by John for a reason. Trees are helpful to determine whether or not the wind is blowing (Eller, 1974:96) and are particularly vulnerable to strong winds (6:13). It may also be that the tree is used metaphorically for human beings, especially "those that dwell on the earth," since trees were commonly used this way in Jewish literature (Ezek. 31:14; cf. Mark 4:32c). The Targums substitute persons for trees in the text of Isaiah (2:13;

14:8; 61:3). Vulnerability to the destructive powers of tribulation is highlighted by the inclusion of the picture of a fierce wind blowing against a tree.

John then *saw another angel ascending from the rising of the sun*. The east, where the sun rose, was the location of Eden (Gen. 2:8; 1 Enoch 32:1-6) and the place of divine revelation (Isa. 41:2). The glory of God entered the east gate of the temple (Ezek. 43:2-4); the messiah was expected to come from the east (Sib. Or. 3:652-56); the star announcing Jesus's birth rose in the east; and the wise men came to visit Jesus from the east (Matt. 2:1-2). Moreover, east was the direction of Palestine from the perspective of Asia Minor. This angel from the rising of the sun would certainly symbolize hope in the context of tribulation.

This angel had *the seal of the living God*. In Revelation, the seal of the living God placed on the righteous is the counterpart of the mark of the beast on the wicked (13:16-17; 14:9-11; 17:5; 19:20; 20:4); "every human bears one of two seals" (Murphy, 1998:219). Boring calls the mark of the beast "a pale imitation of God's marking his servants" (1989:129). Barclay says the reason for the power of this seal is that it is from the living God rather than "the dead gods of the heathen" (1960:2.25; see also Josh. 3:10; Ps. 42:2; Isa. 44:9, 17-18). Although several connotations are possible for the seal, the image of protection seems to fit best the context of tribulation (see TBC, Seal of the Living God). Yet there is no promise here that God's people will escape persecution; indeed, they may even suffer and die. The assurance is that they will be able to overcome tribulation because they have received God's mark. The meaning of the passage is that the 144,000 are those who have declared and continue to declare their loyalty to Christ, knowing that he will be with them in tribulation. Thus, the followers of Christ can face the tribulation knowing that if they overcome they will be protected in the sense that they will be granted a place in heaven with God as part of the great throng that no one can number.

John *heard the number of those who were sealed, one hundred forty-four thousand*. Some argue that the 144,000 are martyrs who receive protection to give their witness. Thus, the symbol parallels the martyrs under the altar in chapter 6 and the two witnesses of chapter 11. Yet the passage does not say they are martyrs; and it presents them on the brink, not as the casualties, of tribulation (v. 3). Dispensationalists believe that the 144,000 are the saved remnant of devout Jews who witness that Christ was the messiah in the tribulation after the saints have been raptured from the earth. This position is not supported in the biblical text; there is no evidence that the church has been raptured; and clearly, all nations, not just Jews, are persecuted (13:7). Moreover, although Walvoord contends that this passage along with Isaiah 11:11-12 is evidence the twelve tribes will be reconstituted (1966:141; see also 2 Esd. 13:39-45), ten of them were dispersed several centuries before the writing of Revelation (cf. Barker, 2000:163-165; Aune, 1998a:461).

A more moderate position than dispensationalism holds that the 144,000 are Jewish people who will become Christians. Malachi argues that the prophet Elijah will return to bring a conversion to the Jewish people (Mal. 4:5-6). Augustine adds that this conversion under the influence of the great prophet Elijah will be to the true messiah, our Christ (*City of God* 20.29). Thus, it is contended that this passage refers to the eventual salvation of Israel. Support for this is found in Paul's contention that, after the period of the Gentiles, God will turn again to Israel (Rom. 11:11-32). However, this position suffers from two of the same criticisms as the immediately preceding one: the inclusion of all nations in the persecution of the beast from the sea (13:7), and the dispersion of ten of the twelve tribes of Israel.

The best interpretation of the 144,000 is that they symbolically represent the Christian church. The dispersion of the ten tribes and the irregularity of the list of tribes that follows seem to indicate that John is not speaking literally of Israel. The meaning is that the followers of Christ are sealed so they can overcome the great tribulation and emerge victoriously as the great multitude in heaven with God. The number 144,000 is clearly symbolic. Twelve is the number both of the patriarchs who gave their names to the tribes of Israel, and of the apostles of Christ the Lamb. When multiplied together to equal 144, they represent the entire people of God under the old and new covenants. One thousand is used in the Hebrew scriptures symbolically of a large quantity (Exod. 20:6; Deut. 1:11; 7:9; 1 Sam. 18:7; 21:11; Ps. 3:6; 68:17; Dan. 7:10). It often designates a division of an army, which adds to the picture that the 144,000 are about to do battle with the forces of the beast (Num. 31:14, 48; Deut. 1:15; 1 Sam. 8:12; 22:7; 2 Sam. 18:1, 4). Of course, they are a strange army because they conquer, not by destroying the enemy, but by being martyred and thus identifying with their leader, the Lamb that was slain.

The 144,000 were *sealed out of every tribe of the people of Israel*. The list that follows is different from any ordering of tribes in the Hebrew scriptures. Dan is missing, and Levi is added in most manuscripts to complete the number 12. Dan replaces Gad in some manuscripts and Manasseh in others. It has been suggested that the deletion of Dan was due to its change to Man, short for Manasseh, but the evidence is weak. It is better to find the reason for the omission in the Hebrew tradition connected with the tribe of Dan. The tribe was associated with idolatry and was thus considered to be unfaithful (Lev. 24:11; Judg. 5:17; 18:30; Jer. 8:16-17). Jeroboam set up two golden calves to be worshiped in Dan and Bethel (1 Kings 12:28-33). Beasley-Murray suggests that the location of the tribe of Dan in the north (Num. 2:25), the direction of darkness, caused the association of Dan with the darkness of idolatry (1974:143). Perhaps out of this connection with idolatry and Jacob's association of Dan with a snake (Gen. 49:17), Hebrew tradition held that Satan was the prince of the tribe of Dan (Test. Dan 5:4-7; 6:1). Christian tradition said the antichrist would come from Dan (Irenaeus, *Adv. Haer.* 5.30.2). The implication of the deletion of the tribe of Dan is that, in the battle between Christ and the antichrist, the unfaithful tribe of Dan is left unsealed (Wall, 1991:118; cf. Aune, 1998a:462-63).

The listing of the tribes is also unusual in including Joseph instead of Ephraim and in mentioning Judah first. Although the tribe of Ephraim was also associated with idolatry (Hos. 4:17–14:9, especially 5:9) and with "accommodation to Roman life" (Thompson, 1998:107), Ephraim's exclusion from this list is probably best explained simply in the substituting of Joseph for his son, Ephraim. The placing of Judah first in the list is more significant and is related to the exclusion of Dan. While Dan was the tribe of the antichrist, Judah was the tribe of Christ (Gen. 49:8-12; Heb. 7:14; Rev. 5:5). In the listing of genealogies in 1 Chronicles 3–7, the sons of Judah are listed after those of David and Solomon and before the offspring of the other patriarchs. Judah is probably placed first in Revelation 7 because it is the tribe of Christ the Lamb.

In any case, the ordering here is different from any other available list of the patriarchs. This may indicate that a symbolic interpretation of the nation of Israel is in order. Nevertheless, it should be noted that the Bible contains about twenty different sequences arranged according to the geographical location of the tribes, the birth order of the patriarchs, the pairing the patriarchs with their mothers, and so forth. Only one list repeats itself, and that sequence does begin with Judah in a geographical order from south to north (Num. 2:3-31; 10:14-28).

Great Multitude 7:9-17

In the second half of chapter 7, the tone changes from tribulation to glory, and the scene changes from earth to heaven. In verses 1-8 the church is pictured on the brink of tribulation; in verses 9-17 it is presented in heaven with God after the persecution is over. Efird says that chapter 7 answers "the question of what happens to those who are martyred in the tribulation" (1989:76).

In this passage, the ones who have overcome tribulation emerge in heaven with Christ, who was martyred and raised to glory before them (Mark 8:31-33; 9:2-8). Because they have been loyal to God and have overcome the tribulation, they are granted a glimpse of their future reward, the promise to those who were sealed in the previous passage. Roloff indicates that this reward is paralleled in the vision of the city of God (1993:96; 7:15a and 22:3; 7:15c and 21:3; and 7:17 and 21:4).

The promise God made to Abraham that his seed would be as numerous as the stars in the sky and the sand of the sea (Gen. 15:5; 32:12; Heb. 11:12) and that he would be the father of many nations (Gen. 17:4-6, 16; also 35:11; 48:19; Rom. 4:16-18; Sir. 44:19) are both fulfilled in this passage (Aune, 1998a:466). John observed *a great multitude that no one could count*. The followers of Christ the Lamb, the seed of Abraham, are the great multitude. That the great multitude is *from every nation, from all tribes and peoples and languages* makes it clear that this group is not limited to Jews but includes the remnant of the Gentiles (Isa. 45:20-25; 66:19-24; Jer. 23:3; Mic. 4:7; Zech. 9:4; 14:16). The size of the multitude and the diversity of the group emphasize the universality of Christ's gospel.

The great multitude was *standing before the throne and before the Lamb*. In Hebrew tradition, persons stood in the presence of the deity. The throne consistently refers to God in Revelation. That the Lamb is in parallel construction with the throne indicates that Christ is on par with God. This is a clear affirmation of the divinity of Christ the Lamb.

Moreover, the great multitude was *robed in white*. White is used symbolically of victory and purity, but in this context probably refers to the glorified heavenly bodies of those who suffer and die in the tribulation. A similar description is given in Revelation of God's people (3:5; 6:11; 7:13; 19:8) and of heavenly beings (4:4; 19:14).

The great multitude also had *palm branches in their hands*. Palm branches are traditional symbols of victory and thanksgiving (John 12:13; 1 Macc. 13:51; 2 Macc. 10:6-7). Here the picture is of the thanksgiving of the great multitude after they have passed through persecution and won the victory. Like Christ, they have conquered the powers of Satan with their witness and now receive their heavenly reward.

This great multitude cried: *Salvation belongs to our God who is*

seated on the throne and to the Lamb. The word *salvation* (*sōtēria*)
means deliverance or preservation. This is not so much a personal
song of deliverance as a praise to God, who enabled the deliverance
(Ladd, 1972:119). It was the suffering and death of Christ the Lamb
that allowed the great multitude to overcome in a similar way. The
thanksgiving of the great multitude is directed to God for preserving
them in tribulation and delivering them from it by enabling their overcoming. This hymn of praise will be repeated at the fall of Satan, the
dragon (12:10-12), and Babylon, the city of evil (19:1-2).

Then the entire court of heaven *fell on their faces before the
throne and worshiped God.* This picture of heavenly worship repeats
Revelation 4:10. Here, they sing: *Amen! Blessing and glory and wisdom and thanksgiving and honor and power and might be to our
God forever and ever! Amen.* Barclay (1960:2.33-34) and Mounce
(1977:172) define each of the terms in the doxology. It is better, however, simply to note that the seven terms of acclamation attributed to
God stress completeness: they represent all the divine characteristics
that could be used to describe God. Six of the seven attributes occur,
but in a different order, in the doxology of 5:12. The use of a definite
article before each of the words indicates the uniqueness of God's portrayal of that attribute, for example, the blessing above all blessings.
Amen is placed at the beginning and end of the list, giving greater
affirmation to each characteristic of God—"so be it."

Following the doxology, one of the elders addressed two questions
to John: *Who are these, robed in white, and where have they come
from?* That the questions are rhetorical is obvious from John's
answer: *Sir, you are the one that knows.* The questioning is a literary device common in the Bible (Jer. 1:11-13; Ezek. 37:3; Amos 7:8-
9; 8:2; Zech. 4:4-14; 6:4-5), which focuses attention on the answer:
These are they who have come out of the great ordeal. Some argue
that they are martyrs, but there is nothing in the passage to limit the
group in this way. They most likely refer to all who remain faithful to
the end of tribulation. The NRSV translation here is curious because
the tense is present. The present tense, "those coming," contrasts
with the two aorists that follow, *have washed* and *made them white,*
and stresses that they are continuously coming out of the great ordeal.
The tribulation is clearly conceived as a prolonged process. The definite article with *great ordeal* indicates a decisive time of intense suffering, the first clear reference to a specific period of tribulation. There
are several possible interpretations of the great ordeal. It may refer to
the persecution of Domitian at the time that Revelation was written
[Persecution during Domitian's Reign], to the suffering of Christians

throughout history, or to a final eschatological tribulation (see TBC, The Great Ordeal).

The ones coming out of the great ordeal *have washed their robes.* Washing is for purity, especially purity so that the person can be consecrated to God (Exod. 19:10, 14; Zech. 3:1-5). Although it is not mentioned in this passage, washing is usually for the removal of sin (Ps. 51:1-7; Isa. 1:18; 64:9; 1 Cor. 6:11). Here washing is done by remaining steadfast in temptation. The aorist tense and the context of verses 9-10 make it clear that the washing is accomplished by God's sending Christ the Lamb to suffer and die as a model for the Christian to follow in personal purification.

As a result of washing their robes, the ones coming out of the great ordeal *made them white in the blood of the Lamb.* The literal meaning here seems strange: how can garments be made white by washing them in blood (see TBC, Washed in the Blood)? The paradox focuses the idea of victory through suffering. The aorist tense points to the once-and-for-all event that was accomplished on the cross by Christ the Lamb to bring about the salvation of humanity (1:5). The suffering and death of the saints allows them to identify with this act of the Lamb (12:11), whose robe is also dipped in blood (19:13), rather than with the beast who shed the saints' blood (6:10) and is punished by a sea of blood (8:7-9; Koester, 2001:98-99). Indeed, Christians wash themselves by being faithful in persecution and even martyrdom and thus participate in the salvation of Christ (1 Cor. 1:30).

The chapter ends with a poem in synonymous parallelism, using a series of Old Testament allusions. Because the saints have been faithful in persecution, they are now *before the throne of God,* meaning they dwell in the presence of God (Lev. 26:11-13; 1 Kings 8:10; 2 Chron. 7:1-3; Ps. 91:1; Ezek. 37:27; Zech. 2:10; John 1:14; Rev. 21:3). The status of those who are in God's presence is clear: they *worship him day and night within his temple.* This means they have true fellowship with God (Gen. 28:16; Isa. 6:5). The allusion here is to temple worship (Ps. 48; 84; Hab. 2:20; Heb. 8:1-2), where the conquerors may reverence God directly without the need for priestly intermediary. Indeed, *the one seated on the throne will shelter them* just as God spread a tabernacle over the people of Israel (Exod. 15:13; 40:34-38; Isa. 4:5-6). God's protection causes them not to be harmed by certain things of this world: *they will hunger no more, and thirst no more; the sun will not strike them, nor any scorching heat.* God's protection will keep them from harm (Ps. 23:4; 91:5, 6; 121:6; Isa. 49:10; Matt. 5:6; John 4:7-15; 6:35; 7:37-38). This is contrasted to the worshipers of the beast who have no rest, day and night, from their fiery torment (14:9-11). The relationship of God to his conquering people is described using the metaphor of a shepherd: *for the Lamb at the center of the throne will be their shepherd, and he will guide them to springs of the water of life, and God will wipe every tear from their eyes.* The imagery of the shepherd emphasizes God's guidance (Exod. 13:21-22; Ps. 5:8; 23:1-3), God's provision (Ps. 23:5-6; 36:8-9; Isa. 40:11; John 21:15-17; Rev. 21:6; 22:1, 17; 1 Enoch 48:1), God's comfort (Isa. 25:8; 40:1, 11), God's compassion (Isa. 40:11; Matt. 9:36), and God's protection (John 10:1-18; 1 John 3:16). Here Christ the Lamb is also the shepherd just as God is the shepherd of Israel. Throughout Revelation, the Lamb ironically rules with the shepherd's rod (2:27; 12:5; 19:15).

This chapter has formed a cushion between the six seals of chapter 6 and the seventh seal of chapter 8. The point is that those who overcome the tribulation of the seal judgments will emerge victorious. First, the conquerors are seen as the 144,000 on the brink of tribulation; then they are portrayed as the great multitude that has come out of the ordeal. The purpose is to encourage the people of God to withstand the tribulation and thus to conquer it.

THE TEXT IN BIBLICAL CONTEXT

The Seal of the Living God

In this passage the servants of God are marked with a seal. Sources of this image are found in the seal placed on Cain to protect him from those who would kill him as he wandered the earth (Gen. 4:8-16), in the mark of blood placed on the doorposts of the Israelites to protect them when the Lord came to take the life of the firstborn in each of the homes in Egypt (Exod. 12:1-13), and in the mark placed by the man clothed in linen on those who mourn over the abominations of Jerusalem to protect them from being killed by armed men (Ezek. 9:1-11). According to the Hebrew scriptures, a rosette of pure gold engraved like a signet with the words, "Holy to the LORD," was fastened on the turban of Aaron so that it rested on the high priest's forehead (Exod. 28:36-38; see also Isa. 44:5). In a similar way, the followers of God wore a phylactory as a distinguishing mark on their foreheads (Deut. 6:8; 11:18; see also Exod. 13:9). Paul interprets the spirit as such a seal placed on the believer (2 Cor. 1:21-22; Eph. 1:13; 4:30).

The seal is used in three ways in the Bible. First, a seal designates authenticity in a number of occurrences. For example, the king gave the signet ring that carried his mark to the person who was entrusted with the king's authority (Gen. 41:42; Esther 3:10; 8:2). Moreover, God places a similar mark on the Son of Man to designate the authentic heir of the authority of God (John 6:27), and followers of Christ are similarly marked as the true people of God (Eph. 1:13-14). Second, a seal connotes ownership. In the ancient world, slaves received a mark of ownership on their wrist or neck (Lucian, *Syr. Dea* 59; Philo, *The Special Laws* 1.58). Likewise, God's followers bear the inscription: "The Lord knows those who are his" (2 Tim. 2:19). Third, a seal is used to guarantee protection. In antiquity, the slave who bore a mark received the protection of the master (Herodotus, *The Persian Wars* 2.113). The mark God placed on Cain protected him from those who would kill him (Gen. 4:15). The mark of blood placed on the doorposts of the Israelites was for protection against the plague on the firstborn of Egypt (Exod. 12:23). Those who mourned the abomination of Jerusalem received a mark that protected them from being killed with the rest of the city (Ezek. 9:4-5). This latter meaning of protection seems to best fit the context of persecution in Revelation.

The Symbolic Israel

Some argue that Israel and the church are distinguished in the New Testament (Rom. 9-11) and that the most natural meaning of the 144,000 from the twelve tribes of Israel in this passage is that they are ethnic Jews. Pate states that God is not yet finished with Israel: "The purpose of the Great Tribulation is to win the nation of Israel to its Messiah" (1998:165; Deut. 4:30; Jer. 30:7; 31:31-34; Ezek. 20:37; 36:22-32; 37:1-14; 39:21-29; Zech. 13:8-9; Dan. 9:24-27; 12:1; Mal. 4:5-6; Matt. 24:15-31; Rom. 11:25-29). Hence, the 144,000 is "a distinct group of Jews who are converted to Christ during the Great Tribulation, which, in turn, evangelizes the Gentile nations—the innumerable multitude" (1998:164-66). In the end times, these Jews and Gentiles will join in worship of God in the restored temple in Jerusalem (Isa. 2:2; 49:6; 56:6-8; Zech. 14:16).

It is better, however, to interpret *the servants of our God* (7:3; also 2:12; 11:18; 19:2, 5; 22:3, 6) and the *people of Israel* (7:4), not literally to be the nation of Israel, but symbolically as the Christian church (Gal. 6:16). Indeed, no literal twelve tribes existed at the time of the writing of Revelation (2 Kings 17; Jer. 16:10-15; Ezek. 47:13; 48:29; 2 Bar. 63). Although one stream of tradition held that at the culmination of all things the nation would be restored (Isa. 49:6; 2 Esd.13:39-50; 2 Bar. 78-87; Test. Moses 3:3-9; Ps. Sol. 17:28-30; 50; 1 QM 2; see also Matt. 10:5-6; 19:28; Luke 22:30), the New Testament affirms that the ultimate climax is realized in the restoration of Israel through the church (Luke 1:68-79; 2:29-32; John 5:43-47; 11:51-52; Acts 2:14-21; 26:14-23; Rom. 9-11; Eph. 2:11-22). John clearly shares this idea of the Christian church as the symbolic Israel (Rev. 1:6; 2:9; 3:9; 5:10; 21:12-14). Moreover, if the 144,000 in chapter 7 is identified with the same symbol in chapter 14, they are not limited to Jews because they are "redeemed from the earth" and "redeemed from humankind" (14:3-4). Furthermore, Paul says that the true Jew is not the one who has received literal, physical circumcision but the one whose heart has been circumcised spiritually through faith in Christ (Rom. 2:28-29; 4:11-16; Gal. 6:15-16; Phil. 3:3-7) and that Abraham's offspring includes those who belong to Christ (Rom. 9:6-8, 24; Gal. 3:29; 4:28-31). Some of the phrases that describe Israel in the Hebrew scriptures—"a priestly kingdom," "a holy nation" (Exod. 19:6), "my chosen people" (Isa. 43:20)—are used by Peter to designate Christians (1 Pet. 1:2; 2:9). Moreover, the New Testament affirms that Jewish Christians are composed of twelve dispersed tribes, thus fitting the description in chapter 7 (James 1:1; 1 Pet. 1:1; cf. Matt. 19:28). Hence, it is best to take the 144,000 to include symbolically both Jewish and Gentile Christians (see TBC on chs. 2-3, The Jews).

Salvation

In the Hebrew scriptures, *salvation* (*yascha*) means "deliverance," "rescue," "safety," and "welfare." It is used of the person whom God helped to win victories over enemies (1 Sam. 4:6, 45; 1 Chron. 11:14; 18:6; Ps. 3:8; 20:6; 38:22; 42:11; 43:5; 44:4; 118:14, 15, 21; Jon. 2:9) and thus becomes the equivalent to the word *conqueror* in Revelation. The difference is that in the Hebrew scriptures victory usually comes through military means, but in Revelation victory is through the suffering of Christ the Lamb.

In the New Testament, *salvation* means "deliverance or preservation in the face of serious danger." When Paul is shipwrecked, he urges those with him to take some food for their survival (*sōtēria*). The author of Hebrews says that building an ark was salvation for Noah and his family (11:7). In a similar way, Christ is portrayed as the salvation of his people from the oppression of this world (Luke 1:46-55). Nevertheless, salvation is used commonly in a more religious sense—the salvation brought only by Jesus Christ through the forgiveness of sins (Luke 1:77; Acts 4:12). In this sense, salvation is based in faith, belief, repentance, confession, instruction, and sanctification (Rom. 1:16; 10:10; 2 Cor. 7:10; 2 Tim. 3:15; 1 Pet. 2:2). Paul says that salvation comes not only from believing in Christ but also from suffering for him (2 Cor. 1:6; Phil. 1:28-29; see also 2 Tim. 2:10). In obedience, the Christians are called to work out their own salvation (Phil. 2:12) and thus avoid the wrath of God (1 Thess. 5:9). Although salvation clearly has a present sense (Luke 19:9; 2 Cor. 6:2), it also has an eschatological significance (Rom. 13:11; Heb. 9:28; 1 Pet. 1:5). Through suffering, Christ became the source of eternal salvation for believers (Heb. 5:9-10). In Revelation, the word *salvation* occurs only in three doxologies of praise to God for what has been accomplished through Christ the Lamb (7:10; 12:10; 19:1).

The Great Ordeal

The great ordeal has its source in the desecration of Jerusalem and its temple by Antiochus Epiphanes (1 Macc. 1:20-62). Jerusalem was recovered by the Maccabees, and the temple was purified. Yet at the death of Judas Maccabeus, "there was great distress in Israel, such as had not been since the time that prophets ceased to appear among them" (1 Macc. 9:27).

The persecution of God's people is used in at least three ways in the Bible—of the persecution that Christians suffer throughout history (John 16:33; 2 Tim. 3:12), of the perennial conflict between God and Satan (Luke 10:18-19; John 16:32-33; Rom. 8:31-39; Col. 1:11-13; Heb. 2:14-18; see also Matt. 12:28-29; Acts 14:22), and of the final, eschatological persecution (Dan. 12:1; Matt. 24:21-22, 29; Mark 13:19; 2 Thess. 2:3-4). The use of the present tense in this passage points to the first two types of persecution. In later parts of Revelation, the eschatological seems more prevalent (Rev. 13:7-8, 13-15). Yet to have a complete understanding of the meaning of the great ordeal, it must be considered in each of these ways.

Washed in the Blood

This passage says that the ones coming out of the great ordeal washed their robes white in the blood of the Lamb. The image emphasizes purity (Dan. 12:10; Rev. 3:4). In the Hebrew scriptures, white and red are opposites (Gen. 49:11-12; Isa. 1:18; Lam. 4:7). Moreover, a life that was evil was compared to a filthy garment, and a pure life was likened to clean clothes (Exod. 19:10, 14; Isa. 64:6; Zech. 3:3-5; see also Exod. 19:10-15). In the New Testament, this cleansing comes through the blood of the death of Christ (Rom. 3:25; 5:9; Eph. 1:7; Col. 1:20; Heb. 9:14; 1 Pet. 1:2, 19; 1 John 1:7). In Revelation, the paradox of being made white through washing in blood is a graphic picture of the spiritual truth that by overcoming tribulation the

Christian's life is purified by the blood of the Lamb, poured out through Christ's death on the cross (Rev. 12:11).

THE TEXT IN THE LIFE OF THE CHURCH

Preserved in Tribulation

This passage clearly teaches that those who conquer the tribulation have a place with God in heaven. Christians who suffer in this world, identify with Christ who suffered and died on the cross. Dirk Philips finds words of encouragement in this passage:

> Be of good courage, and do not turn aside or vacillate, for your deliverance is near, that you who now in manifold ways are tempted and must suffer much, [for] you have whitened your clothes and have washed your robes in the blood of the Lamb, Rev. 7:14. Yes, you are marked on your forehead with the sign of the living God and therefore may not worship that ugly beast, nor receive his sign, that you, I say, will be delivered out of all sorrow and come to eternal gladness, where you will neither hunger nor thirst, and the Lamb which is in the middle of the throne will feed you and lead you to the living fountain of water, and God will dry every tear from your eyes. (1992:424)

So with Christ, those who conquer tribulation will enjoy the blessings and joys of heaven in the presence of God, who sits on the throne. Thus, they need not fear the death that may result from persecution. Menno Simons expressed this confidence:

> Therefore we ought not to dread death so ... Nor should we sorrow so about the friends who have fallen asleep in God, as do they who do not look for a reward of the saints. We should rather joyfully lift our head, gird our loins with the girdle of truth, and be taken up to the heavenly Canaan. And so with our only and eternal Joshua, Jesus Christ, take the awarded inheritance, and so be delivered from the laborious way of our hard pilgrimage, so full of trouble, which we must lead through the trackless, cruel waste, so long as we are in this life. And after that we shall rest in peace. (1956:1058-59)

Others have echoed the words of the early Anabaptists. According to Spurgeon,

> It is impossible that any ill should happen to the man who is beloved of the Lord. Ill to him is no ill, but only good in a mysterious form. Losses enrich him, sickness is his medicine, reproach is his honor, death is his gain. (1870:4.93)

In the words of Rupert Brooke,

> Safe shall be my going,
> Secretly armed against all life's endeavour;
> Safe where all safety's lost; safe where men fall;
> And if those poor limbs die, safest of all.
> (quoted in Wilcock 1975:83)

In 1589 Joost de Tollenaer, along with another man and woman, were apprehended in Flanders. After remaining steadfast in much torment, they were sentenced to death for heresy. Subsequently, in the count's castle, they were strangled. The two men were then suspended from the gallows outside the castle, and the woman was buried. During this time, Tollenaer sent a letter to his daughter in which he said:

> Behold, my dear child Betgen, if you fear the Lord with all your heart, and with all your soul, and with all your strength and ability, your name shall be written in the book of life, and you shall be marked in your forehead with the name of the living God.... Behold, such glorious rewards shall they have; he that overcometh shall inherit all things that God has prepared for His chosen. He shall lead them to the fountain of living waters, and shall wipe away all tears from their eyes. (Van Braght, 1950:1078-79)

Salvation through Suffering

In the Bible, salvation is viewed comprehensively. Yet at many times, this comprehensive view is truncated, and the concept of salvation is limited to one of its aspects. Today, justification is emphasized over the other aspects of salvation—the new birth, regeneration, reconciliation, restitution, and so forth. Thus, the legal aspect of salvation, that Christ's sacrifice has wiped our sin from the record, is stressed at the expense of other aspects—the transformed person, the holy life, restored relationships, and so forth. Such an approach is apparently undertaken in the interest of clarity: in order for the gospel to have meaning to secular people, theological words are abandoned. Thus, the theological content of these words is lost along with the ideas they represent, and salvation becomes only justification. The unbeliever is told only that in salvation Christ wipes out sin, and the concept of radical discipleship is lost.

In Revelation, the aspect of salvation that is brought into focus is that the person must stay true to God and avoid compromise with evil in order to be rewarded with the joys of heaven. While the other aspects of salvation should not be lost, Revelation reminds us of the importance of the steadfast purity of life and of discipleship that will be at odds with the world. In the understandable concern to communicate God's plan of salvation to a modern world, the gospel must not be truncated. To be saved, the Christian must overcome evil and conquer tribulation, to the end of gaining the joys of salvation in heaven with God and the Lamb, who suffered through his death on the cross the persecution that brought our salvation.

Worship in Heaven

In the attempt to treat Revelation as a vast puzzle book, many commentators have focused on a cognitive, or mental understanding. Upon reading the book, it becomes evident that Revelation also speaks to the affect, or feelings. Though it is clear that the reader was meant to understand the enigmatic symbols in Revelation, the plethora of liturgical elements prompt the readers to be inspired through worship and praise. Songs scattered throughout Revelation make it clear that singing is not a minor element. Revelation includes many hymns of joy sung by those that have overcome tribulation and are now with God in heaven.

In addition to providing hymns for worship, Revelation has also inspired hymn writers to compose songs that echo the doxologies of Revelation. Charles Wesley writes:

O Worship the King All Glorious Above.
And gratefully sing his power and his love.
Our shield and defender, the ancient of days.
Pavilioned in splendor, and girded with praise.

So Revelation should be viewed as a resource for worship [Essay: Worship in Revelation]. Christ's suffering and death has brought the salvation of humanity and thus gives meaning to their tribulation and possible martyrdom. This is properly a theological truth to be understood, but it should also be an experiential truth to be grasped by the imagination through music and worship. Indeed, the entirety of Revelation may be seen as a Lord's day worship service (1:10-11).

Revelation 8:1–9:20

The Trumpets

PREVIEW

To understand fully the sequences of judgments in Revelation, it is important to discover how these series are structurally related to each other. In general, the structure of the judgments can be considered to be chronological and related to the literal method of interpretation or reiterative and connected to a symbolic hermeneutic (see Preview to chapter 6).

The first option is to understand the seal judgments to be followed chronologically by the trumpets, which in turn are followed chronologically by the bowls of God's wrath. Certainly, Jewish apocalyptic literature is concerned with chronology (Dan. 11; 1 Enoch 91:12-17; 93). Yet a serious difficulty related to taking the trumpet visions this way is that some elements of Revelation are clearly not chronological.

Almost all commentators agree that the birth of the Messiah in chapter 12 is not an event that occurs between the seventh seal (11:15-18) and the rising of the beast out of the sea (13:1-10). Moreover, five of the seven heads of the monster in 13:1 and 17:10 represent kings that have already died. Even more problematical, some events seem to be specifically in conflict when taken chronologically. For example, the stars have already fallen from the sky (6:13) when one-third of them are said to be darkened (8:12). Moreover, 8:7 says that all the grass is destroyed, but later, in 9:4, the locusts are told not to harm the grass. It should also be noted that some events occur in more than one sequence. The judgment of

Babylon in 16:17-21 is the same as the judgments of chapters 17-18; indeed, the destruction of Babylon is described three times in Revelation (14:8; 18:2; 18:21-24). The seventh element of a judgment sequence marks the completion of one series but has within it the beginning of a new series: the seventh seal concludes the seal sequence but also introduces the trumpets (8:1-5), and the seventh trumpet forms a fitting conclusion, while, at the same time, it marks a new beginning (11:15-19).

All of these difficulties with a chronological interpretation indicate that the judgments are better understood as reiteration. The seals are repeated in the trumpets, which are in turn reiterated in the bowls of God's wrath. Indeed, there is considerable repetition of symbols in Revelation, for example, the vision of the 144,000 (7:2-8 and 14:1-5); the description of the beast (13:1-8 and 17:3-6); the description of Jerusalem (21:1-8 and 21:9-22:5); the announcement of the fall of Babylon (14:8 and 18:2-3; see Barr, 1998:120 on "doublets" in Revelation). This reiteration is reflected in the clear parallels between the first two judgment series. The seventh seal and trumpet each mark an end (6:17; 11:15). Both series are interrupted by an interlude between the sixth and seventh element (7:1-17; 10:1–11:14). Neither the seventh seal nor the seventh trumpet represents a judgment like the other six (8:1-5; 11:15-19).

Some commentators even see in the reiteration an artistic structuring of the entire book of Revelation around the number seven. Caird states: "A rather more plausible suggestion about the structure of John's book is that it consists of several weeks, perhaps even a week of weeks, beginning as it does on the Lord's day (1:10), and ending in the endless Sabbath of the holy city" (1966:105). This structure around weeks is certainly consistent with Jewish thought regarding the interpretation of history (Dan. 9:24-27; 1 Enoch 91:12-17; 93). Ford describes two possible organizations of Revelation: one based on seven series of seven and another on six series of six (1975:46-50). However, no general agreement exists among the commentators on the details, and such structuring seems to force Revelation into a framework that is not clear in the book itself. Indeed, there are four series of seven in Revelation, but the other visions are not numbered. John seems to be making a distinction between the numbered and unnumbered visions; the latter are close-ups of the former. Although structuring the entire Revelation around the numbers seven or six is not convincing, it seems clear that these numbers are key to the book and that Revelation includes considerable reiteration.

Although they contain repetition, it must be recognized that there are distinctions between the seals and trumpets; the reiteration is not total. Wilcock notes that the seals represent persecution of the church, and the trumpets are judgments on the world. As such, he argues that they are the two sides of God's redemption outlined in chapter 5 (1975:88). Schüssler Fiorenza says that, while the seals present judgment on the Roman Empire, the trumpets are judgment on the cosmos (1991:71). Boring demonstrates this cosmic judgment in relation to the trumpet sequence by noting judgment on the land (8:7), sea (8:8-9), rivers (8:10-11), and heavenly bodies (8:12) (1989:136).

In addition to reiteration, two other structural characteristics of this portion of Revelation should also be noted. First, there is a thematic distinction between the first four trumpets and the two that follow, just as in the series of seal judgments the first four were distinguished from the others by being instituted by four horsemen. In the trumpet sequence, the first four judgments arise from the forces of nature, while the fifth and sixth come from God; the first four are on the environment, while the next two are directed at humanity (Matt. 24:13-22). This distinction in the trumpet sequence is made even more obvious by the intrusion between the fourth and fifth trumpet of the interlude that describes the eagle flying in midheaven.

Second, the seventh seal marks both a conclusion to the seal judgments and an introduction to the trumpets, thus serving as a clear transition between the two series. After the sixth seal is opened at the end of chapter 6, chapter 7 forms an interval before the opening of the seventh seal at the beginning of chapter 8. The seventh seal is connected to what precedes as the seventh member of the seal sequence, and it looks forward to the series that follows by introducing seven angels who were given seven trumpets. Indeed, the seventh seal is a suspension of judgment for the purpose of repentance, but it is also clearly the introduction to a new series of judgments. It is a solemn moment preceding the announcement of the startling images that begin in verse 6.

More important than the structural issues are allusions in the trumpet judgments to the Exodus plagues (see TBC, The Exodus Plagues and Trumpet Judgments). The trumpets are more intense than the plagues of the Exodus, but the latter serve as a backdrop for the divine judgment upon those who oppose God's redemption of the saints and the cosmos. Although the Exodus plagues were not usually interpreted eschatologically in the Jewish tradition, the trumpet judgments of Revelation are portrayed as an eschatological Exodus of the faithful (Aune, 1998a:499, 507). Divine guidance is emphasized through the use of passive verbs throughout the passage, with God as the implied agent of the judgments. God uses natural plagues to bring judgment on those who persecuted and slaughtered the faithful saints.

OUTLINE

The Seventh Seal, 8:1-5
Hail and Fire Mixed with Blood, 8:6-7
The Bloody Sea, 8:8-9
The Bitter Waters, 8:10-11
Dark Heavenly Bodies, 8:12
The Eagle in Midheaven, 8:13
The Demonic Locusts, 9:1-12
The Satanic Attack, 9:13-21

EXPLANATORY NOTES

The Seventh Seal 8:1-5

Surprisingly, like the seventh trumpet to follow, the seventh seal was not a judgment. After all the catastrophic events accompanying the other seals, a climax or final judgment would be expected. Instead, nothing happened, and the suspense remained. Like the holding back of the four winds in 7:1-3 and the sealing of the seven thunders in 10:4, the wrath of God seems restrained in this passage. Rowland says that New Testament eschatology is characterized by the anticipation of living in the "penultimate time ... this sense of being 'in between' with the prospect not of release but of disorientation, of destruction and chaos before the new age can come" (1998:615).

Upon the opening of the seventh seal, *there was silence in heaven*. Several interpretations of the silence have been suggested. Some believe it symbolizes a return to the silence that Jewish literature portrays as existing at creation (Rissi, 1966:4-6; Beasley-Murray, 1974:149-50; see also Wis. Sol. 18:14-15; 2 Esd. 7:30; 2 Bar. 3:7). Revelation does present an eschatological renewal of the original creation (2:7; 21:1; 22:2). Yet, there is no evidence of the elements of creation in the present passage. Building on the work done by Knohl establishing that priestly acts in the inner sanctuary of the temple were done in holy silence to avoid the idolatry of giving personal attributes to God (1996:17-30), Wick has argued that the silence in this passage is for the purpose of allowing the temple sacrifices to be offered, here especially, the sacrifice of incense (1998:512-14; cf. Barker, 2000:169). Because incense symbolizes prayer, silence is to prepare for the prayers of the saints to be heard (R. H. Charles, 1920:1.223-24; Beasley-Murray, 1974:150-51; cf. Aune, 1998a: 507). Indeed, these prayers are answered in the judgment of the wicked that follows. Therefore, perhaps the silence is also an awesome suspense that precedes the trumpet judgments. Beale makes the case that judgment is associated with silence in the Hebrew scriptures and tradition (1999:446-50). Glasson compares the silence to "the ominous calm before a terrific storm" (1965:55), and Beasley-Murray calls it a "breathless expectancy for the judgment to fall and the kingdom to come" (1974:149). The silence echoes the words of the prophets: "the Lord is in his holy temple; let all the earth keep silence before him!" (Hab. 2:20; see also 3:3; Zeph. 1:7; Zech. 2:13). This dramatic silence contrasts with the loud singing of chapter 7, emphasizes the importance of the prayers of the saints, and heightens the awfulness of the trumpet judgments. This mixture of images of worship and suspense makes clear again that John is a literary master.

The silence was *for about half an hour*. Roloff asserts that in Revelation the *hour* is used either as "a symbolic designation of salvation" (3:10; 9:15; 14:7, 15) or as "a circumlocution of the brevity of a period" (17:12). Moreover, half of a whole number "signals a situation of crisis and transition." Thus, the *half an hour* designates a period "that according to God's plan was particularly stressed but that is not the end, a transition in that it points beyond itself to something new, something final" (1993:102).

In the midst of silence, John *saw seven angels who stand before God*. The use of the definite article in the original text indicates that this is a specific group. That they stand before God indicates that they are to be identified with the angels of the presence in Jewish literature (Jub. 1:27; 2:1-2, 18; 15:27; see also Isa. 63:9). These are angels who have immediate access to God. There may also be an allusion to the Jewish belief that angels had no knees and therefore must always stand in God's presence (Aune, 1998a:509).

To these seven angels in the presence of God *seven trumpets were given*. Josephus describes the trumpet as a narrow tube, thicker than a flute but broad enough for breath to pass through, a little less than a cubit in length with a bell-shaped end (*Ant.* 3.291). Trumpets are associated with a variety of activities in the biblical tradition (see TBC, The Trumpets). The closest parallel is their use in settings of divine judgment (Ezek. 33:1-6; Joel 2:1; Zeph. 1:15-16). In Revelation the trumpets are connected with tribulation (8:7-12; 9:1-21; 11:15-19). The use of the passive *were given to them* suggests that God is the subject and therefore that the tribulations come from God (8:7, 12; 9:1,15).

Then *another angel*, distinguished from the seven angels, appears on the scene. Elsewhere in Revelation, this phrase describes an angel coming from heaven or located in midheaven (7:2; 10:1; 14:6-9; 18:1). This angel serves as an intermediary between God and humanity, offering to God the prayers of the saints and executing God's will on earth. Indeed, the prayers of the saints play a part in the execution of God's will. Some have argued that this angel is Christ, because angels do not typically serve as intermediaries; however, angels clearly do fulfill this role in the scriptures and in Jewish literature (Dan. 9:20-23; 10:10-14; Heb. 1:13-14; Tob. 12:11-15; 1 Enoch 9; Test. Levi 3:5-6).

This angel had *a golden censer*, an article of worship connected with the temple (Exod. 27:3; 2 Kings 24:13; 2 Chron. 4:22; 1 Esd. 2:13) and especially with the altar of incense (Exod. 37:25-28; 1 Kings 7:50; Heb. 9:4). Indeed, the word used here normally means "incense" (Aune, 1998a:512). Because incense symbolizes prayer and because gold is a valuable metal, the value of the prayers of the saints is stressed in the image of the golden censer.

The angel also *came and stood at the altar*. In the Old Testament, there are two altars—the altar of sacrifice and the altar of incense (Exod. 30:1-10; 40:5; Lev. 4:7; 16:12-13; Num. 16:46; 1 Kings 6:22). Yet, Revelation always speaks of heaven as having only one altar, and the most dominant symbol associated with that altar is not sacrifice but incense (6:9; 8:3-5; 9:13; 14:18; 16:7). Even in chapter 6, where the theme of sacrifice is the clearest, the dominant image is suffering, not sacrifice (cf. T. C. Smith, 1997:98-101). Thus, the two Old Testament altars are merged into one in Revelation, and the dominant image of the altar is prayer rather than sacrificial death, so that the judgment of God is in response to the prayers of the saints rather than to sacrifices (Exod. 3:7-12). In the fifth seal (6:9-11), the blood of the suffering martyrs cries out for justice; here their prayers are offered on the altar of incense.

The same angel was given *a great quantity of incense to offer with the prayers of all the saints*. In Revelation, incense is used symbolically for prayer; as the incense rises so the prayers of the saints go up to God in heaven. In 6:10, similar prayers of the martyrs are described; here, though, it is all the saints who, in the face of tribulation, pray to God that evil be defeated and the will of God triumph. These prayers of the saints are so important to God that the judgments are held up until they are finished (Morris, 1969:120). In the tribulations of life, God listens to the prayers of the saints. Indeed, the trumpet judgments come in response to these prayers. The meaning of the passage is that Christians struggling on earth have confidence that God hears their prayers for the strength to overcome and thus receive salvation.

After the incense offering was made, *the angel took the censer and filled it with fire from the altar and threw it upon the earth.* Fire is a common symbol of the purifying judgment of God (Isa. 6:6; Ezek. 10:2-7; Matt. 3:11-12; 2 Thess. 1:6-9). God's judgment on Sodom and Gomorrah came in the form of fire (Gen. 19:24). Ironically, the censer that offers the prayers of the saints is the same as the one that inflicts God's judgment on the earth, indicating that the judgment of the wicked is brought about by the prayers of the righteous for justice (see Notes on 6:10).

Then, after the angel again filled his censer with fire and threw it on the earth, *there were peals of thunder, rumblings, flashes of lightning, and an earthquake.* The most obvious referent is to the theophany on Mount Sinai (Exod. 16:16). These symbols are used to indicate the judgment of God: thunder is God's voice (Ps. 18:13; 29:3); lightning is God's arrows (Ps. 18:14; 29:7; see also 77:18); and hailstones are God's weapons (Josh. 10:11; Job 38:22-23; Isa. 30:30; Sir. 46:5). The earthquake imagery is included in the seventh element of each of the three series of judgment (11:19; 16:18). Here it announces the seven trumpets, which are the vindication of the faithful saints who call out to God in their suffering.

Hail and Fire Mixed with Blood 8:6-7

The passage now turns to the judgments that ensue when the seven angels who had the seven trumpets made ready to blow them. The first angel blew his trumpet, and hail and fire mixed with blood were hurled to the earth. This first trumpet judgment of hail echoes the seventh plague of the Exodus from Egypt (Exod. 9:22-26; see also Ezek. 38:22). In this hailstorm, however, the hail is mixed with blood, while in Exodus it is mingled with fire (Exod. 9:23-24). This added feature parallels the Exodus plague, which turned the Nile River into blood (Exod. 7:17-18). Blood and fire are common features in descriptions of God's judgment (Joel 2:31; Acts 2:19-20; Sib. Or. 5:377-78). A naturalistic explanation of this phenomenon calls attention to the fact that in semi-tropical storms red desert sand mixed with the wind and hail to give the appearance of blood, and lightning would add the dimension of fire. Such catastrophes remind the reader of the temporal nature of the cosmos and the imminence of the end.

The focus of the passage is on the effect of the storm on vegetation: *a third of the earth was burned up, and a third of the trees were burned up, and all the green grass was burned up.* The fraction *a third* occurs twelve times in the first four trumpet judgments. Fractions in Revelation are a symbol of God's mercy and an invitation to repentance. The meaning is that the trumpet judgments are not completely devastating; they destroy only part of the vegetation upon which humans depend for their sustenance. This is not the final judgment but a warning to repent. Yet the use of fractions does portray the intensification of God's judgment: the fraction one-fourth is used in the seal sequence (6:8) and one-third in the trumpet series. The destruction here is more intense than that caused by the fourth seal.

The Bloody Sea 8:8-9

The trumpet judgments continue: *The second angel blew his trumpet, and something like a great mountain burning with fire, was thrown into the sea.* The relation of this symbolism to Jeremiah's dirge over Babylon connects this passage with the fall of Babylon described in chapters 17–18 (Jer. 51:24-25; see also Exod. 19:16-20; 1 Enoch 18:13-16; Sib. Or. 5:158-160). The symbols may also have been inspired by the eruption of Vesuvius in A.D. 79, which destroyed Pompeii and Herculaneum (see Aune, 1998a:519-20, 527, 531). The result described here is also similar to the geographer Strabo's description of the effect of the eruption of a volcano near the island of Thera (*Geog.* 1.3.16). When Thera, which would have been visible to John at Patmos, erupted in 1573, the sea was tinged with the orange of iron oxide (Glasson, 1965:58).

When the great burning mountain was thrown into the sea, *a third of the sea became blood, a third of the living creatures in the sea died, and a third of the ships were destroyed.* This catastrophe corresponds to the first plague of Exodus (Exod. 7:20-21), but the second trumpet is more destructive than that Exodus plague, in which only the fish die. The death of the sea creatures follows naturally from the turning of the sea to blood; the destruction of the ships, however, does not. Therefore, perhaps a spiritual meaning is intended. While the death of the sea creatures denotes environmental devastation, the destruction of the ships may connote commercial damage.

The Bitter Waters 8:10-11

Then the third angel blew his trumpet, and a great star fell from heaven, blazing like a torch, and it fell on a third of the rivers and on the springs of water. Although it is difficult to literally conceive of a star falling on a third of the rivers and springs (Aune, 1998a:521), a falling star from heaven is a common spectacle in the biblical tradition of the end (Mark 13:25; Rev. 6:13). Moreover, stars are also conceived as living creatures that worship God (Neh. 9:6), fight against humans (Judg. 5:20), and exalt themselves and are cut down (Isa. 14:12-15). It is likely that the symbol of a falling star was inspired by meteors John had observed in the sky.

Readers are told: *The name of the star is Wormwood.* Wormwood denotes a class of plants noted for their bitterness and is used in the Old Testament to symbolize the bitterness of idolatry (Deut. 29:17-18), the punishment of God (Jer. 9:14-15; 23:15; Lam. 3:15, 19), and the lips of a strange woman (Prov. 5:3-4).

As a result of the falling star, *a third of the waters became wormwood.* This judgment does not directly parallel one of the plagues of Exodus, but its result is the opposite of the effect on the bitter waters of Marah, which were made sweet when Moses threw into them a piece of wood (Exod. 15:23-25). Although wormwood was not a deadly poison, in this case *many died from the water because it was made bitter.* A third of the fresh water supply, a necessity for life, was poisoned by the falling star. This judgment may be upon the river deities, which were commonly worshiped; the meaning then would be that these gods are impotent before the eternal God (Morris, 1969:124). In any case, the third trumpet continues the theme of the judgment of God on the forces of nature.

Dark Heavenly Bodies 8:12

When the fourth angel blew his trumpet, *a third of the sun was struck, and third of the moon, and a third of the stars, so that a third of their light was darkened; a third of the day was kept from shining, and likewise the night.* This corresponds to the ninth plague of Exodus (Exod. 10:21-23). Moreover, the prophets used phenomena like these to signify the day of judgment (Isa. 13:10; Ezek. 32:7; Joel 2:1-2, 10, 31; 3:15; Amos 5:18; 8:9; see also Matt. 8:12; Mark 13:24-25). The powers of evil are connected with darkness (2 Cor. 6:14-15; Col. 1:13), while the power of God is associated with the lengthening of the daylight and the provision and intensifying of light (Josh. 10:12-14; 2 Kings 20:8-11; Isa. 30:26; Rev. 21:23; Sir. 46:4). The nature of the restriction of light in this passage is ambiguous: the first part of the verse says that one-third of all heavenly bodies were darkened, but the second half states that one-third of the time there is no light at all. Moreover, this plague is logically impossible for two reasons: the stars have already fallen in the seal judgments (6:13), and the cosmic balance would be completely upset by the darkening of these heavenly bodies. Therefore, although an eclipse or cloud cover could cause limited darkness, a symbolic meaning is probably intended: the darkness of separation from God (Beale, 1999:482). The limited nature of the darkness probably connotes God's mercy and call to repentance in the face of such judgment.

The Eagle in Midheaven 8:13

After the sounding of the first four trumpets, a brief interlude follows in which John observes an eagle flying in midheaven. The solemn appearance of the eagle forms a pause that warns humanity of the more intense devastation to follow. Although the eagle was the symbol of the Roman Empire (2 Esd. 11:1-12:3), that does not seem to explain its use here. The meaning of the symbol is dependent on how the word *aetou* is translated: it can mean either "eagle" or "vulture." If the former is in mind, the emphasis is on protection from harm when one is borne up on, or sheltered by, the eagle's wings (Exod. 19:4; Deut. 32:11; Ps. 17:8; 36:7; 57:1; 61:4; 91:4; Rev. 12:14; see also Ps. 18:10; 2 Bar. 77:17-26). If the meaning is vulture, the picture is of doom, represented by the animal that seeks out corpses to devour (Deut. 28:49; Jer. 48:40; Matt. 24:28; Luke 17:37). The latter meaning, announcing judgment, gains support from Hosea 8:1 where the vulture is also connected with a trumpet. Thus, the appearance of the vulture heightens the terror of the two trumpet judgments to follow.

The bird was *crying with a loud voice as it flew in midheaven,* *"Woe, woe, woe."* The vulture's wings can carry it to the zenith of the sky where all can see and hear the message. The word *woe (ouai)* has an eerie sound—the foreboding voice of doom. It indicates that worse disasters are to follow. Indeed, the structure of Revelation indicates that three judgments should follow, the three woes. The first two are clearly the next two trumpet judgments (9:12). Although the structure would also imply that the third woe is the seventh trumpet (11:14), the final trumpet is not a woe at all but an enthronement of the Lord God almighty (see Notes on 11:14 and the Preview of Chapters 15-16 regarding the identity of the third woe).

The announcement of the eagle was *to the inhabitants of the earth.* This phrase is consistently used in Revelation for those hostile to God (3:10; 6:10; 11:10; 13:8; 17:2) and is set over against the saints of God *[Glossary: The Inhabitants of the Earth].* The plagues fall on the evil society, but like the Israelites in Egypt, the faithful saints who carry God's protective seal are preserved (9:4; see also 1 John 5:18).

The Demonic Locusts 9:1-12

After the one-verse interlude, the trumpet judgments continue. The particular plague that follows reminds readers of the eighth plague of the Exodus (Exod. 10:1-20). Its more explicit source, however, is Joel 1–2 where the Day of the Lord is marked by a plague of locusts. Nevertheless, in these sources the plagues involve real locusts, but in the fifth trumpet they are demonic creatures that resemble locusts.

When the fifth angel blew his trumpet, John saw *a star that had fallen from heaven to earth.* Ancient religions saw the stars as deities (Deut. 4:19; Judg. 5:20; 1 Enoch 86:1). Yet in the present passage, the use of the past perfect indicates that the star represented has already fallen, alluding to the fall of Satan in the prehistoric battle between good and evil (Gen. 6:1-4; Isa. 14:12-15; Luke 10:18; 2 Pet. 2:4; Rev. 12:4; 1 Enoch 6-10; 21:6; 54; 88:1; Wis. Sol. 2:24; 2 Enoch 29:4-5; 2 Bar. 56). In the parallel Canaanite account, the God Athtar (Daystar or Venus), who proposed to take the place of Baal, was unsuccessful and came to earth, where he reigns as "god of it all" (Boring, 1989:136). Rather surprisingly, the satanic fallen star in this passage acted at God's command (Job 38:4-7; 2 Enoch 30:14-15; Test. Sol. 8-18).

This fallen star *was given the key to the shaft of the bottomless pit.* The pit is not a place of torment but one where evil spirits and demons are temporarily detained (Luke 8:30-31) awaiting their final destination in the pit of fire and sulfur (Rev. 20:10). Satan's abode is not systematically designated in the scriptures but is variously stated as the underworld, the air, and heavenly places (Eph. 2:2; 6:12). That God gives the star the key to the pit indicates that God is ultimately in control of the beings who reside there (see TBC, The Bottomless Pit).

When the star *opened the shaft of the bottomless pit,* a swarm of frightful locusts emerged: *from the shaft rose smoke like the smoke of a great furnace, and the sun and the air was darkened with the smoke from the shaft. Then from the smoke came locusts on the earth.* The destructiveness of locusts is understood in scripture to be punishment for sin (Deut. 28:38; 1 Kings 8:37-40). Indeed, the accompanying elements in the passage are not unusual for a locust invasion: a swarm of locusts does look like a cloud and can be thick enough to darken the sun (Joel 2:10).

Some believe that the smoke described here is from the flames of hell. Yet the pit from which the locusts come, located in the under-world, is identified with *Sheol* or *Hades,* a dark, gloomy place, not a place of fire and smoke. The lake of fire, or *Gehenna,* is not identi-fied with the underworld, and indeed, is given no location in scripture.

Therefore, it is better to consider the smoke here to be a realistic description of a locust plague rather than an indication that the locusts emanate from the place of torment.

Yet the plague is clearly to be seen as much more than a locust invasion. The imagery alternates between a locust herd and a cavalry (Job 39:19-20; Joel 2:4). The Hebrew word for locust (*hangol*) is very close to the Arabic word for troop (*hangol*). One referent for the imagery in the passage is the troops of the Parthian army from the East, which later did actually conquer the eastern end of the Roman Empire. Thus, John merges images of a locust herd and a Parthian invasion to describe the demonic army of God's enemies.

Another image is added to the picture when the locusts *were given authority like the authority of scorpions on the earth*. Mounce describes a scorpion in the following manner: "A lobster-like vermin some four or five inches long, it had a claw on the end of a tail that secreted a poison when it struck" (1977:194). Scorpions were considered poisonous beings much like snakes and came to be associated with the forces of rebellion and evil (Ezek. 2:6; Luke 11:12; Sir. 39:29-30). Although the sting of a scorpion is painful, it is rarely fatal. Indeed, to undergo such pain constantly would be worse than death. Hence, the torture of scorpions is a symbol of God's judgment on a rebellious and sinful world.

The locusts *were told not to damage the grass of the earth or any green growth or any tree*. The passive verbs throughout the first five verses of the chapter indicate that the locusts are agents of God. They were told not to damage the foliage, their normal food (Exod. 10:15; Joel 2:3), but instead to attack *only those people who do not have the seal of God on their foreheads*. These are unusual locusts; instead of grass, they attack humans who are not followers of God (TBC, The Locusts). It is clear that, like the Israelites in the Exodus plagues, the faithful saints escape the torment of their oppressors (Exod. 8:22-23; 9:4-6; 10:23; Wis. Sol. 18:1-2). According to the Jewish tradition, the plagues of Exodus served to sanctify the Israelites and punish the Egyptians (Beale, 1999:384-85) in order "to move their hard hearts to repentance" (Smith, 2000:49, 51). This image is reminiscent of Jesus promising his followers power over scorpions (Luke 10:19).

The locusts were allowed to torture those without the seal of God *for five months*. This is approximately the length of the portion of the year that locusts could attack—from early spring to late summer. That they attacked for the entire time emphasizes the plague's considerable duration. It is the length of the flood of Noah's day (Gen.

7:24) and was also used to describe the length of time Gessius Florus terrorized Jerusalem during the Jewish War of the mid-first century (Ford, 1975:149). Although five months describes a long time for such intense tribulation, it is of limited duration, and the mercy of God will intervene to bring it to an end.

As a result of the attack, *people will seek death but will not find it; they will long to die, but death will flee from them.* The intensity of the torment is emphasized by the repetition of the statement. The terrible nature of this torment is made even more clear since death is sometimes seen as positive in the Bible. Indeed, Paul pictures death as a desired blessing (Phil. 1:23), rather than the avoidance of torment (Job 2:9-10; 3:20-22; Jer. 8:3).

In verses 7-10, the locusts are described in considerable detail. They *were like horses equipped for battle* (Job 39:19-21; Joel 2:4-5). Often locusts and horses are compared. For example, an Arab proverb says: the locust has the head of a horse, breast of a lion, feet of a camel, body of a serpent, and antenna like a maiden's hair (Beasley-Murray, 1974:162; Mounce, 1977:196). The description conjures up the opposite of the centaur of Homeric mythology, which has the head of a human and the body of a horse (Ford, 1975:145); here it is the head that is horse-like. Regardless of the source of the idea, the imagery points to a cavalry of horses arrayed for battle.

The locusts also had on their heads *what looked like crowns of gold.* Although there is nothing on the head of a locust that looks like a crown, Mounce points out that the yellow breast of the locust may have suggested the golden color (1977:196). Ford says that the imagery may come from the helmets of the Roman soldiers, which were bronze and burnished with gold (1975:151). If Ford is correct, then these locusts are a parody of the Son of Man, who also has a golden crown on his head (14:14). In any case, the symbol describes a victorious army, an idea that has already been added to the images of locusts and scorpions.

The faces of the locusts *were like human faces.* Although this is not a natural characteristic of locusts, the symbol probably implies intelligence. Humans are generally considered the most intelligent of created beings. These demonic locusts are terrible in appearance but have the intelligence of a human being.

The locusts had *hair like a woman's hair.* Glasson draws attention to the Arab proverb mentioned above that compares locusts' antennae to a maiden's hair (1965:60). However, from the context, it is more likely that the hair has the meaning of strength or ferocity. Samson wore long hair as a source of strength (Judg. 16:13-19). In

ancient cultures long, unbound hair was often characteristic of barbarous peoples. The Parthians, the enemies of the ancient Roman
Empire, were known as fierce warriors who wore their hair long. So
the symbol accentuates, not femininity, but ferocity and strength.

The locusts also had *teeth like lions' teeth*. The locusts in Joel's
vision are described similarly (Joel 1:6). This symbol reinforces the
image of fierceness because the demonic locusts devour with ferocity.
Hence, their destructiveness is highlighted.

Moreover, the locusts *had scales like iron breastplates*. The scaly
bodies of locusts would have reminded the reader of the coat of mail
worn by Goliath (1 Sam. 17:5) and the armor protecting the ele-
phants that accompanied the king's army when it fought against the
Maccabees (1 Macc. 6:43). The meaning is that humans are powerless to protect themselves against such demonically fortified beasts.

The noise of the wings of the locusts *was like the noise of many
chariots with horses rushing into battle*. A locust invasion was,
indeed, accompanied by a rushing sound caused by the beating of
innumerable wings. The image of an army is again evoked by the
description of chariots rushing into battle, destroying everything in
their way (1 Sam. 13:5; 1 Chron. 19:7; Joel 2:4-5).

The locusts *have tails like scorpions, with stingers, and in their
tails is their power to harm people for five months*. Mounce says
that the shift to the present tense at this point adds vividness to the
account (1977:197). The stingers allude to the goads that were used
in the ancient world for floggings (1 Kings 12:11; 2 Macc. 6:30; 7:1)
and connote destruction and death (Hos. 13:14; 1 Cor. 15:56). This
symbol turns the imagery back to the scorpions: the destruction of the
locust is in its mouth; the sting of the scorpion is in its tail. There is
also an allusion to the army of the Parthians, who had the reputation
of being able to shoot a volley of arrows while advancing and retreat-
ing; thus, their sting was also observed to be in their tail. Ford turns
attention again to the centaurs, who in Babylonian mythology were
equipped with the tail of the scorpion (1975:152). Whatever the
specifics of the allusion, the point of the image of the scorpion's tail is
that the demonic locusts are destructive from all directions, front and back.

Finally, the locusts are described as having *as king over them the
angel of the bottomless pit*. That they have a king contradicts
Proverbs 30:27, which says that locusts have no king, but these are
not ordinary locusts but demonic beings. The king of the locusts may
be the demonic angel that unlocked the pit and permitted the locusts
to escape. The meaning is that this catastrophe is directed by the king
of demons.

The name of the king of the locusts *in Hebrew is Abaddon, and in Greek he is called Apollyon.* The word *abaddon* means destruction and is used in the Hebrew scriptures in parallel construction with *Sheol* (Job 26:6; Prov. 15:11; 27:20), death (Job 28:22; see also 31:12), and the grave (Ps. 88:11). Moreover, the lowest part of *Gehenna*, the place of torment in Jewish literature, is *abaddon* (Ford, 1975:145). *Appollyon* also means destroyer, and it occurs as a proper noun only in this passage. There is no doubt also an allusion to Apollo the sun god, which takes on added significance because emperor Domitian liked to be regarded as Apollo incarnate. Indeed, one of the symbols for Apollo was the locust, and Apollo was often thought to bring plagues and destruction. So the image connotes the threat of destruction attached to Emperor Domitian and by extension to all satanic forces arrayed against the saints of God. Indeed, both *abaddon* and *appollyon* describe judgment by the destructive hoard of demonic locusts.

The Satanic Attack 9:13-21

The sixth trumpet judgment is an attack from across the Euphrates River. Although the structure of this plague resembles those of the Exodus, there is no Exodus typology in this passage. The sixth trumpet more closely parallels the fifth that precedes it. It is another attack by satanic creatures on the unfaithful but more intense than the preceding one: the fifth trumpet brings torment; the sixth carries death. The plague in this passage exploits the inhabitants' uneasiness about an invasion by the Parthians—the fearsome horsemen who lived to the east of the Euphrates River. Yet the invaders seem to be less a cavalry than a satanic hoard.

As the passage begins, John says: *the sixth angel blew his trumpet, and I heard a voice from the four horns of the golden altar before God.* Because horns consistently designate power in apocalyptic literature, the horns on the altar are symbolic of the power of God's word. Although the altars of both burnt offering and incense were constructed with horns (Exod. 27:2; 30:1-3), the latter is referred to here. Because the altar of incense is where the prayers of the saints are offered (6:9-10; 8:3-5), the judgment of the sixth trumpet is an answer to the prayers of saints arising from the four horns of the altar of incense.

The voice from the altar instructed *the sixth angel who had the trumpet, "Release the four angels who are bound by the great river Euphrates."* That these angels are bound indicates that they bring an evil force like the four angels that controlled the destructive winds

(7:2). The number of the angels indicates that their destructive activity extends throughout the universe—to the four corners of the earth. These angels correspond to the angels of punishment of apocalyptic literature, who cause the nations of the east to destroy Palestine (1 Enoch 40; 53:3; 56; 62:11; 2 Bar. 6:1-4). Here they are bound at the great river Euphrates much like the Red Sea served as an obstacle for the Israelites when they were delivered from Egypt (Exod. 14:26-29; 15:4). All the great enemies of Israel came from across the Euphrates. The enemy located there in the first century was the Parthians, who serve here as a symbol for the satanic forces that attack the enemies of God's people (see TBC, The Great River Euphrates).

The command to the sixth angel with a trumpet was carried out when *the four angels were released who had been held ready for the hour, the day, the month, and the year*. The four angels are in a state of readiness because they cannot act on their own but only in the time and manner determined by God (2 Esd. 7:106-11; 1 Enoch 81:2; 92:2; Sib. Or. 2:325-38; 3:91-92; 8:424-27). That their release is according to the plan of God is reinforced by the specification of the exact time of their release—*the hour, the day, the month, and the year* (Num. 1:1; Hag. 2:10). When they are released, however, nothing can stop them.

John reports the size of the great army held back at the Euphrates: *The number of the troops of cavalry was two hundred million.* Although some futurists suggest that this number is to be taken literally and argue that it roughly approximates size of the militia of modern China (see Walvoord, 1966:166, note 13), similar references in the Hebrew tradition to infinitely large numbers indicates this number is probably symbolic of the innumerability of the forces (Ps. 68:17; Rev. 5:11; 7:9-17). The extraordinarily large number, perhaps "ten thousand times tens of thousands" (Aune, 1998a:539), indicates that the army has superhuman power (Deut. 33:2; Jer. 6:22-26; Ezek. 38:14-16; Dan. 7:10).

The great cavalry *wore breastplates the color of fire and of sapphire and of sulfur; the heads of the horses were like lions' heads, and fire and smoke and sulfur came out of their mouths*. This is reminiscent of the description of the monster Leviathan (Job 41:18-21) and of the destruction of Sodom and Gomorrah (Gen. 19:24). The imagery lends itself well to interpretations consistent with the normal ways of interpreting Revelation: the futurist sees in the imagery the effects of the employment of modern weapons (Walvoord, 1966:167); the preterist finds the Parthian's breastplates of metal-

rusted, fiery red (Ford, 1975:154); and the idealist observes the "virulent and tenacious" forces of evil (Caird, 1966:123). The grotesque picture of horses with heads of lions spewing from their mouths fire, smoke, and sulfur demands the latter symbolic meaning over a literal interpretation of the passage. The elements connote ferocious, demonic creatures arising out of the abyss to mete out hellish persecution on the unfaithful.

Further description indicates *the power of the horses is in their mouths and in their tails; their tails are like serpents, having heads; and with them they inflict harm.* The most obvious referent for these symbols is Satan, who is characterized as a serpent (Ps. 91:13; Luke 10:19; Sir. 39:30). In ancient mythology, serpents were pictured as having a head at each end (Pliny, *Nat. Hist.* 8.35). Although the futurist might find the referent for the idea of power in both the head and the tail in flame-throwers and tail-bombers (Wilcock, 1975:99), the most obvious source of the image is in the attack of the Parthian horsemen, known for their ability to shoot a volley of arrows as they charged and another in retreat. Yet it may be that the meaning of the attack is symbolic. Instead of the word of God, which is the weapon of the Lamb, the demonic hoards spew the deception of Satan from their mouths, causing humans to continue in their idolatry (Beale, 1999:514-15). In any case, the symbols here intensify the sinister nature of these demonic beings.

The response to this satanic attack is remarkable: *The rest of mankind, who were not killed by these plagues, did not repent of the works of their hands.* In the midst of intense tribulation, the opportunity for repentance is still open. The plagues are both punishment for sin and opportunity for the unfaithful to turn to Christ before the end. In history, humans have been able to deny God and escape, but in the end, judgment will come. Yet in spite of all the torments that have been revealed in the six trumpet judgments, they do not repent. This reminds the reader of the hardening of Pharaoh's heart in the Exodus story (Exod. 7:13, 22; 8:15, 19, 32; 9:7, 12, 34-35; 10:1, 20; 11:9-10; 14:4). Revelation says they do not repent of *the works of their hands,* or the production of idols (Acts 7:41).

The passage elaborates this point that the unfaithful *did not give up worshiping demons and idols of gold and silver and bronze and stone and wood, which cannot see or hear or walk.* In the ancient world, some Jews and Christians believed that worshiping idols was the same as worshiping devils (Deut. 32:17), and others believed that idols were totally impotent but their worship was rebellion against God (Ps. 115:4-7; see TBC, The Worship of Idols). Both of these traditions are addressed in this passage. Idolatry is condemned both because the idols are demonic and because they are impotent. Although these ideas seem contradictory, Revelation teaches that, in contrast to the power of God, demonic idols are powerless.

In spite of the intense judgments on the unfaithful, they *did not repent of their murders or their sorceries or their fornication or their thefts*. These evil practices are part of traditional catalogues of vices (Mark 7:21-22; Gal. 5:19-21; Rev. 21:8; 22:15). Three of them are prohibited in the Decalogue: murders, fornication, and thefts (Exod. 20:13-15; Luke 18:20; Rom. 13:9); the fourth, sorcery, is clearly condemned by the early Christians (Acts 19:11-20). The point of including this list is that, in addition to refusing to give up their idolatry, the unfaithful continue in their immoral practices. Their repentance, then, would involve renouncing both idolatrous beliefs and immoral practices.

THE TEXT IN BIBLICAL CONTEXT

The Seven Angels

At the beginning of chapter 7, a group of four angels held back the winds—four being the number of completion in the natural world. Here, seven angels are described as standing before God. This means they are direct representatives of God—seven being the number of God's completion. These seven angels are the ones who later pour out the seven bowls of God's wrath (15:1-8; 16:1; 17:1; 21:9). It is likely that they are closely connected with the seven spirits before the throne of God (1:4), who are the heavenly counterparts of the churches.

These angels also hark back to the seven archangels of Jewish literature: Suriel, Raphael, Raquel, Michael, Saragael, Gabriel, and Remiel (1 Enoch 20; see also Tob. 12:15). Only two of these archangels are mentioned in the Bible: Michael (Dan. 10:13, 21; 12:1), and Gabriel (Dan. 8:16; 9:21; Luke 1:19, 26), who fight against God's enemies (Exod. 23:20-21; 33:2; 2 Kings 19:35; 2 Chron. 32:21; Matt. 26:53; 1 Macc. 7:41; 2 Macc. 10:29; 11:6; 15:23; 4 Macc. 4:10). In Revelation, their purpose is to accomplish God's judgment by blowing the seven trumpets and pouring out the bowls of God's wrath.

The Trumpets

The most obvious source for the imagery of the seven trumpets is the story of Joshua and the battle of Jericho, where seven priests with seven trumpets march around the city of Jericho seven times on the seventh day (Josh. 6:1-11; see also 1 Chron. 15:24; Rev. 11:19). After this they make a long blast on the trumpets, the people give a great shout, and the wall of the city falls down flat. Then, the seven priests with the seven trumpets go in front of the ark of the covenant into the city.

Gideon also uses trumpets as instruments of war against the Midianites (Judg. 7). After reducing his troops from 32,000, Gideon finally takes just 300 soldiers into battle armed only with trumpets and empty jars with torches inside. Nevertheless, they defeat the Midianites, showing that battles are won, not with large armies and powerful weapons, but by the power of God.

Trumpets are used in a variety of other ways in the biblical tradition. The glory of God is accompanied with the sound of a trumpet (Exod. 19:16-19; 20:18); trumpets are used in connection with military victories (Josh. 6:1-16; Judg. 7:15-23); trumpets celebrate the coronation of the king (1 Kings 1:34,39; 2 Kings 9:13) and are especially associated with the kingship of God (Ps. 47:5-7; 98:6; Zech. 9:14; Ps. Sol. 11:1); trumpets are blasted as an alarm calling Israel to national repentance for sin (Isa. 58:1; Jer. 4:5-8; 6:1,16-17; Ezek. 33:2-6; Joel 2:15-16; Amos 3:6) or to battle (Judg. 3:27-28; Neh. 4:18); and trumpets are used in connection with worship (Lev. 23:24; Num. 10:10; Ps. 98:6) on such occasions as the Jubilee, which marked the end of seven weeks of seven years each (Lev. 25:8-9). In the New Testament, trumpets were associated with the second coming of Christ (Matt. 24:31; 1 Cor. 15:51-52; 1 Thess. 4:16).

In apocalyptic literature, trumpets are a common element in eschatological settings. They announce the judgment of the wicked (Joel 2:1; Zeph. 1:14-16; 2 Esd. 6:17-24; Sib. Or. 4:171-78; Apoc. Abraham 31), the gathering of God's people for protection and salvation (Isa. 27:13; Zech. 9:14-17; Matt. 24:31; Ps. Sol. 11), and the resurrection of the righteous (1 Cor. 15:51-58; 1 Thess. 4:16-17). Revelation follows this tradition of apocalyptic literature in utilizing trumpets to announce the tribulation of the unrighteous and the protection of the faithful.

The Exodus Plagues and Trumpet Judgments

As was suggested in the Preview, the trumpet judgments parallel remarkably the plagues poured out on Egypt before the Exodus of the Israelites:

	Trumpet Judgment	Exodus Plague
Hailstorm	Rev. 8:7	Exod. 9:22-26
Bloody Sea	Rev. 8:8-9	Exod. 7:17-21
Bitter Waters	Rev. 8:10-11	Exod. 15:23-25
Darkness	Rev. 8:12-13	Exod. 10:21-23
Locusts	Rev. 9:1-12	Exod. 10:12-15
Crossing River/Sea	Rev. 16:12-16	Exod. 14:21-31

Yet in each case the trumpet judgments are more intense than those of the Exodus. In the seventh Exodus plague, hail is described as accompanied by fire in a manner that suggests lightning; in the first trumpet judgment, the hail is mingled with blood—a much more gruesome picture. In the first Exodus plague, the bloody sea causes the fish to die; in the second trumpet judgment, the same phenomena destroys ships as well. The bitter waters at Marah during the Israelites' wilderness wanderings are merely not potable; the plague of the third trumpet says the bitter water causes death to many. The ninth plague of Exodus brings darkness for three days, but the fourth trumpet judgment produces a darkening of the heavenly bodies and the accompanying cosmic consequences. The eighth Exodus plague produces a locust herd that completely destroys vegetation, but the locusts of the fifth trumpet are terrifying demonic creatures. After the plagues of the Exodus, the Red Sea is parted for the Israelites to cross but then sweeps back to destroy the Egyptian army; the sixth trumpet is an attack of an innumerable demonic hoard from across the Euphrates River that kills a third of humanity. Thus, the trumpet judgments are similar to the Exodus plagues but more intense.

From this we see that the trumpet judgments of Revelation are portrayed as a new Exodus of God's people and that their intensity points to devastation of cosmic proportions. Yet just as God spared the Israelites, who marked their doors with lamb's blood, and even used these plagues to allow the Israelites to escape from Egypt, so the faithful who are marked with a seal on their foreheads are protected from the trumpet judgments upon the unrighteous, and these very judgments are used to allow the martyrs to escape to heaven where they experience the salvation God has prepared for them.

The Bottomless Pit

The word *pit* (*abyssos*) literally means "unfathomably deep" (Ford, 1975:143). The pit is the lower part of the three-story universe composed of earth, sky, and the pit (Gen. 1:6-8; Deut. 30:11-14), and may be identified with the fountains of the deep (Gen. 7:11; Job

38:16; Ps. 33:7; 107:26); the depths of the earth (Job 28:14; Ps. 71:20; Rom. 10:7); and Sheol, the resting place of both the fallen angels (1 Enoch 18:12-16; 21:9) and the dead (Num. 16:30-34; 1 Enoch 108:6). The pit is the evil counterpart of the heavenly court, which represents the powers of evil personified by the great monsters Tiamat, Rahab, and Leviathan [see TBC on ch. 11, The Beast]. Caird draws attention to the parallel in the Genesis creation account, where the waters above the firmament are divided from the waters of the deep, translated *abyssos* in the Septuagint (1966:118). Uriel, whose name means "fire from God," is the angel in charge of the pit (1 Enoch 19:1; 20:2; 21:9).

Seven of the nine biblical occurrences of the word *abyssos* are in Revelation. The equivalent of *Hades* (Rom. 10:7), the pit serves as a prison for Satan (20:1-3), the beast (11:7; 17:8), and the fallen angels (2 Pet. 2:4). The demons that Jesus drove out of the man in the country of the Geresenes beg him not to order them back into the pit (Luke 8:31). This passage makes it clear that the pit is the abode of demons who come out in the form of locusts to torment the evil ones on the earth.

The Locusts

The locust is a fairly common character in scripture. It is used to symbolize the destruction of trees and fruit due to disobedience (Deut. 28:42), sin (1 Kings 8:37), ingratitude (Ps. 78:46), treachery (Isa. 33:4), and self-indulgence (Amos 7:1; Nah. 3:17). Elsewhere, God's wrath is pictured as a locust herd, and one of the judgments on Israel in the Exodus from Egypt is, of course, a plague of locusts (Exod. 10:1-20).

Moreover, a locust hoard is used metaphorically to describe a military attack. Because Israel did evil, the Lord allowed Midian to prevail over them. Part of the harassment of the Midianites was the destruction of the produce of the land (Judg. 6:1-6). The Midianite destroyers are characterized as being "as thick as locusts" (Judg. 6:5; 7:12).

Joel describes the judgment of God on the people as a military force with the characteristics of a hoard of locusts (Joel 1:4-7). The community is called to lament and return to God before the impending attack (1:8-14). The language Joel uses to describe this Day of the Lord (2:1) foreshadows that of Revelation's fifth trumpet: the darkening of the sky (2:2), the horse-like appearance of the locusts (2:4), the chariot-like sound of the locust herd (2:5), and the clear connection of the locusts to a military attack (2:6-11).

The imagery of the attack of locusts in Joel and Revelation is a powerful portrayal of the force of evil. Yet it alone does not capture evil adequately. Therefore, other symbols like scorpions and chariots are added to intensify the imagery. Taken together metaphors are built up to approximate Satanic power, but language is never adequate to describe spiritual truths. Such metaphorical language is, however, more adequate than direct language for portraying spiritual truths that are not completely comprehensible.

The Worship of Idols

This passage describes idol worship in two ways that are consistent with the Judeo-Christian tradition. First, idols are portrayed at times as devils (Ps. 106:36-38; 1 Cor. 10:14-22), and, in the passage under consideration, the worship of idols is seen as sorcery (see also Mark 7:21-22; Acts 19:18-19; Gal. 5:20; Rev. 21:8; 22:15). A second approach to idol worship is reflected in many passages that present idols as impotent (Deut. 4:28; Ps. 135:15-18; Isa. 44:6-20; Jer. 10:3-5; Dan. 5:4-23; Acts 14:15; 1 Cor. 8:4-6; Sib. Or. 5:77-80). The psalmist describes the impotence of idolatry:

> Their idols are silver and gold, the work of human hands.
> They have mouths, but do not speak; eyes, but do not see.
> They have ears, but do not hear; noses, but do not smell.
> They have hands, but do not feel; feet, but do not walk; they make no sound in their throats.
> Those who make them are like them; so are all who trust in them. (Ps. 115:4-8)

In a manner similar to that in Revelation, the conceptions of idol worship as both demonic and impotent are combined in the Hebrew tradition (1 Enoch 99:7). However idols are conceived, their worship is condemned as rebellion against the true God (Exod. 20:4-6; Deut. 16:21-22; 32:16-18; Jer. 1:16).

THE TEXT IN THE LIFE OF THE CHURCH

The Seventh Seal

One of the great film directors of the twentieth century, Ingmar Bergman, captures very well the awful suspense of *The Seventh Seal* in his black and white film by that name. The action begins with a knight who has returned from the Crusades with a white cross on his chest confronting Death, personified by a man with black clothes and a face that is an inhuman white color. Although Death has come for him, he gains a reprieve by challenging Death to a chess game. The reprieve is threatened when the knight reveals his chess strategy to a priest in a confessional but finds out at the end of the confession that the priest is Death. Over the entire reprieve, the haunting presence of Death is always imminent. There is rumor that a plague is coming and has, indeed, devastated nearby towns. A young girl is executed by burning because she is thought to be a carrier of the scourge. In the end, Death does come to defeat the knight and take him.

Blanketing the entire film is an anxious suspense regarding the expectation of death. There is the death of a victim of the plague, which the characters watch; yet their own death is expected but never actualized. Even in the end, although the characters walk away with Death, we do not see them die. At the beginning of the film, the seventh seal of Revelation chapter 8 is read by a narrator; just before Death takes them away, an actor begins to read about the seven trumpet judgments, which are the seventh seal.

The silence that is the content of the seventh seal may be an anxious, suspenseful silence that anticipates the coming of the seven trumpet judgments. This suspense is captured artistically and effectively by Bergman in his cinematic masterpiece, which keeps the viewer in eerie suspense for a catastrophic death that is always expected but never comes.

The Power of Prayer

The silence brought by the seventh seal also provides a time for the prayers of the saints to be answered. A recurring theme in Revelation is that those who have suffered and died for their faith pray for the justice of God to come and vindicate their martyrdom. This vindication comes in the plagues on those who dwell on the earth—the wicked. Thus, the plagues in Revelation are the result of the prayers of the saints.

It is important to remember that the prayers of the saints have power over the forces of evil. I teach a Sunday school class of about fifteen seventh and eighth graders. At times we keep a prayer chart to guide our prayer time in the class. On the left hand column of the chart are prayer requests and on the right are answers to prayer. On our present chart are such requests as safety for persons in the congregation who are traveling over the Christmas holidays, healing for a grandmother who had recent surgery, and resolution of the present conflict in Bosnia. I am usually more amazed than the students at how the right column fills up with answers to the prayers of the left column. Yet that should not be surprising, because the incense imagery of Revelation communicates that Christ intervenes in the world to prevail over the forces of evil in response to the prayers of the saints.

The Folly of Prediction

In 1988 the world began to become aware of a tragedy that had taken place in Russia's Chernobyl nuclear plant, and although the world did not know until later the extent of that catastrophe, a significant amount of radiation had been released into the atmosphere. In the years that followed, more information came out about the extent of the effect of this nuclear disaster.

In a manner that is all too common, biblical prognosticators related the tragedy of Chernobyl to the symbolism of Revelation, in this case to the third trumpet. The nuclear plant, "blazing like a torch," had made the waters bitter, and "many died from the water." Indeed, some claimed an etymological connection between the words, "Wormwood" and "Chernobyl." It did not seem to matter that the other symbolism did not fit so well. In what sense was the nuclear plant "a great star" that "fell from heaven?" Such inconsistencies in the literal occurrence did not deter some from making predictions about the significance of the Chernobyl incident, which many saw as a literal fulfillment of the third trumpet and a prediction that the eschaton was soon to occur.

Years have now passed, and Chernobyl is rarely mentioned except for an occasional news item about the effects of the disaster on the health of the people in that locality. Chernobyl has given way to other events that inspire prophetic prediction. Indeed, Boyer (1992) has documented hundreds of such occurrences that have been read as indications that the end would be soon. While Revelation makes it clear, particularly in chapter 22, that Christians should anticipate the coming of Christ and the culmination of history, experience has demonstrated clearly that specific predictions based on contemporary events are futile.

Menno Simons recognizes Martin Luther's indulgence in a biblical interpretation similar to the one just described when Luther characterizes Origen as Wormwood. Menno points this out but stops short of agreeing with Luther:

> The great Origen especially, by his philosophy and self-deceit, dealt so shamefully with the Holy Scriptures that Martin Luther in his book *Servum arbitrium* calls him *Spercissimus scripturarum interpres* (that is, the falsest explainer of the Scriptures). And besides, it is said in the notes in Luther's New Testament that this Origen is the great star which fell from heaven, burning like a lamp, and that his name is wormwood. Rev. 8:11. We will leave it to God who and what he is. (1956:279)

The symbols of Revelation are often too artistic and impressionistic to be tied to specific events or persons. The third seal may be speaking of the many Chernobyls that have adversely affected our environment and even the Origens that may have falsely interpreted the scriptures. Therefore, the imagery of Revelation has permanent value if not specific predictive power.

Spiritual Warfare

Spiritual warfare has become a preoccupation of many Christians to the same extent that using events in the modern world to predict the future has dominated the thinking of others. This fascination with spiritual warfare was very evident in a series of fantastically popular novels by Frank Peretti (a good alternative is O'Brien, 1997, in which the battle is fought by love).

The first of Peretti's writings was *This Present Darkness* (1986), a novel about people from a small town in the Midwest who "find themselves fighting a hideous New Age plot to subjugate the townspeople, and eventually the entire human race." The book's cover pictures the town in dark colors with the claws of some demonic being reaching down toward the church, which sits in the midst of the town. The words on the cover announce that enclosed is "much insight into spiritual warfare and the necessity of prayer." Indeed, God's victory is made effectual through believers' prayers.

Although Perretti's novel has value, the Book of Revelation presents a much fuller insight into spiritual warfare and prayer. Chapter 9 describes the forces of evil being unleashed as the angel opens the shaft to the bottomless pit. Peretti is correct to remind us of the power of Satan's forces, since too often we do not really appreciate the reality of evil in the world. What Peretti does not fully appreciate in his captivating novel is what Revelation makes central: Satan and the forces of evil have already been defeated by the victory that Christ achieved on the cross. While with Peretti we should recognize the power that the devil has as the prince of this world, Revelation reminds us that Christians need not fear Satan's power because the victory has been won over evil in the heavenly realm by Michael and the forces of God (Rev. 12:7-9) and in the earthly realm by Christ on the cross.

Revelation 9 and Peretti's novel remind us of the spiritual warfare that is going on between the forces of God and of Satan. Yet this truth cannot be read apart from the message of the rest of Revelation. Perretti could benefit from taking seriously Revelation's message that the forces of evil, powerful as they are, have already been overcome by the forces of God. Therefore, Satan's power extends to "only those who do not have the seal of God on their foreheads" (9:4). Those who have overcome persecution and are protected by the seal of God have nothing to fear from attack by the forces of evil.

Eschatological Fiction

Several years ago, a novel by Bruce Merritt entitled *The Patmos Conspiracy* was published (see my review in Yeatts, 1993). Merritt's book includes fascinating phenomena that he ties to the end of the world: the major movement of the earth's geological plates producing earthquakes on an unprecedented level, the plans of New Era religion, a total oil embargo by OPEC, and the mysterious disappearance of ships in the Persian Gulf. These "historical" events are coupled with the appearance of demonic beings that resemble those of Revelation 9. The historical elements of this novel are somewhat plausible, and the introduction of beings from Revelation is compelling. Herein lies the danger of such literature based on Revelation.

Far more popular, and more obviously fictional, is the *Left Behind* series by Tim LaHaye and Jerry Jenkins (1995-). These novels, featuring beautiful women, successful men, and exciting violent action, tell about what happens after the "rapture," with action focusing around the main characters, Rayford Steele, a commercial airline pilot, and Buck Williams, an international newspaper correspondent. Nicolae Carpathia, the antichrist, claims to be God, profanes the temple, constructs a gigantic smoke-belching image of himself that is worshiped by multitudes, and is killed—only to rise from the dead indwelt by Satan. Pope Peter Mathews is the harlot leader of the Antichrist's one-world faith. False prophet Leon Fortunato is raised from the dead by the Antichrist and compels all to worship the images of Antichrist Carpathia constructed throughout the world. The ten regional potentates of the Antichrist's rule constructed from the permanent members of the United Nations Security Council compose the horns of the beast (Yeatts, 2001).

It must be remembered that novels like this are fiction, not future historical narrative. Yet most conservative Christians are not used to reading religious fiction. Therefore, such novels are read as future history rather than as the imaginary literature that they are. Perhaps a new literary category should be created for such writing called eschatological fiction. This might remind readers of the obvious point that such literature is, indeed, fiction.

The beasts portrayed in the fifth and sixth trumpets, the locusts/scorpions/cavalry/demons, communicate powerfully when interpreted as symbolic evil beings. Evil is, indeed, hideous beyond rational speculation. Nevertheless, when interpreted literally in fictional novels about the end times, such symbols become grotesque at best and misleading at worst. Morbid preoccupation with the demonic beasts of this passage, which are impossible to picture literally, tends to divert the attention of the reader from the important truth of the passage: the forces of Satan, powerful beyond description, have been destroyed by Christ's redemptive activity on the cross. Therefore, if we are faithful to Christ, we have nothing to fear from the evil forces arrayed and portrayed in the plagues of Revelation or in the writings of eschatological fiction.

Revelation 10:1–11:19

The Witness of the Faithful

PREVIEW

Revelation 10:1–11:14 forms an interlude between the blowing of the sixth and seventh trumpets and contains the accounts of the little scroll, the measuring of the temple, and the two witnesses. There was a similar interlude between the sixth and seventh seals, which included the two throngs—the 144,000 and the great multitude. These interludes prepare the faithful for the continuation of persecution: the former consoles the persecuted with the promise of future bliss if they overcome, and the latter speaks of protection for those who are loyal to God in tribulation. Sweet says that the seal interlude seals the faithful against persecution, and the trumpet interlude measures them in preparation for witness (1990:175). Although the two interludes have similar or related images, their settings are different: the seal interlude takes place in heaven, and the trumpet interlude on earth. More specifically, the location of the first part of chapter 11 is Jerusalem.

That Jerusalem's temple seems to be intact has led to one of the most perplexing problems in Revelation. Because the temple was destroyed in A.D. 70, at least two decades before Revelation was probably written, Wellhausen and others have posited that chapter 11 was borrowed from a Zealot source from the time of the Roman siege of Jerusalem—specifically, from the time when troops had taken the city but not the inner court of the temple, which was occupied by the

Zealots. The prophecy in 11:1-2 would then be that, although Jerusalem will be destroyed, this last refuge for God's people, the inner court of the temple, will be preserved from destruction. However, this theory has rather significant shortcomings. It would require that John incorporated a passage that proved false: the entire temple was destroyed in the siege. Caird labels the theory "improbable, useless, and absurd":

> improbable, because, once the outer court had fallen to the army of Titus, not even the most rabid fanatic could have supposed that he would be content to occupy it for three and half years and leave the sanctuary itself inviolate; useless, because, whatever these words might have meant to a hypothetical Zealot, they certainly meant something quite different to John twenty-five years after the siege; and absurd, because of the underlying assumption that John could not have intended these words to be taken figuratively unless someone else had previously used them in their literal sense. (1966:131)

More certainly, the elements of this interlude are heavily borrowed from the prophet Ezekiel; specifically, the eating of the scroll is from Ezekiel's vision in chapters 2-3, which is the prophet's commissioning. Since John has been commissioned twice before (1:9-20; 4:1), this passage might be seen as a reaffirmation of that prophetic call in preparation for intense persecution.

In addition, the interlude answers two questions: How long will it be until the end? And what is the task and fate of God's people until the end comes? The first question is answered in chapter 10 with the words: *There will be no more delay* (v. 6); and the second, in chapter 11: the task of the faithful is to witness even in the likelihood of intense persecution.

OUTLINE

The Announcement of the Little Scroll, 10:1-3a
The Seven Thunders, 10:3b-7
The Eating of the Little Scroll, 10:8-11
The Measuring of the Temple, 11:1-2
The Two Witnesses, 11:3-14
The Seventh Trumpet, 11:15-19

EXPLANATORY NOTES

The Announcement of the Little Scroll 10:1-3a

As the interlude opens, John saw *another mighty angel coming down from heaven.* The description of this angel alludes to the angel

Gabriel, whose name means "mighty one of God" and who appears to Daniel (Dan. 8:16-26; 9:21; see also 10:5; 12:5-13). The angel is one of the three mighty angels in Revelation (5:2; 18:21-24). The word *another* is used to distinguish this angel either from the first mighty angel, who also introduces a scroll, or from the seven angels who blew the seven trumpets. The descriptor *mighty* favors the former identification, and the immediate context of the seven trumpet judgments favors the latter.

The angel was *coming down from heaven.* This glorious activity indicates that the divine being comes from the throne of God. The angel is contrasted with the fallen star of 9:1, who also comes from heaven but with a message of destruction rather than of protection and imminent deliverance. The present participle indicates that coming down from heaven is a permanent characteristic of the angel (18:1; 20:1). The meaning is that the message of this angel is of divine origin. To confirm this, four characteristics of the angel are then presented, which include divine allusions (Job 37; Ps. 18:7-15; Amos 3:8; Zech. 10:1; see also 1 John 3:2) and recall the vision of the Son of Man in chapter 1 and the vision of God in chapter 4.

The first characteristic is that the angel was *wrapped in a cloud.* The cloud, a traditional symbol of the glory of God (Exod. 19:9, 16-17; 33:10; 34:1-5; Num. 11:25; 12:5-9), is associated with the *shekinah,* the presence of the divine in the tent of meeting or the house of the Lord (Exod. 33:9; Num. 14:10; Deut. 31:15; 1 Kings 8:11; 2 Chron. 5:13-14). In this passage it is the clothing of an angel (see Ezek. 18:7, 16). Through this symbol, the divine nature of the message of the angel is highlighted. The word *wrapped* carries the image of putting on a garment (Ps. 109:19) and certainly means that the heavenly being was surrounded by the glory of God's protective presence (see Luke 19:43; Wis. Sol. 19:17; see also 3 Macc. 6:26).

The angel also had *a rainbow over his head.* The rainbow represents the mercy of God. It surrounded God's throne both in John's vision of heaven (4:3) and in Ezekiel's throne vision (Ezek. 1:28). The rainbow effect may have been caused by the shining of the angel's face upon the cloud. Regardless of the cause, the rainbow, as in chapter 4, connotes the mercy that coexists with divine glory.

The third characteristic of the angel is that *his face was like the sun.* Most likely, the symbol alludes to the glory of God, which seems clearly to be the meaning in the shining face of Moses on Mount Sinai (Exod. 34:29-35) and Jesus on the mountain of his transfiguration, where the cloud of God's glory is also present (Matt. 17:1-8). Other suggestions are that the face of God is associated with divine strength

(Dan. 8:18; 10:15-19; Rev. 1:16), divine favor and peace (Num. 6:22-27; see also Ps. 84:11), or divine wrath (Lev. 17:10; Ezek. 14:8; 15:7). Yet the symbol is best associated with glory, and the faithful are promised shining faces as they share God's glory (Dan. 12:3; Matt. 13:43; 1 Enoch 38:4; 39:7; 104:2).

The final characteristic of the angel is that he had *legs like pillars of fire*. In their wilderness journey, the Israelites were led by a pillar of cloud by day and a pillar of fire by night. So, like the cloud, the pillars of fire connote the presence and especially the guidance and protection of God. Just as Israel was guided from Egypt by God's presence (Exod. 13:21-22; 14:19-24), so the faithful are protected by the angel in their suffering. The word translated *legs* here is literally "feet," representing power (Ford, 1975:162); the conquering monarch placed his foot on the neck of the defeated king (Josh. 10:24). Moreover, the Roman tradition refers to the foot or its imprint bringing miraculous healing (Tacitus, *Hist.* 4.81). Thus, the image communicates that God powerfully guides and protects the faithful as they are persecuted for their witness.

This fantastic mighty angel *held a little scroll open in his hand*. This little scroll must be understood in relation to the scroll opened by the Lamb in chapter 5. Some commentators find in the little scroll merely a symbolic reinforcement of John's prophetic call (see Ezek. 2-3; Jer. 1:4-10). Schüssler Fiorenza says John is called to give a "prophetic interpretation of the situation of the Christian community" (1985:54). Yet this interpretation taken alone leaves unexplained the contents of the scroll. Interpreting more specifically, others see the scroll of chapter 5 as Revelation 1-11 and the little scroll here as chapters 12-22. Yarbro Collins says that the major purpose of this section is to introduce chapters 12-22 and to link it to the first half of the book (1991:66). However, this makes nothing of the size of the scrolls: the two halves of Revelation are of relatively equal length. Still other commentators interpret the contents of the scroll of chapter 5 to be the chapters that follow, the judgments of chapters 6–9, and the little scroll to be Revelation 11:1-13. Mounce argues that the little scroll "reveals the lot of the faithful during the final period of Satanic opposition" (1992:51). This interpretation seems to be on the right track, but there is no reason to limit its application to the end of time.

A more comprehensive interpretation, one that is most consistent with the meaning of the scroll in chapter 5, is offered by Caird: the larger scroll contains God's plan of redemption insofar as it applies to Christ's work, and the little scroll describes God's redemption as it applies to the role of the faithful saints (1966:126). Pieters argues that the scroll is like the first scroll but deals with only what can be known by God's people, particularly what applies to them (1954:133-34). Thus, the passage is a prophetic commissioning of the church (see Mark 13:9-13; Luke 24:44-49), which has the duty to bear witness to the word of God (Morris, 1969:136). This witness is the part the faithful play in God's redemption of humanity and the world. In short, it is best to take the little scroll to refer to divine redemption as it relates to God's people, the faithful, who are to bear witness even in persecution and martyrdom.

The important qualifier here is the word *open,* which indicates that the scroll is not hidden, but is disclosed. The perfect participle stresses permanence: it is permanently opened. Christ opened the first scroll (5:1-8), and there is no reason to believe that he is not the agent here also. The two scrolls are linked by the appearance of the *mighty angel* and by allusions to the commissioning of Ezekiel (Ezek. 2:8–3:3). Yet the word used to refer to the scroll in this passage is the diminutive *little scroll* (*biblardion*) rather than the normal *scroll* (*biblion*) used in chapter 5.

The angel then set *his right foot on the sea and his left foot on the land.* This image calls to mind the Colossos of Rhodes erroneously thought to straddle the harbor (Aune, 1998a:556). The emphasis here is on universality: the angel's message is for the whole world. The sea and the land together with the heavens constitute the entire universe (Gen. 1:9-10; Exod. 20:4, 11). Some believe the stress is on the enormous size of the angel (see especially Ford, 1975:158), but it is hard to see why the angel's size is important.

The mighty angel then *gave a great shout, like a lion roaring.* The strong angel in Revelation 5:2 was similarly "proclaiming with a loud voice." The intent is to focus on the depth and intensity of the angel's voice, which would likely be associated with the judgment of God and the human response of fear (Jer. 25:30-32; Hos. 11:10-11; Joel 3:16; Amos 1:2; 3:4-8).

The Seven Thunders 10:3b-7

When the mighty angel shouted, *the seven thunders sounded.* There is a clear allusion here to the Sinai motif, which is linked to trumpets as the present interlude interrupts the trumpet judgments (Exod. 19:16-25; Heb. 12:18-24). Elsewhere, the Lord's voice is compared to thunder and is connected to the glory of God (Ps. 29:3-9; John 12:28-29). Indeed, where thunders are present in Revelation, they announce an appearance of God (4:5; 8:3-5; 11:19; 16:17-21) or a voice from heaven (6:1-2; 14:2; 19:5-8). The definite article indicates that certain seven thunders are in mind, and the context would imply that the thunders are divine judgments (chs. 6-9). So, the seven thunders come from the voice of God through the mighty angel proclaiming judgment on the world. We would now expect seven thunder judgments, like the seven seals, trumpets and bowls, but the thunder judgments do not occur.

When John was about to write down what he observed, he *heard a voice from heaven saying, "seal up what the seven thunders have said, and do not write it down."* This voice is not identified, but the context would indicate that it is still the voice of the mighty angel. In apocalyptic literature, to seal a book means to conceal its contents (Dan. 12:4, 9: see also Matt. 17:9; 2 Esd. 14:18-48). In the New Testament, it is used in this sense only in Revelation (see 22:10); usually the sense intended by sealing is to certify or authenticate. Moreover, to seal something that has not yet been written is unprecedented. Nevertheless, it seems clear that John understood the message of the seven thunders but was asked to conceal it rather than pass it on. Because thunders are associated with the seal, trumpet, and bowl judgments (8:5; 11:19; 16:18), it is a similar sequence of judgments that is being sealed.

But why are the seven thunders concealed? It may be to indicate that their effects are canceled. Roloff argues that they are canceled because the end is so imminent (1993:123); others say that the cancellation is to demonstrate the mercy of God (Hab. 3:2); and still others believe that they are canceled due to the repentance of the wicked (Jer. 18:8; Jon. 3:8-9). An alternative more likely than the image of canceling is that the sealing of the seven thunders signifies the limited character of Revelation (Deut. 29:29: 1 Cor. 13:12; 2 Cor 12:3-5). The book does not contain all of God's judgments because only God knows all that is in store for this world (Matt. 24:36; Mark 13:32). Mounce says that John only writes what God has communicated to him (1992:48). God has other judgments that are not communicated and thus not recorded here. Beasley-Murray says that "the will of God is far greater than ... prophecy is able to express" (1974:173). Therefore, the sealing up of the seven thunders seems best interpreted as indicating that when the tribulations of the seven seals, trumpets, and bowls have been communicated by God to John and ultimately to the reader, there are still more judgments which are not, and perhaps cannot, be communicated to humanity. A corollary of this principle is that Christians should be humble when specifying what is in store for the future because all the information is not available; God has not revealed everything.

Then the mighty angel *raised his right hand to heaven and swore by him who lives forever and ever, who created heaven and what is in it, the earth and what is in it, and the sea and what is in it.* This gesture is the customary way of taking an oath (Deut. 32:40; Dan. 12:7; see also Exod. 6:8; Num. 14:28-30; Ezek. 20:15, 28; cf. Aune, 1998a:564). The object of the oath is God, which adds to its seriousness (Gen. 14:22-23; Ezra 9:6; Ezek. 20:5-8). Beasley-Murray says: "No higher power than this could be invoked when making an oath" (1974:173). Furthermore, that God lives forever and ever is a great comfort to those who are facing persecution and possible death, and that God is the creator of all reminds the reader that the creation is being renewed in the new heaven and the new earth, the reward of those who overcome tribulation (Heb. 11:3).

The words of the oath that the mighty angel took are: *There will be no more delay.* The King James Version translates this phrase: "Time shall be no more." This rendering would indicate that the angel announces the end of time and the beginning of eternity. Nevertheless, the Judeo-Christian understanding of eternity is not the end of time but unending time (Ladd, 1972:144). A better translation of the original is found in the words of the New Revised Standard Version: "no more delay" (Hab. 2:3; Heb. 10:37). The connection of this statement to the rest of the verse, which speaks of the fulfillment of the mystery of God, makes much more sense if the meaning has to do with delay than with the end of time (cf. Aune, 1998a:568).

It should be noted that the passage answers the question *How long?* which was posed by the martyrs under the altar (6:10). Daniel's answer to this question is that "a time, two times, and a half a time" must pass (Dan. 12:6-7; see also 2 Thess. 2:3; Rev. 6:11). Here the answer is: *There will be no more delay* before the end (2 Pet. 3:3-10; see also Luke 12:45-46). The prayers of the saints are about to be answered, the hour of God's deliverance is at hand, the seven thunders have been canceled, the seventh trumpet is about to sound, and the coming of Christ is at hand. Peterson's words are instructive on this point: "'Today is the day of salvation.' Procrastination—the chief mischief introduced by predictors and fortune tellers of all kinds ('if the truth is still in the future, I do not have to deal with it today')—is abolished. We live in an intense, eternal Now" (1988:107). The promise of immediate deliverance should be reassuring to all humans under persecution—those of John's time under the threat of Domitian's rule, those Christians throughout history who face suffering and martyrdom, and those in our time who struggle against evil. Through divine mercy, the end is prolonged for those who need repentance, but for those who are faithful in persecution, God's mercy necessitates that the end will come soon (Matt. 24:22; 1 Cor. 4:1-5; Eph. 1:9-10; Col. 2:2).

The mighty angel's words continue: *but in the days when the seventh angel is to blow his trumpet, the mystery of God will be fulfilled.* The *mystery* does not refer to a secret but to what is revealed only to the faithful (Dan. 2:29-30; Amos 3:7; Rom. 16:25-26; 1 Cor. 15:51-52; 2 Esd. 14:5; 1 Qp Hab. 7.4-5). This revelation of God holds the answer to confusing questions about the purpose of human history: it is moving toward the triumph of God's salvation. The word *fulfilled* is used in the sense of finished (Matt. 24:14; Rev. 11:7; 2 Bar. 85:10): human history is soon finished and God's salvation will appear.

The mystery of God was *announced to his servants the prophets.* The word *announced* (*euangelizōmai*) is used of preaching the gospel (see TBC, Good News). The promise that God will be victorious over the powers of evil though the witness of the faithful is good news. That the gospel is communicated through the prophets is consistent with the definition already set out for the prophet as the one who communicates the word of God (Amos 3:7).

The Eating of the Little Scroll 10:8-11

When John was instructed to take the little scroll from the angel, he told the angel to give it to him, and the angel responded: *Take it, and eat it.* This transaction is remarkably similar to Ezekiel's call (Ezek. 2:8–3:11; see also Jer. 15:16) and to other prophetic acts (Jer. 13:1-11; Ezek. 5:1-12), indicating that it is primarily a reaffirmation of John's prophetic call. To eat the scroll means to assimilate completely its message, to master thoroughly its contents, and to make it part of one's life. Barclay says that this passage is reminiscent of the Jewish practice of teaching the alphabet with letters made of flour and honey, which the student was allowed to eat if he identified the letters correctly (1960:2.69). John's taking the scroll from the angel here parallels the Lamb taking the scroll from the one seated on the throne in 5:7 (Beale, 1999:548). The proclamation of God's message of redemption depends on the faithful responding to their prophetic commission to accept persecution and martyrdom (John 6:52-65; 17:6-19; Rev. 12:11). Because the angel who brings this message is the one who stands on the land and sea, the prophetic commission is universal .

So when John took the little scroll and ate it, he said: *it was sweet as honey in my mouth, but when I had eaten it, my stomach was*

made bitter. This bitterness is not found in Ezekiel. The mouth is associated with physical life and the intake of food, whereas the stomach
is the location of the heart, the seat of spiritual life (John 7:38). The
message of salvation makes the scroll sweet to the mouth, but when
the message is digested in the stomach, it is bitter because of the real-
ization that the plan of God includes not only the sweet ultimate protection of the faithful but also the bitterness of persecution and martyrdom (Koester, 2001:104; TBC, The Bitter-Sweet Scroll). Caird
says it well: "The way of victory is the way of the Cross" (1966:130).

John was then told: *You must prophesy again.* This is a reference
to chapters 12-22, where John will continue to prophesy. Thus, the
present passage serves to connect the two major sections of
Revelation. In addition, the statement gives further support to the
interpretation that the end of chapter 10 is a reaffirmation of John's
prophetic call. John's prophecy is to be *about many peoples and
nations and languages and kings.* This phrase or a close variation
occurs seven times in Revelation (5:9; 7:9; 10:11; 11:9; 13:7; 14:6;
17:15), which intensifies the completeness or universality of the
prophecy. The use of the word *kings* in this rendering of the statement points forward to the kings of the earth, who join forces with
Babylon and commit adultery with the great whore (17:10-12). John's
prophetic message condemns the whole evil world, as the witnesses
of Jeremiah (Jer. 1:10), Christ (Matt. 10:18), and the faithful followers of Christ (Matt. 10:17-18; Mark 13:9; Luke 21:12) convict their
hearers. This phrase refutes the idea that Revelation is for the Jewish
people at the end of time. Indeed, the message is for all times and
places, not just for a specific group of persons at a particular time.

The Measuring of the Temple 11:1-2

Chapters 10-11 speak of the witness of the people of God. The little
scroll symbolizes the responsibility of the Christian to bear witness to
God's redemption, even when that involves suffering and death. Now,
measuring the temple symbolizes the ultimate protection of the faithful who bear this witness. Although they may lose their lives, they will
be protected from eternal death and will have a place in the temple of
God.

As the chapter begins, John says: *Then I was given a measuring
rod like a staff.* The measuring rod was a lightweight reed (*kalamos*),
grown along the Jordan River (1 Kings 14:15; Ezek. 29:6-7; 40:3;
41:8; 42:16-19; Matt. 11:7; Mark 6:8). We are not told who gave it
to him; perhaps it is best to assume that it was the mighty angel of
chapter 10.

John continues: *and I was told, "Come and measure the temple of God.* In Ezekiel's parallel passage, the entire temple is measured (Ezek. 40–48); here only the inner court (*naos*), the altar, and those who worship are included. Moreover, Ezekiel focuses on the details of the temple rather than on persons—those who worship there, the nations, and the two witnesses. Zechariah's vision speaks of measuring Jerusalem (Zech. 2:1-2; see also Rev. 21:15-17), not the temple.

To comprehend this passage, it is necessary to have a basic understanding of the layout of the temple (see Ford, 1975:169, for a more detailed description of the sanctuary). The first temple, indeed, did have inner and outer courts. However, the Herodian temple was composed of three inner courts for the priests, Israelites, and women along with a court of Gentiles outside a wall that separated it from the inner courts (Eph. 2:14-16; Jos., *War.* 5.193-194; *Ant.* 15.417-20).

The measuring of the temple may be interpreted in two ways. Some argue that the temple is measured for rebuilding, which seems to be the meaning to Ezekiel and Zechariah (Ezek. 40; Zech. 2; Rev. 21:15-17). Yet it would be strange for the Hebrew temple to be rebuilt when the message of the New Testament is that sacrifices offered in the temple, which needed to be repeated, were less than adequate and that Christ's death was the perfect once-for-all sacrifice, making animal sacrifices superfluous (Heb. 9:11–10:18). Moreover, Paul says that Christians are the new temple (1 Cor. 3:16-17; 6:19; 2 Cor. 6:16); and in Revelation, Jerusalem refers only to the New Jerusalem, never to the earthly city and its temple (Schüssler Fiorenza, 1991:77). Therefore, it is better to interpret the temple to be symbolically the people of God and the measuring to be for their protection. It must be admitted that the image of measuring is used symbolically in scripture more often for punishment than for preservation (2 Sam. 8:2; 2 Kings 21:13; Isa. 34:11; Jer. 30:11; Lam. 2:8; Amos 7:7-9; Zech. 2:1-12; 1 Enoch 41:1-2; 61:1-5). Yet because the temple was destroyed and no longer literally present when John wrote (Mark 13:2; see also Rev. 21:22) a symbolic interpretation seems appropriate. Moreover, since there are clearly elements of the passage that must be taken symbolically, even commentators who tend toward interpreting the Bible literally admit that the measuring is probably symbolic (Ladd, 1972:150; Walvoord, 1966:176). Nevertheless, Ladd argues that, although the measuring is not for the rebuilding of the Hebrew temple but for preservation, those protected are only Jews (see Matt. 23:37-39; Luke 21:24; Rom. 11:1-2, 26-27). Because there is no evidence in the text for limiting the reference to Jews, it is best to see faithful Christians as the new temple of God that

is protected, not from physical harm, but from spiritual destruction
(see TBC, The New Temple). The saints were sealed for protection in
7:1-8; now they are measured for the same reason.

John was also told to measure *the altar and those who worship
there*. Although Barker changes "worshiper" to "boundary" on the
basis of an emendation to the word likely to occur in a Hebrew original, no such speculation is necessary (2000:73, 187-88). The altar is
certainly used symbolically for the worshiping community, thus preserving the identical meaning of the two parts of this phrase in synonymous parallelism. Measuring the worshipers with a rod suggests a
symbolic interpretation and gives support for interpreting the entire
passage symbolically. The meaning is that God's worshipers will be
protected.

Nevertheless, John was told: *do not measure the court outside
the temple; leave that out*. Although the temple was measured for
protection, the outer court was left out and thus not protected. This
exclusion is captured in the verb (*ekballō*), which means "cast out,"
"expel," or "remove." It seems best to interpret the temple to be the
faithful and the outer court to be the unfaithful. The meaning, then, is
that the faithful who are persecuted physically, economically, and
socially will be protected from spiritual harm, but that the unfaithful
who prosper now will suffer ultimate destruction.

The court outside the temple is to be left out *for it is given over
to the nations, and they will trample over the holy city*. The holy
city in this passage is contrasted with Babylon, the city of evil, and is
used symbolically to represent God's people. The symbolic interpretation is reinforced by the fact that the phrase *holy city* is used in
Revelation only for the New Jerusalem and never for the earthly city
of Jerusalem. The holy city, therefore, most likely refers to the faithful (see TBC, The Trampling of the Holy City). Because *trampling*
usually carries the idea of contempt, it designates the persecutions of
the faithful. So the meaning of this verse is that the evil nations will be
allowed to treat God's people with contempt, but the verse that follows makes it clear that this persecution of the faithful is for a limited
time.

John is told that the holy city will be trampled for *forty-two
months* (11:2; 13:5), a time designation that also occurs in Revelation
as three and a half times (12:14; or days in 11:9, 11), and one thousand two hundred and sixty days (11:3; 12:6). This duration is used
for the trampling of the holy city (11:2), the prophecy of the two witnesses (11:3), the nourishment of the woman in the wilderness (12:6,
14), and the time of the beast's authority (13:5). Hebrew tradition held

that after the Exodus there were forty-two stages in the Israelites' wilderness wandering (Num. 33:5-56). Beasley-Murray argues that this Exodus typology (Exod. 19:4; Deut. 32:10-12) reminds the faithful that "they are pilgrims, having no settled home in this world, and that they are being prepared for life in the inheritance of the kingdom" (1974:205). The more obvious source of the symbol is in the period of Antiochus Epiphanes' desecration of the Temple, recorded in Daniel 9, which lasted approximately three and a half years from A.D. 168 to 165 (see also Dan. 7:25; 8:14; 12:7, 11-13). It should also be noted that the length of Titus's siege of Jerusalem in A.D. 70 was about three and a half months (see Ford, 1975:177). In Revelation, the time period is a symbol of Satan's power exercised by the beast. The reason for the numerical designation of three and half years may relate to the interruption of persecution in midstream, half the completion of seven; the forty-two months may be perfection missing the mark, six times seven. Whatever lies behind the symbolic numbers, the meaning of the passage is clear: Satan's tribulation of the faithful is limited and will soon come to an end.

The Two Witnesses 11:3-14

Two witnesses are introduced with the words: *And I will grant my two witnesses authority to prophecy for one thousand two hundred sixty days in sackcloth.* The word *martys* means "witness or testimony," carrying a legal connotation, but it came to be used in the technical sense of martyr. Boring defines martyrdom as "holding fast to one's Christian convictions when tried before the pagan courts, even to the point of death, thereby giving testimony to the truth of the Christian message" (1989:145). Jesus, the faithful witness (1:5; 3:14; 19:11; 22:20), is the example for Christians, who are called to conquer tribulation (2:17; 2:26-28; 3:12, 21; 12:17; 1 QS 8.1-10) and are reminded by Jesus that, when they bear faithful witness, the end is near (Matt. 24:14).

The choice of *two witnesses* probably has roots in the idea that the agreement of at least two persons was necessary for a testimony to be valid in a court of law (Num. 35:30; Deut. 17:6; 19:15; Matt. 18:16; John 8:17) and that Jesus sent his disciples in pairs to bear witness to the gospel (Mark 6:7; Luke 10:1; Acts 13:2; 15:39-40). Walvoord argues that the use of the definite article indicates that two specific persons are in mind (1966:179; for a more complete enumeration of the possibilities, see Ford, 1975:177-78). Some suggest that the witnesses are Enoch and Elijah because neither died (Gen. 5:24; 2 Kings 2:11; 2 Esd. 6:26; 1 Enoch 90:31), but a more likely pairing is Moses, the giver of the law, and Elijah, the great prophet, who appeared together on the Mount of Transfiguration (Matt. 17:1-9; Mark 9:2-8; Luke 9:28-26). Indeed, Moses was also seen as a great prophet (Deut. 18:15-18; 34:10-12; Hos. 12:13), and the belief became current that Moses did not die (Jude 9). Moreover, Elijah was expected to come before the end to preach to the Gentiles (Mal. 4:5-6; Matt. 17:10-13; Mark 9:11-13; Luke 1:17; also Moses, see Aune, 1998a:600). It has been suggested that the two witnesses, Moses and Elijah, stand allegorically for the law and the prophets. While it is true that Christ's witnesses come with the authority of the law, and prophets to call persons to repentance and faithfulness, it seems that some actual persons are envisioned. The next section will make it clear that, indeed, Moses and Elijah are in the mind of the author (see Aune, 1998a:601-2 for other possibilities).

The passage says that the two witnesses were *wearing sackcloth,* a fabric the prophets donned to communicate mourning due to distress (Isa. 20:2-6; 37:1-3) or penitence (Job 42:6; Dan. 9:3-4; Jon. 3:6-9; Matt. 11:21; cf. 2 Kings 1:8; Zech. 13:4; Mark 1:6). The prophecy of persecution and tribulation causes the witnesses sorrow and motivates them to call persons to repentance (Koester, 2001:108).

How should the appearance of the sackcloth-clad witnesses, Moses and Elijah, be interpreted? A literal and futuristic interpretation is that they are two persons sent to Israel to bring her conversion, when the time of the Gentiles is past. Yet there is no evidence in the passage to limit the witness to Jews. A more idealistic interpretation is that the two witnesses, Moses and Elijah, represent those prophets who come to the church in times of persecution. Mounce combines the first two interpretations by saying that the two witnesses are not limited to two persons but "represent the church in the last days before the end" (1992:54). The best interpretation, however, is that the two witnesses symbolize faithful Christians who bear witness in the world at all times. As two witnesses rather than seven, which would have connoted the complete church, they are the portion of the church that is faithful even unto death. Just as two of the seven churches in Asia, Smyrna and Philadelphia, were portrayed as faithful, likewise the two witnesses represent that portion of the church that is faithful to the point of martyrdom.

The two witnesses are also called *the two olive trees*, an image from the vision of Zechariah, where the reference is to Joshua, the Davidic king, and Zerubbabel, the high priest (Zech. 4:3-14; see also 1 Pet. 2:9). Here, verse 6 suggests that the two olive trees are Moses and Elijah, clear evidence that symbols do not always have the same referents. The plant image is found elsewhere (1 Cor. 3:5-9; 1 QS 8.5; 11.8; CD 1.7; 1 QH 14.15), and the oil of the olive tree is connected to the Holy Spirit (Zech. 4:6, 14; see also Rev. 4:5; 5:6). Hence, the ideas associated with the image of the two olive trees indicates the richness of the image.

The two witnesses are also called *two lampstands*. This image, too, is from Zechariah's vision, where the referents are again Joshua and Zerubbabel. Zechariah describes a lampstand of gold with seven lamps (Zech. 4:2), while Revelation speaks of seven lampstands, which are the complete church (Rev. 1:20). In Revelation, lampstands are faithful Christians who give luminous witness to the divine light of God's presence. The two lampstands, as a portion of the complete church, reinforce the idea that the two witnesses represent the portion of the church that is martyred in tribulation.

Describing the activity of the two witnesses, John says: *And if anyone wants to harm them, fire pours from their mouth and consumes their foes; anyone who wants to harm them must be killed in this manner.* The weapon that the faithful use against their enemies is fire from their mouth. As Christ conquers, not with the violence of the lion, but with the suffering of the lamb, so faithful Christians conquer persecutors, not with violent resistance, but with the testimony they bear in the face of suffering. The singular, *mouth,* may indicate that the testimonies of the two witnesses are identical (Ford, 1975:171). Thus, evil is conquered by the unified word of two witnesses, who represent the portion of the church that is faithful even unto death.

Moreover, these two witnesses *have authority to shut the sky, so that no rain may fall during the days of their prophesying.* This statement suggests that one of the witnesses was Elijah, who had the power to keep rain from falling (1 Kings 17-18; Sir. 48:3-4). Indeed, the New Testament writers reinterpret the drought of Elijah's time to have lasted for three and a half years (Luke 4:25; Jam. 5:17), although its length seems different in the Old Testament account (1 Kings 18:1).

The witnesses also *have authority over the waters to turn them into blood.* Indeed, Moses had this power. When Pharaoh refused to let the Israelites leave Egypt, God enabled Moses to turn the waters of the rivers into blood (Exod. 7:14-24; see also Rev. 8:8-9; 16:3-4). Further alluding to the Exodus, the witnesses have authority *to strike the earth with every kind of plague, as often as they desire.* This refers to the power God gave Moses to enact the plagues (1 Sam. 4:8;

see also Isa. 11:4; Wis. Sol. 16:15-29; 18:5; 19:1-8).

Thus, if two individuals are in the mind of the author, the witnesses are almost certainly Moses and Elijah. The Hebrew tradition held that at the end of time Elijah would return (Mal. 4:5-6; Sir. 48:10; Tertullian, *A Treatise on the Soul*, 50) and God would send a New Moses (Deut. 18:15). John the Baptist became identified with the Elijah that was to come (Matt. 11:14; 17:10-13; Mark 1:2-3; 6:14-16; Luke 1:17; John 1:21). In Revelation, the point is that the faithful, represented by two witnesses, have power like Moses and Elijah, perhaps through the prayers they make to God (Rev. 5:8; 6:10).

When the two witnesses *have finished their testimony, the beast from the bottomless pit* appears on the scene. This is the first mention of the beast in Revelation, but this character will dominate the second half of the book (see TBC, The Beast). In contrast to Christ and the New Jerusalem, which descend from heaven (1:7; 21:10), the beast ascends from the bottomless pit, a parody of the Christ's parousia (see also 9:1; 13:1). Moreover, ascension from the pit is not so much an event as it is an indication of the character of the beast: he continuously comes from the place of satanic evil (Luke 8:26-33; Rev. 9:1-11).

Then, the beast *will make war on them and conquer them and kill them*. The battle between the witnesses and the beast links chapter 11 with the battle between Michael and Satan in chapter 12 and the reappearance of the beast in chapter 13. Like the Lamb, his witnesses make war (Rev. 2:16; 19:11-15), but the strange use of warfare language to describe conflict among three individuals, the beast and the two witnesses, indicates the spiritual nature of the conflict (Aune, 1998a:617). Therefore, as in the parallel war between Michael and the dragon, the attack of the beast on the witnesses is most probably a spiritual rather than a military conflict (Rev. 12:7-12).

There is irony in the use of the verb conquer (*nikaō*) because Revelation has already made it clear that the faithful witnesses are the real conquerors (2:7, 11, 17, 26; 3:5, 12, 21). The irony suggests that it is through their faithfulness in their battle with the beast that the saints conquer. As Christ overcame through his death and resurrection, Christians conquer through faithfulness even unto death. Boring says: "faithfulness does not deliver them from death but causes it" (1989:147).

After the war with the beast, the two witnesses' *dead bodies will lie in the street*. There is no verb in this statement; *lie* is supplied, probably because that is what dead bodies normally do. Despite the translation, the word *bodies* is a collective singular here, indicating the unity of their witness and perhaps that the two witnesses are interpreted symbolically as all faithful Christians. In the Hebrew tradition, unburied bodies were a degradation and their lying in the street a humiliation (1 Kings 13:21-22; 21:24; Ps. 79:2-4; Jer. 8:1-3; 14:16; 16:4; Ezek. 6:5; Tob. 1:16-20; 2:3-8; 2 Macc. 5:10).

The street where their bodies will lie is in *the great city that is prophetically called Sodom and Egypt, where also their Lord was crucified.* This city is hard to identify because it is the great city, Rome; it is Sodom and Egypt; and it is Jerusalem, where the Lord was crucified. It is all of these, and yet limited to none of them. It is the archetypical city of evil, associated with Babylon (16:17–18:24; see also Gen. 11); but it is contrasted with the New Jerusalem, which embodies all that is righteous and pure (Rev. 21:9–22:5). Although the city is not to be identified with any political entity of this world, it has many of the qualities of cities known for evil. Without any other description, *the great city* would mean Babylon, which throughout Revelation represents Rome (16:19; 17:18; 18:10, 16, 18, 19, 21). Rome, in turn, symbolizes the power of the emperor and the blasphemy of emperor worship. In spite of the characteristics that follow, if a particular city is in view, Rome is the choice most consistent with usage in Revelation. Rome was considered "the center of the world" (Friesen, 2001:124).

Sodom and Egypt symbolize hostility to God's faithful and are proverbial for abomination. Sodom treated wickedly the two angels that visited Lot (Gen. 19:1-11) and, as a result, became a symbol for the foolishness and corruption of Judah (Deut. 32:32; Isa. 1:9-10; Jer. 23:14; Ezek. 16:44-52; see also Wis. Sol. 19:14-15). Egypt oppressed and enslaved God's people, Israel (Exod. 1:8-22; Acts 13:17; see also Matt. 2:13-23). Therefore, both cities received the judgment of God (Exod. 7–12).

The city *where also their Lord was crucified* is obviously Jerusalem, which was also known as the great city (Sib. Or. 5.154, 226, 413; see also Pliny, *Nat. Hist.* 5.15), was traditionally the place where prophets die (Luke 13:33; Aune, 1998a:620-621), and was identified with Sodom (Isa. 1:10-11). The death of the two witnesses parallels the passion of Christ, which took place in Jerusalem. The measuring of the temple that follows also connects this passage with Jerusalem. Indeed, Jerusalem has a reputation for evil because she killed the prophets (Matt. 23:37-39) and is described as retaining the evil ways of Egypt (Ezek. 23:27).

Hence, the city described is the personification of the evil of Rome, Sodom, Egypt, and Jerusalem (see TLC, The City of Vanity) together. Caird says: "The city is heir to the vice of Sodom, the tyranny of Pharaoh's Egypt, and the blind disobedience of Jerusalem, but it is not literally to be identified with any of them" (1966:138). It is the city, representing the forces of evil, that persecutes the two witnesses, who give testimony to the lordship of Christ (John 15:20).

While the bodies of the two witnesses lie in the streets for *three and a half days members of the peoples and tribes and languages and nations will gaze at their dead bodies and refuse to let them be placed in a tomb.* Leaving a dead body unburied was an outrage and a dishonor in the ancient world (Aune, 1998a:622). The three-and-a half-day duration, built on the three-and-a-half-year desolation of Antiochus Epiphanes, is changed to days under the influence of the three-day time period that Jesus spent in the tomb. Thus, like the Lamb, whom they serve, the two witnesses lie dead for about three days. Revelation uses this time designation, which carries rich allusions, to indicate that the persecution of the faithful witnesses will be short-lived. The recurrence of the phrase *peoples and tribes and languages and nations* indicates that the ministry of the two witnesses is not limited to Jerusalem or to the Jews, but is universal.

Continuing the theme of verse 9, John says: *and the inhabitants of the earth will gloat over them and celebrate and exchange presents, because these two prophets had been a torment to the inhabitants of the earth.* The phrase *the inhabitants of the earth* is a common idiom in Revelation for the faithless world *[Glossary: Inhabitants of the Earth],* whose consciences are tormented when the two prophets, in the tradition of Elijah (1 Kings 18:17; 21:20; see also John 16:8-11), explain to them the righteousness of God. The faithless gloat over the death of the witnesses whose testimony condemns them. Jesus said the earth would rejoice over his death (John 16:19-20; see also Mark 13:13); now the same people of the earth gloat over the death of his witnesses. Yet the irony is that in the end heaven will rejoice over Satan's defeat (Rev. 12:12), and the witnesses will rejoice over the destruction of the great whore (18:20; see also Esther 9:18-23). Taken together, the images in verses 9 and 10 indicate that, although it will be short-lived, the persecution and humiliation of the faithful witnesses is universal.

Yet this message of universal rejection is not the last word: *But after the three and a half days, the breath of life from God entered them, and they stood on their feet, and those who saw them were terrified.* It was believed that the breath of life, which was in all creatures, left them at death only to return at resurrection (Thompson, 1998:127). Here the breath of life from God certainly refers to the spirit of God or the Holy Spirit (Gen. 2:7; 6:17; 7:15, 22; Ezek. 37:6, 10). The result is that they stand up, striking terror into those who have just rejoiced over their death. The persecutors' terror at the resuscitation of the two witnesses parallels the reaction to the resurrection of the Lord (Matt. 28:4; Luke 24:5, 37). Morris points out the switch to the past tense here, arguing that it indicates that the resurrections of the witnesses are "so certain that he can speak of them in the past" (1969:151). This gives faithful followers of Christ the Lamb confidence that, if they are put to death like the Lamb who was slain, they will also, like the Lord they serve, be resurrected to new life.

John continues his description of the revival of the two witnesses: *Then they heard a voice from heaven saying to them, "Come up here!" And they went up to heaven in a cloud while their enemies watched them.* The witnesses are summoned into heaven like their prototypes, Moses (Deut. 34:5-6; Jude 9; Jos., *Ant.* 4.326) and Elijah (2 Kings 2:11), and even like John the Revelator (Rev. 4:1). Indeed, the ascension of the witnesses to heaven parallels the ascension of Christ (Mark 16:19; Acts 1:9) and alludes to Christ's eventual return from heaven (Acts 1:11; 1 Thess. 4:16-17). This ascension of the witnesses occurs while their enemies watch, just as they watched the passion and resurrection of Christ (John 19:37; see also Rev. 1:7). The passage gives the reader confidence: as Christ was resurrected from the dead, so witnesses who conquer persecution for Christ's cause will arise victorious (1 Cor. 15:51-56).

At the moment the two witnesses were taken into heaven, *there was a great earthquake.* This phenomenon is associated with divine intervention (Exod. 19:18) and marks the end of each of Revelation's judgment sequences (8:5; 11:19; 16:18). Again the parallel between the vindication of the two witnesses and that of their Lord is evident, because an earthquake also accompanied the resurrection of Christ (Matt. 27:54; 28:2). Most likely, the earthquake symbolically represents the impact of the revival of the two witnesses. Caird expresses this clearly: "The death and vindication of the martyrs is itself the earthquake shock by which the great city is overthrown" (1966:139).

The result of the earthquake is that *a tenth of the city fell.* This is the only use of the fraction one-tenth in Revelation, but Revelation has repeatedly used fractions to symbolize God's mercy and call to repentance. Koester says: "The conversion of the nations, rather than their destruction, is God's will for the world (2001:111). Perhaps one-tenth indicates that this catastrophe is not as bad as the seals and trumpets, because one-fourth and one-third are the fractions associated with those judgments.

More specifically, *seven thousand people were killed in the earthquake*. Some have pointed out that this number would have represented about one-tenth of the city of Jerusalem. Yet because the passage describes a spiritual city, which defies restriction to Jerusalem or any earthly city, the number of persons killed is likely symbolic: seven, the number of completion, times one thousand, a large number. The paradoxical meaning is that the destruction is both complete and limited.

As a result of the judgment on the city, *the rest were terrified and gave glory to the God of heaven*. It has already been noted that the terror parallels the reaction to the resurrection of Jesus (see on v. 11). The reaction here is strange, however, because Revelation usually emphasizes the refusal of God's enemies to repent (6:15-16; 9:20-21; 16:9, 20-21). Therefore, some commentators believe the glory given to God may have fallen short of true repentance: they acknowledge God's power but do not place their trust in God (Mounce, 1992:57; Beale, 1999:604-5). Nevertheless, the language used in this passage usually connotes repentance (Josh. 7:19; Isa. 42:12; Jer. 13:16; 1 Pet. 2:12; Rev. 14:6-7; 15:4; 16:9; 19:7-8; 21:24). Ladd argues that, since Gentiles are always portrayed as unrepentant in Revelation, those who repent are Jews, represented by the city of Jerusalem, and this passage thus marks the final conversion of the Jewish people as a whole (1972:159). Yet there is no clear evidence in this passage for limiting the repentance to Jewish people. Therefore, it is best to assume the ministry of the two witnesses results in the repentance of all that remain in the city. According to Schüssler Fiorenza, "while the cosmic plagues (6:12; 8:5; 11:19; 16:18) do not bring about repentance, the prophetic witness of Christians, even unto death, does" (1991:79).

The section concludes with the words: *The second woe is passed. The third woe is coming very soon*. It is not at all clear to what the three woes refer. In the interlude of the eagle, which occurs between the fourth and fifth trumpet, the three woes are announced. Therefore, it would be expected that they would be identified with the last three trumpet judgments (8:13). The announcement after the fifth trumpet that the first woe is passed and two more are to come (9:12) would confirm that expectation. Yet there is no similar note after the sixth trumpet judgment; and indeed, although Beale argues that God's kingdom is a woe on God's enemies because it signals their demise (1999:610), the seventh trumpet is clearly not a woe (11:16-19). Therefore, some have suggested that the referents for the three woes are the three judgment sequences—the seals, trumpets, and bowls.

The difficulties with this are that the woes are introduced as about to begin in 8:13 when the first woe would have been over and the second more than half over. Moreover, two woes are announced as yet to come in 9:12 when the seal judgments and six trumpet judgments have already passed. So it is better to assume that the first two woes are the fifth and sixth trumpet judgments and that the identity of the third woe is uncertain, perhaps the seven bowl judgments (see Preview of Chapters 15-16).

The Seventh Trumpet 11:15-19

After an interlude—since the sixth trumpet—that included the little scroll, the measuring of the temple, and the two witnesses, the seventh trumpet finally concludes that judgment sequence. The passage begins: *Then the seventh angel blew his trumpet, and there were loud voices in heaven, saying, "The kingdom of the world has become the kingdom of our Lord and of his Messiah, and he will reign forever and ever."*

Some words are in order here about the complex structure of the judgment sequences of Revelation because the series of trumpet judgments concludes with the seventh trumpet. At the end of the series of seal judgments, when the reader would have expected the most intense of the catastrophes, the seventh seal was an awful silence (8:1).

When the reader comes to the last trumpet with a similar expectation, what occurs is an even greater surprise than the seventh seal: the seventh trumpet is a heavenly chorus singing praises because the witnesses have conquered and the kingdom of God is at hand. Where the third woe is expected, a hymn of praise occurs. Again the reader comes to the end, but the end is not revealed. Instead, there is a statement of the ultimate truth that God reigns rather than Satan, who seems throughout the catastrophes to be in control. Beasley-Murray points out a connection between the seventh seal and the seventh trumpet: "Following on the silent listening to the prayers of God's people (8:4), the answer to their prayers in the gift of God's kingdom is celebrated" (1974:188). Hence, the last trumpet is one of Revelation's climactic heavenly worship scenes: the jubilant announcement of the arrival of God's kingdom and the rewarding of the saints who have overcome Satan. In the same way that the seventh seal both concluded the seal judgments and announced the seven trumpets (8:2), the seventh trumpet concludes the trumpet judgments and also announces "the destroying of those who destroy the earth"— Satan, the beast, and the false prophet—which is the next topic of the book. So both the seventh seal and the seventh trumpet are important transitional links in the overall movement of Revelation, tying what preceded with what follows. The triumph of Christ and his witnesses over the power of evil removes all obstacles to God's reign.

The past tense, *has become* implies that the arrival of the Lord's kingdom is so certain that it is spoken of in the past; moreover, it makes it clear that the kingdom of God is not limited to a future time period. Rowland argues that the verb should be translated "was" because the kingdom of this world has always been God's, and Satan's "temporary usurpation" of that kingdom is soon to end (1998:643). In any case, Revelation's conception of the kingdom is paradoxical— already but not yet (5:10; 6:16-17; see also John 3:36; 5:28-29; 1 John 5:13, 20). God's redemption has been accomplished in Christ's death and confirmed by the witness' testimony (Phil. 2:9-13), but it awaits final manifestation when Christ comes for his church (Rev. 19:11-21). Ewert says: "The church always lives in the twilight just before the dawn of the eternal kingdom" (1980:21).

The duration of the reign of Christ is *forever and ever.* The word repeated here (*aiōn*) means literally "time" or "age." It came to refer to a very long time—an eternity. Linked with a preposition (*eis*), it is used in the sense of "forever" or "for all eternity." The repeated use of the plural, often occurring in doxologies like this one, emphasizes the idea of eternity (Sasse, *TDNT* 1.198-200; 1:6, 18; 4:9; 4:10; 5:13; 7:12; 10:6; 14:11; 15:7; 19:3; 20:10; 22:5). In contrast to the rule of the emperor, which is temporary, God's rule is eternal, commencing in the present age and continuing into the age to come. This passage assures those who are persecuted that their brief tribulation will be followed by the eternal reign of Christ the Lamb.

After the seventh angel announced the rule of God, *the twenty-four elders who sit on their thrones before God fell on their faces and worshiped God.* As previously noted, the twenty-four elders represent the people of God, the twelve patriarchs symbolizing the Old Testament saints, and the twelve apostles the New Testament followers of Christ. Their purpose here and elsewhere in Revelation is to worship God by singing hymns of praise (4:10-11; 5:8-10; 19:4). The reason for the praise is that God's reign has begun, that the nations who have persecuted the saints have been judged, and that the saints have received their reward.

The song begins: *We give you thanks, Lord God Almighty.* This language was a basis for early Christian worship (Did. 9:2-3; 10:2-4). Boring argues that it is also the basis for John's understanding of suffering and martyrdom (1:8; 4:8; 11:17; 15:3; 16:7, 14; 19:6, 15;

21:22): only a God who is almighty is worth dying for (1989:145). God is further described in the words *who are and who were.* Surprisingly, the plural is used, perhaps to include both the Lord and his Messiah (v. 15). Moreover, there is no future here as there was in 1:4, because the end has come—the kingdom has begun. The emphasis now is on the imminent expectation of the rule of God.

The reason for the gratitude expressed to God is that *you have taken your great power and begun to reign.* The perfect tense, *have taken,* places stress on the permanence of God's reign; the aorist, *begun to reign,* denotes the beginning of an action. Although Satan has power (Luke 4:6-7), the message of Revelation is that Satan's power is terminated by his defeat, commencing the rule of God (12:7-12). The defeat of evil is the action that marked the beginning of the permanent, everlasting kingdom of God.

The song continues: *The nations raged, but your wrath has come.* This statement contains a play on the word *orgē,* which might best be expressed as: "The nations were angry, but God's anger has come" (Acts 4:25; Rev. 6:17). Although Satan and his beast led the nations in rebellion against God, they are put down in preparation for the sovereignty of God. The suffering saints are strengthened by the knowledge that the forces arrayed against God are defeated (Ps. 2:1-6; 98:1-3; 99:1-5).

In preparation for God's kingdom, *the time for judging the dead* arrives. This anticipates the white throne judgment (Rev. 20:11-15). The word *time* (*kairos*) denotes, not a chronology of events, but an appropriate or fitting occasion. Yarbro Collins calls attention to the change in this passage from the focus on the redemption of the world to individual salvation (1991:74). Here individuals are raised to be judged, both the servants of God and the destroyers of the earth. In the end, God's justice prevails.

On the one hand, the judgment is *for rewarding your servants, the prophets and saints and all who fear your name, both small and great.* Emphasis here is on rewarding all those who serve God. The mention of prophets and saints may be to distinguish the martyrs, the prophets, from those who are faithful but escape death, the saints. The categories, small and great, imply that everyone, regardless of earthly stature, is treated fairly in the judgment (see 13:16-17; 19:5, 17-18; 20:12; see also Gen. 19:11). The meaning of the statement is that no Christian need fear judgment because all Christians will receive what is due to them (Rev. 19:8).

On the other hand, the judgment is *for destroying those who destroy the earth.* Caird says that the destroyers of the earth are the four horsemen who through warfare wreaked havoc (6:8); the blazing mountain that destroyed life in the sea (8:8-9); the falling star Wormwood that defiled the waters (8:10-11); the angel of the abyss named "destroyer" (9:11); and the monster that arises from the abyss to kill and conquer (11:7; see TLC, The Destroyers of the Earth). The punishment in this passage fits the sin; the destroyers are destroyed (1 Cor. 3:17; Rev. 9:11). The judgment will occur with the destruction of the beast and the false prophet (Rev. 19:19-21; 20:10) and their followers in the city of Babylon (Jer. 51:24-26; Rev. 18:1-19:4).

After the judgments of the saints of God and the destroyers of the earth, *God's temple in heaven was opened, and the ark of his covenant was seen within his temple.* Hebrew tradition affirmed that the heavenly temple contained an ark that was the prototype for the one housed in the earthly tabernacle and temple (Aune, 1998a:677). The scene here parallels the tearing of the curtain of the temple that accompanied the death of Jesus (Matt. 27:51; Heb. 10:20). The destruction of the earthly temple was announced in verses 1-2; here the heavenly temple takes its place, complete with the ark (TBC, The Ark of the Covenant). Eller says: "Although the temple has been out-moded by Christianity and actually destroyed by the Romans, its real significance has not been lost and desecration is not the last word concerning it; it stands in heaven" (1974:123). The earthly sanctuary is unnecessary because God has defeated the power of evil in the world and is now fully present to comfort the saints in their suffering (Heb. 9:8; 10:19-25; Rev. 21:3-4).

The trumpet judgments end with *flashes of lightning, rumblings, peals of thunder, an earthquake, and heavy hail.* The elements of this description are normal accompaniments of an appearance of God (Exod. 19:16-19; Ps. 18:13; 104:7; Isa. 30:30), and these phenomena of the seventh trumpet are also associated with the seventh seal and bowl (8:5; 16:18).

The climax at the end of chapter 11 seems to bring Revelation to a close. If the rest of the book were absent, this would be a fitting conclusion, but the conclusion is canceled. Caird says that the conclusions reached at the end of each of the series of judgments—the seals, trumpets, and bowls—are canceled to give humanity three opportunities to repent (1966:146; see also Jer. 4:27; Joel 2:13; Amos 7:2-3; Jon. 3:9). Yet the conclusion reached with the seventh trumpet divides Revelation into two distinct parts. In chapters 12–22, new ideas are not encountered; instead, new symbols are introduced for teaching the same truths that were communicated in chapters 1–11.

THE TEXT IN BIBLICAL CONTEXT

Good News

In 10:7, the mystery of God's salvation was announced to the prophets; the Greek word for announced is *euangelizen*, which means "announce good news." A similar phrase was used in the Hebrew scriptures for good news regarding success in battle. The Philistines communicate to their priests and people the good news of the death of Saul (1 Sam. 31:9). After the death of Absalom in battle against David's troops, Ahimaaz desires to communicate to David the "good news" of victory over the enemies (2 Sam. 18:19-20). The word is used in a more limited sense in the New Testament for the good news of salvation. Paul connects it with two key themes of this Revelation passage—the mystery of God and the prophetic tradition (Rom. 16:25; Eph. 3:2-6)—and makes it clear that the good news is divine rather than human (Gal. 5:3; Eph. 3:7-13; Rev. 14:6-7). Thus, salvation is good news to the faithful as they understand the mystery of God communicated by the prophets: through suffering, the faithful Christian participates in Christ's redemption of the world, which will only be fully accomplished when Christ finally appears to make all things new.

The Bitter-Sweet Scroll

The scroll that John was told to eat included the sweet message of salvation and the bitter message of persecution. The psalmist indicates that the fear of the Lord and the words of the Lord are as sweet as honey (Ps. 19:10; 119:103). Jeremiah affirms that God's words are a joy and delight (Jer. 15:16). Nevertheless, it is also clear that, for the faithful, the Lord's message brings suffering and reproach (Jer. 15:17-18; 20:8; see also Matt. 23:37-38; Rev. 8:11). In the parallel passage in Ezekiel, the word of the Lord is associated with sweetness (Ezek. 3:3), but although the scroll does not taste bitter to Ezekiel's stomach as it does to John's, the prophet goes in bitterness to deliver the message to the wicked (Ezek. 3:13). Indeed, Ezekiel associates righteousness with life and turning from righteousness with death (Ezek. 3:20-21; see also 2 Cor. 2:16; 7:8-10).

The New Temple

Ford has a complete discussion of the tradition that the temple in Jerusalem will be rebuilt (1975:173-75). Some of that discussion is useful for understanding Revelation 11:1-3. Because the temple represented the presence of God in Israel, its destruction by the Babylonians meant God was no longer with them (1 Sam. 4:21-22; 2 Kings 24-25; Ezek. 9:3-10). Therefore, Ezekiel described a new temple to replace the destroyed one (see Ezek. 40–48 and Lind's discussion in *BCBC*, 1996, on Ezekiel; see also 10:4-5; 11:23). Haggai and Zechariah added that exiled Israel would return under the leadership of Joshua, the high priest, and Zerubbabel, the governor, who are represented by two olive trees (Zech. 3-4; Rev. 11:4). Later, the idea became current that God (with the Messiah as agent in a few texts) would rebuild a temple loftier than Herod's, not merely for the people of Israel, but for all who repent and worship God (Tob. 14:5-6; 1 Enoch 90:29; 2 Bar. 4; 32:2-6; Sib. Or. 5:414-433; Test. Benjamin 9:2; Ps. Sol. 17:24, 32-33). The Qumran community viewed the earlier temple as unclean and in need of replacement by a temple of the faithful (1 Qp. Hab. 8.8-13; 9.4-5; 12.7-9; 9.12-10.13; 4 Qp. Nah. 1.11-12; CD 1.3; 4.17-18; 5.6-7; 6.11-16; 12.1-2; 20.22-24).

The idea, prevalent at Qumran, that the faithful constitute the temple is also at least implicitly present in the New Testament. In Mark, Jesus judges the misuse of the temple, announces doom upon the temple, and points forward to a new temple for all believers, one made without hands (Swartley, 1981; 165-79; 185-90; see also Geddert, *BCBC*, 2000 on Mark). Jesus uses the image of the temple to refer to his own body (John 2:19-21; Acts 6:13-14). Luke says that God does not live in houses made by human hands but in heaven and earth (Acts 7:44-50). Paul makes it clear that faithful Christians constitute God's temple if the spirit dwells in them (1 Cor. 3:16-17), if they keep separate from the uncleanness in the world (2 Cor. 6:16), and if through faith they give up sinfulness and live in obedience to God (Eph. 2:1-22; 1 Pet. 2:1-10). John adds his theme of conquering through patient endurance by indicating that those who are faithful to the end are part of the temple of God (Rev. 3:10-12; see also 1 Enoch 61:1-5).

The Trampling of the Holy City

In Revelation, Jerusalem is known as the holy city, a designation with considerable history associated with the themes of Revelation—trampling and restoration. The psalmist uses Jerusalem and "the holy city" in parallel construction (Ps. 79:1). The prophet Isaiah anticipates the restoration of those who identify with the holy city Jerusalem, which had been trampled by its adversaries (Isa. 48:2; 52:1; 63:18). At the time of its restoration after the exile, Jerusalem was known as the holy city (Neh. 11:1, 18). Due to the repentance of the people, Daniel also thought that Jerusalem and its cultic practices would be restored after a seventy-year trampling of the sanctuary (Dan. 8:13-14; 9:24; see also 1 Macc. 3:45; 4:60; 2 Macc. 8:2). In the New Testament, Jesus expected that Jerusalem, the holy city (Matt. 4:5; 27:53), would be trampled by Gentiles (Luke 21:24; see also Matt. 24:2; Mark 13:2; Luke 21:6; see also Ps. Sol. 2:2, 19; 8:4). The ultimate word on the holy city, however, is that it will serve as the New Jerusalem, the bride of the Lamb (Rev. 21:1–22:5).

Forty-Two Months, or One Thousand Two Hundred Sixty Days

The duration of the Satanic persecution of the faithful is said to be three and a half years, which is enumerated as forty-two months or one thousand two hundred sixty days. Glasson has a detailed discussion of the source of this symbol in Daniel's reference to the persecution of the Jews by Antiochus Epiphanes, the ruler of Syria (1965:68-70). Daniel divides a week of seven years in half at Antiochus's abomination of desolation, which was probably the setting up of the likeness of the god Zeus in the temple (Dan. 9:27; 11:31; 12:11; for a more detailed account of the events, see 1 Macc. 1:54-61). Daniel believed that this desecration included widespread abandonment of God's covenant (Dan. 11:30-32; 1 Macc. 1:15) and would last for only about three and a half years (Dan. 12:7, 11) before a restoration would occur (Dan 7:21-27; 12). Jeremiah had placed the restoration at seventy years after the exile to Babylon (Jer. 25:11-12; 29:10).

Many of the elements of this passage have been associated in the New Testament with the second coming of Christ: a falling away from the faith (Mark 13:6; 2 Thess. 2:3), the appearance of an abominable ruler (2 Thess. 2:3-4; Rev. 11:7), the desecration of the temple (Matt. 24:15; Mark 13:14; 2 Thess. 2:4), and unparalleled suffering (Mark 13:19). Thus, the New Testament reinterprets the tribulations of Antiochus Epiphanes to apply to the time just before the Messiah comes. The faithful Christian witness learns from this that his persecution will last for only a brief time before Christ will come to destroy the forces of evil and inaugurate the era of peace.

The Beast

The source of the image of the beast that ascends from the bottomless pit seems to be in ancient creation myths like the Babylonian one, which views the creation of the universe as a struggle between Marduk, the creator and god of light, and Tiamat, the dragon, the water monster that represents the original chaos. In the mythical view of creation, God subdued the great ocean monster, imprisoned him deep in the sea, and made heaven and earth out of the two halves of his body (Ps. 74:13; Isa. 27:1; 51:9; Amos 9:3). The beast also has parallels in the sea monsters mentioned throughout the Hebrew scriptures (Gen 1:21; Job 7:12; Ps. 148:7; Amos 9:3; Sir. 43:25), particularly Leviathan, the female beast from the ocean (Job 41; Ps. 74:13-14; 104:26; Isa. 27:1; see also Ezek. 29:3; 32:2-3); Rahab (Job 26:12; Ps. 87:4; 89:9-10; Isa. 51:9-10); and Behemoth, the male from the wilderness (Job 40:15-24; see also Isa. 30:7; 51:9).

From this mythical reservoir comes the beast of Revelation. His closest relatives are the four beasts of Daniel, the first representing Babylon (Dan. 7:2-21), which Revelation takes symbolically for Rome. In Daniel, however, the beast is Antiochus Epiphanes (Dan. 8:9-12), who slaughtered or enslaved 80,000 Jews, constructed an altar to the Olympian Zeus in the holy place, offered pigs on the altar of sacrifice, and the turned the temple into a brothel (Dan. 9:27; 11:31-32; see Barclay, 1960:2.73). Jesus speaks of a desolating sacrilege (Matt. 24:15; Mark 13:14), who leads people astray with false teaching and is associated with the destruction of Jerusalem by Titus in A.D. 66-70 (Matt. 24:3-44; Mark 13:3-27; Luke 21:7-28). Paul's man of lawlessness is a satanic figure who tries to take the place of God (2 Thess. 2:3-4). The Johannine Epistles indicate that an antichrist will come in the last hour, who is a deceiver and denies that Jesus is the Christ from God (1 John 2:18, 22; 4:1-3; 2 John 7). This tradition is the backdrop for the satanic oppressor of the faithful in Revelation, pictured as a beast in chapter 11, a great red dragon who is the devil in chapter 12, the beast from the sea representing the Roman Empire in chapter 13, and the scarlet beast symbolizing Rome in chapter 17. Taken together, they impressively portray the power of evil.

The Ark of the Covenant

The ark of the covenant contained the tablets on which the Ten Commandments were written (Deut. 10:1-5), an omer of manna (Exod. 16:32-34), and Aaron's staff that budded (Num. 17:7-11). It was located in the holy of holies to serve as a symbol of God's presence and a place of atonement for sin (Lev. 16:2-5; 1 Kings 6:19; 8:1-9; 2 Chron. 35:1-6; Ps. 99:1; Heb. 9:3-4). Moreover, it was occasionally carried into battle (Num. 10:35-36; Josh. 6:6-21; 1 Sam. 4:1-11), and it may have been carried away during the reign of Rehoboam by Shishak of Egypt with the "treasures of the house of the Lord" (1 Kings 14:25-26). A more likely possibility is that it was destroyed when Jerusalem was captured by the Babylonians in 586 B.C. (Jer. 3:16). Yet according to Jewish tradition, before the Babylonian invasion, Jeremiah hid the ark safely away in a cave in Mt. Nebo until it would be found during a future restoration of Jerusalem (2 Macc. 2:4-8; 2 Bar. 6:80:1-2). Revelation anticipates the recovery of the ark when the kingdom of God is realized.

A Spiritual Exodus

The trumpet judgments of Revelation are modeled after the plagues of Israel's Exodus from Egypt (Exod. 7-12). Therefore, the seven trumpets are conceived as the spiritual exodus of God's people from this world. The details of the trumpet judgments come from the Egyptian Exodus, but they are clearly spiritualized in Revelation. The locusts become scorpions and horses and, ultimately, demons (Exod. 10:12-15; Rev. 9:1-12); the Red Sea becomes the Euphrates River, which is really an evil force (Exod. 14; Rev. 9:14-15); the Egyptians become Parthian warriors, who are also demons (Exod. 5; Rev. 9:19). Thus the trumpet judgments are not merely events that occur at the end of the world but the spiritual battle that the faithful saints must fight against Satan and his forces to win their exodus from the tribulations of this world.

THE TEXT IN THE LIFE OF THE CHURCH

The Little Scroll and the Cross

Menno Simons did not attach to the statement, "time shall be no more," the sense of resignation that is so popularly associated with the King James Version's rendering of the statement. Menno believed that the Christian should not act as though hope is past but, instead, should live in light of the cross:

> Remember that the angel of Revelation has sworn by the eternal and living God who made heaven and earth that after this time, there shall be time no more.... Therefore comfort not one another with senseless comfort and uncertain hope, as some do who think that the Word will be taught and observed without the cross. I have in mind those who know the Word of the Lord, but do not live according to it. Oh, no! it is the Word of the cross and will in my opinion remain that unto the end. It has to be declared with much suffering and sealed with blood. The Lamb is slain from the foundation of the world.... If the Head had to suffer such torture, anguish, misery, and pain, how shall His servants, children, and members expect peace and freedom as to their flesh? (1956:109-10)

Menno uses the symbol of the little scroll to demonstrate the persecutions Christians can expect when they take up the cross:

> as soon as I had eaten the book that was shown to me, although it was in my mouth sweet as honey, yet it made my belly bitter, for there were written therein lamentations and mourning and woe. While I served the world I received its reward; all men spake well of me, even as the fathers did of the false prophets. But now that I love the world with a godly love, and seek its welfare and happiness; rebuke, admonish, and instruct it with Thy Word, pointing it to Jesus Christ, the crucified, it has become unto me a grievous cross, and as the gall of bitterness. (1956:80)

The scroll in chapter 5 was God's redemption as it applies to Christ the Lamb; the scroll in chapter 10 is the same plan as it applies to faithful Christians. What is sweet about the little scroll is that Christ, through his death and resurrection, brought God's salvation; what is bitter is that the faithful must identify with Christ's redemption by taking up the cross and suffering even unto death. Thus, the message of the interlude is that Christian prophets must give testimony to their faith and be obedient in tribulation. The words of Wall are relevant here: "Temptations are tests of faith in God, since every problem of faith stems from a diminishing confidence in God. The tendency is often to place confidence in the definitions of security and happiness promoted within the surrounding social order" (1991:135). The mission of God's people is to bear witness to the end, which may involve persecution and martyrdom. Although the majority of humankind will not repent and Satan will appear victorious, God will vindicate those who bear witness.

The City of Vanity

The writer and preacher John Bunyan (1628-88), during intermittent imprisonments for preaching, produced the classic Christian allegory, *Pilgrim's Progress* (see Bunyan, 1964). This book and Foxe's *Book of Martyrs* were the two Christian best-sellers of the Victorian age. Bunyan was a Puritan holding a Calvinist view of grace, but he was much closer to the Anabaptists in his view of baptism and the church.

In Bunyan's classic book, Christian and Faithful, on their way to the celestial city, find themselves at the fair in the city of Vanity, which is described with language similar to that used in Revelation to describe Babylon the Great. Shortly after they arrived in Vanity, Christian and Faithful showed themselves different from the inhabitants of Vanity: their dress and speech were different, and they showed no interest in buying Vanity's goods. As a result, the two pilgrims were beaten, smeared with dirt, and placed in a cage. The patience with which Christian and Faithful endured the persecution caused some to be won to their side, but in the end they were found guilty of disturbance and placed in iron cages with their feet in stocks. In the midst of this torment, they remembered that Evangelist had told them they would be treated in this way. Thus, the two pilgrims accepted their situation and waited patiently for their ultimate deliverance.

At their trial, Christian and Faithful confronted charges similar to those made of their Lord Jesus Christ—breaking the rules, disturbing the peace, and dividing the town. Witnesses affirmed that the two were disloyal to the city out of principles of faith and holiness and that the customs of Vanity had nothing to do with those of Christianity. Part of Faithful's answer to the charges was that he was a man of peace.

The verdict was that both Christian and Faithful were guilty and deserved the death penalty. Faithful was tortured and executed by burning at the stake, and at his death Christian saw a chariot with horses transport Faithful into the air and through the clouds. On his way back to prison, Christian sang:

Well Faithful, thou hast faithfully profest
Unto thy Lord: with him thou shalt be blest;
When Faithless ones, with all their vain delights,
Are crying out under their hellish plights.
Sing, Faithful, sing; and let thy name survive;
For though they kill'd thee, thou art yet alive.

Bunyan's story of Faithful and Christian in the city of Vanity is an attempt to update the account of the Revelation's two witnesses. After their testimony, the beast from the bottomless pit attacks and kills them. Later they are revived and taken up in a cloud to God in heaven. Likewise, Faithful and Christian patiently endure the persecutions of Vanity, and although only Faithful dies, both rise above the tribulation to life with God in the Celestial City—Faithful immediately, and Christian at the end of his journey.

Guernica and the Great City

Eller suggests a connection between Picasso's *Guernica* and the devastation of the great city of Revelation (1974:87-92, 115). Just as the painting is both about the violence of Guernica, Spain, at the time of the Spanish Civil War in 1937 and about all other cities where war has brought its destruction, so also Revelation describes Rome, Sodom, Egypt, and Jerusalem and makes them all part of the word painting that Revelation calls Babylon the Great. Picasso, as only the cubist artist with multi-perspective can, views the theme of violence from a variety of perspectives. The bull image may come from the senseless slaughter of the Spanish bullfight rituals; the horse, a traditional symbol of warfare in Revelation as well as in art, adds to the scene of carnage; the bird appears to be a sacrifice connoting the religious significance of the violence of Guernica and all warfare; the variety of human faces in anguish express the emotions associated with violence; the body parts represent the human toll that violence exacts; and so forth. In a similar manner, Revelation views the murderous evil of Babylon through the multi-perspective lens of four ancient cities. Rome symbolizes the idolatry of the emperor cult that forces the person to choose between worship of God or the state; Sodom is associated with the promiscuous sexual immorality of Lot's neighbors who, even when offered his daughters as sexual partners, lusted for the two angelic visitors; Egypt connotes the oppression of Israel's slavery, where they were forced to labor under increasingly difficult conditions; and Jerusalem portrays the spiritual blindness that caused its people to put to death their Messiah, Jesus of Nazareth.

In John's introduction of the city of evil in Revelation 11:7-10 and then its description in chapter 18, we see an artist at work. Chapter 11 describes the evil city Babylon, using multi-perspective images that in only a few words draw on rich associations related to Rome, Sodom, Egypt, and Jerusalem, much like Picasso's *Guernica* looks at the subject of violence from many visual perspectives. Later, in chapter 18, John will use poetry to paint a word picture of the sinful greed of Babylon the Great.

It must be concluded that Revelation is better interpreted as a picture book than as a series of algebra problems *[Essay: Interpretation of Apocalyptic Literature]*. When we ask: What city is to be identified with Babylon? we are asking the algebraic question: What is x? A better question is: What do we learn about the intensity of evil from associating Babylon, the personification of evil, with other great evil political entities? We should not ask: What city is the great city? but What variety of meanings are implied in seeing the great city as Rome? Sodom? Egypt? Jerusalem?

Televisions, Satellites, and Other Anachronisms

The story of the two witnesses has some rather fantastic elements when taken literally. After the beast conquers and kills the witnesses, they lie in the streets for three and a half days, while all of the "peoples and tribes and languages and nations will gaze at their dead bodies."

Popular writers think they have the key to how this passage can be interpreted literally. All the world would be able to actually observe the two witnesses through television signals beamed by satellite. LaHaye makes this point:

> Someone has suggested that the modern medium of television makes possible the fulfillment of Revelation 11:9. The only way in which people all over the world could see two bodies lying in the streets of a city over a three-day period of time would be through the medium of television; in fact, in recent years it has been possible by the launching of television satellites for many parts of the world to view the same sight at the same time. This is one more indication that we are coming closer to the end of the age, because it would have been humanly impossible just a few years ago for the entire world to see these two witnesses in the streets at a given moment of time. (1975:154)

This questionable exegesis focuses an important principle of biblical hermeneutics: the Bible cannot mean what it never meant. Another way of saying this is that the Bible cannot mean what its original author did not intend. To think that John wrote about televisions and satellites is a gross anachronism.

This principle is denied by two groups of commentators from radically different positions. The postmodern interpreters believe that the meaning of a text stands on its own, independent from what its author intended to say. The fundamentalist interpreter, operating out of a literalistic hermeneutic, says that what John communicated was not understood by John but that God communicated something that only we, in the age in which the scripture is fulfilled, can understand. It is rather surprising to find postmoderns and fundamentalists in the same camp; yet they do both agree that the meaning of a text is not dependent on what the author meant.

The problem with these modes of interpretation is that they make the meaning of scripture totally subjective: it means what the reader thinks it means. Because there is no objective measure for how a passage is to be interpreted, the Bible can mean almost anything the reader sees in it. That seems a dangerous way to interpret scripture. Although there are differences among commentators regarding what the author intended a passage to communicate, the use of principles of sound exegesis is a relatively objective way of determining the meaning of a biblical text.

The Destroyers of the Earth

About a year ago, my daughter took a biology course that involved travel to Belize to catalogue vegetation in a remote rain forest. Her purpose was to work for the preservation of the unique life forms found in the area. One day, when she and a colleague were at work, they came across an illegal logging operation. Not only were the workers cutting trees that were marked by government action for preservation, but they had also bulldozed streambeds, destroying plant and animal life. My daughter and her coworkers reported their observation, and government agents raided the operation, handcuffing the loggers and taking them to jail. A troubling side note to the story was that the loggers were mostly Mennonites.

On a much larger scale, the violent and materialistic Babylon of Revelation has destroyed the earth with its war and greed just as the loggers destroyed the land in their search for marketable timber. The promise is that like the small logging operation raided by the government troops, the destroyers of the earth will be destroyed. God's creation is to be preserved, not exploited. Therefore, the destruction of the destroyers is considered an appropriate punishment.

Christ's Great Kingdom

The seventh trumpet, surprisingly, is not a tribulation but an announcement: "The kingdom of the world has become the kingdom of our Lord and of his Messiah." It is important to note that the verb here is in the past tense. God's kingdom is not only something we anticipate in the end, but also what has already occurred when Christ defeated the powers of evil in his death on the cross and resurrection from the tomb. We are to announce with our lives and our words that the kingdom has come. Perhaps one of the most powerful presentations of the presence of the kingdom and our task to make the world aware of it is found in the nineteenth-century post-millennial hymn of H. Ernest Nichol, "We've a Story to Tell to the Nations":

> We've a story to tell to the nations
> That shall turn their hearts to the right,
> A story of truth and mercy,
> A story of peace and light,
> A story of peace and light.

We've a song to be sung to the nations
That shall lift their hearts to the Lord,
A song that shall conquer evil
And shatter the spear and sword,
And shatter the spear and sword.

We've a message to give to the nations
That the Lord who reigneth above
Has sent us his Son to save us
And show us that God is love,
And show us that God is love.

We've a savior to show to the nations,
Who the path of sorrow has trod,
That all of the world's great peoples
Might come to the truth of God,
Might come to the truth of God.

Chorus:
For the darkness shall turn to dawning,
And the dawning to noon-day bright,
And Christ's great kingdom shall come on earth,
the kingdom of love and light.

Revelation 12:1-18

The Woman and the Dragon

PREVIEW

In the structure of Revelation, after chapter 11 has formed an appropriate conclusion, chapter 12 begins anew. Indeed, following the awful cosmic judgments poured out at the blowing of the first six trumpets, the seventh trumpet is the jubilant enthronement of the Lord God Almighty and his Messiah—an appropriate conclusion. If the second half of the book were absent, it might not be missed. Boring summarizes this idea effectively:

> With the sounding of the seventh trumpet in 11:15-19, we were brought (once again!) to the End. All that is supposed to happen at the eschatological victory of God happens: the kingdom comes, God himself comes, the dead are raised, the last judgment is held, the good are rewarded, the corruptors of creation are destroyed, there is a sense of restoration and fulfillment. Chronologically, things can proceed no further: we have been through the final plagues (twice!) and are now at the End. There is a sense in which the document could end here, as the first hearers-readers may well have supposed it would. And yet ... (1989:150)

Chapters 12–14 form an interlude between the blowing of the seventh trumpet at the end of chapter 11 and the pouring out of the seven bowls on the earth in chapters 15–16. The bowl judgments would follow naturally as the contents of the little scroll of chapter 11 much like the seal judgments of chapter 6 were the contents of the scroll that was taken by the Lamb from the right hand of God in chapter 5. Yet, the visions of the woman and dragon (ch. 12), the two beasts (ch. 13), and the Lamb on Mount Zion (ch. 14) intervene.

Chapters 1–11 have affirmed both the redemption of Christ symbolized in the scroll in chapter 5 and the persecution of the faithful portrayed in the seven seal judgments of chapter 6. How can these two realities exist side by side? The answer comes in the war in heaven between the forces of God and Satan (ch. 12), in which Satan is decisively defeated and driven from heaven, and the parallel battle on earth between the two beasts and the saints (ch. 13), which explains why the faithful continue to be persecuted. Chapter 14 then reminds us that the ultimate outcome of these battles will be God's salvation of the faithful. After this, chapter 15 returns to the theme of judgment by introducing a new sequence of seven plagues.

Thus, although some find seven signs in chapters 12–14 (see Morris 1969:155-86; Beale, 1999:621), the section does not include a numbered series of judgments. Instead, it is a symbolic explanation of the causes of the conflicts that were portrayed in the first half of Revelation. It describes why the saints must endure persecution before evil can be overcome. The main conflicts are between God and Satan (ch. 12) and between the saints and the beasts (ch. 13). The battle in the heavenly realm is won by Christ, and the saints complete that victory on earth by being faithful in the face of the assaults of the beast and the false prophet. The result is that the faithful saints are part of the 144,000 exalted with the Lamb on Mt. Zion.

Looking more closely at chapter 12, we see that Revelation does not proceed chronologically, because the event described here is the birth of Christ. This description follows a combat myth widespread in Egyptian, Babylonian, and other cultures of the ancient Near East (see Table): a monster waits to destroy a child about to be born, but the child is born and escapes the monster; in some cases the child destroys the monster. The Greek myth of the birth of Apollo is particularly relevant here. The serpent Python pursued Leto while she was pregnant with Apollo, whose father was Zeus. The north wind, however, came to Leto's aid and took her to the island of Delos where the sea god Poseidon hid her with waves until she gave birth to Apollo, who subsequently killed Python. That the island of Delos was visible from Patmos may explain John's use of this myth. The meaning, then, is that in Christ, not in Apollo nor in the incarnations of Apollo in Augustus and Nero, is the salvation of God's faithful people.

Table 1: Parallel Stories

Culture	Child	Mother	Beast
Egyptian	Horus	Isis	Set-Typhon (Red Dragon)
Babylonian	Marduk	Damkina	Tiamat (7-headed monster)
Persian	Fire	Ahura	Azhi Dahaka
Greek	Apollo	Leto	Python (Red)
Gospels	Jesus	Mary	Herod
Revelation	Christ	Woman	Red Dragon

Although John's is the only story in which the mother is left on earth while the child is exalted to the heavenly realm (Krodel, 1989:237), John probably draws from several or all of these traditions for his account of the woman and the dragon (see also Barker, 2000:200-211, 320-21, who sees the woman, and later the Holy City, as the Queen of Heaven). Like preachers today, John used stories current in the culture of his listeners to portray the religious truth of the victory of the forces of God over those of Satan in the super-cosmic battle between good and evil.

Some might find it troubling that John is dependent on ancient mythology, but John's borrowing has precedent. Isaiah, for example, seems to draw on the same mythological tradition to provide a dragon that symbolizes the persecution of God's people (Isa. 27:1; see also Gen. 3:14-15). Moreover, myth should not be limited to the non-factual but should include all ancient tales that interpret the present. Roloff defines myth as:

> a narrative portrayal of primordial proceedings between gods, demonic powers, and heroes, which wishes to provide information regarding the origin and essence of the world, the place of human beings in it and the genesis of the relationships and norms that define their existence. Myth seeks to explain what is now and what is experienced as real in that it interprets it as a consequence of an event between supernatural beings. (1993:142)

Caird says that "all genuine convictions require a mythology" to influence human conduct (1966:148). In this chapter, John uses myth to communicate divine truths in terms his audience would understand.

The major truth communicated in chapter 12 is that Satan's persecution of the faithful is explained by the universal struggle between the powers of good and evil, which has already been won through the death and resurrection of Christ the Lamb. The struggle refines the faithfulness of the saints, and the Lamb's victory gives the faithful confidence to patiently endure without compromising (Beale, 1999:621-24).

OUTLINE

The Birth of Christ, 12:1-6
The War in Heaven, 12:7-12
The Rest of the Woman's Offspring, 12:13-18

EXPLANATORY NOTES

The Birth of Christ 12:1-6

As chapter 12 begins, John reports that *a great portent appeared in heaven*. The word *portent (sēmeion)* does not occur in Revelation 1–11 but is used several times in the second half of the book (13:13-14; 15:1; 16:14; 19:20) and quite frequently in the Gospel of John, where it is commonly translated "sign." Ford notes that the word occurs seven times in Revelation, three times with reference to heaven and four times related to earth. This calls to mind the numerology of the ancient world, which understood three to represent perfection in the divine realm and four to symbolize completion in the physical world *[Essay: Gematria]*.

The common translation of *portent (sēmeion)*, "sign," designates something that points beyond itself (Murphy, 1998:277). It is associated with the divine (Gen. 1:14; 9:12-17), is paired with power *(dynamis)* and wonders *(terata)* (Exod. 7:3; John 4:48; Acts 2:19-22), and is used both of signs associated with the coming of the Christ (Isa. 7:10-14; Matt. 24:3, 30; Luke 21:7-28; see also Matt. 16:1; Mark 8:11) and with signs performed by Satan (Rev. 13:13-14; 15:1; 16:14; 19:20).

The woman is a good portent in Revelation, where the word occurs nineteen times (2:20; 9:8; 12:1, 4, 6, 13, 14, 15, 16, 17; 14:4; 17:3, 4, 6, 7, 9, 18; 19:7; 21:9)—nearly as often as the title Lamb. This woman parallels the bride (19:7-8; 21:9), contrasts with the whore (17:3-6, 18; 18:16), and is the counterpart of the mighty angel (10:1).

A number of interpretations of the woman are possible. Caird makes a compelling case that she is the goddess Roma, the queen of heaven (1966:148). Although there probably is an allusion to the goddess of Rome in the symbol, it does not seem to be the dominant image. A quite literalistic and biblical interpretation is that the woman is Mary, the mother of Jesus (Matt. 2:1-15), but John's woman is a superhuman, heavenly being. Two other interpretations see the woman as a community, and maybe both carry a measure of truth (see TBC, The Woman). It may be that the woman is the Hebrew people and the point of the symbol is that the Christ is born out of the Jewish community. Or the woman may represent the faithful community of Christians against whom Satan's wrath is directed. It is best to take the woman as referring to both the people of Israel and the faithful Christians, because Revelation makes no clear distinction between Israel and the church.

The description of the woman has parallels in the vision of Joseph in the Genesis narrative (Gen. 37:9), the beloved woman of the Song of Solomon (6:10), and the holy city of Revelation (Rev. 21:10-11); but it is contrasted with Revelation's great whore (17:4), the city of Babylon (18:16). Moreover, symbols associated with the woman here are related by Jesus to the *eschaton,* his second coming (Matt. 24:29-30; Mark 13:24-25; Luke 21:25).

The first element of the description of the woman is that she was *clothed with the sun* (Judg. 5:31; Sir. 26:16). Ford argues that this may be a parody of the sun goddess or an allusion to the portrayal on coins of the rays of the sun emanating from emperor's crown. She further indicates that the word translated *clothed (periballō)* may also mean "to throw up a rampart around" (1975:188). Usage elsewhere in Revelation, however, supports the image of clothing (7:9; 10:1; 11:3; 17:4; 18:16; 19:8, 13). Thus, the meaning of the symbol is that the woman is clothed in glory and majesty (Ps. 104:1-2; Isa. 60:1; Rev. 21:22-23).

The woman also appeared *with the moon under her feet.* Coins from the time of Tiberius picture former Emperor Augustus and his wife Livia as the sun and the moon. This symbol then communicates that the woman has dominion over the rulers of this world.

In addition, the woman wore *on her head a crown of twelve stars.* This may be a reference to the twelve stars of the zodiac (Wis. Sol. 13:1-2; Philo, *Life of Moses* 2.122-26; Jos., *Ant.* 3.186; Aune, 1998a:681), but a more direct connection is certainly to the twelve patriarchs of Israel (Rev. 7:4-8). In Joseph's dream the stars represent his brothers (Gen. 37:9; see also Test. Naphtali 5:1-8, where Levi becomes like the sun and Judah like the moon). Moreover, there were twelve stones on the breastplate of Aaron, Israel's great high priest. By extension, there is here probably also an allusion to the twelve apostles of Christ (21:10-14). Thus, the twelve stars are the Hebrew people represented by the twelve patriarchs and the faithful followers of Christ symbolized by the twelve apostles.

Following the description of the woman comes the affirmation: *She was pregnant*. Boesak indicates that pregnancy brings an end to hopelessness, appealing to biblical examples of Sarah, Rebekah, Rachel, and Hannah (1987:80). The prophet Isaiah compares the arrival of God's judgment and deliverance to childbirth (Isa. 7:14; 26:16-17; 54:1; 65:23; 66:7-13; see also Mic. 4:9-10; 5:3; Matt. 24:8; John 16:21). Certainly, the story of the birth of Jesus, the supreme deliverer and judge, is also close to mind (Matt. 1:18-23).

The pregnant woman *was crying out in birthpangs, in the agony of giving birth* (Gen. 3:16). More generally, the language is used of crying out in desperation (Rev. 18:18-19), perhaps to Yahweh for salvation (Ps. 22:5; 34:6, 18; Rev. 6:10). The present tense may indicate the prolonged nature of the birthpangs (Ford, 1975:197). The woman was crying out *in the agony of giving birth*. Although the word translated *agony* is nowhere else used of childbirth, it is connected in 4 Maccabees with martyrdom (Ford, 1975:189).

In addition to the woman, *another portent appeared in heaven: a great red dragon*. The word *dragon* is used of the sea monster, who represents the kingdoms that oppose Israel. Here the dragon is clearly Satan, who persecutes God's people (Beale, 1999:632-34). Revelation pictures Satan on a throne in heaven (12:7; 13:6; Eph. 2:2; 6:12). The meaning here is that Satan is behind any persecution of the faithful. In the words of Paul: "For our struggle is not against enemies of blood and flesh, but against the rulers, against the authorities, against the cosmic powers of this present darkness, against the spiritual forces of evil in the heavenly places" (Eph. 6:12).

The description of the dragon that follows connotes a terrible, frightful monster and parallels the description of the beast from the sea (13:1). The *red* color calls to mind the red horse of the seal judgments (6:4) and the scarlet beast ridden by the great whore (17:3). There is likely an allusion to the red beasts of other ancient cultures—the Babylonian snake and the Egyptian Typhon (Ford, 1975:199). The color suggests the blood shed by this devilish dragon (John 8:44; Rev. 6:4).

The *seven heads* of the dragon parallel the seven-headed Canaanite Leviathan (Ps. 74:14; Test. Abraham 17:14), the one hundred-headed Egyptian Typhon, and the multiple-headed Greek Hydra. Later the seven heads are identified as seven kings of Babylon (see Explanatory Notes on 17:9-11).

The *ten horns* are characteristic of Daniel's fourth beast, where they probably represent ten rulers of the Greek empire from Alexander the Great to Antiochus Epiphanes (Dan. 7:7-8, 20, 24). In Revelation, horns represent political power, and the number ten connotes great power (Rev. 5:6; 17:12-14; see also Matt. 4:9).

The *seven diadems on his heads* are royal crowns that symbolize the sovereignty of a king (Esther 1:11; Isa. 62:3; Rev. 13:1; Sir. 11:5; 47:6; Wis. Sol. 5:16-17; see also Pliny. *Nat. Hist.* 8.33). The passage seems to be saying that Satan is completely sovereign. Although there is a sense in which Satan rules in this world, Revelation 19:12 reminds us that Christ has many diadems and thus even more power than Satan. The implication is that the dragon's claim to authority is blasphemous. In this vein, Wall speaks helpfully of "evil's most fundamental idolatry: the promotion of secular power over what belongs to the creator God and God's exalted Lamb" (1991:160).

The dragon's *tail swept down a third of the stars from heaven and threw them on the earth.* This act of the dragon alludes to the fall of Satan from heaven along with his angels (Luke 10:18; John 12:31; 16:11; Jude 6; 1 Enoch 6-12) and to the little horn of Daniel's beast (Dan. 8:10). That he swept a third of the stars from heaven indicates his awesome power, but the fraction also symbolizes the limited nature of this power in comparison to that of Christ (Rev. 8:7-12; see also John 12:23, 31). It is interesting to note that what happens in heaven is an explanation of earthly realities: Satan is behind the tribulations that the faithful suffer.

Following the descriptions of the woman and the dragon, the drama begins: *Then the dragon stood before the woman who was about to bear a child, so that he might devour her child as soon as it was born.* This story has roots in the enmity placed between the woman and the serpent after the Fall (Gen. 3:15) as well as alluding to Pharaoh's edict to kill Israelite baby boys at the time of the birth of Moses (Exod. 1:15-2:10) and to Herod's plot to kill the baby Jesus (Matt. 2:13-16). Ladd states succinctly the meaning of the story: "Here is the ultimate purpose of Satan: to frustrate the work of Christ" (1972:169).

The woman then *gave birth to a son, a male child,* who is the fulfillment of the Hebrew scriptures (Ps. 2:7; Isa. 7:14; 9:6; Jer. 20:15; Acts 13:33). The repetition of the gender seems to be for emphasis and may imply royalty.

The one born *is to rule all the nations with a rod of iron* (Ps. 2:7-9; Mic. 5:2-4; Rev. 2:27; 19:15). The reason that the dragon Satan wants to destroy the child is that the Christ who is born will destroy the dragon (Heb. 2:14; Rev. 11:18) and his works (1 John 3:8) and assume his authority (Isa. 9:6). Yet it is crucial to note that the word for *rule* is the verbal form of shepherd (*poimainein; see* Matt. 2:6). Boring captures the sense this word gives to the passage: "'Shepherd all the nations with a rod of iron' is not a picture of brute force but of the future absolute and universal rule of the Messiah. If Revelation teaches anything, it is that the power by which God brings the kingdom is the power of suffering love revealed on the cross" (1989:153). Christ rules through suffering love, and the faithful participate in that rule through overcoming persecution (Rom. 1:4).

As the story continues, the woman's *child was snatched away and taken to God and to his throne.* The word translated *snatched away (arpazō)* is used in connection with both the activity of Satan (Matt. 13:19; see also Acts 23:10) and the second coming of Christ (1 Thess. 4:17); there is also an unmistakable allusion to the binding of Satan (John 12:31-32; Acts 2:33-36; Col. 2:15; Heb. 2:14-15; Jude 23; Rev. 12:7-11). Here it refers to the ascension of Christ to the throne of God (Luke 9:31, 51; Acts 1:9), which, with his birth, represents the entire ministry of Christ (Phil. 2:5-11; 1 Tim. 3:16).

The *throne,* which is usually occupied by God, is a symbol of sovereignty. Through his victory over Satan, Christ ascends to God's throne to participate in the divine rule (Rev. 3:21; 5:6). The emphasis is on thwarting Satan's plot to overthrow God's plan (Mark 1:13; Rev. 2:13).

After her child was safely born and ascended to heaven, *the woman fled into the wilderness,* the location of her evil counterpart, the whore (17:3). The wilderness is where God protected and sustained Israel (see TBC, The Wilderness) and thus symbolizes the refuge of the faithful in tribulation (Jer. 2:2). Revelation's two witnesses, Moses (Exod. 2:15) and Elijah (1 Kings 17; 19:3-8), both made similar treks into the wilderness (Beale, 1999:643). In the wilderness, the woman *has a place prepared by God* (John 14:2-3; Rev. 12:14). This detail, which reflects Revelation's emphasis on the care of God for the faithful, is not found in other mythical stories (Sweet, 1990:197). The meaning is that, although persecuted and even killed for their witness to a hostile world, the faithful will ultimately be protected and saved by God.

In the place prepared by God, the woman *can be nourished for one thousand two hundred sixty days.* The idea of nourishment calls to mind the manna and quail provided in Israel's wilderness wanderings. The provision here is for the time of the witness of the martyrs (11:3). One thousand two hundred sixty days is the brief period of time associated by Daniel with the abomination that Antiochus Epiphanes brought to Jerusalem in the second century B.C. (Dan. 8:14; 12:11, 12). The message is that the faithful will be nourished and strengthened by God during the brief but intense tribulation and martyrdom that comes on the earth (7:1-8; 11:1-2).

It should be noted that the themes of protection and suffering alternate in Revelation. A statement of protection (7:1-8; 11:1-2; 12:6) precedes each period of suffering (7:13-17; 11:3-13; 12:11).

The War in Heaven 12:7-12

The war described in verses 7-12 is a spiritual battle in heaven between God and Satan (see Roloff, 1993:142-43). Caird says: "Michael's victory is simply the heavenly and symbolic counterpart of the earthly reality of the Cross" (1966:154). It gives to the faithful the confidence that the struggle they are encountering on earth has already been won in the heavenly spiritual world by Christ's death and resurrection.

The connection of this passage to what precedes is not clear. The only common character is the Satanic dragon who appears here with his demonic forces to fight against Michael and his angels (cf. Matt. 25:41; Eph. 6:12; 1 Enoch 40:7). Christ's enthronement in the preceding section makes this victory of Michael's forces possible. The point of verses 1-6 is the strife between Christ and Satan; the point of verses 7-18 is that the conflict is soon over and the victory won.

The message in verses 7-12, then, is that Christians should be faithful to the end. Michael's victory means Satan is a defeated enemy. Glasson describes the tribulations endured by the faithful as the "final convulsions of a conquered foe" (1965:75). The question raised in this section is: Why do the faithful suffer? The answer is: Because they are faithful. Faithful saints expect persecution precisely because they are followers of the crucified Christ (John 15:20; Jas. 4:4).

The section begins with the announcement: *war broke out in heaven* (2 Macc. 5:1-4; Sib. Or. 3:796-808; Asc. Isa. 7:9-11). It may seem surprising to find Satan in heaven, but in the Hebrew scriptures, Satan has free access to heaven (Job 1:6-12; 2:1-6) and, indeed, seems to be the public prosecutor in the heavenly court (Zech. 3:1-2). Therefore, his defeat is legal, not military. In the New Testament, Satan is the enemy of God and leader of the forces of evil. Thus, the faithful on earth are reminded that the superhuman adversary causing their persecution has already been defeated in heaven.

The description of the war in heaven follows: *Michael and his angels fought against the dragon*. Michael, whose name means "one like God," is the chief of the seven archangels and a principle figure in apocalyptic literature. According to Sweet, Michael is "perhaps the most important figure in contemporary Judaism after God" (1990:200). Daniel portrays him as the protector who will liberate Israel from Persian oppression (10:13-14, 20-21; 12:1; see also 1 Enoch 9:1-3; 10:11-22). Later, Michael becomes the protector of the righteous (1 QM 17.7-8) and the archangel who disputed with the devil over the body of Moses (Jude 9). Here he is introduced abruptly, and the battle begins.

In response to Michael, *the dragon and his angels fought back, but they were defeated, and there was no longer any place for them in heaven*. The second verbal form in this segment literally means "they had no strength" (Gen. 32:28; Ps. 13:4; Dan. 7:21), and the third clause indicates their complete defeat (Rev. 20:11; 1 Enoch 40:7). Such a resounding victory over Satan in the heavenly, spiritual realm serves as a great source of comfort to the faithful who are doing battle with the forces of evil in the earthly, physical world (Rom. 16:20; Heb. 2:14-15).

The great dragon is then described as *that ancient serpent, who is called the Devil and Satan, the deceiver of the whole world*. There is no doubt left about his identity: he is at the same time the serpent that tempted Adam and Eve in Eden (Gen. 3; see also Isa. 27:1; Rom. 1:21; Wis. Sol. 2:24); Satan, the great adversary and accuser (see TBC, Satan); the devil, the Greek counterpart of this great accuser or slanderer (see TBC, The Devil); and the deceiver of the whole world (John 8:44; 2 Thess. 2:9-10; Rev. 16:14; 20:3, 7-8, 10). The great enemy who accuses the faithful in the court of heaven is a formidable but defeated foe.

Then the dragon *was thrown down to the earth, and his angels were thrown down with him*. The cognate *(ballō)* of the word translated *thrown down (ekballō)* is associated with punishment (Matt. 3:10; 5:29; 13:41-42, 48-49; John 15:6). The punishment here is that the defeated Satan with his angels is banished to the earth; later he will be driven from the earth to the pit (Rev. 20:1-3) and finally to the lake of fire and sulfur (Rev. 20:10).

The New Testament portrays Satan as the ruler of this world (John 14:30; 16:11; Eph. 2:2), which means he has great secular authority (Rev. 2:9, 13, 24; 3:9). Yet the devil is also the leader of the demonic army that fights against the armies of God and therefore must be defeated before God's rule can be established (John 12:31-32). Nevertheless, that great defeat has already been accomplished through the death and resurrection of Christ (John 12:31-33; Col. 2:13-15). Beasley-Murray says Satan's descent to earth has several implications: he no longer accuses humans before God, the extent of his influence over history is limited, his power over the church has ended, and his time is short (1974:202). So faithful Christians continue with confidence the struggle on earth against the followers of Satan that has already been won in heaven by the Lamb that was slain.

The idea of a prehistoric cosmic fall of Satan is an attempt to solve the problem of evil (Isa. 14:12-20; Luke 10:18; 1 Enoch 9-10; 2 Enoch 29:4-5), a problem that has baffled every theistic religion. The best suggestion is that evil is the result of humanity going against God but that, even before humans were present, evil existed. Perhaps, since evil is irrational by nature, it should be no surprise that humans cannot understand it and that no rational explanation can be completely satisfying. Revelation gives a clear statement of the reality of demonic influence but no adequate rational explanation of the presence of evil.

What follows instead is a hymn celebrating the sovereignty of God and victory of Christ (Rom. 8:33-34), one of seven heavenly anthems in Revelation (4:8-11; 5:9-13; 7:10-12; 11:15-18; 12:10-12; 15:3-4; 19:1-8). Introduced by the words, *Then I heard a loud voice in heaven, proclaiming*, this hymn of the suffering faithful is sung because Satan has been defeated. Although the identity of the loud voice is uncertain (Rev. 6:1; 10:1-7; 19:5), the occurrence of the phrase, "our comrades" *(adelphōn)*, in verse 10, makes it likely that the voice belongs to one of the faithful, perhaps one of the saints under the altar in 6:9-11 (Ladd, 1972:172).

The song begins with the clause: *Now have come the salvation and the power and the kingdom of our God and the authority of his Messiah*. A common expectation in the New Testament (Matt. 26:64; John 12:31; Rom. 5:11; 8:1; Rev. 14:13), this salvation is the accomplishment of God and Christ, and the kingdom symbolizes the sovereignty that belongs to them alone (7:10; 19:1).

In order for salvation and the kingdom to come, *the accuser of our comrades has been thrown down, who accuses them day and night before God*. Here the imagery changes from the battlefield to the courtroom, where the dragon is the accuser of the saints, who are defended by Michael (Beale, 1999: 661-63). The dragon's constant activity is highlighted (Rev. 14:10-11; see also 4:8; 7:15), but his ultimate downfall is the last word (John 14:30; Rom. 8:34-35). The one who tirelessly tormented the faithful has been overcome by the salvation won in Christ.

The reason the dragon has been thrown down is that *they have conquered him*. The inclusion of the pronoun *autoi* is probably for emphasis—the faithful themselves have conquered the dragon, and the aorist tense of the Greek verb indicates that the saints' victory is complete (Morris, 1969:162; see TBC, Conqueror and Conquerors).

Yet it must be remembered that the victory of the faithful is ultimately *by the blood of the Lamb* (John 1:29; Rom. 3:24-25), that is, by Christ's death and resurrection (1:5; 5:9; 6:9-10; 7:14; 22:14). Through the blood of Christ, the dragon's power is broken and Christ's reign begins (Luke 10:18; John 12:31-32). Christ is enthroned in heaven with God; what remains is for evil to be defeated on earth (1 Cor. 15:24-26; Eph. 6:12-17; 1 Pet. 5:8-9).

The saints' victory also comes *by the word of their testimony*. In the super-cosmic battle between God and Satan, the Lamb's blood can only defeat the forces of evil through the faithful witness of the saints (2 Cor. 12:9-10; Phil. 4:13). Caird says: "The power of evil may be absorbed by innocent suffering and neutralized by forgiving love. If the world is to hear and accept God's amnesty, there must be witnesses; and if evil is to burn itself out to the bitter end, their testimony must be the testimony of suffering" (1966:157).

It should also be noted that in this witness there is no fighting or resistance of evil by the faithful. Indeed, the saints *did not cling to life even in the face of death*. A major principle of following Christ is self-renunciation (Luke 24:26); love and obedience are more important than life itself (Matt. 10:39; 16:25-26; Mark 8:34-36; Luke 9:23-27; John 12:25; Rev. 14:13-14). Through losing one's life, the faithful martyr identifies with Christ's death and wins the victory over Satan (1 Cor. 2:6-8; Phil. 2:6-11; Col. 1:15-20; 2:15; Rev. 1:9; 2:10; 5:9-13).

In response to the call to faithful witness in the face of death, the saints are exhorted: *Rejoice then, you heavens and those who dwell in them!* It is the saints in heaven that rejoice at the witness of the faithful on earth (Isa. 49:13). The word for heaven occurs often in Revelation but only here in the plural. The word *dwell (skēnē)* regularly translates the Hebrew *shekinah,* and thus connotes God's presence (7:15; 13:6; 21:3).

In contrast to the rejoicing in heaven, there is *woe to the earth and the sea, for the devil has come down to you with great wrath*. While the heavenly kingdom rejoices, woe is pronounced on the kingdom of the beast (13:1-10). The reason for the woe is that, although evil has been eradicated from heaven, it is present with great intensity on earth. Although the wicked believe the descent of the devil to be a great blessing, it is really the worst plague (Sweet, 1990:202; see also 2 Thess. 2:8-12; Rev. 9:12; 11:14; 14:9-11).

The reason that the devil has come in such wrath is *because he knows that his time is short.* The word for *time (kairos)* here does not relate to chronology but to the time that is appropriate to the devil, later specified as forty-two months (13:5). The devil's persecution of the faithful is the final intense attack before his destruction (1 Pet. 5:8-10). Eller says that Satan is acting with desperation "like a chicken with its head cut off." He elaborates:

> As we see the tantrums and traumas growing ever more wild and reckless, it is *not* an indication that Evil is growing in strength and about to take over. Quite the contrary, it is evidence that the dragon already has been decapitated and can't last much longer. This knowledge, of course, does not change . . . the reality of the damage he can wreak; but it does enable us the better to stand up under them. Through John, the word of God comes to us: "Hang in, fellow! Hang in! You've got it won, just stay in there until the bell! And the final bell, we are assured, will ring *soon!*" (1974:129)

The fate of the faithful has been secured by the victory of Christ; yet they must endure for a short time.

This hymn proclaims as an anthem in the Lord's day worship (1:10) that the heavenly battle between Michael and the dragon signals the victory of Christ, whose death and resurrection are the ultimate source of Michael's victory. The nature of the battle with the dragon will be described in the attacks of the two beasts in chapter 13.

The Rest of the Woman's Offspring 12:13-18

The passage that follows is both a continuation of the story of verses 1-6, telling what happens after the woman flees into the wilderness, and an elaboration of the hymn in verses 10-12, explaining why the faithful still suffer even though Satan is defeated. Much Exodus typology is present in the passage: Pharaoh's pursuit of the Israelites (Exod. 14:8), their escape on the eagle's wings (Exod. 19:4), and the opening of the earth to swallow the family of Korah (Num. 16:32-33) have parallels here.

The story of the woman and the dragon continues: *So when the dragon saw that he had been thrown down to earth, he pursued the woman who had given birth to the male child.* Because the dragon can no longer attack the child Christ, who has ascended to heaven, he directs his efforts at the woman, the mother of the people of God. The word translated *pursued (diōkō)* also means "persecute" (Acts 9:3-5). This persecution is the final tribulation of God's faithful followers (11:2-3; 13:5-8).

Against this attack, *the woman was given the two wings of the great eagle.* There is certainly here an allusion to the escape of the Israelites from oppression in Egypt (Exod. 19:4; Deut. 32:10-12). The passive verb implies that her escape is provided by God (Ps. 74:12-15; Isa. 40:30-31; Test. Moses 10:8-9). The eagle symbolizes the divine power, which protects and ultimately delivers God's people from the attack of the evil one.

The reason the eagle's wings were given to the woman is *so that she could fly from the serpent into the wilderness, to her place where she is nourished for a time, and times, and a half a time.* The duration here is three and a half years (Dan. 7:25; 12:7), which is equivalent to forty-two months (11:2; 13:5) and to one thousand two hundred sixty days (11:3; 12:6), which are used elsewhere in Revelation (see Notes on 11:2). The admonition in this passage is for the faithful to withstand persecution because, after a little time, they will be relieved (John 16:33).

After the woman was taken into the wilderness, *from his mouth the serpent poured water like a river after the woman, to sweep her away with the flood.* In the thinking of the ancient world, the sea was refuge for the water monster, the personification of evil (Ps. 18:4; 74:13; 124:4; Ezek. 29:3; 32:2; Rev. 21:1; Test. Asher 7:3). A more literal referent may be to the flooding of the Nile River (Exod. 14:21-29; 15:12). Whatever the referent, the flood is the persecution of the serpent (Ps. 18:4-6; 32:6; Isa. 43:2). That the river comes from the serpent's mouth alludes to his lying and deception (Matt. 24:24; 2 Thess. 2:9-11; Rev. 2:9, 13-14; 3:9; 13:11-17).

In response to the serpent's attack, *the earth came to the help of the woman; it opened its mouth and swallowed the river that the dragon had poured from his mouth.* This alludes to the pre-cosmic conflict between the earth and the sea. Here the earth is perceived as a person, much like Mother Earth. Indeed, two strong feminine images dominate this section as "Mother Earth" rescues the "Queen of Heaven" (Barr, 1998:112, 125). Elsewhere the earth is said to swallow Cain (Gen. 4:11); the Egyptians (Exod. 15:12); and Korah, Dathan, Abiram, and their comrades (Num. 16:30-33; 26:10; Deut. 11:6; Ps. 106:17). The meaning of the earth coming to the support of the woman is that God protects his people against Satan's persecution (Ps. 32:6; Isa. 50:2). Even nature fights on behalf of God's people (Barclay, 1960:2.106-7; Ps. 68).

When his attack was thwarted, *the dragon was angry with the woman, and went off to make war on the rest of her children, those who keep the commandments of God and hold the testimony of Jesus.* The major interpretative issue here is the identity of the children, literally seed *(spermatos),* an image usually associated with the male parent (Aune, 1998a:708). Some see the rest of her offspring to be Gentile Christians: the Jewish Christians are sealed in chapter 7, while the Gentile Christians endure the ordeal of Satan's attack in chapter 12 (Glasson, 1965:76). Others argue that the rest of the woman's offspring refers to individual Christians on earth, distinguished from the heavenly saints who are sealed for protection (Ladd, 1972:174; Beale, 1999:677; Rom. 8:28-30; Heb. 2:10-13). The best interpretation is probably to view the seed as Christ, and the rest of the offspring to be the faithful who obey the divine commandments and give testimony in the face of persecution and death but are promised that they too will in the end be delivered by God from the Satanic attack (Dan. 3:5-6, 17-18; Matt. 16:18; Rev. 1:9; 6:9; 12:11; 13:9-10; 14:12; 20:4).

THE TEXT IN BIBLICAL CONTEXT

The Woman

There is considerable biblical precedent for taking the woman to represent a community. The Hebrew scriptures portray God's people as both a beautiful woman faithfully covenanted to God (Ezek. 16:8-14; Hos. 2:19-20) and a faithless whore (Jer. 3:6-10; Ezek. 16:15-22). The community that the woman represents is most likely either the Hebrew people of God or the community of faithful Christians. In favor of the former is that the scriptures call her mother Zion (Isa. 66:7-11; 2 Esd. 10:7, 44), the wife of Yahweh (Isa. 54:5, 6; Jer. 3:20; 31:32), and the mother of Israel (Isa. 1:8; 26:17-18; 49:20-21; 50:1; 54:1; Hos. 4:5; Mic. 4:9-10; Sir. 48:18-19; 2 Esd. 9:38–10:59). This nation of Israel gave birth to the Christ (Rom. 9:4-5) to whom, in turn, the saints are betrothed (2 Cor. 11:2; Eph. 5:25-27; Rev. 19:7-8; 21:2, 9). Thus, by extension, the woman may also be the mother of the faithful church. Paul says that Jerusalem above is the mother of Christians, who are the Israel of God (Gal. 4:26; 6:16). The woman is best seen as a symbol of Israel, who is the mother of those faithful to her offspring Christ. This positive portrait of the feminine gender is an important balance and antidote to the negative feminine imagery often emphasized in contemporary writings (Pippin, 1999).

The Great Red Dragon

In Revelation, the great dragon represents Satan (see Rev. 20:2; also TBC on ch. 11, The Beast). In Babylonia, the beast from the sea is Tiamat (abyss), and the beast from the land is Kingu (serpent). In the Hebrew tradition, the dragon imagery is also used to describe Israel's enemies, Egypt (Isa. 30:7; Ezek. 29:3-5; 32:2) and Babylon (Jer. 51:34). Out of this background, Satan emerges as an angelic enemy of God (1 Chron. 21:1; Isa. 14:12-20). An evil person is called a child of Belial, an evil spirit later identified with Satan (1 Sam. 1:16; 2:12; 25:17, 25; 2 Sam. 16:7; 1 Kings 21:10, 13; 2 Cor. 6:15). Although in the Old Testament Satan is not called a dragon, many see the dragon as related to the serpent of Genesis 3 (Exod. 7:8-12; Deut. 32:33; Ps. 91:13). Drawing on the rich Hebrew tradition, the dragon in Revelation 12 symbolizes the archenemy, the persecutor of the faithful people of God (John 15:20-21). This enemy is an empire in chapter 13 and an emperor in chapter 17 (for a thorough description of this combat theme in ancient mythology, see Forsyth, 1987).

The Wilderness

The wilderness was originally a place of sin (Lev. 16:10, 20-22), wild animals (Isa. 13:21-22; 34:13-15; Mark 1:13), and unclean spirits (Luke 11:24). Yet it came to be the location of protection (1 Kings 19:1-8; Song Sol. 3:6-8; 8:5), provision (Exod. 16:4-8; Isa. 40:3-5; Hos. 2:14-15), and discipline (Deut. 8:2-10). Moses fled to the wilderness for protection from Pharoah (Exod. 2:15). After Israel's exodus from Egypt, the people found refuge in the wilderness of Sinai (Exod. 19:1-4). Elijah fled to the wilderness for sustenance during a drought (1 Kings 17:1-9). In the second century B.C. during the oppression of Antiochus Epiphanes, many fled to the wilderness with the false hope of protection (1 Macc. 2:29-38). John the Baptist prepared for ministry by living in the wilderness (Luke 1:80; 3:2-3). In the first century A.D., the Jerusalem church fled to Pella to escape the Roman invasion (Eusebius *Eccl. Hist.* 3.5; see also Mark 13:14-20), and it appears that the Qumran community anticipated a similar flight (1 QS 8.12-14).

In Revelation the wilderness has a double meaning. It is the location of Babylon, the great whore (11:1-3), and in this sense it symbolizes the tribulation and suffering of the faithful. Yet the allusion to the trip of Mary and Joseph to Egypt after the birth of Christ paints the wilderness as a place of protection (Matt. 2:13-15). Similarly, the faithful are promised protection in the wilderness during their time of tribulation in their eschatological exodus.

Satan

The word *Satan* is the transliteration of the Hebrew word for adversary or accuser (Num. 22:22; 1 Sam. 29:4; 1 Kings 11:14, 23). Its personification is the accuser of Job (Job 1:6-12; 2:1-6), Joshua the high priest (Zech. 3:1-2), and the wicked (Ps. 109:6). In the New Testament, Satan becomes the tempter (Matt. 4:10; Mark 1:13; Luke 4:8; 1 Cor. 7:5), the deceiver (2 Cor. 2:11; 11:14; 2 Thess. 2:9-10), the one who thwarts the work of God (1 Thess. 2:18), and the evil one (Matt. 6:13; 1 Tim. 5:15). He causes illness (Luke 13:16; 2 Cor. 12:7); takes away the word of God from its hearers (Mark 4:15); and seduces Judas (Luke 22:3; John 13:27), Peter (Luke 22:31), Ananias (Acts 5:3), and Christians (2 Cor. 2:11). Certainly, Satan is a formidable adversary for faithful saints.

The Devil

The Greek word for devil, *diabolos,* means accuser or slanderer (1 Pet. 5:8) and translates the Hebrew *Satan* in the Septuagint (Job 1:6-11; 2:1-7; Zech. 3:1-2; see also 1 Enoch 40:7; Jub. 1:20; 10:1). The two words, *devil* and *Satan,* are paired in Revelation (Rev. 12:9; 20:2) and are used interchangeably for the one who tempts Jesus (Matt. 4:1-11; Luke 4:1-13); seduces Judas (John 6:70-71; 13:2); imprisons the faithful (Rev. 2:10); causes illness (Acts 10:38), sin (1 John 3:8-10), and death (Heb. 2:14); and takes away the word of God (Luke 8:12; see also Matt. 13:39). This powerful enemy of the saints (Acts 13:10; Eph. 6:11; 1 Pet. 5:8) is a murderer and liar (John 8:44) who tempts the faithful and leads them astray (1 Tim. 3:6-7; 2 Tim. 2:26). Revelation tells us that the devil and Satan will be bound and prohibited from deception (20:1-3). Such reassurance effectively undergirds the faith of the persecuted.

Conqueror and Conquerors

Verse 11 says that the faithful conquer the dragon Satan with the Lamb's blood and testimony. The word *conquer (nikaō; nikos),* which means "to win," or to "defeat," denotes victory and superiority. The Septuagint uses the word for success in battle (2 Sam. 2:26; 1 Esd. 4:5), against serpents (Wis. Sol. 16:10), or in disputes (2 Macc. 3:5). In 4 Maccabees, the righteous are also said to be victorious over their emotions (6:33; 13:7) and enemy assaults (6:10) and to receive the divine rewards of victory (7:3). The word refers to the overthrow of a superior opposing force, although that success may not be public. Only God, who is unconquerable, can bring such a victory. God is victorious (1 Chron. 29:11; 2 Macc. 13:15) through Israel (2 Macc. 10:38). The only occurrence of the verb in the Synoptics is in connection with the overpowering of the strong man (Luke 11:22), where the parallel accounts have "tie up" (*deō*; Matt. 12:29; Mark 3:27). The verb describes the victory of the servant of God (Matt. 12:20; see also Isa. 42:1-4). John's Gospel speaks of Jesus conquering the world (16:33); Paul refers to Christ's victory over death (1 Cor. 15:54-57).

In Revelation, the idea of conquering is used for the provisional victory of the beast over the two witnesses (11:7), the campaign of first horseman (6:2), and the beast's triumph over the saints (13:7). Yet the ultimate and definitive victory goes to the Lamb (5:5; 17:14) and to the saints who fight with him (12:11; 15:2; 21:7). Christ the Lamb has conquered the kingdom of this world (11:15). The saints are recognized repeatedly in the refrain, "he who overcomes" (2:7, 11, 17, 26; 3:5, 12, 21). The saints conquer by the blood of the Lamb (1:5; 5:9; 12:11), with the word of their testimony (2:13; see also 3:14), and through not clinging to life in the face of death (Matt. 10:28; 16:25-26; Rowland, 1998:650). The Christian conquers through following Christ's pattern of enduring suffering without compromise and thus participates in Christ's own victory. Indeed, Caird says: "The Conqueror is one who follows Christ along the road which leads to victory; or rather, because Christ comes in all his victorious power to those who open the door to him, the Conqueror is one in whom Christ wins afresh his own victory, which is also God's victory" (1966:58). The one who shares in Christ's suffering also shares in Christ's victory. Those who follow Christ in patiently enduring persecution are rewarded by reigning and judging with God in the kingdom (Matt. 19:28; Luke 22:28-30; John 16:29-33; 1 Cor. 6:2; 2 Tim. 2:11-13). Although the true conqueror is Christ the Lamb, who has won the victory over the powers of evil by his death on the cross, the saints are also conquerors through faithfulness in tribulation and even martyrdom (Bauernfeind *TDNT* 4.942-45).

Indeed, there is a sense in which the victory of the saints is present already (1 John 2:13-14; 4:4; 5:4-5). We are told that Christ has already won the victory and been enthroned with God (Acts 2:34; Rom. 8:32-36; Eph. 1:20-22; Col. 3:1; Heb. 1:3; 8:1; 10:12; 12:2; 1 Peter 3:21-22). His kingdom is in progress. Although there is a sense in which we do not need to wait for the parousia to reign with Christ, the completion of Christ's reign will take place at his second coming.

Yet the method of conquering is not typical. The powerful Roman

Empire conquered through armed violence, but the Lamb overcame through submission to suffering and death. Barr discusses this contrast:

> A more complete reversal of value would be hard to imagine.... [T]he Lamb is the Lion. Jesus is the Messiah, but he has performed his messianic office in a most extraordinary way, by his death. Yet his death is not defeat, for it is just this that makes him worthy to open the scroll revealing the will of God. Jesus conquered through suffering and weakness rather than by might. John asks us to see both that Jesus rejects the role of Lion, refuses to conquer through supernatural power, and that we must now give a radical new valuation to Lambs; the sufferer is the conqueror, the victim the victor (1984:41).

Richard Hays says that the followers of Jesus imitate him through enduring and "bearing prophetic witness against the violence, immorality, and injustice of an earthly empire that claims the authority that rightly belongs to God.... They imitate Jesus' example of powerless suffering and refuse to succumb to the illusion that power equals truth" (1996:176).

The biblical sense of *conquer* is captured in the anthem of the civil rights movement: "We shall overcome someday." The peaceful freedom marchers who sang this prevailed over the violence and oppression of racism. Richard Hays affirms: "No one can enter imaginatively into the world narrated by this book [Revelation] and remain complacent about things as they are in an unjust world (1996:183-84).

The Rest of the Woman's Offspring

The Explanatory Notes argued that the rest of the woman's offspring are faithful followers of Christ "who keep the commandments of God and hold fast to the faith of Jesus" (14:12). The remnant theology of the Hebrew tradition maintained that, regardless of the tribulations that come, God would have a remnant that would be obedient and faithful (2 Esd. 6:25; 7:28; 12:34; 13:23-24, 48; 1 Enoch 83:8; 2 Bar. 29:4; 40:2).

The word translated "offspring" *(sperma)* is rooted in the Genesis narrative. After the Fall, God places enmity between the serpent and the offspring of the Eve (Gen. 3:15). Later, God promises Abraham as many offspring as the dust of the earth, the sand of the sea, and the stars of the heavens (Gen. 13:15-16; 15:5; 22:17-18; Rom. 9:27). Abraham is also assured a land for his inheritance (Gen. 15:18). Although God warns that Abraham's offspring will be oppressed (Gen. 15:13), they will also be a blessing to all the nations of the earth (Gen. 22:18). Later, Paul interprets the offspring of Abraham to include Christ (Gal. 3:16) and his followers who are heirs to Abraham, not through the law, but through faith in Christ (Rom. 4:13; Gal. 3:27-29). Thus, it seems quite appropriate to see the offspring of the woman to be Christ and those who are faithful to him. Indeed, in Revelation 12 the child of the woman is Christ, and the rest of her offspring are those who are faithful to Christ through the attack of the satanic dragon.

THE TEXT IN THE LIFE OF THE CHURCH

The Devil and the Church

In the premodern world, the devil was conceived as a personal being with a human likeness. Indeed, the world was filled with myriads of demonic beings whose purpose was to deceive and overcome the Christian. Anything that was not of God was thought to be demonic and was warded off by making the sign of the cross, placing hideous gargoyles on buildings, or even practicing exorcism. The power of the devil struck fear into the hearts of many followers of Christ who were afraid they might spend eternity in hell.

The best portrayal of this view of demonic evil may be *Dante's Inferno*, in which an individual named Pilgrim is led through hell. There he observes people being punished for their sins and their refusal to repent; he experiences angry devils armed with hooks and pitchforks, attacking serpents, boiling pitch, groans of torment, and a horrible stench. In the last canto, when the levels of hell have been descended to the center of the earth, Pilgrim encounters the "king of the vast kingdom of all grief," a gigantic beast with three faces and two mighty bat-wings larger than the sails of a ship. The description of the devil is hideous:

> In each of three mouths he crunched a sinner with teeth like those that rake the hemp and flax, keeping three sinners constantly in pain;
> the one in front—the biting he endured was nothing like the clawing that he took: sometimes his back was raked clean of its skin. (*Inferno*, 244)

With the advent of the modern world and enlightenment rationalism, emotional fear of Satan abated and the power of the devil to deceive Christians was evaluated rationally. Some concluded that the modern person could no longer believe in a personal devil; his only continued usefulness was perhaps to personify in mythical terms the prevalence and persistence of evil forces in the world. Others who wished to affirm a personal devil redefined the being in rational terms. In the late seventeenth century, John Milton's devil says that the spiritual world of heaven and hell are a construction of the mind:

> The mind is its own place, and in itself
> Can make a heaven of hell, a hell of heaven.
> (*Paradise Lost,* 1.254-55)

C. S. Lewis's *Screwtape Letters* describes a devil that is calculating and reasonable, who sees emotion as more vulnerable than reason and gives logical principles and methods for undermining the Christian's commitments and relationships (1943:18, 20-23). Here the modern devil is a reasonable and rational being.

In the postmodern era, there is a renewed willingness to reconsider the reality of the demonic and even the validity of occult practices. The reaction of the traditional Christian community has been to focus on the demonic and even to see its acceptance in the broader community as evidence of increased activity on the part of the devil. What has come to be almost an obsession with the demonic among conservative Christians seems to have its genesis in works like Hal Lindsey's phenomenally popular *Satan Is Alive and Well on Planet Earth* (1972). This book categorizes phenomena that the author attributes to the activity of the devil, concluding with a description of how the Christian should respond to this onslaught of the demonic.

Each of these responses to the devil are defective. The fear of the premodern age lacks an understanding that Christ has, indeed, definitively won the battle over the devil. The rational approach of the modern world does not understand that evil is insidious and even irrational. The fascination with the demonic as an alternative spirituality acceptable in a postmodern world fails to understand that the devil has great power to create destruction but has ultimately been made impotent by Christ's death and resurrection.

Revelation teaches that the power of the devil *appears* to dominate in this world, but because the defeat of the dragon has already taken place in heaven, the faithful are confident that his power is short on earth and that they will ultimately win the cosmic battle. In short, the devil is a powerful but defeated foe.

Menno Simons on the Dragon

Early Dutch Anabaptist leader Menno Simons interpreted the dragon in a totally spiritual sense:

Since then this old crooked serpent, which from the beginning has been proud and arrogant and false, a cruel murderer, has been put under the feet of Christ and His church, and must endure and see his lying seed destroyed and trampled underfoot through the revealed truth; therefore he gnashes his teeth and breathes out the accursed, infernal breath of heresy through his prophets and preachers in the most frightful manner. He casts out of his mouth the terrible streams of his tyranny, by means of the rulers and mighty ones of the earth, at the glorious woman pregnant with the Word of the Lord, in hope of exterminating and destroying her seed. But God be eternally praised, who has protected her against the red dragon and has prepared a place in the wilderness for her. (1956, 324-25)

It is appropriate to include in this connection a prayer from Menno that draws on the imagery of the dragon:

O Lord! Dear Lord! Grant that the wrathful dragon may not entirely devour Thy poor little flock, but that we, by Thy grace, may in patience conquer by the sword of Thy mouth; and may leave an abiding seed, which shall keep Thy commandments, preserve Thy testimony, and eternally praise Thy great and glorious name. Amen, dear Lord. Amen. (1956, 742)

They Can Only Kill Us

The principle of not clinging to life in the face of tribulation is demonstrated in the activity of certain young blacks in the days of apartheid South Africa. Allen Boesak reports that in response to black youths' nonviolent resistance, government troops killed children and forced young people to be aware that they needed to be willing to give their lives for the cause of the birth of the new South Africa. The youths responded with the words: "They can only kill us." Boesak elaborates: "Their only power is the power to destroy. They can never last. If the church as a whole in South Africa does not learn that now, soon it will have nothing to teach" (1987:83-84).

This does not mean that the faithful renounce life or seek martyrdom. Boesak continues:

We get even angrier at those who, while hiding behind the guns of the oppressor, accuse us of seeking to become martyrs. There is no way to explain this to those who will never understand what it means to know that life may be all one has, but it is not all there is. We love life because it is a gift of God, we protect it from the destroyers of the earth because it is sacred, and yet we are willing to give it up for the sake of others because giving it thus is a gift of God too. (1987:89-90)

Nevertheless, there is a sense in which suffering, if not death, is inevitable if one is to be a faithful follower of Christ. Alan Paton introduces to his readers a middle-class black man who cautiously decides to join the South African struggle for freedom because: "When I go up there, which is my intention, the Big Judge will say to me, Where are your wounds? and if I say I haven't any, he will say, Was there nothing to fight for? I couldn't face that question" (1981:66-67).

Revelation 13:1-18

The Two Beasts

PREVIEW

The second vision of the interlude between the seven trumpets and the seven bowls is of two beasts, one from the earth and another from the sea. Ramsay reports that in the language and art of first-century Asia Minor, foreign products were "of the sea," and native beings emerged from, or reclined on, the earth (1904:103-4). Therefore, the beast from the sea most likely symbolizes the Roman Empire, which was considered foreign in Asia and communicated with the province by sea; while the beast from the land is the worship of the empire, which was not imposed from Rome but grew up in the province and was enforced by high priests of Asia and local officials called asiarchs (Friesen, 2001:30, 41-43; see Entering the World of Revelation: Getting Our Bearings).

The source of the beast imagery lies in ancient Near Eastern cultures (TBC on ch. 11, The Beast). The two beasts, created on the fifth day (Gen. 1:21; 2 Esd. 6:49-52; 1 Enoch 60:7-10; 2 Bar. 29:4) are destroyed by God in a primeval struggle (Ps. 74:13-14; Isa. 27:1). The beast symbolism in the ancient world came to designate political empires; for example, the apocalypse of Esdras uses the eagle to symbolize Rome (2 Esd. 11:1–12:51). Nevertheless, a more direct antecedent of two beasts comes from Daniel 7.

The two beasts also help to complete the symmetry of Revelation; for many of the symbols of good in Revelation, there are corresponding evil counterparts:

GOOD	EVIL
One seated on throne (ch. 4)	Dragon (ch. 12)
Lamb (ch. 5)	Beast from sea (13:1-10)
Seven Spirits (1:4; 3:1; 4:5; 5:6)	Beast from land (13:11-18)
Two witnesses (ch. 11)	Two beasts (ch. 13)

Moreover, there is a stark contrast between the symbols connected with the Lamb and the beast from the sea (see Aune, 1998a:726 for similarities between the two symbols).

LAMB	BEAST
On Mount Zion (14:1)	On sea (13:1)
Authority from God (5:7)	Authority from Satan (13:2)
Mark of slaughter (5:6)	Mortal wound (13:3)
Homage to God and Lamb (5:12)	Homage to Dragon (13:4)
Ransomed saints (5:9)	Makes war on saints (13:7)

This contrast is also captured in a word play on Lamb *(arnion)* and beast *(thērion)*.

The identity of the beast is one of the most disputed issues in Revelation. Futurists have speculated endlessly on such diverse possibilities as Mohammed, Frederick II, Luther, Napoleon, Hitler, Henry Kissinger, and Saddam Hussein. Yet preterists, searching the historical context of Revelation, have reached no consensus. Caird puts forward Caligula's statue erected in the holy of holies as evidence that "though we cannot say that Caligula is the Antichrist, he undoubtedly sat for the portrait" (1966:166). Tacitus's description of Nero makes him a likely candidate (*Annals* 15.29, 44, 74). Barker has even speculated that the beast from the earth was Josephus (2000:236-39).

With the introduction of these two beasts, the trinity of evil is now complete: Satan (dragon), the 'antichrist' (the beast from sea), and the false prophet (the beast from land). Although the pairing of the Holy Spirit with the false prophet is less evident in Revelation than the other two trinitarian contrasts, the purpose of the Holy Spirit is to glorify Christ (John 16:13-14), while the false prophet glorifies the beast (Rev. 13:12). Wall further develops the symmetry: "On the one hand, when the Evil One gains dominion over those who bear his mark (13:17-18) the result will be their death (13:11-16). On the other hand, when God is allowed to rule over those who bear the Lamb's name (14:1), the result will be their eternal life (14:2-5)" (1991:160).

The focus of this chapter is on the short duration of Satan's attack on the faithful through the two beastly emissaries, the first operating by force and the second through deception (Barr, 1998:126-27). Banished from heaven, Satan focuses his last intense persecution on the faithful offspring of the woman, using the two horrible beasts for the dreadful purpose.

OUTLINE

The Beast from the Sea, 13:1-10
The Beast from the Earth, 13:11-18

EXPLANATORY NOTES

The Beast from the Sea 13:1-10

The chapter divides into two sections, each beginning with the words *And I saw,* a common introductory clause in Revelation, occurring seven times in chapters 13–15 (13:1, 11; 14:1, 6, 14; 15:1, 2). Yet attempts to divide the chapters into seven corresponding sections seem strained.

[Although a variant reading in Revelation 12:18 has little impact on the meaning of the text, it does affect where the chapter break is to be placed. The difference is in the pronoun subject of the sentence. The best external evidence, including a ten-leaf, third-century papyrus fragment of Revelation and Codices Sinaiticus, Alexandrinus, and Ephraem, supports "and he took his stand on the sand of the sea" *(kai estathē).* The other reading is "and I took my stand on the sand of the sea" *(kai estathēn).* The earliest witness to the latter reading is a sixth-century uncial manuscript. The significance of this textual variation is that, if the pronoun is "he," it refers to the dragon, and the verse should be taken with chapter 12; but if the reading is "I," the referent is John, and the verse should be attached to chapter 13. The former is clearly the best choice, which is the motivation for the NRSV translation: *Then the dragon took his stand on the sand of the seashore.* Yet, inexplicably, the NRSV translators place 12:18 in the paragraph that begins chapter 13. Although this translation preserves the correct meaning of the words, the verse should be connected to chapter 12.]

What John saw was *a beast rising out of the sea.* The imagery of the sea has roots in the Red Sea of the Exodus, which guided the Israelites but drowned her enemies (Wis. Sol. 10:18-19). Moreover, it parallels the sea upon which the great whore sits (17:15) and parodies the heavenly sea (4:6). In Revelation the sea is also related to the bottomless pit, the abode of evil and chaos (9:2; 11:7; 17:8).

As stated in the Preview, it is best to take the beast from the sea to be the personification of the Roman Empire (2 Esd. 11:1) because Rome's communication with the province of Asia was by sea. The terms of power associated with the beast point to Rome, but they are also similar to those used of the dragon in chapter 12. Rome embodies, at the same time, the powers of both the Roman Empire and Satan. The dragon (Satan) uses the beast (the Roman Empire) to persecute God's people.

Some expect the beast to be a particular person who will appear to help bring the end. Yet the Johannine Epistles speak of many antichrists, a term not used in Revelation, but in 1 John 2:18; 2 John 7; cf. 1 John 4:2-3. Indeed, rather than limit the beast to symbolizing the first-century Roman Empire or an end-time world ruler, it may be better to broaden the imagery to include all forces that work against Christ. Thus, whatever the specific referent, the meaning is that persecution of Christians comes from rulers of this world who are ultimately counterfeit christs.

The beast from the sea is described as *having ten horns*. The horns of Daniel's fourth beast are ten kings that arise from the Seleucid dynasty preceding a little horn, Antiochus IV Epiphanes, who overthrew Jerusalem and desecrated the temple (Dan. 7:7-8, 24-26; 11:30-36). In Revelation, the ten horns seem to connote the Parthian rulers who threatened Rome from the east (Rev. 17:12). As a characteristic of the beast, the ten horns draw on the power associated with the Seleucid dynasty and the Parthian threat to symbolize political power used against the faithful.

The beast had *also seven heads*. The four beasts of Daniel 7 also had a combined seven heads—four leopards, a lion, a bear, and a terrifying monster (Glasson, 1965:79-80). Later in Revelation, the referents of the seven heads are specified as seven kings (see Explanatory Notes on 17:9-11). Nevertheless, the most clear connection is to the seven-headed dragon of Revelation 12, which symbolizes Satan. A more tenuous allusion may be to the seven hills of Rome. This kaleidoscopic imagery communicates that evil worldly forces arrayed against the faithful, which are as powerful as the Seleucid kingdom and Roman Empire, have their source in Satan.

On the horns of this beast from the sea *were ten diadems*. The diadem is a royal crown signifying the sovereign power of the beast, which is, though, only a shadow of the power of Christ, who has many diadems on this head (Rev. 19:12). Mounce suggests that the placement of the crowns on the horns, the symbol of power, rather than on the heads, the seat of rationality, indicates that the sovereignty "rests on brute force" (1977:250). The power of the beast, symbolized in its horns, comes from the dragon Satan.

On the heads of the beast *were blasphemous names*. Blasphemy is slandering of God through word or deed (Dan. 7:25; Matt. 24:15; 2 Thess. 2:4; Rev. 17:3-6). Here the blasphemy probably refers to inscriptions on coins carrying the likeness of Roman emperors along with names like "divine" *(divus)* and "God" *(theos)*. Ford reports: "Julius Caesar, Augustus, Claudius, Vespasian, and Titus were officially declared divine at their death; the latter three used the title *Divus* on coins during their lifetime" (1975:220). The most explicit claim to deity is attributed to Domitian, who proclaimed himself "our Lord and God" (*dominus et deus noster; see* Suet., *Domitian* 13; Martial, *Epigrams* 5.8; 10.72). Such titles were certainly considered blasphemous by Jews and Christians (Exod. 20:7; Luke 4:8).

A more detailed description follows: *And the beast that I saw was like a leopard, its feet were like a bear's, and its mouth was like a lion's mouth.* In Daniel, four ancient empires are represented as four beasts: the first, the lion, is Babylon, who brought desolation to Jerusalem and its temple (Jer. 27:16-22); the second, the bear, symbolizes Media; the third, the leopard, connotes Persia; and the fourth, "a terrifying and dreadful and exceedingly strong being," represents the kingdom of Satan (Dan. 7:3-8). Jewish writings identify Daniel's fourth beast with Rome (2 Esd. 12:11; Abodah Zarah 2b; Shebu'oth 6b). All four of Daniel's beasts are from the sea. John combines into two the characteristics of Daniel's four beasts to connote the epitome of evil. Revelation employs these powerful beasts and the kingdoms they represent as symbols for the Roman Empire, and, indeed, for all evil political regimes that oppose the kingdom of God. Barclay says it well: "For John the Roman Empire was so satanic and terrible that in itself it included all the evil terrors of the evil empires which had gone before. It was, as it were, the sum total of all evil" (1960:2.109-10; see also Lederach in *BCBC,* 1994, on Daniel).

To this beast *the dragon gave ... his power and his throne and great authority.* The source of the beast's power is Satan (2 Thess. 2:9), which parallels God's sharing divine authority with Christ (Rev. 3:21; 12:5, 10). The sense of this clause is that to worship the beast is really to worship Satan. Yet if Satan has been defeated, what power does he have to give? A major paradox of the New Testament is that Satan, though fallen, still has great power and authority (see TBC, The Authority of the Devil).

The description of the beast continues in greater detail: *One of its heads seemed to have received a death-blow, but its mortal wound had been healed.* Although some would find in this image Emperor Caligula's recovery from a serious illness (Suet., *Caligula* 14; *Dio's Roman History* 59.8.1-3; Philo, *The Embassy to Gaius* 14-21), John's audience would more likely have connected it with the death of Nero, who may have committed suicide in A.D. 68 by stabbing himself in the throat (Suet., *Nero* 49). Nero's satanic nature received confirmation for Christians in the story that snakes had been found guarding his cradle (Tac., *Annals* 11.11; see Barclay 1960:2.116-19). After Nero's death, the rumor spread that he was still alive or had come back to life *[Essay: Nero Redivivus Myth]*. Although an objection to applying the *Nero Redivivus* myth to this passage is that the entire beast died, not just one emperor, the death of Nero did have a catastrophic effect on the empire that led to the unstable reigns of three emperors in the next two years. Indeed, the peace was not restored until the reign of Vespasian. Whatever its historical referent, there may also be here an allusion to the resilience of evil: whenever an evil ruler with beast-like characteristics is defeated, another takes its place. Moreover, the healed wound of the beast is the counterfeit of the death and resurrection of Christ the Lamb. Whereas Christ's resurrection is permanent and has universal implications, the beast's recovery lasts only for a brief time (Beale, 1999:689).

The populace eagerly embraced this beast: *In amazement the whole earth followed the beast*. The amazement is due to the military power of the beast (Rowland, 1998:657). To the first readers of Revelation, this worldwide following of the beast would be connected with the rise of the destructive power of Rome under Emperor Domitian. More generally, it reminds persons of all time periods that they must choose to be either among the few who are God's children or the masses who follow the evil one (1 John 5:19).

To follow the beast, the whole earth *worshiped the dragon, for he had given his authority to the beast*. Because the beast receives power from the dragon, there is universal worship of Satan. While Christ causes people to worship God (Rev. 1:6), the beast diverts worship from God to the Roman Empire. The imperial cult involved sacrifice, incense, and prayers (Yarbro Collins, 1991:93). For Christians to practice such acts of worship in honor of the beastly Roman emperor would be blasphemy, idolatry, and even Satan worship (1 Cor. 10:20).

Then the whole earth *worshiped the beast, saying, "Who is like the beast, and who can fight against it?"* Clearly a parody of the doxology to the Lamb (Rev. 5:2, 9-10, 12-13) and similar doxologies to God (Exod. 15:11-12; Ps. 35:10; 89:6-8; 113:5; Isa. 40:25; 44:7; Mic. 7:18), this contributes to Revelation's symmetry: instead of worshiping the Lamb, who rules with God, they worship the beast, who received authority from the satanic dragon. The irony is that, although they worship the beast for its fighting power, the beast's army lost the war against Michael's forces in heaven and will be overcome by the armies of the Lamb (17:14; 19:11-16). The obvious answer to the two questions posed in this verse is: "Christ the Lamb" (Koester, 2001:126).

Perhaps as a result of confidence gained from the acclamation of its followers, the *beast was given a mouth uttering haughty and blasphemous words*. This arrogant speech calls to mind Antiochus IV Epiphanes, who also blasphemed God and curtailed temple worship in the second century B.C. (Dan. 7:8, 11, 20, 25; 11:36; 1 Macc. 1:20-28). The passive verbs in verses 5-7 indicate that the beast's power was imputed by the dragon or allowed by Christ. This power is used here to blaspheme God, probably by attributing divine titles to the emperors (Rev. 19:13, 16), or more generally by giving to the beast loyalty that should only be rendered to God.

The beast *was allowed to exercise authority for forty-two months*. This period is equivalent to three and a half years and one thousand two hundred sixty days, all durations of the beast's authority in Revelation (see Notes on 11:2). The sense here is that God, who has ultimately allowed the beast and Satan to execute authority, will terminate that privilege after a limited period of time.

Then the beast *opened its mouth to utter blasphemies against God, blaspheming his name*. The Law clearly condemns blaspheming the name of God (Exod. 20:7; Deut. 28:58-59; see also Matt. 5:34-35; Test. Moses 8:5). Because the name was thought to be equivalent to the person (Ps. 111:9; Luke 1:49), blasphemy against the name of God was considered equivalent to blasphemy against God. Thus, the participial phrase repeats for emphasis the sense of the main clause. The blasphemy is in the deification of the beastly Roman empire (2 Thess. 2:4). Certainly, to regard any political state as supreme over God is blasphemy.

The beast also blasphemed God's *dwelling, that is, those who dwell in heaven*. The word *dwelling (skēnē)* translates the Hebrew *shekinah*, "tabernacle," which came to represent the presence and glory of God (Exod. 29:45; Lev. 26:11-12; Rev. 21:3; see also Isa. 57:15; Ezek. 37:26-27; Rom. 8:11; Phil. 3:20; Heb. 11:13-16; 13:14; Rev. 7:15). Although a variant reading includes "and" before *those who dwell in heaven,* distinguishing between God's *dwelling* and *those who dwell in heaven*, the external evidence overwhelmingly favors the omission of the conjunction, thus yielding the reading: "God's dwelling, that is, those who dwell in heaven." Thus, the reference is primarily to a people rather than a place. Those that dwell in heaven are the faithful (Eph. 2:6; Col. 3:1), who are God's dwelling (Rev. 11:1-2).

The beast was also *allowed to make war on the saints and to conquer them.* Again the beast functions with God's permission. Analogous to this is the divine permission given for Christ's enemies to condemn him to death. Nevertheless, as was the case with the accusers of Christ, the beast's conquering is an illusion; the true victors are the faithful saints, the followers of Christ the Lamb (11:7, 11; 12:11, 17). The primary referent for the conqueror of the saints in the context of Revelation is emperor Nero, who had executed Christians, and Domitian, who was expected to continue the persecution of Nero. In such persecution, the saints are confident of victory if they bear obedient and faithful witness.

Nevertheless, the beast *was given authority over every tribe and people and language and nation.* Its universal authority (Dan. 3:5-6) is a parody of the authority of the Lamb (5:9-10; 19:6-8; 22:1-5). Some argue that, because Nero never ruled the entire world, this passage anticipates an end-time antichrist who will have such authority. Yet this may be a hyperbolic statement of the widespread power of Rome. Moreover, the Romans did consider their power to be worldwide, and the language here seems to refer to Rome. Harrington speaks of the *orbis Romanus,* the universal extent of Rome's rule (1993:139).

The beast worshipers, *all the inhabitants of the earth,* are contrasted with the followers of Christ called in verse 6 "those who dwell in heaven." The former are specified as *everyone whose name has not been written from the foundation of the world in the book of life of the Lamb that was slaughtered.* The book of life was the civic register of all good citizens (see TBC on ch. 20, The Books), and since it belongs to the Lamb here, it is a register of those faithful to Christ (Phil. 4:3; Rev. 3:5-6; 20:12, 15; 21:27). The reference to the slaughter of the Lamb indicates that it is through the death of Christ that persons become enrolled in the book of life (5:9-10).

The passage can be read in one of two ways. First, it may mean the names were written in the book of life before the foundation of the world, which would lend credence to the argument that the passage is a statement of predestination (Eph. 1:4; see Beale, 1999: 702-3). Second, the sense may be that the Lamb was slaughtered from the foundation of the world, a common idea in the biblical tradition (Acts 2:23; 1 Pet. 1:18-21; 1 Enoch 62; Test. Moses 1:14) that seems to have been accepted by Menno Simons (1956:109) and other sixteenth-century Anabaptists (van Braght, 1950:470, 1033). To paraphrase the words of Barclay, redemption is older than creation (1960:2.125; see also Matt. 25:34). The word order of the passage clearly favors the latter interpretation.

An Old Testament quotation is introduced with the familiar declaration: *Let anyone who has an ear listen.* In the letters to the churches, this statement is used either to introduce the promise to the conqueror (Rev. 2:7, 11, 17) or as a conclusion (Rev. 2:29; 3:6, 13, 22).
Here it is a warning preparing for the following prophetic oracle (see
also Matt. 11:15-16; Mark 4:9). Mounce translates it: "Now hear this"
(1977:256)! The reader is to listen carefully to the poetic statement:
*If you are to be taken captive, into captivity you go; if you kill with
the sword, with the sword you will be killed.* Although the Greek
text is uncertain and its meaning paradoxical, at the very least this
paraphrase of Jeremiah says that sin brings its own punishment (Jer.
15:2; 43:11). Because the sins spoken of here are related to killing
and taking captives in war, the verse is a strong statement of nonre-
sistance.

The section ends with the injunction: *Here is a call for the
endurance and faith of the saints.* As has been noted before, the
word for *endurance (hypomonē)* is not a passive bearing of persecution, but its courageous acceptance and transformation into victory.
Yet the saints are called to faithful endurance rather than to
vengeance. Jesus showed how to accept peacefully and without retaliation the persecution that inevitably follows the decision to choose
the Lamb (John 18:11). So God's faithful are called to accept tribulation without violent resistance because justice for their persecutors will
be enacted by God.

The Beast from the Earth 13:11-18

The second half of the chapter begins like the first: *Then I saw another beast that rose out of the earth.* Although all of Daniel's beasts
come from the earth (Dan. 7:17), the closest parallel is with
Behemoth, the earth monster (Job 40:15-24). The beast from the
earth is also related to both the beast from the sea (2 Esd. 6:49-52;
1 Enoch 60:7-10; 2 Bar. 29:4; see also Baba Batra 74a), and the
dragon, who controls both the sea and the earth through his beastly
emissaries (Rev. 12:12). If the first beast symbolizes political power in
service of the dragon, the second represents religious authority
demanding allegiance to that satanic rule. Later, this beast will be
called the false prophet (see TBC, The False Prophet).

Although some see this beast as organized religion supporting the
eschatological Antichrist (see Ladd, 1972:182-83), it is better to find
the referent for the symbolism in the worship of the emperor. Unlike
the Roman Empire that came to Asia by sea, emperor worship grew
up in the province, that is, from the earth (see Ramsey, 1904:103-4).

The local priests fanned belief in the emperors' divinity, built temples to them in each city of the province, and organized the cult into dioceses (Acts 19:31). This false religion worships the state instead of God. Barclay comments: "When a Church compromises with the world, it becomes the world, and ceases to be a Church—and Christ is betrayed again" (1960:2.128).

The beast from the earth *had two horns like a lamb*. Daniel's ram had two horns (Dan. 8:3-4), and the beast from the sea had ten (v. 1); the latter counterfeits Christ the Lamb (Matt. 24:24; Rev. 5:6). Shockingly, Beasley-Murray calls it the lamb of Satan (1974:216). Because the horns of the beast symbolize power, the worship of the state, and particularly emperor worship, are counterfeit Christianity with a power apparently like Christ's.

This false Christ showed its true nature when it *spoke like a dragon*. The word *dragon* is equivalent to serpent, and the allusion to Eden is obvious (Gen. 3:14-15; Rev. 12:9). Although the beast from the earth looked like the Lamb, it spoke with the deceitfulness of Satan. Emperor worship was satanic, and the advocacy of the worship of the state in any context is, in modern terms, like a wolf in sheep's clothing.

The beast from the earth *exercises all the authority of the first beast on its behalf*. As the faithful saints exercise the authority of Christ, which came from God (Rev. 5:6-7), so the dragon gave authority to the beast from the sea (Rev. 13:4), who passes that authority on to this beast from the earth. Employing this authority, the second beast *makes the earth and its inhabitants worship the first beast, whose mortal wound had been healed*. This contrasts with the Holy Spirit's influencing persons to worship God and the Lamb. Although some feel that this worship refers to an anticipated religious system that will force persons to worship an eschatological antichrist, a more likely referent, in the context, is to the imperial cult, which caused the people of the province to worship the state. The Roman Empire did not enforce this cult, but its provincial representatives who accommodated to the ideas of the Roman world did (see Friesen, 1993, for documentation of the imperial cult in Ephesus). Rowland says that Revelation demands resistance to this accommodation: "Emperor worship had become part of the fabric of life, and John's vision in effect demands of readers that they unravel that fabric and weave a new fabric of living in which the persistent, even casual, participation in state religion and the social conventions that surround it form no part" (1998:658). Pilgrim (1999) places Revelation's ethic of resistance in the context of Paul's ethic of subordination to the state and Jesus' ethic of critical distancing from the state.

To verify its power, the beast from the earth *performs great signs, even making fire come down from heaven to earth in the sight of all.* The Roman emperors honored astrologers that performed such feats (Justin, *Apol.* 1.26; Irenaeus, *Adv. Haer.* 1.23.1; Eusebius, *Eccl. Hist.* 2.13). Moreover, these evil sorceries that the beast performs are a parody of the signs performed by Christ's followers (see TBC, Good and Evil Signs). The particular sign here is to "bring down fire," which is the same phenomenon caused by the divine counterpart of the beast from the earth, the Holy Spirit, on the day of Pentecost (Acts 2:3-11). The use of the present tense indicates that the beast performs these signs habitually. That the two witnesses in Revelation 11 have similar power implies it is available to the suffering faithful.

Through these signs, the beast from the earth *is allowed to perform on behalf of the beast [from the sea], it deceives the inhabitants of the earth.* The great signs of this beast come, not from divine power, but from deception, imitating Satan, the great deceiver (Rev. 12:9; 19:20; 20:3, 8; cf. 2 Thess. 2:3-10, and Elias, *BCBC,* 1995:277-80). Yet only the unfaithful inhabitants of the earth are deceived (Rev. 6:10; 11:10; see also 13:8; 17:8), not the faithful saints (Matt. 28:18-20; Mark 13:22).

This beast deceives the unfaithful by *telling them to make an image for the beast that had been wounded by sword and yet lived.* Here is a clear allusion to Christ, who was also *wounded* and *yet lived* (Rev. 2:8; see also Rev. 13:3, 12). The beast from the earth is the wicked counterpart of the Holy Spirit, who reveals Christ, the image of God (2 Cor. 3:18; 4:4; Col. 1:15), to the faithful, who, in turn, are conformed to that image (Rom. 8:29). Because the phrase, *for the beast,* is dative *(tō thēriō)* rather than genitive, the emphasis is on the image, not as a likeness of, but as a shrine *for* the beast, similar to the ones constructed for Nebuchadnezzar (Dan. 3:1), Beliar (Asc. Isa. 4:1-13), and the Roman emperor of John's day (Murphy, 1998:309; see also Aune, 1998a:762-64). This beast provides instruction for worshiping the first beast, a practice clearly forbidden in the Decalogue (Exod. 20:4-5; see also 32:8; Mark 13:14; Acts 17:29).

The beast from the earth *was allowed to give breath to the image of the beast [from the sea] so that the image of the beast could even speak.* In the first century, likenesses of the emperors spoke through ventriloquism. Lucian describes a crane and long tube that were attached to a canvas likeness of Asclepius so that questions addressed to the god could be answered in a life-like manner (*Alex.* 26). The breath given to the image of the beast is an evil counterpart of the breath of life that revived the two witnesses (11:11; Thompson, 1998:141), and its speech parodies Christ, the Word of God (John 1:1-18).

The beast from the earth went so far as to *cause those who would not worship the image of the beast [from the sea] to be killed.* Daniel's friends, Shadrach, Meshach, and Abednego, refused to worship the likeness of Nebuchadnezzar even when threatened with death (Dan. 3:4-7, 11, 15; Lederach, *BCBC,* 1994:78-87). Moreover, there is some evidence that death was the penalty for refusal to worship the Roman emperor (Pliny, *Letter* 10.96; see also Caird 1966:177). Because Jesus affirmed that only God should be worshiped by the faithful (Matt. 4:10; see also Rom. 1:25), all are faced with a choice to worship the beast or remain true to the end (2 Thess. 2:1-12).

The beast from the earth also *causes all, both small and great, both rich and poor, both free and slave, to be marked on the right hand or the forehead.* The language of the passage includes everyone (6:15; 11:18; 19:5, 18; 20:12). Just as the Lamb's followers have his name on their foreheads (7:3-9; 9:4; 14:1-5), so the beast worshipers are marked as such (14:9-10; 16:2; 19:20; 20:4). The word *mark (charagma)* is the technical term for the imperial stamp on documents. A corresponding stamp was issued for worshiping the emperor and was necessary to function economically in the empire (see Ramsay, 1904:110-11). This mark is the evil counterpart of the seal of the redeemed; and taken together, they communicate the spiritual reality that all must declare loyalty either to God and the Lamb or to Satan and the Beast (7:2; 14:1).

The result of the issuing of this stamp is *that no one can buy or sell who does not have the mark, that is, the name of the beast or the number of its name.* This practice probably has its closest connection to the certificates that were at times issued to persons who worshiped the emperor and were then necessary for buying and selling. Moreover, coins and bills of sale were marked with the imperial stamp, which caused some Jewish Zealots to reject the use of Roman currency and to mint their own to avoid handling coins with blasphemous divine names attributed to the emperor (Murphy, 1998:312-13). The meaning of this passage is that the faithful must refuse to give allegiance to the emperor even when harassed economically.

To determine the identity of this beast whose worship is necessary for economic survival *calls for wisdom.* The number that follows identifying the beast is only intelligible with divine understanding (1 Cor. 2:6). John then challenges the reader: *let anyone with understanding calculate the number of the beast, for it is the number of a person.* The word *calculate* alludes to the ancient practice of gematria, or communicating ideas through numbers (Yoma 20a; Nazir 5a; Sanhedrin 22a; Ukzin 3.12; Irenaeus, *Adv. Haer.* 5.30). The letters of both the Hebrew and Greek alphabets served as number systems, with each letter designating a successive numerical equivalent (see tables 2-3 below). For example, Deissmann reports that in the graffiti of Pompeii is the statement, "I love her whose number is 545" (1965:277). This love-struck man added the numerical equivalents of the letters in the name of the object of his affections to arrive at the number.

Table 2. Greek Numerals

GRE.	ENG.	NUM.	GRE.	ENG.	NUM.	GRE	ENG.	NUM.
α	a	1	ι	i	10	ρ	r	100
β	b	2	κ	k	20	σ	s	200
γ	g	3	λ	l	30	τ	t	300
δ	d	4	μ	m	40	υ	u	400
ε	e	5	ν	n	50	φ	ph	500
–	–	6	ξ	x	60	χ	ch	600
ζ	z	7	ο	o	70	ψ	ps	700
η	ē	8	π	p	80	ω	ō	800
θ	th	9	–	–	90	–	–	900
						á	å	1000

Table 3. Hebrew Numerals

HEB.	ENG.	NUM.	HEB.	ENG.	NUM.	HEB.	ENG.	NUM.
א	a	1	י	y	10	ק	q	100
ב	b	2	כ, ך	k	20	ר	r	200
ג	g	3	ל	l	30	שׁ	sh	300
ד	d	4	מ, ם	m	40	ת	th	400
ה	h	5	נ, ן	n	50			
ו, וֹ	w, o	6	ס	s	60			
ז	z	7	ע	e	70			
ח	ch	8	פ, ף	p	80			
ט	t	9	צ, ץ	Ð	90			

Specifically, the beast's *number is six hundred sixty-six.* Although the meaning of the number may have been obvious to John's readers, it was uncertain to Irenaeus in the second century, who gives three possibilities (see *Eccl. Hist.* 5.30.3). More significantly, Irenaeus notes that some writers and manuscripts have the variant 616 instead of 666. Based on gematria, the addition of the numerical equivalents of the Greek letters in Caligula's name, Gaios Kaisar, yields a total of 616 (g = 3 + a = 1 + i = 10 + o = 70 + s = 200 + k = 20 + a = 1 + i = 10 + s = 200 + a = 1 + r = 100). Nevertheless, the best solution for the number 666 uses a transliteration of the name Nero Caesar into Hebrew letters and numerals. Because the Hebrew alphabet has no vowels, the name Nero Caesar transliterated from the Latin to Hebrew would be *nro qsr.* Adding the equivalents of these letters (see Table 3. Hebrew Numerals: n = 50 + r = 200 + o = 6 + q = 100 + s = 60 + r = 200), the total is 616, which accounts for the variant reading mentioned by Irenaeus. The corresponding accusative case in Latin (objective in English), *nron qsr* (Neron Caesar) adds to 666 (+ n = 50). Thus, the name Nero(n) Caesar accounts for both the common reading 666 and the variant 616. Bauckham uses a similar process to demonstrate that the Hebrew transliteration of the Greek word *beast* (*thērion*: th = 400 + r = 200 + y = 10 + o = 6 + n = 50) yields 666 (1993a:388-89). And Malina and Pilch have suggested that the letters of a Hebrew word *shlshwl* (sh = 300, l = 30, sh = 300, w = 6, l = 30), meaning "dragon or crawling beast," add up to 666 (2000:177). Nevertheless, if a specific person is in mind, Nero is the best identification of the beast through gematria.

Nero was a particularly violent person, who murdered many, including his own mother. Indeed, Suetonius quotes a piece of graffiti from first century Rome that said:

> Count the numerical values
> Of the letters in Nero's name,
> And in "murdered his own mother":
> You will find their sum is the same. (*Nero* 39)

This quotation illustrates both the beastly reputation of Nero and the popularity of the use of gematria. Nero was the first emperor to persecute and even behead, crucify, and burn Christians. Thus, he is a particularly appropriate candidate for the designation 666.

Yet this interpretation is not without its difficulties. First, the spelling for Nero's name here is unusual, although it may have support in the Qumran discoveries as Murabba'at (DJD, II, 101, plate 29, line 1; Bauckham, 1993a:388; Barker, 2000:233; cf. Beale, 1999:719-20). Second, some think John's audience would have had difficulty understanding this transliteration into Hebrew; nevertheless, Aramaic words like *maranatha* (1 Cor. 16:22) and *abba* (Rom. 8:15; Gal. 4:6) were understood by Greek-speaking Christians, and Hebrew words are used elsewhere in the text of Revelation, e.g., Apollyon (9:11), Harmagedon (16:16), Hallelujah (19:1-8), and Gog and Magog (20:8). Indeed, Yarbro Collins reports: "Foreign languages were often used to make the reference even more esoteric" (1991:97), so Nero cannot be ruled out on this basis.

Nevertheless, the reader need not turn to the complicated processes of gematria to arrive at a tenable referent for 666. Indeed, this would be the only clear example of gematria calculation in Revelation (though Bauckham proposes more instances [1993a:389-407]), where most of the numbers have symbolic significance; and if John would have had a Hebrew spelling in mind, he might have noted this in the text (9:11; 16:16). Moreover, the wisdom needed to understand the number is not mathematical aptitude but spiritual discernment (Beale, 1999:720-28). Hughes suggests that the number be understood symbolically, because 666 is the "number of a person," six represents humanity falling short of the divinity implied in the complete number seven, and the three-fold repetition 666 suggests a human counterfeit of the holy Trinity (1990:154-55).

Those who read Revelation in the context in which it was written at the end of the first century would have interpreted the beast from the sea to be the Roman Empire led by Domitian, who was thought to be Nero reborn. In turn, the beast from the earth was emperor worship, through which the citizens of the empire were compelled to call Domitian "Lord" and "God." Although these are the best referents for the beastly symbols, their meaning can apply to any time when the state assumes power that should be God's. The spirit of the beast is present when any state demands complete allegiance, whether that state be communist, Nazi, or capitalist; the spirit of the beast from the earth is present in any church that advocates allegiance to such a government, whether that church be the orthodox church of Russia, the state church of Nazi Germany, or ultra-patriotic fundamentalism in the United States. This passage warns the faithful that refusal to give such allegiance may mean death.

THE TEXT IN BIBLICAL CONTEXT

The Antichrist

The beast has many names in the biblical tradition. Daniel calls the Seleucid ruler, Antiochus IV Epiphanes, "the abomination that desolates" because he desecrated the temple in Jerusalem by setting up an altar to the Greek god Zeus and abolishing regular offerings (Dan. 8:11-14; 9:27; 11:30-36; 12:11; 2 Macc. 6:2). Paul speaks of the lawless one who exalts himself above other gods, declaring himself to be God (2 Thess. 2:3-10; Elias, BCBC, 1995:277-80). In the synoptic apocalypse, Jesus describes a desolating sacrilege and horror of false christs and prophets (Matt. 24:24; Mark 13:6, 14, 21-22). In Revelation, a trinity of the dragon, the beast, and the false prophet perform signs, deceive many by causing them to worship the beast and receive its mark, and eventually are cast into the lake of fire and sulfur (Rev. 16:13-14; 19:20; 20:10).

The Beastly Mosaic

John creates of Daniel's beasts (Dan. 7:3-8) a single beastly mosaic. Resembling the cubist tradition of Picasso, it is built on animal traits used symbolically throughout the Bible. The first aspect of the symbolic painting is the lion, which is used for leaders of an oppressing city (Zeph. 3:1-3; Zech. 11:3), for all evil attacks (2 Tim. 4:17-18), and even for the devil himself (1 Pet. 5:8). The second image in the mosaic is a leopard who swiftly pursues its prey (Hab. 1:8), rips apart the transgressors (Jer. 5:6), and mangles those who forsake the Lord (Sir. 28:23). The third element is a bear who steals lambs from the flock (1 Sam. 17:34) and mauls children to death (2 Kings 2:24). In Revelation, this composite of awful elements is brought together to describe what no single image can fully portray, the demonic character of the beast from the sea.

The Authority of the Devil

One of the major paradoxes of the New Testament is that the devil, though defeated, has great power in this world. In Revelation the devil is conquered by Michael and thrown from heaven to earth (12:7-12). Later, he is bound and cast into the pit so that he can no longer deceive the nations (20:3). Finally, he is condemned to the lake of fire and sulfur, his final abode (20:10). Yet throughout the New Testament, we find the devil actively working with great power. If the devil is fallen; what then is the nature of his present power?

Jesus makes it clear that the devil is the ruler of this world (John 12:31; see also Rev. 2:13) and that his kingdom has great strength (Matt. 12:26-29; Mark 3:23-27; Luke 11:18-22). In the story of the temptation of Jesus, the devil has authority over the kingdoms of this earth to give them over to whomever he pleases (Matt. 4:8-9; Luke 4:5-8). Yet to Paul, the devil's authority is also spiritual: "The god of this world has blinded the minds of the unbelievers, to keep them from seeing the light of the gospel of the glory of Christ, who is the image of God" (2 Cor. 4:4). This verse, while recognizing the awesome influence of the devil, also implies that the power of God in Christ is more glorious. Moreover, Jesus affirms the ultimate truth about the devil: that he will be judged and condemned (John 16:11).

Christians and the Government

If the beast is the Roman Empire, then the attitude in Revelation toward the government of Rome is quite hostile and seems to be at odds with the one found in other parts of the New Testament. An investigation of the relationship between the New Testament church and the Roman government should be instructive for developing a proper Christian attitude toward the state in any time period.

Although Jesus insisted that God be followed above all else, he seemed to have no hostility to the state, and he affirmed giving the emperor his due (Matt. 22:15-22; Mark 12:13-17; Luke 20:20-26). Paul thought that the governing authorities were instituted by God for the good of the citizens and therefore should receive honor, respect, and revenue (Rom. 13:1-7). Moreover, Paul took refuge from persecution with Roman officials (Acts 16:19-40) and appealed to his Roman citizenship for protection from the authorities (Acts 22:25-30). The pastorals advocated subjection to, and prayer for, kings and authorities (1 Tim. 2:1-2; Titus 3:1). Peter accepted human authority and honored the emperor (1 Pet. 2:13-17).

By John's time, however, the Roman government under Domitian was perceived to be demonic, much like the Seleucid dynasty under Antiochus IV Epiphanes in the time of Daniel (Dan. 11:20-39). Temples to the goddess Roma and to the Roman emperors had been erected in all the cities Revelation addressed, and emperor worship was enforced by local priests throughout the Roman province. This was further complicated by the fact that Christians could become wealthy participating in the commerce of Rome. No wonder John saw the beastly Roman Empire to be empowered by Satan.

Perhaps what the faithful can learn from the New Testament teaching on the Christian and the state is a proper balance reflected in the words of Jesus: "Give therefore to the emperor the things that are the emperor's, and to God the things that are God's" (Matt. 22:21; Mark 12:17; Luke 20:25). When the government functions to the benefit of its people and asks nothing the Christian cannot provide, then the faithful can support the government and even take pride in citizenship. Nevertheless, when the government is exploitive of its people and asks for the worship and exclusive allegiance of the people, it must be treated by the faithful as the arm of Satan.

The Example of Peter

In Revelation, the faithful are exhorted not to seek revenge against, or to compromise with, the persecutor. Peter serves as an example of one who tried both options and demonstrated their futility. Peter promised to remain faithful to Jesus even if it meant death (Matt. 26:33-35); nevertheless, in Gethsemene he took a sword to defend Jesus and himself (Matt. 26:51). Jesus rebuked him, speaking words very similar to Revelation 13:9-10: "All who take the sword will perish with the sword" (Matt. 26:52). After this attempt at revenge, Peter tried the option of compromise. He denied Christ and ran away (Matt. 26:69-75). When he came to his senses, he repented of his cowardice. Revelation teaches that the proper response to persecution is neither retaliation nor compromise but faithful endurance, which turns violence into victory. This is also the clear counsel of 1 Peter 2:11–4:19 to believers facing abuse (Waltner, *BCBC*, 1999, on 1 Peter: 82-154).

The False Prophet

Jesus warned his followers to beware of false prophets that would come performing signs and leading the elect astray (Matt. 7:15; 24:24; Mark 13:22; see also 2 Cor. 11:13-15; 1 John 4:1). In Revelation, the beast from the earth is identified as the archetypical false prophet, who along with the dragon and the beast from the sea compose the trinity of evil (16:13; 19:20; 20:10). The false prophet is the demonic counterpart of the third person in the holy Trinity because it carries out tasks that are counterfeit to those of the Holy Spirit, performing signs and inspiring worship (19:20; see also 2 Thess. 2:9). Peter exhorts the faithful to discern false prophets by their destructive opinions, denial of Christ, licentious ways, and greed (2 Pet. 2:1-3).

Good and Evil Signs

The signs performed by the beast from the earth to cause persons to worship the beast from the sea are a parody of the signs performed by Christ's faithful followers (2 Cor. 12:12; Rev. 11:5-6). The New Testament church witnessed sorcerers like these (Acts 13:6-12; 16:16; 19:13-20; Did. 16:3-4), who, like the magicians of Pharaoh, used signs to prove divine power (Exod. 7:11, 22; 8:7; Acts 2:19; 2 Cor. 10-13 [13:1-5]; 2 Thess. 2:9; Heb. 2:14; 2 Esd. 5:4; Asc. Isa. 4:10; Sib. Or. 3:63-70). Yet the Law cautions that even prophets promising "omens or portents" that actually come true may be testing one's allegiance to God (Deut. 13:1-3). Furthermore, Jesus warns that false messiahs and prophets will perform such signs (Matt. 24:24; Mark 13:22), and Paul says the lawless one will have similar powers (2 Thess. 2:9-10). Jesus cautions that not everyone who does signs is of God, but only those who do the will of God (Matt. 7:21-23). In Revelation the faithful saints are called to be vigilant in discriminating between the signs from God and those from the false prophet of Satan.

THE TEXT IN THE LIFE OF THE CHURCH

The Demonic State

The New Testament instructs the faithful to give government the allegiance that is its due. Indeed, Romans 13 indicates that such authorities are instituted by God. Yet Revelation 13 stresses that governments demanding allegiance due only to God are demonic. Rowland reminds readers that these demands can be subtle:

> In John's vision, the task of the beast that arises out of the land is to persuade ordinary people that what they see in the first beast is normal and admirable, so that any deviation or counterculture is regarded as strange and anti-social and, therefore, to be repudiated. John's vision helps to unmask these processes and is a pointed reminder of the ease with which the powers of evil can seduce us. Despite the widespread assumption that it was evil men like Hitler, Stalin, and Pol Pot and their supporters who were responsible for crimes against humanity, they would not have been able to commit atrocities without the tacit support of ordinary people (including many Christians), who kept their noses clean, maintained a low profile, and avoided at all costs being seen as "political." (1998:660)

More specifically, when the state demands that citizens carry out violent activities that are contrary to the law of God, the faithful will refuse and even resist. Speaking of human government, Wilcock declares:

> [The saints] will not take up the sword to overthrow it.... But neither will they worship at its shrine, and be swayed by its talk of "patriotism," and give it "the clerical blessing it so much desires." They reserve the right to criticize, and to discern continually between the state functioning properly *under* divine authority, and the state acting illegitimately *as* divine authority." (1975:124)

Yoder makes the important point that this refusal to take up the sword is not a strategy to manage or transform the demonic state but to renounce worthy goals when they cannot be attained by peaceful means:

> The point is not that one can attain all of one's legitimate ends without using violent means. It is rather that our readiness to renounce our legitimate ends whenever they cannot be attained by legitimate means itself constitutes our participation in the triumphant suffering of the Lamb. (1972:244)

The Powers

Wink (see especially 1992:3-10) contributes to an understanding of the two beasts by insisting that the powers of this world are not merely spiritual beings but real political entities (the United States, Russia, etc.), economic systems (capitalism, socialism, communism, etc.) and cultural ideals (the American Dream, male supremacy, etc.). The demonic spirituality of the Roman Empire of the first century was emanating from a real political institution. Indeed, Satan and his beasts have power only as they embody themselves in individuals or institutions. The spirituality of institutions implies that they can be redeemed: institutions were good but are fallen and need redemption. The demonic Roman Empire and the powers of racism, sexism, militarism, and materialism can be conquered by the faithful.

Wink argues that the ancient world and the biblical writers understand the physical and spiritual to be equally real. Each earthly phenomenon has a spiritual counterpart. The dragon represents Satan, guardian angels represent churches and persons, beasts represent empires, and the New Jerusalem represents the people of God. The powers have both physical and spiritual dimensions. This ancient view was supplanted by gnosticism's focus on the spiritual and denial of the physical as evil, false, and corrupt. Many Christians today evidence a modern variation of this view when they assume that the powers are spiritual beings alone. The modern world, however, offers another view, informed by enlightenment materialism that denies the spiritual, regarding it as projection and illusion. Spiritual powers are ignored as prescientific, and the world is represented as dominated by what can be seen and felt. A third option is represented by theologians in the modern world who preserve the spiritual world in a materialist context by assuming that there are both physical and spiritual realms but that they are totally unrelated and do not interact. This view, the position of theological liberalism, protects the religious from the challenge of the sciences. Wink argues for another position that adapts the ancient worldview of the Bible to the modern world. He argues that all phenomena have both an inner spiritual and an outer physical aspect.

Wink's model has enormous implications for understanding the symbols of Revelation. The war in heaven in chapter 12 is both the conflict between the spiritual powers of God and Satan in heaven, and between the faithful and the Roman Empire on earth. The beast from the sea is both a spiritual force against the soul of the saints, and the Roman government or the oppressive government of Russia or America—or any regime that takes on demonic force. The beast from the earth is both a spiritual prophet bent on the destruction of souls, and the Roman religious propagandists for the empire or even pro-pagandists for nuclear armaments or the oppression of minorities and women. The demonic powers of Revelation are both frighteningly physical and alarmingly spiritual.

The Two-Sides of Nonviolence

The paradoxical poetic statement of verse 10 seems to reject violence as an option for responding to oppression. Allan Boesak, speaking of nonviolence from a South African perspective, finds "no justification in the biblical message for the use of violence" and agrees with the early church when it refused "to participate in the emperor's military," saying: "It is not lawful for me to fight." Nevertheless, he questions the hypocrisy of advocating nonviolence to the Latin American and African struggles for liberation but "not the violence of the 'just war.'" He insists on applying the "condemnation of the use of violence" to German and U.S. armies as much as to African revolutionaries:

> Again, I do not say that their interpretation is necessarily wrong, but I do protest against the simple, pietistic exegesis which prescribes non-vio-lence for one group of Christians while saying not a word about the vio-lence of those who have forgotten what it means to be oppressed, and who in their own history have never hesitated to take up arms. (1987:102)

The Mark of the Beast

Throughout history, rulers have demanded allegiance that should only be given to God by requiring their subjects to wear a mark similar to that spoken of in Revelation. When the sixteenth-century Anabaptists were confronted by church rulers who forbade them to be rebaptized and penalized such actions with death, they viewed themselves to be "devoured by the awful beast which rose up out of the sea" (van Braght, 1950:450). During an interrogation aimed at making him reveal who had baptized him, Hans de Vette told his accuser: "John's Revelation speaks of a beast, which rose up out of the sea; you may belong to that race" (621). Moreover, Hans Vermeersch viewed receiving the sacrament of the church to be receiving the mark of the beast and exhorted God's elect to refuse it (631-32).

In more recent years, Nazis branded prisoners on the wrists with a number, and Boesak reports that, in a similar manner, the South African Defense Force branded the hands of township residents with indelible ink to indicate that through interrogation they were found not guilty of illegal acts (1987:103-104). Revelation prepares the faithful by reminding them that if they resist giving ultimate allegiance to rulers they may suffer and even face martyrdom.

Gematria

The explanatory notes argue that the number 666 may be understood through the use of gematria, a practice common at the time Revelation was written (see tables 2 and 3). Yet the practice has also been used in one form or another to the present. In the early centuries of the Christian era, the Sibylline Oracles used gematria on the Greek name of Jesus *(iēsous)*, computing as follows: i (10) + ē (8) + s (200) + o (70) + u (400) + s (200) = 888 (Sib. Or. 1:324-30; see Table 2. Greek Numerals in Notes above). Using this practice, initials of emperors from Julius to Vespasian total 666: K(Caesar), S(Sebastos/Augustus), T(Tiberius), G(Gaius/Caligula), K(Claudius), N(Nero), G(Galba), O(Oespasianos/ Vespasian) (see Sib. Or. 5:12-50). Moreover, a particular abbreviated combination of Domitian's titles from coins, Imperator Caesar Domitianus Augustus Germanicus *(Autokrator Kaisar Dometianus Sebastos Gernamicus*—a kai domet seb ge), has been calculated to total 666. In a similar manner, the name of Gaios Kaisar adds up to the variant 616. Considering a word rather than names, *deny (arnoume)*, in Greek adds to 666. The uninitiated person can very quickly verify these calculations using the Greek numeral system (see table 2). Omitting all other letters and using the common u = v equivalent, the Roman numerals in the name *Vicarivs Filii Dei* (The Vicar of the Son of God), a Latin designation for the pope, adds up to 666 (Sanders, 1918:96).

Gematria is even used today to arrive at popular conclusions about the number 666. Boyer reports a simple identification associated with the fact that each of the names of Ronald Wilson Reagan had six letters, and further notes that Reagan changed the street number of his California mansion from 666 to 668 (1992:276). Using multiples of the number 6 to let a = 6, b = 12, c = 18, d = 24, and so forth, the writer Church found "Mark of Beast," "sun" and "moon," "people" and "sin," "New York City," "computer," and several combinations of words related to the devil and hell to add up to 666 (in van Impe, 1983:115-16). Such a scheme used during World War II made a = 100, b = 101, c = 102, d = 103, and so on; with those equivalencies, the name "Hitler" adds up to 666 (Barclay, 1969:2.131). One of my students simply took the alphabet backwards, assigning z = 100, y = 101, x = 102, w =103, and so on, finding that my name, "Yeatts," works out to 666. I trust the reader sees the absurdity of this practice.

Revelation 14:1-20

Interlude of Encouragement

PREVIEW

Chapter 14 brings encouragement in the midst of tribulation (see Isa. 10:33–11:11; Joel 2:32; Mic. 4:6-7; 2 Esd. 2:42-48). These alternating themes of encouragement and tribulation, found throughout Revelation, keep before the reader the ultimate bliss of the faithful saints who overcome persecution. Chapters 12–13 focus on the dragon and the beast, chapter 14 on God and the Lamb. A slightly different way of looking at the context is to view chapter 12 as Christ's conflict and victory over Satan in heaven, chapter 13 as the earthly parallel struggle with the demonic forces of evil on earth, and chapter 14 as the final victory of the faithful over their earthly persecutors. Boring says that chapters 12–13 "let us see how things presently *are*" with Satan and the beast in charge, while chapter 14 "let[s] us see how things *finally* are" in the hands of God and the Lamb (1989:168). Wall's words capture this idea:

> Every single item of John's account of his vision is a deliberate contrast to what he has just described as the reign of evil in chapter 13: the oppression has been exchanged for liberation, evil for good, suffering for celebration. John's explanation of his vision, then, establishes the conditions for the eschatological reversal of history's painful circumstances. (1991:178)

Similar contrasts occur within chapter 14 itself. The announcement of the bliss of the 144,000 with the Lamb on Mt. Zion (vv. 1-4) is followed by the wrath of God on those who worship the beast (vv. 6-11), and the blessed rest of the saints (vv. 12-13) is closely trailed by the fate of the unfaithful in the great wine press of the wrath of God (vv. 14-20). Moreover, the contrast is continued in the chapters that follow: the hosts worshiping God in heaven (15:1-5) are contrasted with the pouring out of the seven bowls of God's wrath on the inhabitants of the earth (15:6-16:21).

These contrasts confront the reader with a choice between following the beast or being faithful to the Lamb. Peterson summarizes this choice quite well:

> We choose: we follow the dragon and his beasts along their parade route, conspicuous with the worship of splendid images, elaborated [sic] in mysterious symbols, fond of statistics, taking on whatever role is necessary to make a good show and get the applause of the crowd in order to get access to power and become self-important. Or we follow the Lamb along a farmyard route, worshiping the invisible, listening to the foolishness of preaching, practicing a holy life that involves heroically difficult acts that no one will ever notice, in order to become, simply, our eternal selves in an eternal city. It is the difference, politically, between wanting to use the people around us to become powerful (or, if unskillful, getting used by them), and entering into covenants with the people around us so that the power of salvation extends into every part of the neighborhood, the society, and the world that God loves. (1988:132-33)

Such a choice is continuously before the reader of Revelation.

Chapter 14 echoes other portions of Revelation as well. The vision of the Lamb on Mt. Zion in verses 1-5 reminds the reader of the vision of the Lamb and the Scroll (ch. 5) and anticipates the New Jerusalem (21:1–22:5). In verses 6-11, angels announce the eventual fall of Babylon (chs. 17–18) and foreshadow the rider on the white horse who comes to make war and judge (19:11-16).

However the passage fits into the structure of Revelation, the setting of chapter 14 is in heaven with the Lamb and his faithful followers, who have emerged victorious from tribulation. The chapter begins with the vision of the faithful upheld by the Lamb, continues with an announcement to fear and worship God, and ends with the fearful and glorious coming of the Son of Man. These sections should encourage the faithful in their resistance of Satan and the beast with the knowledge that the Lamb will be present to strengthen them and that catastrophes will not ultimately harm them. Indeed, in the end, the followers of the beast will, like their master, be destroyed; and the faithful will, through their persecution, complement Christ's work in redeeming the world.

OUTLINE

The Lamb and the 144,000, 14:1-5
Three Angelic Voices, 14:6-13
The Harvest and the Wine Press, 14:14-20

EXPLANATORY NOTES

The Lamb and the 144,000 14:1-5

The first vision in chapter 14 is of the faithful supported by the Lamb, their reward for a consistent witness in persecution. It is contrasted to the fate of the beast worshipers in the preceding chapter, who renounce their commitment to God. Thus, the passage encourages God's people to resist their enemies through the Lamb, who gives them strength.

John opens the chapter with the words *Then I looked*, which adds dramatic effect to the passage (4:1; 6:2, 5; 7:9; 14:14; 19:17). When John looked, *there was the Lamb, standing on Mt. Zion!* The Lamb Christ, who finds a place by the heavenly crystal sea (15:2), is contrasted to the beastly antichrist, who stood on the sand of the earthly sea (17:1-8). Moreover, while the Lamb resides on the mountain, the beast's abode is the bottomless pit (11:7; 17:8).

Various interpretations have been given for Mount Zion. Walvoord believes it is the site of the earthly millennial reign, not the heavenly eternal reward (1966:213-14; see also Krodel, 1989:260-61). Instead of an earthly location, Harrington sees Zion as the "heavenly counterpart of earthly Jerusalem" (1993:147; see also Heb. 12:22). Schüssler Fiorenza says that Zion is neither in heaven nor earth but "an eschatological place of protection and liberation" (1991:87). Other interpreters take Zion symbolically to mean the "salvation community" (Roloff, 1993:170; Wilcock, 1975:132; see also John 4:20-24; Eph. 2:6), or the victory of the saints (Ladd, 1972:189). The location of the Lamb is most likely on the heavenly Zion, which indicates his firm foundation in the spiritual realm (see TBC, Mount Zion).

With the Lamb on Mt. Zion *were one hundred forty-four thousand.* Probably the same 144,000 as were sealed from the twelve tribes in chapter 7, they are contrasted with the followers of the beast in chapter 13. In both places the 144,000 is best understood as the faithful symbolic Israel (see TBC on ch. 7: The Symbolic Israel). Schüssler Fiorenza calls them "the community of the Lamb"

(1991:88). If that is the case, then the meaning of the passage is that the faithful share in the Lamb's victory.

The 144,000 *had his name and his father's name written on their foreheads.* This engraving most likely refers to the "seal of the living God" (3:12; 7:2; 9:4) and is contrasted with the mark on the foreheads of the followers of the beast (13:16-17). To have God's name on one's forehead is to be consecrated to serve God (3:12; 22:4); to bear the beast's counter-image is to be devoted to the service of Satan.

Then John *heard a voice from heaven like the voice of many waters.* Such a voice is a common element of the visions of Revelation (1:10; 4:1; 10:4, 8; 11:12; 12:10; 14:13; 18:4; see also 16:1, 17; 21:3). The comparison to many waters should remind the reader of powerful waves crashing against the shore (Barclay, 1960:2.136; see also Ezek. 1:24; 43:2; Rev. 1:15; 19:6). The power of the voice from heaven, presumably the voice of God, is highlighted.

The voice was also *like the sound of loud thunder.* This image is associated with the presence of God in Revelation (4:5; 8:5; 11:19; 16:18; 19:6; see also Ezek. 1:24; Rev. 6:1). Barclay argues that the metaphor means that the voice of God is unavoidable and unmistakable (1960:2.136). More specifically, thunder is almost always associated with the judgment of God.

Yet the voice from heaven *was like the sound of harpists playing on their harps.* In Revelation, harps are associated with heavenly temple music (5:8-12; 15:2-4). Although the voice of God is terrible in its judgments, this image reminds the faithful that it also soothes their troubled spirits, a characteristic of music, especially that produced by harps.

When the harpists play, the faithful 144,000 *sing a new song before the throne and before the four living creatures and before the elders.* The new blessing in God's deliverance of the faithful requires a new response of gratitude in the recipients of that blessing as they break forth in song (Exod. 15:1-18; Ps. 33:1-3; 40:1-3; 96:1-3; 98:1; 144:9-11; Isa. 42:10; Rev. 5:9-13; 7:14-17; 15:3-4). The point is that those faithful in tribulation will be delivered by God, and this passage is an expression of their gratitude for that salvation.

Regarding the new song, John states: *No one can learn that song except the 144,000.* This parallels the name that no one could know (2:17; 19:12) and carries with it the idea of mystery (17:5, 7; 1 Cor. 2:6-9). The faithful servants of God are given the ability to understand and rejoice over the mystery of their deliverance (10:7).

It is significant that the 144,000 *have been redeemed from the earth* because it indicates that the group is not limited to Jews but includes all humanity. The word *redeemed* means "purchased" or "ransomed" (5:9-10) and refers to the faithful who have been purchased from slavery to the beast (13:4, 17). The faithful are not removed from the earth but are separated from its influence by the redemption of the Lamb of God (John 17:15).

One of the most difficult passages in Revelation states: the redeemed 144,000 are *those who have not defiled themselves with women, for they are virgins.* Although the word *virgin* means one who has never engaged in sexual intercourse, it is also used for those who are chaste (2 Cor. 11:2; cf. Aune, 1998a:811-12). The most clear parallel to this symbol in Revelation is the bride of Christ the Lamb, who must be a virgin (19:7-8; 21:2-9). Although the defilement spoken of may have its source in the Levitical requirements (Lev. 15:16-21), its primary referent in Revelation is to having relations with the great whore (17:1-2; see also 2:20-23).

The literal interpretation of virginity has been affirmed in several ways. First, in the second and third centuries, believers sometimes were married spiritually but not physically. The present passage may be advocating this practice for a select group of faithful Christians. Second, virginity may be referring to the sexual abstinence temporarily required for fighting in holy wars (Deut. 20:1-9; 23:9-11; 1 Sam. 21:5; 2 Sam. 11:11). The meaning would be that the conflict with Rome is a holy war, so participants should abstain from sexual relations. The implication that the virgins are male in this passage would be consistent with this interpretation. Third, the passage may allude to intercourse with temple prostitutes. On this view, the interpretation is literal, but the meaning is metaphorical referring to the apostasy that such intercourse with pagan religions entails. The fourth and most likely literal interpretation is that the passage is advocating celibacy, a practice seemingly exalted above marriage by both Jesus and Paul (Matt. 10:37-38; 19:10-12; Luke 14:26-27; 18:29; 1 Cor. 7:1-7; see also Barclay 1960:2.139 on the Acts of Paul and Thecla 11 and Acts of the Martyrs 12th Apoc. 304) and advocated by early Christians. Indeed, Marcion established a church of celibates, and Origen castrated himself to ensure celibacy. Such celibacy grew out of the idea that commitment to Christ should supersede all other attachments. It should be noted, however, that celibacy was never required of all Christians (Murphy, 1998:316).

Nevertheless, although a literal interpretation is possible, the metaphorical is more likely (see Lam. 2:10 LXX, Philo, *On the Cherubim* 49-50; *On the Posterity of Cain and His Exile* 134; *Questions and Answers on Genesis* 4.95, 99; *on Exodus* 2.3, 46).

The metaphorical meaning is reinforced both by the fact that nowhere else in scripture are sexual relations referred to as defilement (see 1 Tim. 4:3; cf. 1 Cor. 7; see also TBC, Virgins) and that the passage is limited to male virginity. So the reference is to spiritual virginity—faithfulness, obedience, and holiness (Matt. 5:8; Mark 7:20-23). The 144,000 are virgins in that they remain faithful by avoiding the idolatrous practices of the whore Babylon (Rev. 14:8; 17:1-6; 18:3, 9; 19:2). The meaning is that those who are faithful to Christ must abstain from social intercourse with the world and its beastly representative.

These virgins *follow the Lamb wherever he goes*. The virgins are the holy counterpart of those who follow the beast (13:3). The present tense connotes that it is the character of the virgin saints to continuously follow the Lamb, to do what the Lamb does rather than turning aside to follow the beast. There is irony here that, although sheep are known for their ability to follow (John 10:1-6), here the Lamb is the one followed. Moreover, the Lamb serves as a model for the saints in his faithful discipleship unto death.

The followers of the Lamb *have been redeemed from humankind as first fruits for God and the Lamb*. The symbol has its basis in the Old Testament sacrificial ritual where the first fruits belonged to God and represented the entire harvest (Exod. 23:19; 34:22; Lev. 23:9-21; Num. 28:26; Deut. 26:1-11; Neh. 10:35-37; Prov. 3:9; Jer. 2:3). The image is applied here to Jesus, whose resurrection was the first fruits of the dead (1 Cor. 15:20-23). When the faithful share in the suffering of Christ, they complete the harvest Christ began (Matt. 10:38; Mark 8:34; Jas. 1:18).

Because the redeemed were the first fruits, *in their mouth no lie was found; they are blameless*. Lying, the chief characteristic of the devil, the beast, and their false prophets (Isa. 9:15; Jer. 14:14; 20:6; 23:25-32; 27:8-22; 29:21; Zech 13:3) and followers (Rom. 1:24-25; Rev. 21:8, 27; 22:15) is not found in the followers of God and the Lamb (Ps. 32:2; Isa. 53:9; Zeph. 3:9, 12-13; 1 Pet. 2:22). The saints are, indeed, to emulate Christ the Lamb by being faithful (Eph. 1:4; 5:25-27; Phil. 2:15; Col. 1:22; 1 John 1:5-10; 3:5-6; Jude 24; Rev. 14:5) and therefore a ceremonially pure offering to God (Exod. 12:5; Lev. 23:12; Heb. 9:13-14; 1 Pet. 1:19).

Three Angelic Voices 14:6-13

Following the vision of the Lamb and the 144,000 virgins on Mt. Zion is a series of three visions, each introduced by different angels speaking with loud voices and announcing, in turn, an eternal gospel, the fall of Babylon, and the eternal torment of fire and sulfur.

John begins the section with the words: *Then I saw another angel flying in midheaven.* The use of angels to announce judgment is common in Revelation, especially in the trumpet sequence (chs. 8–9; 11:15-19; see also 10:1) and in the chapter under consideration where six such angels appear (vv. 6, 8, 9, 15, 17, 18). Yet it is not clear to what previous angel *another* refers here because there is no clear referent in preceding material. Perhaps the word is simply used to be consistent with the five other occurrences of *another angel* in the chapter.

The angel in midheaven had with him *an eternal gospel to proclaim to those who live in the earth—to every nation and tribe and language and people.* The word *eternal* occurs only here in Revelation, but it is used frequently in other Johannine writings, where it is connected with *life* (John 3:15-16, 36; 4:14, 36; 1 John 1:2; 2:25). The meaning is that the gospel is permanently valid (Friedrich, *TDNT* 2.735). The eternal gospel of Christ the Lamb is contrasted with the temporary rule of the emperor, which was also called good news in contemporary writings (Sweet, 1990: 225; Ford, 1975:247). Although this is the only occurrence in Johannine literature of the noun *gospel* (the verbal form occurs here also and in 10:7), it is elsewhere associated with the words of Christ addressed to sinners who repent (Mark 1:15; Acts 14:15; see also John 3:16; 2 Thess 1:9-10; 1 Tim. 1:15). Moreover, Jesus connects the spread of the gospel with the coming of the end (Matt. 24:14; Mark 13:9-13).

The angel then *said in a loud voice: "Fear God and give him glory for his hour of judgment has come."* The context indicates that this command is given to those who dwell on the earth (v. 6), the beast worshipers (v. 9). It is a call for them to fear God and repent in order to avoid the judgment that will be described in verses 8-11 (see also Matt. 3:1-2; Mark 1:14-15; Luke 12:4-5; Rev. 15:4; cf. Beale, 1999:753). Even the beast worshipers will eventually worship the One *who made heaven and earth, the sea and the springs of water.* In Revelation, the availability of water, which is essential for physical life, is associated with eternal life (7:17; 21:6; 22:17); and the desert, where that water is not available, is associated with spiritual death (12:6, 14; 17:3). Thus, the ecological preservation of God's creation is, in this passage, related closely to spiritual salvation.

The next vision of this section is introduced with the words: *Then another angel, a second, followed, saying, "Fallen, fallen is Babylon the great!* The fall of Babylon is repeated seven times in Revelation (14:8; 16:17-21; 17:1-18; 18:1-3, 4-8, 9-20, 21-24) and is described in detail in chapters 17–18. Babylon is first mentioned in the Bible as Babel, the archetypical expression of human pride in opposition to God (Gen. 11:1-9; see also 10:10). Interestingly, this is the first mention of Babylon in Revelation (11:8; see also 1 Pet. 5:13). Babylon was the first great empire to destroy Jerusalem and its temple in 586 B.C. In Revelation, Babylon symbolizes Rome, the second empire to accomplish the same abomination in A.D. 70 (2 Esd. 3:28-31; 2 Bar. 10:1-3; 11:1; 67:7; Sib. Or. 5:143-59). Not surprisingly, Babylon becomes symbolic of all great evil forces arrayed against the people of God. The prophets announce the fall of Babylon (Isa. 21:9-10; 24:19-20; Jer. 50:2; 51:6-10; 2 Bar. 13; Sib. Or. 5:434-46). Later, Babylon the Great had a major role in the apocalyptic writings of both Daniel and Revelation (Dan. 4:28-33; Rev. 14:8; 17:1–18:24). So certain is the demise of Babylon that its fall is spoken of here as a completed action (Fekkes, 1994:88).

The reason given for the fall of Babylon is: *She has made all nations drink of the wine of the wrath of her fornication.* Divine punishment is often described as the wicked drinking the wrath of God (Job 21:20; Ps. 75:8; Isa. 51:17-23; Jer. 25:15-29; 51:6-7; Rev. 16:19; 18:6; 19:15), an image thought by some to be inconsistent with the biblical picture of divine love. Yet God's wrath is the natural result of evil actions; those who resist the eternal gospel by refusing to repent bring God's wrath upon themselves (Wis. Sol. 11:16; 12:23). *Fornication* here symbolizes the seductive influence of materialism and sensuality best exemplified in Israel's Queen Jezebel (2 Kings 9:22; Isa. 1:21; 23:16-17; Nah. 3:4; Rev. 17:1-6). Because Rome seduced nations with her wealth and pleasures, she called down the wrath of God upon herself. It should be noted that *wine* also symbolizes the blood of the saints (Rev. 17:2, 6), who, in contrast, are pure and without blame. The nations are punished for their persecution of God's faithful people, who are vindicated by God's judgments. So the wrath of God is not so much an emotional outpouring of divine vengeance as a display of divine justice.

The final vision of this section is introduced by the words: *Then another angel, a third, followed them crying with a loud voice, "Those who worship the beast and its image, and receive a mark on their foreheads and on their hands, they will also drink the wine of God's wrath, poured unmixed into the cup of his anger."* This command not to worship the beast is a serious warning against those who become unfaithful in the face of persecution (Eph. 2:1-3; Rev. 3:8-10). That the wine is unmixed means that the wrath of God is full strength and undiluted (Aune, 1998a:833). The word *wrath (thymos),* used often in Revelation (14:10, 19; 15:1, 7; 16:1, 19; 19:15) but only once elsewhere in the New Testament for God's wrath (Rom. 2:8), is passionate rage. *Anger (orgē),* the more frequently used word, is more tempered and controlled. The presence of both in this passage intensifies the reality. The wrath of God in the bowl judgments of chapters 15–16 has the redemptive purpose of purging the seductive materialism of Babylon (John 3:36; Rom. 1:18; 3:5-6; 12:19; Col. 3:6) before the kingdom of chapters 20–22 can come in its fullness (Ps. 9:7-8; 110:5-7).

The judgment of those who worship the beast is that *they will be tormented with fire and sulfur in the presence of the holy angels and in the presence of the Lamb.* Sulfur makes a hot, persistent fire that burns "with peculiarly acrid and noxious fumes" (Metzger, 1993:78). If *holy angels* is a designation for God (Beasley-Murray, 1974:226; see Matt. 10:32-33; Mark 8:38; Luke 12:8-9; Heb. 4:13), the punishment of those who worship the beast is observed by God and the Lamb. Other writings indicate that the righteous will be among those who watch (2 Thess. 1:7-10; 2 Esd.7:35-38, 76-87; 1 Enoch 27:2-4; 48:9; 90:26-27; 2 Bar. 30:4). If so, in a significant reversal of fortunes, Christians observe the torment of their persecutors.

From the fire, *the smoke of their torment goes up for ever and ever.* This is certainly an allusion to the burning of Sodom and Gomorrah (Gen. 19:28; Jude 7) and, in Revelation, of Babylon (19:3). It is contrasted to the incense smoke of the continuous worship of heaven (19:3) and of the prayers of the saints (5:8; 8:4). In Hebrew thought, *forever and ever* means "aeons of aeons" and may not mean "everlasting" but merely an indefinitely long time (Rev. 4:9; 15:7). In the torment, *[t]here is no rest day or night for those who worship the beast and its image and for anyone who receives the mark of its name.* This is a parody of the scene in heaven where unceasing praise to God is sung (4:8), and it contrasts to the experience of those who die in the Lord (14:13). While the unfaithful are in constant torment, the saints rest from their tribulations.

The torment is *a call for the endurance of the saints.* The saints, who instead "will reign for ever and ever" (22:5), are not to gloat over the eventual fate of the wicked but to remain faithful until their vindication comes (6:9-11). In a letter to Governor Pliny of Bithynia in Asia Minor, Emperor Trajan said: Christians who deny "that they are Christians, and make the fact plain by their actions [that is, by worshiping Roman gods] shall obtain pardon" (*Letter* 10.96). Schüssler Fiorenza says: "In contrast, the threat of eternal punishment made in Revelation warns Christians and non-Christians alike not to worship idols and not to participate in the imperial cult" (1991:90). The saint's faithfulness is a witness to a doomed world (Caird, 1966:188).

Specifically, the saints who endure are *those who keep the commandments of God and hold fast to the faith of Jesus,* bringing into focus obedience and loyalty (12:17). In Revelation, the word *faith* is rare and always means "faithfulness" (2:13, 19; 13:9-10; 14:12). Eternal torment, the price of apostasy, is far worse than the temporary suffering associated with obedience and faithfulness (Mounce, 1977:277).

After the call for endurance, a beatitude follows: *And I heard a voice from heaven saying, "Write this: Blessed are the dead who from now on die in the Lord."* The meaning of *from now on* is somewhat ambiguous (John 13:19; 14:7). It may carry the sense of either "soon" (Wall, 1991:187; see Matt. 23:39; 26:64) or "assuredly" (Beasley-Murray, 1974:227). It is also not certain to what the phrase should be connected: it seems to mean that those who die from now on are blessed, but Morris may be correct to take it to mean that the *rest for labor* is from now on (1969:183). The beatitude at least means that those who are faithful in persecution will receive rest.

This beatitude, one of seven in Revelation (1:3; 16:15; 19:9; 20:6; 22:7, 14), indicates, ironically, that those who die in the Lord are the truly blessed. Specifically, for the ones who are faithful, death is not a tragedy but a blessing that brings rest from the labors of enduring persecution. Indeed, such a death bears witness to the death and resurrection of Christ (Rom. 8:18; 1 Thess. 4:13-18; Rev. 1:18). The more specific nature of the blessedness of those who die in the Lord is in the words that follow: *"Yes," says the Spirit, "they will rest from their labors...."* Labor here is the toil and tribulation associated with following the Lamb (Rev. 2:2). This rest of the faithful (Matt. 11:28; Heb. 4:3, 9-10) comes in answer to the prayers of the saints (Rev. 6:9-11) and contrasts with the beast worshipers, who have no rest (Rev. 14:11).

The reason the faithful are able to rest is that *their deeds follow them.* Although the New Testament is often thought to exalt faith and grace over deeds and works, Jesus emphasizes acts of service (Matt. 25:31-46; Luke 6:35), and Revelation stresses faithfulness rather than faith, endurance rather than assurance, and obedience rather than grace (2:13; 3:8, 15; 14:4; 20:12-13; see also 1 Cor. 15:58; 2 Esd. 7:77; 1 Enoch 38:2; 41:1; 2 Bar. 14:12). Barclay says that Revelation is concerned with character instead of deeds (1960:2.150; see also Prov. 16:2; 21:2), but that is not consistent with Revelation's consistent reference to deeds. Mounce is probably more correct to assert that there is no real separation between character and actions (1977:278). The point of the passage is that faithfulness is more important than life (2 Cor. 5:6-8; Phil. 1:21-24) and unfaithfulness more tragic than death (Rom. 8:38-39).

The Harvest and the Wine Press 14:14-20

Two more angels announce visions (see Joel 3:9-14), the first a grain harvest (vv. 14-16; see also Isa. 63:1-6; Hos. 6:11) and the second a wine press (vv. 17-20; see also Jer. 51:33; Lam. 1:15). The former is the harvest of the faithful, and the latter the reaping of the unfaithful. This section contains parallels to Jesus' parables (Matt. 13:24-30, 36-43, 47-50; Mark 4:26-29) and the synoptic apocalypse (Matt. 24:31; Mark 13:26-27).

As the vision begins, John says: *Then I looked, and there was a white cloud.* In the scriptures, clouds are the vehicle of travel for God (Ps. 18:11-12; 104:3; Matt. 17:5) and Christ (Acts 1:9-10). In Revelation, the two witnesses go up into heaven on a cloud (11:12), and here Christ comes to judge on a white cloud. Moreover, white is the color of Christ and his followers (19:11, 14). At the parousia, Christ is expected to come on the clouds (Mark 13:25-27; 14:62; Acts 1:11; Rev. 1:7).

As the vision continues, *seated on the cloud was one like the Son of Man,* a common eschatological symbol of salvation in Daniel and Johannine literature (Dan. 7:13-14; 8:15-18; 10:16-21; John 5:27-29; Rev. 1:13; see also 2 Esd. 13; 1 Enoch 46:2-4). Some argue that the Son of Man is the seventh angel in chapter 14 (vv. 6, 8, 9, 14, 15, 17, 18; see also Dan. 8:15-17; 10:16, 18). Slater mentions that *Son of Man* may "describe heavenly beings in human likeness," "be a symbol of the faithful," or designate an archangel—Gabriel or Michael (1999:69-70, 72-74). Yet it seems better to take the Son of Man to be Christ rather than an angel, because in the New Testament the designation is never used of an angel, and it would be strange for Christ to be commissioned to reap by an angel (Matt. 13:37, 41, 49), even a messenger from God (Murphy 1998:327). Moreover, in similar passages in Revelation, Christ is clearly in mind (1:7, 13, 16; 19:11-16; see Dan. 7:13-14; Mark 13:26; 14:62).

The one like a son of man came *with a golden crown on his head, and a sharp sickle in his hand.* This is the victor's crown *(stephanos)* given to the one who conquers through suffering and martyrdom (Rev. 12:11). The *sickle* is a harvest tool, which symbolizes the role of a judge (Joel 3:13-14; Matt. 3:12; Mark 4:29; Luke 3:17; Rev. 3:21).

Another angel came out of the temple, calling with a loud voice to the one who sat on the cloud. That this angel comes from the temple indicates that he comes from God's presence to instruct Christ to harvest the earth (Isa. 17:5; Jer. 51:33; Matt. 13:30; Mark 4:29) and that only God knows the time of the judgment (Mark 13:27, 32-37; Acts 1:7; Rev. 6:9-11).

Then the angel told the one on the cloud: *Use your sickle and reap, for the hour to reap has come, because the harvest of the earth is fully ripe.* That the earth is ripe means that it is the right moment for judgment. Some argue that the harvest is the judgment of the wicked (Isa. 63:3-6; Jer. 51:33; Ezek. 15:6; Matt. 13:36-43; 2 Bar. 70:2). Yet it seems more consistent with the imagery to take the harvest as the gathering of the faithful into heaven (Hos. 6:11; Matt. 9:37-38; Mark 4:26-29; 13:26-27; Luke 10:2; Rev. 14:4; 2 Esd. 4:35). The word for harvest or reaping *(therismos/theridzō)* is never used in the Septuagint for mowing down enemies (Caird, 1966:190). Therefore, the harvest of the faithful for reward contrasts with the wine press of judgment on the unfaithful.

The passage ends with the words: *So the one who sat on the cloud swung his sickle over the earth, and the earth was reaped.* No details regarding the reaping are given; only its certainty is really important.

The wine press imagery seems to change the focus from the faithful to the wicked. Caird argues that the passage describes the death of the martyrs (1966:192-93). While it is true that divine judgment comes in answer to the prayers of the martyrs for salvation, it is difficult to see the imagery of this passage to refer to the righteous.

The vintage begins with another angel who is virtually identical to the angel of the wheat harvest: *Then another angel came out of the temple in heaven, and he too had a sharp sickle.* This angel also comes from the presence of God and is one of the angels associated with the sickle of judgment (Matt. 13:39-42). In a somewhat puzzling image, the sickle here is used in a harvest of grapes (Joel 3:13).

The reader is told: *Then another angel came out from the altar, the angel who has authority over fire, and he called with a loud voice to him who had the sharp sickle.* This is probably the same altar on which the martyrs are offered, and this judgment is in answer to the prayers offered up as incense from this altar (6:9-11; 8:3-5). Clearly, the angel is associated with the judgment of the wicked (Isa. 63:2-6; Lam. 1:15; Joel 3:13; Matt. 18:8-9; Luke 9:54; John 15:6; 2 Thess. 1:6-8).

One of the angels tells the other: *Use your sharp sickle and gath-*

er the clusters of the vine of the earth, for its grapes are ripe."
Although the vine fairly consistently represents the people of God (Ps.
80:8-19; Isa. 5:1-10; Jer. 2:21; Lam. 1:15; Ezek. 17:1-10; 19:10-
14; Hos. 10:1; John 15:1-7), the image of the wine and grapes used
for the wicked is not without precedent (Deut. 32:32; Isa. 51:17;
63:2-6; Joel 3:13; Rev. 14:10; 18:6; 19:15). Indeed, the context
seems to require that the wine press symbolizes the punishment of the
unfaithful.

The order of the second angel is carried out by the first: *So the
angel swung his sickle over the earth and gathered the vintage of
the earth, and he threw it into the great wine press of the wrath of
God.* This task is carried out later by Christ (19:15). Elsewhere, the
punishment of the great whore, the symbol for unfaithful Babylon, is
that she drink the blood of the saints and the martyrs until she is intox-
icated (17:6; see also Jer. 51:39, 57). It is notable that *the wine press
was trodden outside the city.* The literal picture is of workers trampling grapes with their feet in a trough that led the juice away to a
basin underneath where the wine was collected. The city is most likely Jerusalem, which has often been associated with judgment (Joel
3:2; Zech. 14:1-4, 12-14; Rev. 11:8). That the wine press was trodden outside the city relates to the idea that nothing unclean could
enter the New Jerusalem (21:27), and more especially to the practice
that capital punishment was commonly administered outside the city
gates (Joel 3:12-13). Indeed, Christ, the ideal of those who suffer for
their faith, was crucified outside the city of Jerusalem (Heb. 13:12).
The implication may be that the judgment of the wicked is accomplished by the one who was also killed outside the city.

As a result of the judgment, *blood flowed from the wine press,
as high as a horse's bridle.* Instead of juice, blood flowed from the
grapes (Gen. 49:11; Deut. 32:14; see also 2 Esd. 15:35-36; 1 Enoch
100:3). This flowing of blood is a terrible contrast to the river of life
(Sweet, 1990:232; 22:1; see also Ezek. 47:1-12). The blood flowed
for a distance of about 200 miles. The number can be taken literally to denote approximately the length of Palestine. Yet not enough
people have lived on earth to supply this much blood (Eller,
1974:144). Therefore, a better meaning is derived from the literal
translation, "one thousand six hundred stadia." Four, the number of
the physical universe (7:1; 9:14-15; 20:8), squared and multiplied by
the very large number, one hundred, produces the desired 1600.
Ironically, forty, another number that when squared equals 1600, was
a traditional number for punishment (Num. 14:33; Deut. 25:3; Acts
1:3). Sixteen hundred contrasts with 144,000, the other squared

number in Revelation, which symbolizes those who are sealed from persecution by God (Rev. 7:4; 14:1). The meaning of the number used in this passage is that God will finally judge the physical world with great power.

THE TEXT IN BIBLICAL CONTEXT

Mount Zion

This is the only occurrence of Mount Zion in Revelation. Thought to be the highest of the world's mountains (Isa. 2:2; Mic. 4:1; see also Ps. 48:1-2; Ezek. 17:22), Zion is the location of the Yahweh's rule (Isa. 24:23; Mic. 4:7); the city of the great King (Ps. 2:6; 48:2), the Holy One (Isa. 60:14), and the living God (Heb. 12:22); God's residence and resting place (Ps. 132:13-18; Isa. 8:18); a sanctuary (Ps. 20:2); a holy mountain where the Messiah king comes to judge (Ps. 2:5-6; Jer. 25:30); a foundation stone (Isa. 28:16); the place of the announcement of the Day of the Lord (Joel 2:1); the source of the surviving remnant of Assyrian and Babylonian aggression (2 Kings 19:30-31; Obad. 17); and the location of the Lord's judgment and deliverance (Isa. 24:21-22; 59:20; Joel 2:32; 3:16; Zeph. 3:16-17; 2 Esd. 13:25-40; 2 Bar. 40) and eschatological reign (Ps. 146:10; 149:2; Isa. 24:23; 52:7; Obad. 21; Mic. 4:7; Zech. 14:9). For Paul, Mt. Zion contrasts with Mt. Sinai, where the law of condemnation was given (Rom. 3:20; 2 Cor. 3:7-9). Here what is in mind is the heavenly Mount Zion (Heb. 12:22-24), the place of God and the Lamb, which is contrasted with the sea abode of the serpent and the beast.

Virgins

Used often in connection with Zion (2 Kings 19:21; Isa. 37:22; Jer. 14:17; Lam. 2:13; see also Jer. 18:13; Amos 5:2), virginity, and especially its converse, prostitution and adultery, usually carry symbolic, metaphorical meanings (Exod. 34:15; Deut. 31:16; Judg. 2:17; 8:27, 33; Jer. 3:20; Ezek. 16; Hos. 1-3; 9:1). Israel is called both a virgin and a harlot (2 Kings 19:21; Jer. 3:6; 18:13; Lam. 2:13; Hos. 2:5; 5:4). The prophets viewed the Sinai covenant as marriage (Jer. 2:2-3; Hos. 2:14-20) and idolatry as adultery or fornication (Ezek. 16, 23), a theme that Paul continues (2 Cor. 11:2). In Revelation, sexual intercourse with Babylon, the great whore, symbolizes idolatry, especially that associated with materialism (Rev. 17:2, 4; 18:3, 9; see also 14:8; 19:2); and marriage represents faithfulness to God (21:2, 9; 22:17). One of the major arguments for taking virginity metaphorically in this passage is that marriage is nowhere else in scripture described as defilement, but instead is placed in high regard (Gen. 2:18-24; Matt. 19:4-6; 1 Cor. 7:4-5; Eph. 5:22-33; Heb. 13:4). The apostles married (Mark 1:30; 1 Cor. 9:5), and holiness is compared to marriage (Matt. 25:1-13; John 3:29; Eph. 5:25-27; Rev. 19:7-8; 21:2).

To Die in the Lord

The Hebrew scriptures do not include a clear picture of what happens to those who die. For example, the prophet Isaiah seems to both deny and affirm life after death:

> The dead do not live; shades do not rise—because you have punished and destroyed them, and wiped out all memory of them. (Isa. 26:14; see also 38:18-19)

> Your dead shall live, their corpses shall rise. (Isa. 26:19; see also 25:8)

Daniel presents the first clear affirmation of life after death:

> Many of those who sleep in the dust of the earth shall awake, some to everlasting life, and some to shame and everlasting contempt. Those who are wise shall shine like the brightness of the sky, and those who lead many to righteousness, like the stars forever and ever. (Dan. 12:2-3)

In the New Testament, eternal life is more clearly affirmed (John 5:24; 11:25-26). Paul asserts that humans will live eternally because Christ died and rose from death (1 Cor. 15:3-8, 12, 17-18, 20-28; Rom. 14:8-9). In addition to resurrection at the time of death, Paul teaches that Christ will return to earth to usher the faithful immediately into eternal life (1 Thess. 4:13-18). The nature of this existence is determined by the judgment of God (Rev. 20:11-15), but those who die in the Lord can be confident that they will be eternally with God and Christ (Rev. 22:1-5).

Fire and Sulfur

Yet Revelation speaks also of those who do not die in the Lord. Fire and sulfur is the traditional symbol for divine judgment in the Hebrew scriptures (Ps. 11:6; Isa. 30:33; 34:8-10; Ezek. 38:21-22), calling to mind particularly the destruction of Sodom and Gomorrah (Gen. 19:24-28; see also Deut. 29:22-24; Isa. 13:19; Jer. 50:40; Luke 17:28-30). In Revelation, the devil and the beast and their followers are all condemned to fire and sulfur by God and the Lamb (19:3, 20; 20:10, 15; 21:8; see also Mark 9:43-45; Luke 16:19-31).

Two different Greek words are translated "hell" in English versions of the Bible. The more common is *hades,* the equivalent of the Hebrew *sheol,* or the place where all the dead go to await the resurrection with no implications of torment or suffering, except in the story of the rich man and Lazarus (Luke 16:23). Yet the Greek word for hell, with a meaning closer to the "fire and sulfur" of Revelation is *gehenna,* which alludes to the valley of Hinnom, the boundary between Judah and Benjamin southwest of Jerusalem, where at times human sacrifice by fire was carried out in worship of Baal or Molech (2 Kings 16:1-4; 21:6; 23:10; 2 Chron. 28:3; 33:6; Jer. 7:31-32; 19:5-7; 32:35). It came to designate the place of fire and eternal torment (2 Esd. 7:36; 1 Enoch 27:1-2; 48:9; 54:1-6; 56:3-4; 90:26-28; 2 Bar. 59:10; 85:13-15).

Except for James's discussion of its effect on the tongue (Jas. 3:6), all occurrences of *gehenna* in the New Testament are in the words of Jesus, mostly in Matthew's gospel. The reader is warned that *gehenna* is a liability for the person who calls another a fool (Matt. 5:22), that it is better to lose an eye or hand than to be cast into *gehenna* (Matt. 5:29-30; 18:8-9; Mark 9:42-48), that Pharisees in their zeal make their converts twice as much a child of *gehenna* as they were before they were evangelized (Matt. 23:15), and that the person who can kill should not be feared as much as the one who can cast into *gehenna* (Matt. 10:28; Luke 12:5). After undiplomatically calling the scribes and Pharisees snakes and vipers, Jesus asks: "How can you escape being sentenced to hell [*gehenna*]?" (Matt. 23:33). *Gehenna* is also implied in the fire that is the destination of those who do not bear fruit (Matt. 7:19), the weeds in the parable of the sower (Matt. 13:30), the goats in the Jesus' judgment of the nations (Matt. 25:41), as well as in the outer darkness where the man with no wedding garment (Matt. 22:13) and the worthless slave in the parable of the talents (Matt. 25:30) are cast. Whether the exact nature of this punishment is fire or darkness, it causes victims to weep and gnash their teeth (Matt. 8:12; 13:42, 50; 22:13; 24:51; 25:30; Luke 13:28; see also Ps. 112:10; Sib. Or. 2:290-310).

Without using the word *gehenna,* Paul speaks of destruction from which the wicked cannot escape (1 Thess. 5:3; see also Heb. 10:27). Moreover, the second epistle of Peter warns that sinning angels will not be spared judgment of the darkness of hell, the only reference in the Bible to *tartarus,* a Greek place of punishment located below *hades* (2 Pet. 2:4). In addition, Jude announces that the inhabitants of Sodom and Gomorrah and nearby cities will suffer the punishment of eternal fire (Jude 7; cf. Charles, *BCBC,* 1999, on 2 Peter/Jude:233, 294-98).

Although not used in Revelation, the concept of *gehenna* is behind the lake of fire and sulfur (19:20; 20:10; 21:8; see also 14:10).

Universalism and Limited Salvation

Some persons insist that the intense punishment of fire and sulfur contradicts the teachings of the Bible regarding the nature of God and the fate of humanity. A loving and all-powerful God would certainly ensure that all of humanity would eventually be saved. Indeed, a variety of scriptures do seem to support universal salvation (see Boring, 1989:226-27). God promises Abraham that all the families of the earth will be blessed through him (Gen. 12:1-2). The psalmist indicates that all nations shall come, bow down, and glorify God (Ps. 86:9). The prophet Isaiah speaks of all nations streaming into Zion (Isa. 2:2-4) and all people seeing the glory of God (Isa. 40:5) and sharing an eschatological feast on Mount Zion (Isa. 25:6-10). Paul speaks of all things being one day united in Christ (Eph. 1:10). Revelation says that at the coming of Christ everyone will see him, even those who pierced him (1:7). Indeed, in the end, all things will be made new (21:5), all nations will worship God (15:4), all the creatures in the universe will sing praises to God (5:13), and the nations and the kings of the earth will be found in the holy city (21:22–22:3).

Nevertheless, a similar array of passages speaks of salvation being limited to the faithful. Isaiah affirms that the inhabitants of the earth will be punished for their iniquity (Isa. 26:20-21) and that all flesh will be judged by God in a manner that involves punishment in unquenchable flames of fire (Isa. 66:15–16,24). In this same line, Jesus speaks of those who do not care for others as destined for eternal punishment (Matt. 25:31-46). Similarly, John's gospel condemns the disobedient to the wrath of God (John 3:36). Paul indicates that the justice of God requires that the unfaithful "suffer the punishment of eternal destruction, separated from the presence of God" (2 Thess. 1:6-10). Indeed, Revelation speaks of those who worship the beast and those not written in the book of life as destined for the lake of fire and sulfur (14:9-10; 20:15).

Thus, many scriptures can be listed for both universal and limited salvation. Indeed, in two contiguous verses, John's gospel says that God sent his Son so that those who believe in him might be saved and so that the world through him might be saved (John 3:16-17). Perhaps Ramsey Michaels' words are instructive here: "Christianity preaches a universal gospel of salvation, but not a gospel of universal salvation" (1997:257). His point is that all are invited but not all choose to come.

THE TEXT IN THE LIFE OF THE CHURCH

Hell and Divine Punishment

In this passage we encounter the torment of fire and sulfur, which has troubled the church since Renaissance humanism and Enlightenment rationalism seemed to rule it out as a primitive and offensive idea. A Jewish student studying the Gospel of Matthew in one of my university classes said: "Jesus repeatedly tells his followers, if they do not do what he says, they will burn in hell; the Torah is much more humane than this."

Nevertheless, many Christians continue to hold the traditional view that all those who have not appropriated God's salvation will be condemned to everlasting conscious punishment (see Morris, 1984:369-70; also TBC, Fire and Sulfur). The Bible asserts that sin will be punished (Dan. 12:2; Matt. 10:15; John 5:28-29; Rom. 5:12-21) for the duration expressed in the word *age (aiōn/aiōnion)*, which is used of the eternal age to come (Matt. 12:32; 18:8; 25:41, 46; Rom. 11:36; 16:26; 2 Cor. 11:31; 2 Thess. 1:9; 1 Tim. 1:17). Other words of Jesus like "unquenchable fire" (Mark 9:43, 47-48; Luke 3:17) and "where their worm does not die" (Mark 9:47-48) can be adduced in support of a hell of eternal conscious punishment.

Arguably, this has been the position of most Christians throughout church history. In the second century, Clement of Rome says: "For if we do the will of Christ, we shall gain repose; but if not, nothing shall save us from eternal punishment, if we neglect His commandments" (2 Clem. 6:7). In the same century, Polycarp told his persecutors: "You threaten with the fire that burns for a time, and is quickly quenched, for you do not know the fire which awaits the wicked in the judgment to come and in everlasting punishment" (*Martyrdom* 11.2). Eighteenth-century American theologian/preacher Jonathan Edwards said:

> The body will be full of torment as it can hold.... They shall be in extreme pain, every joint of 'em, every nerve shall be inexpressible torment. They shall be tormented even to their fingers' ends. The whole body shall be full of the wrath of God. Their hearts and their bowels and their heads, their eyes and their tongues, their hands and their feet will be filled with the fierceness of God's wrath. This is taught to us in many scriptures. (quoted in Gerstner, 1980:56, n.37)

Yet Nels Ferre says that such descriptions of Hell "make God a tyrant," Hitler by comparison "a third degree saint, and the concentration camps ... the king's picnic grounds" (1951:228). In a similar vein, Hans Küng asks: "What would we think of a human being who satisfied his thirst for revenge so implacably and insatiably?" (1984:136). Because of such concerns regarding the traditional view, some Christians have turned to a position at the other extreme, universalism, which argues that all will be saved whether or not they have accepted God's salvation. Some believe that there is simply no distinction made among persons in the afterlife, while others believe that the love of God is so strong that, in the end, all persons will surrender and be saved. Holding the latter position, Origen contended that all persons would eventually be conquered by God's goodness (see Crouzel, 1989:265).

Christian history has also produced at least three intermediary positions between the extremes of eternal conscious punishment and universal salvation. Some persons agree with the traditional view but take the fire of hell to be metaphorical speaking of spiritual punishment. Crockett points out that both Matthew and Jude describe hell as eternal fire (Matt. 3:10, 12; 5:22; 18:8-9; 25:41; Jude 7) and blackest darkness (Matt. 8:12; 22:13; 25:30; Jude 13), two conflicting ideas. To add to the ambiguity, Jewish writers describe the wicked, instead of burning eternally, as being burned and then eaten with worms (Judith 16:17; Sir. 7:17); one writer even uses both fire and ice to describe hell (2 Enoch 10:2). Crockett further indicates that fire makes more sense as punishment for beings with physical bodies than for spiritual beings like the devil and his angels (Matt. 25:41) and concludes that a hell of fire and brimstone is a hyperbolic and picturesque way of speaking of the seriousness of rejecting God's salvation in Christ. In support, he appeals to Jesus' common employment of hyperbole (Matt. 7:5; 19:24; Mark 6:23; 11:23; Luke 9:60) and to the New Testament writers' regular use of fire symbolically (Luke 12:49; 1 Cor. 3:15; 7:9; Jas. 3:5-6). Moreover, he maintains that such a position was or is held by such luminaries as Martin Luther, John Calvin, Charles Hodge, Kenneth Kantzer, and Billy Graham (1992:30, 44-45, 51, 61).

A second medial position is the purgatorial view, which holds that, although the eternal fate of either heaven or hell is decided at death, there is an intermediate place, where persons who have died with guilt are purified in preparation for eternal life with God. Moreover, persons in this life can aid the cause of the dead through prayers and good deeds. Although individuals do not stay in purgatory permanently, the place remains until the last judgment (Hayes, 1992:91-118).

The scriptural evidence for the purgatorial view is somewhat sketchy and indirect. The clearest support for the doctrine is in 2 Maccabees, a book from the second century before Christ, considered canonical by the Roman Catholic Church, which speaks of prayer and atonement for the sins of those who have died in battle (2 Macc. 12:39-45). A passage in the Protestant canon used to support the purgatorial position is Jesus' words regarding blasphemy against the Holy Spirit, which he says will not be forgiven, "either in this age or in the age to come" (Matt. 12:31-32). This carries the implication that other sins might be forgiven in the next world. Support for purgatory is also found in Paul's use of the metaphor of a building to suggest that some persons will be saved "through fire" (1 Cor. 3:10-15).

Admittedly, the biblical support for this position is sketchy, and the New Testament texts expressing confidence in God's provision in Christ for our salvation (Rom. 8:1, 31-39; 1 Cor. 15:54; 2 Cor. 5:1-8; Phil. 1:21-22; 3:20-21; Col. 1:13-14; 1 Thess. 4:13-18) and those favoring salvation by grace through faith rather than good works (Rom. 3:28; 5:1-5; Gal. 2:21) seem to speak against it. Nevertheless, purgatory received very early support in the tradition of the church, to which Roman Catholic interpreters are more likely to appeal than are Protestants. In the second century, Perpetua placed considerable confidence that her prayers would hold Dinocrates, her dead brother, in the abyss (*Martyrdom of Perpetua and Felicitas* 2.3), and Augustine prayed for his mother Monica after her death (*Confessions* 9.13). Moreover, Cyprian of Carthiage believed that purgatory was appropriate for persons whose courage lapsed in persecution (*Letter* 55.20), and Augustine argued that although it is possible to be purged either in this life or the next, some would suffer eternal punishment (*Enchiridion* 18; *City of God* 21.13). The Council of Trent formalized the doctrine of purgatory, affirming that "between death and the general resurrection" the living can benefit the departed souls through prayers, good works, and celebration of the Eucharist (see Hayes, 1992:113).

The final position between eternal, conscious punishment and universalism is annihilationism, which affirms that God is perfect and cannot look on sin, so it must be eternally banished from the divine presence, but which rejects the cruelty of eternal punishment and interprets hell as a symbolic way of speaking about annihilation. The idea of God punishing persons eternally is thought to be inconsistent with divine justice. Yet those freely choosing to reject Christ's salvation are not tormented eternally but cease to exist at death. C. S. Lewis called hell the "outer rim where being fades away into nonentity" (1965:115).

Unlike the purgationists, annihilationists appeal primarily to biblical evidence. The Hebrew scriptures speak of the wicked ending in destruction that involves the termination of existence (Ps. 37:1-2, 9-10, 20, 38; Mal. 4:1). Jesus' image of hellfire is that, although the fire is unquenchable, those cast into it are destroyed like weeds rather than burned eternally (Matt. 3:10, 12; 10:28; 13:30). Even passages that speak of eternal punishment do not affirm that individuals are placed there permanently (Matt. 25:46; see also Jude 6-7). More convincing evidence for annihiliationism comes from Paul, who never speaks of hellfire but uses the image of eternal death and destruction as the fate of wicked (Rom. 1:32; 6:23; 1 Cor. 3:17; Gal. 6:8; Phil. 1:28; 3:18-19; 2 Thess. 1:6-10). The author of 2 Peter seems to speak of punishment for false prophets and sinful angels until the day of judgment after which they will be destroyed (2 Pet. 2:1-10; 3:7).

Often the debate about hell becomes emotional, and opposing views are treated as heresy. The variety of views presented here should not be seen as ways of undermining the biblical teaching on the subject but as sincere attempts on the part of Christians committed to biblical revelation to interpret passages that are difficult to explain in light of the benevolent nature of God.

The Seven Bowls of God's Wrath

PREVIEW

Chapters 12–14 form an interlude between the seven trumpets and the seven bowls of God's wrath. The interlude is connected to what follows by the contrast of the bloody ocean from the winepress of God's wrath (14:20) with the sea of fire where the faithful worship God (15:2; Caird, 1966:196-97).

As Revelation progresses, its structure becomes more complex. The seven seals and seven trumpets have passed, and the last series of plagues, the seven bowls of the wrath of God, begins. Mounce says the judgment "revealed by the seals and announced by the trumpets is now executed by the bowls" (1977:284).

The structural relations among the numbered visions are quite interesting. The seals, trumpets, and bowls are related in the ways they are introduced. Chapter 5 reports that a scroll with seven seals is given to the Lamb before the judgments are poured out as these seals are broken; in the midst of the eerie silence of the seventh seal in Revelation 8:1-5, the seven trumpets are announced before being sounded in sequence to initiate each of the seven trumpet judgments; and the heavenly celebration of chapter 15 serves as a preface to the seven bowls of God's wrath, which are poured out on the earth to bring the seven last plagues.

The trumpets and bowls are connected structurally in a more complex manner. The interlude between the fourth and fifth trumpets announces three woes (8:13), which would seem to be the last three trumpet judgments (9:12, 14). Nevertheless, the seventh trumpet is not a woe but an announcement of the advent of the kingdom of God (11:15-19). Therefore, the third woe is postponed and perhaps is to be identified with the seven bowls. If so, just as the seventh seal is not a judgment but announces the trumpet judgments (8:1-2), so the seventh trumpet is not the third woe but anticipates the seven bowl judgments, which are that woe.

To move from structural to more literal concerns, the bowls referred to here are flat utensils used as saucepans or drinking cups. In the Hebrew scriptures they are associated with God's wrath (Ps. 75:7-8; Isa. 51:17; Jer. 25:15-16; Ezek. 23:33-35; Hab. 2:16; Rev. 14:8, 10; 16:19). In Revelation, they are also the vessels that held the incense that was the prayers of the saints (5:8; see also 8:3-4). Thus, the bowls of wrath are, in a sense, God's answers to the prayers the saints offered requesting their vindication and relief from the persecutions they were undergoing.

The bowls here are also called "plagues," a word carrying a clear allusion to the Exodus narrative. The bowls of God's wrath are the final plagues accompanying the eschatological exodus from this world of those who conquered the beast and his followers, as the Israelites conquered Pharaoh and their oppressors in the deliverance from Egypt. Indeed, these bowl judgments recapitulate in a seven-fold sequence the plagues of the Exodus (see Lev. 26:21 and Table 4 below); Exodus imagery dominates throughout chapters 15–16. Boring points out some of the more obvious parallels (1989:173):

Egypt	Rome
Pharaoh	Caesar
Plagues	Bowls
Red Sea	Euphrates River
Song of Moses	Song of the Lamb
Tabernacle	Tent of Witness
Hardening of Pharaoh's Heart	Refusal of Repentance

Moreover, the bowls of God's wrath repeat with remarkable consistency the judgments of the seven trumpets (see Table 4 below). The first trumpet and bowl are on the earth; the second element of each sequence turns the sea to blood; the third pair affects the rivers; the fourth influences the sun; the fifth produces darkness; the sixth includes an attack of troops from across the Euphrates River; and the seventh brings "lightnings, rumblings, peals of thunder, and an earthquake." It seems indisputable that the bowls of God's wrath are not a unique sequence but a reiteration of the trumpet judgments.

Table 4. Exodus Imagery in Revelation 15–16

	Exodus Plagues (Exod.)	Trumpet Judgments (Rev.)	Bowl Judgments (Rev.)
Hailstorm	9:22-26	8:7	16:17-21
Seas/Rivers to Blood	7:17-21	8:8-9	16:3, 4-7
Bitter Waters	15:23-25	8:10-11	
Darkness	10:21-23	8:12-13	16:10-11
Locusts	10:12-15	9:1-12	
Crossing Sea/River	14:21-31	9:13-19	16:12-16
Sores	9:10-12		16:2
Sun Scorches			16:8-9
Lightning, etc.		11:15-19	16:17-21
Frogs	8:1-15		16:12-16

There are differences, however. For example, no interludes follow the fourth and sixth bowls as would be expected from observing the seal and trumpet series. Instead, there is an interlude after the third bowl resembling the prelude to the seal sequence (chs. 4–5). Moreover, although it is not clear from the NRSV translation, a further distinction is made between the first three bowls and the last four in that the former are poured out into *(eis)* and the latter on *(epi)* creation, a distinction that seems more structural than semantic.

A more substantive uniqueness of the bowl judgments is that they are more intense and universal than the trumpets. The trumpets affect part (one-third) of creation (8:7-12), while the bowls bring universal destruction (16:3, 20). As the climax approaches, the intensification of tribulation makes the deliverance of the faithful more glorious.

Interestingly, the plagues only fall on those who wear the mark of the beast (16:2). As the Exodus plagues were on the Egyptians but the Israelites were spared, so in the eschatological exodus the calamities are on the faithless and disobedient, but those who were faithful in persecution are protected by God from the plagues. Although there is no evidence that the saints will be "raptured" out of the great tribulation, there is clear evidence of their protection in the midst of the final judgment.

Chapters 15–16 complete three sets of seven judgments—seven seals, seven trumpets, and seven bowls. These are not chronological but different ways of looking at the same judgments. Each one is complete but open-ended. In the words of Caird, "Because [John] had learnt his theology at the foot of the Cross, he knew that an end could also be a beginning" (1966:210). Furthermore, the judgments are meant not so much to describe a sequence of catastrophes as to teach the theological truth that the wicked will be punished and God's people delivered from tribulation.

Now that the three series of seven judgments are complete, it is important to note that in each one repentance is emphasized (2:16, 21; 3:19; 9:20; 14:6-7). Even in the final judgments of the bowls of God's wrath, when the end is imminent and God's purpose inevitable, repentance is available (15:3-4; 16:8-9; 18:4).

OUTLINE

The Song of Moses, 15:1-4
The Tent of Witness, 15:5-8
The Seven Bowls, 16:1
The Sores, 16:2
The Sea into Blood, 16:3
The Rivers into Blood, 16:4
Interlude of the Angel of Waters, 16:5-7
The Scorching Sun, 16:8-9
The Agonizing Darkness, 16:10-11
The Drying of the Euphrates, 16:12-16
The Earthquake and Hail, 16:17-21

EXPLANATORY NOTES

The Song of Moses 15:1-4

As chapter 15 begins, John *saw another portent in heaven, great and amazing.* The word *portent (sēmeion)* connects this section with the preceding interlude where the woman clothed with the sun (12:1) and the great red dragon (12:3) are called portents (see note on 12:1). The seven bowls of God's wrath point to the anger of God against wickedness, which is brought to a close with this series of *great and amazing* plagues.

The portent is the *seven angels with seven plagues, which are the last.* The word translated *plagues (plēgas)* in this section means a "blow" or "stroke" or the resulting wound or bruise. It is reserved for the bowl judgments in Revelation, which stresses their awfulness and relates them closely to the Exodus plagues. With the plagues mentioned here, *the wrath of God is ended.* Used only twice in connection with God elsewhere in the New Testament, the word *wrath (thymos)* connotes a "passionate anger," or "rage" (14:19; 15:1, 7; 16:1), in contrast to the more common *orgē,* meaning "anger," or "indignation" (6:16-17). The two are occasionally used together in Revelation (14:10; 16:19; 19:15). The purpose of the wrath of God is "to remove sin, evil, lovelessness, and godlessness from the world ... in the elimination of evil altogether" (Walhout, 2000:160). The emphasis here is not the chronological end of God's wrath, although it may indicate that divine judgment is not eternal (Ps. 77:7) and that God's actions are, therefore, justice and not vengeance. Rather, the focus is on the completion of God's wrath; this sequence is the climax of the most complete manifestation of God's justice. Beale captures this idea well: "The full portrait of God's wrath will be finished when all the bowl visions have been painted on the heavenly canvas" (1999:788).

Then, John *saw what appeared to be a sea of glass mingled with fire.* In the vision of heaven, the sea symbolized the separation or holiness of God (4:6). The hymn to the holiness of God sung there (4:8) parallels remarkably verses 3-4 in the present context. The red color of fire calls to mind the Red Sea, especially in light of the plethora of allusions to the Exodus in this context. Yet the more profound meaning is probably connected to the connotation of purification associated with fire. God's wrath purifies the wicked like the persecution purifies those who are faithful to God.

Next John saw *those who had conquered the beast and its image and the number of its name.* These words connect the present passage with the interlude between the judgments of the trumpets and bowls. Identical to the 144,000 of chapter 14, those who conquered the beast are the faithful who withstood his persecution and, through suffering and martyrdom, prevailed over the powers of evil. The verb here is the same as the one used for the Lamb's conquering through death on the cross (5:5) and is, by contrast, a present tense here indicating that it is the habit of the faithful to continuously conquer the beast. As with their leader, the Lamb, the saints conquer through suffering and even martyrdom. Through their death, the faithful frustrate the beast whose purpose was for them to cave in to persecution. In the words of Barclay, "It was the very fact that they had died that made them victors. If they had remained alive by being false to their faith, they would have been the defeated" (1960:2.155). Though the victory, by all appearances, belongs to Satan and the beast and their followers, it is actually God and the saints who have conquered.

These conquerors were *standing beside the sea of glass with harps of God in their hands.* Literally, they stood upon *(epi)* the sea like the Israelites who stood on the Red Sea in their deliverance from Egypt. Here they find themselves in God's presence, perhaps sharing the divine holiness symbolized by the sea (see 4:6) and receiving God's protection from the plagues that are about to appear. Possession of the harps of God indicates that they participate in heavenly worship (Ps. 81:1-2; 144:9; Amos 5:21-24; Rev. 5:8; 14:2).

Moreover, the conquerors sing the song of Moses, the servant of God, and the song of the Lamb:

> Great and amazing are your deeds,
> Lord God the Almighty!
> Just and true are your ways,
> King of the nations!
> Lord, who will not fear
> and glorify your name?
> For you alone are holy.
> All nations will come
> and worship before you,
> for your judgments have been revealed. (15:3-4)

After the Exodus, the Israelites sang the song of Moses by the Red Sea, celebrating their victory over Pharaoh and the Egyptians (Exod. 15:1-18). Subsequently, it has been sung in every synagogue service, stamping it eternally into Jewish awareness. The song of Moses in this passage is treated through Hebrew parallelism as equivalent to the song of the Lamb, which was sung beside the heavenly sea, celebrating the triumph of Christ and the faithful over the beast; and it stands in stark contrast even in language with the worship of the dragon by his followers in the previous section (13:3-4). The song in this passage celebrates Christ as the new deliverer whom the faithful follow across the sea of persecution into the new heavenly promised land. It is sung before the final deliverance occurs because the salvation of the faithful is so certain.

Although the song of Moses and the Lamb is a mosaic of Old Testament expressions (see TBC, Song of Moses and the Lamb), it bears little resemblance to the song of Moses in Exodus 15. The song of Moses focuses on the demise of the enemies of Israel, while the song here centers on the conversion of the world (Koester, 2001:142). Therefore, some argue that Deuteronomy 32 is a closer parallel to this passage than Exodus 15. If so, the celebration is for God's faithfulness (v. 4), which is recounted from Jacob to Moses. Regardless of its background, the song draws from Old Testament imagery to emphasize the justice and holiness of God, who brings the seven last plagues, rather than the torment of the wicked or the achievements of the faithful. The intentions and mighty acts of God are perfect, especially the judgments of the bowls of God's wrath.

The last verse of the song seems to conflict with Revelation's consistent theme of the refusal of the wicked to repent (9:20-21; 16:9, 11). Perhaps the reference is to recognition of God's power rather than to repentance. Nevertheless, the angel with the eternal gospel in the preceding interlude called for repentance (14:6-7), and repentance may have also occurred in response to the trumpet judgments (11:13). Thus, there is no reason to reject the plain sense of the passage: that all nations repent and worship God.

The Tent of the Witness 15:5-8

After the conquerors finished their song, *the temple of the tent of witness in heaven was opened.* This tent is the heavenly counterpart of the sanctuary that Israel used before the temple was built (see TBC, The Temple of the Tent of the Witness). The earthly tent was constructed to model the heavenly sanctuary (Ford, 1975:257), which was also filled with God's glory. Clearly, the context of this passage, like the one before it, is worship. The witness contained in this tent is most likely the Torah, which was kept in the ark located in the tent/temple (see TBC on ch. 11, The Ark of the Covenant). The purpose of its presence is to ensure that the judgments that follow are consistent with the Law and grow out of God's faithfulness to the covenant witnessed in the Torah.

After noting the tent of the witness, John observes that out of the temple came the seven angels with the seven plagues, robed in pure bright linen, with golden sashes across their chests. That the angels come from the temple indicates their divine origin and that the plagues are from God. This rare description of angels parallels closely that of the Son of Man in chapter 1, and emphasizes their priestly function in this continuing picture of heavenly worship. Although there is significant support for a variant reading of "linen" *(linon)* as "stone" *(lithos),* linen makes better sense with the modifier *katharon,* which means "clean," or "pure," rather than the NRSV's "bright" (Metzger et al., 1971:756). Translated thus, the modifier emphasizes the holiness of the angels who pour out the bowls of God's wrath (see Matt. 28:3; Mark 16:5).

After the seven angels, the next character to appear on the dramatic scene was one of the four living creatures. These creatures are intermediaries before God and on behalf of the physical universe (4:6; 5:6; 7:11; 14:3; 19:4) and were responsible for opening the first four seals so that their horsemen could ride forth to deliver judgments to the earth (6:1-8). That the last plagues are from one of the living creatures implies they will affect the whole physical universe.

This living creature gave the seven angels seven golden bowls full of the wrath of God. These bowls were broad, shallow vessels used for drinking and libations or as receptacles for the ashes of the dead. Although the connection with the ashes of the dead is appropriate in the context of the last plagues, an allusion that is even more appropriate in this context so completely saturated with worship imagery is the liturgical utensils used in the temple (Exod. 27:3; Num. 7; 1 Kings 8:4). Specifically, they remind the reader of the golden bowls of incense that are the prayers of the saints (Rev. 5:8; Jos., *Ant.* 3.143). Again it is clear that the judgments of the bowls come in response to the prayers of the saints. To continue the liturgical picture, priestly angels carry bowls of incense from the tent of the witness to pour on the earth. The one who lives forever and ever is God, not divine wrath. The meaning is that, in contrast to Satan, the beast, and evil itself, which are transient, God is always able to protect and vindicate those who remain faithful.

As the scene ends, the temple is filled with smoke from the glory of God and from his power. Smoke is a usual symbol for the dwelling place of God (Exod. 19:18; Isa. 4:5; 6:1-4; see also Ezek. 10:3-4; 44:4). The point is that the judgments are God's activity. Because of the power and glory of God, no one could enter the temple until the seven plagues of the seven angels were ended. As in the giving of the

Law on Mount Sinai, the glory prohibits anyone from coming close (Exod. 19:21-25; see also 40:34-35; 1 Kings 8:10-11; 2 Chron. 7:1-3). The meaning, then, is that no one can intercede to stop God's inevitable judgment.

The Seven Bowls 16:1

After the introduction of chapter 15, the pouring out of the bowls of God's wrath begins with John's word: *Then I heard a loud voice from the temple telling the seven angels....* Although Farrer contends this is not God's voice because it speaks of God in the third person (1964:175), it is likely the voice of God because the previous verse declared no one was allowed to enter the temple (15:8; see also Isa. 66:6; Rev. 10:4, 8).

God's voice commands the seven angels: *Go and pour out on the earth the seven bowls of the wrath of God.* The Hebrew tradition witnesses to a seven-fold punishment for sin (Lev. 26:18, 21, 24, 28; Ps. 79:12). Here the last plagues, poured out on the earth from the seven bowls (Ps. 69:24; Jer. 10:25; 42:18; 44:6; Zeph. 3:8; cf. Acts 2:17, 18, 33; Titus 3:6), although terrible (Heb. 10:31), have the positive effect of purging creation from evil in preparation for the New Jerusalem (21:1–22:6; see also Gen. 3; Isa. 24:5-6; Rom. 8:18-25). Indeed, the seven bowls poured out on the earth are in answer to the prayers of the saints represented by bowls with incense rising to the Lamb (Koester, 2001:147).

The Sores 16:2

The first bowl judgment brings *a foul and painful sore.* The noun here means an "abscess," or "ulcer." Although the parallel to the boils in Exodus 9:10-12 is obvious (see also Deut. 28:27, 35; 2 Kings 20:7; Job 2:7-8; Luke 16:19-21), there is no similar judgment in the trumpet sequence. The first adjective *(kakos)* means bad in the sense of evil, and the second *(poneros)* denotes a painful sickness. If the sickness is leprosy, as seems quite possible, then it carries the implication of ceremonial defilement (Lev. 13; Num. 5:2-3; 12:10-15; 2 Kings 5; 15:5).

The sore *came on those who had the mark of the beast and who worshiped its image.* The sore on the body parallels the mark of the beast and is an appropriate punishment for the person bearing it. A repeated theme in the judgments of Revelation, especially the bowls, is that, as the Exodus plagues fall on the Egyptians but not the Israelites, so the bowl judgments affect only the beast worshipers who wear his mark, and those who worship the Lamb and bear his seal are exempted (14:9-11). The corollary is that all persons must serve either the Lamb or the beast, and that the latter comes with disastrous results (20:15; 21:8; 22:15).

The Sea into Blood 16:3

After the plague of sores, *[t]he second angel poured out his bowl into the sea, and it became like the blood of a corpse, and every living thing in the sea died.* Perhaps inspired by the bloody naval battles of the time (Ford, 1975:271; see Jos., *War.* 3.522-531), this judgment has parallels in both the Exodus plagues (Exod. 7:17-21) and the trumpet series (Rev. 8:8-9) but is more catastrophic than either. The Exodus counterpart affected only the Nile River and Egypt; this bowl judgment affects at least the Mediterranean and the entire Roman Empire, which depended on the sea for its economic well-being. Thus, this bowl judgment parallels the judgment on Babylon, which destroys its sea trade (18:17-19). While the second trumpet killed only one third of the living creatures in the sea, the second bowl defiled the essential water supplies, causing the death of all sea life. That the sea became like the blood of a corpse means literally that it had coagulated and symbolically that, like the leprosy of the preceding verse, it caused all that contacted it to be unclean (Gen. 9:4; Num 5:2-3).

The Rivers into Blood 16:4

The third bowl judgment is similar to the second: *The third angel poured his bowl into the rivers and springs of water, and they became blood.* The corresponding third trumpet turned a third of the rivers bitter, causing some death (8:10-11; see also Ps. 78:44). Those who shed the blood of the saints now are awash in blood (6:10; Koester, 2001:149). Like the preceding bowl judgment, this one may have implications for the profit made by Babylon through commerce on the waters (18:11-19). Although the effect of the third bowl is not stated, it can be assumed to be more intense than the parallel trumpet because its effect is not muted by the use of fractions and because the other bowls evidence increased intensity.

Interlude of the Angel of Waters 16:5-7

In the interlude that follows the pouring out of third bowl of God's wrath, the *angel of the waters* speaks. In Jewish literature, each element of nature has a corresponding angel (Ps. 104:4; Heb. 1:7;

1 Enoch 61:10; 66:1-3; see also 1 Enoch 60:11-24). Revelation has already introduced angels of wind (7:1) and fire (14:18). Here, the angel of the waters addresses God: *You are just, O Holy One, who are and were, for you have judged these things.* The phrase *who are and were* is based on Exodus 3:14 and is reminiscent of earlier visions (1:4, 8; 4:8), but the omission of the future tense is no doubt because the future has come, the end is near (see also 11:17). The words of the angel stress God's justice, a common theme in the Hebrew scriptures (Ezra 9:15; Ps. 51:4; 119:137), which is emphasized repeatedly in Revelation, especially in the hymn of the preceding chapter (15:3-4).

The basis for God's justice is: *because they shed the blood of the saints and prophets, you have given them blood to drink. It is what they deserve!* While the saints are the faithful in general, the identity of the prophets is more difficult to determine. They may be those given the gift of prophecy in the New Testament church (Acts 11:28; 13:1; 21:10-11; 1 Cor. 12:28; 14:3; Eph. 4:11) or, more likely in this context, the subgroup of the faithful who are martyred. The point here is that the plagues of blood are particularly appropriate because, in divine justice, the punishment fits the crime (Gen. 9:6; Isa. 49:26; Luke 12:48; Rom. 1:24-32; Wis. Sol. 11:15-16). Those who shed the saint's blood deserve to have their drinking water changed to blood, an idea present in the chapters that both precede and follow this vision (14:8, 19-20; 17:6). On a somewhat different note, Wall affirms: "The blood-plague envisions God's righteous judgment of a people who have rejected the blood of the Lamb" (1991:198). The exclamation addressed to the beast worshipers, *It is what they deserve!* contrasts with the one that earlier described Christ: "You are worthy!" (5:9, 12).

With additional words of affirmation for God's justice, John hears *the altar respond, "Yes, O Lord God, the Almighty, your judgments are true and just!"* Although many nonhuman creatures speak in Revelation, this is the only place where an altar speaks. It may be the voice of the angel of the altar (14:18), but no one except God was allowed into the temple (15:8). The voice from the altar most likely comes from the souls of the martyrs under the altar, who cried out for justice (6:9-10; see also 9:13); the series of bowl judgments is the answer to their prayers (8:3-5). Here the words of the souls under the altar repeat the song of Moses and the Lamb, which also stressed the theme of divine justice (15:3-4; see also 19:2). The theme of justice is emphatically affirmed by the word *Yes* (Aune, 1998a:888).

The Scorching Sun   16:8-9

Following the interlude, *[t]he fourth angel poured his bowl on the sun, and it was allowed to scorch them with fire.* The fourth trumpet produced the opposite of this bowl—darkness (8:12). The use of the word *scorch* twice as a verb *(kaumatizō)* and once as a noun *(kauma)* in verses 8-9 emphasizes the intensity of the heat. Apocalyptic literature commonly speaks of the destruction of the earth by fire (Sib. Or. 2:196-213; 4:171-78; 8:225-28; Pseudo John 14). Although cosmic destruction by fire is rare in the Bible (see 2 Pet. 3:10), canonical writings speak of fire in connection with judgment (1 Cor. 3:13; 2 Pet. 3:7). Here, creation is not consumed but only tortured.

The result of this bowl is that they were scorched by the fierce heat, but they cursed the name of God, who had authority over these plagues, and they did not repent and give him glory. This passage makes explicit what the verb *allowed (edothē)* in the previous verse implied: that the judgment comes with divine permission and even authority. The awful judgment here provides a stark contrast with the fate of the faithful (7:16-17; 21:4). The refusal to repent, repeated in verses 11 and 21 (see also 9:20-21), reminds the reader of the hardening of Pharaoh's heart in the Exodus story (Exod. 7:3, 22; 8:15). The tragic response of blasphemy, instead of repentance (11:13), is the sin unto death (1 John 5:16) and indicates identification with the beast (13:1, 5-6). Indeed, the three series of judgments have little effect on the consciences of the wicked.

The Agonizing Darkness   16:10-11

The description of the last three bowls, which parallel the final trumpets, begins with the words: *The fifth angel poured his bowl in the throne of the beast.* This plague is again not on the faithful (see Exod. 10:23) but on the beastly Rome, which symbolizes all that is hostile to God's faithful people.

The result is that *its kingdom was plunged into darkness.* This corresponds to the ninth plague of Exodus (Exod. 10:21-23) and the fourth trumpet, where the darkness is caused by the smoke of the abyss associated with the onslaught of locusts (9:1-2). This may allude to the plunging of the Roman Empire into a chaos of darkness after the suicide of Nero (Caird, 1966:204) or the darkness that folllowed the crucifixion of Jesus (Matt. 27:45; Mark 15:33; Luke 23:44; Aune, 1998a:890). Moreover, darkness is a common metaphor for association with evil and Satan, and for separation from God (Beale, 1999:824).

In response, the *people gnawed their tongues in agony, and cursed the God of heaven because of their pain and sores, and they did not repent of their deeds.* Darkness alone would not cause this response; the mention of pain and sores implies that this is a response to all the plagues, intensified by the darkness (Wis. Sol. 17:1–18:4). Although the people recognize the God of heaven as the source of the plagues (see Rev. 11:13), again they refuse to repent, which is remarkably still an option even during the last plagues.

The Drying of the Euphrates 16:12-16

The sixth bowl of God's wrath is a battle much like the corresponding sixth trumpet only more obviously historical and political (6:2; 9:14). It is, however, also a plague of frogs; and as such, it parallels the second Exodus plague (Exod. 8:1-15).

The plague begins: *The sixth angel poured out his bowl on the great river Euphrates, and its water was dried up.* The Euphrates River, the largest river in the region—which, unlike most rivers in the Near East, was never known to dry up (Aune, 1998a:890-91)—formed the eastern boundary of the land promised in God's covenant with Abraham and his seed (Gen. 15:18; Deut. 1:7-8; Josh. 1:3-4). The heathen were thought to live outside the boundaries of this land. The action here reminds the reader of the drying up of the Red Sea in the Exodus from Egypt (Exod. 14:21) and the Jordan River in the conquest of Canaan (Josh. 3:7-17; see also 2 Kings 2:8). Israel's scriptures expected the Exodus miracles to be repeated when the people returned from exile (Isa. 11:15-16; Zech. 10:10-12; 2 Esd. 13:39-47).

The reason given for the drying of the Euphrates is *to prepare the way for the kings from the East.* Although Isaiah promised the waters would dry up for Israel's return from Assyria (Isa. 11:15-16), and Titus recruited from beyond the Euphrates for the Jewish War that culminated in the fall of Jerusalem in A.D. 70 (Ford, 1975:273), the most clear referent for the imagery in this passage is no doubt the expected return of Nero from the East *[Essay: Nero Redivivus Myth].* Because the Euphrates River protected the Roman Empire from invasion by the feared Parthians, the kings of the East probably allude to the Parthian regional rulers.

Although the imagery so far has been quite political and historical, what follows is more grotesque: *And I saw three foul spirits like frogs coming from the mouth of the dragon, from the mouth of the beast, and from the mouth of the false prophet.* Some have argued that verses 13-16 form an interlude between the sixth and seventh bowls, which would conform to the pattern of the seals and trumpets. Yet the sixth bowl would be shorter than the corresponding elements of the other series. Moreover, it is better to see the verses as an expansion, describing a battle connected with the drying up of the Euphrates, similar to the fifth and sixth trumpet judgments (9:1-21).

The frog appears only here and in connection with the Exodus plague in the biblical record (Exod. 8:1-15; Ps. 78:45; 105:30; see also Wis. Sol. 19:10). That the frogs were foul alludes to their being ceremonially unclean and thus anathema in this setting of worship (Lev. 11:10-11). This uncleanness is reinforced in the blasphemy that comes from the mouths of the frogs in the form of propaganda on behalf of the trinity of evil—the dragon, the beast, and the false prophet. The dragon is Satan, the evil counterpart of God the Father (12:9), and the beast from the sea parallels God the son (13:1-10). The false prophet introduced here is the inspiration of demonic spirits (Deut. 13:1-5; Zech. 13:2; Matt. 10:1; Mark 1:23; 13:22) and counterfeits the Holy Spirit, the inspiration of all true prophets. The false prophet is identified with the beast from the land (13:11-18; see also Rev. 19:20; 20:10) and parallels Pharaoh's magicians in the Exodus story, who were also able to produce frogs (Exod. 8:7). Foretold by Jesus (Mark 13:22) and witnessed by the church (Acts 13:6-12), the false prophet is the propagandist for the lawless one (2 Thess. 2:9-12) or antichrist (1 John 2:22; 4:3; 2 John 7). The third person of the evil trinity is the false prophet par excellence.

In addition, the evil trinity is here compared to frogs. The imagery of frogs may connote "their endless croaking" and its futility as compared to the glory of the divine trinity (Mounce, 1977:299). Yet Zoroastrianism, the dominant religion of Persia before the seventh century B.C., seems a better source for the imagery. In that tradition, animals were divided into good and evil categories, similar to the Hebrew clean and unclean animals, and the deity associated with the evil animals was the frog. Zoroastrianism saw the frog as "the bringer of plagues, and the agent of Ahriman, the power of darkness, in his struggle against Ormuzd, the power of light" (Barclay, 1960:2.169). Regardless of the source of the imagery, these frog-like demons serve a function similar to the locusts of the fifth trumpet plague (9:1-11).

The frogs of the sixth bowl of God's wrath are *demonic spirits, performing signs.* In the same way that the locusts of the sixth trumpet were not really locusts, but demonic beings, the entities in this bowl are frog-like demons. They work signs in support of the evil trinity just as the false prophet did miracles in support of the beast (13:13-15) and the magicians in Egypt worked wonders for Pharaoh

(Exod. 7:22; see also Matt. 24:24; 2 Thess. 2:9-10).

In addition to performing signs, the demonic spirits *go abroad to the kings of the whole world.* Although there is debate concerning whether or not the kings of the whole world are identical to the kings of the east, the former, inspired by the demonic trinity and perhaps by the spirit of Nero (Caird, 1966:206), gather kings from the whole world against God (Ps. 2:2-3; Joel 3:2; Zeph. 3:8; Zech. 14).

The demonic spirits *assemble them for battle on the great day of God the Almighty.* The four possible interpretations of this war correspond to more general theories of interpreting Revelation (see Entering the World of Revelation: Interpreting Revelation). The preterist argues that the battle is between the Parthian regional rulers and the Roman Empire of John's first-century context. The idealist believes the battle is symbolic of the spiritual warfare between God and Satan that has already been won through Christ's death on the cross but continues between the faithful and their persecutors. The futurist emphasizes the presence of the definite article and sees this as the eschatological battle between God and the forces of evil on the Day of the Lord. The dispensationalist might see this as the war of liberation of the redeemed Jewish remnant, left after the rapture as a witness during the seven years of tribulation on the earth preceding the millennial rule of Christ. Some combination of the first three positions seems best: the passage draws on the imminent conflict between Rome and the Parthians to symbolize the permanent conflict between God and Satan, which manifests itself in the persecution of the faithful by evil individuals and institutions, and which may, indeed, escalate as the eschaton approaches.

Verse 15 is thought by many interpreters to be a parenthesis or even an interpolation because the content seems to be an intrusion into the thought of the passage and there is a shift from the third to first person. Yet it could be asked how something so out of place would have found its way into the text. Moreover, is it such an intrusion? It abruptly reminds the hearers that they must be prepared for the great day of God Almighty. Parenthetical statements are quite common in Revelation, especially in the letters to the churches (2:5, 16; 3:3; see also 14:13). Thus, assuming the verse to be an insertion is unnecessary. With the end near, it functions both as an admonition to be awake and as a promise of blessedness on the watchful.

The verse reintroduces the motif of Jesus as thief: *See, I am coming like a thief!* These are the first words of Jesus in Revelation since the letters to the churches in chapters 2–3. The emphasis in the motif of Jesus as a thief is on the uncertainty of the time of his coming (see

TBC, Coming Like a Thief). The image speaks against those who would predict the time of the parousia. Eller addresses those date-setters: "Christians ... are not supposed to know ahead of time about the 'when' of the end; the plea is rather for what we have been calling 'perpetual expectancy'" (1974:149). The message is: Be awake.

John follows with a blessing on the vigilant: *Blessed is the one who stays awake and is clothed, not going about naked and exposed to shame.* This is the third beatitude in Revelation (1:3; 14:13; 16:15; 19:9; 20:6; 22:7,14; see also Luke 12:37-39). The result here of not being awake is that one might be caught naked, a shameful experience in the ancient world as well as today (Ezek. 23:26-27; see also 2 Cor. 5:1-5; Did. 16:1). The image may be of a soldier who is not prepared for attack so that he is forced to waste time clothing himself or to run away naked in disgrace (Bruce, 1969:657; see Amos 2:16; Mark 14:51-52).

Returning to the theme of battle, the evil trinity assembled the kings of the whole world *at the place that in Hebrew is called Harmagedon.* Found nowhere else, the etymology of Harmagedon is uncertain. *Har* clearly means mountain. *Magedon* seems related to Megiddo, a geographical location between the Sea of Galilee and the Mediterranean on the north side of the Carmel Ridge where the road from Egypt to Damascus traversed through a strategic pass connecting the plain of Palestine with the valley of Esdraelon. Yet, while the final battle in the Old Testament is placed near Jerusalem, the location of Megiddo is a two days journey away (Beale, 1999:838). More important than its location is that Megiddo was mentioned several times in the Hebrew scriptures in connection with violent battles (see TBC, The Great Battlefield at Megiddo). Although it is plausible that such a place would be the venue for the final battle of the Day of the Lord, there is a major difficulty: Megiddo is a valley, not a mountain. Michaels says that Harmagedon is like referring to "Death Valley Mountain" (1997:189). Indeed, this is the only mention of Mount Megiddo in the Bible or Jewish literature (Jeremias, *TDNT* 1.468). Perhaps the reference is to a forty-foot tel located in the valley or to Mount Tabor (Judg. 4:12, 14) or to nearby Mount Carmel (1 Kings 18:20-46). Although the latter is particularly appealing because of its association with false prophets in contest with Elijah, such references are strained translations of Harmagedon. Difficulties related to the transliteration of *Harmagedon* have led some to attempt more symbolic readings through emending the Hebrew letters of *Harmagedon*. The most convincing emendation is to *har mo'ed,* Mount of Assembly, a reading made more attractive by its allusion to the word *assemble* in verse 14 and Isaiah's reference to "the mount of assembly" (Isa. 14:12-13). Caird argues for an emendation that would read "the marauding mountain" (1966:207; see also Jer. 51:25; Rev. 8:8). Neither of these is convincing, however, and it is probably best to think that the great historic battle ground in the valley of Megiddo was transformed into Mount Megiddo under prophetic expectations related to the final battle (Isa. 14:13; Ezek. 38:8, 21; 39:2, 4, 17; Dan. 11:45).

This Old Testament place of battle seems an appropriate symbolic location for the final battle between God and Satan and a fitting counterpart for Mount Zion (Heb. 12:22-24; Rev. 14:1; 21:10). Yet no battle is fought, and Glasson may be correct in saying that the battle awaits 19:19-21 (1965:93). Nevertheless, it is more likely that the final battle is not literal but symbolic, and that the message related to the symbol of Harmagedon as the final battle is that in the end the heavenly victory of God over evil will be achieved on earth. In any case, even in the battle of Armageddon, "the saints do not fight for or with God" nor do they "become co-executors of God's punishment upon the wicked" (Pilgrim, 1999:177).

The Earthquake and Hail 16:17-21

The content of this passage forms a literary bridge by including both a final dramatic conclusion to the Bowls of God's wrath (chs. 15–16) and a prologue to the Fall of Babylon (chs. 17–18). It begins in a now familiar manner: *The seventh angel poured his bowl into the air, and a loud voice came out of the temple, from the throne, saying, "It is done!"* Although pouring out the bowl into the air may be a literal reference to causing the hailstorm to form in the upper atmosphere, more likely, the air is a reference to the domain of demons (Eph. 2:2; 6:12). That the loud voice is from the throne identifies it as God's. Yet the words *It is done!* parallel Jesus' last words on the cross (John 19:30) and mark the end, not chronologically, but in the sense of completion: God's justice is complete (11:17-18). There will be no new series of seven judgments.

These climactic words are followed by *flashes of lightning, rumblings, peals of thunder, and a violent earthquake.* These elements accompany the seventh seal (8:5) and trumpet (11:19; see also 4:5; Exod. 9:24; Jos., *War* 4.286-87), but here the earthquake is emphasized as in other pictures of the end (Isa. 13:13; 24:17-20; Hag. 2:6-7; Zech. 14:4; Mark 13:8; Heb. 12:26-27; Rev. 11:13; Test. Levi 3:9). The phrase *such as had not occurred since people were upon the earth* echoes the responses to the Exodus plagues (Exod. 10:6,

14; 11:6; see also Joel 2:2; Matt. 24:21; Mark 13:19). An earthquake like this one was unusual even in a time of frequent earthquakes.

As a result of the earthquake, the *great city was split into three parts*. Carrington sees here an allusion to the three-fold division of Jerusalem under the leadership of Simon, Eleazar, and John after the invasion of Titus (1931:266; see also Jos., *War* 5.1-4). It is more likely in this context that the division of the city into three parts is related to the evil trinity mentioned in the previous section (Michaels, 1997:190n). Although the great city is Jerusalem in 11:8, here it is most certainly Rome, as it is in the more complete description of the fall of Babylon to follow (18:10, 16, 18, 19, 21). In this passage, not merely a tenth (11:13), but the whole city is destroyed. Such a proleptic announcement of an event elaborated later is quite common in Revelation (6:12-17; 11:15; 14:14-20; 15:2-4). Indeed, the fall of Babylon has already been announced in 14:8 (see also Dan. 2:31-45; 4:14; 5:24-28; 7:11-12).

Along with Rome, *the cities of the nations fell*. These are the cities ruled by the kings of the earth. Thus, the satellite cities that supported and received sustenance from Rome also come to ruin (17:12-14; 18:9). Beale summarizes: "It is not just Rome or some later great capital of evil that is decimated but all the world's cultural, political, economic, and sociological centers. They fall because they are part of the Babylonian world system" (1999:843).

The source of the punishment on Babylon is clear from the words that follow: *God remembered great Babylon and gave her the wine-cup of the fury of his wrath*. The Greek practice of drinking wine from bowls sheds light on the combination of images used (Barr, 1998:132). There is irony, though, in the idea that those who forgot God are remembered by God. The method of remembrance raises the problem associated with the fury of God, which is to some degree ameliorated by the contention in Revelation that God's wrath toward Babylon is fair because she committed spiritual fornication by worshiping the beast (14:8-11; 18:2-3).

Before the fury of God *every island fled away, and no mountains were to be found*. The island imagery may have been suggested by John's imprisonment on Patmos, and the mountains by the tradition of Rome being built on seven hills (Caird, 1966:209). In apocalyptic literature, the mountains commonly disappear along with other cosmic catastrophes that prepare for the new heaven and new earth (Hag. 2:6-7; Zech. 14:10; Rev. 20:11-21:2; 1 Enoch 1:5-6; Assumption of Moses 10:1-2, 4-7). That the islands and mountains already disappeared in the sixth seal (6:12-14) gives further support to the idea that the visions of Revelation are artistic rather than chronological (see Barker, 2000:278, for symbolic interpretations in the Hebrew tradition of both mountains and islands). Perhaps the most interesting idea here is that it is the earth that is being prepared for the rule of Christ (5:10; 11:15; 15:4; 20:4-10).

The seventh bowl of God's wrath ends with *huge hailstones, each weighing about a hundred pounds, dropped from heaven on people.* The first trumpet was also a plague of hail (Rev. 8:7). Moreover, this judgment echoes the seventh plague of the Exodus from Egypt (Exod. 9:22-26), and the Exodus tradition includes a rather dramatic military victory followed by a divine hailstorm at Beth-Heron (Josh. 10:11). Indeed, in the Hebrew tradition hailstorms are a symbol of God's judgment on the enemies of God and Israel (Isa. 28:2; Ezek. 13:11-13; 38:22; Wis. Sol. 5:22). The hailstones may have been suggested by the stones launched from catapults during Titus's attack on Jerusalem (Ford, 1975:265; see Jos., *War* 5.268-74). In this passage they symbolize the ultimate defeat of Babylon, the great tormenter of God's people.

In response, the people of Babylon *cursed God for the plague of hail, so fearful was that plague.* Refusal to repent is the common response to the bowl judgments (16:9, 11; cf. 11:13; 15:4). Here the inhabitants of Babylon, like their leader the beast, cursed the God who sent the plagues (13:1, 5-6; 17:3).

THE TEXT IN BIBLICAL CONTEXT

The Plagues

The use of the word *plague* to describe the bowls of God's wrath connects these judgments semantically to the Exodus plagues (15:1, 6, 8; 16:9, 21; see also 21:9; 22:18; Janzen, BCBC, 2000, on *Exodus*: 114-153). Indeed, the same word is used in the Septuagint for the last, most catastrophic plague of Exodus (Exod. 11:1-9). In the Holiness Code, plagues are the fate of those who do not obey the law (Lev. 26:1-2, 18, 21, 23, 24, 27-28; see also Deut. 28:15-68). The word translated "plague" in Revelation described the suffering and pain of Isaiah's servant (Isa. 53:3, 4, 10; also 1 Clem. 16). In Luke's gospel, the word describes the beating of the man subsequently ministered to by the Good Samaritan (Luke 10:30). In Revelation, the attack of the throngs from across the Euphrates (Rev. 9:18, 20) and the destruction of Babylon (18:4, 8) are called plagues, along with the bowls of God's wrath.

The Song of Moses and the Lamb

In this passage, rife with Old Testament allusions, the song of Moses and the Lamb certainly has the most clear connections to the Hebrew scriptures. The title, song of Moses, reminds the reader of Exodus 15, where the Israelites, after being saved from the Egyptians and the Red Sea, which served as the watery grave for their pursuers, sang a song of praise for God's miraculous deliverance. Yet, the song of Moses and the Lamb seems in some ways to be closer to Deuteronomy 32 than to the song of Moses.

> For I will proclaim the name of the Lord;
> ascribe greatness to our God!
> The Rock, his work is perfect,
> and all his ways are just.
> A faithful God without deceit,
> just and upright is he. (Deut 32:3-4)

Moreover, the song of Moses and the Lamb is a mosaic of Old Testament expressions.

> *Great and amazing are your deeds* (Ps. 92:5; 98:1; 111:2; 139:14)
> *Lord God the Almighty* (Gen. 17:1; 35:11; Exod. 6:3; Ps. 68:14; Ezek. 10:5)
> *Just and true are your ways* (Deut. 32:4; Ps. 145:17)
> *King of the nations! Lord, who will not fear and glorify your name?* (Jer. 10:6-7; Mal.1:6, 11, 14)
> *For you alone are holy* (1 Sam 2:2; Ps. 99:3, 5, 9; 111:9)
> *All nations will come and worship before you* (Ps. 86:9; Isa. 2:2-4; 66:19-21; Jer. 16:19; Mic. 4:2)
> *for your judgments have been revealed* (Exod. 6:6; 7:4; 12:12; Ps. 98:2)

John's dependence on the Hebrew scriptures is indeed impressive.

All the Nations Shall Come

The last verse of the song of Moses in the present passage appears to teach that God's salvation is available to everyone. The psalmist expresses the theme clearly: "All the nations you have made shall come and bow down before you, O Lord, and shall glorify your name" (Ps. 86:9). The prophets concur with this theme: according to Isaiah, God says, "All flesh shall come to worship before me" (Isa. 66:23); and Malachi repeats twice in one verse that God's "name is great among the nations" (Mal. 1:11). The book of Isaiah also describes the salvation of the nations in terms of their rejecting violence: "They shall beat their swords into plowshares, and their spears into pruning hooks; nation shall not lift up sword against nation, neither shall they learn war any more" (Isa. 2:4).

Paul's letters continue this Old Testament theme, stating that God "set forth in Christ, as a plan for the fullness of time to gather up all things in him, things in heaven and things on earth" (Eph. 1:9-10; see Yoder Neufeld, BCBC, 2002, on *Ephesians*: 49-52); declaring that God exalted Christ "so that at the name of Jesus every knee should bend, in heaven and on earth and under the earth, and every tongue should confess that Jesus Christ is Lord, to the glory of God the Father" (Phil. 2:10-11); and affirming that "God was pleased to reconcile to himself all things, whether on earth or in heaven, by making peace through the blood of his cross" (Col. 1:20). Revelation caps this theme by saying that the leaves of the tree of life are for the healing of the nations (Rev. 22:2). The Bible certainly affirms that the saints of God will not be limited to any ethnic group but will be composed of all nations and peoples.

The Temple of the Tent of the Witness

This passage speaks of the tabernacle, the worship place for Israel in the wilderness before they settled in the promised land and erected a permanent temple in Jerusalem. Constructed according to a careful description given by God (Exod. 25-27; see also 38:21; Acts 7:44 Heb. 8:5) and tended by the Levites (Num. 1:50-54; 18:1-8), the tabernacle symbolized the presence of God with the Israelites (Exod. 33:7-11; see also 1 Kings 8:10-11; Isa. 6:4; Ezek. 44:4) through the accompanying cloud by day and fire by night that directed them through the wilderness (Exod. 40:34-38; Num. 9:15-23; 10:11). Initially the ark of the covenant was located in the tabernacle until a temple was constructed in Jerusalem (Exod. 25:10-22; 32:15; Deut. 10:5; 1 Kings 8:6-9; see TBC on ch. 11, The Ark of the Covenant).

Darkness and Light

During the fifth bowl judgment, the kingdom of the beast is plunged into darkness. An investigation of the scriptural uses of darkness reveals that it is certainly not only an eschatological judgment but also the characteristic of Satan in his ever-present opposition to Christ's mission. Indeed, the mission of Christ is a continual confrontation of the forces of darkness. The world before Christ is darkness and the "shadow of death" (Matt. 4:16; see also Isa. 8:19-22), and humans are in this darkness because of their evil deeds (John 3:19) and hatred of one another (1 John 2:11). Specifically, those who take Jesus into custody before his crucifixion are under the "power of darkness" (Luke 22:53). Jesus, the light coming into the darkness (John 1:5) and into darkened human hearts (2 Cor. 4:6), rescues humans from the power of Satan by transferring them into the light of God (Acts 26:17-18; Eph. 5:8; Col. 1:13). Although the faithful are no longer in darkness (1 Thess. 5:4-5), the struggle with evil continues (Eph. 6:12). In that struggle, the saints are to "proclaim the mighty acts of him who called you out of darkness into his marvelous light" (1 Pet. 2:9). Thus, the story of salvation is portrayed as the confrontation between darkness and light.

The Battle of the Great Day of God the Almighty

The idea of a final battle between kings with their nations and God with the anointed has deep roots in the biblical tradition (Ps. 2:2-3). Isaiah and Jeremiah saw this battle to be the result of God's anger against those who reject divine instruction and arrogantly practice violence and oppression (Isa. 5:18-30; 13:4-22; Jer. 6:1-8). Zephaniah says this battle on the Day of the Lord will be a terrible time of "distress and anguish," "ruin and devastation," and "darkness and gloom" (Zeph. 1:14-18). Joel calls the people to repent in order to avoid the judgment that is coming on the nations (Joel 2:11; 3:2, 9-15). Zechariah describes this battle in considerable detail as a time of suffering for Jerusalem but also as a time when they will be defended by God (Zech. 14). Ezekiel 38-39 is the most memorable prophecy of this final battle between Israel and Gog of the land of Magog, where weapons of "pestilence and bloodshed," "torrential rains and hailstones," and "fire and sulfur" are used against Gog (Ezek. 38:22). In the New Testament this eschatological battle is spiritualized to speak of God's judgment against those who reject the word of God (John 12:48; cf. 6:39) and of God's testing the righteous with fire (1 Cor. 3:13; Phil. 1:10; 2 Pet. 3:11-12).

Coming Like a Thief

Christ as thief is perhaps the strangest metaphor in the New Testament. Although Jesus does refer to thieves in the more conventional way (Matt. 6:19-20), there is only one characteristic of a thief that can properly be attributed to Christ: the uncertainty associated with his coming. Christ refers to himself as thief to emphasize that the faithful must be ready because the Son of Man will return at an unexpected hour (Luke 12:39-40; see also Matt. 24:42-44; Matt. 25:13;

Mark 13:32-37; Acts 1:6-7). Paul adds to uncertainty the idea of deception when he says that Christ will return when the wicked feel peace and security (1 Thess 5:2-5). Peter stresses the importance of disclosing Christ's coming because it will usher in the Day of the Lord when the earth will be dissolved with fire and all will be disclosed (2 Pet. 3:10). Although the image is connected to the parousia elsewhere, the connection is not so clear in Revelation. In the letter to Sardis, the coming of Christ is promised if the Sardians refuse to wake up and repent, a contingency not usually associated with the second coming (Rev. 3:3). In the present context, the thief imagery is connected with the battle of the Day of the Lord God Almighty (Rev. 16:15).

The Great Battlefield at Megiddo

The location of the "battle on the great day of God the Almighty" is a place called Harmagedon (Rev. 16:14, 16). As the Explanatory Notes indicate, it is likely that this location has some connection with Megiddo, the great battleground in the Hebrew scriptures.

After twenty years of oppression at the hands of the Canaanites, the judge Deborah commissioned Barak to engage Sisera, the commander of Canaanite King Jabin's army, at Mount Tabor. Barak agreed only if Deborah would accompany him. She assented but warned Barak that he would not be honored because the victory would go to a woman. Actually, God won the battle by throwing Sisera's troops into panic, resulting in the complete destruction of the Canaanite army. In his flight, Sisera was killed, indeed, by a woman named Jael, who drove a tent peg through his head with a hammer (Judg. 4:4-24; see Brensinger, BCBC, on *Judges*: 61-75). After the battle, Deborah and Barak sang the following words:

> The kings came, they fought;
> then fought the kings of Canaan,
> at Taanach, by the waters of Megiddo;
> they got no spoils of silver.
> The stars fought from heaven,
> from their courses they fought against Sisera. (Judg. 5:19-21)

In contrast to this great victory of Israel, two kings of Judah met terrible military deaths in Megiddo. After killing Joram in Jezreel to carry out his commission to destroy the house of Ahab, Jehu ordered his troups to shoot Judah's King Ahaziah, an ally of Joram. The wounded Ahaziah subsequently fled to Megiddo and died there (2 Kings 9:1-28). After Josiah was defeated and killed by Pharoah

Neco, servants carried the dead king from Megiddo to Jerusalem for burial (2 Kings 23:28-30).

Stories like this are most likely what caused Jeremiah to say that Jerusalem's inhabitants "mourn for their king as one mourns for an only child, and weep bitterly over him, as one weeps over a firstborn. On that day, the mourning in Jerusalem will be as great as the mourning for Haddad-rimmon in the plain of Megiddo" (Zech. 12:10-11). It is probable that these traditions related to Megiddo, especially the death of Judah's great king Josiah, caused the place to be associated with the final battle on the day of God Almighty.

THE TEXT IN THE LIFE OF THE CHURCH

Salvation through Christ

Revelation teaches that it is Christ who, through his death and resurrection, has won the victory over Satan and the beast. Moreover, the present passage says that all nations will come and worship before God. What does this mean for the scope of salvation? How can it be that salvation is only through Christ and yet that all nations will come to worship God? There are at least four positions on this issue (see Okholm and Phillips, 1996, which is basis for most of the information in this section). The traditional view, sometimes called *exclusivism,* emphasizes the first principle but ignores the second, believing that only those who have accepted God's salvation through Christ will be saved and that those who do not will be damned. Considerable biblical material supports the view that salvation is only through Christ. Speaking to a Jewish audience about the resurrection of Christ, Peter says: "There is salvation in no one else, for there is no other name under heaven given among mortals by which we must be saved" (Acts 4:12). When asked by a Philippian jailor what he must do to be saved, Paul replies: "Believe on the Lord Jesus, and you will be saved, you and your household" (Acts 16:31). Later, in the epistle to the Romans, Paul says: "if you confess with your lips that Jesus is Lord and believe in your heart that God raised him from the dead, you will be saved" (Rom. 10:9). Speaking of condemnation rather than salvation, John's gospel affirms: "Those who believe in him are not condemned; but those who do not believe are condemned already, because they have not believed in the name of the only son of God (John 3:18). Perhaps the clearest support for the exclusivist position is also in the Fourth Gospel, where Jesus says to Thomas: "I am the way, and the truth, and the life. No one comes to the Father except through me" (John 14:6). Although exclusivists believe with good support that no one comes to God except through Christ, they often do not treat adequately the equally biblical idea that eventually all things will come together in the kingdom of God.

In reaction to the pessimism of the traditional view regarding the fate of the majority of humanity, enlightenment humanism led to a *pluralist* position, affirming that many religions when followed sincerely lead to God. Hick (in Okholm and Phillips, 1996:29-59) argues that the major religions contain a similar structure of salvation, whether it is called redemption (Judaism and Christianity), submission (Islam), or enlightenment (Eastern religions). Moreover, love and kindness are taught in many religions, and Christians do not, on average, differ in moral goodness from non-Christians. Hick denies the uniqueness of Christ in salvation on the evidence that Christ did not claim to be divine in passages that scholars agree are authentically from Jesus. If Jesus is merely a human being, then he is not unique among the religious prophets who have all served similar functions in their respective traditions. The pluralist position could affirm the idea that all nations will eventually worship God, but not the truth that salvation comes only through the death and resurrection of Christ.

Because both the exclusivists and pluralists seem to ignore at least one clear biblical teaching, two medial viewpoints have been considered. McGrath (in Okholm and Phillips, 1996:151-80) outlines the *particularist* position, which agrees with the exclusivists that salvation is only in Christ, but places the fate of those who have not heard of Christ in the hands of God. This view also shares with exclusivism the belief in a sharp distinction between general and special revelation. John Calvin differentiated between knowledge of God as creator and redeemer; Martin Luther between "the hidden God of creation and law (*Deus absconditus*)" and "the revealed God of covenant and gospel (*Deus revelatus*)" (Okholm and Phillips, 1996:165). The former, in each case, is open to all religions but is not salvific; the latter, available only in Christ, leads to salvation. Moreover, particularists affirm against the pluralists that careful investigation indicates there are indeed major differences among the various religions in their structures of salvation. For example, the Christian scriptures state that Jesus died on a cross, which the Qur'an denies. More importantly, various religions have different concepts of salvation: the Homeric tartarus, the Christian heaven, and the Buddhist nirvana. And most important, as was noted by the exclusivists, Christianity affirms that salvation comes only through Jesus Christ. Finally, the particularists raise a question regarding the contention of the pluralists and inclusivists that all will eventually come to Christ: Does "all will be saved" mean "all *must* be saved" (Okholm and Phillips, 1996:177)? Is it possible for a person to reject the invitation to salvation? This line of logic would seem to lead to a radical divine predestination of salvation for all. Although universal salvation is ruled out, particularists indicate that there may be surprise at who will be saved, appealing to Jesus' statement regarding the Ninevites, the queen of Sheba, and the inhabitants of Tyre, Sidon, Sodom, and Gomorrah (Matt. 10:15; 11:22; 12:41-42). Particularists believe that God is not limited to human effort, but persons who did not hear about Christ may be led to God through prevenient grace. In the words of an old hymn:

> I sought the Lord, and afterward I knew
> He moved my soul to seek him, seeking me;
> It was not I that found, O Savior true;
> No, I was found by Thee.

A second medial position, *inclusivism,* agrees with the pluralists that all nations, even from other religious traditions, indeed come to God, but affirms with the particularists that this salvation is through the work of Christ. For example, Pinnock (in Okholm and Phillips, 1996:95-123) asserts that both general and special revelation are salvific and both have their origin in Christ, that God's salvation is open to all regardless where or when they live or lived, that the Holy Spirit is at work among all people drawing them to God, and that God may even use the positive aspects of other religions to call persons to himself. Inclusivists appeal to biblical passages that speak of the wideness of God's salvation (Ps. 22:27; 65:5; 1 Tim. 2:3-4; Rev. 14:3; 22:2). The Johannine writings in particular emphasize the universal scope of Christ's work (John 1:9; 3:16-17; 10:16; 12:32; 1 John 2:2). Moreover, the Bible has several examples of persons coming to salvation outside of the Judeo-Christian tradition. Abraham seems convinced that Melchizedek, the King of Salem, worships the God of Israel through the Canaanite god, *El Elyon* (Gen. 14:17-24). The pagan Abimelech acts more like a follower of the God of Israel than Abraham (Gen. 20:1-18). Cornelius, a Gentile god-fearer teaches Peter that God has witnesses in all religious traditions (Acts 11:16-17). Perhaps due to this strong biblical evidence, the inclusivist position has not been without its proponents. John Wesley believed that God communicates inwardly to those who have not heard about Christ: "We have great reason to hope, although they lived among the Heathens, yet were quite another spirit; being taught of God, by his inward voice, all the essentials of true religion" (1986:7.197). Moreover, C. S. Lewis contends that adherents to other religions can be Christians unknowingly: "There are people in other religions who are being led by God's secret influence to concentrate on those parts of their religion which are in agreement with Christianity, and who thus belong to Christ without knowing it" (1967:176).

The four positions as they relate to the two biblical concepts of salvation in Christ alone and the salvation of all nations may be diagramed in the following manner:

Salvation:	In Christ Alone	Of All Nations
Pluralism	No	Yes
Inclusivism	Yes	Through Christ
Particularism	Yes	No Opinion
Exclusivism	Yes	No

Armageddon

Under the symbol of Armageddon, "the battle on the great day of God the Almighty" receives its most political/historical treatment. Therefore, attempts have repeatedly been made to tie this symbol to contemporary events. For example, Dwight Wilson cites quotations from the World War I era (1977:36):

> The time cannot be far off when Russia's millions, augmented by the armies she will gather from these among the nations, will be thrown by their rulers into Palestine in order to destroy the nation of the Jews. (*Our Hope,* August 1916)
>
> The most striking sign of the times is the proposal to give Palestine to the Jews once more.... November 2, 1917 was a red-letter day in the world's history when the British Foreign Secretary addressed his now famous letter to Lord Rothchild on this subject. (*Our Hope,* July 1919)

Referring to the title of his book, Wilson concludes, "'Armageddon Now!' has been the premillennarians' cry since 1917—to what avail?"

The symbol has also been a favorite of many leaders. Since the 1940s, Armageddon has been tied most closely to the nuclear arms race. In his book *March to Armageddon,* Powaski (1987) uses the image to present a fine sketch of the twentieth-century arms race from Roosevelt's Manhattan Project, to Truman's employment of nuclear weapons in Hiroshima and Nagasaki and the subsequent Cold War, to Eisenhower's arms control, to Kennedy's Limited Test Ban Treaty, to

Johnson's Strategic Arms Limitation Talks, to Nixon's Salt I and Detente, to Carter's Salt II, to Reagan's rearmament. Powaski's discussion could now be extended to the fall of Soviet communism during the Bush administration and the expectations related to the year 2000 during the Clinton administration.

Perhaps the most popular recent references to Armageddon were by American President Ronald Reagan. After being told of a leftist coup in Libya, Reagan responded:

> That's a sign that the day of Armageddon isn't far off.... Everything is falling into place. It can't be long now. Ezekiel says that fire and brimstone will be rained upon the enemies of God's people. That must mean that they will destroyed by nuclear weapons. (cited in Boyer, 1992:142)

Later he told a lobbyist for Israel:

> You know, I turn back to your ancient prophets in the Old Testament and the signs foretelling Armageddon, and I find myself wondering if we're the generation that's going to see that come about. I don't know if you've noted any of those prophesies lately, but believe me, they certainly describe the times we're going through. (ibid.)

A more out-of-the-mainstream person who was attracted to Armageddon imagery was David Koresh, the leader of the Branch Davidians, who saw himself as the one preparing the world for Armageddon. He believed that the tribulation had already begun and that he had been called to open the seven seals. He told his followers that they would migrate to Israel to convert Jews, thus triggering the international conflict that would lead to an invasion by the U.S. army. In this battle of Armageddon, Koresh would be the angel preparing the world for the New Jerusalem (Bromiley and Silver, 1995:58).

A particularly embarrassing prediction regarding Armageddon is portrayed in the title of Hal Lindsey's book, *The 1980s: Countdown to Armageddon*. Addressing the fig tree passage (Matt. 24:32-34), he asserts in capital letters: "WE ARE THE GENERATION HE WAS TALKING ABOUT!" (1980:181). After summarizing contemporary events that reflect Armageddon imagery and indicate the end is near, Lindsey concludes: *"The decade of the 1980's could very well be the last decade of history as we know it"* (1980:8, author's emphasis). Such faulty speculation should caution others against similar predictions.

Revelation 17:1-18

The Great Whore

PREVIEW

Chapter 16 marked the end of Revelation's numbered visions—the seven seals, seven trumpets, and seven bowls. Caird says that the numbered visions present panoramas of judgment and the unnumbered visions give close-ups of some aspects of that panorama (1966:211). This distinction describes particularly well what happens in the transition between chapters 16 and 17 of Revelation. The seventh bowl (16:17-21) is a panoramic view of the fall of Babylon; chapters 17–18 give detailed, close-up pictures of that fall. The book comes to a climax at the end of chapter 16 with the final judgment of the seventh bowl. What follows is not a new event; all is finished with the words, "It is done!" (16:17). Roloff calls what follows "an enlargement photograph" (1993:193).

The fall of Babylon has already been announced twice in Revelation (14:8; 16:19). Here we learn the details related to that fall, the victory over the systemic evil symbolized in Babylon the Great. This destruction of evil is the climax of Revelation: the victory of Christ and his followers, and the establishment of the New Jerusalem. The fall of Babylon is the judgment that brings the destruction of evil (chs. 17–18); the ascent of the New Jerusalem is the salvation that brings the eternal preservation of all that is good (ch. 20–22). Hence, Revelation portrays good and evil again in perfect symmetry. This is not a strict dualism, however, because the outcome is never in doubt: evil Babylon will ultimately be destroyed (Barker, 2000:226).

There is a difference in the way the fall of Babylon is portrayed in chapters 17 and 18. Chapter 17 is a narrative that announces the fall and identifies the characters in the drama, the whore and the beast; chapter 18 is a poetic dirge or lament sung over the fallen city. Peterson sees here another parallel to the Exodus story, suggesting that, similarly, Exodus 14 is a narrative description of the judgment of Egypt and the salvation of Israel, and Exodus 15 a song celebrating these events (1988:144). Thus, the Exodus from Egypt forms a positive counterpoint to the fall of Babylon.

As with much of Revelation, the imagery of Babylon's fall is from the Old Testament. Indeed, the predominance of Hebrew material has led many commentators to suspect that the bulk of the chapter is from a Jewish source. The source theory might explain the alternation of the imagery for the beast between kings and kingdoms (Beasley-Murray, 1974:250; see also Dan. 2:36-45; 7:17-18, 23-27 and Lederach, BCBC, 1994, on *Daniel*; 2 Esd. 13:25-50). If the source theory is true, the chapter refers to the Jewish persecutions of A.D. 66-70, and the phrase "the saints and martyrs of Jesus Christ" (v. 6) was added, along with verse 14, to give the passage a Christian flavor.

In addition to the major source in the Hebrew tradition, a subordinate source for the great whore image may be found in the Roman culture (Barclay, 1960:2.187-188). Temple prostitutes were a common religious temptation in the culture of John's day. More specifically, Messalina, the wife of Emperor Claudius, who lived as an empress by day and a common prostitute by night, may have sat for the portrait of Revelation's great whore (Juvenal, *Satires* 6.118-132; see Tac., *Annals* 11.31; cf. Aune, 1998b:929).

Wherever the awful image in Revelation comes from, it is manifestly clear that the whore symbolizes the worship of Rome. Yet the reader must ask: Why add a great whore to the symbol of the beast in describing Rome? What is gained by including this repulsive creature? The whore of Babylon is the counterpart of the bride referred to in connection with the New Jerusalem (19:7; 21:2, 9): the whore's blasphemy of God contrasts with the bride's faithfulness to God (Mulholland, 1990:277). Again there is symmetry between good and evil: on the one hand, the beast with his whore, which is the city of Rome, and on the other hand, the Lamb with his bride, which is the New Jerusalem.

But the question might still be asked: why add such a lurid symbol? Perhaps Flannery O'Connor provides the best answer:

The novelist with Christian concerns will find in modern life distortions which are repugnant to him, and his problem will be to make these appear as distortions to an audience which is used to seeing them as nat-

ural; and he may well be forced to take ever more violent means to get
his vision across to this hostile audience. When you can assume that your
audience holds the same beliefs that you do, you can ... use more normal
ways of talking to it; when ... it does not, then you have to make your
vision apparent by shock—to the hard of hearing you shout, and for the
almost blind you draw large and startling figures. (1988:805-6)

This explanation, although written about twentieth-century audiences,
appears a convincing reason for introducing the symbol of the whore
in John's writing.

This image of the fornicating city has been interpreted to be either
historical Rome or symbolically what Rome represents. Some see
Babylon as the goddess Roma and the Rome of John's day that
seduced others to the idolatrous worship of the emperor. Others see
Babylon as a timeless symbol of spiritual whoredom that seduces persons from God to the worship of violence and materialism. Mounce
describes the great whore as "a dominant world system based on
seduction for personal gain over against the righteous demands of a
persecuted minority" (1977:307).

Although chapter 17 introduces the great whore, the surprising
twist in the chapter is that most of the content describes the beast,
who has already received extensive treatment (11:7; 13:1-10). John
is greatly amazed by the whore, but it is the beast that is explained to
him. Perhaps the point is: to understand the whore, observe the beast.
Eller contends that the whore is the outward manifestation of the
world, and the beast is the spiritual reality behind her worldliness
(1974:158). In addition to being surprising, the presentation of the
beast in this chapter contains considerable ambiguity: it is both an
empire and a line of rulers. Yet such ambiguity is not unusual in
Revelation. This beast has its roots in the ten-horned beast of Daniel
7:7-8 and in the eagle of 2 Esd. 11–12 and is a parody of Revelation's
Lamb that was slaughtered (5:6) but is alive (1:18; 13:14).

A final caution should be noted in approaching this chapter, which
vividly portrays Babylon as both woman and whore. The one who
sees this as justification for either stereotyping women as evil or for
taking offense at the evil portrayal of the female gender should note
that the beast is male. So Revelation is not discriminating, portraying
the evil city both as male beast and female whore, each contributing
significantly to the total portrait but neither giving basis for derogato-
ry gender stereotypes (see TLC on ch. 19, Women in Revelation).

The content of the chapter clearly falls into two sections, the vision
(vv. 1-6) and its interpretation (vv. 7-18), a pattern also found in
Daniel 7 and 2 Esdras 13. Yet the irony of Revelation 17 is that the

vision is more lucid than the interpretation. Indeed, the latter seems to raise more questions than it answers.

OUTLINE

The Whore on the Scarlet Beast, 17:1-6
The Interpretation of the Whore and Beast, 17:7-18

EXPLANATORY NOTES

The Whore on the Scarlet Beast 17:1-6

The vision of the whore on the scarlet beast begins with a verse that ties what precedes to what follows: *Then one of the seven angels who had the seven bowls came.* This is perhaps the seventh angel that in the preceding passage announced the fall of Babylon in the final bowl of God's wrath (16:17) and also perhaps the angel that will show John the bride, the antithesis of the whore in the vision that follows (21:9). Such connecting symbols have become common in Revelation.

This angel then announces to John the theme of chapters 17 and 18: *"Come, I will show you the judgment of the great whore."* The verb translated "show" also introduces the bride in 21:9 (see also John 5:20; 1 Tim. 6:15; 1 Clem. 35:12; Barn. 5:9). The one introduced is the major symbol of the chapter, the great whore *(pornē),* the personification of Babylon, which parallels Isaiah 47 and Jeremiah 51, and serves as a negative counterpoint for the personification of wisdom in Proverbs 9. The symbol carries the sense of *porn,* the root of both *whore,* her vocation, and *fornication (porneia),* her activity. This root carries today the sexual imagery of its literal meaning in Revelation. Yet the apocalypse uses *porn* metaphorically to connote idolatry, and by extension economic perversion, because the whore offers herself for money (see Ortlund, 1996, for a discussion of the use of the symbol "whoredom" throughout the Bible).

That the great whore is *seated on many waters* reminds the reader of the beast that arises from the sea (13:1-10). Jeremiah describes Babylon as by many waters (Jer. 51:12-13), alluding to the ancient city's irrigation system that directed the waters of the Euphrates so as to facilitate the river's contribution to the wealth of the city. Yet here the reference is to Rome, the New Babylon, who is seated on the waters in the sense that she has power over the nations. Later, in verse 15, the waters are identified with "peoples and multitudes and nations and languages" (Isa. 8:7-10; Jer. 47:2; Ezek. 29:9-10). These waters contributed to the economic power of Rome by serving as the conduit for commercial wealth to flow into the city. This is the maritime equivalent to the often-repeated statement: All roads lead to Rome.

The great whore is the one *with whom the kings of the earth have committed fornication, and with the wine of whose fornication the inhabitants of the earth have become drunk*. The kings of the earth are Rome's political and economic subjects, who are dependent on the material goods they receive from Rome and therefore accept her idolatry and immorality (16:14; 17:18; 18:9-10). Thus, their relations with the whore are economic and commercial (Ezek. 16; Jos., *Ant*. 14.110-11). That the kings are from the earth indicates that Rome's economic influence has spread throughout the world. These kings of the earth who fornicate with the whore are the antithesis of the 144,000 who are virgins (14:4) and who marry the Lamb (19:7-8). The woman is a whore because she seduces the kings of the earth to idolatry and the inhabitants of the earth from the worship of God (Jer. 2:20-31; 13:27; Ezek. 16:15-22; Nah. 3:4) to intoxication with the economic prosperity of Rome (Beale, 1999:849). The passage speaks powerfully of Rome's materialistic influence throughout the world.

To show John the great whore, the angel *carried [him] away in the spirit into the wilderness* (Isa. 19:22; Jer. 51:26, 29, 43). As in introductions to previous visions in Revelation, the phrase *in the spirit* refers to a visionary state that brings true spiritual insight (1:10; 4:2; see also Ezek. 3:14; 37:1; 40:1-2; 2 Cor. 12:2-3); its presence in the vision of the holy city (21:10) heightens the contrast between the whore and the bride.

The location of the vision in *the wilderness* reminds the reader of Jesus' encounter with Satan in that venue (Matt. 4:1-3; see also Luke 1:80). The wilderness was a desolate place where unclean animals and evil spirits lurked (Isa. 13:19-22; Luke 11:24) "an earthly analogue to the abyss" (Thompson, 1998:159). This wilderness where John views the great whore is the counterpart of the mountain where he is taken to observe the Lamb's bride, the New Jerusalem (21:10; see also Exod. 3:1-6). Yet the wilderness is at the same time a place of protection (12:6, 14), in this case from the great whore. A literal mind may also be bothered by the ambiguity regarding the location of the woman: is she in the wilderness or on the waters, two rather conflicting images (see also 12:13-17)? The experienced reader of Revelation has likely grown accustomed to such ambiguity of symbolism. The wilderness is probably simply a place of protection from which the faithful can see the destruction of the great whore and reflect in seclusion on her nature and their relationship to her (see Morris, 1969:205).

In the wilderness, John sees *a woman sitting on a scarlet beast*, the beast from the sea, which was previously described as having *seven heads and ten horns* (13:1; cf. to the Lamb in 5:6). The color *scarlet* has a double meaning: it alludes to the dress of the woman who shares the splendor of the evil beast (v. 4) and to the blood of the saints and witnesses (v. 6). Secondary allusions may be to the color of Satan, the red dragon (12:3), and by contrast to the white dress of the 24 elders (4:4) and the 144,000 (7:9; see also Ps. 51:7). Perhaps the most difficult interpretive issue is to distinguish between the referents for the woman and the beast. If the woman is the city of Rome and the beast the Roman Empire (Krodel, 1989:292), the meaning here is that the city receives economic and political support from its vast empire.

The scarlet beast on which the woman rode *was full of blasphemous names*. In Revelation 13:1, the heads (emperors) of the beast have these names; here the whole beast (empire) is covered with them. The latter indicates that the whole Roman empire sanctioned the divine titles, like "God," "Savior," and "Lord," inscribed on buildings, monuments, and coins. Surely, the chief characteristic of the beast and the empire for which he stands is blasphemy.

Turning again from the beast to the woman, John describes her lavish apparel. The colors of her clothing, *purple and scarlet,* came from expensive dyes, the purple processed from shellfish and the scarlet from female insects (Morris, 1969:205-6). Although the clear connotation of the colors relates to their association with wealth, it may also be significant that purple is connected with royalty (Judg. 8:26; Dan. 5:7) and scarlet with sin (Isa. 1:18). The woman is also bedecked with *gold and jewels and pearls.* The gold here points forward to the golden cup of abominations and impurities in the following verse and contrasts with the golden crowns of the twenty-four elders (4:3-4), the golden bowls of incense that are the prayers of the saints (5:8; 8:3), and the golden altar (9:13). The reference to pearls, which were thought to be of great value (Job 28:18; Matt. 7:6; 13:46), anticipates their reappearance in the gates of the New Jerusalem, the antithesis of Babylon the whore (21:21). In general, the woman was dressed like a whore (see also 18:16; Judg. 8:26). Her clothing is not appropriate for a faithful woman (1 Tim. 2:9-10; 1 Pet. 3:3-4), and it stands in stark contrast to the fine linen of the bride (19:7-8) as well as the woman clothed with the sun (12:1) and the heavenly beings who wear white robes (3:18; 6:11; 7:9; 19:14).

The whore is *holding in her hand a golden cup full of abomi-nations and the impurities of her fornication.* The Septuagint used *abominations* to refer to the abomination of desolation in Daniel. In Revelation, the term refers to the abomination of worshiping Rome to gain her benefits. Although the woman looks beautiful and seductive, inwardly she is hideous and depraved (cf. Prov. 7:4-27).

On the whore's *forehead was written a name.* There is probably here an allusion to the custom of Roman whores putting their names or the names of their owners on headbands. The name on the whore's forehead is called a *mystery.* This does not mean that it is a puzzle, but that it is revealed through the prophets to the faithful (1:20; 10:7; Dan. 2:29-30; Rom. 11:25; 1 Cor. 2:6-7; 15:51; Eph. 3:3-6; Col. 1:25-27; 2 Thess. 2:7). Indeed, the meaning of this mystery is clear: Babylon is Rome (cf. T. C. Smith, 1997:115-16, who believes Babylon refers to Jerusalem).

The actual name written leaves little doubt that the whore's inscription is closer to the mark of the beast than to the seal of God: *"Babylon the great, mother of whores and of earth's abomination."* By contrast, Christ the rider on the white horse wears a name on his thigh, "King of kings, Lord of lords" (19:16). Although Babylon refers to Rome, it also designates any city that is a true abomination (see TBC, Babylon the Abomination). As the mother of whores, Babylon entices her children to join in her adultery, which involves all forms of abomination, including the idolatrous worship of Rome.

Indeed, John saw that the whore was *drunk with the blood of the saints and the blood of the witnesses to Jesus.* Taken literally, the whore is in violation of the prohibition of Leviticus 17:10 (Rowland, 1998:681). The phrase *drunk with blood* was in common use among Roman writers to describe their emperors (Suet., *Tiberius* 59; Pliny, *Nat. Hist.* 14.28; see also Jos., *War* 5.344). Isaiah employs it to refer to both Israel's oppressors (1 Kings 16:31) and the response of God to that oppression (1 Kings 18:4; see also Isa. 34:5-6; 49:26). The metaphor is one of John's favorites to depict the tribulations of the saints in Revelation. That the persecutors were drunk indicates they reveled in their tortures; that the saints shed their blood indicates they refused to deny Christ even under persecution (11:7-10; 12:17; 14:12; 20:4; see also 13:7, 10; 16:6; 18:24; 19:2).

Although Ford argues that the word *witness* is not used in the sense of "martyr" in the New Testament (1975:279), it seems to carry that connotation in Revelation (1:5; 2:13; 3:14; 11:3). If Ford is correct, it is not evident how the words *saints* and *witnesses* are to be distinguished. Although Aune argues for their equivalence

(1998b:937), it is best to take *witness* in the sense of "martyr" here. The combining of violence and seduction in the image of the whore indicates that Rome's wealth was based on violence against her enemies. Robert Smith addresses a similar problem today: "The churches must stop playing chaplain to the Pentagon and Wall Street, stop sprinkling holy water on tanks and banks" (2000:36, 82).

John's response to seeing the whore was to be *greatly amazed*. The passage does not clarify why John is amazed. He may be puzzled at the strange sight of the whore or shocked at her wickedness. Swete says that he is surprised because, expecting to observe the fall of Babylon (16:17-21), he sees a woman on a beast (1908:218). Beale is most likely correct to see the amazement as "shock, fear, and perplexity" (1999:862-63). Whatever the reason for the amazement, it serves as a transition device leading into the interpretation of the vision that follows.

The Interpretation of the Whore and Beast 17:7-18

Completing the literary connection with what precedes, the angel asks the rhetorical question: *Why are you so amazed?* Daniel experiences a similar emotion when asked to interpret visions for Babylonian Kings Nebuchadnezzar and Belshazzar (Dan. 4:19; 7:15, 28; 8:15-19, 27). The angel here assures John that he will reveal *the mystery of the woman, and of the beast with seven heads and ten horns that carries her*. Again the parallel to the interpretations of Daniel's visions is obvious (Dan. 2:19-49; 4:9-29; 5:13-29; 7:16-27; see also 2 Esd. 12:10-30).

The angel's interpretation begins with the words: *The beast that you saw was, and is not, and is about to ascend from the bottomless pit and go to destruction.* This clause introduces two elements that will be seen throughout the interpretation that follows: *saw* is repeated in verses 12, 15, and 18; and *is not*, in verses 8b and 11. The latter is a blasphemous variation on the title for God (1:4, 8; 4:8) reminding the reader that the Lamb is God (1:17-18; 2:8) and the beast is a parody of God. Yahweh, the "one who is," contrasts with the beast, "who is not." The entire picture is reminiscent of the head of the beast that died and revived (13:3, 12, 14). Behind the image is the *Nero redivivus* myth, the beast being the personification of the Roman empire in Emperor Nero, who had died, but whose imminent return was expected *[Essay: Nero Redivivus Myth]*. Nero's death and *redivivus* parallels Christ's crucifixion and parousia. The beast's ascending from the bottomless pit, the evil counterpart of heaven (2 Pet. 2:4; Jude 5-7; 1 Enoch 10:4-6,11-14; 18:11-16; Jub. 5:6-11), is a caricature of the descent of Christ from heaven at the end. The use of the present tense indicates that the beast repeatedly arises from the abyss: it is his character to do so (11:7). Eller is correct to assume the truth of the passage is that the disappearance of evil is always an illusion (1974:157-58): when it appears that evil "is not," look out! Despite his persistence, though, the eventual fate of the beast is destruction (19:20; 20:10; see also Matt. 7:13; Phil. 3:19; 2 Pet. 3:7). This destruction that follows the ascension of the beast from the bottomless pit is contrasted with the salvation brought by the ascension of Christ the Lamb from the cross into heaven (Heb. 10:39). The beast goes to destruction; Christ lives forever and ever. Although the rule of the beast is temporary, the kingdom of the Lamb is eternal.

John is not the only one amazed at the sight of the beast: *the inhabitants of the earth, whose names have not been written in the book of life from the foundation of the world, will be amazed when they see the beast, because it was and is not and is to come.* The book of life here alludes to the book of the living, which recorded the righteous and holy (Ps. 69:28; Isa. 4:3). Although this verse and 13:8 seem to imply predestination, the rest of Revelation is clear that humans determine their own eternal fate (3:5; 20:11-15; 21:27; see also TBC, Predestination). The phrase *is not* implies no persecution at present; *is to come* affirms its return. Because the verb *come (parestai)* is from the same root as *parousia*, the return of the beast is the evil antithesis of the second coming of Christ (1 Cor. 15:23; 1 Thess. 2:19; 1 John 2:28).

The most ambiguous part of the vision begins with the words: *This calls for a mind that has wisdom: the seven heads are seven mountains on which the woman is seated.* In a manner analogous to the revelation of mysteries to the faithful, the identity of the beast is discovered using wisdom (13:18; 1 QH 7.26-27). The first identification of the seven heads of the beast is that they are seven mountains, a courageous revealing of the beast's identity, because it was commonly thought that Rome was built on seven hills (Sib. Or. 2:18; 13:45; 14:108; Suet., *Domitian* 4; Virgil, *Aeneid* 6.783; *Georgics* 2.535; Martial, *Epigrams* 4.64; Cicero, *Letter to Atticus* 6.5; Ovid, *Tristia* 1.5.69; cf. Beale, 1999:870). Boring insightfully says that Rome became Babylon after destroying Jerusalem and its temple in A.D. 66-70 just as Babylon had in 586 B.C. (1989:180; see 1 Pet. 5:13; 2 Esd. 3:1-3). The obvious reference to Rome here indicates that John was using symbols, not to hide his message, but to make it more clear and complete.

The second identification of the seven heads of the beast is that *they are seven kings,* who appear to be Roman emperors or perhaps stand for all the emperors of Rome. There is little agreement regarding the identification of the specific emperors intended in the passage (see TLC, The Seven Heads of the Beast). Yet the overall meaning of the complex symbol is lucid: the present ruler, who persecutes the faithful, will endure for only a little while before being supplanted by the eternal kingdom of God (Dan. 7:13-14). The imagery may be confusing, but the meaning is clear and comforting to the faithful.

The uniqueness of the seven kings is that *five have fallen, one is living, and the other has not yet come; and when he comes, he must remain only a little.* The word *fallen* set beside *living* in the next clause indicates that the five kings have died (see Aune, 1998b:949). Revelation suggests that the evil powers of the past have been replaced by one who *is living* and is the sixth in the sense that he participates in the 666. Yet just as the sixth trumpet and bowl were followed by a seventh and last judgment that was short, so the present king will be replaced by one who will *remain only a short time.* In other words, the end is near.

The last king in the sequence is *the beast that was and is not, it is an eighth but it belongs to the seven and it goes to destruction.* The phrase *is not* may be explained in terms of the persecutions of the first century: in the early 60s, Nero killed Christians in the arenas; in the early 70s, Titus destroyed Jerusalem and its temple; in the 80s, there had been no significant persecution *(is not),* but the 90s brought the expectation of its renewal under Domitian (see Yarbro Collins, 1991:129). The wording *eighth but it belongs to the seven* seems to refer to *Nero redivivus,* the expectation that emperor Nero, one of the seven, would return perhaps in the person of Domitian (Sib. Or. 4:119-24; 5:33-34, 363-69; Asc. Isa. 4:2-4; Eusebius, *Eccl. Hist.* 3:20; Tertullian, *Apol.* 5.4; Pliny, *Panegyricus* 53; Juvenal, *Satires* 4.38-40; Martial, *Epigrams* 11.33; Tac., *Hist.* 2.8-9; Suet., *Nero* 57; see also Dan. 8:8-9, 22; Rev. 13:3, 12, 14; cf. 11:7-13). Mounce notes that the eighth is not "one of the seven," but *belongs to the seven,* suggesting that the beast is not a human ruler but the supernatural power that lies behind all evil rulers (1977:316). Whatever the designation of the beast and the other kings, the point is that all earthly political powers will be destroyed. The kingdoms of this world must fall to prepare for the kingdom of God.

After explaining the symbol of seven kings, the angel interprets a similar image: *the ten horns that you saw are ten kings who have not yet received a kingdom.* In Daniel, this symbol designates the ten rulers that succeeded Alexander the Great (Dan. 7:7, 24). Here the ten kings are likely the kings of the East (16:12)—either the Parthians, who are linked in tradition with the reappearance of Nero (Beasley-Murray, 1974:258), or more generally, the "client kings" who ruled the regions on behalf of Rome (Aune, 1998b:951). Futurists counter that the ten kings are eschatological figures, presently identified with the European nations. It seems best to interpret the ten kings symbolically in terms of the image of *ten horns*. Because the horn is consistently a symbol of power, ten horns symbolize complete power in the political realm and represent all powers arrayed in support of the beast. The meaning, then, is that there will be considerable extension of the beast's authority. If this symbolic interpretation is correct and the ten horns do not submit to individual identification, perhaps attempts in the previous verse to identify the seven heads of the beast as kings or kingdoms were misguided, and the symbolic interpretation should be accepted.

The reign of the ten kings is then described. They *receive authority* from the beast, which he obtained from the dragon Satan (13:2, 4), *for one hour,* the short period of time that will in the next chapter designate the duration of the judgment of Babylon (18:10, 17, 19). The kings, in turn, *are united in yielding their power and authority to the beast.* The ten kings, literally, "have one mind," and, in the words of Morris, "are willing collaborators" with the beast (1969:212).

These ten kings then *will make war on the Lamb, and the Lamb will conquer them.* The beast has already waged war on the faithful (11:7-13; 13:7); here, through his ten horns, he attacks the Lamb. In the battle of Armageddon, the weapons of warfare were the words of blasphemy that poured from the mouths of the evil trinity (16:13-14). By implication, then, the Lamb will win this battle, not with military weapons, but with his blood and the witness of the faithful (12:11; see also 17:14; 19:11; Wis. Sol. 3:5-8; Test. Joseph 19:8). Indeed, this battle is the earthly parallel of the battle already won by the Lamb on the cross (see 6:1-2; 19:19-21; cf. 1 Enoch 91:12; 98:12).

The reason for the victory is that the Lamb is *Lord of lords and King of kings.* These titles are given to the Babylonian god Marduk, who conquered the monster Tiamat (Beasley-Murray, 1974:259); to king Nebuchadnezzar (Ezek. 26:7; Dan. 2:37); to the God of Israel (Deut. 10:17; Ps. 136:2-3; Dan. 2:47; 2 Macc. 13:4; 3 Macc. 2:2; 1 Enoch 9:4; 63:4; 84:2); and, with some variation, to Roman Emperor Domitian (Suet., *Domitian* 13). In Revelation, Christ is given universal dominion (19:16; see also 1 Tim. 6:15-16) because he has conquered through his death and resurrection (see 1:5; 3:21; 5:5).

The Lamb's victory over the beast is shared by *those with him [who] are called and chosen and faithful*. Whereas the words *called* and *chosen* are not found elsewhere in Revelation (but see Matt. 22:14), the adjective *faithful* is used for both the saints (2:10, 13; 15:14) and Christ the Lamb (1:5; 3:14; 19:11). Yet the three words are related and relevant to the message of Revelation: the chosen confirm their call by being faithful. Hence, the saints participate with the Lamb in conquering the beast through their faithful witness in the face of tribulation.

The angel continues the interpretation of the vision: *The waters that you saw, where the whore is seated, are peoples and multitudes and nations and languages*. It has already been noted that this symbol alludes to the irrigation system of Babylon, but the interpretation here applies to Rome, as it had to other world powers (Isa. 8:7-8; Jer. 46:7-8; see also Ps. 29:10). The vast throngs represented by the waters are the economic basis for Rome's trade and security (Beale, 1999:882). These *peoples and multitudes and nations and languages* are contrasted with the "called and chosen and faithful" of the preceding verse; Revelation teaches the universality of the faithful (5:9; 7:9) and of the heathen (10:11; 11:9; 13:7; 14:6; 17:15).

The angel then describes division in the ranks of evil: *And the ten horns that you saw, they and the beast will hate the whore*. With traditional graphic metaphors, Revelation describes the destruction of Rome by the beast and his ten subordinate rulers (Isa. 49:26; Ezek. 16:35-41; 23:25-31; Hos. 2:2-7; Mic. 3:1-3). With the phrase *make her desolate*, literally "make her a desert," the image changes from the waters back to the wilderness, using a word from the phrase "desolating sacrilege" (Luke 21:20). That she is *naked* contrasts with the luxurious clothes she formerly wore (v. 4). The beast and its ten horns then *devour* the whore, like the wild dogs that ate the flesh of the idolatrous Queen Jezebel (2 Kings 9:30-37; see also Jer. 10:25; Ezek. 39:4,17-20; Zeph. 3:3). The beast and his confederates will, in turn, be devoured like the whore (Rev. 19:17-21). Finally, the tormenters of the whore will *burn her up with fire*, the traditional punishment for harlotry (Lev. 21:9; cf. 18:8-9; Josh. 7:15; Jer. 38:18, 23). No doubt this is also an allusion to the suspicion that Nero set fire to Rome in A.D. 64 (Tac., *Annals* 15.38-41). The entire picture is one of mutiny—the beast (emperor) and his horn (provincial rulers) turning against the whore (city of Rome; see Ezek. 38:21; Hag. 2:22; Zech. 14:13). More symbolically, Rome's power of seduction has become disgusting, like a whore who is destroyed by her clients.

God's role in the whore's destruction is then stated: *For God has put it into their hearts.* The irony here is that God speaks to the hearts of the beast and ten kings to *carry out his purpose by agreeing to give their kingdom to the beast.* This statement has a repetition of the words that might literally be rendered "to carry out his purpose and carry out the same purpose," and that serves to emphasize God's influence on the actions of the beast and his cohorts. The *words of God* refer to the divine purposes related to the fall of Babylon (14:8; 16:19; 18:8), which *will be fulfilled* (10:7; 15:1, 7-8; Luke 18:31; 22:37; Acts 13:29) as evil destroys itself (Mark 3:23-26). Yarbro Collins says this passage "shows one of the inherent flaws of the will to power. It does not unite; it divides" (1991:122). Indeed, it affirms that the internal division of evil is God's will.

The identification of the whore is again made evident: *The woman you saw is the great city,* a phrase that unmistakably identifies Rome (11:8; 16:19). The *kings of the earth,* over whom Rome rules, are those who mourn the burning of Babylon (18:9; cf. 21:24) and later join the beast to war against the Lamb (19:19), not the kings of the East, who execute God's purpose in judging the whore (16:12). Thus the symbol alludes to the ten kings of this chapter (17:12-14, 15-17) but anticipates the mourning over Babylon of chapter 18.

THE TEXT IN BIBLICAL CONTEXT

The City as Whore

The city as a woman has roots in the Hebrew image of Zion/Jerusalem as both virgin daughter (Isa. 37:22; Lam. 2:13) and mother (Isa. 66:6-13). The relationship between God and Israel is spoken of as a marriage, with Israel as the wife who rejects her husband God to commit spiritual whoredom by worshiping other gods (Isa. 1:21; Jer. 2:20; 3:1, 6, 8-10; 5:7; Hos. 2:5; 3:3; 4:15; see Guenther, *BCBC,* 1998, on Hosea). Her despicable conduct is exemplified in the archetypical whore Jezebel, who seduced Ahab to worship the Baals (1 Kings 21:25-26; 2 Kings 9:22; Rev. 2:20). In a similar manner, idolatrous cities are called whores: Tyre (Isa. 23:15-17), Ninevah (Nah. 3:4-5), Samaria (Ezek. 23:1-10; see also Jer. 2:20-37), and Jerusalem (Ezek. 23:11-21, see also 16:15-52; Jer. 13:27). Wilcock says: "The hills of Rome, the streams of Babylon, the seas of Tyre, are all called in to illustrate different aspects of" the great whore of Babylon (1975:168-69).

Nevertheless, the harlot Jerusalem of Ezekiel 16 seems to be the model for the portrait of Babylon in Revelation. In her original state before her harlotry, God says: "I pledged myself to you and entered into a covenant with you ... and you became mine" (Ezek. 16:8). The clothing of Ezekiel's Jerusalem resembles closely that of Revelation's Babylon: "You were adorned with gold and silver ... fine linen, rich fabric, and embroidered cloth" (Ezek. 16:13). Like the woman of Revelation, she became a whore. Ezekiel makes it clear that the whoredom symbolizes idolatry, stating that she made "colorful shrines" from her clothes, repeating twice that she "built ... a platform and made ... a lofty place in every square" (Ezek. 16:24, 31) and explicitly referring to her "abominable idols" (Ezek. 16:36). Because Jerusalem plays the whore for Egypt, Philistia, Assyria, and Chaldea (Ezek. 16:26-29), her divine judgment is similar to that pronounced on Revelation's Babylon: God will "uncover your nakedness to them" and "they will strip you of your clothes ... and leave you naked and bare," "stone you and cut you to pieces with their swords," and "burn your houses" (Ezek. 16:37-41). In spite of Jerusalem's idolatry, God repeats, "I will establish/remember my covenant" (Ezek. 16:60, 62), and affirms, "I forgive you all that you have done" (Ezek. 16:63).

Another prophecy that is relevant to Revelation's image of the great whore is the allegory of the sisters Oholah and Oholibah in Ezekiel 23 (see Lind, *BCBC,* 1996, on Ezekiel:194-203). At the beginning, that chapter states: "Oholah is Samaria, and Oholibah is Jerusalem" (Ezek. 23:4). The allegory identifies Samaria's idolatry: "Oholah played the whore" and "defiled herself with all the idols of everyone for whom she lusted," especially Assyria and Egypt (Ezek. 23:5-8). In a manner similar to Revelation's judgment of Babylon by the beast and the ten kings, Ezekiel says of Samaria that God "delivered her into the hands of her lovers, into the hands of the Assyrians," who "uncovered her nakedness" and "killed her with the sword" (Ezek. 23:9-10). Oholibah, her sister Jerusalem, was even "more corrupt than she in her lusting and whorings" (Ezek. 23:11). Her whoring, too, symbolized the idolatry of Jerusalem in the lusting after the "images of the Chaldeans" (Ezek. 23:14). God addresses Oholibah in judgment, as he does Babylon in Revelation, saying that he will cause her lovers, the Babylonians, to "cut off your nose and your ears ... and your sons and your daughters, and your survivors shall be devoured by fire" (Ezek. 23:25). Judging both Oholah and Oholibah, God brings "an assembly against them" to "stone them," "cut them down," "kill their sons and their daughters, and burn up their houses" to judge their "sinful idolatry" (Ezek. 23:46-49).

John clearly draws on the descriptions of the whore cities of the Hebrew scriptures to paint his picture of Babylon the Great, who is symbolically the city of Rome. Because she committed adultery by her idolatrous worship of the luxurious abominations of imperial Rome and her shedding the "blood of the saints and the blood of the witnesses to Jesus" (Rev. 17:4-6), the beastly empire and its allies turn on her to "make her desolate and naked," "devour her flesh and burn her up with fire" (Rev. 17:16).

Babylon the Abomination

The name of the whore is, "Babylon the great, the mother of whores and of earth's abominations." The word "abominations" is equivalent to the Hebrew term for idol, *bosheth,* and is inserted by the Chronicler in place of *Baal* in the word *Ishbaal* (2 Sam. 2:8-11) to make "Ishbosheth" (1 Chron. 8:33; 9:39; Beasley-Murray, 1974:252, n.2). The entire name, and specifically the use of the word "abominations," is reminiscent of the "abomination of desolation," a phrase associated in Daniel with the slightly more than three-year occupation of Jerusalem by the Seleucids and their ruler Antiochus IV Epiphanes (Dan. 9:27). Antiochus's blasphemous rule was remembered for his curtailing of temple worship and erecting an altar to Zeus in the temple (Dan. 11:31; 12:11). First Maccabees records many other abominations of Antiochus: inducing the Jews to worship idols and profane the Sabbath; building altars in the towns of Judah upon which unclean animals, including swine, were sacrificed; tearing up and burning the books of the law and condemning to death anyone who possessed a copy of the Law or adhered to its precepts; offering sacrifice on the altar of burnt offering; killing women who had their children circumcised; and hanging the children from their mother's necks (1 Macc. 1:41-61). Jesus says that a similar abomination will precede the flight of Judeans to the mountains, perhaps the flight to Pella during the invasion of Titus (Matt. 24:15; Mark 13:14). Jesus speaks of the abominations that will precede the end of the age, and Revelation describes the blasphemous idolatry of the whore Rome, who worshiped the luxury of its imperial government and persecuted those who refused to participate in such idolatry.

Predestination

A possible interpretation of the latter part of Revelation 13:7 is that the names of the faithful were written in the Lamb's book of life before the foundation of the world; the language of 17:8 more clearly supports that meaning. Thus, these verses could be used in defending the doctrine of predestination; that is, persons are elected by God before creation to be either saved or lost. How is this reconciled with the repeated theme of Revelation that persons must choose to worship the beast or the Lamb?

Two considerations related to predestination in Revelation and the Christian scriptures must be kept in mind. First, the names of sinners are blotted out of the book of life (Exod. 32:32-33; Rev. 22:19), but those of the faithful are not (Rev. 3:5). Hence, to see God's choice at creation as irrevocable is out of keeping with clear biblical teaching. Second, the emphasis in the New Testament is not on predestination but on the offer of salvation to all by repentance and forgiveness of sin through the Lamb (John 1:29; 3:16; 1 Tim. 2:1-7; Rev. 2:5). Although there are passages that can be interpreted as supporting predestination (Rom. 8:28-30), the New Testament message as a whole calls all persons to repentance and salvation. Presenting a balanced view of the relationship between God's election and human response, Caird says that for John "salvation is from start to finish the unmerited act of God. But he constantly qualifies it with an equally strong statement of human responsibility" (1966:168).

THE TEXT IN THE LIFE OF THE CHURCH

The Seven Heads of the Beast

The passage describing the seven heads of the beast has intrigued Christians throughout history, perhaps because it appears to be a puzzle, and it resembles similar passages in Daniel 2 and 7. Although it is misleading to consider the words to be a puzzle, many Christians have treated it that way and have spent hours trying to solve the puzzle.

Most have considered the seven kings to be Roman emperors, but a confusing variety of identifications have been suggested, depending on what emperor is the first and whether or not the three emperors after Nero, who ruled for a total of only eighteen months, are included. The emperors that are candidates for inclusion in John's designations are:

Julius Caesar	Died 44 B.C.
Augustus	31 B.C.–14 A.D.
Tiberius	14-37 A.D.
Caligula	37-41 A.D.
Claudius	41-54 A.D.
Nero	54-68 A.D.
Galba	June 68–murdered 15 Jan. 69 A.D.
Otho	suicide 17 Apr. 69
Vitellius	killed in war with Vespasian 20 Dec. 69
Vespasian	69-79 A.D.
Titus	79-81 A.D.

Domitian	81-96 A.D.
Nerva	96-98 A.D.
Trajan	98-117 A.D.

Perhaps the most common configuration is achieved by beginning with Augustus, the first to be designated "prince" of the empire (Tac., *Annals* 1.1). The "five fallen" would then be Augustus, Tiberius, Caligula, Claudius, and Nero. The three weak emperors, Galba, Otho, and Vitellius are then skipped. Bruce says that the short terms of these rulers made them relatively insignificant from the viewpoint of provinces like Asia (1969:658). Roman historian Suetonius calls their rules "rebellions" (*Vespasian* 1; see also Sib. Or. 5:35). Yet they were emperors, and leaving them out is troubling. The "one ... living" would be Vespasian, which presents a major problem, because Revelation was most likely written during the reign of Domitian, not Vespasian *[Essay: Dating of Revelation]*. R. H. Charles posits that John may have adapted a Jewish source from Vespasian's rule (1920:2.69). Caird suggests that possibly John was exiled to Patmos and received the visions during Vespasian's reign but wrote them down later, during Domitian's rule (1966:218). The emperor that is "yet to come" and will "remain only a little while" would be Titus, who did reign for only a few years and was known to be in critical condition (Ford, 1975:281; see also *Dio's Roman History* 66.26). The "eighth" that "belongs to the seven" then would be Domitian, who was considered to be Nero reborn (Tertullian, *Apol.* 5.4; Juvenal, *Satires* 4.37-38; Pliny, *Panegyricus* 53). The major problem with this scheme is that the passage would imply that Domitian "is not," although he was likely the ruler when John wrote. It seems best to assume that John wrote this, and perhaps 11:1-2, during the rule of Domitian but from the perspective of Vespasian's reign, much like Daniel was perhaps written in the time of Antiochus Epiphanes in the second century B.C. about the kings who ruled Babylon in the sixth century B.C.

The uncertainty of these designations of emperors is emphasized by the plethora of alternative orderings. A relatively common option is to start with Nero, the first ruler to persecute Christians, and include the short rules that followed: Nero, Galba, Otho, Vitellius, Vespasian, Titus, Domitian, and Nero reborn. Another possibility is to begin with the first emperor, Julius (Sib. Or. 5:12-15; see also Jos., *Ant.* 18.2.2; Suet., *Vespasian* 1). Rist then limits the list to those declared divine by the senate: Julius, Augustus, Claudius, Vespasian, and Titus along with the present emperor, Domitian, and the future Neronic antichrist (1957:495). Also beginning with Julius, Schüssler Fiorenza includes among the "fallen" those who died violent deaths: Julius (assassinated), Caligula (assassinated), and Nero (suicide), followed by Domitian, and then Nerva and Trajan (1991:97); perhaps also Claudius (poisoned) and Titus (murdered by Domitian). Krodel starts his list, instead, with Caligula, the first to personally claim divinity and the first to rule after the crucifixion of Jesus: Caligula, Claudius, Nero, Vespasian, Titus, Domitian, a short reign, and Nero reborn (1989:297). Table 5 shows the various configurations:

Table 5. The Seven Emperors

Begin with:	First "Emperor"	First to persecute saints	Julius (Divine)	Julius (violent death)	First to claim divinity
"fallen"	Augustus	Nero	Julius	Julius	Caligula
	Tiberius	Galba	Augustus	Caligula	Claudius
	Caligula	Otho	Claudius	Claudius	Nero
	Claudius	Vitellius	Vespasian	Nero	Vespasian
	Nero	Vespasian	Titus	Titus	Titus
"is"	Vespasian	Titus	Domitian	Domitian	Domitian
"little while"	Titus	Domitian	Antichrist	Nerva	Short Reign
"eighth"	Domitian	Nero reborn		Trajan	Nero Reborn

A completely different method for designating the kings is to identify them with kingdoms rather than Roman emperors. The word "fallen" applies better to kingdoms than to emperors. Although Daniel uses "kings" to designate kingdoms (see Lederach's notes on Daniel's kingdoms: 148-78), it must be remembered that the present passage reads "kings" (basileia), not "kingdoms." In any case, the most convincing configuration of kingdoms is to consider among the five fallen to be all the kingdoms that ruled Israel: Egypt, Assyria, Babylonia, Persia, and Greece. Rome is then the one that is. Any attempt then to identify "little while" and "eighth" is hazardous.

A viable alternative to these proposals holds that John did not intend to identify either emperors or kingdoms, but instead to communicate symbolically truths about political power. The "seven kings" represent completion as seven normally does and as the number twelve does in 2 Esdas 11–12. That "five have fallen" means that most of the world's political power has already passed. The power that "is living" will "remain only a little while" and will be replaced by the "eighth" that "belongs to the seven and goes to destruction." The meaning is that the faithful are expecting a crisis that will focus all the earth's power arrayed against them, but the end is near.

This treatment of the king/kingdoms exemplifies how the church has interpreted apocalyptic literature. Some have found the referents for the symbols in the rulers during the time when Revelation was written, others identify the referents in historical kingdoms that lead up to the eschatological kingdom of God, and still others find the meaning, not in literal kings or kingdoms but in ideas that apply to all people everywhere. Perhaps each of these ways of interpreting apocalyptic writing has something valuable to communicate (see Entering the World of Revelation: Interpreting Revelation).

Revelation 18:1-24

The Fall of Babylon

PREVIEW

Chapter 18 is another description of the fall of Babylon, this time in the form of a magnificent dirge or lament. This great piece of literature is full of Old Testament allusions (see TBC, Lament over Babylon), leading some to believe it was part of an earlier Jewish source, perhaps from the time of Titus's destruction of the temple in A.D. 66-70 that provided material for both chapters 17 and 18 (see Glasson, 1965:101-2; Beckwith, 1919:724; Aune, 1998b:983-84). Although Babylon is literally the fallen city, the imagery could easily apply to Rome's massacre of the Jews and destruction of Jerusalem. Indeed, no distinctly Christian material is included apart from "apostles" in verses 20 and 24. Nevertheless, the tone of the chapter is consistent with Revelation 13 and could have been composed by the revelator. If John did use a source, he applied the symbols to faithful Christians under Roman persecution.

In addition to being a lament or taunt song, chapter 18 may exemplify at least two other genres. Aune identifies it as a prophecy following the oracular form, which includes the threat of God's judgment and the reason for the fulfillment of the prophetic expectation (1983:284-85). Morris calls the chapter "a summary of all prophetic oracles on the doom of unrighteous peoples" (1969:214). Richard, instead, finds here a trial scene (1995:134). The three forensic words used (*krima:* 17:1; 18:20; 19:4; *krisis:* 18:10; 19:2; and *krinein:* 18:8, 20, 19:2, 11) anticipate the final judgment (11:18; 19:11; 20:4, 12, 13).

It is remarkable to note that no description is given in chapter 18 of the details of the destruction of Babylon. Indeed, attempts to construct a chronology of the fall have led to confusion: past, present, and future tenses are used without consistency, and the demise (v. 2-3) is followed by a call to flee (v. 4-5), which is in turn followed by a prediction of destruction (v. 8)—the opposite of what would be expected chronologically (Krodel, 1989:305-6).

The author is more concerned with the attitudes of those observing the fall. Only one verse narrates Babylon's fall (17:16); the twenty-four verses of chapter 18 describe the significance of that fall (Krodel, 1989:301). Caird contrasts Revelation 4 with the present passage: in the former, God is described through the hymns of the worshipers; in the latter, Babylon's fall is seen through the laments of her supporters (1966:227).

The implication of chapter 18 is that Rome's supporters believed even God could not bring down Babylon the Great (Ps. 10:4, 11, 13; Obad. 3-4). This attitude reminds the reader of the overwhelming pride expressed by the classical Greek *hubris* that precedes the downfall of tragic heroes (Prov. 29:23; Isa. 47:8-9; Ezek. 28:2; Zeph. 2:15; Luke 14:11). In the case of Rome, luxury and wealth and their attendant greed and injustice caused spiritual poverty (Rev. 3:17). Boesak says it well:

> The wealth Rome is so proud of is not a sign of God's blessing or Rome's hard work, it is directly related to the oppressive military might and economic exploitation that are the hallmarks of that society. The wealth of Roma Mater was built on the continued exploitation of weaker nations, on the robbing of the colonies, and on slave labour. It was the power of the beast that made possible the wealth of Rome. (1987:110)

The reason for the destruction of Babylon is her idolatrous worship of material goods, which must be eliminated in preparation for the establishment of the New Jerusalem. Therefore, the author is not so much gloating over the victory of the saints as rejoicing over the destruction of the evil equivalent of Babylon, imperial Rome. John exalts over the burning city because he is describing the doom of a great enemy of God's people—and, in fact, of the power of evil itself.

That the fall of Babylon has already been announced in Revelation three times as an accomplished fact (14:8; 18:2; see also 17:16) is a problem for those who insist that Revelation is chronological. The content compels the reader to see the apocalypse, not as chronological events, but as ultimate realities. The reality here is the inevitability of the fall of the rule of materialistic evil, Babylon, in preparation for the righteous kingdom of God, the New Jerusalem.

It should be emphasized again that this chapter is not an outcry of revenge or a gloating at the destruction of the enemy but a rejoicing at the triumph of God's justice. The emphasis summarized in verse 3 is on the justice of the condemnation of Babylon and, symbolically, Rome. The kings whom Rome seduced into idolatrous worship of the state will fall with her. The merchants whom Rome has enlisted to exploit her subjects and entice them to the worship of mammon will suffer her economic collapse (see 6:5-6; Caird, 1966:223). This is not vindictiveness but fairness.

Of course, it is clear by now that the whore Babylon stands for Rome, the antithesis of the bride Jerusalem, which symbolizes the faithful. Yet Babylon implies more than Rome: she is all powers that oppose God's purpose. Eller says it well:

> So make "Babylon" Babylon; John's picture is accurate—it fell! Make "Babylon" Rome; right again—it fell! Make "Babylon" New York or Washington or Las Vegas or Hollywood (or a combination of all of them); still right—they will fall, you can depend on it! And in the end, worldliness will fall finally and completely. Where? In "Babylon," of course; but how and when and where John doesn't presume to tell us—that is in God's hands, where it belongs! (1974:155)

OUTLINE

The Announcement of Babylon's Fall, 18:1-3
The Faithful Called to Come Out of Babylon, 18:4-8
The Laments over Babylon, 18:9-20
The Disappearance of Babylon, 18:21-24

EXPLANATORY NOTES

The Announcement of Babylon's Fall 18:1-3

The dirge begins with the appearance of *another angel* that is not identified and is probably to be distinguished from the angel that interpreted the vision in the preceding chapter (17:1, 7). Indeed, Revelation contains a confusing plethora of unidentified "other angels." That John sees the angel coming from heaven indicates both that the angel is from God and that John is located on earth.

The angel has *great authority,* a phrase also used of the beast (13:2). In Revelation, authority *(exousia)* is attributed to God (16:9), Christ (12:10), the faithful (2:26; 11:6; 22:14; see also 20:6), and the forces of evil (6:8; 9:3, 10, 19; 13:2, 4, 5, 7, 12; 17:12-13). Although angels, like humans, usually "receive" rather than "have" authority (but see 14:18), Mulholland's conclusion that the angel must be Christ is unwarranted (1990:284). The angel's authority is its power to destroy Babylon.

From the angel's appearance, *the earth was made bright,* likely because the angel has just come from the presence of God. In Revelation, the term *splendor (doxa)* is an attribute of God (4:9, 11; 5:13; 7:12; 11:13; 14:7; 15:8; 19:1, 7; 21:11, 23; see also 16:9) and Christ (1:6; 5:12). The implication is that all heavenly beings share in the divine splendor.

The angel then *called out with mighty voice,* as might be expected of an angel with "great authority" (see also 10:1). Other angels in Revelation have loud voices (5:2; 7:2; 14:7, 9, 15, 18; 16:17). With the mighty voice, the angel announces: *Fallen, fallen is Babylon the great!* This repeats the message announced three times already in Revelation (14:8; 16:17-19; 17:15-18; see also Isa. 13:19-22; 21:9; Jer. 51:8). The great city of evil has, in divine reality, fallen; and here her destruction is again manifested.

Babylon's demise is elaborated, using the images of demons and grotesque birds and beasts. The Greek aorist verb *has become* indicates that Babylon's destruction has already in reality occurred. The word translated "dwelling place" occurs only here in the New Testament, but is often used in the Septuagint for God's abode in heaven (1 Kings 8:39, 43, 49; 2 Chron. 30:27; Ps. 76:2 [75:3]; see also Dan. 2:11; Nah. 2:11-13). In this passage it serves as an antithesis to the sanctuary of the faithful (21:10, 22; Exod. 15:17; see also Ps. 107 [106]:4, 7). The presence of *demons* stresses that there are only evil spiritual beings, no humans, in the city (Jer. 9:11). The word *haunt* is regularly translated "prison" or, in the verbal form, "guard" (Isa. 21:11-12). The adjective *foul* means "unclean" or "unholy," is used of evil spirits (16:13), and serves as a contrast to "holy city" (21:27). The phrase *foul and hateful bird ... beast* echoes the proscriptions of the law (Lev. 11:2-45; Deut. 14:3-21) and calls to mind many Old Testament descriptions of judgment (Isa. 13:21-22; 34:11-15; Jer. 9:10-11; 50:39; 51:36-37; Zeph. 2:14-15; see also Luke 11:24-26). Mounce says that the reference here and in Isaiah 13:21 is to satyrs, demonic creatures that resemble hairy goats (1977:323). The point is that Babylon/Rome will become a wasteland like Sodom and Gomorrah (Isa. 13:19; 34:9; Jer. 50:40). Instead of being the habitation of kings, merchants, and sailors, the city will be inhabited by demons, and unclean birds and beasts. Thompson says: "In short, the city is transformed into a ... 'wilderness'" (1998:167).

The reasons for Babylon's ruin are then elaborated. That *all nations have drunk* indicates that the effect of her corruption is universal. The word for "wrath" *(thymos)* connotes the passion of God's wrath (14:8, 10; 16:19; see also 12:12) against the *fornication* and idolatry of worshiping the beast (17:2, 4-6; see also 13:4; Isa. 23:17). Specifically, *the kings of the earth,* or Babylon's allies, *have committed fornication with her, and the merchants of the earth have grown rich from the power of her luxury.* The noun translated "power" occurs as a verb in verses 7 and 9, but there is no clear equivalent elsewhere. It carries the idea of "excessive luxury and self-indulgence with accompanying arrogance and wanton exercise of strength" (Beckwith, 1919:713). The sexual immorality of Babylon is a metaphor for her extravagent materialism (see also vv. 9, 16, 17, 19; Aune, 1998b:988-90).

The Faithful Called to Come Out of Babylon 18:4-8

This section division is marked by a change of speaker indicated by the phrase *another voice from heaven* (10:4, 8; 11:12; 14:2, 13). The location of the voice in heaven and the words *my people* in the next verse both might suggest that the voice is God's, but the reference to God in the third person in verses 5, 8, and 20 makes that unlikely. The voice is probably an angel speaking on behalf of God.

The voice says: *Come out of her, my people, so that you do not take part in her sins.* The language recalls the flight of the Jews to Pella during the fall of Jerusalem in A.D. 66-70. Separation became a traditional element of apocalyptic literature (12:6, 14; see TBC, Come Out of Her) and, according to Wall, of the Johannnine community (1991:215). Yet this is probably a symbolic refusal to practice idolatry rather than a literal command to leave Rome (John 17:15). Paul makes the distinction that it is not possible to leave the world but that its sin can be avoided (1 Cor. 5:9-11; 2 Cor. 6:14-18; Eph. 5:11; see also Augustine, *The City of God* 18.18). The passage speaks of moral, not geographical separation (Sweet, 1990:268; see also Boring 1989:189). Revelation exhorts the faithful to resist the values and lifestyle of Rome outlined in the letters to Ephesus, Pergamum, and Thyatira (Yarbro Collins, 1991:127). The call is to be God's people, refusing to compromise in a sinful, materialistic world (Hos. 2:23; Rom. 9:25-26; 1 Pet. 2:10); "it is impossible to serve both Rome and the Lamb" (Thompson, 1998:175).

The faithful are told to flee *so that you do not share in her plagues.* The call to repentance in the face of the punishment to come is common in Revelation (9:20; 16:9, 11). From the nature of the destruction that follows, the punishment is likely political and economic reversal (Wall, 1991:214; Luke 1:51-53).

The plagues upon Rome are appropriate, *for her sins are heaped high as heaven.* The most common translation of the verb *(kollaō)* is "piled up," and the image is that the pile of sins is so high that God can see them (Gen. 11:4; 18:20-21; Ezra 9:6; Jer. 51:9). Whatever the meaning of the verb, the sins mentioned are drunkenness and sexual immorality, which, in this context, are used metaphorically for economic imperialism (Michaels, 1997:203).

Due to the heaping up of Babylon's sins, *God has remembered her iniquities.* The use of *iniquities (adikēma),* rather than "unrighteousness" *(adikia),* may refer to "unjust deeds" that transgress specific commandments *(dikaiōma)* of the law (Ford, 1975:297). In any case, Babylon is not getting away with her sins (16:19); God forgives (Jer. 31:34; Heb. 10:15-18), but also remembers (Exod. 2:24; 1 Kings 17:18).

Indeed, God calls for justice: *Render to her as she herself has rendered.* This command has its origin in the *lex talionis* (see TBC, Render as She Has Rendered), which the Hebrew scriptures apply to Babylon (Ps. 137:8; Jer. 50:15, 29; 51:24; see also Ps. 28:4). The meaning is that the punishment must fit the crime: render as she has rendered (Rev. 16:5-6). Here, Rome deserves retribution for destroying Jerusalem and its temple. Nevertheless, it is certainly not the faithful that are to render this judgment; they are called to leave, and elsewhere to repay only by suffering. Indeed, like Christ the Lamb, the victims slay the victors precisely by *not* taking the sword (Michaels, 1997:204-5); and divine judgment is actively carried out by worldly agents, the beast and his ten kings (17:12, 16-17).

Yet John here seems to go beyond *lex talionis* to demand: *repay her double for her deeds; mix a double draught for her in the cup she mixed.* The *cup* symbolizes God's judgment of fornication, the symbol for idolatry (14:8-10; 17:4; 18:3). The double retribution is based on the Hebrew law (Exod. 22:4, 7, 9) but is used by Jeremiah as an Old Testament idiom indicating payment in full (Jer. 16:18; 17:18; see also 50:15, 29; Rev. 11:13; 16:18). Hughes explains this by saying that double "is not twice as much as the offense, but the exact equivalent, in the same way as a person who looks exactly like someone else is called his double" (1990:191). Beale supports this interpretation by speaking of the "difficulty of putting twice as much into Babylon's cup, which has already been described as 'full' (17:4)" (1999:901). So the connotation is not revenge but justice: Rome reaps what she sows.

The justice on Babylon is summarized: *As she glorified herself and lived luxuriously, so give her a like measure of torment and grief.* As in verse 3, the verb translated *lived luxuriously* refers to sensual existence. Sweet contends that it carries the meaning, "flaunted her power" (1990:269). The noun *torment* is used for the judgment of fire and sulfur (14:10-11; see also 9:5), and by way of contrast, *grief* is something God will wipe away in the New Jerusalem (21:4).

Babylon's arrogant luxury and power are captured in the words: *Since in her heart she says, "I rule as a queen; I am no widow and I will never see grief."* The verb *rule (kathēmai)* was translated "sit" throughout chapter 17 and refers to Babylon's authority over the waters (v. 1), the scarlet beast and its ten horns (v. 3), the seven kings (v. 9), and peoples and multitudes and nations and languages (v. 15). That she is not a widow indicates she is secure (Isa. 47:7-10), perhaps economically (17:4). Mounce says that it connotes success in war in the sense that no husbands have been lost (1977:326; Aune, 1998b:996).

Because of Babylon's luxury and hubris, *her plagues will come in a single day.* A few manuscripts read "a single hour" in conformity with verses 10, 17, and 19 (but see Isa. 47:8-9). Whatever the duration of time, the point is that Babylon's destruction is inevitable (Isa. 3:16-17; Dan. 5). Wall says that the brief duration of time connotes the "frailty of secular power" when compared to its divine counterpart (1991:215). The plagues on Babylon are three-fold: *pestilence (thanatos)* is the word for "death" (2:23), *mourning (penthos)* echoes the previous verse, and *famine (limos);* famine and *thanatos* were used in the seal judgment of the black horse (6:5-8). The specific manner of judgment is that Babylon *will be burned with fire* (17:16; Jer. 50:31-32; 51:25, 30, 32, 58; see also Ezek. 23:25; 1 Cor. 3:13; 2 Pet. 3:12), the traditional punishment for prostitution (Lev. 21:9; see also Jub. 20:4). The entire judgment gives credence to the statement: *mighty is the Lord God who judges her.* The sense is forensic: Babylon is receiving her sentence for judgment that has already been administered (11:13; 16:18-19; 17:16). The point is that God, not Babylon, is mighty; the eternal Rome will be brought down in a single day.

The Laments over Babylon 18:9-20

Modeled on the dirges of Isaiah 23 and Ezekiel 26-28, this section could be divided into individual laments over Babylon by the three groups whose prosperity depended on her symbolic double, Rome. The kings of the earth (vv. 9-10; Isa. 23:8-12; Ezek. 26:15-18;

27:35) are the rulers of Asia who mourn the loss of the political power that allowed them to live luxuriously. The merchants of the earth (vv. 11-17a; Isa. 23:2-3; Ezek. 27:12-24, 36) lament the loss of the economic power that brought them great profit. The sailors on the sea (vv. 17b-19; Ezek. 26:16-18; 27:25-35) decry the collapse of the maritime power that permitted them to transport their goods. The description of the power and wealth of Babylon/Rome makes her fall more tragic by contrast (see Barclay, 1960:2.200-204 on the extravagance of Rome). All this power was lost *in one hour,* a phrase that punctuates each dirge (vv. 10, 17, 19). Yet the sorrow at the destruction of Babylon/Rome is selfish: the mourners' material prosperity is at stake. If Babylon vanishes so rapidly, the wealth of her dependents will perish just as suddenly (Beale, 1999:913-14).

The *kings of the earth, who committed fornication and lived in luxury with her* are not the ten kings that join the beast to make war against Babylon (17:12-14, 16-17) because here they are on her side. Instead, they are kings she has conquered who are now allies (17:2, 18). In their deep sorrow for Babylon's fate, they *will weep and wail,* the loud wailing that is the response of all three groups who lament Babylon's fall (vv. 15, 19; see also Ezek. 27:31). The reason for their sorrow is that *they see the smoke of her burning* (v. 18; 14:11; 19:3). The reader is here reminded of the destruction of Sodom and Gomorrah (Gen. 19:28; see also Isa. 34:10; Ezek. 28:18). In the ancient world, smoke signaled destruction of a city (Mounce, 1977:327). The emphasis here is on the city's total economic and political collapse.

To observe the burning city, the kings of the earth *will stand far off, in fear of her torment,* a refrain repeated in the two subsequent laments (vv. 15, 17). Those who were compromising with Rome for economic benefits now keep their distance (Murphy, 1998:372-73). Followers of Jesus similarly keep a safe distance during his passion (Matt. 26:58; 27:55). Perhaps here they are avoiding the intense heat of the burning city (Bruce, 1969:659). Nevertheless, what is manifestly clear is that they offer no assistance to their ally.

From a distance the kings of the earth say: *Alas, alas, the great city,* a refrain repeated in the laments to follow (vv. 16, 19). The word of exclamation *(ouai),* best translated "Woe!," has an eerie, ominous sound in Greek and is doubled for emphasis. The exclamation is made on behalf of *Babylon, the mighty city!* The focus here is on the political and economic power of Rome, which is quickly eclipsed by God: *For in one hour your judgment has come* (17:12-14; 18:8, 10, 17, 19).

In the second lament of the section, *the merchants of the earth weep and mourn for her.* The verbal forms are present participles, in contrast to the future tense verbs in verse 9, which may connote immediacy, persistence, or both. Indeed, the merchants' lament is the longest, perhaps because they are the most affected by economic collapse (Pliny, *Nat. Hist.* 6.26). The merchants wail *since no one buys their cargo anymore.* Clearly, their motives are selfish and economic: they are losing the benefits reaped from Rome's considerable wealth. According to the Talmud, "Ten measures of wealth came into the world: Rome received nine, and all the world one" (Kiddushin 48b). Mounce describes the opulent wealth of Rome:

> At one of Nero's banquets the Egyptian roses alone cost nearly $100,000. Vitellius had a penchant for delicacies like peacocks' brains and nightingales' tongues. In his reign of less than one year he spent $20,000,000, mostly on food. One Roman, after squandering an immense fortune, committed suicide because he could not live on the pittance which remained—about $300,000. (1977:329; for a more detailed account, see Barclay, 1960:2.201-4; Aune, 1998b:998)

Verses 12-13 are a catalogue of Rome's wealthy cargo (Acts 21:3). Ezekiel provides a similar list of the wares of Tyre (Ezek. 27:1-24; see also 16:10-13). The present catalogue reflects Roman commerce of the first century (see Barclay, 1960:2.205-10; Caird, 1966:226; Beasley-Murray, 1974:267; Ford, 1975:298-99; Mounce, 1977:329-30; Aune, 1998b:998-1001; Pliny, *Nat. Hist.* 6.26; 12.84) and is arranged with somewhat similar items in six groups of four in most, the former the number of evil (13:18) and the latter the number of completion in the physical world (4:6, 8; 5:6, 8, 14; 6:6; 7:1-2, 11; 9:13-15; 14:3; 15:7; 19:4; 20:8). The arrangement is as follows:

> Precious metals: gold, silver, jewels, and pearls
> Fine raiment: fine linen, purple, silk, and scarlet
> Decorative articles: all kinds of scented wood, all articles of ivory,
>   all articles of costly wood, bronze, iron, marble
> Spices: cinnamon, spice, incense, myrrh, and frankincense
> Foods: wine, olive oil, choice flour, and wheat
> Beasts: cattle and sheep, horses and chariots.

The catalogue ends with *slaves—and human lives.* The former word *(sōmatōn)* is literally "bodies" and carries the connotation of human livestock (1 Chron. 5:21); the latter *(psychas)* is often translated "souls" but the root meaning is *lives* (Ezek. 27:13). It should be noted that slaves were crucial to the profit of Rome and her provinces for the cheap labor they provided. The catalogue includes slaves last because they were considered to be of least account and were sold for domestic labor or to serve in brothels (see Barclay, 1960:2.210-11). The first-century Roman Empire supported her luxury on the sweat of 60,000,000 slaves (Mounce, 1977:331). The point made in this passage is that the commodities listed have been placed ahead of humans lives (see Matt. 16:26). In short, material goods were valued more than God or humanity.

The loss of material luxuries is then summarized: *The fruit for which your soul longed has gone from you, and all your dainties and your splendor are lost to you, never to be found again!* Fruit is considered metaphorically a sign of prosperity (22:2; see also Ezek. 47:12), and its lack an indication of destruction (Jer. 48:32). The word *dainties* refers to oily and fatty foods, and *splendor* to clothing and decorations; together they designate exotic luxuries (Morris, 1969:220). Note that the city symbolically possesses a *soul,* contributing to its personification.

Verses 15-16a are composed mostly of images repeated from the lament of the kings of the earth. The *fine linen* forms an antithesis to the clothing of the bride, the New Jerusalem (19:8, 14), but the garb of the great city also simulates that of the great whore: *purple and scarlet, adorned with gold, with jewels, and with pearls!* (17:4; see also 21:10-14; Ezek. 28:13). In short, González and González are accurate in their paraphrase: "The good life is gone" (1997:120).

The final lament is by all the sea traders. The word translated *shipmasters* means "steersmen" or "pilots," *seafarers* translates the noun place used with a present participle meaning "to sail," and the word *sailors (naytai)* is the basis for its cognate, *nautical* (Acts 27:27; see also Ezek. 27:27-29). These words together refer to *all whose trade is on the sea* (Ps. 107:23; Ezek. 27:25).

The sailors *stood far off and cried out as they saw the smoke of her burning.* Much of this statement is repeated in the other two laments (see vv. 9-10, 15). The imperfect tense of the second verb denotes a continuous "crying out." The entire picture is reminiscent of the fire of Rome in A.D. 64 (Tac., *Annals,* 15.38-41; Caird, 1966:227).

The question *What city was like the great city?* is unique to this lament and echoes Ezekiel's lament over Tyre, the great naval power of his day (Ezek. 27:32). The contrast of the power of Tyre and Rome with the power of God is unmistakable in both Ezekiel and Revelation.

The elements of verse 19 are scattered throughout all the verses of the earlier laments except the catalogue of cargo (vv. 12-14). Two new ideas here are that the sailors *threw dust on their heads,* a sign of intense grief, and that *all who had ships at sea grew rich by her wealth,* a statement of economic dependence. Beasley-Murray calls the latter the idolatry of "gross materialism and mammon worship" (1974:268).

The exclamation that follows calls the reader to an exaltation that anticipates the next chapter (19:1-10). The outburst *Rejoice!* (12:12; Deut. 32:43; Jer. 51:48) contrasts strikingly with the mournful "Alas!" of the laments. The phrase *O heaven* addresses those who live there and contrasts with the "inhabitants of the earth," Revelation's designation for the wicked *[Glossary: Inhabitants of the Earth].*

The list *saints and apostles and prophets,* an enumeration of the only distinctly Christian elements in the chapter, contrasts with the kings, merchants, and sailors. To distinguish among the former three is difficult, but Beasley-Murray suggests that *saints* is the inclusive term, and that *apostles* are the New Testament saints and *prophets* their Old Testament equivalent (1974:268). Together they represent all the faithful who are now in heaven observing the destruction of their great oppressor, Babylon. These three groups are the winners. Their faithfulness and martyrdom brought the fall of Babylon, which was, in turn, their personal vindication. Mulholland asserts: "Every drop of blood of the saints, apostles, prophets ... joins with the blood of the Lamb to seal God's victory over the Beast" (1990:288).

The victory is stated in legal terms: *God has given judgment for you against her.* The verb *has given judgment (ekrinen)* and the noun *judgment (krima)* are both here; the literal sense is: "judged your judgment," emphasizing the justice of the fall of Babylon. The law of malicious witness is probably in mind (Deut. 19:16-19), and the witness given was in the face of death (6:9).

The Disappearance of Babylon 18:21-24

As is common in Revelation, the section division is marked by the appearance of an angel. The *mighty angel* also came on the scene in connection with each of the two scrolls (5:2; 10:1-2). The fall of Babylon consummates God's redemptive purpose as symbolized in the scrolls (Caird, 1966:230-31). Here, the angel *took up,* not a scroll, but *a stone like a great millstone* (Neh. 9:11; Jer. 51:63-64). That the angel *threw [the millstone] into the sea* reminds the reader of the censer containing the prayers of the saints thrown onto the earth to bring the seventh seal (8:4-5), and of the mountain hurled into the sea to initiate the second trumpet judgment (8:8-9).

The action of the angel is then explained: *With such violence*

Babylon the great city will be thrown down. The word for *violence* occurs only here in the New Testament. The words *will be found no more* contain a double negative along with the word *eti,* usually translated "yet," connoting considerable emphasis, a construction repeated six times in this section (see Ezek. 26:21; 27:36).

The violent destruction of Babylon is followed by an eerie silence: *the sound of harpists and minstrels and of flutists and trumpeters will be heard in you no more; and an artisan of any trade will be found in you no more; and the sound of the millstone will be heard in you no more.* The tone here is reminiscent of what followed the eruption of Vesuvius in A.D. 79 (Caird, 1966:231). The point is that Babylon's destruction will be so complete that there will be no more signs of life. The artists will no longer create and perform on their instruments. "The stilling of the creative arts tells of God's absence," says Wall (1991:218; see Isa. 5:12; 24:8). In dramatic contrast to the preceding verse, the *millstone* here is a metaphor for commercial activity, the making of bread, which is necessary for the preservation of life. In short, all creative and business activities are destroyed in Babylon's demise (Matt. 24:37-39; Luke 17:26-30). Whereas the luxury items of the wealthy were destroyed in the preceding section, life's simple pleasures enjoyed by all but the destitute cease here (González and González, 1997:122-23).

The images of desolation continue: *the light of a lamp will shine in you no more; the voice of bridegroom and bride will be heard in you no more; for your merchants were the magnates of the earth, and all nations were deceived by your sorcery.* At night slaves escorted their masters with torches (Mounce, 1977:334). The point is that there is neither entertainment nor productive work at night. The wedding imagery symbolizes merriment (Jer. 7:34; 16:9; 25:10). The merchants, who merited the longest lament of the section, are here called *magnates,* connoting arrogance because of their supposed greatness. Their economic and commercial power promoted the idolatry of luxurious materialism, which Revelation considers to be *sorcery* (see Sib. Or. 3:350-55; 4:145-48; 5:162-65; 8:9-18). Indeed, Duff assserts that in the first century wealth attained through commerce was seen to be corrupt (2001:69). The word for *sorcery (pharmakeia)* reflects the seductive and deceptive activities of the dragon (12:9) and the beasts (13:3; 5-8, 12-18) and alludes to Rome's practice of magic (see 9:21; 21:8; 22:15; Isa. 47:8-13; Nah. 3:4; Aune, 1998b:1010). Yet Rowland is correct to apply this term to the commerce and culture of the wicked city: "Readers will be in for a rude shock if they think that there is a neutral character to all the activity of trade, commerce, and socializing. Such commercial and cultural activities are described as 'sorcery'" (1998:694).

The chapter ends with a focus on the faithful: in Babylon *was found the blood of prophets and of saints* (Jer. 25:10; 51:49; Matt. 23:25-37; Luke 11:47-51; Rev. 16:6; 17:6; 19:2). This contrasts with what was not found in Babylon in verses 21-23. Here prophets are most likely a subclass of saints (see v. 20). The reference may be particularly to the massacre of Christians under Nero and to the anticipated renewal of that persecution under Domitian, when the faithful would again be slaughtered like their master, the Lamb that was slain.

The phrase *all who have been slaughtered on earth* seems like an overstatement. Yet when Babylon is viewed as symbolic of all cities of evil, the meaning is clear. Rome also served as a focus for satanic evil (Tac., *Annals* 13.39-41; *Agricola* 30, in Krodel, 1989:309), and Jesus describes Jerusalem in similar manner (Matt. 23:34-35). The word *slaughtered (esphagmenōn)* is used of both the Lamb and the martyrs (1:5; 5:6, 9; 6:9; 7:14; 12:11; Heb. 12:24). Their innocent blood, which cried for just vindication (Gen. 4:10; Rev. 6:10; 2 Macc. 8:3-4), has been satisfied with the destruction of Babylon.

In sum, the main point of these chapters on the fall of Babylon (chs. 17–18; see also Dan. 2, 7) is that when all the political powers of the world have fallen—and they will—God's kingdom survives. Harrington says that "greed, exploitation, and oppression are a cancer that will undermine and destroy every empire" (1993:184). Yet it is not the role of the faithful to rise up and overthrow Babylon through force. Instead, Boring reminds the reader what Revelation communicates repeatedly: "The ultimate power of the universe is the power of God manifest and effective in the self-sacrificing power of the Lamb" (1989:188).

TEXT IN BIBLICAL CONTEXT

Lament over Babylon

The description of Babylon in this passage is drawn from a wide variety of Old Testament texts. Isaiah announces the destruction of Babylon, which he calls a "virgin daughter" (Isa. 47). Jeremiah affirms that Babylon will be punished in the process of Israel's restoration (Jer. 50–51). Indeed, the destruction of Babylon is directly compared to the fate of Sodom and Gomorrah (Isa. 13:19-21). Yet God's judgment is not limited to Babylon but is applied to Ninevah (Nah. 3; Zeph. 2:13-15), Samaria (Amos 5-6), Jerusalem (Jer. 13-14), and even to all nations (Isa. 34; see also 14:24-16:14; 20:1; 21:17). Perhaps the most complete picture of God's judgment on another nation is the description of the fall of Tyre in Ezekiel 26–28, where ironically, Babylon is the destroyer (see also Isa. 24 and Ezek. 23).

Come Out of Her

The injunction to escape Babylon and avoid her doom is based on similar injunctions of the prophets (Isa. 48:20; 52:11-12; Jer. 50:8-9; 51:6, 9, 45; Zech. 2:6-7). Moreover, the theme of being "called out" is quite common in the biblical tradition, beginning with God's call to Abraham: "Go from your country and your kindred and your father's house to the land that I will show you" (Gen. 12:1). Later, Abraham's nephew Lot and his whole family are called to escape quickly from Sodom before the Lord destroys the city (Gen. 19:12-23). After their wilderness sojourn, the Israelites are warned to come away from the dwellings of Korah, Dothan, and Abirim before the earth opens up and swallows their families and goods because of their revolt against Moses (Num. 16:23-26). Jesus picks up the escape theme when he warns the inhabitants of Judea to flee to the mountains from the "desolating sacrilege" (Matt. 24:15-16; Mark 13:14). Spiritualizing the theme, Paul calls his readers to "come out ... and be separate from" unbelievers (2 Cor. 6:14-18) and to "take no part in the unfruitful works of darkness" (Eph. 5:11). The author of the Pastorals extends the idea slightly: "Do not participate in the sins of others; keep yourself pure" (1 Tim. 5:22). Certainly, the theme of separation is imbedded in the very fabric of Scripture.

The Great Millstone

To demonstrate prophetically the imminent fall of Babylon, a mighty angel takes what appears to be a great millstone and hurls it into the sea. Then the angel affirms: "With such violence Babylon the great city will be thrown down, and will be found no more" (v. 21). Drawing on imagery that Nehemiah uses to describe the fate of the Egyptians in the Exodus (Neh. 9:11), this mighty angel is performing a prophetic act that announces the destruction of Babylon, the great city of evil that symbolizes Rome (Sib. Or. 5:155-61).

Such prophetic activity has a rich tradition among the Hebrews. The prophet Ahijah tore the new garment he was wearing into twelve pieces, giving ten to Jeroboam, saying: "See I am about to tear the kingdom from the hand of Solomon, and will give you ten tribes" (1 Kings 11:29-32). God told Isaiah to walk naked and barefoot for three years because the king of Assyria would take the Egyptians captive "naked and barefoot, with buttocks uncovered, to the shame of Egypt" (Isa. 20:1-6). God told Jeremiah to buy a linen loincloth and hide it in a cleft of rock by the Euphrates River. Subsequently, God told him to retrieve the loincloth, which was ruined and useless, like the people of Israel and Judah (Jer. 13:1-11). Later, God told Jeremiah to fill every wine jar as a symbol that the people—"the kings who sit on David's throne, the priests, the prophets, and all inhabitants of Jerusalem"—would be filled with drunkenness and destroyed (Jer. 13:12-14). On another occasion, God instructed Jeremiah to break an earthen jug, symbolizing that Jerusalem would fall to her enemies as punishment for her sin and idolatry (Jer. 19:1-13). Jeremiah was led by God to buy a field at Anathoth from his cousin Hanamel and to give the deed to Baruch, instructing him to place it in an earthenware jar for a long time to affirm that property could again be purchased in Judah (Jer 32:6-15). God instructed the prophet Ezekiel to depict the siege of Jerusalem by Babylon on a brick; to lie on his side three hundred days to symbolize the number of years that Israel would be punished; to eat a barley cake baked on human dung, and later cow's dung, to symbolize that the people of Israel would "eat their bread, unclean, among the nations"; and to cut his beard with a sharp sword and divide the hair—one-third to be burned with fire, one-third struck with the sword, and one-third scattered to the wind—to demonstrate the fate of Israel (Ezek. 4:1-5:4; see Martens, *BCBC,* 1986, on Jeremiah, and Lind, 1996, on Ezekiel for the above texts).

The naming of children was also a common prophetic act. Isaiah named his son *Maher-shalal-hash-baz* ("The spoil speeds, the prey hastes"), to demonstrate that "the wealth of Damascus and the spoil of Samaria would be carried away by the king of Assyria" (Isa. 8:1-4). The prophet Hosea named his children prophetically significant names: "Jezreel," to indicate that God would "break the bow of Israel in the valley of Jezreel" for shedding the "blood of Jezreel" (Hos. 1:4-5); "not pitied" because God "will no longer have pity on the house of Israel or forgive them" (Hos. 1:6); and "not my people," because Israel is not God's people and Yahweh is no longer Israel's God (Hos. 1:9; see Guenther, *BCBC,* 1998, on Hosea:41-47).

Prophetic acts like this are not uncommon in Revelation. Each of the elements of the numbered judgment series is introduced by opening one of the seals of a scroll (ch. 6; 8:1-5), blowing of a trumpet (8:6–9:21; 11:15-19), or pouring out of a bowl onto the earth (ch. 16). The act of the Lamb receiving the scroll symbolically affirms his implementing its contents through affecting God's salvation (ch. 5).

The measuring of the temple prophetically enacts its preservation (ch. 11). In the chapter that follows, the wedding supper of the Lamb is the prophetic act that inaugurates the kingdom of God (19:1-10).

Perhaps the closest parallel to the prophetic millstone that heralds the fall of Babylon in the passage under consideration is when Jeremiah's book containing the catastrophes that would come upon Babylon was read in the city and then tied to a stone and thrown into Euphrates to "rise no more" as punishment for Babylon's idolatry and killing of the people of Israel (Jer. 51:47-64). In its use as part of a more elaborate prophetic act, the rock also symbolizes God—"their rock is not like our Rock" (Deut. 32:31). Jesus uses the metaphor of a millstone in connection with stumbling blocks, saying that it would be preferable for anyone who would place a stumbling block before "these little ones who believe in me" to have a millstone attached to his neck and be drowned in the sea (Matt. 18:6-7; Mark 9:42; Luke 17:2).

In the present passage, the millstone symbolizes the fall of Babylon. In an eerie and dramatic symbolic event, the millstone sinks to the bottom of the sea never to be seen again, just as Babylon, the great city that persecuted the faithful, and its symbolical equivalent, the great Roman Empire, are permanently destroyed (see Aune, 1998b:1008-9, on millstones).

The Day the Music Died

Dancing to instruments of joyous music was connected to the success of the Israel's united Davidic dynasty (2 Sam. 6:5). The prophet Isaiah, however, saw that musical celebration had continued without accompanying "deeds of the Lord" (Isa. 5:12); so he prophesied that God's judgment would come and quiet the music (Isa. 24:3, 8-9). Isaiah affirmed, however, that when God is again appropriately worshiped, Israel's enemies will be destroyed and the music heard again (Isa. 30:29).

Jeremiah uses language echoed in Revelation 18 to describe, three times, the effects of the destruction of Babylon: God will bring to an end "the sound of mirth and the sound of gladness, the voice of the bridegroom and the voice of the bride, the sound of the millstones and the light of the lamp," "for the land shall become ... a waste" (Jer. 7:34; 16:9; 25:10-11). Ezekiel ironically employs the same language to speak of Babylon's destruction of Tyre (Ezek. 26:13). Appropriately, the prophets picture the time of destruction as the cessation of the sound of music.

THE TEXT IN THE LIFE OF THE CHURCH

The Fall of Babylon

Because Babylon is without doubt symbolic of Rome, the announcement of the fall of Babylon in Revelation 17–18 speaks, at least immediately, of the fall of the Roman Empire. Indeed, the literal event, which did not take place for more than three centuries after Revelation was written, did have an immense effect on the church. Therefore, the passage under consideration had relevance as it anticipated the literal demise of the empire, and a brief review of the process of that demise would be instructive (see Perry, 1985:143-46, 167-69, the basis for much of the information in this section).

During the reign of Emperor Marcus Aurelius toward the end of the second century, the empire was politically stable and economically prosperous, much like the Babylon of Revelation; but in the third century, she was plagued by a greedy military that had little loyalty to Rome. Encouraged by this situation, the Germanic peoples penetrated Italy and engaged the Roman armies. To obtain funds and supplies for the military effort, the cities of the empire were pillaged and destroyed. The resulting increase in disloyalty caused economic production on behalf of the empire to dry up. Its spiritual life also declined as the disenchanted populace turned to the mysticism of the mystery religions to alleviate their suffering.

In the later third and early fourth centuries, emperor Diocletian tried to bring stability to the empire through tight discipline, and later Constantine attempted the same through the toleration and adoption of Christianity. Yet the demise of the empire came soon, not by the invasion of the Parthians, as the first-century empire feared, but by the invasion of Germanic peoples. Forced into northern Italy by the Mongol Huns, the Goths defeated the Roman legions and ensured a place for themselves in the empire. Rome was further weakened by the deterioration of roads and the dwindling of the trade that brought luxuries into Rome during John's day. Rome fell progressively under the control of the Germanic soldiers. Finally, Rome was sacked by the Goths in A.D. 410 and the Vandals in A.D. 455. In 476 the invaders overthrew Emperor Romulus and placed a German on the throne.

For the Christian church the significance of the fall of the Roman Empire, forecast in Revelation 17–18, was immense. Saint Augustine of Hippo, who studied the Latin classics in Carthage, wrote his *City of God* during the time when Rome was collapsing. He addressed the pagans who blamed the tragedy on Christianity, charging that the Christians undermined the empire by refusing to serve in the army.

Augustine's *City of God* responded to the Roman crisis much like Plato's *Republic* addressed the Greek empire's struggle between Athens and Sparta. Augustine said that the city of this world is not the ultimate concern of the Christian because the ideal state can never be actualized on earth, but only in heaven. Therefore, the destruction of the Roman Empire should not overly disturb the Christian, because Christianity cannot be identified with any political entity. Specifically, Augustine believed Rome's disintegration to be unimportant because it did not affect the Christian, who is ultimately a citizen of heaven. The success of Christianity is not tied to the material progress of Rome or any other empire of this world. The Christian is not ultimately a citizen of any government, but only of the kingdom of heaven. Thus, Augustine, in thinking about the event anticipated by Revelation 17-18, laid the basis for the two-kingdom ideal that has become central to Anabaptist theology.

Whore Worship

Revelation 18 describes the destruction of Babylon the great whore, who is condemned primarily for fornication. The metaphor of fornication carries the sense of seducing persons to the worship of the beastly empire of Rome. Yet it is interesting that the sins of Babylon are not primarily spiritual, but material and economic. The seduction is to buy into the luxurious life that the Roman Empire can provide its adherents. Rowland says: "International trade can be a form of cultural promiscuity by which one power exploits and drains the resources of many others. In extravagance and luxury lies the hidden a cost in human lives and societies" (1998:696).

Kraybill has demonstrated that at the end of the first century Christians in the province of Asia could live quite well by participating in the trade that Rome made possible. It seems that Asia Minor exported olive oil and wine in return for grain imports (Kraybill, 1996:16; information here is dependent on this source). According to Kraybill, "Christians had ready access to the ships, docks and guild halls that serviced Rome's enormous appetite.... Some first-century Christians had wealth or social connections that would have enabled them to move in circles of political and economic influence" (16). It seems that it was possible for citizens of the provinces to make a fortune on the commerce of the empire and accumulate considerable wealth, property, and even slaves (Rev. 3:17). Indeed, there is indication that inhabitants of provinces like Asia moved "into social and political positions once reserved for Roman aristocrats" (69). Thus, Kraybill believes that John did not write Revelation out of personal poverty or oppression; rather, out of identification with the poor, John believed that the faithful "no longer could participate in an unjust commercial network thoroughly saturated with idolatrous patriotism" (23). Labeling this mutually advantageous relationship "fornication," John "condemns it as immoral, self-serving and idolatrous" (58). Kraybill argues that John's admonition to "come out" meant that they should "withdraw immediately" or "share in Rome's guilt and her punishment" (16). Although Revelation does seem to reflect the anticipation of persecution, it clearly gives evidence that Christians were faced with the economic temptation to give in to the seduction of material wealth, which John portrays as "whore worship."

Most likely, the first-century Christians believed, as Christians today do regarding the American Dream, that one did not need to sell out to Rome to reap its benefits. Compromise was seen as expedient, and being a member of the Roman middle class more attractive than membership in God's kingdom (Wall, 1991:217). This certainly seems to have been the predicament of the church at Laodicea (3:14-22). It was thought that one could be successful financially and still be a good Christian—indeed, perhaps an even more effective Christian. Revelation is addressing precisely this issue, and the answer is: Do not practice "whore worship." Peterson captures this idea quite well: "The great danger that the world poses for us is not in its gross evils, but its easy religion. The promise of success, ecstasy, and meaning that we can get for a price is Whore-worship. It is the diabolical inversion of 'you are bought with a price' to 'I can get it for you wholesale'" (1988:147).

Turning to the modern world, the materialistic pursuit of whore worship is grossly evident and devastating in the extensive trafficking in drugs and pornography. Yet it is just as present, if more subtly so, in a number of "legitimate" enterprises. Nike's payment for Michael Jordan's advertising, a sum commensurate to all the workers in the factories that make the shoes, is whore worship. The use by a major cigarette company of Joe Camel commercials to seduce the young to begin to smoke, a habit that will likely lead to disease and a shorter life, is whore worship. The Nestle company's ads in underdeveloped countries aimed at convincing mothers that using formula is more modern than breast feeding, even though it is far less beneficial to the infants, is whore worship. Truly economic gain is as enticing today as it was in the first century when Revelation was written. The materialistic world provides the attraction of "the bird held by the glittering eye of the snake" (Wilcock, 1975:166).

The Two Suppers

PREVIEW

The celebratory mood of the first half of chapter 19 is signaled by the command, "Rejoice over her!" (18:20). The victory song of this chapter is a "counter-scene" to the lament over the fall of Babylon in chapter 18 (Eller, 1974:172). The persons involved in the dirge in chapter 18, the kings, merchants, and sailors, are contrasted with those praising God in chapter 19: the great multitude, the twenty-four elders and four living creatures, and the voice from the throne (Mounce, 1977:336). Such striking contrasts of heavenly praise and earthly persecution have, of course, become quite common in Revelation:

Praise	Persecution
4:1–5:14	6:1-17
7:1–8:5	8:6–9:21
10:1-11	11:1-14
12:1-18	13:1-18
14:1-20	15:1–16:21

Similar contrasts occur in this section: the judgment of the whore (chs. 17–18) leads to the millennial kingdom of God (20:1-6) and the defeat of Gog and Magog (20:7-10) to the establishment of the New Jerusalem (21:1–22:5).

Focusing on the sections of praise, the heavenly hymns of 19:1-10 have striking parallels with many earlier interludes of joy in the midst of judgment (7:9-17; 12:10-12; 15:2-4). Specifically, the heavenly vision of chapters 4–5 includes many elements of 19:1-10—the phrase "after this," the appearance of the twenty-four elders and four living creatures, the heavenly voice, and the throne. Yet the closest parallel is with the announcement of the kingdom of God in the seventh trumpet (11:15-19).

loud voices	11:15	19:1
forever and ever	11:15	19:3
reign	11:15, 17	19:6
twenty-four elders	11:16	19:4
power	11:17	19:1
small and great	11:18	19:5
judge	11:18	19:2

Thus, the kingdom was announced proleptically in the seventh trumpet (11:15-19), just as the fall of Babylon (chs. 17–18) was anticipated by the seventh bowl (16:17-21).

Two praise hymns in Revelation 19:1-10, each introduced by the statement, *I heard what seemed to be the voice of a great multitude,* serve as a bridge linking chapters 17–18 to 19:11–22:5. Looking back, verses 1-5 praise God for the judgments that brought the fall of Babylon; looking forward, verses 6-10 celebrate the wedding supper of the Lamb in anticipation of the New Jerusalem. Thus, 19:1-10 serves both as conclusion to the dirge, praising God for the judgment of the whore, which avenges the blood of the faithful, and as introduction to the second coming of Christ, which heralds the arrival of the kingdom of God. The note of praise dominating the first ten verses of chapter 19 is not the jubilant gloating of the faithful over the fall of Babylon but their reverent rejoicing for the destruction of evil, which heralds the victory of God's justice. Peterson captures the tone of the saints when he says, "Four hallelujahs pull us from the edge of gloating ... to the act of worship where we are humble and adoring in the presence of the Glory" (1988:149).

The material that follows these hymns of praise describes seven stages in the coming kingdom, each introduced by the words *Then I saw:*

The Rider on the White Horse (19:11-16)
The Supper of God (19:17-18)
The Destruction of the Beasts (19:19-21)
The Millennium (20:1-3)
The Defeat of Gog and Magog (20:4-10)
The White Throne Judgment (20:11)
The Lake of Fire (20:12-15)

Yet Boring is without doubt correct to assume that these stages are "no calendarization of the End, but a tour through an eschatological art gallery" (1989:194-95).

The first of these stages is perhaps the most impressive account of the coming *(parousia)* of Christ in the Bible (see also Matt. 25:31-46; 1 Thess. 4:13–5:11; 2 Thess. 1:5–2:12). Yet it contains no details of what will occur at Christ's appearing, only word pictures. Indeed, the emphasis is not on the event but the reality that Christ will return. The truth is that in the end we meet a person, Christ, who as in the beginning was God (Boring, 1989:197). Here, Christ appears as judge and warrior. The theme of judgment is common in the New Testament (Matt. 13:41-42; 25:34, 41; Rom. 2:5; 2 Thess. 1:5-12). Yet, the warrior is more rare and is used here ironically. From the first ten verses of the chapter, the reader expects a bridegroom to appear, but instead there is a warrior. Given that turn of events, the expectation is that the warrior will annihilate the enemies with weapons of destruction, but Christ appears with only the sword of the Word of God. Such transformations from warlike to peaceful images have come to be expected in Revelation. The clearest parallel is chapter 5 where the lion of the tribe of Judah becomes the Lamb that was slain.

Indeed, Christ here is the antithesis of the warrior of chapter 6; the only common symbol is the white horse (6:2). As was just mentioned, instead of the bow of warfare, Christ carries the sword of his mouth. Moreover, instead of the victor's crown *(stephanos)*, Christ wears the royal diadem *(diadēmata)*. Instead of bringing war, famine, and death, Christ brings justice, righteousness, and redemption (Eller, 1974:176).

A further note should be emphasized about this and other battles in Revelation. To perceive them to be literal is to do damage to apocalyptic imagery; these battles describe ultimate realities. One such reality is that the victory Christ won on the cross will be fully realized in his *parousia*, when he comes to wage a spiritual battle in which Satan will be defeated to prepare for his binding in chapter 20.

OUTLINE

Praise for Judgment of the Great Whore, 19:1-5
The Marriage Supper of the Lamb, 19:6-10
The Rider on the White Horse, 19:11-16
The Supper of God, 19:17-18
The Destruction of the Beasts, 19:19-21

EXPLANATORY NOTES

Praise for Judgment of the Great Whore 19:1-5

The beginning of the chapter is marked by the statement: *After this I heard what seemed to be the voice of a great multitude in heaven.* Although the great multitude may be an angelic host (5:11-12; 7:11-12; 12:10; see also Heb. 12:22), the reference to salvation and the blood of God's servants makes it more likely that these are the faithful in heaven who have come out of the great tribulation (7:9-10; 13:17; 15:2-5).

The multitude says, *Hallelujah!* a transliteration of two Hebrew words—*hallal,* meaning "praise," and *Jah,* the truncated form of *Yahweh.* In the Old Testament, the word occurs only in numerous psalms, although the phrase "praise the Lord" occurs frequently. Eleven psalms are introduced by *hallelujah* (106, 111, 112, 113, 117, 135, 146-50); and six, called the Hallel Psalms, are associated with Passover and deliverance from Pharaoh and Egypt (Ps. 113-18). In Revelation the word *hallelujah* is also associated with God's salvation, this time from the beast and Babylon.

The praise of God continues: *Salvation and glory and power to our God.* Such three-fold praise is common in Revelation (4:9, 11; see also the seven-fold praise of 5:12; 7:12). Salvation includes both the inauguration of God's redemption (5:1-10; 7:10) and the judgment of all that hinders God's rule (Matt. 6:13; Rev. 12:10; Hughes, 1990:196-97). Yet God's salvation is also personal, involving a change of values that transfers citizenship from fallen Babylon to the New Jerusalem (Mulholland, 1990:291; see Col. 1:13-14). Such salvation is what brings hope in the midst of catastrophe (Peterson, 1988:152).

The reason God is to be praised is that *his judgments are true and just* (14:8; 15:3-4; 16:5-7). The point here is that *he has judged the great whore,* who receives a just sentence because she *corrupted the earth with her fornication* (17:1-5; 18:3). The word *corrupted* carries the sense of "seducing to bring ruin," appropriate for the great whore. Barclay perhaps says it best: "The worst of all sins is to teach others to sin" (1960:2.219).

For this woman who seduced persons into sin, God *has avenged on her the blood of his servants.* The word *avenged (ekdikeō),* meaning to procure justice (Deut. 32:43; 2 Kings 9:7; see also Rev. 2:20-22; 16:5-7; 1 QM 1.5-7; 4.6-7), also occurs in connection with the martyrs' prayer (6:10). Because idolatry is viewed as equivalent to murder (9:20-21; 13:13-15), the punishment of death is a just response to the prayers of the martyrs for such retribution (6:9-11). The servants here are all the faithful who through persecution at the hands of the whore share in the blood of martyrs and in the cross of Christ (2:13; 11:3, 7-8; 17:6; 18:24; see also 2 Macc. 7:37-38; 4 Macc. 6:28-29).

The praise is then repeated: *Once more they said, Hallelujah!*— literally, "the second voice said, Hallelujah!" The repetition resembles a liturgical antiphon. Similar reiteration occurs in the Hallel Psalms and the song of Miriam (Exod. 15:1, 21). Here it emphasizes the theme of the justice of God's judgment of the whore.

The second hallelujah is followed by the statement: *The smoke goes up from her for ever and ever.* Although this is reminiscent of the burning of Sodom (Gen. 19:24-28; Rev. 11:7-8) and Tyre (Isa. 34:9-10; see also 13:19-22) and perhaps of the fire of hell (14:11; 20:10; see also 9:2; Matt. 3:12; Mark 9:43), the primary allusion is no doubt again to incense of the prayers of the saints (5:8; 8:3-4), which are answered in the burning of the whore. Her destruction was caused by the beast and its ten horns (17:16; 18:8, 9, 18, 21-24). Ironically, the mythic eternal Rome *(Roma aeterna)* burns for forever and ever (Beale, 1999:929).

In the continuing scene of praise, *the twenty-four elders and the four living creatures fell down and worshiped God who is seated on the throne* (4:8-11). Common in the praise hymns of the early chapters of Revelation (4:4-11; 5:6-14; 6:1-7; 7:11-14; 11:16; 14:3; 15:7), these two groups have not been seen since 14:3 and 15:7 respectively, and will not appear again *[Glossary: Twenty-Four Elders, Four Living Creatures]*.

The saints join the physical universe in worshiping God, *saying, "Amen. Hallelujah."* The word *amen* coupled with *hallelujah* concludes the fourth book of the Psalms (Ps. 106:48) and is an affirmation of the praise of God (1:6-7; 5:14; 7:11-12). The reference to *all you his servants* indicates the universality of the message to all the faithful (1:1; 2:20; 7:9-17; 10:7; 11:18; 19:18; 22:3). The words *all who fear him* speak, not of terror, but of the reverence appropriate for God's sovereignty. The designators *small and great* indicate that in the worship of God social class distinctions are obliterated (see also 13:16; 19:18; 20:12). The point is that all the faithful join in the song of praise to God for judging the whore.

The Marriage Supper of the Lamb 19:6-10

This section begins with the same words as the preceding: *Then I heard what seemed to be the voice of a great multitude.* Although not identified here or in 19:1, the multitude is probably the 144,000, which are described with similar language (14:1-2). That the voice of the multitude was *like the sound of many waters and like the sound of mighty thunderpeals* conjures up the awesome torrent of a majestic waterfall or a shocking crack of thunder (1:15; 6:2; 7:4; 14:2; 18:2; 19:1; cf. 17:15). The voice is *crying out, Hallelujah!*

The reason for the summons to praise issued by the great multitude is that *the Lord our God the Almighty reigns.* The theme of God's sovereignty repeats the thrust of verses 1-3. There the focus was on God's judgment of the great whore; here the blessing of God's kingdom is announced. Yet the announcement is proleptic awaiting—in the narrative—the return of Christ and the chaining of Satan, like the earlier proleptic announcements of the fall of Babylon (14:8) and the arrival of the kingdom of Christ (11:15). The verb *reigns (ebasileysen)* is an aorist that denotes the initiation of action at a point in time. Ortlund suggests that the tense should be treated like a present or as ingressive: "has entered on his reign" (1996:162, n.60). Although God always reigns, that reign is recognized here and is the reason for the emotional outburst (11:15-17; Ps. 93:1; 97:1; 99:1). The word *Almighty (pantokrator),* literally means, in this context, that God controls all (see Notes on 1:8). There is here a clear allusion to the titles of Emperor Domitian—"Lord," "Lord and God" (Suet., *Domitian* 13; Martial, *Epigrams* 5.8; 10.72). Hence, the suggestion is that God, not Rome, has all power, and that all earthly power will be defeated and Christ's reign established.

The basis for the great multitude to *rejoice and exult and give [God] the glory* is that the *marriage supper of the Lamb has come.* This theme anticipates the final vision of the New Jerusalem (20:11-22:5) in the same way that the summons to rejoice in 18:20 anticipated the celebration in this chapter. Although the marriage supper seems to be an eschatological banquet after the forces of evil are defeated and Christ's kingdom established (Matt. 8:11), the actual marriage supper of the Lamb is nowhere described. Therefore, it is likely not an event but a symbol of the joyful, intimate, and indissoluble fellowship between Christ and the faithful. The faithful saint awaits the parousia in the same way as a pure betrothed bride anticipates her wedding (Mounce, 1977:340).

Nevertheless, the word translated *bride* here is literally "woman" *(gynē),* rather than the normal word for bride *(nymphē)* (18:23; 21:2, 9; 22:17). This symbol makes a significant contribution to the symmetry of Revelation's imagery. On the one hand, the bride is an equivalent image to the New Jerusalem and stands for the saints (Matt.

23:37; Rev. 14:4); on the other hand, the whore is Babylon, composed of the unfaithful "inhabitants of earth" (17:1-6).

The bride, who symbolizes the faithful, *has made herself ready* with righteous deeds and good works (2:2, 19; 3:1, 8, 15; Eph. 2:10). In a real sense, she is responsible for her own purity (2 Cor. 5:15; 1 John 3:3). Yet, *to her it has been granted to be clothed with fine linen, bright and pure,* which indicates that her purity is imputed (2 Cor. 3:18). These two apparently contradictory ideas, that the faithful are responsible for their own holiness (Gen. 35:2; Isa. 52:1; 2 Cor. 7:1) and that purity is a gift of God (Zech. 3:4; see also Rev. 13:5) are both true (Isa. 61:10; Phil. 2:12-13; 1 John 2:2-3). Earlier the great multitude that no one could number washed their own robes, which were made white by the blood of the Lamb (7:14). The paradoxical truth is that the faithful are responsible to be pure and do good works, but their salvation is ultimately given as a divine gift. In any case, the garments of the bride resemble Christ (Matt. 17:2; Luke 9:29) but contrast with the glittering clothes that symbolize the luxurious wickedness of the whore (17:3-4; 18:16).

To clarify what has been implied: the bride's *fine linen is the righteous deeds of the saints.* The saints' wedding garments for the Lamb's marriage supper are their good works (3:5, 18; 5:8; 6:11; 7:9, 14; 14:4-5, 12; 16:15). Morris suggests that the word *deeds* means a judgment or decree (15:4; Rom. 1:32; 5:16) and that its reference here is not to good works but is the "sentence of justification" (1969:227). Yet Paul uses the word to denote an act of righteous obedience (Rom. 5:18-19), and the plural *deeds* suggests concrete acts, not a general state of justification (Ortlund, 1996:163, n.64). Mounce says it well: "The bride's garment is woven of the innumerable acts of faithful obedience by those who endure to the end" (1977:340).

Parenthetically, an angel now appears to say: *Write this.* Although the word *angel* is not in the Greek text, it is implied that the words are spoken by the interpreting angel (1:11; 17:1; 21:9). The command to write is not without precedent in Revelation (1:11, 19; 14:13; 21:5; see also 10:4); here what is to be written is the fourth of Revelation's seven beatitudes (1:3; 14:13; 16:15; 19:9; 20:6; 22:7, 14). The blessing is placed on those *who are invited to the marriage supper of the Lamb.* The word *invited (keklēmenoi)* echoes the "called" *(klētoi)* and "chosen" *(eklecktoi)* who follow the Lamb (17:14) and is a perfect participle, emphasizing the permanence of the invitation to the Lamb's marriage supper. The point of the beatitude is: *"you are invited!"* (Eller, 1974:173; see also Matt. 22:3; Luke 14:15-17). Then the angel affirms the beatitude's importance: *These are true words of God.* Later, the witness of Revelation is similarly confirmed by God (21:5; 22:6; see also 1 Tim. 4:9; 2 Tim. 2:11; Titus 3:8).

In response to the angel's invitation to the marriage supper, John *fell down at his feet to worship him* (22:8-9; see also Dan. 2:46). In the Hebrew tradition, angels were not worshiped (but see Num. 22:31), and Christians evidenced respect for angels but not worship (1 Cor. 11:10; Gal. 1:8; Heb. 1:7, 13-14; 2:5; 2 Pet. 2:11). Nevertheless, angel worship seems to have been evident in certain circles (Col. 2:18; Heb. 1:4-14; Test. Levi 5:5; Apoc Zeph. 9:3; Asc. Isa. 8:4-15; Justin Martyr, *Apol.* 1.6; cf. Acts 10:25-26; Aune, 1998b:1036). The verb *worship (proskyneō)* means to "bow down," or to give the authority that is only due to God. Schüssler Fiorenza captures its meaning in contemporary words: "'Don't salute the flag, salute God;' or 'Don't pledge allegiance to the state, pledge it to God'" (1991:103). Surprisingly, even John is tempted to idolatry, the sin condemned most often in Revelation. The angel addresses him abruptly: *You must not do that!*

The reason the angel says that John should not worship him is: *I am a fellow servant with you and your comrades who hold the testimony of Jesus* (Acts 10:25-26; 14:11-18; Rom. 1:26-27). John is a fellow servant *(syndoulos)* with the angel in the sense that they share the same prophetic task: to communicate and interpret God's word, not to reveal it (John 15:26-27). Instead of worshiping the angel, John is told: *Worship God!* (4:6-11; 5:14; 7:11, 15; 1:16; 14:7; 15:4; 19:4; Deut. 6:13; Matt. 4:10; Luke 4:8). Sweet insightfully notes the trinitarian structure of this verse (1990:281): *Worship **God**! For the testimony of **Jesus** is the **spirit** of prophecy.* Although the New Testament does not include a fully developed doctrine of the Trinity, its seeds are imbedded in passages like this (see also 1:4-6).

The Rider on the White Horse 19:11-16

This passage is one of the clearest descriptions of the second coming in the New Testament. The fall of Babylon in chapters 17-18 prepares for the appearance of Christ to establish the kingdom. Again the reiteration of earlier conflicts, so characteristic of Revelation, is demonstrated here. The victory celebration of verses 1-10 is followed by renewed conflict in verses 11-21. Moreover, nearly all elements of the passage are repeated from preceding chapters (5:1-14; 12:5,10-12; 14:6-20; 16:13-16; 17:12-14).

The section begins with a familiar clause: *Then I saw heaven opened.* The door of heaven opened in 4:1; here heaven itself opens (11:19; 15:5; see Ezek. 1:1; Matt. 3:16; Mark 1:10; John 1:51; Acts 10:11; 2 Bar. 22:1). The perfect participle *opened* denotes an event with continuing effects. What John saw was a *white horse* whose rider here is clearly Christ; in chapter 6 the rider is just as clearly not Christ (see Notes on 6:1-2). At this point, the purpose for opening heaven is to prepare for the glorious coming of Christ.

The rider on the white horse is *called Faithful and True.* Applied commonly to God in the Hebrew tradition (Exod. 34:6-7; Deut. 7:9; 32:4; Isa. 49:7; Rev. 6:10; 3 Macc. 2:11; Jos., *Ant.* 11.55; 1 QM 13.9), the two designators are virtually synonymous (1:5; 3:7, 14; 15:3; 21:5; 22:6; John 14:6). The word translated *faithful* is the common word for faith *(pistis).* Here it means, not "to believe," but "to be trusted," as it does in every occurrence in Revelation. In the Hebrew world, truth *(alēthinos)* does not refer to correspondence with reality as it does to the Greeks, but instead, to reliability (Ladd, 1972:253; Jer. 10:10; John 1:17). Christ, the trusted and reliable follower of God, is the supreme example for his faithful followers.

If faithfulness and truth are his qualities, Christ's activity is that *in righteousness he judges and makes war.* Both verbs are present tense, implying activity already in progress and permanent; they refer to habitual activity, not one-time events. Throughout most of the Bible, God is the one who judges (Ps. 45:4-6; 96:13; Isa. 11:4; John 3:19; Rev. 16:5-7; 19:2; 3 Macc. 2:3; 1 QM 11.14) and makes war (Exod. 15:3; 1 QM 12.10-11; 19.2-4; see also Rev. 2:16; 17:14). Yet the mixed metaphor is quite instructive; in Christ's battles the only weapons are words of judgment (12:7-12; Joel 3:16). This is not a military battle but the "wordy battle of the lawcourt" (Caird, 1966:240). Moreover, the rider's actions are done in righteousness, a distinctive characteristic of the Messiah (Isa. 11:3-6; Acts 17:31; Heb. 1:8). In contrast to the evil war of the beast (11:7; 13:7), Christ's judgment reflects the righteousness and justice of God (Ps. 72:2; 96:13). Indeed, Christ's judgment enacts God's salvation through the elimination of all evil so that the kingdom can come.

As the description of the rider continues, it becomes more similar to the vision of the Son of Man in 1:16-20. *His eyes ... like a flame of fire* (Dan. 10:6; Rev. 1:14; 2:18) symbolize the perfect knowledge of the Christ who comes in judgment (Isa. 33:14; 1 Cor. 3:13; Heb. 4:13). Christ is able to "'see through' all pretense and to penetrate the depths of the human heart" (Beasley-Murray, 1974:279; see 2:23). Christ also has *on his head ... many diadems.* In contrast to the victor's crown *(stephanos),* the diadem *(diadēma)* is the royal crown worn by the king or emperor (Isa. 28:5; 62:3). In the ancient world a ruler would wear more than one crown to show that he was sovereign over several countries (Metzger 1993:91; see 1 Macc. 11:13). Like his title, the King of kings, Christ's many crowns (19:12) indicate sovereignty over all the kingdoms of the earth (1:5; 17:14; 19:16; 1 Tim. 6:15) and contrast with the seven diadems of the dragon (12:3) and the ten diadems of the beast (13:1), who have considerable, but limited, authority. Ladd sums up the truths behind this symbol: "The coming of Christ will mean the public manifestation and the universal enforcement of the sovereignty which is already his by virtue of his death and resurrection" (1972:254; see Acts 2:36; 1 Cor. 15:25-28; Phil 2:9-11; Rev. 5:6-14).

The next symbol associated with Christ is mysterious: *he has a name inscribed that no one knows but himself.* The name contrasts with a similar name on the forehead of the great whore (17:5). In Semitic thought, the name refers to the essence of the person; and because Christ's name is secret, the depths of his character cannot be fully comprehended (Matt. 11:27; Luke 10:22). Christ's names are revealed: "Faithful and True" (v. 11); "Word of God" (v. 13); "King of kings and Lord of lords" (v. 16). Michaels correctly notes with irony that "we already have more names here than we know what to do with" (1997:214n). Bruce, therefore, suggests that the name that no one knows is still another name, one not mentioned in this passage (1996:661). Some think the name is *Yahweh,* which was not to be pronounced except once a year when the high priest entered the holy of holies. Farrer notes an interesting connection with the diadem imagery: the priest wore the consonants of God's name YHWH on a gold plate on his forehead (1964:198). Yet others think the name is Jesus, which was thought to be powerful and was used to heal. It is more likely the name is one that appears in the passage, perhaps King of kings and Lord of lords. Whereas before this time Christ's names could not be known, when he returns, they will be fully comprehended (1 Cor. 13:12; Phil. 2:9-11; Asc. Isa. 9:5). Furthermore, the faithful anticipate that they will share in Christ's glory because they wear a name indicating their connection with the Lord (2:17; 3:12; 14:1).

The rider on the white horse also wears *a robe dipped in blood.* The verb for *dipped* is the perfect passive participle of the word *baptism.* The tense indicates that the dipping is the permanent result of the one-time event of the cross of Christ. Indeed, consistency with other texts in Revelation seems to require that the blood is Christ's (1:5; 5:6, 9; 12:11; 13:8). Thus, a new transformation has taken place: the military Christ has become the crucified Christ. Boring says that such a transformation is "not absurd for one who can define 'conquering' as 'dying' and 'Lion' as 'Lamb.' It is analogous to the idea that Christians wash their garments and make them white in the blood of the Lamb" (1989:196; 7:14). Although this interpretation seems inconsistent with the wine press, where the blood is that of the wicked (14:18-20; see also Isa. 63:1-6), the rider there is not bloodied (Eller, 1974:176). Another interpretation that can be related to the preceding one is to see the blood as that of the martyrs, who are already bloody from their great ordeal (7:14). Caird declares: "The Rider bears on his garments the indelible traces of the death of his followers, just as he bears on his body the marks of this own passion." Even though the persecution seems to be the defeat of the faithful, it is really the ingathering of the saints, which turns the slaughter of faithful into the defeat of their enemies (1966:243-44). As has already been seen many times in Revelation, the blood of martyrs parallels the marks of Christ's slaughter. Yet if it is the blood of the martyrs, there is irony here because they are covered not with blood but with pure linen, like the saints who are washed white in the blood of the Lamb. Although the symbolism is complex, the message is clear: the blood of Christ has won the victory for the saints over their persecutors; Christ has been bloodied in the process of washing the martyrs clean.

It has already been mentioned that one of the names of the rider on the white horse is *The Word of God,* which connects Revelation to other Johannine writings (John 1:1, 14; 1 John 1:1) and may indicate a common author or tradition. Because in the New Testament, the Word of God is Christ (2 Cor. 2:17; 4:1-6; see also Col. 1:15-20), the phrase clearly identifies the rider (1:2, 9; 20:4). Slater notes that this title "presents Christ as more than a witness but also as *the* full manifestation of the divine plan in human form ... as the sovereign Lord of the universe" (1999:220-21).

It is likely that the phrase *armies of heaven* has connections with the designation Lord of Hosts *(Yahweh Sabaoth).* Yet the clothing of the armies, *fine linen, white and pure,* makes it clear that they are not literally an army at all, but the martyrs or faithful saints, the 144,000 (1 Thess. 3:13; see also Rev. 2:10; 3:21; 3:4-5; 4:4; 6:11; 7:9-17; 14:4-5; 19:8; 22:14). Their white garments and *white horses* identify them with Christ and symbolize the victory of those who are faithful to death and perhaps also their purity and holiness (Aune, 1998b:1060).

The description continues: *From his mouth comes a sharp sword.* Although the words conjure up violent images (Isa. 11:4; 2 Thess. 2:8), even in the Old Testament the image is softened to refer to refinement (Isa. 49:2). In the New Testament, the *sword* is symbolically the word of God (Eph. 6:17; Heb. 4:12; Rev. 1:16; 2:12, 16). Certainly, the context in Revelation indicates that the only weapon Christ will use to defeat his enemies is the sharp sword of the word of God (v. 21). In a similar way, the faithful saints conquer by the word of their testimony (Rev. 12:11). Friesen summarizes Revelation's message related to this final war: "The only real victory in Revelation is the sacrifical death of Jesus. . . . Victory belongs to the victim. Even the final confrontation with the Beast is not really a battle: the name of the 'warrior' is the Word of God; his only weapon is the sword of his mouth; no fighting is recounted; the only blood mentioned is the warrior's, shed before the confrontation. Imperialism finally meets its match: resolute weakness" (2001:216). As with the war of Armageddon, there is no battle here; the victory has already been won by Christ on the cross (Isa. 11:1-5; Rev. 19:20). According to Wall, "The point of biblical battles is not to defend militarism; the point is to defend the faithfulness of God" (1991:232).

With the sharp sword of the Word of God, Christ will *strike down the nations.* This weapon is used only against the nations, not the dragon, the beast, and the false prophet (Fekkes, 1994:121). The verb for *striking down* is used elsewhere of God's judgment (Exod. 9:15; Num. 14:12; Deut. 28:22; 2 Kings 6:18; Isa. 11:4; Hos. 6:1; 2 Macc. 9:5; Ps. Sol. 17:24-25; War Scroll 5-6), but here Christ's weapon is the Word. This is evangelism, not warfare; conversion, not slaughter.

After Christ's enemies are struck down, *he will rule them with a rod of iron.* It is surprising to note that this is the only future tense verb in the section, probably under the influence of Psalm 2. The final battle is not a future event but the permanent truth of Christ's victory through the cross. The *rod* here is of *iron* indicating the strong, unbreakable nature of Christ's rule (Ps. 2:9; Isa. 11:4). Yet, as in similar passages, the word *rule (poimanō)* is the verbal form of "shepherd" (Rev. 2:26-27; 12:5). With a rod, the shepherd defended his sheep, but the shepherd image also connotes gentle care (7:17; cf. Zech. 13:7; Matt. 26:31).

Although violence has been muted to this point in the symbols related to the final battle, the divine wrath intensifies in the statement *he will tread the wine press of the fury of the wrath of God the Almighty* (14:8-11, 19-20; Isa. 63:3-6). The imagery is strengthened by the use of both *fury (thymos)* and *wrath (orgē)* in the same sentence. The *wine press* is Babylon's judgment for killing the saints and martyrs (v. 13; 2 Thess. 1:5-10; Rev. 18:6; Sib. Or. 2:249-51).

The description of the rider concludes with the revelation of the mysterious name of Christ: *On his robe and on his thigh he has a name inscribed, "Kings of kings and Lord of lords."* A sword was commonly pictured as hanging on the thigh (Caird, 1966:247; Exod. 32:27; Judg. 3:16, 21; Ps. 45:3; Song Sol. 3:8; Homer, *Iliad* 1.190; *Odyssey* 11.231; Virgil, *Aeneid* 10.788). Here, instead, a name is written, probably on the fold of dress that lay on the rider's thigh (Barclay, 1960:2.235-36). A statue in Ephesus reflected the practice of portraying the emperor riding a horse with his name on his thigh (Cicero, *Oration against Verres* 4.43; Justinus 15.4-5). The significance of the name on the thigh is captured by Wall, who describes it as roughly equivalent to wearing a company coat or team jacket, identifying the person's community (1991:232; 13:16-17; 14:1). The great irony of the passage is that the name no one knows is displayed for all to see. The meaning is that Christ, not the emperor, is the ruler with all power. John's high Christology comes through again here in this declaration of Jesus' divinity through applying to him titles that the Old Testament reserves for God (Deut. 10:17; Dan. 2:47; 1 Tim. 6:15; Rev. 1:5; 17:14; 1 Enoch 9:4; see also 1 Cor. 8:5-6; Phil. 2:9).

The Supper of God 19:17-18

When John repeats the words *Then I saw,* what he sees is *an angel standing in the sun.* The literal designator, one angel, distinguishes this being from the heavenly multitude in 19:1. That the angel stands *in the sun* may refer to its splendor, but the sun is also a good vantage point from which to address the birds.

Then, *with a loud voice* the angel standing in the sun *called to all the birds that fly in midheaven* (8:13; 14:6-7). Most likely vultures (Matt. 24:28; Luke 17:37; see also 1 Sam. 17:44, 46; Isa. 18:6), the birds are summoned with the words: *Come gather for the great supper of God* (Matt. 22:1-4; Rev. 3:20). This hideous meal of dead flesh is contrasted with the glorious marriage supper of the Lamb in the opening verses of the chapter. The word *supper (deipnon)* occurs in Revelation only in these two passages (see 19:9). The conflict that follows was proleptically described in the battle of Armageddon (16:12-16), and the imagery comes from Ezekiel's vision of the battle of Gog and Magog (Ezek. 20:7-10; 39:1-20; see Lind, *BCBC,* 1996 on Ezekiel: 313-21; also Isa. 34:6-7; Jer. 46:10; Zeph. 1:7-9). However, again, no literal battle is described, and the spiritual warfare that ensues is fought, not by demonic and angelic beings, but by real persons who align themselves with the beast or Lamb (Eph. 6:10-12). Moreover, the outcome of the "battle" is so certain that scavenger birds are summoned in advance to devour the corpses of God's enemies, the beast and its allies.

The menu of the supper of God is elaborated in greater detail: *the flesh of kings, the flesh of captains, the flesh of the mighty, the flesh of horses and their riders—flesh of all ... both small and great* (Lev. 26:27-30; Deut. 28:53; 2 Kings 6:28-29; Jer. 19:9; Ezek. 5:10). The plural of *flesh* with the definite article could be translated "corpses" (see 17:16). The variety of persons listed and the collective *all* imply that no one is left out (6:15; 13:16; 17:15; 20:12). Yet, noting that the faithful are excluded, Beasley-Murray says that it refers, not to everyone, but to "all kinds of men" (1974:283). Richard is certainly right to note that the theme of eschatological reversal is present (Ezek. 39:17-20; Zeph. 1:7-9): "Those who are normally victims to be sacrificed (birds and wild animals) are invited as persons to eat in the sacrifice, while those who normally do the sacrificing (heroes, princes, and warriors) are involved in the sacrifice as victims" (1995:147). Indeed, the passage presents the reader with a choice of suppers: the saints have chosen by their faithfulness to attend the marriage supper of the Lamb; while the inhabitants of the earth, who refuse God's continual offer of repentance, have chosen for themselves the supper of God described here. The emphasis of this passage is that the fate of the latter group is total destruction.

The Destruction of the Beasts 19:19-21

In this section, the setting of warfare intensifies: Then I saw the beast and the kings of the earth with their armies gathered to make war against the rider on the horse and against his army. Because they are gathered in anticipation of war, the kings here seem to be the ten horns of the beast (17:3, 7, 12-14, 16; see also Ps. 2:2) rather than those earlier called the "kings of the earth" (17:2; 18:3, 9). Yet because, as elsewhere in Revelation, there is no description of warfare, Boring concludes that there is no battle in John's theology except for the one that took place on the cross (1989:199-200).

The "battle" ends with the capture of *the beast* and the *false prophet*. To John, the beast was the Roman Empire (13:1-10) and the false prophet the provincial leaders of the empire cult (13:11-18). In the realm of timeless truths, the beast is political power that has become satanic, and the false prophet is religion organized in support of that demonic secular power. The trinity of evil—the dragon, the beast and the false prophet—are associated also with the battle of Armageddon, which anticipates the conflict here (16:12-14).

As in chapter 13, the false prophet is described as the one who

had performed ... the signs by which he deceived those who had
received the mark of the beast and those who worshiped its image
(13:11-18). Both the beast and the false prophet *were thrown alive*
into the lake of fire that burns with sulfur. Later, they will be joined
there by the devil (20:10), Death and Hades (20:14), those not written in the book of life (20:15), and the ones who evidence traits not
consistent with faithfulness to God (21:8). First mentioned here (but
see 14:10-11; Dan. 7:11; 1 Enoch 54:1-2; 2 Enoch 10; Asc. Isa.
4:14), the lake of fire is the equivalent of *gehenna,* the place of punishment for the wicked. Sulfur is a yellow substance found in the valley of the Dead Sea that burns with an intensely hot and putrid flame
(Mounce, 1977:350; Gen. 19:24; Num. 16:33; Deut. 29:23; Job
18:15; Isa. 30:33; 34:9; Ezek. 38:22; Luke 17:29; Rev. 9:17-18;
14:10; 20:10; 21:8). Ironically, the beast from the *sea* is thrown into
the *lake* of fire (Mulholland, 1990:304).

The final battle concludes with the words: *And the rest were*
killed by the sword of the rider on the horse, the sword that came
from his mouth; and all the birds were gorged with their flesh. The
rest are the armies of the beast and the ten kings of the East (17:12-
14), who are struck down in spiritual warfare by Christ's sword, the
Word of God (Isa. 11:4; John 12:47-49; 2 Thess. 2:8; Heb. 4:12).
That they are denied burial and eaten by birds adds to their humiliation (Aune, 1998b:1068). Bruce addresses the issue of spiritual warfare in a helpful manner: "The analogy of Scripture discourages the
idea that Christ, having conquered thus throughout preceding ages,
will change His weapons for the final struggle and have recourse to
those which he rejected in the day of temptation in the wilderness"
(1969:661). Christ's weapon here and throughout scripture is the
Word of God, which can torment hearers by convicting them of sin
and judging their deeds (Rowland, 1998:701). This battle is equivalent
to the vintage of the wine press (14:17-20) and the battle of
Armageddon (16:12-16). The complete destruction of all the forces of
Satan prepares for the complete reign of God. Eller says it well:
"From here on out, it's God all the way" (1974:179).

THE TEXT IN BIBLICAL CONTEXT

The Marriage Supper of the Lamb

The marriage supper is the celebration of the faithful because the
great whore, who shed the blood of the saints, has been judged
(18:20). The metaphor of supper as celebration is established in the
Hebrew tradition. After all rejoicing has been terminated by a great

desolation (Isa. 24:4-13), Isaiah speaks of a celebration with "rich food" and "well-aged wines," when the unnamed ruthless oppressing city is destroyed (Isa. 25:1-2, 6-7). Moreover, the wedding supper in Revelation reminds the reader of Psalm 45, a royal wedding psalm in which the kingly husband is God. The theme is later given eschatological overtones as Israel is "gathered from the four quarters of the world" to "eat with the Messiah, and the gentiles will eat with them" (3 Enoch 48A:10; 2 Bar. 29:3-8). Jesus says that suffering can now be accepted with rejoicing because it means the faithful are in a long and great prophetic lineage of persecution (Matt. 5:12).

Indeed, Jesus expands this theme considerably in comparing the kingdom of God to a wedding banquet. To this banquet God the King invites not only Gentiles but everyone his servants can find (Matt. 22:1-10; see also Luke 13:29). Luke's version of the story includes among the invited "the poor, the crippled, the blind, and the lame" (Luke 14:15-24). Interestingly, the ones who reject the invitation are killed (Matt. 22:5-6); and the one not wearing the wedding robe, which in the context of Revelation means not doing righteous deeds, is condemned to "outer darkness" (Matt. 22:11-14).

John's gospel uses the occasion of a wedding supper at the beginning of Jesus' ministry to demonstrate his power (John 2:1-11). When the wine gives out, Jesus tells them to fill the jars with water. When they do, the water in the jars becomes much better wine than was the depleted supply.

In a variation on the wedding supper theme, Jesus compares the eschatological supper with the bread and cup he shared with his disciples at their last meal together. Jesus speaks of a messianic banquet where he will again eat bread and drink wine with his disciples (Matt. 26:26-29; Mark 14:22-25). Then, in words reminiscent of Revelation, those who are faithful in trial will share the meal together with the Old Testament saints in God's kingdom (Matt. 8:11; Luke 13:29) and, subsequently, sit with Christ on thrones of judgment (Luke 22:28-30). Paul makes holiness a prerequisite for sharing in Christ's meal (1 Cor. 11:27-32).

The Bride of Christ

In the Old Testament, Israel is called the bride of God. The prophets used the image to describe the original mutual devotion of God and Israel (Jer. 2:2; Ezek. 16:6-15). Indeed, in the Hebrew tradition, the love story recorded in the Song of Solomon has been viewed as an allegory of the relationship between God and Israel.

Yet in the Old Testament, the bride Israel is often faithless (Jer.

2:1-5; Ezek. 16:16-52; Hos. 2:1-13). Isaiah calls her a whore who has turned from justice and righteousness to murders (Isa. 1:21). Jeremiah reports that the Lord says Israel broke the covenant they enjoyed when God was her husband (Jer. 31:32). Yet, turning from wrath to compassion, God receives Israel back (Isa. 50:1ff.; 54:5-6; Jer. 3:11-14; Hos. 2:14-23) and great celebration ensues (Isa. 61:10). Even her restoration is symbolized as a marriage (Isa. 62:5).

The New Testament expresses union with Christ in terms of a bridegroom and his bride (Mark 2:19-20). Yet in Jesus' wedding parables, the invited guests are the focus, not the bride. Like Old Testament Israel, those invited refuse to come so that others are, in turn, invited (Matt. 22:1-14; Luke 14:15-24). Perhaps more relevant to the context of Revelation is the parable of the wise and foolish virgins, the latter of which are not ready when the bridegroom comes for them (Matt. 25:1-13). In contrast, John's gospel asserts that for the one who stands and hears Christ the bridegroom, there is reason for great joy (John 3:29).

Paul focused more directly on the wedding as a symbol of the relation of Christ to the church. Nevertheless, unlike the Old Testament's relationship between God and faithless Israel, the church is regarded as a faithful bride. Paul insists that marriage is an indissoluble union (Rom. 7:1-4). Thus, it is an appropriate image for the unity of the Lord and his faithful saints (1 Cor. 6:17; 2 Cor. 11:2). Moreover, corporately, Paul portrays the faithful church as a wife that Christ loves (Eph. 5:25-27, 32).

The Parousia

While the second coming of Christ has already in Revelation been presented through the image of a harvest (14:14-20) and the concept appears like bookends at the beginning and end (1:7; 22:20), Revelation 19:11-21 is the apocalypse's clearest description of the coming of Christ. Therefore, it will be instructive now to investigate what the rest of the New Testament says about the parousia.

Although the coming of Christ is a theme that pervades virtually the entire New Testament, Jesus himself cautions against those who predict it from the signs around them. Immediately before Jesus' ascension into heaven his disciples ask him a final question: "Lord, is this the time when you will restore the kingdom to Israel?" Jesus' last statement to his disciples answers this question emphatically: "It is not for you to know the times or periods that the Father has set by his own authority" (Acts 1:6-7). To those who point to wars, famines, and earthquakes, suggesting that these are signs of his coming, Jesus says his followers should not be led astray, because these are not the end but the "beginning of birthpangs" (Matt. 24:3-8; Mark 13:5-8; Luke 21:8-11). Jesus' point is that the saints should not anticipate being taken out of the world by Christ but should endure torture and hatred to the end as a testimony to the nations (Matt. 24:9-14; Mark 13:9-13; Luke 17:25; 21:12-28). Indeed, Jesus cautions that his followers be considerably skeptical about those who announce that the Messiah has come (Matt. 24:15-26; Mark 13:14-23; Luke 17:20-21). Yet he comforts them with the knowledge that they will not be fooled because, in contradiction to the "secret rapture" taught by so many popular writers and speakers, his coming will be evident for all to see (Matt. 24:27-31; Mark 13:24-27; Luke 17:22-24; 21:25-28). Those who point to the fig tree passage as evidence for predicting that the kingdom is near (Matt. 24:32-35; Mark 13:28-31; Luke 21:29-33) overlook the words of Jesus that follow: "But about that day and the hour, no one knows, neither the angels of heaven, nor the Son, but only the Father" (Matt. 24:36; 25:13; Mark 13:32). Jesus further confounds his listeners by following his description of persecutions with the word that happiness and prosperity will continue right up to the second advent of Christ (Matt. 24:37-42; Luke 17:26-37). Clearly, Jesus does not want us to speculate about when he will come but to be constantly awake and ready through living a faithful and holy life (Matt. 24:42-44; Luke 21:34-36). Advice concerning his second coming can be summarized best in Jesus' own words: "Keep awake therefore, for you do not know on what day your Lord is coming.... Therefore you also must be ready, for the Son of Man is coming at an unexpected hour" (Matt. 24:42, 44; Mark 13:33; see also Luke 21:34-36). Jesus then proceeds to tell two parables that demonstrate the uncertain time of his coming and the need to be ready (Matt. 25:1-30; Mark 13:34-37).

Paul provides the traditional imagery surrounding Christ's return. After the "lawless one" who deceived the saints is destroyed (2 Thess. 2:3–12), with an archangel's call and the sound of the trumpet of God, Christ will descend from heaven accompanied by the faithful dead (1 Thess. 4:13-16). Then the saints who are alive on the earth will rise into the clouds to meet their Lord (1 Thess. 4:17-18). Yet Paul affirms with Jesus that the "times and seasons" of this coming are unknown: it will be like a thief in the night (1 Thess. 5:1-2; Rev. 3:3; 16:15). Furthermore, Paul is consistent with his Lord in stating that there will be "peace and security" right up to the time of the parousia (1 Thess. 5:3). Again, the advice to the church is not to speculate when Christ will come, but instead, to be awake and vigilant (1 Thess. 5:6-11).

Elsewhere, Paul turns to theoretical reflection on the parousia. Rooting the second coming of Christ in the death and resurrection of Jesus (1 Cor. 15:20-23), he states that the parousia will be a time when the dead will be raised (1 Cor. 15:51-52); and he confirms Jesus' teaching that what is really important is to prepare for the second coming by being faithful and blameless (1 Cor. 1:7-9; see also 1 Tim. 6:14-15). Although Paul notes that those who do not "know God" and "obey the gospel" suffer "eternal destruction, separated from the presence of the Lord" (2 Thess. 1:8-9), he comforts his readers with the knowledge that it is God through Christ who strengthens them so that they can, indeed, be holy and blameless when Christ comes (1 Thess. 3:13; 5:23; 2 Thess. 2:1-2).

Other New Testament writers add to our knowledge of the second coming of Christ. Contrary to the theme of judgment in Revelation's passages on the parousia, Hebrews asserts that it will be a time, "not to deal with sin, but to save those who are eagerly waiting for him" (Heb. 9:28). In a similar vein, the author of the first epistle of John says that we followers of Christ can have confidence rather than shame when Christ comes (1 John 2:28). The reason for this confidence is that "we will be like him, for we shall see him as he is" (1 John 3:2). Finally, James exhorts the faithful to patient anticipation of this great event (Jas. 5:7).

THE TEXT IN THE LIFE OF THE CHURCH

Liturgical and Literary Expressions

In our time, the treatment of Revelation as a blueprint for the end of the world has caused many Christians to overlook the vast resources for worship to be found in the book. Hymns and poems that lend themselves to use in worship are included throughout, with 19:1-10 probably the most clear and sustained liturgical anthem in the entire book. Indeed, although it does not share much language with Revelation 19, the "Hallelujah Chorus" from Handel's *Messiah* may be the best commentary on this section of Revelation (Michaels, 1997:210-11).

Moreover, the bride image of chapter 19 has stimulated the creative energies of the hymnwriters. For example, Samuel John Stone's hymn "The Church's One Foundation" includes the verse:

From heaven he came and sought her
To be his holy bride.
With his own blood he bought her
And for her life he died.

Although the glorious chorus of the first half of Revelation 19 has generated poetic words of inspiring praise, the awful account of the second coming in verses 11-21 has inspired poetry of quite a different tone. The image of Christ conquering through his word inspired Martin Luther to write:

> And though this world, with devils filled,
> Should threaten to undo us,
> We will not fear, for God hath willed
> His truth to triumph through us.
> The Prince of Darkness grim
> We tremble not for him;
> His rage we can endure,
> For lo! his doom is sure;
> One little word shall fell him.

Perhaps the most well-known poem on the second coming is by William Butler Yeats, but it inspires horror rather than praise:

THE SECOND COMING

> Turning and turning in the widening gyre
> The falcon cannot hear the falconer;
> Things fall apart; the centre cannot hold;
> Mere anarchy is loosed upon the world,
> The blood-dimmed tide is loosed, and everywhere
> The ceremony of innocence is drowned;
> The best lack all conviction, while the worst
> Are full of passionate intensity.
> Surely some revelation is at hand;
> Surely the Second Coming is at hand.
> The Second Coming! Hardly are those words out
> When a vast image out of *Spiritus Mundi*
> Troubles my sight: somewhere in the sands of the desert
> A shape with lion body and the head of a man,
> A gaze blank and pitiless as the sun,
> Is moving its slow thighs, while all about it
> Reel shadows of the indignant desert birds.
> The darkness drops again; but now I know
> That twenty centuries of stony sleep
> Were vexed to nightmare by a rocking cradle,
> And what rough beast, its hour come round at last,
> Slouches towards Bethlehem to be born?

Hence, the alternation of blessing and judgment in Revelation has inspired contrasting creative expressions. In Revelation 19 the first ten verses focus on the praise of those experiencing God's mercy, and the last eleven center on the fate of those who taste the divine judgment.

To see these polarities in a single chapter is particularly striking.

Indeed, the contrast of God's mercy and judgment in Revelation 19 has inspired Anabaptist writers. Menno Simons refers to the last verse of this chapter in a paragraph that demonstrates toward his enemies both a wish for God's mercy and an expectation of their apparent stubborn refusal of divine initiative.

> Would to God that he and his preachers, together with all the papists and monks, who are guilty of innocent blood, might find mercy and grace before the eyes of the great and Almighty God, in the day when the fearful sound of the last trumpet shall resound, and that the innocent blood of which they are the cause might not be counted against them! This I could wish from the bottom of my heart. But if they continue in their present mood and do not turn from ungodliness, then, says the Spirit of God, the fiery pool will be their reward and part. Rev. 19:21. (1956:714)

Women in Revelation

The women in Revelation have, at times, been used to reinforce gender stereotypes, whether of the evil whore or the spotless bride. To counteract this, Talbert points out that there are four women in Revelation (1994:86-87; see Friesen, 2001:186 for the suggestion of a fifth woman, the earth, *gē,* in 12:16). In the usual symmetry of Revelation, two of the women are evil and two are good. A brief summary of each may bring a balanced look at gender in Revelation (cf. Duff, 2001:16, 107-9, who argues that Revelation buys into the gender stereotype of the day that women had difficulty controlling their appetites for food and sex; Pippin, 1999, where Revelation and biblical apocalyptic generally is viewed as misogyny; and Carey, 2001:97, who calls for rejection of the misogyny of Revelation).

The first woman encountered is Jezebel, the archetypical idolatress. As a character in the Hebrew Bible, Jezebel was the daughter of Ethbaal, the king of the Sidonians, who married Ahab, the king of Israel, but remained devoted to the Phoenician god Baal and supported prophets of the cult (1 Kings 16:31-33; 1 Kings 18:19; see also 11:8). Revelation picks up on the idea that Jezebel promoted "harlotries and sorceries" (2 Kings 9:22). The letter to Thyatira condemns the church there because they "tolerate that woman Jezebel, who calls herself a prophet and is teaching and beguiling my servants to practice fornication and to eat food sacrificed to idols" (2:20). Christ promises to throw her on a bed and to condemn those who commit fornication with her to great distress and even death unless they repent (Rev. 2:22-23). The sin of Jezebel was certainly more than fornication; it was toleration of idolatrous practices like eating food offered to idols and participation in the sexual orgies associated with pagan religion. So Jezebel was clearly a seductress that tempted the faithful to practice idolatry.

The second woman in Revelation is the mother of the Messiah, who symbolizes God's people. Unlike the harlot Jezebel, the woman is divinely "clothed with the sun, with the moon under her feet, and on her head a crown of twelve stars" (12:1). Yet she is pregnant, with the serpent waiting to devour her child (12:4). After she gives birth to a son "who is to rule all the nations with a rod of iron," the child is taken to the throne of God, and the woman to the wilderness, where she is nourished during the time of tribulation on the earth (12:5-6). This woman certainly serves as a glorious picture that counteracts the evil one portrayed by Jezebel and the whore that follows.

The third woman in Revelation is the great whore, who commits fornication by causing the kings of the earth to give blasphemous worship to Babylon, symbolizing the beastly Roman Empire (17:1-3). She is dressed garishly in whore's clothes, carries a cup of fornication from which she imbibes until she is drunk, and wears on her forehead the name "mother of whores" (17:4-6). The sight is so macabre that John is amazed to see her.

The fourth woman in Revelation, the bride, the wife of Christ the Lamb, symbolizes the faithful and wears "fine linen, bright and pure," which are the "righteous deeds of the saints" (19:8). If the whore was the fallen city of Babylon, the bride is the glorious New Jerusalem descending from God in heaven (21:2). Like the magnificent mother of the Messiah, the New Jerusalem is decked in jewels and pearls (21:11-21) and has no impurities (21:27).

If the reader is keeping score, there are two evil and two good women in Revelation. Revelation does not play to gender stereotypes that either glorify or vilify women but is true to life in presenting both good and bad representatives of both genders.

Revelation 20:1-15

The Millennial Kingdom

PREVIEW

In chapter 19 the subordinate powers of evil, the beast and the false prophet, were destroyed, leaving only the dragon Satan. As a result of the earlier war in heaven, Satan was banished from the celestial realm (12:9). Chapter 12 made clear that Satan's fall from heaven was the result of Jesus' birth, passion, and exaltation. In the present passage, Satan is removed from the earth through a two-step process: first he is bound (vv. 1-3); then he is cast into the lake of fire (vv. 7-10). Yet, as Beasley-Murray correctly notes, there is no great struggle between Christ and Satan, "the supreme antagonists of history"; an angel curtails the devil's power at the command of God (1974:284).

Revelation seems here to be particularly dependent on the ordering of Ezekiel:

	Ezekiel	Revelation
Defeat of the Enemy	ch. 35	19:17-21
Resurrection/Kingdom	chs. 36-37	20:4-6
Gog/Magog	chs. 38-39	20:7-10
New Temple/Jerusalem	chs. 40-48	21:1-22:5

The Hebrew tradition includes a final battle, similar to the one in verses 7-10, in which God appears to destroy miraculously Israel's oppressors and establish a divine rule of peace and security (Isa. 66:15-23; Dan. 11; Zech. 14; 2 Esd. 13:58; Sib. Or. 3:657-731;

Barn. 15). In these passages, the deliverance of the faithful comes, not through weapons of warfare, but through the Lord's direct intervention.

Moreover, it is crucial for interpreting chapter 20 to remember that the teaching of Revelation is closely tied to the theology of the rest of the New Testament, especially to the death and resurrection of Christ (1 Cor. 15:20-28). The parousia brings to fruition what has been present since Christ died on the cross and rose triumphant from the grave, winning the victory over death (Rev. 1:6). The events of Revelation 20 fulfill the prayer uttered first by Christ and then by his faithful followers: "Your kingdom come. Your will be done, on earth as it is in heaven" (Matt. 6:10).

Again, literary features contribute to the theological impact of the passage. First, chapter 20 continues the remarkable symmetry of good and evil in Revelation. Those faithful to the Lamb are rewarded with participation in the millennial kingdom of God (vv. 4-6), while those who are not faithful receive the judgment of the lake of fire (v. 15). Second, the use of time heightens the contrast between the suffering and reward of the saints. Michaels points out that the references to time related to the tribulation of the faithful are relatively short: three and a half days (11:9, 11), five months (9:5), one thousand two hundred sixty days (11:3; 12:6), and forty-two months (11:2; 13:5); by contrast, the millennial kingdom is a lengthy thousand years (20:2, 4, 5, 7). The point of the contrast is that the sufferings of the saints are insignificant when compared to the bliss of their reward (Michaels, 1997:220-21; see Rom. 8:18; 2 Cor. 4:17; Rev. 12:12).

Finally, it should be noted that Revelation 20 is arguably the most controversial chapter in the book. Caird calls it a "paradise of cranks and fanatics on the one hand and literalists on the other" (1966:249). Perhaps the reason for controversy is that the chapter raises many difficult—and even unanswerable—questions. Is the setting of the chapter on earth as verse 1 announces or in heaven where most of the characters—the angel (v. 1), the resurrected souls of the martyrs on thrones (v. 4), God on the throne (v. 11), and the dead, great and small (verse 12)—would likely be located? Will all the saints be martyred in the end (v. 4), or if not, how will saints living at the time of the parousia be resurrected when they have not yet died? Because it would appear that the armies of the kings of the earth were killed and eaten by vultures (19:21), from where do the armies of Gog and Magog come? Are they human, military forces, or a demonic army (9:1-11; 16:13-16)? Do they attack the saints? What is the reason for releasing Satan after a one-thousand-year reign of Christ? What bliss does the millennium bring that would warrant postponing heaven for a thousand years? Perhaps Eller is correct to conclude that the reader of Revelation should "quit fussing with details and look to the central truth involved"—the importance of faithfulness in anticipation of participation in the kingdom of God (1974:181-83; see also Caird, 1966:249; Mounce, 1977:351). What is clear from this chapter is a progression that is common in apocalyptic literature: the reign of Christ, the resurrection of the dead, and the last judgment.

OUTLINE

The Binding of Satan, 20:1-3
The Millennium, 20:4-6
The Release of Satan, 20:7-10
The Great White Throne, 20:11-15

EXPLANATORY NOTES

The Binding of Satan 20:1-3

The passage begins in the typical manner for this part of Revelation: *Then I saw an angel coming down from heaven.* There is probably an allusion, by contrast, to the star angel of 9:1, who released locusts from the bottomless pit (see also 10:1-3; 18:1-2). Here the angel has the task of overcoming evil to inaugurate the millennial kingdom. The contrast in the mission of the two heavenly beings is heightened by the indication in 9:1 that the star fell, whereas in 20:1, the angel descended. The latter verb is also used for the descent of the New Jerusalem from heaven in 21:2 (Ford, 1975:329).

The angel that came down from heaven was *holding in his hand the key to the bottomless pit and a great chain.* The bottomless pit is the permanent abode of the devil and his evil comrades (Luke 8:31; 2 Pet. 2:4; Jude 6; Rev. 11:7; 17:8; Jub. 5:6; 1 Enoch 88:1). The word *chain (halysin)* could be translated "handcuffs" or "leg irons" (Ford, 1975:329; see Mark 5:3-4; Acts 12:6-7; Eph. 6:20), and the key that unlocks it belongs to Christ (1:18). Together, the key and chain symbolize the curtailing of Satan's power.

Indeed, the angel *seized the dragon, that ancient serpent, who is the Devil and Satan.* The one who inspired the beast and false prophet to persecute and deceive the faithful saints is now spiritually restrained from his evil pursuits. As in 12:9, we have here all Revelation's names for the great leader of the realm of evil. The *dragon* is the primeval beast who made war on the saints but was defeated by Michael and his angels in the great war in heaven (12:7-8). The *serpent* was the deceiver of Eden who poured water from his mouth to sweep away the woman who had given birth to the Messiah (12:15). The *Devil* was the accuser or slanderer of the saints who was intent on deceiving the faithful before the end (12:12). All these roles of the evil one are terminated here by the work Christ has already accomplished on the cross (Rom. 8:34; Rev. 12:9). In a sense, this is the reversal of the fall of Genesis 3.

After seizing Satan, the angel binds the great perpetrator of evil *for a thousand years.* The act is certainly not for punishment (Isa. 24:21-22; 1 Enoch 10, 18), but for restraint (Matt. 12:24-29; Mark 3:22-27; Luke 11:15-23; Jub. 48:15). Moreover, the binding of Satan may not be a future event but a result of the crucifixion and resurrection of Christ (Matt. 12:29; Luke 10:17-18; John 12:31-32; 16:11; Col. 2:15; Heb. 1:3; 2:14-15; 12:2; Rev. 12:4-6; cf. Matt. 13:41; 1 Cor. 15:24-28). The saints take part in Satan's restraint through their commitment to faithfulness, thus serving to limit the devil's influence in the world (Efird, 1989:113; see Luke 10:17-19). If this interpretation is correct, the thousand years refers to the present church age rather than a future expectation.

After the angel bound Satan, he *threw him into the pit, and locked and sealed it over him, so that he would deceive the nations no more, until the thousand years were ended.* Sealing is often for confinement (Dan. 6:17; Matt. 27:66; Bel and Dragon 11, 14; Jos., *Ant.* 10.258; cf. Rev. 7:2-4; 10:4; 22:10), and in this case, it is to curtail Satan's deception (vv. 3, 8, 10). The verb *deceive* carries the connotation of seduction and is used of the activity of Jezebel (2:20; see also 17:2; 18:3, 9). Deception is the very character of Satan (12:9) and the main activity of the false prophet (13:14; 19:20). The object of this deception is the nations, which in Revelation include all persons (5:9; 7:9; 10:11; 11:2, 18; 14:6, 8; 17:15; 18:3, 23) who in the end are won over by God (15:4; 21:3; 22:2; see also Matt. 24:14; 28:19-20; Mark 13:10; Luke 2:29-32; Rom. 10:12-13). The presence of the nations is confusing here, because this group was annihilated in the previous passage (19:11-21). Yet we have learned not to demand chronological consistency from Revelation.

Richard calls the restraint of Satan a "high security operation" (1995:149), which includes his being *seized (ekratēsen), bound (edēsen), thrown* down *(ebalen), locked* up *(ekleisen),* and *sealed (esphragisen).* These elaborate measures indicate to some that Satan must be rendered completely inactive during the millennial reign of Christ (see Mounce, 1977:353; Walvoord, 1966:291-92). Yet the passage only confirms that Satan is kept from deceiving the nations,

which probably does not include prevention of all of Satan's power
but only his active aggression against the faithful and his inciting the
nations to persecute Christians (see Ladd, 1972:262). Hendricksen
takes the binding of Satan to mean that he cannot prevent the missionary outreach of the church (1982:226). Whatever the exact
nature of Satan's binding, the devil has been given a death blow,
reminding both him and his antagonists that he is playing a losing
game (Mulholland, 1990:306). Satan's imminent demise encourages
the faithful to live in anticipation that the kingdom of God is at hand.

After the thousand years are over, Satan *must be let out*. This
verb here implies that God is the actor. Yet it should not be assumed
that the word *must (dei)* constrains God in some way; it simply indicates that God's will is being accomplished (Mark 8:31; 13:7; Luke
24:26, 44; Rev. 1:1; 4:1; 10:11; 11:5; 13:10; 17:10; 22:6; see also
Dan. 2:28; Matt. 26:42). Beasley-Murray properly notes the clear
parallel between Genesis 3 and the present passage: creation leads to
the Fall, as the parousia is followed by the release of Satan
(1974:291). Yet this section ends with the consolation that Satan's
release is only for *a little while* (2:21; 6:11; 10:6; 12:12; 19:17-21).

The point of the release of Satan is to highlight the resilience of
the power of evil. Mounce's words are particularly apropos here:
"Apparently a thousand years of confinement does not alter Satan's
plans, nor does a thousand years of freedom from the influence of
wickedness change man's basic tendency to rebel against his creator"
(1977:354).

The Millennium 20:4-6

The theme of the release of Satan was introduced proleptically in
verse 3 and will be developed in verses 7-10. In the meantime, John
*saw thrones, and those seated on them were given authority to
judge*. The background for this passage is Daniel 7, where the
Ancient One sits eternally with the "holy ones of the Most High" on
thrones (Dan. 7:9, 13-14, 22, 26-27; see Lederach, *BCBC*, 1994,
on Daniel). Contrary to the belief of those who expect an earthly reign
of Christ, the setting for this passage is apparently heaven, because all
of the forty-seven occurrences in Revelation of *thrones*, except those
occupied by Satan and the beast, (2:13; 13:2; 16:10) are in heaven
(1:4; 3:21; 4–5, 7; 8:3; 11:16; 12:5; 14:3, 5; 16:17; 19:4-5; 20:11;
21:5; 22:1-3). Although in the Greek text there is no subject of the
second clause, the implied subject is *those seated on [thrones]*, most
likely the saints who have remained faithful in tribulation. As is quite
common in Revelation, the source of their authority, although again

not specified, apparently is God (cf. 13:7, 15). Most commentators believe that the judgment given to the faithful is either to share in divine judgment of the world (Matt. 19:28; Luke 22:29-30; 1 Cor. 6:2-3) or to act as judges reigning over the empire of the beast (Dan. 4:17; see also Eph. 2:6; 2 Tim. 2:12; Rev. 3:11; 5:10). Yet Richard argues that their judgment is the "power to do 'justice'" (1995:150-51; 17:1; 18:20) or, in the words of Barclay, the ability to "redress the balance of this world" (1960:2.247). The meaning of judgment that is most consistent with the language of the text, however, is that the saints who occupy these thrones receive a favorable judgment from God because of their faithfulness (1:6; 2:26-27; 7:4-10; 11:1-2). Thus, the expulsion of Satan in the previous passage is the fulfillment of the promise to those who have been faithful in the tribulation (6:9-12).

In addition to thrones, John *saw the souls of those who had been beheaded for their testimony to Jesus and for the word of God.* The verb *beheaded (pelekizō)* occurs only here in the New Testament, and the noun form *(pelekys)*, which does not occur in the New Testament, designates the double-edged axe used for execution during the Roman Republic (Eusebius, *Eccl. Hist.* 2.25, witnesses that the apostle Paul died thus), but replaced by the sword in the empire (Jos., *Ant.* 14.125; Diodorus of Sicily 19.101.3; cf. Polybius, *Histories* 1.7; see also Aune, 1998b:1086). Here, though, it symbolizes all the ways the saints were martyred (14:13; 18:24). The word translated *testimony (martyria)*, indeed, need not be limited to literal martyrdom but can include the witness of all the saints who remain faithful. The *testimony to Jesus* is a subjective genitive: Jesus is the content of the testimony affirmed by the faithful (6:9-11). As has been noted repeatedly, their testimony in the face of persecution and even death (7:13-17; 11:3-13; 12:11, 17; 13:8; 14:4-5) parallels the redemptive suffering and death of Christ (1:2, 5, 9; 2:8; 3:14).

The ones beheaded for their testimony *had not worshiped the beast or its image and had not received its mark on their foreheads or their hands.* The primary referent here is to the mark of the beast, which the false prophet enticed people to take (13:12, 15-16; 14:9-11; 16:2; 19:20). Although, literally, the passage describes two groups, the martyrs and the faithful, the conjunction *and (kai)* connecting the two clauses likely indicates that both groups, not just the martyrs, are on thrones ruling with Christ (Wilcock, 1975:191-92). Michaels insightfully says that persons are not martyrs because they are killed, but killed because they are faithful (1997:225; 14:4; 17:14). Nevertheless, although the reign of Christ is not limited to martyrs, the passage does give them special consideration (Ladd, 1972:263-64).

Thus, it is most likely that the faithful saints, both living and dead, that *came to life and reigned with Christ a thousand years.* The verb, *came to life (ezēsan),* seems to imply that those who *reigned with Christ* had died, leading some to affirm that in the end all are martyred (see Morris, 1969:237; Mounce, 1977:355-56; Rev. 13:15). This line of reasoning, which limits the kingdom to those who are killed during the last generation of church history, contradicts the universal nature of the church in Revelation (chs. 2–3; 5:9; 14:1-5; Beasley-Murray, 1974:294) and the message of the rest of the New Testament that the kingdom is composed of all Christians, living and dead (Mark 13:27; 1 Cor. 15:51-52; 1 Thess. 4:16-17). Indeed, there is no reason to limit *came to life* to resurrection from the dead. Efird is probably right to translate it "lived" and to assert that it refers to the state of living, not the event of resurrection (1989:115). Indeed, the martyrs have already come to life spiritually and are living with Christ in heaven (6:11; 11:11-12). Moreover, John always uses *life* as the abundant life that characterizes the New Jerusalem (Eller, 1974:186). Whatever the nature of the *coming to life* described here, Christ's bodily resurrection, affirmed throughout scripture, gives his followers confidence they will also be resurrected in the flesh (Ladd, 1972:265). The essence of this text is that ultimately the destination of the martyrs is not death but resurrection.

One of the most difficult passages in Revelation is the parenthetical statement: *(The rest of the dead did not come to life until the thousand years are ended).* Although this verse is not found in several ancient manuscripts, most notably Codex Sinaiticus, it cannot easily be rejected, because it is present in almost all texts. The most literal rendering would say that the rest of the dead are those who were not martyred, which would mean that the millennium is reserved for those who die for their faith. Another option is to interpret the rest of the dead as the unbelievers, a reading that allows all of the faithful to participate in the millennium. It is perhaps best not to be too literal in our interpretation of the kingdom and too rigid about who is included in which resurrection.

Following the parenthetic statement, the thought of verse 4 is continued with the affirmation: *This is the first resurrection,* a concept found nowhere else in scripture (but see Rom 8:9-11; 1 Cor. 15:22-24). Some would take the first resurrection to be physical, just as the first death is physical. Although there is no second resurrection in scripture, some think it is implied (see 20:12-13) and affirm that there are two bodily resurrections. The most literal interpretation is that the first resurrection is for martyrs and the second for all the *rest of the dead,* believers and unbelievers (see Morris, 1969:238). Others who accept two bodily resurrections would see the first as for the saints and the second for the unbelievers (see Ladd, 1972:268; John 5:29). Yet it may be that the first resurrection does not necessitate a second. Those who hold this position believe either that the overcomers are first in the sense of being a "foretaste" or "guarantee" of the reign of Christ (Sweet, 1990:289), the first group to experience resurrection and its blessings (Ford, 1975:350; Wall, 1991:239; see 1 Cor. 15:23), or first in the sense that the resurrection has not already happened (Boring, 1989:208; see 2 Tim. 2:18).

In the face of this confusing array of interpretations, it is probably most consistent with the rest of the biblical record to interpret the first resurrection spiritually to be belief and commitment to faithful service of Christ (John 5:24; 11:25-26; Rom. 6:4; 2 Cor. 1:21-22; Eph. 2:1, 5-6; Phil. 3:20; Col. 2:12; 3:1; 1 John 5:11-12; Rev. 14:13); the second resurrection, then, is the general resurrection to eternal life (Dan. 12:2; John 5:28-29; Acts 24:15; Phil. 3:10-11, 21). Thus, the first resurrection is not a chronological event but a state of being committed to God and Christ (Efird, 1989:115).

The fifth of Revelation's seven beatitudes then follows (see also 1:3; 14:13; 16:15; 19:9; 22:7, 14): *Blessed and holy are those who share in the first resurrection.* As is typical of the stylistic structure of Revelation, there is no description of the millennium here (see 21:9–22:5), but only a blessing on persons participating in the first resurrection, paralleling the introduction of the marriage supper of the Lamb (19:9). Those who share the first resurrection also are called *holy (hagios),* the adjective most commonly used in Revelation to denote the faithful people of God (5:8-9; 8:3-4; 11:18; 13:7, 10; 14:12; 16:5; 17:6; 18:20, 24; 19:8; 22:11, 21). Elsewhere it designates God (4:8; 6:10; 15:4), Christ (3:7), angels (14:10), and the city of Jerusalem (11:2; 21:2, 10; 22:19).

The promise to the resurrected ones is that *the second death has no power* over them (2:11), meaning that they will be exempted from eternal punishment in the lake of fire. The New Testament reflects the rabbinic idea of two deaths: the first is physical death elaborated in verse 4 (Rom. 5:12-21; 1 Cor. 15:21-22; 2 Cor. 5:14; Heb. 9:27; Rev. 11:7-10), and the second is separation from God and the eternal destruction of the lake of fire mentioned in verse 14 (John 5:29; Eph. 2:5; Rev. 19:20; 20:10, 14-15; 21:8). Beale argues for an interesting chiasm of death and resurrection: the first death is physical, and the second spiritual; the first resurrection is spiritual, and the second physical (1999:1005-7). It is interesting to note that physical death continues until the end of the millennium, when *Death and Hades* are finally destroyed (20:14). The promise of this beatitude is that those who die for their faithfulness will escape eternal death.

Instead of finding themselves in the lake of fire, the faithful *will be priests of God and of Christ, and they will reign with him a thousand years.* The priestly character of the saints refers to their role in calling the world to worship God through Christ (Heb. 9:14; 1 Pet. 2:5; Rev. 14:1-5; 22:3-4). The *reign* of the faithful symbolizes their participation in God's rule through Christ over the powers of the world (Rom. 8:18-25; 1 Cor. 4:8; 6:2-3; Rev. 1:5; 11:15; 12:10-11; 15:3; 17:14; 19:16; 22:5). The paradox is that the rule of the saints is both already (Mark 1:15; Luke 11:20; 17:21; 22:28-30; Eph. 1:20; 2:4-6; 5:5; Col. 1:13; 1 Thess. 2:12; Rev. 1:6; 5:9-10) and not yet (Matt. 19:28; Mark 14:25; 1 Cor. 6:3, 9-10; Gal. 5:21; 2 Thess. 1:5). The priestly worship and kingly rule of the faithful saints are treated together in Revelation (1:6; 5:9-10; see also Exod. 19:6; 1 Pet. 2:9).

The Release of Satan 20:7-10

The defeat of Satan in this passage follows as a natural sequel to the victory over the other two members of the trinity of evil, the beast and the false prophet: *When the thousand years are ended, Satan will be released from his prison* (see v. 3; 2:10). The Hebrew roots of this story are in Ezekiel 38–39. One of the mythological parallels to this action is the Babylonian legend in which Tiamat is to be released at the end of history to again be defeated by Marduk as he was at the beginning. At the end of history, according to Revelation, the devil is allowed to make one last effort to deceive the nations at the time immediately preceding Christ's return, which finally brings Satan's onslaught to an end (2 Thess. 2:3-10). The action here corresponds to the devil's persecution of the church after his earlier expulsion from heaven (12:13-17). Satan's revival in this section is the "counterpart to the beast's death, healing, and return" (Sweet, 1990:291; see 13:3; 17:8-11). The purpose of Satan's release is to provide "a testing time for Christians" to prove the validity of their faith (Barclay, 1960:2.246). Moreover, the event symbolizes the persistence of Satan's deceptive activity and the stubbornness of humanity.

Some scholars suggest that the uncertainty of the language in this verse gives support to the contention that the millennium is symbolic of an indefinite period of time. Morris argues that the conjunction *when (hotan)* carries the meaning of "whenever," connoting uncertainty (1969:238). Efird relates this contingency to the faithfulness of the saints, contending that apostasy leads to the loosing of Satan, and faithfulness keeps evil under control (1989:116). Moreover, the verb *ended (telesthē)* carries the sense of goal rather than chronology, and the subjunctive mood both here and in verse 3 indicates an indeterminate period. Therefore, one thousand years is probably used, not as a chronologic unit, but as a period of human history (Ps. 90:4; Eccles. 6:6; 2 Pet. 3:8).

After Satan's release, he *will come out to deceive the nations at the four corners of the earth, Gog and Magog, in order to gather them for battle; they are as numerous as the sands of the sea.* Consistent with his character, Satan will come out to deceive nations (12:9; 20:3; see also 13:13-15; 19:20), who this time are both Gog and Magog (Ezek. 38:2-3) and, more universally, all the nations from the four corners of the earth (Isa. 11:12; Ezek. 7:2; Rev. 7:1) and are "as numerous as the sands of the sea" (Gen. 22:17; Josh. 11:4; Judg. 7:12; 1 Sam. 13:5; cf. Ezek. 38:16). Satan's deception is that he will gather them for battle as he did the frog-like spirits at Armageddon (16:13-16). Although Mounce distinguishes this battle from the two before the millennium (1977:362), Revelation probably does not report a chronological sequence of battles, but instead, the repetition of conflicts symbolizes the resilience of evil. Indeed, this "final" battle (Zech. 14:1-11; Sib. Or. 3:663-74) is the same conflict as Armageddon (16:14-20), the battle of the ten horned beast and the Lamb (17:14), and the battle of the rider on the white horse (19:19-21). One reason to believe that the battle repeats earlier warfare relates to the participants. Because the human armies perished in the earlier battles (16:12-16; 19:17-21), who is left to fight? To see the battles as reiteration makes this discrepancy evaporate.

The description of this battle is apparently dependent on Ezekiel 38–39 (see Lind, *BCBC*, 1996, on Ezekiel). Following the restoration of Israel (Ezek. 33–37), Ezekiel's army from the nations of the earth is destroyed with fire and sulfur (38:8, 22; 39:6). Yet Ezekiel describes Gog as the prince of the people of Magog: "Gog, of the land of Magog, the chief prince of Meshech and Tubal" (Ezek. 38:2-3; 39:1; see also LXX of Amos 7:1). Elsewhere in the Bible, Gog and Magog are mentioned only in genealogies (Gen. 10:2; 1 Chron. 1:5; 5:4). Later in Jewish tradition, however, they become two geographical locations (Sib. Or. 3:319, 512; Jerusalem Targum on Num. 11:27; Deut. 32:39; Palestinian Targum on Exod. 40; Num. 24:17; Eduyoth 2.10; Abodah Zarah 3b; Buskoth 7b). Moreover, in amplification of prophecy related to Gog and Magog, they become leaders, who in apocalyptic literature symbolize forces of evil (Morris, 1969:239).

The interpretations of Gog and Magog differ predictably along literal/symbolic lines. Some believe that Magog is an actual city that will attack the people of God in the end times. Although the word *battle (polemos)* can be used figuratively of strife and quarreling, it does connote real armed conflict. Yet the location of Magog has been problematic: Ezekiel believed Gog to be the prince of Meshech and Tubal, which are located in Asia (Ezek. 38:1); and at least one Jewish source roughly contemporary with Revelation locates the land of Gog and Magog in Ethiopia (Sib. Or. 3:319-20). Furthermore, futurists, without any etymological evidence, seem to place Meshech and Tubal somewhere in Russia (e.g. Moscow and Tobolsk). However, it seems better to take Gog and Magog symbolically. The Tel el-Amarna tablets use Gog symbolically for the northern nations (Beasley-Murray, 1974:297). Specifically, Josephus identifies Magog with the Scythians, a threat that occupied the area to the north (*Ant.* 1.123). Whatever the specific referent, Gog and Magog most likely represent archetypical enemies, symbolic of all that is hostile to God's faithful saints. This attack is not from specific nations to the north but innumerable hordes from all corners of the earth (Beasley-Murray, 1974:297; 2 Esd. 13:5; 1 Enoch 56:5-8; Sib. Or. 3:662-668). Whatever the meaning of Gog and Magog, the point of the battle is to remind the faithful that the end of the world is in the hands of God, not Satan (Morris, 1969:236).

The battle began as the innumerable forces of Satan *marched up over the breadth of the earth and surrounded the camp of the saints and the beloved city*. The verbs in this passage are aorists, denoting completed action, as though the outcome of the battle is already certain. The *breadth of the earth* is certainly not meant literally but metaphorically connotes the universal scope of the battle (Isa. 8:8; Hab. 1:6; Sir. 1:3). The image of the *camp of the saints* recalls Israel's nomadic wilderness habitat (Num. 2:2-34; 9:23; Heb. 11:9, 13). Schüssler Fiorenza indicates that the camp implies protection "from the last assault of all demonic and evil powers" (1991:108; see Ezek. 38:10-13; Heb. 13:11-13). The *beloved city* here proleptically announces the New Jerusalem, which awaits more detailed description in the next chapter (21:10–22:5; see also 3:12; 11:2). Taken together, the city and camp describe God's faithful saints, who are not promised escape from the onslaught of the evil one, but divine protection as they overcome the worst that Satan can throw at them. Mulholland says it well: "They are not safely 'whisked away,' 'raptured' to heaven, so as to escape the final action of God. God's people are the very focus of the action" (1990:306-7).

In the consummation of the last battle, *fire came down from heaven and consumed* the "armies" of Satan. The intervention of God with fire is a traditional biblical image (Gen. 19:24-28; Deut. 4:24; 2 Kings 1:10-12; Ezek. 38:22; 39:6; Luke 9:54; 2 Thess. 1:6-8; Heb. 12:29). While the image of "coming up" *(anabēsan)* describes the destructive actions of the demonic, "coming down" *(katebē)* is used of the salvific actions of God (Richard, 1995:149). As we have seen at least twice before in Revelation (16:12-16; 19:17-21), the "final battle" is no battle at all. Instead, God intervenes on behalf of the faithful in a fantastic manner, in this case with fire from heaven (cf. 11:5 with 13:13). The emphasis here is not on the defeat of a human army but on the annihilation of the devil and his followers. Weaver's words are powerful: "When confronted with the fullness of the victorious Lord and the reign of God, the resistance of evil simply melts away" (1994b:491).

The battle moves quickly to conclusion (see 12:9; 20:1-3): *the devil who had deceived them was thrown into the lake of fire and sulfur, where the beast and the false prophet were* (19:20). The elimination of evil marks the climax of Revelation; the demise of the evil trinity is completed with the destruction of the ultimate enemy, Satan. It is difficult to visualize how spiritual beings like Satan, the beast, and the false prophet can *be tormented day and night forever and ever* in a literal fire (14:10-11). The issue is complicated by the fact that the lake of fire was originally planned, not for beings with corporal bodies that would be affected by physical torment, but for the devil and his angels (Matt. 25:41; see also 1 Enoch 18:11-19:2; 21:1-10). Therefore, the lake of fire and sulfur may symbolize a spiritual punishment that would be more appropriate for the evil trinity; but if so, it is no less torment for all who are consigned there. This final annihilation of the devil opens the way for the kingdom of God, but the general resurrection must precede this joyous consummation.

The Great White Throne 20:11-15

The great white throne is perhaps the most impressive description of final judgment anywhere (Dan. 7:9-14; 2 Esd. 6:17-20; 1 Enoch 47:3; 90:20; 2 Bar. 24:1). Although there are several judgments in Revelation (e.g. 14:14-20; 19:17-21), John seems more interested in the impact of judgment on human responsibility than in distinguishing a chronology of judgments. Thus, reiteration is likely at work; John only knows of one judgment—and it includes everyone (Boring, 1989:210).

At the beginning of the scene, John *saw a great white throne and the one who sat on it*. The throne is *great* in the sense of being authoritative and powerful and *white* in the sense of being victorious and glorious (1 Kings 10:18; Matt. 17:2; 1 Cor. 15:24-28; 1 Enoch 18:8). The white throne parallels the white horse, which represents the judgment of Jesus (19:11; cf. 6:2). In Revelation, though, the one who sits on the throne and exercises absolute dominion is God (4:2-11; 5:1, 7, 13; 6:16; 7:10, 15; 19:4; 21:5). Thus, the white throne judgment teaches that a higher court than Rome is handing down sentences (Boring, 1989:211).

Upon the appearance of the one who sat on the great white throne, *earth and the heaven fled from his presence, and no place was found for them*. In the last judgment, even nature, which is itself fallen, recoils from God's holiness because there is no place for corruption in the holy city to come (Isa. 34:2-4; 40:8; Rom. 8:19-22). The perceptive reader will note that finally all evil has been destroyed: Babylon (18:1-24), the beasts (19:20), the dragon (20:10), Death and *Hades* (20:14), and now the earth. It should be noted that the Bible seems ambiguous about the future of earth, indicating both that the world will perish (Ps. 102:25-27; Isa. 51:6; Matt. 24:35; Mark 13:31; Luke 16:17; 1 Cor. 7:31; 2 Cor. 4:18; Heb. 1:10, 12; 2 Pet. 3:7, 10, 12-13; 1 John 2:17; Rev. 6:14; 16:20) and that creation will be renewed (Isa. 11:6-9; 65:17-18; Matt. 19:28; Acts 3:21; Rom. 8:21). Despite this ambiguity, what is certain is that the end of the earth, as it presently is, prepares for the new heaven and new earth (21:1).

After the disappearance of heaven and earth, John *saw the dead, great and small, standing before the throne*. Although Revelation speaks of death both spiritually and physically (1:5; 1:17-18; 2:8; 3:1; 11:13; 14:13), that they were *standing* indicates physical death is in mind and resurrection has occurred. The phrase, *great and small* (11:18; 13:16; 19:5, 18), stresses that at death all will be judged. Indeed, the New Testament insists on the universality of judgment (Matt. 25:32; John 5:28-29; Rom. 14:10; 2 Cor. 5:10; 2 Tim. 4:1; 1 Pet. 1:17; 4:5; see also Dan. 12:2). Barclay says: "The judgment seat of God will be the great leveller" (1960:2.251).

When all were gathered for judgment, two *books were opened*. The first, which Metzger calls the book of merit (1993:96), is a record of all deeds performed, both good and evil, and symbolizes God's omniscience and human responsibility. Walvoord finds judgment on the basis of works to be unacceptable and insists that it is not for salvation but rewards in heaven (1966:306-7). Yet he admits that the wicked are here condemned to the lake of fire on the basis of their works, and there is no mention in the passage whatsoever of rewards. We must, therefore, conclude that the final judgment involves everyone and takes account of human deeds done in this world. Yarbro Collins is certainly consistent with this passage when she says, "Each deed is of ultimate significance and must be accounted for" (1991:142). Then the second *book was opened, the book of life,* which contains, not the deeds, but the names of the faithful. In contrast to the first book, Metzger calls this the book of mercy (1993:96). It is the citizenship roll of the New Jerusalem, which includes the names of faithful saints who have overcome the persecution of Satan (3:5; 21:27). Although the previous book affirmed that in the final judgment deeds do matter, this one reminds us that God's mercy is ultimately our basis for salvation. The Lamb's book of life tells the faithful that, when judged by God, Christ's death is the only basis for acquittal.

Surprisingly, the reader is once more warned against resting on the grace of God and ignoring good deeds: *the dead were judged according to their works, as recorded in the books.* Indeed, the sentiment of this clause regarding the importance of good works is repeated again in the next verse. How do we reconcile this emphasis on works with the doctrine of salvation by faith? Perhaps the church has often had too weak a doctrine of faith. Although the Bible elsewhere affirms that salvation is not through works, Revelation clearly affirms that faith does not come without works. Richard reminds those who emphasize correct doctrine over proper behavior that in Revelation "it is orthopraxis that saves us, not orthodoxy" (1995:158). Yet to those who would overemphasize works salvation, Mounce's words are an important corrective: "The issue is not salvation by works but works as the irrefutable evidence of a ... relationship with God" (1977:366). Perhaps, paradoxically, Richard and Mounce are both correct: the inclusion of both the books of deeds and the book of life in Revelation points in that direction. Indeed, the books remind us of two paradoxical truths that must be kept in tension to avoid distorting the biblical teaching on judgment: human works and deeds do matter to God when it comes to determining who is saved, but salvation cannot be earned and only comes through the death of Christ by which the names of the faithful were inscribed in the Lamb's book of life.

For the purpose of judgment, *the sea gave up the dead that were in it.* Although death is pictured as a great sea and the source of demonic forces (Ps. 18:4, 16-17), probably more relevant to this passage is the importance of burial to the Hebrews (1 Kings 13:21-22; 14:11; Jer. 8:1-2; Tob. 2:3-7) and the tradition that those who drowned at sea would perish (see 1 Enoch 61:5). Bruce observes: "In some Jewish circles resurrection was thought of as possible only for those buried on dry land" (1969:663). The meaning of this segment of text is certainly captured well by Swete: "The accidents of death will not prevent any of the dead from appearing before the Judge; sea and land will alike deliver up their tale" (1908:272-73).

Following the example of the sea, *Death and Hades gave up the dead that were in them, and all were judged according to what they had done.* The word *all* refutes the contention of some that this is just the resurrection of the wicked. Moreover, if *Death* includes the righteous, then the parallel construction of this passage necessitates that *Hades* is a universal grave until all are brought to judgment (Morris, 1969:241; Acts 2:27, 31). Indeed, this passage affirms that all, the wicked and the righteous, are judged and that no one escapes (Heb. 9:27; cf. Aune, 1998b:1103).

After they gave up their dead, *Death and Hades were thrown into the lake of fire.* Death, the last enemy, was destroyed by Christ on the cross (1 Cor. 15:26-28; 2 Tim. 1:10). So we witness here the "death of Death" (Boring, 1989:213). Moreover, if death is to be destroyed, then *Hades,* the temporary abode of the dead, is no longer necessary and is therefore cast into the lake of fire where the demonic creatures were thrown (19:20; 20:10). All this purging of evil is preparation for the New Jerusalem (21:8, 27). Nevertheless, as is the case with many passages related to the lake of fire, this one is difficult to take literally. How can death be cast into some physical chamber? Ladd is no doubt correct to take the lake of fire in this passage as symbolic for the complete destruction of death and the grave (1972:274; 1 Cor. 15:54-55; Rev. 21:4). Morover, perhaps Death and Hades should be taken as evil powers instead of places (Barker, 2000:366).

The *second death* is then identified as *the lake of fire.* The first death is physical (Heb. 9:27), the second spiritual and eternal (Matt. 10:28). Alford says: "As there is a second and higher life, so there is also a second and deeper death. And as after that life there is no more death, so after that death there is no more life" (1861:729).

Finally, the destiny of the inhabitants of the earth (13:8; 17:8) is announced: *anyone whose name was not found written in the book of life was thrown into the lake of fire.* Those included here are the ones who have not chosen to follow Christ or have not remained faithful to that choice (Deut. 30:19; John 5:40; 8:24; 1 John 5:12; Rev. 3:5; 21:8,27; 22:14-15). Although humans are judged according to their deeds, Ladd correctly notes: "Salvation is to be found alone through the Lamb of God" (1972:274; see Rom. 3:10).

THE TEXT IN BIBLICAL CONTEXT
The Resurrection

The ancient Hebrews saw the blessings of God to Israel to be focused on this life (Isa. 11:1-10). The only clear picture of resurrection to new life came from Daniel: "Many of those who sleep in the dust of the earth shall awake, some to everlasting life, and some to shame and everlasting contempt" (Dan. 12:2; see also Isa. 25:7; 26:19). Later, some Jewish writings focused on resurrection of the faithful only (1 Enoch 46:4-8; 58:2-5; 83:1-84:6; Ps. Sol. 3:9-12), while in others all the dead are raised (2 Esd. 7:31, 37; 2 Bar. 50:1–51:6; Test. Benjamin 10:8; Asmpt. Moses 41:2-3).

In the New Testament, the Jewish conception of resurrection was appropriated by Jesus (Matt. 22:29-32; 24:31; Mark 12:24-27; Luke 20:34-36; John 5:25-29; see also Matt. 20:19; Mark 10:34; Luke 18:33) and those who knew him (Matt. 9:18; John 11:24). Furthermore, the writers of the New Testament epistles rooted the resurrection of humanity in Christ's resurrection (Rom. 14:9; 1 Cor. 15:12-20; Phil. 3:10-11; Heb. 9:27-28; 1 Pet. 1:3-5; see also John 11:25-26), and they expected both a spiritual body (1 Cor. 15:52) and an eternal habitat (1 Thess. 4:17).

Revelation clearly has the most complex doctrine of resurrection in the New Testament. As with the epistles, the resurrection of Christ (Rev. 1:5, 18; 2:8; cf. 13:14) forms the basis for the expectation of the faithful witnesses that, if they die in tribulation, resurrection will follow (11:11-12). Subsequent to that resurrection, the faithful are promised rest from their labor (14:13), the defeat of their accuser (12:10) and oppressor (15:2; see also 2 Thess. 2:8), a crown of life (2:10), a place with Christ on his throne (3:21; see also 2 Cor. 5:8; Phil. 1:21, 23), and redemption and bliss on Mt. Zion (14:1-4). Moreover, the present passage envisions that the faithful will reign with Christ for a thousand years (20:4, 6), although elsewhere that reign is forever (11:15; see also Dan. 7:14, 27).

The Judgment

Revelation has already recorded at least three judgments: the harvest of the faithful and the vintage of the earth (14:14-20), the judgment of the beasts (19:20), and the great white throne judgment of the dead (20:11-15). Indeed, some commentators find in scripture a series of seven judgments, including the judgment of the nations (Matt. 25:31-40), the judgment of believers (2 Cor. 5:10), and the judgment of unbelievers (Rev. 20:11-15; see Scofield, 1945:1351). Yet the Bible is more interested in the fact of judgment than in a chronology of judgments (Ladd, 1972:271; John 12:31; Rom. 2:6-11). Indeed, all judgments are likely one (Dan. 12:2; John 5:28-29; Rom. 14:10; 2 Cor. 5:1; Heb. 4:12-13; Jude 6), which both condemns the wicked (Isa. 13:6-22; 2 Pet. 3:7; Wis. Sol. 3:10-19) and rewards the righteous (Isa 14:1-4; Wis. Sol. 3:1-9).

It must be admitted, though, that the Bible is ambiguous regarding who does the judging. Consistent with Revelation, God is sometimes portrayed as the one on the throne (Isa. 6:1), who judges everyone (Rom. 14:10; Heb. 12:23) based on the books that are opened (Dan. 7:9-14), and gives rewards to those who serve him (Matt. 6:4) and punishments to the ones who lack mercy (Matt. 18:35). Surprisingly, the more likely administrator of judgment in the New Testament is Christ (John 5:22, 27), who judges both the living and the dead (2 Tim. 4:1) on behalf of God (Matt. 19:28; John 5:30; Acts 17:31). Christ's judgment is based on whether or not the person has done the will of the Father (Matt. 7:21-23; 2 Cor. 5:10), cared for the unfortunate (Matt. 25:31-48), and remained faithful to the end (Rev. 3:21; see also 1 Enoch 45:3; 55:4; 61:8).

The solution to this ambiguity is to be found in Revelation 22:1, 3, where God and Christ are on the throne together. It is not that God judges at certain times and Christ at others, but that when one is judging so is the other. Mounce strikingly demonstrates the unity of Father and Son in judgment by comparing two parallel passages from Paul (1977:364): although the language is virtually identical, the judge is God in Romans 14:10, and Christ in 2 Corinthians 5:10 (see also John 5:22; 8:16). Whoever the judge, the faithful are reminded that they will participate in the judgment (Matt. 19:28; 1 Cor. 6:2; see also Jer. 1:10; Hos. 6:5).

The Books

The word translated "scroll" *(biblion)* occurs twenty-three times in Revelation (Moulton and Geden, 1926:147). At least three books in the Hebrew tradition could be referents for *biblion* in the text of Revelation. The most obvious is the book of life, which has roots in the list of all those who lived in the city of Jerusalem (Isa. 4:3). The implication is that to be alive is to be written in the book, and to be dead is to be blotted out (Ps. 69:28; 139:16). Later, the book of life was thought to contain only the names of those who reverence God

(Mal. 3:16) and do righteousness (Ps. 69:28; 1 Enoch 47:3; 104:1), while excluding those who sin without forgiveness (Exod. 32:32-33). This book is given eschatological connotations in the concept that only those whose names are in the book will be delivered from judgment (Dan. 12:1). Yet Jeremiah introduces mercy into the process by asserting that those who know God are forgiven of their sin, which is then not remembered against them (Jer. 31:34; cf. Rev. 18:5). In the New Testament, Jeremiah's theme of forgiveness and mercy is elaborated (1 John 2:1-2), and having one's name written in heaven (Luke 10:20) is based on belief in Christ (Matt. 10:32-33; Mark 8:38; John 3:36; 5:24) and faith in God (Rom. 3:22-26; 5:1-2; see also Phil. 4:3; Heb. 12:23). Yet the teaching of Revelation is that the names of those who remain true to God in persecution will be included in the book of life (Rev. 3:5), which has been kept by God from the creation of the world, but that those who give in to persecution will be blotted out of the book (3:5; 13:8; 17:8; 20:12; 21:27), punished in the lake of fire (20:15), and excluded from the holy city (21:27).

A second book with roots in the Hebrew scriptures is the book of deeds, a record of the names of individuals along with their works (Esther 6:1; Dan. 7:10; Mal. 3:16; 1 Enoch 81:1-2; 107:1; 2 Bar. 24:1). Similar to the Persian annals (Esther 2:23; 6:1), it includes both sins and righteous deeds (2 Bar. 24:1), written on heavenly tablets (Jub. 30:20, 22) to be remembered as criteria for the final judgment (Dan. 7:9-10; 12:1; 2 Esd. 6:20; 1 Enoch 90:20; 2 Bar. 24:1). At the great white throne, judgment is on the basis of the deeds that are recorded in such a book (Rev. 20:12). Yet this document is closely related to the book of life, because inclusion in the New Jerusalem is based on avoidance of impure practices so that one is included in the book of life (Rev. 21:27).

A third book in the Hebrew tradition is the book of judgment, which describes the oppression that will come to God's people (Isa. 65:6-7; 2 Esd. 6:17-24; 1 Enoch 106:19). This book serves as a backdrop for the judgments of the sealed book in chapter 6, and the judgments that come as a result of the opening of the books before the great white throne (20:12). In the kaleidoscopic imagery of Revelation, it is often difficult to know which of the three meanings of *biblion* is in the mind of the author.

Good Works

Although the previous section noted that the book of life introduces God's mercy and forgiveness into the theme of judgment, the passage under consideration unmistakably emphasizes judgment on the basis of works. Twice the idea is repeated in verses 12-13. Indeed, the theme of the importance of good deeds runs throughout the biblical tradition. In the story of Sodom and Gomorrah, Abraham addresses God, reflecting on the fate of the righteous and the wicked: "Far be it from you ... to slay the righteous with the wicked, so that the righteous fare as the wicked! Far be that from you! Shall not the Judge of all the earth do what is just?" (Gen. 18:25). The Psalms affirm the righteousness and equity of the judgment of God (Ps. 96:13; 98:9; see also 1 Enoch 103:4) and add that the judgment of the righteous is based on deeds (Ps. 28:4; 62:12; see also Prov. 14:14; 24:12). Perhaps Jeremiah summarizes this tradition when, referring to both "those who trust in the Lord" and "those who trust in mere mortals," the prophet says that God will "test the mind" and "search the heart" to judge the "fruit of their doings" (Jer. 17:10).

Perhaps even more surprising than the tradition of judgment by works in the Hebrew scriptures is the continuation of the theme in the New Testament. In John's gospel, Jesus affirms that belief in God is the work his followers are to perform (John 6:28-29). At the end of his Sermon on the Mount, the emphasis on good deeds is even more explicit as Jesus affirms the importance of doing what he has taught, using three metaphors: the broad and narrow gate (Matt. 7:13-14), the trees with good and bad fruit (Matt. 7:17-20; Luke 6:43-45), and the wise and the foolish (Matt. 7:24-27; Luke 6:48-49). Here, he drives home the importance of hearing and acting on his words (Matt. 7:24; Luke 6:47) by indicating that it is not those who say, "Lord, Lord," who will enter the kingdom, but "only the one who does the will of my Father in heaven" (Matt. 7:21-23; see also Luke 6:46-47). In the parable of the talents, Jesus makes the point that in the kingdom of heaven, persons will be rewarded for their good stewardship of resources, and those evidencing poor stewardship will be "cast into outer darkness where there will be weeping and gnashing of teeth" (Matt. 25:14-30; see also Luke 19:11-26). Perhaps Jesus' teaching is best summed up in his words: "For the Son of Man is to come with his angels in the glory of his Father, and then he will repay everyone for what he has done" (Matt. 16:27).

In spite of Paul's emphasis on faith as basis for human justification before God (Rom. 3:20, 27-28; Gal. 2:16; 3:10; Eph. 2:8-10; see also Titus 3:4-5), he also affirms that, on the day of judgment, God will test human works with fire (1 Cor. 3:12-15) so that those who do good receive eternal life with "glory and honor," and those who are self-seeking and do wickedness receive "wrath and fury ... anguish and distress" (Rom. 2:5-11). Paul's letters to the Ephesians and Colossians affirm this idea, stating clearly that God will reward on the basis of what has been done (Eph. 6:8; Col. 3:23-25). As a result, Paul exhorts his beloved Philippians: "Work out your own salvation with fear and trembling; for it is God who is at work in you, enabling you both to will and to work for his good pleasure" (Phil. 2:12-13). Later, in the same book, Paul says that it is those who work together with him whose names are in the book of life (Phil. 4:3). Paul's teaching can be summarized in words similar to those of Jesus: "God's righteous judgment will be revealed. For he will repay according to each one's deeds" (Rom. 2:5-6; cf. 2 Cor. 5:10; see also 1 Pet. 1:17).

This biblical tradition of the judgment of works is especially evident in Revelation. Throughout the letters to the churches, Christ follows the words, "I know your works," with some specific information about the faithfulness of the congregation in the city addressed (Rev. 2:2, 19; 3:1, 8, 15). The purpose for this may be found in John's words to the church in Thyatira: "All the churches will know that I am the one who searches the minds and hearts, and I will give to each of you as your works deserve" (2:23; see also 2:26). Moreover, the followers of the beast are condemned for not repenting of their deeds (9:20; 16:11), and the 144,000 saints on Mount Zion are those who endure to the end by keeping the commandments of God and remaining faithful to Jesus (14:1-5, 12). Similar to the words of Jesus and Paul, Revelation concludes that at the parousia Christ will "repay according to everyone's work" (22:12).

THE TEXT IN THE LIFE OF THE CHURCH

The Millennium

The source for the millennium is the Old Testament Day of the Lord (Amos 5:18-20). Israel thought that the Messiah would come to vindicate her and destroy her enemies, but Amos proclaimed that the Day of the Lord would be a day of justice—the reward for all righteousness and the punishment of all evil. Daniel develops the idea in more detail by describing four major kingdoms of this world that will be overthrown by the eternal kingdom of God, which, in turn, will never be destroyed (Dan. 2:44; 7:14, 27; see also 1 Enoch 91:12–93:14; 2 Bar. 40:1-3; Sib. Or. 3:46-62).

The Jewish tradition elaborated this kingdom into the reign of the Messiah, "the anointed one," which was thought to be in this world and focused on Mt. Zion (2 Bar. 30:1-5; 39:3–40:4). In preparation for this reign of righteousness, the powers of evil are to be bound, and all injustice, oppression, and sin cleansed from the earth (1 Enoch

10:1-11:2; 21:6; 91:1-19). Indeed, the Apocalypse of Baruch predicts that manna will once again come down from heaven, and the earth will bring forth produce in an abundance never known before: "The earth will also yield fruits ten thousandfold. And on one vine will be a thousand branches, and one branch shall produce a thousand clusters, and one cluster will produce a thousand grapes" (2 Bar. 29:3-8; see also Sib. Or. 3:741-61). Moreover, among other miraculous benefits, "health will descend in dew, illness will vanish, and fear and tribulation and lamentation will pass away ... and joy will encompass the earth" (2 Bar. 73:1-10; see also Sib. Or. 3:767-84).

It was usually thought that the kingdom of the Messiah would be of limited duration, but there was considerable difference of opinion regarding its length (see Beasley-Murray, 1974:288-89; Ford 1975:353)—40 years based on Deuteronomy 8:2 and Psalm 90:15, 400 years based on the same Psalm passage and on Micah 7:15 (see 2 Esd.7:28-29), or 70 years based on Isaiah 23:15. A particularly popular option was to combine the Sabbath rest on the seventh day of creation (Gen. 2:2) with Psalm 90:4 (see also 2 Pet. 3:8) to arrive at a 1000-year Sabbath following the 7000 years of history and preceding an unending 8000th year (1 Enoch 93:3-10; 2 Enoch 32:2–33:2; Barn. 15; Sanhedrin 97a,b). Rabbi Eleazar ben Hercanus had already in A.D. 40 predicted that the kingdom of the Messiah would be 1000 years (see Jub. 1:29; 23:26-31).

Although the messianic kingdom was a common idea in Jewish circles at the time of the second generation of the church, the millennium was a minor point in the theology of the New Testament, mentioned only in Revelation 20. Fourteen chapters of Revelation are devoted to the three and a half years of tribulation (6:1–18:24), while only three verses (20:3-6) are given to the 1000 years of the millennial kingdom (Boring, 1989:202).

Later, however, the millennium became a major part of the speculation of the church. In the first four centuries, a thousand-year sabbatical reign of the faithful on this earth, complete with the rebuilding of a New Jerusalem and many physical and spiritual blessings, including the peaceful coexistence of all creatures, was expected before the new world would be established (Papias in Eusebius, *Eccl. Hist.* 3.39; Justin, *Dialogue with Trypho* 80-81; Irenaeus, *Adv. Haer.* 5.28.3; 5.32.1; 5.33.3; Tertullian, *Against Marcion* 3.24; Dionysius in Eusebius, *Eccl. Hist.* 7.24; Cerinthus in Eusebius, *Eccl. Hist.* 3.28; 7.25; Barn. 15:4-9; Lactantius, *Institutes* 7.14; Hippolytus, *Com. on Dan.* 2:4; Jerome, *Com. on Isa. 60:1*). Even then, some objected to a literal millennial kingdom (Justin, *Dialogue with Trypho* 80;

Eusebius, *Eccl. Hist.* 3.39; 7.24); Origen, *On First Principles* 2.11.2-3; Ambrose, *Homily on Ps. 1:54*). After Augustine, the church accepted the idea of a spiritual reign of Christ between the incarnation and the parousia (*City of God* 20.7-17; 22.30). Yet belief in a literal reign on earth has persisted to the modern day in sectarian groups (e.g., Reeves, 1976; Emmerson and McGinn, 1993; Wainwright, 1984:21-103; Klaassen, 1999:23-45). In the nineteenth century, many evangelical scholars saw the church as bringing in the kingdom, and twentieth-century dispensationalism revived the idea of a literal reign initiated by the second coming of Christ.

Three Millennial Views

Interpretations of the millennium have fallen generally into three camps. The prefixes related to the views designate when Christ is expected to come. Thus, *postmillennialists* believe that Christ will return *after* the millennium. Proponents of this position, including Daniel Whitby in the seventeenth century, Jonathan Edwards and Charles Finney in the eighteenth century, and the great Princeton scholars of the nineteenth and early twentieth centuries, Charles Hodge and B. B. Warfield, contend that Christ will establish the millennium on earth through the church. The millennium then designates the triumph of the gospel proclaimed by Christians to the end of the earth, making the world progressively better until the millennium is inaugurated without the coming of Christ. It should be stressed that the millennium takes place, not through the efforts of humanity, but through the divine activity of God using the church. After the millennium, of literally one thousand years or symbolically a long duration, Christ will appear to raise the dead, judge the world, and inaugurate the new order:

Postmillenialism

Spread of Gospel–> Millennium–> Parousia–> Judgment–> Eternal Realm

Some biblical passages speak in favor of this view. Jesus says explicitly: this good news of the kingdom will be proclaimed throughout the world, as a testimony to the nations; and then the end will come" (Matt. 24:14). Moreover, Jesus' parables of the mustard seed and the yeast emphasize the spread of the gospel (Matt. 13:31-33; Luke 13:18-21). Finally, in the great commission, the *locus classicus* text of postmillenialism, Jesus says to his followers: "All authority in heaven and on earth has been given to me" so that you will "[g]o therefore and make disciples of all nations" remembering "I am with you always, to the end of the age" (Matt. 28:18-20).

The most serious deficiency of postmillenialism lies in the theme running throughout the New Testament that Christians are to "keep awake" because no one knows when Christ will come (Matt. 24:42-43; 25:13; Mark 13:32-37; Luke 12:35-38). Of course, this alertness is absurd if one thousand years, or a long period of time, must pass before Christ will return. Another difficulty of this position is that the world has not become increasingly better in the moral realm.

The second alternative interpretation is *premillennialism*—Christ will return *before* the millennium. Here the millennium is not the work of the church but is only actualized with the second coming of Christ. While historical premillennialism has its roots in the church fathers—Justin, Tertullian, Irenaeus, and so forth, the modern dispensational brand of premillennialism began with John Nelson Darby and the Plymouth Brethren in the nineteenth century and has been popularized in the twentieth century by C. I. Scofield's *Reference Bible* (1945) and Hal Lindsey's best-selling *The Late Great Planet Earth* (1970), and in the twenty-first century by LaHaye and Jenkins (1995-).

In contrast to the previous position, premillennialism holds that the world will become increasingly more corrupt, culminating in a "great tribulation" of seven years. Premillennialists differ on whether or not a rapture, separate from the parousia, will occur at this point. While the historic premillennialists thought that Christians would experience the tribulation, dispensationalists believe that the church will be surprisingly and instantaneously raptured to avoid the great tribulation. A variation on the pretribulation rapture is that Christians will go through the first three and a half years and be raptured before the worst outpouring of God's wrath in the second half of the tribulation. Premillennialists agree on the remainder of the outline. A parousia will occur as Christ comes to reign physically from his throne in Jerusalem for literally a thousand years. Then Satan will be released for the final conflict, and subsequently, the ungodly will be resurrected for final judgment in preparation for their eternal consignment to either heaven or hell.

Premillennialism

Corruption–> (Rapture?)–> Tribulation–> Parousia–> Millennium–> Release of Satan–> Judgment of Ungodly–> Eternal Realm

The strongest argument in favor of this view is that it takes scripture, and particularly Revelation, quite literally and chronologically: the tribulation (6:1–16:20), the parousia (19:11-16), the millennium

(20:4-6), the release of Satan (20:7-10), the resurrection and judgment (20:11-15), and the eternal city (21:1-22:5).

The argument against premillennialism in general is that, although the overall scheme is consistent with Revelation, the details come from diverse sources and imply connections that are not in the text. A seven-year tribulation occurs nowhere in scripture except in Daniel 8:14, which can just as easily be interpreted as three and a half years, the usual period of tribulation in scripture (Dan. 7:25; 12:5-12; Rev. 11:2-3; 12:6). The idea of a separate resurrection before the millennium is based on the supposition that the first resurrection requires a second, although there is no second resurrection in the text (20:5-6). Indeed, a literal reading of Revelation 20:5 says that the resurrection following the millennium is the first resurrection, and the idea of a separate resurrection is contradicted by Jesus in John 6:40: "I will raise them [all believers] up on the last day." A more trivial difficulty of premillennialism is that it requires believers inhabiting glorified bodies to live together in the present world with unbelievers with physical bodies (Beale, 1999:1016-17).

Addressing the dispensational pretribulational rapture variation of premillennialism, two separate eschatological appearances of Christ are based on Paul's statements regarding Christ coming "with" and "for" his saints (1 Thess. 3:13; 4:13-18). This distinction, based tenuously on Paul's use of pronouns, is found nowhere in Revelation. Moreover, although there is a coming of Christ before the final bowls of God's wrath (14:14-20) and another after the tribulation (19:11-21), no rapture occurs in Revelation 4–5, where dispensationalists would expect it. Indeed, the saints are present on earth throughout Revelation and are exhorted to patiently endure tribulation to receive their reward (11:18; 13:7-10; 14:12; 16:6; 17:6; 18:24; 19:8).

The third way the church has interpreted this passage is represented by the *amillennialists,* who believe there is no literal earthly millennium of one thousand years, but instead, that the millennium is a spiritual portrayal of the church age. This position, first clearly espoused by Augustine, has been affirmed throughout history by the church's leading interpreters. Amillennialists are neither optimistic nor pessimistic but realistic about the future of this world, taking their cue from the parable of the sower (Matt. 13:24-30, 36-43). Moreover, the millennium is not a physical kingdom of literally one thousand years but is the extended period between Christ's first advent when he was born in a manger, died on the cross, and arose from the grave, and his second advent when he will come to judge the dead and establish the kingdom of God. Although some amillennialists believe the millennium symbolizes the spiritual reign in heaven of the martyrs, most see it as the spiritual state of faithful saints on earth during the church age. In his death on the cross, Christ bound Satan, not to keep him from persecuting the saints but to assure the faithful that they can overcome his deception. The first resurrection is conversion, which delivers the sinner from the power of the devil and inaugurates the spiritual state of commitment and confidence in the face of tribulation while the second resurrection is not mentioned in scripture.

Amillennialism

Law of Sin and Death	Conversion	Millennium	*Parousia*	
Law of Sin and Death ->	First Resurrection	Saints in Tribulation ->	Second Resurrection	-> Eternal Realm

Much biblical evidence can be marshaled in favor of elements of this position. Jesus explicitly says he is not establishing a physical kingdom: "My kingdom is not from this world ... my kingdom is not from here" (John 18:36), and the number one thousand, designating the temporal duration of the kingdom is certainly used symbolically in the Bible (Job. 9:3; Ps. 50:10; see also Ps. 90:4; 2 Pet. 3:3-9). Moreover, resurrection is described as the spiritual event that happens at the time of belief (Eph. 2:4-7; see also John 5:25), and the last days are said to begin with Jesus (Heb. 1:2) and Pentecost (Acts 2:16-21; cf. John 6:39-40, 44, 54-55; 11:24; 12:48). In addition, Christ's reign is portrayed as already in process (1 Cor. 15:20-28; Rev. 5:9-10), and Jesus' ministry brings the kingdom of God by causing Satan to be bound (Matt. 12:28-29; Mark 3:27; see also John 12:31-33; Rev. 20:2) and to fall from heaven like lightning (Luke 10:17-20; 11:20-23). Weaver says that although "premillennialists interpret the chapter as predicting a future, historical reign that will culminate in a great battle ... in which evil is dealt a final, violent defeat ... [a]ctually, however, Revelation 20 compares the rule of evil with the reign of God, from the perspective of a victory already accomplished—the resurrection" (1994b:491). The major difficulty related to the amillennial position is that it spiritualizes ideas often assumed to be literal and is difficult to refute because of this emphasis on symbolic interpretation.

In sum, all views believe Christ is coming again, and the Bible warns against speculation regarding the timing of that parousia. Indeed, immediately before Jesus left this earth and ascended into heaven, when his disciples ask, "Lord, is this the time when you will restore the kingdom to Israel?" he responds: "It is not for you to know the times or periods that the Father has set by his own authority" (Acts 1:6-7). Moreover, Paul warns: "Now concerning the times and the seasons, brothers and sisters, you do not need to have anything written to you. For you yourselves know very well that the Day of the Lord will come like a thief in the night" (1 Thess. 5:1-2).

Revelation 21:1–22:21

The Heavenly City

PREVIEW

The last two chapters of Revelation are composed of the final vision of the book, followed by somewhat random closing exhortations. The first creation has disappeared (20:11), the last judgment has followed (20:12-13), and the wicked have gone to their punishment (20:15). Nothing remains but the eternal reward of the saints, using the images of the New Heaven and Earth and the New Jerusalem. The importance of these chapters, particularly 22:1-8, is affirmed by Beasley-Murray, who calls it "the climax not only of the Book of Revelation, but of the whole story of salvation embodied in the Bible" (1974:305).

The city imagery found here has roots in the Hebrew tradition of the New Jerusalem and the Greek understanding of the *polis,* the political city-state (see TBC, The Holy City). Boring notes that Old Testament salvation history is the account of cities from their construction immediately after the fall from Eden (Gen. 4:17) to the expectation of the eternal bliss of the New Jerusalem, which actually contains elements of the original Garden, such as the tree and river of life (Gen. 2:9-10; Rev. 22:1-2). He also indicates that eternal destiny, according to the Bible, is not in the Greek Elysian fields or the Native American happy hunting grounds, but in a city with which those addressed by Revelation in the seven cities in Asia could identify (1989:219-20). Likewise, contrary to the Greek idea of an eternal soul floating ungrounded throughout eternity, the Bible promises a resurrected body inhabiting a renewed earth (see TBC, The New

Heaven and New Earth). Swete says that the word *new (kainos)*, which permeates Revelation, "suggests fresh life rising from the decay and wreck of the old world" (1908:275).

There are two general ways that the New Jerusalem has been interpreted (see Malina, 2000 for an alternative view of an astrological city married to a cosmic lamb). Some see it as describing the millennial kingdom rather than the eternal state of heavenly bliss because the city does not seem to be purged of all evil. The nations are in the city; and dogs, sorcerers, and fornicators are immediately outside (22:15). Yet the order of Revelation would force those who believe in a literal millennium, by their own literalistic hermeneutic, to place this kingdom after the final judgment following the millennium, a chronological impossibility. So most commentators from all perspectives see the New Jerusalem as the eternal heavenly city. John nowhere else mentions a millennial city, and the dimensions recorded here seem to indicate a city that transcends earthly conception. Therefore, Revelation probably uses earthly language to describe symbolically the eternal state of the community of faithful saints who conquer the beast. Indeed, these people of the New Jerusalem are the faithful parallel to the evil followers of the beast who inhabit Babylon, the symbol of the demonic Roman Empire (Lilje, 1957:259).

The parallels between the visions of the city of Babylon in chapter 17 and the New Jerusalem here are noteworthy (see Farrer, 1964:212). After identical introductions of the two cities (17:1; 21:9), the pure bride (21:11) is contrasted with the abominable whore (17:5). Both figures have the name of their Lord/lord on their foreheads (17:5; 22:4), but the names of those comprising the bride are written in the book of life (21:27), while the followers of the whore are not named there (17:8). Surprisingly, the kings of the earth are associated with both cities (17:15-18; 21:24). Mulholland concludes that the implication of this Fallen Babylon/New Jerusalem counter-image is that the proper response to Babylon is not accommodation or compromise but "corporate obedience to God" and "powerful confrontation with the world" (1990:347-48). In the characteristic symmetry of Revelation, the New Jerusalem is also contrasted with the lake of fire. The emphasis in this passage is on the community whose destination is the New Jerusalem. While the image of the city stresses a community of faithful saints, the number twelve, a factor of virtually every other number recorded in this last vision, symbolizes the people that comprise the city (21:12-14, 15-17). Although the emphasis is on the conquerors, Revelation demands justice on behalf of the whole earth, not just saints (Schüssler Fiorenza, 1991:119-20; see 6:9; 15:4; 18:20).

The structure of the last two chapters of Revelation is somewhat confusing. The chapter divisions certainly do not correspond to any break in thought, so the two chapters are considered together here. Yet Wilcock has proposed a helpful structure for the section, taking 21:1-8 as a seven-point introductory outline for what follows (1975:199; cf. Schüssler Fiorenza, 1991:109; Farrer, 1964:215):

God's City (21:2 // 21:10-21)
God's Dwelling (21:3 // 21:22-27)
God's World Renewed (21:4-5a // 22:1-5)
God's Word Validated (21:5b // 22:6-10)
God's Work Completed (21:6a // 22:11-15)
God's Final Blessing (21:6b-7 // 22:16-17)
God's Final Curse (21:8 // 22:18-19)

Sweet also notes structural parallelism between the first three chapters of Revelation and the last two. The Son of Man vision of chapter 1 is followed by the letters to the churches in chapters 2–3 just as the vision of New Jerusalem in 21:1–22:5 is followed by many echoes of the letters to the churches in 22:6-21 (1990:301).

Before looking at the passage in detail, the theme of prophecy, which is central in chapter 22 and has considerable implications for interpreting the entire book, should be considered (see Aune, 1989:103-16). The Hebrew prophet was one who communicated a unique message from God for people of his time. Prophecy was common in first-century Palestine (Matt. 7:15-20), and prophets were a significant group in the New Testament church (1 Cor. 12:28-29; Eph. 2:20; 3:5; 4:11; 1 Thess. 5:20). A company of prophets formed around Paul and Barnabas (Acts 13:1). In its introduction and conclusion, Revelation identifies itself as a prophecy (1:3; 22:6-7, 9-10, 18-19; see also 10:11), and both true and false prophets are mentioned in the book (2:20; 11:3, 6, 10; 16:3; 19:20; 20:10). Prophets are also spoken of in connection with other groups of Christ's followers: servants (10:7; 11:18), saints (11:18; 16:6; 18:20, 24), and apostles (18:20).

Although John never directly calls himself a prophet (1:3; 19:10; 22:6, 9-10, 18-19), Revelation clearly stands in the lineage of Old Testament prophecy (note title of Bauckham, 1993a and discussion in 1993b:115-25). John sees himself as being possessed by the Spirit of God when he speaks words attributed to Christ in the first person; these chapters as well as his extended discourses resemble those of the Old Testament prophets. Thus, although Revelation is primarily an apocalypse, evidences of other genres like prophecy and epistle are also present.

OUTLINE

The New Heaven and the New Earth, 21:1-8
The New Jerusalem, 21:9-27
The Presence of God, 22:1-5
Worship God! 22:6-11
Christ Is Coming Soon! 22:12-17
Stern Warning 22:18-19
Come, Lord Jesus 22:20-21

EXPLANATORY NOTES

The New Heaven and the New Earth 21:1-8

The last vision of Revelation begins as John *saw a new heaven and a new earth*. The word *heaven* here is equivalent to "sky," indicating that the new heaven has continuity with the present cosmos (3:12; 11:12; 21:10). Newness here carries with it the idea, not of a spiritual existence, but of a new creation of the material world (Gen 1:1; 2 Cor. 5:17; Gal. 6:15; Eph. 2:10; 4:24). Indeed, salvation includes the entire universe because all of creation must be renewed to serve as an appropriate abode for the faithful saints. Thus, the Bible places humanity in a restored heaven and earth from which evil is banished and the righteous reign supreme, rather than in a spiritual realm separate from the physical (Dan. 12:3-4).

To prepare for the new heaven and earth, *the first heaven and the first earth had passed away*. Their disappearance was anticipated in 20:11-14 (Mark 13:31; 1 Cor. 7:31; 1 John 2:17; Rev. 7:1-2; 12:12). Yet the more intriguing phenomenon here is that *the sea was no more*. The Hebrew tradition regarded the sea as a hostile force that God brought under control in creation (Job 38:8-11; Ps. 89:9; see also Isa. 57:20-21; Amos 9:3), an idea rooted in the Babylonian legend of Tiamat, the sea monster, who was subdued by the god Marduk in the creation of the world (TBC on ch. 11, The Beast). Moreover, Barclay says: "The Egyptians saw the sea as the power which swallowed up the waters of the Nile, and left the fields sterile and barren and unfruitful for want of water" (1960:2.254; see also Plutarch, *On Isis and Osiris* 32). In scripture, the sea monster Leviathan, conquered by God in the creation of the universe (Job 26:12-13; Ps. 74:13-14; Isa. 51:9), was expected to be similarly annihilated in the New Creation (Isa. 27:1). Additionally, Daniel's four beasts came from the sea (Dan. 7:3), and in Revelation, the sea is the abode of the first beast (13:1; see also 11:7; 12:12), the great whore (17:1), and the dead (20:13). Indeed, the sea was a common symbol of separation. Ladd calls it "the dark, the mysterious, and the treacherous" force that threatened "tiny ships" that navigated the Mediterranean (1972:276; see Ezek. 28:8). This brutality of the sea is out of keeping with the perfection of the new earth and therefore must be destroyed (Sib. Or. 5:155-61, 447-48; Test. Levi 4:1).

After observing the new heaven and new earth, John *saw the holy city, the new Jerusalem*. While the new heaven and earth point to a new cosmos, the New Jerusalem speaks of a new society (Richard, 1995:161; 14:1-4; 15:2). It is interesting to note that Revelation describes a "new" Jerusalem, not a rebuilt, restored city (Murphy, 1998:409). The word *holy (hagios)* here is the normal word for saints in Revelation (5:8; 8:3; 11:18; 13:7, 10; 16:6; 17:6; 18:20, 24; 19:8; 20:6, 9; 22:11) and highlights their holy and renewed lives (Rom. 12:2; 2 Cor. 6:16-18). Moreover, the destiny of the saints in the holy city is set over against those who are condemned to the lake of fire (21:8, 27). Beasley-Murray calls Revelation *A Tale of Two Cities ... The Harlot and the Bride* (1974:315); whereas historically Babylon destroyed Jerusalem, here the tables are turned.

The New Jerusalem is then described as *coming down out of heaven from God*. Because the city descends again in verse 10, this verse is no doubt a proleptic anticipation of the more elaborate description later. Indeed, the implication is that the city's character is closely bound to its divine origin. God is the architect and builder of the city (Heb. 11:10), which is, in turn, holy and separate unto God (Isa. 52:1-2).

The New Jerusalem was *prepared as a bride adorned for her husband* (parallels 21:9-10; see also 2 Esd. 10:25-28). The bride here is the New Jerusalem, the faithful saints; and the husband is Christ, the Lamb. Their relationship, announced in the marriage supper (Rev. 19:7-8), symbolizes the intimate union between God and the saints, who identify with the Lamb through faithfulness in tribulation (John 3:29; 2 Cor. 11:2; Eph. 5:25-32). While the woman in chapter 12 represents the saints ultimately protected from the suffering they experience, the bride in chapter 21 represents the same saints rewarded for their faithfulness finally in the presence of God (Beale, 1999:1045-46).

Next, John heard *a loud voice from the throne*. Being from the throne, the voice is either God's or that of a messenger speaking on behalf of God (9:13; 11:12; 12:10; 16:1, 17; 18:4; 19:1, 5; see also 4:2, 9; 5:1, 7; 6:16; 7:10, 15; 19:4). The significance is that God has the last word in Revelation (Murphy, 1998:415). The loudness of the voice starkly contrasts with the silence in the dirge over the fall of

Babylon (18:23). The words recall the earlier hymn to the 144,000 (7:15-17).

The voice said: *See, the home of God is among mortals* (Ezek. 48:35). The word *See* might be best translated, "'Now hear this!' or 'Attention!'" (Raber, 1986:299). What is announced with such fanfare is the presence of God. The word translated *home* and the verb *dwell* that follows are both forms of the same Greek word *(skēnē),* which translates the Hebrew "tent" or "tabernacle" *(mishkan),* where God dwelt in the wilderness. Moreover, its verbal form has the same consonants as the Hebrew *shekinah,* which commonly symbolizes the presence and glory of God (Exod. 25:8; Lev. 26:11; Ezek. 37:27; Zech. 2:11; Pirke Aboth 3.9; see also 1 Kings 8:10-11). This communion between God and humanity was lost in the Fall (Gen. 3:8-10), but throughout history God has endeavored to renew the relationship (Ps. 23:4; 46:4-11; Song 6:3; Isa. 41:10: Jer. 30:11; Heb. 11:16). The supreme effort was the divine incarnation in Christ who "tabernacled among us" *(eskēnōsen:* John 1:14; see also Isa. 7:14; 8:8-10; Matt. 1:23; John 1:1-5; 2 Cor. 5:16-21; Eph. 2:22; 1 John 4:7-21). Buildings and churches are superfluous when Christ dwells with his people (Rowland, 1998:730). In the New Jerusalem, God descends from heaven to earth to live eternally with the faithful.

The idea of the presence of God is repeated in the words: *He will dwell with them as their God; they will be his peoples, and God himself will be with them.* Although some manuscripts have the singular "people," there is slightly better evidence for the plural (Metzger et al., 1971:765). Indeed, in Revelation the faithful are composed of peoples from all races and cultures (Rev. 10:11; 11:9; see also Isa. 56:7; John 10:16; Rom. 9:24-26; Gal. 3:28; but see Lev. 26:11-12; Jer. 7:23; 11:4; 22:2; 24:7; 30:22; 31:33; Ezek. 36:28; 37:12, 23, 27; Hos. 1:9; 2:23; Joel 2:27; Zech. 2:13; 8:8; 1 Pet. 2:10).

When God dwells with his people, *he will wipe every tear from their eye. Death will be no more; mourning and crying and pain will be no more, for the first things have passed away.* Because God is present, evil and all that comes with it is eradicated. The words *no more* echo the dirge over Babylon, where it is happiness and prosperity that vanish (18:21-23). The *first things* here are those associated with the first heaven and the first earth (Isa. 42:9; 43:18-19; 2 Cor. 5:17) like sorrow, (Exod. 3:7-8; Isa. 35:10; 51:11; 65:16-19; Jer. 31:16; Matt. 5:4) and death (Isa. 25:6-8; 1 Cor. 15:24-26; Phil. 3:10). Indeed, the effects of the fall from Eden are reversed (Gen. 3:16-19; see also Rom. 5:12; 1 Cor. 15:26, 54-56; Heb. 2:14-15; 9:27; 2 Esd. 8:53-54; 2 Enoch 65:10; 2 Bar. 21:23). Most important, the martyrdom that threatens the faithful is *no more* (Efird, 1989:119; see 7:13-17).

Summarizing, *the one who was seated on the throne said, "See, I am making all things new"* (Isa. 43:18-19; Matt. 19:28). God's speaking confirms the theme of the passage by giving "vocal proof of the abolition of distance between God and man" (Sweet, 1990:299). The divine words conclude that all things have become new—creation, heaven and earth, people, and Jerusalem. The old age, dominated by the dragon Satan, is giving way to God's new age of *shalom* (see Schüssler Fiorenza, 1991:123).

An imperative follows: *Write this, for these words are trustworthy and true* (parallels 3:14; 19:11; 22:6). *Write* probably serves to emphasize the words that follow (Michaels, 1997:238n; 1:11, 19; 14:13; 19:9). Indeed, if the speaker is still God, divine affirmation of the message is significant; Revelation can be trusted because God is reliable (1 Cor. 1:9; 10:13; 1 Thess. 5:24; Heb. 6:18; see also 2 Tim. 2:13). John writes because "the words ... are as true as they are tremendous" (Swete, 1908:279).

The declaration *It is done!* reminds the reader of the words of God in creation (Gen. 2:1-2) and of Jesus on the cross (John 19:30; see also Rev. 16:7). Actually, the verb is in the third person plural, "They are done!" *(gegonan),* referring to what has been revealed. The perfect tense is either consummative, indicating that revelation is now finished, or intensive, emphasizing that the results of revelation continue. In God's drama of salvation, victory has reached its culmination.

The images that follow speak of God as the goal and source of all (1:8). Because *alpha and omega* are the first and last letters of the Greek alphabet, they connote the eternal nature of God (Isa. 44:6; 48:12; 1 Tim. 1:15; 4:9; 2 Tim. 2:11; Tit. 3:8). Revelation attributes the same designation to Christ, again affirming his divinity (1:8; 22:13). The phrase *beginning and end* indicates that God is the source *(archē;* John 1:1) and the goal *(telos;* Rom. 10:4; 1 Tim. 1:5) of creation. Boring says it well: "God does not merely bring the End. God is the End" (1989:215). It is interesting to note that these designations for God and Christ come at both the "beginning and end" of Revelation (1:8, 17; 21:6; 22:13).

This God, the origin and source of all, offers the blessed promise: *To the thirsty I will give water as a gift from the spring of the water of life* (Isa. 55:1; Rev. 22:1,17; cf. Rev. 7:16-17; see also Ps. 36:9; 65:9; Zech. 14:8). In ancient times, water was scarce and was therefore sold as a commodity; here, it is a free gift (Ps. 63:1; Isa. 43:19-20; 44:3) because the price has been paid by Christ (1 Cor.

6:19-20; 1 Pet. 1:18-19; see also John 4:10-14; 6:35; 7:37-39). The water of life probably refers, not to the sacrament of baptism, but to the spiritual thirst that is a prerequisite for complete satisfaction of the desire for God (see Ps. 42:1; cf. Jer. 2:13; 17:13; Rev. 3:17). This free cup of the water of life contrasts with the whore's "golden cup of the wine of impure passion" (Ladd, 1972:279; 17:4; 18:3). Yet even those who practice the vices that follow in verse 8 are welcome to come to the water (Hughes, 1990:226; 1 Cor. 14:23-25; 1 Tim. 1:15; 1 John 1:7).

Although the offer is open to all, God proclaims: *Those who conquer will inherit these things.* The language here echoes the promises to the conqueror in the letters to the churches (2:7, 11, 17, 26-28; 3:5, 12, 21; see also 15:2). Although the subject here is singular, it can be understood as a collective plural (Aune, 1998b:1129). The present participle *(nikōn)* connotes that conquering is a continuous and constant struggle. All are invited to the water of life; yet only those loyal to the end will inherit the new heaven and earth.

These faithful saints are promised: *I will be their God and they will be my children.* Their *God* replaces the expected "their father" (see Lev. 26:12; Zech. 8:8; Rev. 21:3). John's gospel speaks of God as father only of Jesus (1:6; 2:15; see also Ps. 2:7; 89:26-28; Matt. 3:17; 17:5; Luke 1:32; John 1:14, 18; John 20:17; Heb. 1:2, 5); and humans derive their status as children of God through Christ, the true son of God (Beasley-Murray, 1974:313-14). The future tense here implies that this status in the family of God is fully realized in the final resurrection.

Contrasted to the promise to the conquerors that they will be children of God is the parallel lake of fire destiny for seven categories of the unfaithful: *the cowardly, the faithless, the polluted, the murderers, the fornicators, the sorcerers, the idolaters, and all liars.* In the Greek culture, lists like this were formulated to teach ethical behavior (Murphy, 1998:414). Each of the vices in this list relates to endurance in face of persecution (Mark 13:13), representing all those who compromise by giving allegiance to the beast (see Mark 7:21-23; Luke 18:11; Rom. 13:13; 1 Cor. 5:9-11; 6:9-10; 2 Cor. 12:20; Gal. 5:19-21; Eph. 4:31; 5:3-5; Col. 3:5, 8-9; 1 Tim. 1:9-10; 6:4-5; 2 Tim. 3:2-5; Titus 1:16; 3:3; 1 Pet. 4:3; Rev. 9:21; 13:1-15; 22:15). The vices contrast with the righteous deeds that are the garments of the bride (19:8).

The reason these vices are to be avoided is that those practicing them will find *their place ... in the lake that burns with fire and sulfur* (19:20; 20:10, 14). This is not a statement of the destiny of the wicked, who have already been cast into the lake of fire (20:15) but a warning to the faithful to endure to the end. The contrasting water images of this passage indicate that, rather than drinking the water of life, those who give in to persecution are thrown into the lake of fire (Wall, 1991:249), *which is the second death* (20:6).

The New Jerusalem 21:9-27

Revelation now unites the themes of the marriage supper of the Lamb (19:7) and the descent of the New Jerusalem (21:2) in a detailed description of the holy city/bride, which stands in stark contrast to the splendor of Babylon the whore (see Beale, 1999:1118-19). The latter has been overthrown, and the former established eternally (Isa. 1:21-23; 62:1-5). Based on Ezekiel 40–48, which was written immediately after the destruction of the Jerusalem temple in 586 B.C., this passage speaks of the magnificent return of the city of Jerusalem out of heaven. The purpose of the vision is to exhort the wicked to repent and the saints to be faithful in order to participate in the glory of the holy city rather than in the destruction of Babylon.

The section opens when *one of the seven angels who had the seven bowls full of the seven last plagues* addresses John. The words here are almost a literal repetition of 17:1 (see also 4:1; 15:1; 16:1), which intensifies the comparison between Babylon and the New Jerusalem (17:18). Yet the passages that follow this similar introduction are not parallel at all, heightening the difference between the fates of those who follow the whore to share in the destruction of Babylon and those who with the bride participate in the New Jerusalem of eternal bliss. The two contrasting passages are announced by the same angel, who both judges Babylon and blesses Jerusalem.

In this case, the angel says: *Come, I will show you the bride, the wife of the Lamb.* The opening word *Come* is an adverb used as an imperative (Matt. 19:21; John 11:43; Acts 7:3). The word *wife* *(gynē)* denotes any adult female (Matt. 9:20; 1 Tim. 2:11), who may also be a *bride* (Gen. 29:21 LXX; Matt. 1:20; Rev. 19:7; cf. 21:2). Beale suggests that the bride/wife distinction between engagement and marriage may symbolize the "already but not yet" nature of the kingdom of God (1999:1148). The emphasis here, though, is upon the relationship of the bride/wife to her husband (see Isa. 54:5; Hos. 1-2; Matt. 25:1-13; John 3:29; 2 Cor. 11:2). The husband is designated as *Lamb* seven times in the last two chapters of Revelation (21:9, 14, 22, 23; 22:1, 3). It is surprising that the angel promises to show John the bride but actually reveals the city of Jerusalem. Indeed, the bride vanishes until the end of Revelation (22:17). The mixed metaphor of the woman/city, so characteristic of the Babylon/whore material in chapters 17–18, is abandoned to focus on the magnificence of the city Jerusalem.

After the angel announces the bride/wife of the Lamb, John says: *in the spirit he carried me away to a great, high mountain and showed me the holy city Jerusalem coming down out of heaven from God.* The phrase *in the spirit* refers to a visionary state (1:10; 4:2; 17:3). The angel carried John away, not bodily, but through a vision (Morris, 1969:248). Although there is certainly an allusion here to Moses' experience on Mt. Sinai (Exod. 19-33; see also Ezek. 40:2; 1 Enoch 24-25; Jub. 4:26) and the mountain would have reminded readers of the home of God (Isa. 2:2-3; 14:12-14; Ezek. 28:14-16; Mic. 4:1-2; 1 Enoch 25:3), the mountain here is no doubt Zion (Ps. 2:6; 48:1-2; 74:2; 97:8; Isa. 8:18; 46:13; 52:1; 59:20; 60:14; Joel 2:1; 3:17; Heb. 12:22; Rev. 14:1; Jub. 4:26). Mountains were thought to be appropriate locations for visions because of their proximity to the divine world (Aune, 1998b:1151). By contrast, John's observation point for viewing Babylon the whore was the wilderness (17:3; see also Matt. 4:8-10; 17:1). Farrer's point that "Old Jerusalem was a hill-top town" gives a historical reason for the introduction of the mountaintop vantage point (1964:214). In this passage, Jerusalem is called *holy* rather than new (see Gal. 4:26; Phil. 3:20; 2 Esd. 10:27; 2 Bar. 4:3). As in verse 2, the present tense indicates that Jerusalem is continuously *coming down,* so that its action here need not be a separate event from 21:2. Moreover, the descent of the New Jerusalem may be easily contrasted with Babylon (Babel), which tried to exalt itself by going up to heaven (Gen. 11:4).

The holy city descending from heaven is *the glory of God* (Ezek. 43:2-5; see also 10:18; Zech. 2:1-5; John 12:38-41; Rev. 4:9-11; 15:8; cf. Rev. 17:4), which is here portrayed in the analogy of the radiance of precious gems (Ezek. 1:26-28; see also Rev. 18:1). The word *radiance* denotes a light-giving body (Gen. 1:14-16; Phil. 2:15; see also Isa. 60:1, 19; Dan. 12:3; Wis. Sol. 13:2). The most striking feature of the city is its radiance (Morris, 1969:249). The *very rare jewel* that is compared to the glory of God is identified as the *jasper,* which was an opaque stone (see on 4:3), but here glitters *clear as crystal* (see Ezek. 1:22). The point is that God's presence radiates throughout the city (Ps. 46:5; Isa. 60:1; Ezek. 43:5; 48:35; 2 Cor. 3:18), making the sun unnecessary (v. 23). Murphy points out an interesting irony: "God does not depend on humans for his glory, but if they give him glory, they receive salvation. Rome does depend on humans for its glory, but if they give it glory, they receive condemnation" (Murphy, 1998:418).

The radiant city *has a great, high wall with twelve gates, and at the gates twelve angels.* This verse provokes the question: If the gates of the city are always open and the presence of God eliminates the need for protection (see Isa. 54:14; Zech. 2:5), why have walls? The walls probably *"mark off* the holy community from 'outsiders'" (Boring, 1989:223; 21:8, 27; 22:15). Indeed, the wall is not for security (Isa. 26:1-2; Tacitus, *Hist.* 5.8-12; see also Jos., *War* 7.3-4) but to separate it from those outside as a holy city (Isa. 54:11-14).

John describes further the twelve gates of the city: *on the gates are inscribed the names of the twelve tribes of the Israelites.* The *gate* may refer to a tower above the gate, perhaps leading to a castle (Barclay, 1960:2.268; see also *Herm., Sim.* 9.2-18). Like the twelve stars of 12:1, the names inscribed on the gates indicate that the city includes the Old Testament people of God (Matt. 19:28; Luke 22:30). The symbol of the twelve tribes is closely tied to the 144,000, who are sealed out of those tribes (7:1-8).

The twelve gates of the New Jerusalem are arranged in the following manner: *on the east three gates, on the north three gates, on the south three gates, and on the west three gates.* Numbers 2 describes the configuration of the encampment of the Israelite tribes around the tent of the meeting just as the gates inscribed with their names here surround the New Jerusalem (see also Ezek. 42:16-20; 48:31-35; 1 Enoch 33-36). Among the many commentators noting that East-North-South-West is the exact reverse of the ordering of the zodiac, Caird says this order was used to discourage association of the city with the zodiacal cycle (1966:272; see Ford, 1975:343; also 1 Enoch 72-82; Berakoth 32b; Jos., *Ant.* 3.181-87; Philo, *Life of Moses* 2.124-26). A more helpful consideration for interpreting the passage is Mulholland's affirmation that the *three gates* on each side of the city symbolize "perfect, unhindered access to the New Jerusalem" (1990:323). Indeed, there is a parallel here to Jesus' invitation: "People will come from east and west, from north and south, and will eat in the kingdom of God" (Luke 13:29; see Wilcock, 1975:208; see also Isa. 49:12).

In addition to having twelve gates inscribed with the names of the twelve tribes of Israel, *the wall of the city has twelve foundations, and on them are the twelve names of the twelve apostles of the Lamb* (Heb. 11:10). These foundations may have been oblong masonry blocks like those supporting the Herodian temple (Ford, 1975:333). Yet the names of the apostles on these foundations confirm Hughes's contention that "the holy city is a structure of redeemed persons, not inanimate blocks of stone" (1990:227). Mentioned only twice elsewhere in Revelation (2:2; 18:20), the twelve apostles with their names inscribed on the foundations were eyewitnesses of the life and teachings of Jesus (Matt. 10:1-4; Mark 3:14-19; Luke 6:13-16; 1 Cor. 15:5), and their preaching was the foundation of the church (Matt. 16:17-19; Luke 11:49; Gal. 2:9; Eph. 2:20). Slater points out that this image clearly links the historical Jesus with the christological Lamb (1999:198).

John continues to describe his vision: *The angel who talked to me had a measuring rod of gold to measure the city and its gates and walls* (Ezek. 40-43; Zech. 2:1-5; Rev. 11:1-2). In chapter 11, John was instructed to measure the temple; here an angel measures the holy city, which needs no temple (v. 22). In this case, the measuring is not for preservation as in chapter 11, but to demonstrate the glory and perhaps the holiness of the city (cf. Beale, 1999:1072-73).

The measurement determines that the *city lies foursquare, its length the same as its width*. To the ancient Hebrews, the cube was the architecturally complete shape and therefore appropriate to represent the holiness of the temple (Ezek. 41:4, 13-15, 21; 42:15-20; 43:16; 45:2; 48:15-20, 30-35; see also Herm., *Vision* 3.2.5; Baba Batra 75b). The Greeks also believed the square to be the perfect shape and the good man to be "four square" (Plato, *Prototoras* 339B; Aristotle, *Nicomachean Ethics* 1.10; *Rhetoric* 3.11). Indeed, Babylon (Herodotus, 1.178), Ninevah (Diodorus of Sicily 2.3.2), and Nicea (Strabo, *Geog.* 12.4.7) were built in the form of a square or rectangle. But a cube-shaped city is difficult to conceive literally, and it most likely connotes symmetry and perfection. Even more important to interpreting the shape of the city is that it corresponds to the cube-shaped holy of holies in the temple, which was twenty cubits on a side and overlaid with gold (1 Kings 6:19-20; 2 Chron. 3:8-9; see also Exod. 27:1; 28:15-16; 30:1-2; 39:8-9). Thus, the city is the holy of holies, symbolizing God's presence and the city's purity (Ezek. 48:35; Acts 17:24; Rev. 3:12; 21:18, 21). Instead of the holy of holies, which was limited to a high priest once a year on the Day of Atonement, all have free access to God in the holy city (Heb. 4:16; 7:19; 9:12; 10:19-22).

More specifically, the angel measured the city with his golden rod to be *fifteen hundred miles; its length and width and height are equal*. The NRSV translators rendered the original 12,000 stadia as 1,500 miles, roughly the distance from New York to Houston. To speak in terms of geography that John would have appreciated,

Mulholland specifies that, if the 1,500-mile city were centered on Patmos, it would reach from Rome to Jerusalem and cover the Roman Empire from north to south; in short, the New Jerusalem descends to supplant the Roman Empire, the Babylon of John's day (1990:325). It may be, however, that the size of the city is not meant to be taken literally but merely to transcend earthly possibilities and add to the magnificence of the city. Ewert says: "John nearly breaks the bonds of language to describe what he saw in the vision" (1980:156). The vast number indicates there is room in the city for everyone (see also 7:9-17).

Although the conversion into 1,500 miles is literally accurate, the rich symbolism of 12,000 stadia is totally lost. The number is constructed from the numerical designator of the people of God (12) squared, times a very large number (1000), connoting the perfection of God's faithful saints (Eph. 2:20-22; 1 Pet. 2:5). The dimensions of the city parallel the 12,000 sealed from each tribe who occupy the city (7:4-7). Moreover, a cube of 12,000 stadia on each of its 12 edges totals 144,000 stadia, the number that symbolizes the faithful saints who overcame the great tribulation, still another parallel with chapter 7 (7:4; see also 14:1-7; Farrer, 1964:217). In short, the symbolic meaning of the dimensions of the cube-shaped city is the splendor and perfection of the New Jerusalem (Ezek. 37:26-28).

The angel also measured the wall of the city: *one hundred forty-four cubits by human measurement, which the angel was using* (see Herodotus's calculation of the size of Babylon's wall in royal cubits 1:178). It is not clear whether 144 cubits, or its equivalent 216 feet, is the thickness or height of the wall, a disproportionate number in either case. If height is in mind, a 216-foot wall around a city 1500 miles high is unbelievably puny (cf. v. 12). By comparison, the wall of Babylon was 300 feet high, and the walls of Solomon's porch 180 feet high (Barclay, 1960:2.271). Considering thickness rather than height, if the wall is the height of the city, its dimensions would be 300 feet high for each inch thick, far too thin to support itself. Barclay is probably correct to assume that the disproportionately small wall around a magnificently large city suggests that "limitation is nothing in comparison with inclusiveness" (1960:2.272). Yet as before, the measurements are perhaps not to be taken literally but to represent the number of the people of God (12) times itself (144), connoting the communion of the Old and New Testament saints in the holy city.

The description of the building materials of the city is nearly as overwhelming as the dimensions: *The wall is built of jasper, while the city is pure gold, clear as glass.* The temples of Solomon

(1 Kings 6:20-22) and Herod (Jos., *War* 5.222-26) and the throne room of heaven are similarly described (Rev. 4:6; 15:2; cf. 7:14; 18:16). The verb *built* is a compound, meaning "inlaid." The *jasper* designates the glory of God (see on Rev. 4:3; also see v. 11). Calling into question a literalistic interpretation, Eller asks: "Would pure gold even stand up as a construction material?" He concludes that such literalism obscures the intended meaning of the image—"Beautiful! beautiful! beautiful!" (1974:198). The literalism also seems to break down when the gold is described as *clear as glass*. Yet, ancient glass was usually dark, and clear glass was particularly precious (Morris, 1969:251). In any case, both the jasper and the gold reflect the glory of God's presence in the holy city (4:3, 6; see also Heb. 1:3).

In even more magnificent detail, the vision continues: *The foundations of the wall of the city are adorned with every jewel; the first was jasper, the second sapphire, the third agate, the fourth emerald, the fifth onyx, the sixth carnelian, the seventh chrysolite, the eighth beryl, the ninth topaz, the tenth chrysoprase, the eleventh jacinth, the twelfth amethyst* (see Ford 1975:335-36, Mounce 1977:382-83 for descriptions of stones; see Ford 1975:343 for tribal correspondences with zodiacal signs; see Barclay 1960:274 for correspondence between zodiacal signs and precious stones). The word *adorned* echoes the description of the simple clothing of the bride (Sweet, 1990:305-6; 19:8, 14) and contrasts with the false riches of "the mart of Babylon" (Farrer, 1964:220; 17:4; 18:12-13, 16; see also 3:17-18). Although adorning the foundations rather than the gates as would be expected in connection with Old Testament imagery, this verse draws heavily on the description in Exodus of the jewels of the square, golden breastplate of the high priest (Exod. 28:15-21; 39:8-14; see also Isa. 54:11-12; Ezek. 28:12-13; Tob. 13:16; Wis. Sol. 18:24; Jos., *War* 5.228-37). Furthermore, the list begins in Revelation with the jasper, the stone of Judah, the tribe of Christ the Lamb (see Rev. 5:5-6; 7:5), who is also the chief cornerstone of the city (Farrer, 1964:219).

The magnificent description of the city continues: *the twelve gates are twelve pearls, each of the gates is a single pearl*. Rabbinic prophecies contend that the gates of Jerusalem will have gems and pearls thirty cubits square with openings ten by twenty cubits (Morris, 1969:253; Baba Batra 75a; Sanhedrin 100a). Although Barclay reports that Julius Caesar gave Servilia a pearl worth 65,250 British pounds (1960:2.275), the city certainly witnesses to a magnificence that far transcends the present world ("from what oysters would one get pearls large enough to stand as a city's gate!" [Barr, 1998:113]).

It reflects the glory of God, which cannot be described objectively, but only in extravagant language, based on the beauty of precious pearls (Job 28:18; Matt. 7:6; 13:45-46; 1 Tim. 2:9; Rev. 17:4; 18:12; Baba Batra 146a).

The *street of the city* is pictured as the entire city was in verse 18: *pure gold, transparent as glass* (1 Kings 6:30). Although the word *street* is singular and may refer to the main street or the city square (Aune, 1998b:1166), it is probably a collective noun indicating that all the streets of the city are golden. In a context where the streets were muddy and dusty, gold pavement would be especially rewarding (Metzger, 1993:101). The word *transparent*, unknown elsewhere in the Greek Bible, is used by Josephus to describe the stream Moses produced out of the rock (*Ant.* 3.37). Mounce's summary of the imagery presented here is effective: "The overall picture is of a city of brilliant gold surrounded by a wall inlaid with jasper and resting on twelve foundations adorned with precious gems of every color and hue" (1977:383).

Because the presence of God permeated the city, John *saw no temple in the city*. In contrast, Ezekiel included a four-chapter discussion of a restored temple (Ezek. 40-43; see also 2 Bar. 6:1-7). Although Aune sees here an "anti-temple and anti-priestly polemic ... of early Judaism" (1998b:1166), to be without a temple was usually unthinkable in Jewish tradition (Matt. 24:2; Mark 13:2; Luke 21:5-6). It is interesting to note that Ezekiel's words were written after the first destruction of the temple in 586 B.C. (Ezek. 37:24-28), and Revelation's after its second destruction in A.D. 70 (Yarbro Collins, 1991:145).

Yet the reason there is no temple in the New Jerusalem is that *its temple is the Lord God the Almighty and the Lamb* (see Notes on 1:8, *Almighty*). The Lamb shares in God's deity through suffering on the cross (Rev. 1:5-6; 2:28; 3:21; 5:6-10; 12:10-11). Together, God and the Lamb fulfill the need for a temple, which symbolized the presence of God (Exod. 25:22; 1 Kings 6:11-13; Jer. 3:15-17; Ezek. 11:16; 43:1-9; Zech. 14:20-21: Mark 14:58; John 2:21; 4:21; 2 Cor. 6:16; Rev. 7:15; 11:1-2, 19; 15:6, 8). Common eschatological speculation regarding the literal rebuilding of the temple in Jerusalem and the restoration of animal sacrifices is superfluous because the city of God is the temple, and the death of Christ on the cross is the only adequate sacrifice (Heb. 2:17; 8:13; 9:26; 10:12). Indeed, the city is not bricks and mortar, but people; the faithful saints are the temple where God resides (Acts 17:24; 1 Cor. 3:16-17; 6:19; Eph. 2:21-22; Rev. 3:12). A "face-to-face intimacy" with God replaces the mediation of the temple and its priests (Eller, 1974:199).

Another consequence of the presence of God and the Lamb in the New Jerusalem is that *the city has no need of sun or moon to shine on it, for the glory of God is its light, and its lamp is the Lamb.* Although today the moon is known to reflect light, in the ancient world the sun and moon were both thought to be luminaries. As such, they are rendered superfluous by the illumination of God's glory (Isa. 60:19-20; see also Ps. 36:9; cf. Rev. 16:10; 18:23; 2 Esd. 7:39-42) and the lamp of the Lamb, who is the light of the world (John 8:12; see also Matt. 17:2; Mark 9:2-3; Luke 9:28-29; John 1:4, 9, 14, 18; 3:19; 12:35; 17:5; 2 Pet. 1:17). These heavenly bodies do not cease to exist but are simply unneeded (Beasley-Murray, 1974:327).

Perhaps the most difficult interpretive issue related to the holy city is raised by the assertion: *The nations will walk by its light, and the kings of the earth will bring their glory into it.* The nations are not included among the saints in Revelation (11:2, 9, 18; 19:15) but are condemned as those seduced by the whore (14:8; 6:15-17; 18:3, 9-10, 23; 19:15; 20:3), deceived by Satan (20:2-3, 7-8), and agents of Babylon (2:26; 11:2, 18; 14:8; 19:15; 20:3). Yet these nations come in and out of the city! Because nothing unclean is allowed in the city (v. 27), the nations must have repented of their idolatry and become servants of the Lamb (see Isa. 2:2-4; Rev. 7:9; Tob. 14:6; 1 Enoch 10:20-22). Now rather than as oppressors, the nations come in submission to God and the saints (15:4; see also Ps. 2:1-3, 8-9; 72:10-11; 86:9; Isa. 49:6; 55:5; 56:6-8; 60:3, 10-16; 66:19; Jer. 3:17; 16:19; Dan. 7:14; Mic. 4:1-4; Zeph. 2:11; 3:9; Zech 2:11; 8:22; Rev. 2:26-27; Tob. 13:11; 1 Enoch 48:4-5; Ps. Sol. 17:34). Instead of receiving material wealth from Babylon, they bring glory to the New Jerusalem (Hag. 2:7; Test. Levi 18:9; Test. Judah 25:5; Test. Naphtali 8:4; Test. Asher 7:3). Moreover, the *kings of the earth*, who also committed fornication with the whore (17:2, 18; 18:3, 9), were earlier devoured by vultures and destined for the lake of fire (16:14; 19:17-21). Yet here they are ruled by Christ (1:5; 6:15-17; see also Ps. 2:1-3). This passage describes a worldwide revival of those who once served the beast (see Isa. 60:3, 11; cf. Beale, 1999:1097-98). Eller makes a startling conclusion: "If 'the kings of the earth' can find their way to redemption, then it's a possibility for anyone!"—even Hitler, Cain, or Judas (1974:204).

Nevertheless, this passage does raise a serious problem: the presence of the *nations* and *kings of the earth* in the New Jerusalem (22:2; 14-15) after they would appear to have been confined to their eternal punishment (20:15; 21:8; see also 22:2). While the presence of such reprobates in the city gives some rationale for the belief in universal salvation, Revelation's references to punishment in the lake of fire (19:20; 20:10, 14-15; 21:8) and the prohibition of anything unclean from the city (21:26) prevent such a conclusion. Yet at least two universalizing principles are evident in this passage: first, the offer of repentance is always open, even to the very end; and second, there will be surprises regarding who is included in God's salvation—some unexpected persons will populate the eternal city.

This theme of the openness of the city to all is reinforced by the words that follow: *Its gates will never be shut by day*. The gates of the Jerusalem temple were routinely closed at dusk after the evening sacrifices and opened again at dawn to permit the morning sacrifices. Yet this seems unnecessary in a city where the light of God shines incessantly (Fekkes, 1994:100 n79, 272). Although the heavenly city does have walls, they are not for exclusion, since the gates are always open (Isa. 60:11). With evil destroyed, the gates need not be shut for security (20:10, 14-15; 21:8). The picture speaks of complete freedom from the persecutions that have dominated the saints' life on earth and an open welcome to all who wish to repent and enter the city.

Because the gates will not be shut by day *and there will be no night there* (see v. 23; Isa. 60:19-20; Zech. 14:7), they will remain open permanently. The meaning is that all the darkness of evil is banished (see Matt. 6:23; 8:12; 22:13; 25:30), all that is not part of the bright radiance of God (Ps. 139:11; Isa. 30:26).

The exalted image of the city is further reinforced by the words: *People will bring into it the glory and the honor of the nations. But nothing unclean will enter it, nor anyone who practices abomination or falsehood, but only those who are written in the Lamb's book of life* (on the first clause, see Notes for v. 24 above; see also TBC on ch. 20, The Books). Although nations and kings of the earth come to the city with their gifts, nothing unclean or abominable is allowed to enter (see Josh. 7:10-13; Isa. 35:8; 52:1; Rom. 1:18). Clearly the city has become the temple (Fekkes, 1994:99-100). The word translated *unclean* means "common," the word for *abomination* refers to the idolatry of worshiping the beast, and *falsehood* is the main characteristic of those who are excluded from the city (22:15; see also 21:8). Rowland points to the irony of this passage: "Even though the gates of the city are left wide open, some people will remain outside" (1998:720).

The Presence of God 22:1-5

Revelation 22:1-5 forms the climax for the vision of the previous chapter. The theme of the passage is eternal life in a paradise restored. The last things are like creation, but the end surpasses the beginning (Beasley-Murray, 1974:330; Gen. 2:8-17; see also Isa. 51:3; Joel 3:18; 1 Enoch 26:1-2).

The chapter begins as John continues to report on what he saw: *Then the angel showed me the river of the water of life, bright as crystal.* The theme of the river of life permeates the Judeo-Christian tradition (Ps. 1:3; 36:9; 46:4; 65:9; Prov. 10:11; 13:14; 14:27; 16:22; Isa. 41:18; Jer. 2:13; Zech. 14:8; John 4:10-14; Rev. 7:17; 21:6; 22:17; 1 Enoch 96:6; 2 Enoch 8:5; 1 QS 4.21). In Ezekiel 47:1-12 a river flows from the temple to the Dead Sea, which is brought to life by the flow. The theme of death to life is clear; in the New Jerusalem death is abolished and eternal life is a present reality. This life comes through what Christ has accomplished in his suffering, death, and resurrection to new life (John 7:37-39).

The crystal clear river of life is *flowing from the throne of God and of the Lamb.* That the river flows from the throne indicates God is the source of life. Although the Lamb is paired with God twice in the preceding paragraph (21:22-23), Christ on the throne is unusual in Revelation (3:21; 12:5; see also 5:6; 7:17; 2 Cor. 5:10). To have God and the Lamb on a single throne is difficult to visualize but symbolically indicates their unity and shared sovereignty (John 10:30; Gal. 3:20; 1 Tim. 2:5).

Perhaps the most difficult idea to visualize here is that the river flowed *through the middle of the street of the city.* The issue is whether this phrase is to be taken with verse 1, placing the river in the middle of a broad city street with trees on either side, or with verse 2, implying that the river and street are side by side with trees between (cf. Barker, 2000:330). The former paints a better literal picture. Whatever John saw in the vision, the meaning is clear: in the city eternal life is central and available to all. This is likely a counter-image of the martyrs dying in the middle of the street of the city in 11:8 (Michaels, 1997:246).

Another statement that is difficult to visualize follows: *On either side of the river is the tree of life with its twelve kinds of fruit, producing its fruit each month.* Although *tree* is singular, the plural is used in Ezekiel 47:7, and the picture seems to be of a line of trees on either side of the river. The lack of an article indicates a collective noun as in the statement: "Both banks were planted with oak" (Farrer, 1964:222). The image is from the creation story of the garden of

Eden (Gen. 2:9; Ezek. 31:8-9). Although Adam and Eve were not allowed to eat from the tree of life (Gen. 3:3, 6, 17-19, 22-24), here there is free access to its fruit, eternal life (2 Esd. 7:53 [124]; 8:52; 1 Enoch 25:4-5; 32:3-6; 2 Enoch 8:3-4; Test. Levi 18:10-11). The image probably means twelve successive harvests. Both the water and the tree of life symbolize that in the New Jerusalem the faithful saints will have free access to life—eternal and abundant.

More specifically, *the leaves of the tree are for the healing of the nations.* It might be asked why the nations need to be healed if they are in the New Jerusalem. Because these are the nations that identified with Babylon (21:24) and nothing unclean is allowed in the city (21:8, 27; 22:15), their healing is necessary (7:17; 21:4; see also 2 Chron. 30:20; Hos. 6:1). This healing symbolizes the lack of sickness, suffering, and death in the city. Persecutions and afflictions of the present age are now over.

Because of the healing of the nations, *[n]othing accursed will be found there anymore.* The word for *accursed* occurs only here in the Greek Bible (but see Isa. 24:4-6; Zech. 14:11; Rom. 5:12-21; 8:18-25; Rev. 21:8, 27; 22:15). The language may echo the barring of humans from Eden (Glasson, 1965:121; Gen. 3:1-6, 14-17; see also Gen. 4:10-14); in this case, Eden's curse is reversed through the work of the Christ the Lamb (Gal. 3:13). The point is that there is no sin or abomination in the city.

The reason for this purity is that *the throne of God and of the Lamb will be in it, and his servants will worship him.* The throne has become a central symbol in Revelation emphasizing that God and the Lamb rule the world, not Caesar and the Roman Empire (cf. 1 Enoch 45:3; 51:3; 61:8; 62:3, 5; 69:29). The singular pronoun is used for God and the Lamb, again stressing their unity (Beasley-Murray, 1974:332; see also 11:15; see also 14:1). The word translated *worship* literally means "serve" (7:14-15; see also Deut. 10:12; Rom. 12:1; Phil. 3:3), an activity to be expected of *servants.* According to Ewert, this indicates that heaven is not a place of idle leisure but of "meaningful existence" where saints serve and worship God (1980:169).

The goal of this service is that *they will see his face and his name will be on their foreheads* (see TBC, The Vision of God). The servants that are all now priests with direct access to God bear the divine name on their foreheads in the same way that the high priest had "Holy to the Lord" on his forehead (Exod. 28:36-38; see also Jos., *Ant.* 3.187; Philo, *Life of Moses* 2.114-15). The word *name,* which occurs thirty-six times in Revelation, signifies character or ownership

(2:3, 13, 17; 3:1, 4-5, 8, 12; 6:8; 13:1, 6, 8, 17; 14:1, 11; 15:2, 4; 16:9; 17:3, 5, 8; 19:12, 13, 16; 21:12, 14). Those who see God retain the divine likeness on their faces (1 Cor. 15:49; 2 Cor. 3:18; 4:6; 1 John 3:2). The word for *foreheads* occurs only in Revelation, especially in the counter-images of the seal of the living God (7:3; 9:4; 14:1) and the mark of the beast (13:16; 14:9; 20:4; see also 17:5). The meaning is that the saints belong to God and reflect the divine character.

Changing the subject a bit, John returns to the image of light: *And there will be no more night; they will need no light of lamp or sun.* The passage expands on 21:23, echoing the creation of light in Genesis 1:3-5 (see also Gen. 1:26; 9:1-7; Isa. 60:19-20; Zech. 14:6-7; John 1:4-5; 9:4-5), and implying that the darkness of evil has been abolished (John 3:19; 21:23; Rom. 13:12; Tob. 7:1-8). The reason that there is no more need for a lamp or the sun is that *the Lord God will be their light.* The brightness of the city contrasts with the darkness of Babylon, the kingdom of the beast (16:10; 18:23), and alludes to the sun and moon under the feet of the mother of the Messiah (12:1). Although the new creation may also include a sun and other natural lights, the brilliant presence of God makes them superfluous (Beale, 1999:1115; 1 Cor. 15:20-28).

The vision concludes with a common biblical theme: *they will reign forever and ever.* The saints reign with God as king (17:14; 19:16) and with Christ as co-ruler (1:6; 2:27; 3:21; Luke 22:28-30; Rom. 8:17; 2 Tim. 2:12). The question is: Reign over whom? The unfaithful have been converted or condemned to the lake of fire. Yet again, this is to insist on a literal chronology. The point is not to specify who are the subjects of the saints' reign but to affirm its eternal duration (cf. 20:4-6; Dan. 7:18, 27; 12:3; Rev. 1:6; 5:10; 11:15). Schüssler Fiorenza adds an important point: "Not oppressive rulership and subordination but the life-giving and life-sustaining power of God characterizes God's eschatological reign and empire" (1991:113). On this blissful note, John's visions come to a close.

Worship God! 22:6-11

In the final section of Revelation, John returns to the epistolary format of chapters 1–3. There are no more intricate apocalyptic visions, but instead, loosely structured warnings and exhortations that resemble the conclusions of other New Testament epistles (R. H. Charles, 1920:2.211-15 for a tenuous reconstruction). The main theme is the coming of Christ: the statement *I am coming soon* is repeated three times in this chapter (vv. 7, 12, 20; see also v. 10) but occurs else-

where in Revelation only once in the letter to Philadelphia (3:11; see
also 2:16). The present tense indicates that Christ's coming is a permanent reality: Christ is always coming soon. Three subordinate
themes are the authenticity of the book (vv. 6, 9, 16, 18-19),
Revelation as prophecy (vv. 6-7, 9-10; see also the Preview), and the
encouragement of the faithful (vv. 7, 12, 14).

The most confusing aspect to this final section is the difficulty of
knowing who is speaking any given time. God? Christ? An angel?
John? Perhaps it is best to say that God in Jesus Christ speaks, sometimes through an angel (see Beasley-Murray 1974:334-35). Happily,
this ambiguity does not significantly affect the meaning of the passage.

Words of authentication begin the section, indicating the genuineness of what is recorded in Revelation (1:1-3; 3:14; 19:9, 11; 21:5).
The reason Revelation is *trustworthy and true* is that *the Lord, the
God of the spirits of the prophets, has sent his angel to show his
servants what must soon take place.* In a chain-like pattern similar to
the prologue, the word originates from God, whose spirit inspires the
prophets to send an angel with a message for the servants of God (1:1-
2). The phrase *spirits of the prophets* makes it clear that Revelation is
a prophecy sent by the spirit of God (1 Cor. 14:32; 2 Pet. 1:21;
1 John 4:1-3). Michaels is certainly right to connect this phrase with
the seven spirits that symbolize the Holy Spirit in Revelation
(1997:250n; 1:4; 4:5; 5:6). The *servants* may be equivalent to the
prophets or, more generally, to all faithful saints. The word *must* indicates the certain fulfillment of God words (1:1; see 2 Cor. 6:2).

The content of what is to be fulfilled is communicated in the words
of Christ: *See, I am coming soon!* The emphatic *See! (idou)* reminds
the reader of a prophetic oracle. The adverb here is translated "quickly" in the Gospels (Matt. 5:25; 28:7-8; Mark 16:8; Luke 15:22; John
11:29), but in Revelation it always carries the sense of *soon* (Rev.
2:16; 3:11; 22:7, 12, 20). Yet Mounce rightly emphasizes that this
announcement is not "an infallible timetable" but an "urgent expectation" (1977:391). Indeed, faithful saints always live in anticipation of
Christ's coming by overcoming persecution.

The sixth of Revelation's seven beatitudes follows: *Blessed is the
one who keeps the words of the prophecy of this book* (v. 7). This
is the explicit admonition to faithfulness in the face of persecution only
alluded to in the previous verse. The word *keeps* means "observes" or
"fulfills"; the present tense indicates that the words of Revelation are
to be continually practiced in life. The true prophet is the one who
leads the person into obedience to God.

John returns to the theme of authentication with the affirmation *I, John, am the one who heard and saw these things*. Here, John himself asserts that what he has written is what he saw and heard from God (1:1, 9; see also Rom. 16:25-27). In the words of Wilcock, "What John says is what God has said ... the classical doctrine of the inspiration of Scripture as a whole" (1975:215).

After hearing and seeing what he recorded in Revelation, John recounts: *I fell down to worship at the feet of the angel who showed them to me; but he said to me, 'You must not do that! I am a fellow servant with you and your comrades the prophets, and with those who keep the words of this book. Worship God!'* This is a repetition of what happened in 19:10 (see Notes there). Its repetition emphasizes the passage's rebuke of idolatry—a dominant theme of Revelation. The recurrence emphasizes the majesty of what John heard and saw, and the shocking truth that even the one who receives this spectacular message can go astray (Morris, 1969:258-59). This should be a solemn reminder for faithful saints to *keep the words of this book* (1:9; 19:10; cf. Acts 10:25-26).

In the disjointed manner that characterizes this section, John returns to the imminence of Christ's coming as he reports the instructions of the angel: *Do not seal up the words of the prophecy of this book, for the time is near.* This statement is unique in apocalyptic literature, where writers are usually instructed to hide the book for a future fulfillment (1 Enoch 1:2; 90:20; 104:11–105:2; 2 Enoch 33:5-11; 35:1-3; see also Rev. 10:4), although the explicit "motif of sealing a revelatory book in order to preserve its secrets until the eschaton" is found only in Daniel and Revelation (Aune, 1998b:1216). For example, the context of the book of Daniel is sixth-century B.C. Babylon under King Nebuchadnezzar, but the message is for the second-century oppression of Seleucid ruler Antiochus IV Epiphanes. Therefore, Daniel is told to seal up the book for fulfillment some four hundred years later (Dan. 8:26; 12:4, 9; cf. Isa. 8:16). By contrast, Revelation's fulfillment is immediate, so John is told not to seal it up. This means that the message of Revelation is for the seven churches addressed in the book, who were under imperial Rome and were threatened by its idolatrous emperor worship that had become widespread in Asia. John is told not to seal up his message because its fulfillment is near.

If that is true, the major question that arises is: Was John wrong? Apparently, Christ did not appear to relieve the oppression of Rome, although Emperor Domitian's persecution did indeed end with his death in A.D. 96 (Efird, 1989:125). Rather, John seems to be using the first-century context to teach universal truths. The urgency of fulfillment is not chronological but moral (Bruce, 1969:665). In other words, the angel insists that the book not be sealed because the faithful saints must always live as though their lives will soon come under the scrutiny of a just God, rather than because fulfillment is chronologically imminent. Peterson says:

> People who are preoccupied with the future never seem to be interested in preparing for the future, which is something that people do by feeding the poor, working for justice, loving their neighbors, developing a virtuous and compassionate life in the name of Jesus. They want to predict the future. Prediction becomes a substitute for action. (1988:193)

The imminence theme continues with the words: *Let the evildoer still do evil, and the filthy still be filthy, and the righteous still do right, and the holy still be holy.* In the context of evil, righteousness, and holiness, the word *filthy* carries the meaning of moral defilement (Zech. 3:3-4; Jas. 2:2; Test. Judah 14:3). In Daniel the sealing of the book is until some have been purified of such defilement, although there is recognition that the wicked will continue to do wickedness (Dan. 12:9-10; see also Ezek. 3:27). In contrast, John's prophecy is for the immediate future; therefore, everyone is to remain as is, both righteous and wicked. Although the passage seems to be saying that there is no further opportunity for repentance (Matt. 25:10; Luke 13:25), verse 17 makes this interpretation unacceptable (see also 2:4; 3:3, 19). The point is to emphasize necessity of choice: in the end, all must accept the consequences of their deeds. As evil intensifies, the faithful increase their commitment and the wicked fail to understand (Beasley-Murray, 1974:338; 9:20-21; 16:11; 16:21-22; 20:15; 21:8). Thus, the passage is not religious determinism but a call to put life in order before it is too late (Caird, 1966:284; Matt. 3:2; 4:17; Mark 1:15; Rom. 13:11-14; Jas. 5:8; 1 Pet. 4:7).

Christ Is Coming Soon! 22:12-17

Christ's second coming is announced in the words: *See, I am coming soon; my reward is with me, to repay according to everyone's work.* The initial clause is repeated here for emphasis (see Notes on v. 7). The judgment of works reiterates the theme of the white throne judgment (see Notes on 20:12). The word *reward* literally means "wages," that is, what is due to a person for work done (Isa. 40:10; Matt. 5:12; 10:41-42; Luke 6:35; 2 Pet. 2:12-16; Rev. 11:18; see also Ps. 28:4; 62:12; Jer. 17:10; Rom. 2:6-10; 2 Cor. 5:10; Col. 3:23-25; 1 Clem. 34:3). Moreover, the reward is for everyone: to the faithful, the joy of citizenship in the holy city; and to the unfaithful, condemnation to the lake of fire. Yet *work* here is singular, focusing particularly on loyalty. Ladd describes this work as "patience in tribulation, steadfastness under persecution, faithfulness to Christ" (1972:292; 13:10; 14:12). The imminence of the coming of Christ should evoke, not "elaborate charts and timetables," but "repentance from sin and faithfulness to the Lamb" (Wall, 1991:263).

John follows his declaration of the imminent parousia with Christ's words of self-authentication. The designators, *the Alpha and the Omega* (see Notes on 1:8; 21:6), *the first and the last* (see Notes on 1:17; also Isa. 41:4; 44:6; 48:12) and *the beginning and the end* (see Notes on 21:6; also 1:5; 3:14; Jos., *Ant.* 8.2.2), are used elsewhere only of God and all carry the same meaning: that Christ is eternal. While John's gospel emphasizes that Christ the Word worked with God in the beginning to create the world (John 1:1), Revelation here stresses that the last thing will be Christ's return (see Phil. 1:6; Heb. 12:2).

The last of the seven beatitudes of Revelation follows (1:3; 14:13; 16:15; 19:9; 20:6; 22:7): *Blessed are those who wash their robes, so that they will have the right to the tree of life and may enter the city by the gates* (see Notes on 7:14 for the washing of robes). In contrast to 7:14, where the aorist is used (see also 3:4; 1 Cor. 6:11; 1 John 1:8-9), here *wash* is a present participle denoting continuous action: the faithful continuously wash their robes by remaining undefiled by worship of the beast. This washing is necessary because nothing unclean can enter the city (21:27).

In contrast to those who have access to the city, *[o]utside are the dogs and sorcerers and fornicators and murderers and idolaters, and everyone who loves and practices falsehood.* In the ancient world, the dog was not a pet that sat on its owner's lap but, in the words of Barclay, "the street scavenger, homeless and savage and mangy and thieving" (1960:2.290). The Bible uses the dog to symbolize a male temple prostitute (Deut. 23:18), the unclean (Matt. 7:6), outsiders (Matt. 15:26; Mark 7:27), evildoers (Ps. 22:16), and Judaizers (Phil. 3:2). The passage specifies seven types of sinners representing all sins that are outside the city (see Notes on 21:8; see also 21:27).

From what has preceded, *outside* would seem to refer to the lake of fire (20:13-15; 21:8). Yet Ladd admits that, taking the passage literally, its reader finds two groups—the faithful in the New Jerusalem and the unregenerate nations living outside but "influenced by its presence, walking in its light, and bringing their glory to the city"

(1972:284-85). Because evil is not allowed in the city (21:27), however, it must be necessary for those outside to repent in order to have access to the open gates of the New Jerusalem, a repentance that is available to the very end.

The topic returns to the authentication of the message: *It is I, Jesus, who sent my angel to you with this testimony for the churches.* These words identify the messenger as from Christ (see Acts 9:5; 22:8; 26:15), while in verse 6 God sent the angel—again stressing the unity of God and Christ. Although ambiguous in English, the pronoun *you* here is plural in Greek, indicating that this is a corporate message to the churches, specifically the seven churches of Asia. The designation *church* occurs repeatedly in chapters 1–3, mostly in the letters to the churches, and elsewhere only here (Michaels, 1997:254n). Caird believes the *testimony* of Jesus for the churches is also the church's testimony in the sense that she is called to a "self-sacrificing witness" (1966:286). Jesus then introduces for further authentication two self-designators (see Notes on 2:28; 5:5): *the root and the offspring of David* reflect Christ's humanity, and *the bright morning star* his divinity (Bruce, 1969:666: Matt. 22:41-44; Mark 12:35-37; Luke 20:41-44; Rom. 1:3-4).

Verse 17 contains four exhortations, and a major issue is the identity of the one addressed by the word *Come.* Although the coming of Christ is a theme of the section (22:7, 12, 20), the last two admonitions are manifestly not to Christ. If a break is placed between verses 16 and 17, the first two may be addressed to Christ and the last two to the world (Beasley-Murray, 1974:343-44). Nevertheless, because Jesus is emphatically the speaker in this section, he cannot also be the one addressed; and all four admonitions are, therefore, surely directed to the wicked and the unfaithful. First, the *Spirit and the bride say, "Come."* The former is the Holy Spirit that communicates through the spirit of prophecy to the churches (2:7, 11, 17, 29; 3:6, 13, 22; see also John 14:16-17; 15:26-27), and the bride is the community of the faithful (18:23; 19:7-8; 21:2, 9). The Holy Spirit and the saints together issue the invitation to come to Christ. Second, *let everyone who hears say, "Come."* Beasley-Murray distinguishes between the bride (the church) and everyone (the individual saints), asserting that the one who hears is a member who listens as Revelation is read in the churches (1974:345). Yet the hearer must share the invitation with others who have not yet come. Third, *let everyone who is thirsty come.* Everyone who thirsts for righteousness is invited to Christ (Matt. 5:6; see also Isa. 55:1; John 4:10-14; 6:35; 7:37-38; Rev. 7:16-17; 21:6). Fourth, *Let anyone who wishes take the water of life as a gift.* The water of life is from the river in the holy city and symbolizes immortality (Rev. 22:1-2). That it is a gift indicates that eternal life is free, purchased by the cross of Christ.

Most likely, these four exclamations are invitations to the wedding banquet. It should be noted that *"Come!"* is a present imperative throughout, indicating that the appeal is continuous. The task of the faithful, then, is not to wait for the end but to prepare for the banquet by remaining faithful.

Stern Warning 22:18-19

John now turns abruptly to a serious threat: *I warn everyone who hears the words of the prophecy of this book: if anyone adds to them, God will add to that person the plagues described in this book; if anyone takes away from the words of the book of this prophecy, God will take away that person's share in the tree of life and in the holy city, which are described in this book.*

The word translated *warn (martyrō)* means "witness" or "testify" (vv. 16, 20; 1:2); Hughes suggests that it is the obverse of "blessed" (1990:240: 1:3; 22:7). The *plagues* are the bowl judgments (Wall, 1991:272; 15:1-16:20). Hence, the punishment fits the offense; the person who tampers with the prophecy receives the judgment of the same prophecy.

This warning has roots in a variety of biblical passages (Deut. 4:2; 12:32; 29:19-20; Prov. 30:6; Gal. 1:6-9; 1 Enoch 104:10; 2 Enoch 48:7-8). Moreover, in days before the printing press and copyright laws, it was common to end a letter with a warning against tampering with its message. The problem is illustrated by Tertullian, who accused Valentinus of perverting his text with additions and alterations (*Against Heresies* 38). Moreover, Eusebius says that a lost letter of Irenaeus contained the following in an appendix:

> I adjure thee whoever thou art, that transcribest this book, by our Lord Jesus Christ, and by his glorious appearance, when he shall come to judge the quick and the dead, to compare what thou last copied, and to correct it by this original manuscript, from which thou hast carefully transcribed. And that thou also copy this adjuration, and insert it in the copy. (*Eccl. Hist.* 5.20.2)

The Letter of Aristeas similarly warns the translators of the Hebrew scriptures into Greek "that a curse should be laid, as was their custom, on anyone who should alter the version by any addition or change to any part of the written text, or any deletion either" (vv. 310-11).

Yet it must be noted that the admonition here is not related to the

mistakes of copiers but to the distortions of hearers. Several significant variant readings occur in the last sentence of Revelation, despite
this warning (Barr, 1998:144n). John seems more concerned that the
copier will maliciously alter the sense of the text than that he will make
a mistake in copying the wording. Hence, this is not an exhortation
to literalism or a condemnation of the historical study of the Bible, but
an authentication of the message against "deliberate distortions and
perversions" (Ladd, 1972:295) and deceptive false teachings (Beale,
1999:1151). Moreover, the emphasis is really on obedience
(Michaels, 1997:259; Deut. 4:2; 12:32; Rev. 22:7,9). Faithfulness to
the Bible is best demonstrated by obeying it and teaching it faithfully.

Come, Lord Jesus 22:20-21

For the third time in the section, the imminent coming of Christ is
affirmed: *The one who testifies to these things says, "Surely I am
coming soon"* (see Notes on v. 7). Mulholland thinks the three-fold
repetition connotes divine perfection (1990:340). The *one who testifies (ho martyrōn)* here is Christ, the faithful witness (1:5; 3:14),
and *surely (nai)* means "yes" (1:7; 14:13; 16:7; see also 2 Cor. 1:20).

The response to the announcement of Christ's coming is: *Amen.
Come, Lord Jesus!* (1 Cor. 16:22; Did. 10:16; see also 1 Cor.
11:26). The exclamation is equivalent to the Aramaic phrase *maran
atha,* "Lord Come!" Boring points out that these are Christ's "last
words before his actual appearance as history's Judge and Redeemer"
(1989:225). Indeed, the theme of Christ's coming is a fitting consummation to the Bible.

Yet Revelation ends with a brief epistolary benediction: *The grace
of the Lord Jesus be with all the saints. Amen.* Thus, like its introduction (1:4), the book concludes in the form of a letter rather than
an apocalypse. The word *grace (charis)* occurs only here and in the
Prologue (1:4), and the designation *Lord Jesus* only in this passage.
The phrase *all the saints* includes not just the churches in Asia but all
the faithful from all times and throughout the world (7:9, 14).

THE TEXT IN BIBLICAL CONTEXT

The New Heaven and New Earth

Many Christians see the present world as so evil and unjust that it must
be destroyed in preparation for a spiritual existence of bliss and righteousness. Yet Revelation speaks of the future world as a new heaven
and new earth, which sounds more like the restoration of this world

than its demise. This issue focuses a major disagreement among Christians: while they agree that all things will be new, they differ on whether that will involve the destruction of this world or its renewal. The Bible seems to support both ideas.

On the one hand, a few passages point to the annihilation of this world. Although the psalmist speaks of the world wearing out and being replaced like an old garment (Ps. 102:26), Isaiah's images are more violent, describing the skies rolling up like a scroll, heavenly bodies drying up like fig or grape leaves, and people dying like gnats (Isa. 34:4; 51:6). The most violent end to the earth is anticipated in the second epistle of Peter: "The heavens will pass away with a loud noise, and the elements will be dissolved with fire" (2 Pet. 3:10; see also vv. 7, 11-13).

Yet by far the more common biblical image is the transformation of the present world into a new heaven and new earth. Isaiah's description seems particularly to underlie this idea in Revelation (Isa. 66:22). The nature of the renewed creation is probably best described by Isaiah in terms of *shalom* (Isa. 11:1-9) and justice (Isa. 42:3, 9). More specifically, the prophet's words clearly are the roots of Revelation's description of joy and delight and of the absence of death and want in the new heaven and earth (Isa. 65:17-25). The concept of a renewed creation continues in the apocryphal and pseudepigraphal literature (Wis. Sol. 19:6), where the concept of transformation rather than destruction is made even more explicit (1 Enoch 45:4-5; 72:1; 91:14-16; 2 Bar. 3:4-9; 32:6; 44:12; 57:2; Jub. 1:29; 4:26; cf. 23:18) and renewal is described in terms similar to the first creation (2 Esd. 7:29-44, 75; 2 Enoch 8:3-4).

In the New Testament, although Jesus speaks of heaven and earth passing away (Matt. 5:18; 24:35; Luke 16:17), he seems to perceive this in terms of renewal rather than destruction (Matt. 19:28; see also Acts 3:21). Paul personalizes the "new creation" (Eph. 2:10; Col. 3:1-4), speaking of the "redemption of our bodies" (Rom. 8:23), the transformation into God's image (2 Cor. 3:18), and the renewal of the inner nature (2 Cor. 4:16-18). But Paul also speaks of all things united in Christ (Eph. 1:10; Col. 1:20), and 2 Corinthians 5:17 suggests a new creation for those "in Christ."

Therefore, Eller properly refers to a continuity between the old and new heaven and earth, what can be called "the *consummation* of history—not a junking of history in order to start over with something entirely different" (1974:195). Carroll adds to this the idea that the cosmos along with humankind awaits God's judgment and justice. Indeed, humans will be judged for either their abuse of God's creation or their participation with God in the re-creation of the cosmos (2000:256-60; see 11:18). Indeed, Revelation anticipates, not the annihilation of this world, but its renewal and restoration into the new heaven and earth.

The Vision of God

One of the most blessed statements in Revelation is: "They shall see his face" (22:4). In the words of Ewert, "All the bliss of eternity seems to be condensed in that phrase" (1980:161). In ancient times to see God meant death: "You cannot see my face; for no one shall see me and live" (Exod. 33:20). Nevertheless, Jacob did see God and lived, which was considered unique (Gen. 32:30). Moses was allowed to see only the back of God, and yet his face shone so brightly that no one could look upon him (Exod. 33:23; 34:29-35). All of this may have given rise to the custom that to see the king was a privilege denied one not in good favor (2 Sam. 14:24; Esther 7:8). Although God's likeness could not be seen physically, God was spiritually present, offering comfort and strength to Israel (Gen. 12:3; 17:7; Exod. 3:12; 6:7; 29:45; Lev. 26:3-13; Num. 15:41; Deut. 29:10-13; 2 Sam. 7:24; Isa. 52:8; Zech. 9:14-15). The prophets, however, emphasized that this spiritual presence was conditioned on the obedience of the people (Jer. 7:23; 11:4; 24:7; 31:1, 31-34; Ezek. 11:20; 34:24; 36:26-28; 37:23-27; Zech. 2:10-13; 8:8), and the actual presence of God was promised to those who were righteous (Ps. 11:7; 17:15; 24:3-6; 2 Esd. 7:98; Test. Zebulon 9:8). This physical presence of God was the great hope and reward of all the saints of God (Ps. 42:2; Matt. 5:6, 8; Rev. 21:23).

The New Testament unites the Old Testament idea of the divine presence with the incarnation of God in Christ: "If you know me, you will know my Father also" (John 14:7, 9; 17:3). Moreover, Jesus is given the name, Emmanuel, "God is with us" (Matt. 1:23; see also Isa. 7:14; Zech. 8:23). Those who are pure of heart will see God (Matt. 5:8), and Christ's followers will share the throne in glory (Matt. 19:28). Yet Paul adds that holiness is the prerequisite for seeing God (2 Cor. 6:16; see also Heb. 12:14); hence, the vision is always incomplete in this world (1 Cor. 13:12). Nevertheless, seeing God is connected with being like God (2 Pet. 1:4; 3:18; 1 John 3:2-3), and Revelation promises those saints who are faithful to the end that they will see God's face and experience the divine presence (4:1-11; 7:15-17).

The Words of the Book

The warning in Revelation 22:18-19 is one of the strongest biblical statements regarding tampering with the words of scripture. Some have seen this as encouraging a literalistic interpretation of the Bible. The passage that has the closest relationship to Revelation's warning is Matthew 5:18, where the emphasis is on endurance, not inspiration. Yet the Bible has much more to say about inspiration than about literalism. The important thing is that the truths of the Bible are from God.

The idea that God spoke through the Hebrew scriptures is assumed in the New Testament (Matt. 19:4-5; Acts 4:25-26). The concept of inspiration is present in the formulae introducing Old Testament quotations throughout the Gospels, "this was to fulfill," which reveals a high regard for the Old Testament scriptures. Yet Christ places his authority above the Hebrew Bible in his repeated use in the Sermon on the Mount of the words, "You have heard that it was said ... But I say to you ..." (Matt. 5:21, 27, 33, 38, 43). Jesus also insists that all things have been revealed to him by God the Father (Matt. 11:27) and that, in turn, these truths will be revealed to humans by the Holy Spirit (John 14:26). Moreover, the apostle Paul issues commands on the authority of God (1 Cor. 14:37; cf. 7:10, 12, 25).

The text most often mentioned regarding the authority of the Bible is 2 Timothy 3:16-17: "All scripture is inspired by God and is useful for teaching, for reproof, for correction, and for training in righteousness, so that everyone who belongs to God may be proficient, equipped for every good work." The word for "inspired" literally means "God-breathed." It must be remembered that this passage is likely speaking of the Old Testament, the "scriptures" when the New Testament was in process. Perhaps the most important caution in using this passage to support biblical authority is that it is really more about the usefulness of scripture for training in righteousness and equipping for good works than about the authority of the biblical text.

I Am Coming Soon!

The imminent coming of Christ is a theme rooted in the Hebrew scripture's messianic expectation (see Mowinckel, 1954, for further elaboration). Originally a political ruler who would restore the fortunes of Israel in this world, the messiah came to be an eschatological figure that would destroy Israel's enemies and establish God's rule universally. These expectations are rooted in Isaiah's prophecies about a Davidic king: "His authority will grow continually, and there shall be

endless peace for the throne of David and his kingdom. He will establish and uphold it with justice and with righteousness from this time
onward and forevermore" (Isa. 9:7; see chs. 9, 11-12). Although the
suffering servant prophecies of deutero-Isaiah were taken by the
Jewish tradition to apply to the nation of Israel, Christians have consistently applied them to the Christ (Messiah): "He was despised and
rejected by others; a man of suffering and acquainted with infirmity;
and as one from whom others hide their faces he was despised, and
we held him of no account" (Isa. 53:3; see 42:1-4; 49:1-6; 50:4-11;
52:13–53:12). Daniel speaks of the Son of Man ("one like a human
being" in the NRSV): "To him was given dominion and glory and kingship, that all peoples, nations, and languages, should serve him. His
dominion is an everlasting dominion that shall not pass away, and his
kingship is one that shall never be destroyed" (Dan. 7:13-14; see
vv. 23-27; 10:14-21).

The theme of the coming of the Christ is central to the New
Testament (TBC on ch. 19, The Parousia). Jesus begins his ministry
with the announcement that his kingdom is near (Matt. 4:17; Mark
1:14-15) and then travels about, proclaiming the kingdom and insisting that this proclamation is the reason that he has come (Matt. 4:23;
9:35; Mark 1:38; Luke 4:43; 8:1). Moreover, Jesus makes it clear
that his followers must keep awake and watch because he is coming
to establish the kingdom at an unexpected hour (Matt. 24:42-44;
25:1-13; Mark 13:35-37; Luke 12:35-40). Paul raises the expectation of saints by describing what will happen at Christ's return:

> For the Lord himself, with a cry of command, with the archangel's call and
> with the sound of God's trumpet, will descend from heaven, and the dead
> in Christ will rise first. Then we who are alive, who are left, will be caught
> up in the clouds together with them to meet the Lord in the air; and so
> we will be with the Lord forever. Therefore encourage one another with
> these words. (1 Thess. 4:16-18)

In spite of the excitement that this passage may generate, James
counsels the patience of a farmer waiting for a good crop (Jas. 5:7).
Yet Revelation raises its readers' anticipation level by insisting that the
appearance of Christ to bring the end of the age and inaugurate the
heavenly kingdom will come soon (1:1-2, 7; 3:3; 16:15).

The difficulty in the statement of Christ's coming soon is its apparent nonfulfillment. Perhaps, the best way to resolve the difficulty is to
live with the paradox that Christ's coming is already but not yet. It is
soon in the sense that Christ's reign was inaugurated in his death and
resurrection (Matt. 10:23; 16:28; Mark 9:1), but it is yet to be con-

summated in the parousia of Christ, which the faithful await with urgent anticipation (22:7, 12, 16).

Heaven

In the Old Testament, heaven (Hebrew, *shamayim*; Greek, *ouranos*) was part of the physical universe—the equivalent of "sky." Heaven was fixed or material, like a dome (Gen. 1:6-8; Exod. 24:10; Ps. 19:1; 150:1; Dan. 12:3; 1 Enoch 14:9-12; 71:5) stretched out (Ps. 104:2; Isa. 40:22; 44:24; 45:12; 48:13; 51:13, 16; Jer. 10:12; 51:15; Zech. 12:1). Heaven had windows (Gen. 7:11; 2 Kings 7:2, 19; Isa. 24:18; Mal. 3:10), foundations (2 Sam. 22:8), and pillars (Job 26:11). The Hebrew concept of universe was tiered, with water above heaven (Gen. 1:7), the dome of heaven (Gen. 1:8), the earth, (Gen. 1:9), and the waters under the earth (Gen. 1:10; see also Exod. 20:4; Ps. 115:15-17). Yet while heaven was a physical place for the Hebrews, the Hebrew Bible does not reflect the Babylonian conception with levels of heaven. The phrase "heaven of heavens" occurs, but only as a means of overstatement and never as a description of the heavenly realm (Deut. 10:14; 1 Kings 8:27; 2 Chron. 2:6; 6:18; Neh. 9:6; Ps. 148:4). So the Hebrew scriptures describe heaven in physical terms, with little idea of multiple heavens.

Not surprisingly, God has a close relation to heaven: God created heaven (Gen. 1:1; 2:4; Ps. 33:6; Isa. 42:5; 45:18), the divine dwelling place (Gen. 11:1-9; 19:24), where God sits among the heavenly council (1 Kings 22:19; Job 1:6-7). Therefore, heaven is the source of all God's blessings (Gen. 49:25; Deut. 33:13; 1 Kings 8:35), including steadfast love and faithfulness (Ps. 89:2; 119:89-90). Yet God has other dwelling places, such as Sinai (Exod. 19; 34:1-9), the ark (Josh. 3; 6:1-14; 1 Sam. 4), the tabernacle (Exod. 40:34-38), and the temple (2 Chron. 7:1-3). So even in the Old Testament, God is not confined to heaven.

The New Testament understanding of heaven is rooted in the Hebrew scriptures. The physical emphasis is still present in the idea that heaven is God's residence in the skies (Mark 6:41; Luke 9:16; 18:13; John 17:1; Acts 1:11). Moreover, heaven and earth are spoken of as two realms of the physical universe; both were created by God (Acts 4:24; 17:24; Rev. 10:6), both will someday pass away (Matt. 5:18; Mark 13:31; Luke 16:17; 2 Pet. 3:5-7; Rev. 20:11), both stand under God's lordship (Matt. 11:25; Luke 10:21; Acts 7:49), and both, in the end, will be restored by God's salvation (Rom. 8:19-25; 2 Pet. 3:13; Rev. 21:1). Again, God is closely related to heaven, being called the God of heaven (Rev. 11:13; 16:11). In addition, heaven is the throne of God (Matt. 5:34; 23:22; Acts 7:49; Heb. 8:1), and the word *heaven* is used as a substitute for God throughout the Gospel of Matthew (see also Luke 15:18, 21).

Nonetheless, in contrast to the Hebrew scriptures, the New Testament portrays heaven as the place through which Jesus ascended to the abode of God, not part of the physical world, but far above the heavens (John 3:13, 31; Eph. 4:9-10; Heb. 7:26). That is where Jesus is now (Acts 3:20-21; Heb. 9:24; Rev. 13:6) and the place from which he will return on the clouds (Mark 14:62; 1 Thess. 1:10). Although heaven is outside the physical universe, this spiritual, divine realm is occasionally open to humanity through a vision (Acts 7:56; Rev. 4:1) or a direct revelation of the divine (Matt. 3:16-17; Mark 1:11; Luke 3:21-22; John 12:28). Furthermore, heaven is where human salvation is determined and provided (Luke 10:20; Col. 1:5; Heb. 12:23; 1 Pet. 1:3-5).

Occasionally in the New Testament, heaven occurs in the plural. For example, Paul speaks of souls going into the third heaven (2 Cor. 12:2). Although to make rigid designations of what these three heavens are would be to say more than the scriptures do, the first heaven may be the dome or sky, the second may refer to the intermediary heavens spoken of in Ephesians 4:10, and the third is most likely the spiritual realm where God and Christ reside with the angels (Matt. 18:10; 22:30; Mark 12:25; 13:32; Heb. 1:5-14). These multiple heavens seems to communicate the majesty, power, and blessing of the heavenly realm.

So in general, the Bible speaks of two kind of heavens. The first is part of the physical universe, the dome that can be seen from earth. The second is in the spiritual world, where angels minister to God and Christ, and which is the source of salvation and blessing.

THE TEXT IN THE LIFE OF THE CHURCH

New Heaven and New Earth

Christians often think of eternal existence in a spiritual place called heaven, which is quite distinct from earthly life. Some believe that, like the Greek concept of the immortal soul, their spirits will float away to a place beyond the sky. Yet Revelation pictures the eternal reward as occurring in a new heaven and new earth. As the physical body will be resurrected and glorified at the last day, so the creation will be renewed to make an appropriate place to serve as the reward for the faithful.

There is an ecological lesson in this comparison of the physical body to the creation. Christians believe that they should take care of their bodies and not be involved in sins like fornication because they are temples of the Holy Spirit, and their physical bodies contaminate or sanctify the body of Christ (1 Cor. 6:19). The idea behind this is that these physical bodies will be resurrected for eternal life; there is a continuity between the physical bodies of the present world and the glorified bodies of the eternal realm.

In a similar manner, Christians should take care of this universe because in the end it will be renewed to serve as their eternal abode. The next world is not a spiritual place totally different from the present cosmos, but a transformed new heaven and earth that is continuous with, and quite similar to, this world, except that it is purified and glorified like the resurrected physical bodies. Therefore, like Christians take care of their physical bodies because they are temples of the Holy Spirit, they should take care of God's creation because it will be renewed to be the eternal new heaven and new earth.

The New Jerusalem

Another surprise for many Christians is to find that the Bible begins and ends in cities. Immediately after Cain killed his brother Abel and received a mark of protection from God, he built a city and named it after his son Enoch (Gen. 4:7). Throughout the Bible the focus is on great cities: Ninevah, Babylon, Jerusalem, Antioch, Rome, Ephesus. And finally, the passage under consideration indicates that the final reward for faithful saints is a city—the New Jerusalem.

Today we are used to perceiving the city as crumbling and dangerous. My wife and I have been living for two years in North Philadelphia, the poorest and most dangerous part of the fifth largest city in the United States. As we walk around our community, we see more signs of fallen Babylon than the New Jerusalem—abandoned houses, vermin, drug dealers, and prostitutes. Yet Revelation says that we will live eternally in a renewed city. The reason is no doubt that the city symbolizes community. It is hard to live in the city without relating to people. The New Jerusalem will be a community of the faithful saints of God. Revelation describes in fantastic and hyperbolic language the nature of existence in the New Jerusalem. Many writers have followed suit, trying to do justice to the glory that awaits those who are faithful to the end. For example, George MacDonald has done so in prose:

> Into the pool [of light] began to tumble a small cataract of shredded rainbows, flashing all the colours visible to the human eye—and more. The

stream that flowed from it ... a silent motionless tempest of conflicting yet
utterly harmonious hues, with foamy spray of spikey flashes and spots that
ate into the eyes with their fierce colors ... There pulsed the mystical glow-
ing red-heart and lord of colours; there the jubilant yellow-light crowned
to ethereal gold; there the wide-eyed spirit blues—the truth unfathomable;
there the green that haunts the brain—storeland of Nature's boundless
secrets ... All the gems were there—sapphires, emeralds, and rubies; but
they were scarce to be noted in the glorious mass of new-born, every
dying colour that gushed from the fountains of the light-dividing dia-
monds. (quoted in Peterson, 1988:180)

In poetry, Bernard de Cluny's "De Contemptu Mundi" captures well
the beauty of John's New Jerusalem.

> Jerusalem the golden,
> With milk and honey blest!
> Beneath thy contemplation
> Sink heart and voice oppressed.
> I know not, O I know not
> What joys await us there;
> What radiancy of glory,
> What bliss beyond compare.
> O sweet and blessed country,
> The home of God's elect!
> O sweet and blessed country
> That eager hearts expect!
> Jesu, in mercy brings us
> To that dear land of rest:
> Who art, with God the Father
> And Spirit, ever blest.
> (Trans. by John Mason Neile and quoted in Metzger, 1993:101)

Yet as beautiful and faithful to Revelation as these literary render-
ings are, it must be stressed that the New Jerusalem is not a spiritual
concept but a real city, like New York, Nairobi, Mexico City, or Tokyo.
In this sense, the ideal of the New Jerusalem invades the present.
Christians are not called in scriptures to await the kingdom of God but
to make it present on this earth. What would that mean? Mulholland
has asked this question in a particularly relevant and prophetic way:

> What would it mean to have the "Witness of Jesus" in the militaristic mad-
> ness of nuclear proliferation? What would it cost individuals and the
> church? What would it mean to have the "Witness of Jesus" in an indul-
> gent consumer society? What would it cost? What would it mean to have
> the "Witness of Jesus" in the horribly destructive holocaust of abortion on
> demand? What would it cost? What would it mean to have the "Witness
> of Jesus" in a culture whose broken sexuality spawns the poisonous
> destructiveness of pornography? What would it cost? (1990:348)

These questions point to a goal that will certainly not be reached in this present world, but it is the ideal that Revelation calls each faithful Christian to strive toward. In the words of Yarbro Collins, "The new city is not simply identical with the church at any particular time and place. The particular christian community and the church as a whole, however, ought to be a reflection of this glorious vision" (1991:150).

Adding to or Taking away from the Words

The warning in 22:18-19 has been taken, along with 2 Timothy 3:16, as support for the inspiration of scripture. Because the Bible is the inspired word of God, no one should add to or take away from its words. It has even been used to support the doctrine of verbal plenary inspiration, that is, that the words of the Bible are directly from God. The Revelation text appears to speak of the apocalypse itself. By extension both passages have been applied to the entire canon of scripture. How have they been understood by the church?

Almost all Christians have believed that God has in some way been revealed to humanity through the Bible. It is important to stress that the primary way God was revealed, though, was not through a book but through a person, Jesus Christ. Christians believe that "the word became flesh and lived among us" (John 1:14). This has led theological liberals and those espousing neo-orthodoxy to argue that revelation is not primarily the propositional truth of scripture but the relational truth that comes through faith in Christ. The corollary of this assertion is that the Bible is not equal to revelation but includes revelation within it. Revelation is broader than the Bible; the scriptures witness to a truth that is ultimately beyond human comprehension. Moreover, some of the Bible may not be inspired, and some material not in the Bible may be divine truth. Such a relational revelation has the positive effect of avoiding the worship of the Bible, but it does not address the question: In what sense is the written revelation of God in the Bible inspired?

Martin Luther and the Reformers answered this question with their doctrine of *sola scriptura,* the sole authority of the scriptures. The emphasis was on the uniqueness of the Bible as a source of authority. The Anabaptists took this to its logical conclusion by insisting that the Bible was *the* guidebook for life; nothing else was necessary, and few things were permitted—perhaps a hymnbook, but never a novel. Most Protestants have accepted Luther's theory, though not stating it as strongly as this Anabaptist example. The Bible has the standard by which all other authorities—church tradition, reason, science, experience—are judged.

In the modern world, the uniqueness of the scripture was less important than its formal accuracy. Therefore, the doctrine of *inerrancy* was born. This doctrine has traditionally meant that the Bible is absolutely without error in everything it literally says. The basis for the theory of inerrancy was factual logic: if the Bible is the inspired word of God, then it is logical that scripture is inerrant. It might be noted that this is the same sort of argument that was used by the Roman Catholic Church for the bodily assumption of Mary: because Mary was the mother of God, then it is logical that she not experience death. In the case of inerrancy, adherents argue, the inspiration of the Bible implies its inerrancy. The major strength of this position is that it instills confidence that the words of the Bible are from God. One problem with this theory, though, is that it does not account well for the formal errors and variant readings of scripture. The inerrantist addresses this difficulty by insisting that only the autographs were inerrant, a statement of faith that cannot be tested because these original copies are not available. The more significant problem with this theory is that it states more than the Bible says about itself. The Bible logically should be the source for a theory of its own authority. Yet the Bible does not claim to be inerrant.

Therefore, the category of *infallibility* has been posited and has become popular even with some who want to be considered inerrantists. Traditionally, infallibility has meant that the Bible is absolutely trustworthy in areas that it intends to teach. The biblical writers intended to teach about matters of theology, morality, and faith. Yet in other areas the Bible may not be without error. For example, the Bible may not be a textbook of science teaching that the world was created in seven days or that the universe is covered by a dome with stars attached like figs to a tree; the Bible may not be a history textbook reporting exact genealogies or the accurate number of persons that accompanied Moses in the wilderness; it may not be a textbook of sociology approving of slavery and polygamy and enforcing a subordinate position for women; it may not be a textbook of psychology establishing the use of a rod or even a sword for the discipline of children. The advantage of this position is that it takes seriously what the Bible says about its authority. The Bible speaks of trustworthiness, endurance, and usefulness—not inerrancy (Matt. 5:18; 2 Tim. 3:16). The weakness is that the movement from inerrancy to infallibility may begin a slippery slope that in the end leads one to ask: Is the Bible an authority on anything at all?

The two positions, inerrancy and infallibility, agree that God is revealed in the words and propositions of scripture; they both believe in propositional truth. Yet differences have grown up over the type of book that the Bible is. Is it a textbook of natural science, history, and the social sciences, or a book of faith teaching truths about God and the importance of serving God?

Maranatha

Many things have been said about the second coming in this commentary. Perhaps, however, something remains to be said about the Christian's expectation of its occurrence. In the 1970s, there was a preoccupation with the second coming, likely due to the publication of books like *The Late Great Planet Earth*, movies like *A Thief in the Night,* and songs like "You've Been Left Behind." In each of these, the emphasis is on the terror of the possibility of being left behind. Many young adults who grew up on this eschatological diet report that as children they came home from school to find their parents absent and were terrified that Christ had come and they were left behind. Surprisingly, as much emphasis as Revelation places on the parousia, this notion of terror is largely absent. There is a tribulation of the saints in Revelation, but the message is that Christ will come to free the faithful from their present oppression and bring them into the bliss of the kingdom. The reaction to Christ's coming in Revelation is not fear of being left behind but *maranatha,* "Our Lord, come!" (1 Cor. 16:22).

Nevertheless, Ewert is certainly correct to admonish that we are not to be idle in expectation of Christ's coming: "To expect a friend for dinner does not have to do so much with a mental state as doing the appropriate things in preparation for his coming" (1980:180, 182). When I was once asked, "What would you do if you knew that Christ would come tomorrow?" I responded: "I would go to the college and teach." The expectation of the coming of Christ should cause us to be faithful where God has called us.

An Early Anabaptist Confession

"Come, Lord Jesus" was probably one of the earliest statements of faith in Christ. As such it has informed all subsequent affirmations of Christians. Indeed, the Anabaptist articles of Christian doctrine drawn up in Amsterdam in 1630 assert faith in the coming of Christ and the bliss attending that event:

> Finally, we believe also, that our Saviour Jesus Christ, forever blessed, shall visibly come again in the clouds, like as He ascended before ... glorious and magnificent, with the power and glory of all His angels ... Jesus

Christ, blessed forever, will then, with the sound of the trumpet call forth and cause to arise from the earth, all the great number of the dead who from the beginning of the world up to the present day have lived, died, and sown their bodies in the earth to corruption.... And after those who then will be still living, will have been changed to immortality in the twinkling of an eye, the general multitude of all mankind will be placed before the holy throne of God, where the books of conscience shall be opened, and also another book, which is the book of life; and the dead shall be judged according to that which is written in these books, that every one may receive in his own body, either good or evil, according to what they have done or how they have lived here....

Then shall the blessed of God abound in heavenly joy, so that with angelic tongues and heavenly voices they will begin to sing with all the saints of God the new song, giving unto Him who sitteth upon the throne, and unto the Lamb, praise, honor, glory, and blessing, for ever and ever. Amen. (van Braght, 1950:38)

Outline of Revelation

THE VISION OF CHRIST   **1:1-20**

An Apocalyptic Title	1:1-3
An Epistolary Address	1:4-8
The Context of the Vision	1:9-11
The Vision of Christ	1:12-16
The Response to the Vision	1:17-20

THE SEVEN LETTERS   **2:1-3:22**

The Letter to Ephesus: Testing False Teaching	2:1-7
The Letter to Smyrna: Faithful in Tribulation	2:8-11
The Letter to Pergamum: The Cost of Compromise	2:12-17
The Letter to Thyatira: The Toleration of Evil	2:18-29
The Letter to Sardis: The Spiritually Dead	3:1-6
The Letter to Philadelphia: An Open Door of Opportunity	3:7-13
The Letter to Laodicea: The Poverty of Riches	3:14-22

THE VISION OF GOD   **4:1-11**

The Throne	4:1-2
The One Seated on the Throne	4:3-6a
A Response of Praise	4:6b-11

THE LAMB AND THE SCROLL   5:1-14

The Introduction of the Scroll	5:1-4
The Lamb's Opening of the Scroll	5:5-7
Hymns to Christ's Redemption	5:8-14

THE SEALS   6:1-17

The Rider on the White Horse	6:1-2
The Rider on the Red Horse	6:3-4
The Rider on the Black Horse	6:5-6
The Rider on the Pale Green Horse	6:7-8
The Martyrs under the Altar	6:9-11
The Great Earthquake	6:12-17

THE TWO MULTITUDES   7:1-17

144,000	7:1-8
Great Multitude	7:9-17

THE TRUMPETS   8:1–9:20

The Seventh Seal	8:1-5
Hail and Fire Mixed with Blood	8:6-7
The Bloody Sea	8:8-9
The Bitter Waters	8:10-11
Dark Heavenly Bodies	8:12
The Eagle in Midheaven	8:13
The Demonic Locusts	9:1-12
The Satanic Attack	9:13-21

THE WITNESS OF THE FAITHFUL   10:1–11:19

The Announcement of the Little Scroll	10:1-3a
The Seven Thunders	10:3b-7
The Eating of the Little Scroll	10:8-11
The Measuring of the Temple	11:1-2
The Two Witnesses	11:3-14
The Seventh Trumpet	11:15-19

THE WOMAN AND THE DRAGON   12:1-18

The Birth of Christ	12:1-6
The War in Heaven	12:7-12
The Rest of the Woman's Offspring	12:13-18

THE TWO BEASTS   13:1-18

The Beast from the Sea	13:1-10
The Beast from the Earth	13:11-18

INTERLUDE OF ENCOURAGEMENT   14:1-20

The Lamb and the 144,000	14:1-5
Three Angelic Voices	14:6-13
The Harvest and the Wine Press	14:14-20

THE SEVEN BOWLS OF GOD'S WRATH   15:1–16:21

The Song of Moses	15:1-4
The Tent of Witness	15:5-8
The Seven Bowls	16:1
The Sores	16:2
The Sea into Blood	16:3
The Rivers into Blood	16:4
Interlude of the Angel of Waters	16:5-7
The Scorching Sun	16:8-9
The Agonizing Darkness	16:10-11
The Drying of the Euphrates	16:12-16
The Earthquake and Hail	16:17-21

THE GREAT WHORE   17:1-18

The Whore on the Scarlet Beast	17:1-6
The Interpretation of the Whore and Beast	17:7-18

THE FALL OF BABYLON   18:1-24

The Announcement of Babylon's Fall	18:1-3
The Faithful Called to Come Out of Babylon	18:4-8

The Laments over Babylon   18:9-20
The Disappearance of Babylon   18:21-24

THE TWO SUPPERS   19:1-21

Praise for Judgment of the Great Whore   19:1-5
The Marriage Supper of the Lamb   19:6-10
The Rider on the White Horse   19:11-16
The Supper of God   19:17-18
The Destruction of the Beasts   19:19-21

THE MILLENNIAL KINGDOM   20:1-15

The Binding of Satan   20:1-3
The Millennium   20:4-6
The Release of Satan   20:7-10
The Great White Throne   20:11-15

THE HEAVENLY CITY   21:1–22:21

The New Heaven and the New Earth   21:1-8
The New Jerusalem   21:9-27
The Presence of God   22:1-5
Worship God!   22:6-11
Christ Is Coming Soon!   22:12-17
Stern Warning   22:18-19
Come, Lord Jesus   22:20-21

Essays

ANABAPTIST INTERPRETATION OF REVELATION Anabaptist eschatology has reflected the beliefs of the evangelical church in general. Yet the uniqueness of the Anabaptist interpretation of Revelation lies in its martyr theology (see Correll, 1956:2.247). The great battle between God and the forces of Satan is being fought in this world by martyrs.

Many of the early Anabaptists interpreted the symbols of Revelation literally, applying them to Catholic and Protestant church leadership. In South Germany, Michael Sattler identified the seven heads and ten horns of the beast with the Roman church hierarchy. In Zurich, Anabaptists identified Zwingli with the red dragon of Revelation (Clasen, 1972:119). They believed that the suffering of the sixteenth century was evidence that they were in the last days. Thomas Müntzer predicted that the second coming would occur on Pentecost, 1528 (Klaassen, 1981:316-17), and during the time of the German Peasant's War in 1526, Hans Hut predicted: "The final and most terrible times of this world are upon us" (quoted in Liechty, 1994:64). Other Anabaptist leaders rejected such speculations. Balthasar Hubmaier said:

> Concerning this I very strongly opposed Hans Hut and his followers when they hoodwinked the simple people by claiming a definite time for the last day, namely next Pentecost. They convinced them to sell their property and leave wife and child, house and field behind, and are now without means of support. Thus the poor people were convinced to follow him by a seductive error which arose out of ignorance of Scripture. (Quoted in Klaassen, 1981:324)

During the sixteenth century, Anabaptist thinking separated into violent and quiet eschatology (Littell, 1958:102-3). Following Joachim of Fiore, Melchior Hoffman divided history into three parts and predicted that the end would come in 1536. He taught that in 1533 the godless of Strasbourg would be massacred and the 144,000 followers of Hoffman would go out to witness

Christ's return (Clasen, 1972:119). All of this would come about, not by human force, but by divine intervention (Krahn, 1981:100). He affirmed the city of Münster to be the millennial commonwealth; and one of his successors, Jan of Leyden, proclaimed himself to be the Davidic Messiah (Rowland, 1998:540). Bernhard Rothmann called Münster the center of the kingdom and advocated violent overthrow of the enemy: "They will make plowshares and hoes into swords and spears. They shall choose a captain, fly the flag, and blow the trumpet. They will incite an obstinate and merciless people against Babylon" (quoted in Klaassen, 1981:335). By the end of the sixteenth century, only a few made eschatological predictions and violent eschatology faded out.

Most Anabaptists accept what has been called quiet eschatology. Menno Simons and Dirk Philips represent this approach to Revelation. Menno clearly identified the antichrist with the Roman church (Klaassen, 1981:342). Yet he saw the kingdom of God as spiritual (Keeney, 1968:180). He believed, on the basis of scripture rather than world events, that Christ would come from outside history to judge the world and that resurrection is personal like the resurrection of Jesus (185, 186). This view was quite prevalent in Anabaptist circles for two centuries.

However, there were persons that, although not violent, expected a literal millennial reign of Christ on this earth. For example, in the 1890s Claas Epp Jr., a Russian Mennonite farmer and preacher, believed that the tribulation was imminent and would be particularly threatening to Mennonites' pacifistic exemption from the military. Epp led six hundred Mennonites from the Volga River area of Southern Russia hoping to find refuge in Turkestan and to meet the Lord there in 1889. Disappointed in that expectation, some found their way to North America (Belk, 1976). In the late nineteenth century, churches in the Anabaptist tradition rejected even more the literalist approach to Revelation. Perhaps through accommodation with the ideas of the mainline church, the second coming, resurrection, and judgment were given more symbolic interpretations. Nevertheless, the tragedies of the twentieth century (e.g., world wars, economic depression, arms race) led to a revival of evangelical eschatology. Until 1960, premillennialism and dispensationalism received increasing emphasis among Anabaptist-related churches (Correll 1956:2:248). Since then these eschatological views have waned; eschatological hope is more broadly conceived, emphasizing fulfillment now-in-Christ, but consummation yet-to-come.

APOCALYPTIC LITERATURE The most accepted definition of apocalyptic literature at present is:

> "Apocalypse" is a genre of revelatory literature with a narrative framework, in which a revelation is mediated by an otherworldly being to a human recipient, disclosing a transcendent reality which is both temporal, insofar as it envisages eschatological salvation, and spatial insofar as it involves another, supernatural world. (J. J. Collins, 1979:9)

Within apocalyptic literature, the manner of revelation is through visions, epiphanies, otherworldly journeys, angel interpreters, and secret books; the recipient receives revelation from a venerable person, usually identified pseudonymously as from the other world, through discourse or dialogue; the content of revelation includes eschatological predictions about the final outcome of human history, a temporal review of history, or a spatial journey into other worlds (see Collins, 1979:5-18, for an expanded treatment of these characteristics and the typology that follows).

Based on these characteristics, a paradigm of types and subtypes of apocalyptic literature has been constructed. There are two types—those with symbolic visions interested in primordial events or historical development (I), and those with otherworldly journeys interested in cosmological speculation about eschatological persecution and judgment (II). Three subtypes have also been delineated—those that include a review of history through recollection or prophecy after the fact (a); those that include cosmic or political eschatological transformation with no review of history (b); and those that include only individual eschatology, personal resurrection, judgment of the dead, and otherworldly regions and beings with no review of history or cosmic transformation (c).

How does the Book of Revelation fit into this typology of apocalyptic? Revelation comes through symbolic visions of otherworldly beings, Christ and angels, but with only minimal reference to otherworldly journeys. Its content is primarily eschatological because it speaks of cosmic transformation, resurrection, and personal afterlife but has no complex review of history. Therefore, Revelation is categorized best as IIb, including symbolic visions with a concern for cosmic eschatology, although its somewhat less obvious concern for individual eschatology gives it some of the flavor of the category IIc.

ASTRAL PROPHECY Malina and Pilch (2000) contend that the visions of Revelation have their roots in the Babylonian knowledge of astrology that was embedded in the social context of the Mediterranean world (2, 23). Like his fellow astral prophet "brothers" and "sisters" (31), John travels to the sky through "altered states of consciousness" to observe and reveal "celestial secrets" (3-4, 37, 41-44, 70, 216). God the Almighty, who controls the cosmos from the throne constellation "above the vault of the fixed stars" (34, 51, 72), communicates with the earth through such things as thunder (38) and the provision of manna from the sky (56). Angels are "sky servants" who carry out divine tasks (31), and the spirits are "non-visible celestial entities" that personify the power of the sky (34). The lamb is the constellation Aries (63, 88-89, 94), which has a twisted neck, implying that it too has been slaughtered (93). The numbers of Revelation have connections with zodiacal imagery, e.g., seven planets, twelve signs of the zodiac (14-19). The seven golden lampstands are planets (38, 40); the removal of a lampstand would upset the stability of the cosmology (52). The son of man is a constellation: the "sevenstarred Bear [constellation is] in his right hand" (46), and the sword coming from his mouth makes his idenfication likely either Perseus or Orion (38-39). The twenty-four elders or "decans" are "celestial beings on astral thrones marking off twenty-four segments of the horizon" and "embracing the whole cosmos in the course of one night and one day" (73, 83-35). The four living creatures are "the constellations along the celestial equator" which "circumscribed the whole vault of the sky": Leo (lion), Taurus (bull), Scorpio (human face), and Pegasus (the flying eagle) (76-77, 85-86). The seven torches of fire are the seven stars near the pole that make up the constellation Ursa Major (76, 96). Satan is the sky servant before God's throne, who was driven to the earth by God's forces led by the "chief sky servant Michael" (54-55). The morning star is Venus (56, 59, 231). The hymns of Revelation are the music that fills the cosmos (96-97, 180-81). The sky temple descends as the New Jerusalem to earth at the place of the destroyed earthly Jerusalem (70). The first four seal judgments are brought by comet horses: the white horse is Jupiter, the red horse is Mars, the black horse is Mercury, and the pale green horse is Venus (100-101; see also 106-11). In the fifth seal, the sun becomes black and the moon the color of blood (101), and in the sixth seal the sun and moon darken and the stars fall from the sky, which rolls up like a scroll, indicating that "God has nothing more to say" (102-3). The Altar in heaven is a constellation in the Milky Way (102, 112). The number 144,000 is related to the twelve signs of the Zodiac (117), and their "white robes are sky garments" (118). The trumpets and bowls are comets that emanate from the Altar constellation with Sagittarius and the Centaur on either side (106, 128). The locusts resemble ancient pictures of a centaur constellation (131), and the abyss is located in the southern sky (134, 233). The sky referent for the Euphrates is the River of Orion (138). The mother of the Messiah corresponds to the constellation of the Pregnant Woman (155). The dragon Scorpio swept a third of the stars from the southern sky, which is "generally devoid of stars" and a "region known for falling stars" (156-57). The war in heaven between Michael and the dragon is a sky war between Orion and Scorpio (159-66). The beast from the sea is the constellation Cetus, "the traditional Sea-monster" (169, 174), and the beast from the land is a "constellation in the southern sky called simply 'the beast'" (172, 176). The seven kings are the planets (212). The "patron and protector" of Babylon was known to be Aphrodite/Venus (203). The bride is related to Venus, and the marriage of the Lamb corresponds to the constellation named "The Wedding of the Gods" (226-27, 251-53). Gog and Magog have connections with the dark planets Ascender and Descender (234-37).

Although treating Revelation as an astral prophecy may help to explain many allusions that lie behind the text, it is difficult to see astrology as the primary referent to the symbols in the book. The primary meanings of the symbols are more likely found in the social/political world of John and the spiritual/heavenly world where God resides.

AUTHORSHIP OF REVELATION Revelation itself communicates several important things about its author. First, the author's name is John (1:1, 4, 9; 22:8). Given this claim, Revelation is unusual, and perhaps even unique, among apocalypses. With the possible exception of Daniel (see Lederach, *BCBC*, 1994, on Daniel), all Jewish-Christian apocalypses were written under false names *[Essay: Pseudonymity]*.

Second, the author was clearly a Palestinian Jew. Hebrew seems to be his native language; he writes in a very Hebraic form of Greek. For example, nearly three-fourths of the sentences in Revelation begin with "and" *(kai)*, a common Hebraic practice (Aune, 1997:146). Moreover, he is steeped in the Hebrew scriptures. There are more allusions to the Old Testament in Revelation than in any other New Testament book. About 278 of the 404 verses in Revelation have allusions to the Old Testament (Swete, 1908:cxl; see also Westcott and Hort, 1988:184-88 (Appendix); R. H. Charles, 1920:1.lxviii-lxxxii). Yet there are no direct quotations (cf. Fekkes 1994:62, 70). Revelation's author was also familiar with extra-biblical Jewish literature—The Wisdom of Solomon, 2 Esdras, 1 and 2 Enoch, 2 Baruch, the Testaments of the Twelve Patriarchs, the Sibylline Oracles, and the Greek Septuagint, and Aramaic Targums (Sweet, 1990:40). All this points to a person who was intimately familiar with the writings of the Hebrew tradition—probably a Palestinian Jew.

Third, the author was most likely a Christian who lived in Asia near the churches addressed because of the intimate knowledge about them revealed in Revelation (see Notes on chs. 2–3). Clement of Alexandria speaks of John's ministry in Ephesus and the surrounding area:

> Listen to a tale, which is not a tale but a narrative, handed down and committed to the custody of memory, about the Apostle John. For when, on the tyrant's death, he returned to Ephesus from the isle of Patmos, he went away, being invited, to the contiguous territories of the nations, here to appoint bishops, there to set in order whole churches, there to ordain such as were marked out by the spirit. (*Who Is the Rich Man That Shall Be Saved?* 42)

Moreover, Revelation shows knowledge of other Christian writings. The affinities with other Johannine writings are impressive; and there are clear connections with several of the Pauline Epistles, especially 1 Corinthians, which was written from Ephesus; Ephesians; Colossians, written to Christians in a city close to Laodicea; and 2 Thessalonians (Sweet, 1990:40; for the argument that the author need not have been a Jewish Christian, see MacKenzie, 1997).

Fourth, the author calls himself a prophet (10:11; 19:10; 22:6, 7, 9, 10, 18, 19). As a prophet, he had a message from God to communicate to his fellow Christians. He was influenced by the classical Hebrew prophets, but he wrote in the context of Christian prophets like the Nicolaitans (2:6, 15).

If the statement that the author's name is John is taken seriously, the identity of this John must be determined. Several persons named John are mentioned in the Bible. Although John the Baptist was beheaded in A.D. 28-29, Ford claims that Revelation is a production of John the Baptist and the Baptist community. She believes that chapters 4-11 originated with John the Baptist himself, that most of chapters 12-22 were written by a disciple of the Baptist, and that chapters 1-3 and a few other passages were from a Jewish-Christian redactor (1975:28-37; see also T. C. Smith, 1997:93-95). The limited acceptance of this impressively argued but unconvincing thesis makes refutation of it here seem unnecessary. John Mark, whom tradition says wrote the Gospel of Mark under the direction of Simon Peter, is also unlikely to be the author of Revelation. Dionysius considers and rejects this possibility (Eusebius, *Eccl. Hist.* 7.25). The styles of Revelation and Mark show little resemblance, and there is no tradition that connects John Mark with exile to Patmos. John, the father of Simon Peter would certainly have died long before the end of the first century, and there is no evidence to connect John, the member of the Sanhedrin mentioned in Acts 4:6, with Revelation.

This leaves John the son of Zebedee, the disciple of Jesus, among those mentioned in the Christian scriptures, as the most likely candidate for the authorship of Revelation. Barker argues that, although the earliest form of Revelation may have been the Book of the Lord mentioned in Isaiah 34:16, and other early forms that have their source in the temple liturgy interwoven with pre-Christian and Christian prophetic interpretations—some from Jesus himself—its final form is from the Beloved Disciple, who was a follower of

John the Baptist, was the one known later as the elder, and perhaps was a high priest and certainly a prophet, but who may or may not have been the son of Zebedee (2000:10, 57, 64, 67, 72, 76, 78-79, 95, 99, 124, 289).

The major argument in favor of the authorship of John, the disciple, is rooted in tradition. The earliest witness is found only about forty years after Revelation was written in Justin Martyr, who asserts that Revelation was written by "John, one of the apostles of Christ, who prophesied by a revelation that was made to him" (*Dialogue with Trypho,* 81). That Justin lived in Ephesus and spent his youth in Smyrna gives his witness even more credence. At the turn of the second century, Irenaeus, who claims to have heard Polycarp, the martyr from his home town of Smyrna, speak of conversations with John (Eusebius, *Eccl. Hist.* 5.20), says that John, the disciple of the Lord, was the author of Revelation (*Adv. Haer.,* 3.11.1, 4.20.11, 5.26.1, 5.35.2). Other church fathers also give their support to this thesis—Clement of Alexandria (*Who Is the Rich Man Who Shall Be Saved?* 42; *Miscellanies* 6.13), Hippolytus (*de Ant.* 36), Tertullian (*Against Marcion* 3.14.24), Origen (*Commentary on John* 1:22, 5:3; see also Eusebius, *Eccl. Hist.* 6.25; see T. C. Smith, 1997:91 for traditions about John in Ephesus). Indeed, the idea that Revelation was written by John, the disciple of Jesus, was generally accepted by the church until the rise of modern historical-critical scholarship.

Yet there have been some compelling arguments against the traditional view of authorship. As early as the end of the second century, the Alogi believed Revelation to have been written by Cerinthus, a Gnostic who taught that the coming of Jesus would introduce a thousand-year period of sensuous pleasure before the end. The argument that the Gospel of John and Revelation were not written by the same person was made as early as the third century by Dionysius, the bishop of Alexandria. His symbolic method of interpretation contrasted to the literal reign of Christ found by some in Revelation. He pointed out that there were two monuments to persons named John in Ephesus and believed that Revelation may have been written by one referred to as John the Elder rather than John the apostle. By raising questions about authorship, he also raised doubts about the authority of Revelation, saying that Revelation includes "barbarous idioms" and "solecisms" (Eusebius, *Eccl. Hist.* 7.25). Indeed, Revelation's authority was disputed until it was affirmed to be sacred literature in A.D. 367 by Athanasius in his Easter letter (Yarbro Collins, 1984:27-28). Even then it was not universally accepted in the Eastern Churches until the sixth century.

Caird refutes the appeal to tradition in support of John's authorship, contending that second-century traditions about the apostles are clearly unreliable (1966:4). Irenaeus seemed to confuse James, the apostle, and James, the brother of Jesus (*Adv. Haer.* 3.12.14-15); and Polycrates, the bishop of Ephesus, misidentified the two Philips, the apostle and the evangelist (Eusebius, *Eccl. Hist.* 3.31). The latter mistake was also made by Papias, the bishop of Hierapolis, the city where Philip lived when he died (Eusebius, *Eccl. Hist.* 3.39). Caird's point is that tradition regarding which John wrote Revelation cannot be taken with complete confidence.

Indeed, there are other traditions that argue against authorship by John the disciple. Dionysius affirmed that Revelation was written by another John, and Papias contended that the author was John the elder (Eusebius, *Eccl. Hist.* 3:39; 7.25). There is also a tradition, considered by a number of later writers to be from Papias in the early second century, that John was martyred before A.D. 70 (R. H. Charles, 1920:1.xxxviii, xlv-l). There is so much conflicting opinion about this tradition that it cannot be taken too seriously. In general, it must be concluded that tradition regarding the authorship of Revelation is ambiguous.

Perhaps the most convincing argument against authorship by John the disciple is the great difference between the language and diction of Revelation and the Gospel of John (see R. H. Charles, 1920:1.xxix-xxxii; Beasley-Murray, 1974:34). The Gospel is written in excellent Greek; Revelation is composed with an abundance of Hebraic idioms. On the basis of these Hebraisms and the fact that more than half of Revelation's sentences follow the Hebrew practice of begining with "and" *(kai),* Barker argues for a Hebrew or Aramaic original (2000:73). Although the terminology of Revelation differs from the Gospel of John, there are many common terms (Schüssler Fiorenza, 1985:93-101; Beale, 1999:35) and some similarity of message (Rowland, 1998:515-17). Yet the relatively new Greek student can readily see the linguistic difference between the two books by attempting to read them in the original language. The Gospel reads quite easily, with a minimum of unfamiliar words; Revelation is difficult, with many unfamiliar words. The argument is that the same person could not have written both the Fourth Gospel and Revelation.

Another compelling argument that Revelation was not written by John the son of Zebedee is that the author does not appear to be an apostle. It has already been noted that he calls himself a prophet. If he were an apostle, even one of the Twelve, he would have been likely to mention this to give authority to his writing, although Worth maintains that the credentials of a prophet would be more important than an apostle for the author of a book like Revelation (1999:88). In any case, when describing the inscription on the foundations of the New Jerusalem, he refers to the apostles in a strange way if he is one of them (21:11-14).

Finally, there is a difference in the theology of salvation described in the Fourth Gospel and in Revelation. The Gospel stresses salvation being actualized in the present (John 4:13-14; 6:35-40; 10:10); Revelation emphasizes the future aspect (Rev. 21:1–22:5). Furthermore, in the Gospel salvation occurs through belief and trust (John 1:12-13; 3:16-18; 14:1-3); in Revelation it is tied to perseverance and overcoming the forces of evil (Rev. 7:9-17; 12:10-12).

As a result of these arguments questioning the authorship of Revelation by John the disciple, several possible theories have been suggested. First, it may be that Revelation was written by an unknown person and, at least implicitly, attributed to John the disciple *[Essay: Pseudonymity].* According to Epiphanius, the Montanists of the second century were the first to propose this theory in an attempt to discredit Revelation as a false writing by attributing it to the heretic Cerinthus rather than to the apostle John *(Panarion,* 51.3.3-6). Eusebius calls Cerinthus a heretic who expected a literal reign of Christ on this earth *(Eccl. Hist.* 3.28). Irenaeus says that Cerinthus lived with John in Ephesus *(Adv. Haer.* 3.3.4). Some accept the hypothesis first proposed by Eusebius that the author was John the Elder *(Eccl. Hist.* 3.39), and R. H. Charles thinks that the book was written by a Palestinian Jew named John the prophet, who moved to Asia Minor (1920:1.xxxviii-xxxix).

Another theory of authorship is that the difference in style between the Gospel and Revelation is because John the son of Zebedee wrote Revelation in A.D. 67-68 during the reign of Nero and the Gospel some thirty years later during the reign of Domitian at the end of the century. The point is that in the interim he developed a better Greek style. However, on the basis of the argument made below in the essay on the Dating of Revelation, it is more likely that Revelation was written at the end of the century.

A related theory is that John the disciple developed one style for the Gospel and another for Revelation. Kraft believes that the author created a liturgical style reminiscent of the Psalms but not spoken anywhere (1974:16). Yet the language of Revelation is not so much a different style of Greek as the language of a person who "while he writes in Greek, he thinks in Hebrew" (R. H. Charles, 1920:1.cxliii).

Perhaps the most compelling theory, which keeps the two books closely tied to John the disciple and yet accounts for the differences, is that Revelation was written in John's own hand but that the Gospel was transcribed by a student of John (see Brown, 1979, and Culpepper, 1975, on the Johannine school; and Schüssler Fiorenza, 1985:85-113, for the impact of the Johannine school upon the Gospel and Revelation of John and for a variation on this theory that attributes the authorship of Revelation to a member of the Johannine school). The use of scribes was quite common, and appeal to this practice maintains that the ideas in both books come from John, who was a disciple of Christ.

Regarding the unity of Revelation, it has been argued that the book is a composite work because the extensive use of Semitic words indicates a Hebrew source, the repetition of ideas and symbols indicate a combining of sources, and the recurring hymns come from a Hebrew liturgy. It is more likely that the Semitisms reflect an author who thought in Hebrew and wrote in Greek, that the repetitions are due to a stylistic tendency in apocalyptic literature, and that the common vocabulary of the hymns and the discourses indicates that the former were created by the author. Therefore, although Revelation seems clearly to have been influenced by the Hebrew scriptures, Jewish apocalyptic literature, and Babylonian, Persian, and Greek mythology, it is most likely a unity produced at one time by one author (see Aune, 1997:cvii-cxxxiv for a complete treatment of this issue).

CANONICITY AND ACCEPTANCE OF REVELATION Evidence of the acceptance of the Book of Revelation in the Western church comes quite early. In Rome in A.D. 150, Justin Martyr names the book and its author, the apostle John (*Dialogue with Trypho* 81). In A.D. 170, the Muratorian Canon says that the Apocalypse of John was universally recognized in Rome (Swete, 1908:cx). Irenaeus (*Adv. Haer.* 3.11.1; 4.20.11; 5.35.2), Tertullian (*Against Marcion* 3.14.3), Hippolytus (*de Ant.* 36), Clement of Alexandria (*Who Is the Rich Man Who Shall Be Saved?* 42; *Miscellanies* 6.106-7), and Origen (*Commentary on John* 5.3) accept Revelation as scripture. In the fourth century, Eusebius says that some accept it as canonical, but he and others refer to it as a questioned book (*Eccl. Hist.* 4.26). His attitude may have been influenced by the use of the book by millenarians, who believed in a literal reign of Christ on the earth. Overall, though, Revelation was accepted early in the West. Evidence of this is found in the words of St. Jerome: "The Apocalypse of John has as many secrets as words. I am saying less than the book deserves. It is beyond all praise; for multiple meanings lie hidden in each single word" (*Letter* 53.9; translated in Caird, 1966:2).

To the church in the East, Revelation was unknown for four centuries. It was not included in the Peshitto Version of the New Testament in the fifth century. Yet in the fourth century, Athanasius recognized Revelation, and the Council of Carthage listed it as canonical. The Third Council of Constantinople in the seventh century accepted it as part of the scripture of the Eastern church. Nevertheless, the text and imagery of Revelation is absent from the hymns and liturgy of the Syrian church throughout its history. Therefore, Revelation was not accepted as readily in the Eastern church tradition (Gwynn, 1897:c-civ; R. H. Charles, 1920:1.cii; Beckwith, 1919:341-43; Swete, 1908:cxvi-cxvii).

During the time of the Reformation, Revelation came into question in the West. Luther added the Epistle of James and the books following in an appendix to his commentary but separated them from the rest of the canon. He rejected Revelation because of what he called the author's hubris and because he thought it obscured Christ for the ordinary believer. Indeed, in his 1522 *Preface to the Revelation of Saint John,* Luther said: "My spirit cannot accommodate itself to this book. For me this is reason not to think highly of it: Christ is neither taught nor known in it" (*Luther's Works* 35:399). Zwingli could not accept Revelation because its considerable use of angels encouraged what he considered an immature, pious mysticism, and its liturgical format was too close to the Catholic mass. He says: "With the *Apocalypse,* we have no concern, for it is not a biblical book .... I can, if I so will, reject its testimonies" (quoted in Barclay, 1960:1.1). Calvin did not voice an opinion on Revelation; he did quote from it, but his commentaries exclude it.

So, there have been diverse attitudes toward Revelation in the history of the church. No other book in the Bible has aroused such love and such hatred. The same is true today. On the one hand, in Umberto Eco's novel *The Name of the Rose,* a monk, while attempting to find out who is responsible for a series of murders occurring in a monastery, is asked whether or not the Book of Revelation might have the solution to the murders. He responds: "The Book of John offers the key to everything!" (1980:303). On the other hand, George Bernard Shaw, in his *The Adventure of the Black Girl in Search for God,* calls Revelation "a curious record of the visions of a drug addict which was absurdly admitted to the canon under the title of Revelation" (1933:93).

Indeed, Revelation has been loved and hated by Christians. It has served as a paradise for fanatics who give their own peculiar interpretation to the symbols of the text. Yet it has also been rejected by many Christians as either confusing or unintelligible. Caird sums up the situation well when he says: "In modern times scores of commentaries have been written on it so diverse as to make the reader wonder whether they are discussing the same book" (1966:2).

CHARACTERISTICS OF APOCALYPTIC LITERATURE In order to begin to understand how to interpret Revelation, it is important to comprehend the nature of apocalyptic literature. First, the genre of apocalyptic is generated by social and historical circumstances. Revelation has 82 of the 250 occurrences of the word *earth (gē)* in the New Testament, and therefore is not otherworldly but rooted in earthly circumstances (Boring, 1986:268). Charlesworth thinks that Revelation grows out of the experience of "the oppressed and persecuted" (1987:21). To its author, the world is so evil that God must intervene. The Hebrew prophets thought that the present world could be reformed, but the apocalyptists knew that the world was so evil that it could only be redeemed by the intervention of God. So Revelation shares a dualistic division between this present evil world and the future blessed kingdom of God.

Therefore, the affirmation that apocalyptists make in times of crisis is that Christians are to remain faithful. In fact, Efird argues that the reason the good are persecuted is because they are good. Since the world is now dominated by evil, the good can expect to be mistreated. Faithfulness, not unfaithfulness, will be persecuted. When evil has run its course, God will intervene, destroy the evil one, and restore the good to power (1989:21-23). Yet Revelation never counsels the Christian to take up arms against the persecutor. The message of apocalyptic literature is to remain faithful in historical and political evil circumstances.

Second, apocalyptic literature is dominated by allusions to Hebrew, Babylonian, Persian, and Hellenistic literature. It was mentioned in the section on authorship that Revelation alludes often to the Hebrew scriptures. Its affinities with the Babylonian and Persian mythologies and with the Homeric epics should also be recognized.

Third, the language of apocalyptic literature is poetic, metaphoric, and symbolic. The words *like* or *as (hōs)* and *something like* or *as if (homoios)* occur often in Revelation (1:10; 1:13, 14; 4:6-7; 5:6; 6:6); and metaphorical language is also employed (1:12; 5:6). The book of Revelation is more an inspired picture book than a philosophical treatise.

Fourth, the tone of apocalyptic literature is distinctive—at the same time optimistic and pessimistic. Revelation is pessimistic about the present age but optimistic about the age to come when God's redemption in Christ will be fully actualized.

Fifth, apocalyptic emphasizes transcendence—otherworldly beings and regions. Revelation portrays the intervention of angels and demons as messengers of God and Satan.

CHRISTOLOGY OF REVELATION Revelation has a wealth of titles for Christ: faithful witness, firstborn of the dead, ruler of the kings of the earth (1:5); Alpha and Omega (1:8; 21:6; 22:13); who walks among the seven golden lampstands (1:13; 2:1); Son of Man (1:13; 14:14); who has eyes like a flame of fire (1:14; 2:18); whose feet are like burnished bronze (1:15; 2:18); one who holds the seven stars (1:16; 2:1); who has the sharp two-edged sword (1:16; 2:12); who has the seven spirits of God and the seven stars (1:16; 3:1); first and last (1:17; 2:8; 22:13); who was dead and came to life (2:8); Son of God (2:18), holy one, true one, one who holds the key of David, who opens and no one will shut, who shuts and no one opens (3:7); Amen, faithful and true witness, origin of God's creation (3:14); lion of the tribe of Judah, root of David (5:5; 22:16); Lamb (5:6, 8, 12, 13; 6:1, 16; 7:9, 10, 14, 17; 12:11; 13:8; 14:1, 4, 10; 15:3; 17:14; 19:7, 9; 21:14, 22, 23; 22:1, 3); King of Kings, Lord of Lords (17:14; 19:16); faithful and true (19:11); the beginning and the end (21:6; 22:13); and so forth (see Johns, 1998:189-93, for a discussion of the political overtones of these titles and for the case that Revelation is "a subversive resistance manual"; Weaver, 1994a:279-81; 2001:20-33, 73-74, for a treatment of the Christus Victor theme in Revelation; and Slater, 1999, for consideration of the christological images Son of Man, Lamb, and Divine Warrior).

Indeed, Revelation has the highest Christology in the New Testament (see Beasley-Murray 1947:23-29). John places Christ on par with God; the two names are used synonymously (3:21; 6:16; 7:9, 10, 17; 14:1; 21:22, 23; 22:1, 3). As a Jew, John was an inflexible monotheist; placing Christ on par with God shows Christ's unique position and marks the beginning of Trinitarianism. John also adds the Holy Spirit to this Godhead at least by implication (1:4-5; 19:10; 22:17). Thus, John lays the basis, in a rudimentary form, for future formulations of the doctrine of the Trinity.

COMPOSITION OF REVELATION Revelation says that John recorded visions he saw on the Lord's day. It is best to believe that God gave the visions to John and then, through the Holy Spirit, guided their recording in the words of the text. It seems most likely that the transcription of the visions into words was done immediately, rather than after John's return to Ephesus. Because some of the visionary descriptions are difficult to imagine, Christ with "eyes ... like a flame of fire" and "from his mouth ... a sharp, two-edged sword," Boring may be correct to say: "In their present form the visions are literary compositions based on John's [Lord's day] visionary experience, not merely descriptive reports of what he 'actually' saw and heard" (1989:27).

DATING OF REVELATION A minority of scholars have suggested a date for the writing of Revelation during the time of Nero or immediately thereafter (Robinson 1976:221-53; Wilson, 1993:587-605; Barker 2000:xi). A case for this date (A.D. 60s) can be made based on internal evidence. Revelation 11:1-2 describes a measuring of the temple, which may presuppose a time when the temple was still standing, and the destruction of the city by a great earthquake in 11:13 does not reflect how the city actually fell; both passages thus seem to pre-date the historic destruction of Jerusalem in A.D. 70. Moreover, the number 666 in chapter 13 may be a designation for Nero. In addition, the chronology in the list of kings in 17:9-11 may imply that Revelation was written shortly after the death of Nero (see Barker, 2000, for a comprehensive treatment of Revelation's symbols in the context of the time of the Roman occupation and destruction of Jerusalem and its temple in A.D. 70). Turning to external evidence, the reign of Nero is the only time during the first century when widespread persecution of Christians has been clearly documented *[Essay: Persecution during Nero's Reign]*. Furthermore, Clement of Alexandria speaks of John, after returning from Patmos, chasing a young man, an incredible feat for a man in the advanced stage of life demanded by a date at the turn of the first century (*Who Is the Rich Man That Shall Be Saved?* 42). Indeed, Jerome interprets a tradition from Tertullian to mean that John died with Peter and Paul in Rome under Nero's persecution (*Against Jovinian* 1.26).

Yet these arguments are not convincing evidence for the early date. Both the temple and the rule of Nero could have been recalled in a vision some years after each had ceased to exist in the objective world. Although the material in Revelation does not focus on one date, it seems that much of its imagery most naturally finds referents during the reign of Domitian. Although Aune compromises by affirming that the first edition of Revelation comes from Nero's time and the final one from at least as late as the reign of Domitian and probably Trajan (1997:lviii), the later date of about A.D. 95-96 has been accepted by most scholars.

External evidence witnesses to the later date. In the second century, Irenaeus said: "The apocalyptic vision ... was seen no very long time since, but almost in our day, towards the end of Domitian's reign" (*Adv. Haer.* 5.30.3, see also 2.22.5, 3.3.4). In the third century, Victorinus affirmed: "When John said these things, he was in the island of Patmos, condemned to the labour of the mines by Caesar Domitian" (*Commentary on the Apocalypse of the Blessed John* 10.11, see also 17.10); and Eusebius believed that John was banished to the island of Patmos during the rule of Domitian (*Eccl. Hist.* 3.18, see also 3.20, 3.23). This tradition has been accepted throughout most of church history.

Turning to internal evidence, the attitude toward Rome reflected in the book points to a later date. Other New Testament books reflect the positive attitude toward Rome evidenced in the middle of the first century. In Acts, the Roman officials are presented as protecting Christians from persecution (16:35-40; 18:12-17; 22:22-30; 23:12-35; 25:10-11). Both Paul and Peter say that Christians should be subject to Roman rulers (Rom. 13:1-7; 1 Pet. 2:13-17). Yet the picture of Rome presented in Revelation is quite different. She is Babylon, the great persecutor of the people of God (Rev. 17-18). It is therefore likely that Revelation was written later than the writings of Luke, Paul, and Peter, when the attitude toward the Roman government had worsened.

Another argument for the later date for Revelation grows out of the use of Babylon as a reference for Rome. Rome and Babylon were the two forces that destroyed the temple (Yarbro Collins, 1984:57-58). Destruction of the place of worship was the grossest of offenses committed against the people of Israel. As a result of the temple's destruction in 586 B.C., Babylon became a name symbolic of evil in the Jewish tradition (2 Esd. 11-13; 2 Bar. 1-12; Sib. Or. 5:434-48). In Revelation, the city of Rome is symbolized in the word *Babylon,* probably because Rome also destroyed the temple in A.D. 70. Therefore, Revelation could not have been written during the reign of Nero because the temple had not yet been destroyed.

The spiritual state of the seven churches addressed in Revelation also argues for a date sometime after their conversion under Paul in the fifties. Revelation says that false teachings of the Nicolaitans, Balaam, and Jezebel have grown up in the churches. The Asian Christians are portrayed as in a state of decline from their original conversion as a result of the ministry of Paul in Ephesus. Indeed, there is no reference, directly or indirectly, to Paul or his ministry. Moreover, Paul says that all of the Christians in Asia have turned against him (2 Tim. 1:15). Although the authorship and date of this declaration from the Pastoral epistles is in question, it appears clear that some time has elapsed since the conversion of the Asian Christians in the A.D. 50s. Furthermore, according to Polycarp, the bishop of Smyrna in the early second century, the church in that city did not exist until after Paul's ministry (*Letter to the Philippians* 11); and Laodicea, which is described as rich, was completely destroyed by an earthquake in A.D. 60-61 (Mounce, 1977:35). Certainly, the book of Revelation could not have been written much before the end of the first century.

Thus, it can be concluded that the best date for the writing of Revelation is during the reign of Domitian about A.D. 95-96. There is, however, considerable debate regarding the actual extent of Domitian's persecution *[Essay: Persecution during Domitian's Reign]*. Although persecution of Christians at this time may have been overstated, it seems indisputable that the poor and powerless experienced potential—and, to some extent, actual—persecution during the time of the writing of Revelation *[Essay: Persecution in Revelation]*. It is to those persons that Revelation is addressed.

DISPENSATIONALISM A scheme of interpreting the Bible based on the teachings of Scofield, Lindsey, Pentecost, Walvoord, and others who divide history into seven dispensations. As it relates to eschatology, it is traditionally a futurist position that accepts the premillennial scheme but believes that a rapture will remove Christians from the earth before the great tribulation, which will literally come on the earth. Because Christians are no longer present, the "saints" on earth during Revelation's great tribulation are those converted by Jewish witnesses after the rapture. Thus, dispensational eschatology is synonymous with the pretribulational, premillennial return of Christ. It emphasizes Revelation 1:19, arguing that Revelation chapter 1 describes "what you have seen"—the past; chapters 2–3 describe "what is"—the present dispensation; and chapters 4–22 describe "what is to take place after this"—the future after the rapture. Moreover, they take the letters to the churches as describing seven distinct dispensations of church history.

A more progressive dispensationalism has appeared in recent years, integrating preterist and historicist interpretations into its scheme. Progressive dispensationalists emphasize the "already/not yet eschatological tension" (Pate, 1998:135). Agreeing with classical dispensationalists' stress on Revelation 1:19, progressives see a twofold rather than a threefold division between the present age (chs. 1–3) and the age to come, which has "already" begun in heaven (chs. 4–18) but "not yet" dawned on earth (chs. 19–22; Pate 1998:137). Progressive dispensationalists agree with preterists that the background of Revelation 6–18 is the first-century conflict between Caesar and Christ and with historicists that the conflict between Satan and God operates throughout history. Nevertheless, "progressive dispensationalists believe that the final fulfillment of these chapters awaits the time of Christ's return" (146). Progressive and classical dispensationalists also agree that Christians are raptured before the great tribulation and avoid its travail; that the tribulation saints, the 144,000, are "a select group of Jews who are converted to Christ during the Great Tribulation, which, in turn, evangelizes the gentile nations—the innumerable multitude" (165); and that, although Gentiles have been incorporated into God's people through faith, "God is not yet finished with Israel, for one day he will restore that nation to himself and Jesus Messiah" (175). Thus, progressive dispensationalists maintain continuity with their classical counterparts while recognizing the validity of certain claims of preterists and historicists.

EMPERORS AND EMPEROR WORSHIP Revelation seems to indicate that its context includes pressure to worship the Roman emperor and the crisis that this posed for Christians. Tacitus reports that the first temple to Rome was built in 195 B.C. in Smyrna (*Annals* 4.56) and the first temple to the divine Caesar in Pergamum in 29 B.C. (4.37). Emperor worship reached a crescendo under Caligula (Jos., *Ant.* 18.261; Suet., *Caligula* 22), and by the end of the first century A.D. all cities in Asia had temples for the worship of Rome and her emperors. Johns summarizes the influence of emperor worship on Asia Minor, concluding: "There is little question that the province of Asia was the world leader in the imperial cult" (1998:154-57). Pilgrim summarizes the case in even stronger language: "Asia Minor was a veritable hotbed for the imperial cult" (1999:148; see Barclay 1960:1.22-24 and Worth 1999:116-18 for a summary of how each emperor of the first century understood the practice of emperor worship).

Traditionally, it has been thought that Domitian (A.D. 81-96) was the worst of the first-century emperors, insisting on his own divinity, demanding caesar worship, and persecuting Christians who did not participate. More recent scholars have questioned this assessment, emphasizing that it goes back to second-century apologists for the reforms of Trajan, who wished to contrast the good Emperor Trajan with his predecessor, Domitian *[Essay: Persecution during Domitian's Reign]*. Yet coins from 20-18 B.C. bearing a bust of Augustus and a representation of his temple and carrying inscriptions like ROM..ET.AUGUST witness to the presence of emperor worship early in Asia; and inscriptions on the temple in Ephesus, probably built during the reign of Domitian, evidence the divinization of the emperor's family (Friesen 2001:29, 46). That Christians were compelled to worship the emperor several decades after Revelation was written is documented in a letter from Pliny the Younger to Caesar Trajan, who evidently executed Christians and forced those who denied being Christians to invoke the heathen gods and offer worship, wine, and frankincense before a statue of the Caesar (*Letter* 10.96; see also *Mart. Pol.* 8). Nevertheless, Thompson gives convincing evidence that Domitian was not the cold-blooded persecutor of Christians that he was formerly thought to be (1990:109-15). Perhaps the pressure to worship the emperor during the reign of Domitian was more subtle and seductive than open and oppressive. Because Christians were becoming more affluent due to the trade that was prevalent throughout the empire, it may have been their materialism and expectation of wealth, more than outright persecution, that seduced Christians to worship the emperor (Kraybill, 1996:117). Yet, the memory of past persecution under Nero, and its reality in the second and third centuries, make it likely that the expectation of tribulation was present during the reign of Domitian (Yarbro Collins 1984:84-110). Friesen (2001) documents considerable provincial and municipal imperial cult activity with its attendant temples, festivals, officials, coins, and calendar woven into the religious and governmental culture of late-first-century Asia. Christians would naturally resist this usurpation of God's rightful authority and Rome's use of military force in support of imperial religion (208).

GEMATRIA The practice, common in the first century, of hiding meaning in numbers is called gematria. For example, in Revelation the number three is used to indicate the spiritual world—the completion of the Godhead. Although the Trinity is not explicit, this number three is seen in the repetition of "holy, holy, holy" (4:8) and in the threefold designator for God in 1:4-5. The number four is used for the physical world, especially for something universal or worldwide (Beale, 1999:59). This is reflected in the four living creatures that represent the animate universe (4:6-9; 5:6, 8,14; 6:1, 6; 7:11; 14:3; 15:7; 19:4) and the four corners of the earth representing the physical universe (7:1; 20:8). When three and four are added together, the result is seven, the number of completion used throughout Revelation. When the numbers three and four are multiplied together, the result is twelve, the number that represents the diversity of the people of God—the twelve tribes symbolizing the Hebrew people of God (21:12-14), and the twelve apostles God's

New Testament people (7:5-8; 21:12, 14). When the two twelves are added together, twenty-four is obtained, the number of elders that represent the entire heavenly people of God (4:4, 10; 5:8, 14; 7:11; 11:16; 19:4). When these twelves are multiplied together and then multiplied by the large number 1000, the result is 144,000, which represents all of the redeemed who have conquered and are receiving their reward in heaven with God (7:4; 14:1-5). Many other numbers are used in this symbolic way in Revelation. Understanding them illuminates the meaning of the book.

GENRE OF REVELATION   The Greek word *apocalypse (apokalypsis)* means to "uncover," "unveil," or "reveal." The most recent definition of apocalyptic literature does not characterize it as completely distinct from other types of literature like prophecy and wisdom as it was once portrayed. Yet the definition provides a constellation of ideas that seem unique to the literature known as apocalyptic *[Essay: Apocalyptic Literature]*.

The Book of Revelation is congruent with this definition of apocalyptic. Revelation comes through symbolic visions of otherworldly beings, Christ and angels. Its content is primarily eschatological because it speaks of cosmic transformation, resurrection, and personal afterlife. Although Revelation has no complex journey into the heavenly realm and no clear review of history, it does fit most aspects of the definition of apocalyptic literature.

Some have argued that the form of Revelation is a letter and that it therefore is best categorized in the epistolary genre (Boring 1989:5-8). Indeed, Revelation was to be read aloud in the seven churches of Asia (1:3) after the manner of the Pauline epistles. It does seem that Revelation is occasional literature written to the specific time, place, and situation of the Asian churches. Therefore, those who believe that Revelation is a prediction of the modern historical situation are certainly wrong. Yet, although there are elements of an epistolary format in the introduction and conclusion of Revelation, this format is quite superficial. Even the material in chapters 2–3 never circulated as independent letters, nor do they follow an epistolary form.

Others have affirmed that Revelation is primarily prophecy (Beasley-Murray, 1974:19-23; Schüssler Fiorenza 1985:135-40). According to Aune, Revelation was communicated to the churches by a group of prophets in Asia (1989:103-16). If Revelation is prophecy, its main purpose is to proclaim God's word to the Asian churches and to interpret the present situation in terms of God's revelation, like Jeremiah during the oppression of Nebuchadnezzar and Daniel during the persecution of Antiochus IV Epiphanes. Revelation is not long-range prediction of end-time events, but prophetic proclamation of God's message that, in the end, evil will be defeated and good will triumph. Although the message is consistent with that of the prophets, the language and imagery of apocalyptic literature is used to communicate this message (168-70). The formula for introducing visions is the apocalyptic "after this I saw" rather than the prophetic "thus says the LORD."

So, it seems clear that Revelation is primarily apocalyptic literature. It certainly does not contain all apocalyptic characteristics (e.g., pseudonymity, review of history), but it adheres to the apocalyptic form (e.g., angelic mediators, visions, heavenly ascent). Its closest parallels are other apocalypses. So Revelation contains some elements of the epistolary form, shares the purpose of the prophets, but has most affinity with apocalyptic literature (cf. Bauckham, 1993b, 1-17; Carey, 1999:103-6).

GNOSTICISM In the first century, which was permeated by Hellenistic thought, Gnosticism was prevalent. Two of its main doctrines were individual salvation through spiritual knowledge *(gnōsis)* and devaluing of the material world. The gnostic Christians believed that Jesus was a revealer of divine truth that brought salvation. His body was a temporary lodging that he left immediately before his death. Such a belief about the material world and the body led to two radically different thought systems: *asceticism,* the denial of the body; and *libertarianism,* indifference to what is done in the body.

This latter belief lies behind the doctrine of the Nicolaitans, Balaam, and Jezebel referred to in Revelation 2–3. They encouraged persons to "eat food sacrificed to idols and practice fornication" (2:14, 20). Because the meat served at pagan dinner parties had often been sacrificed to idols, Christians had scruples against eating it. Paul said: if an unbeliever invites you to a meal, "eat whatever is set before you without raising any question on the ground of conscience" (1 Cor. 10:27). Yet he advocated abstention if eating violated the conscience of another person. Perhaps the Asian Christians had forgotten Paul's qualification. Moreover, the gnostic encouraged sexual promiscuity, with Corinthian Christians thinking that sexual intercourse was as natural as eating (1 Cor. 6:13). Paul, of course, does not encourage this belief. John's reactions to these gnostic Christians is clear: one must be ready to suffer and even die rather than entering into these questionable practices. Separation from the world and refusal to compromise with its practices must be total. (This section is based on Sweet 1990:32-35, who includes a more complete description of gnosticism. See Aune 1997:149, 195, who calls into question the connection between Gnosticism and the Nicolaitans). For fuller discussion of Gnostiscism, see *Essays* in BCBC volumes: Martin on Colossians, 1993: 289-90; Yoder Neufeld, on *Ephesians,* 2002: 346-47.

HISTORY OF THE INTERPRETATION OF REVELATION For the first four centuries, Revelation was usually interpreted in a literal and futuristic manner. Although none of his writings have been preserved, it seems clear that Papias, who lived in the late first and early second centuries, believed in a literal reign of Christ on earth (Eusebius, *Eccl. Hist.* 3.39). Although admitting that "many who belong to the pure and pious faith, and are true Christians, think otherwise," Justin Martyr affirmed the common view in the middle of the second century that there would be a literal kingdom of the saints centered in Jerusalem. After the 1000-year kingdom was complete, a general resurrection and judgment would follow (*Dialogue with Trypho* 80-81). Irenaeus agreed with Justin, but included more detail: the beast is an antichrist that will come from the tribe of Dan, whose character is represented in the number 666; the kingdom will come on this earth; and humans will actually be raised (*Adv. Haer.* 5.30-36). Tertullian (*Against Marcion* 3.25) agreed with this literal, futuristic method of interpretation. Yet Victorinus introduced the recapitulation theory, that the movement of Revelation is repetitive rather than linear, and was the first to use the idea that Nero had not died but would return again (*Commentary on Revelation* 8:2-3) *[Essay: Nero Redivivus Myth]*.

Due to the delay of the coming of Christ, the literal interpretation of Revelation came into question. In the early third century, Origen gave allegorical interpretations to the symbols (*On First Principles* 2.11.2-5). Methodius continued to use Origen's principles in the early fourth century (see

Symposium 8.4-13 for an allegorical interpretation of the story of the woman and the dragon in Revelation 12). With the reign of Constantine, the Roman Empire could no longer be seen as the beast. Indeed, Eusebius seems to believe that the eschatological hope was fulfilled in the victory of Constantine (*Eccl. Hist.* 10.9). The most comprehensive spiritual reading of Revelation was by Ticonius, a Donatist. In the fifth century, Augustine followed this spiritualizing method (*The City of God* 20.6-21), asserted that the first resurrection is of the soul and the second of the body, argued that the 1000 years represents the entire duration of this world, and posited that the kingdom of Christ referred to the church. The Augustinian position continued to dominate until the beginning of the thirteenth century.

In Joachim of Fiore, interpretation of Revelation took a new turn. Because Christ did not come after 1000 years of church history as expected, the church became complacent and worldly. Joachim showed how the symbols of Revelation predicted in detail the course of human history and indicated that a new age of the Holy Spirit was about to come. In the early fourteenth century, Nicholas of Lyra saw Revelation's visions as predicting the pattern of church history to the end of the world (1997:12-13).

From the sixteenth century to the present, several methods of interpretation have emerged. According to the Protestants, Revelation gives an overview of church history that is directed against the Roman church. Accordingly Luther believed the pope to be the antichrist. In turn, Catholics found Luther to be the antichrist and the Protestant sects to be the false prophet. Anabaptists found both Catholic and Protestant leaders in the symbolism of the beast. Yet the position that rose to prominence during this time found the symbols of Revelation in the first-century context of the book.

In reaction to this tendency, some have turned again to a futurist approach. Daniel Whitby, Jonathan Edwards, and Charles Finney expected a new age would arrive on earth preceding the coming of Christ. John Nelson Darby placed the symbols of Revelation totally in the future, introduced by the imminent coming of Christ. Darby's dispensationalism became very popular in the twentieth century *[Essay: Dispensationalism]*. He focused on the role of the Jewish people in God's plan for the future and postulated a rapture, which would precede the tribulation spoken of in Revelation.

In the nineteenth and twentieth centuries, critical approaches also dominated the study of Revelation. Historical criticism stressed the preterist approach of finding the meaning in the situation at the time when Revelation was written. Literary criticism investigated the relationship of Revelation to other similar literature, the rhetorical and liturgical techniques used, and the structural outline of the book. Moreover, social science techniques were used to analyze the psychological attitudes of the persons in the community that produced Revelation and the situations of injustice that gave rise to these feelings. Several political responses to Revelation emerged from these social scientific approaches. Liberationists saw Revelation as a challenge to the oppressive political structures of this world and a hope for a new society. A variation on this was that Revelation was seen to unmask the controlling ideology of the principalities and powers of this world (Ellul 1977; Stringfellow 1973, 1977; Wink 1992). Reconstructionists advocated the establishment of the rule of God on earth through the imposition of a political system based on the Law of Moses. (This section depends on McGinn, 1987:527-41; Beckwith, 1919:318-34; and Wainwright, 1993:185).

THE INFLUENCE OF REVELATION Given the importance of its message and the forcefulness of its symbolic imagery, the minimal influence of Revelation on other apocalyptic literature is remarkable. The book had no influence on fifteen of the twenty subsequent Christian apocalypses. Revelation's lack of influence is even more remarkable in light of two other facts: later Christian teachings are rooted in apocalypticism, and subsequent apocalypses do depend on other New Testament writings such as Paul, Matthew, and John (Charlesworth, 1987:39-40). In light of this, it is difficult to understand why the influence of Revelation is so minimal.

Although Revelation did not have great impact on other apocalypses, it has had an immense impact on many aspects of Western culture. It has served as a basis for great works of art like Michelangelo's *Last Judgment* in the Sistine Chapel and Hubert and Jan van Eyck's *Adoration of the Lamb* in the Ghent altarpiece. Handel's great oratorio *The Messiah* was inspired at points by Revelation. Literature too has received inspiration from Revelation— George Eliot's *Romolo,* Edmund Spenser's *Faerie Queen,* D. H. Lawrence's *Apocalypse,* Dante's *Divine Comedy,* Thomas Hobbes's *Leviathan,* John Milton's *Paradise Lost,* and Martin Luther King's *We Shall Overcome.*

INTERPRETATION OF APOCALYPTIC LITERATURE If the Book of Revelation is apocalyptic literature, it is different from other types of biblical literature and should be interpreted in a manner consistent with its genre. There are several principles to be kept in mind when interpreting Revelation.

First, assume it was understandable to the audience addressed. John wrote Revelation to the churches in Asia and said, "Let anyone who has an ear listen to what the Spirit is saying to the churches." The language here makes it clear that John intended that the hearers understand the message of Revelation. Certainly the first-century members of the churches in Asia had the advantage of sharing common symbols with the author; they would have understood the meanings of the symbols better than we do today. Perhaps the example of the political cartoon helps us understand how that is true. Whenever persons in North America today see the symbol of the eagle or the maple leaf, they understand them to refer to the United States or Canada, respectively. Moreover, within the United States, the elephant and the donkey are readily identified as the Republican and Democratic parties. Yet to someone in another place and time, these symbols might mean something else or nothing at all. Moreover, a cartoon communicates by exaggeration (Beasley-Murray, 1974:16-17). Likewise, language of apocalyptic writing may exaggerate reality to communicate spiritual truth. While the referents for the symbols in Revelation may not be so clearly related to one specific entity as the symbols in political cartoons, the cartoons do show us how symbolic language operates. In order to comprehend the symbols of Revelation, one must understand how they functioned for the persons to whom Revelation was written— the first-century people from the churches in the Roman province of Asia (cf. Rowland, 1998:506).

Second, determine the meaning of the symbols. Apocalyptic literature uses symbolic language to explain the unexplainable. Psychologist Michael Polanyi says, "We can know more than we can tell, and we can tell nothing without relying on our awareness of things we may not be able to tell" (1964:x). In a related way, Paul says: "Likewise the Spirit helps us in our weakness; for we do not know how to pray as we ought, but that very Spirit intercedes with sighs too deep for words" (Rom. 8:26). John finds symbolic language to be more adequate for communicating spiritual truths because symbols can communicate when literal words are inadequate.

Third, when searching for the meaning of the symbols, the imagination may be a more adequate tool than reason. Revelation is a symbolic picture book. Beasley-Murray says: "John's visions of the end are those of an impressionist artist rather than the pictures of a photographer" (1974:23). Artists understand paintings not so much with their minds as with their imaginations (see Eller, 1974:87-92, for an excellent treatment of artistic imagination based on Picasso's painting *Guernica*). Moreover, when interpreting a picture, the artist is more likely to search for a multiplicity of meanings than for a single referent. Archibald MacLeish said: "Anything can make us look; only art makes us see" (quoted by Peterson, 1988:14). Johns gives a helpful summary of the distinction between a "steno" symbol, which has a clear referent that exhausts its meaning, and a "tensive" symbol, which carries a variety of associations and meanings (1998:139). Although Revelation does have some symbols that seem referential (1:20; 13:18; 21:8), most of its imagery is clearly tensive.

Unfortunately, however, many interpreters have been more likely to treat Revelation like a gigantic algebra problem than like a series of paintings. The procedure has been to find the value of x—whether that value is the person who is the beast, the groups of nations that compose the ten horns of the beast, or the meaning of 666. The artist is more likely to find many meanings in a great painting. Rowland says: "We should not ask of apocalypses what do they mean? Rather, we should ask, How do the images and designs work? How do they affect us and change our lives?" (1998:523). It has been convincingly argued that Revelation contains little theology that is unique to the New Testament, but instead it communicates traditional theology in an alternate way. In symbolic language, the Christian message comes through with more power than would be possible through reasoned argumentation.

NERO REDIVIVUS MYTH   After Emperor Nero killed himself, the empire was plunged into civil war. In this time of near chaos, a myth grew up that he had not died at all but had gone to live with the Parthians, the feared armies to the East of the empire, across the Euphrates River (Suet., *Nero* 57; Dio Chrysostom, *Orations* 21.10). It was thought that Nero would return with the kings of the East to overthrow the Romans. According to the *Sibyline Oracles*:

> Then the strife of war being aroused will come to the west, and the fugitive from Rome will also come, brandishing a great spear, having crossed the Euphrates with many myriads. (4.137-39; see also 4:119-29)

> Then he [Nero] will return declaring himself equal to God. But he will prove that he is not. (5:33-34; see also 5:93-110, 137-54, 214-27, 361-85)

The Roman historian Tacitus comments in passing that "the armies of Parthia were all but set in motion by the cheat of a counterfeit Nero" (*Hist.* 1.2; see also 2.8-9; *Dio's Roman History* 63.7; 66.19.3^b-3^c). Indeed, at least three Neronic pretenders arose (see Aune, 1998a:738-39). Some thought that Emperor Domitian was *Nero Redivivus*, "Nero Reborn." Melito of Sardis called Domitian a "second Nero" because of his persecution of the church (Eusebius, *Eccl. Hist.* 3.17). Tertullian implied that Emperor Domitian was, indeed, *Nero redivivus,* calling him "somewhat of a Nero in cruelty" (*Apol.* 5.4; see also Eusebius, *Eccl. Hist.* 3.20; Juvenal, *Satires* 4.38-40). Wilson argues that the pretenders claimed to be Nero himself, not Nero reborn, and that nowhere in the first century was *Nero Redivivus* ever identified with Domitian (1993:599). Yet the myth does seem to be reflected in the language of Revelation.

NICOLAITANS The name of this group indicates they were probably followers of someone named Nicolas. The most likely candidate is the proselyte of Antioch mentioned in Acts 6:5. Tradition says that he became a gnostic and condoned immorality. Irenaeus indicates that his followers lived in unrepentant indulgence (*Adv. Haer.* 1.26.3; 3.11.1). Hippolytus says that Nicolas "departed from correct doctrine, and was in the habit of inculcating indifferency of both life and food" (*The Refutation* 7.24; see also Tertullian, *Against Marcion* 1.29; *Prescription of Heretics* 33). Clement of Alexandria says the Nicolaitans "indulge in unrestrained license" (*Miscellanies* 3.4; see also 2.20). The actual impact of this teaching is unclear, however, since Eusebius argues that the heresy was short-lived in Ephesus (*Eccl. Hist.* 3.29).

Yet it may be that the name does not refer to the leader of the group but to its character. Nicolas may be a compound word composed of the Greek words *nikon* meaning "to conquer" and *laos* meaning "people." This may explain the connection with the followers of Balaam mentioned in the letter to Pergamum (2:14) because Balaam may also be a compound of the Hebrew words *bela* meaning "to conquer" and *ha'am* meaning "people." The names are ironic because they are used for groups that compromised with evil rather than overcoming it.

Indeed, the group clearly taught immorality and loose living. They probably accepted the gnostic idea that the body was unimportant and therefore it did not matter what they did with it (Efird, 1989:54-55). The Nicolaitans may have combined this with Paul's teaching of Christian liberty, which they took to mean license to do whatever they pleased (1 Cor. 6:12-20; Gal. 5:13; see Barker, 2000:99 for the unlikely suggestion that the Nicolaitans were followers of Paul). This was in direct contradiction to the decision made at the Jerusalem Council (Acts 15:28-29).

PERSECUTION DURING DOMITIAN'S REIGN Most of the evidence for widespread persecution under Domitian is from the writings of Eusebius (*Eccl. Hist.* 3:17-20), Pliny the Younger (*Letter* 10:96-97), Tertullian (*Apol.* 5), and *Dio's Roman History* 67.14. The latter mentions Domitian's execution of his cousin, Flavius Clemens, and the banishment of his wife, Domitilla, the niece of Domitian. Thompson agrees that these writers do document the proclaimed divinity, tyranny, and megalomania of Domitian (1986:153-54), but he claims that there is no evidence that Domitian insisted on divine status more than the other emperors of the time (158-59). He further argues that Christians in Asia enjoyed peaceful and prosperous times during Domitian's reign:

> Some were probably slaves and down-and-outers, but many were free artisans and small traders, wealthy enough to travel around the Roman

empire, own slaves, and live in houses large enough to hold congregations of Christians. A typical Christian congregation in one of the seven cities to which John writes probably consisted of people from various classes and statuses, men and women, bond and free, with those of greater affluence serving somewhat as patrons to the others. (1990:7)

Thompson further points out that Antipas is the only martyr documented in Revelation, (cf. 6:9-11) and that Polycarp is only the twelfth in Eusebius's list of martyrs in the cities of Smyrna and Philadelphia (*Eccl. Hist.* 4.15). Therefore, he concludes that persecution for John was not sociopolitical, but mythical, involving the forces of good and evil rather than Rome and the provinces (1986:166; cf. Beale, 1999:6).

Nevertheless, it seems indisputable that persecution was both present and imminent. Rowland notes that toward the end of Domitian's rule there was harassment of Jews and Christians, the tax imposed on all Jews after the destruction of the temple in A.D. 70 was extended, and certain members of Domitian's court were charged with atheism because of Jewish or Christian sympathies (1998:684; see also Lohse, 1976:220-21). Evidence of Jewish persecution by Romans comes from archaeological findings such as the skeletal remains at Givat ha-Mivtar. Charlesworth describes these as follows: "A little boy died from an arrow wound to the skull, an old woman succumbed when her skull was smashed, a teenaged boy was probably burned to death on the rack, and a man in his thirties suffered crucifixion" (1987:21). Moreover, Christians also suffered at the hands of the Roman rulers. There is evidence that Domitian proclaimed himself *Dominus et Deus Noster,* "Our Lord and God" (Suet., *Domitian* 13; Martial, *Epigrams* 5.8; 10.72; *Dio's Roman History* 67.5.7; 67.13.4; Dio Chrysostom, *Orations* 45.1), although Wilson points out that this evidence is not from the time of Domitian himself (Wilson, 1993:596). That Domitian was regarded as divine in Asia Minor is evidenced by the huge statue that has been found in archaeological digs in Ephesus, which seems to have been destroyed upon the emperor's death (Roloff, 1993:9-10). Clement of Rome, a contemporary of Domitian, speaks of "the sudden and successive calamitous events which have happened to ourselves" and "being persecuted" after suffering "terrible and unspeakable torments" (1 Clement 1, 7). Pliny the Younger witnesses that at the time of Trajan (A.D. 112) Christians were sought out, examined, and even executed if they did not renounce their Christian allegiance (*Letter,* 10.96-97). Beale speculates that the reason for this is that "Roman policy ... became increasingly intolerant toward explicit Christian nonparticipation in the political-religious life of Greco-Roman society" (1999:9). Schüssler Fiorenza argues: "John views Roman power as exploitative, destructive, and dehumanizing because he and some of the Asian communities have experienced poverty, banishment, violence, harassment, and assassination," concluding that there was no justice for poor and powerless Christians. To this situation Revelation provides "the vision of an alternative world and power in order to strengthen Christians in their 'consistent resistance' *(hypomonē)* to the oppressive power of the Roman empire" (1985:4, 8; see also 24-25).

It seems clear that the Christians were in conflict with at least three groups—Jews, Gentiles, and Romans. After the war of A.D. 66-70, Jews became more exclusive, eliminating all heretics, especially Christians, from the synagogue (Sweet, 1990:28; Pate, 1998:139-40). Bitterness between

Christians and Jews was particularly intense in Asia Minor (Hemer, 1986:38, 66). Barrett quotes a "test benediction" from the Jewish Prayer Book at the close of the first century:

> For the renegades let there be no hope, and may the arrogant kingdom soon be rooted out in our days, and the Nazarenes ... perish as in a moment and be blotted out from the book of life and with the righteous may they not be inscribed. Blessed art thou, O Lord, who humblest the arrogant. (Quoted in Barrett, 1961:167)

Christians were also accused by Gentiles of "hatred of the human race" due to their exclusivism, of arson as scapegoats to blame for the fire of Rome, of incest because they celebrated a "love feast" with "brothers" and "sisters," of cannibalism because they ate flesh and blood in their communion service, and of atheism because they did not worship the Roman gods. Regarding Roman oppression, Suetonius asserts that Domitian imposed a tax on Jews and Jewish sympathizers (*Domitian* 12). According to Pliny the Younger, those accused as Christians were executed if they refused to renounce their faith (*Letter* 10.96).

Sordi is probably correct that although there were political implications, the charges against Christians were fundamentally religious (1986:4-5). Sweet indicates that because the Christians could not give obeisance to the emperor, they were considered atheists (1990:31). The concern was probably to maintain public order and preserve the authority of the empire and its worship. In this context, Yarbro Collins concludes that Revelation "was written to awaken and intensify Christian exclusiveness, particularly vis-à-vis the imperial cult" (1984:73).

PERSECUTION DURING NERO'S REIGN   Sordi maintains that Christians were treated with benevolence until about A.D. 62 and that some members of the ruling classes and aristocracy became sympathizers (1986:26-27). Christians were considered to adhere to a "new and mischievous religious belief," charged with "hatred of the human race," and blamed for the fire of Rome, which may have been started by Nero himself (Tac., *Annals* 15.44; Suet., *Nero* 16; cf. Sordi, 1986:30-33). In the words of Tacitus (A.D. 54-120), "So in order to drown the rumor, Nero shifted the guilt on persons known to the people as Christians, and punished them with exquisite tortures." Caird argues that at about this time it may have been discovered that the Christians were not a sect of Judaism but a new religion. Therefore, they would no longer have benefited from the special status *(religio licita)* given to Jews in the empire (1966:22-23). In A.D. 65, large numbers of Christians were killed in ways that even distressed the Romans:

> Covered with the skins of beasts, they were torn by dogs and perished, or were nailed to crosses, or were doomed to the flames and burnt, to serve as nightly illumination when daylight had expired. Nero had offered his gardens for the spectacle, and put on a show in the Circus, mingling with the people in the dress of a charioteer or standing up in a chariot. Hence, even for criminals who deserved extreme and exemplary punishment, there arose a feeling of compassion, for it was not, as it seemed, for the public good, but to glut one man's cruelty, that they were being destroyed. (*Annals,* 10.44)

Later tradition says that Peter and Paul were killed during this persecution in Rome (Eusebius, *Eccl. Hist.* 2.25; 3.1; Acts Peter 36-41 [7-12]); Acts Paul 11; also 1 Clem. 5; Irenaeus, *Adv. Haer.* 3.1.1). Although the *Sibylline Oracles* capture a popular attitude toward Nero, calling him "the man who slew his mother" (5:361-68), Johns is probably correct to assert: "Nero's persecution, though intense, was localized. It is highly unlikely that it reached to the provinces in Asia Minor" (1998:154). Yet it may be that persecution in Rome caused John to anticipate its expansion to the rest of the empire (Beale, 1999:12).

PERSECUTION IN REVELATION It appears clear from the text of Revelation that persecution was indeed evident and expected (2:10-11; 7:13-14; 11:7-9; 12:11; 16:6; 17:6; 18:24; 19:2; 20:4-6; see also 1:9; 2:2-3, 13; 3:8-10; 6:9-11; 7:9-17; 11:1-13; 12:1-17; 13:1-18; 14:13; 17:1-6; see Murphy, 1998:7-11 on persecution in the New Testament). John himself was sent to Patmos as a prisoner (1:9), and his hearers are told to imitate Christ by persevering and conquering in the face of tribulation (1:5-9; 2:10-11, 17, 26-28; 3:5, 10, 12, 21; 7:13-14; 12:10-12; 14:1-5). Revelation specifies that at least one person died for his faith—Antipas of Pergamum (2:13). The issue worth dying for was idolatry, the refusal to worship the emperor. Charlesworth focuses two questions that have relevance for the first-century Christians: "Why should the Christian continue to be willing to die at the hands of Rome...? Why should the Christian continue to suffer and be willing to die for Christ who seems to be powerless?" (1987:26). These questions confront Christians at all times when persecution for the faith seems imminent.

PSEUDONYMITY After the great prophets, it was thought that God's unique revelation to the people had come to an end. The only way that God could speak was through some individual from the ancient past. Hence, for a person in the first century to communicate God's word, it was necessary to write under the name of some great hero in the past. Typically, during a time of crisis, a treatise would be written for the writer's own day but attributed to a great person in ancient Israel. The book might include the words "seal this up," because the message is for the distant future, which was in reality the present. Many noncanonical apocalyptic books were written in this manner— 2 Esdras, 2 Baruch, 2 Enoch, Testament of Levi, Apocalypse of Abraham, Apocalypse of Zephaniah. Indeed, nearly all of the noncanonical apocalyptic books were written pseudonymously (the possible exception being the *Shepherd of Hermas*).

To our modern minds, there seems to be something dishonest about pseudonymous authorship. We are taught that plagiarism is the worst offense that a writer can commit. Such a moral standard would have been unknown in the ancient world. Pseudonymity was not thought to be committing an offense against the false author but giving honor to that author and authority to the words declared to be written under the author's name. It is invalid to apply the criteria of modern writing to the ancient world; pseudonymous authorship was considered acceptable and completely within the bounds of moral practice. Metzger says: "Since the use of the literary form of pseudepigraphy [writing under a false name] need not be regarded as necessarily involving fraudulent intent, it cannot be argued that the character of inspiration excludes the possibility of pseudepigraphy among the canonical writings" (1972:22).

In any case, Revelation clearly was not written under a false name. Several reasons for this conclusion are: the letter form necessitates that the writer be known to the recipients; Revelation does not include a historical review like those written after the fact in other apocalypses; and there is no attempt to establish that John was an apostle and thus worthy of being heard (Barr, 1998:161-62). Thus, Revelation seems not to be pseudonymous.

STRUCTURE OF REVELATION The structure of Revelation is primarily artistic. It uses reiteration; the series of visions tend to repeat elements. Yet there is development. In each series, intensification brings the end closer. Schüssler Fiorenza says: "The dramatic narrative of Rev. can best be envisioned as a conic spiral moving from the present to the eschatological future" (1985:5).

The artistic form of Revelation is built around the number seven *[Essay: Gematria]*. Furthermore, scholars have found seven series of seven or six series of six elements in Revelation (Ford, 1975:46-50). Perhaps more convincing is Ellul's five interrelated series of seven (1977:36-50). It is certainly clear that the major series are interrelated. The first six elements of each series (seals, trumpets, and bowls) bring an event of judgment, and the seventh launches the subsequent series.

Although attempts to structure Revelation around series of seven may seem strained, clearly there are many sevens in Revelation: seven seals (6:1-17; 8:1-5), seven trumpets (8:6–9:21; 11:15-19), seven bowls of God's wrath (16:1-20), seven scenes of God's triumph (19:11-16, 17-21; 20:1-3, 4-6, 7-10, 11-15; 21:1–22:5), seven beatitudes (1:3; 14:13; 16:15; 19:9; 20:6; 22:7, 14), sevenfold praise (5:12), seven categories of people (6:15), seven references to the altar (6:9; 8:3, 5; 9:13; 11:1; 14:18; 16:7), and seven affirmations of Christ's coming (2:16; 3:11; 16:15; 22:7, 12, 17, 20).

Eller points out that another evidence of the artistic structure of Revelation is that each of the series of seven judgments follows a similar pattern. The first four judgments are interrelated and follow each other immediately. Between the fourth and fifth there is a break in the pattern. The fifth judgment is more elaborate, and the sixth marks an intensification of the torment. After the sixth judgment, there is an interlude, which has two parts. The seventh is then an intervention by God to bring the judgments to an end (1974:83-84). The pattern could be visualized in this manner:

1-2-3-4 / 5 / 6 / Interlude A/B / 7

Although Eller's pattern does not exactly match each of the sequences of judgment, Revelation's general outline does reveal an artistic arraignment.

A final evidence of artistic structure in Revelation is the dialectic nature of its symbolism. Nearly every major positive symbol has a negative counterpart. For example, the Trinity—God the Father, Son, and Holy Spirit (1:4-5)—has its corresponding trinity of evil—the dragon, the beast, and the false prophet (19:20-20:2). The mother of the Messiah (12:1-17) corresponds to the great whore (17:1-18), and the New Jerusalem (21:1-22:5) to fallen Babylon (18:1-24).

TRANSMISSION OF REVELATION Revelation has been preserved in relatively few ancient manuscripts. Codex Sinaiticus from the fourth century and Alexandrinus from the fifth are complete, but many of the earliest manuscripts are severely mutilated (see Aland, 1989:96-102, 107-28). Moreover, Weiss says that there are 1,650 variants in Revelation's approximately 400 verses (in Beckwith, 1919:411). In short, Revelation has been transmitted by the fewest manuscripts of any New Testament book and those manuscripts are in the poorest condition when compared with those of other books of the New Testament.

WORSHIP IN REVELATION Worship is certainly central to Revelation. Gloer contrasts Revelation's hymns of worship to similar hymns of the imperial court which serve as a parody of the hymns of Revlation. This makes it evident that the hymns are not incidental to the content of Revelation. They focus a central message of Revelation that all must choose to worship God or the emperor. Gloer concludes: "Music plays a larger role in the Apocalypse than in any other New Testament writing."

Majestic hymns punctuate the tribulation scenes, reminding the reader that the persecution of Satan is not the last word but that God's salvation will prevail. The language is magnificent:

> Worthy is the Lamb who was slaughtered to receive power and wealth and wisdom and might and honor and glory and blessing! (5:12)
> Salvation belongs to our God who is seated on the throne, and to the Lamb. (9:10b)
> They will hunger no more, and thirst no more; the sun will not strike them, nor any scorching heat. (7:16)
> The kingdom of this world has become the kingdom of our Lord and his Messiah, and he will reign forever and ever. (11:15b)
> Great and amazing are your deeds, Lord God the Almighty! Just and true are your ways, King of the nations! (15:3b)
> Hallelujah! For the Lord our God the Almighty reigns. (19:6b)

In chapters 4–5 rhyming endings suggest liturgical intention and possible use: the threefold "holy" *(hagios)* in 4:8 is echoed by three refrains that are initiated by "worthy" *(axios)* in 4:11; 5:9, 12. The repetition of the number three indicates the completion of the holiness and worthiness of God and the Lamb. God is praised in these hymns because of his actions in history, and the worshipers' response is to do the works of God (Rowland, 1998:595; see also 1 John 3:18). Thus, worship is tied closely to active service.

Revelation has also served as the inspiration for many of the church's favorite hymns (see Koester, 2001:33-35). From the descriptions of God and Christ at the beginning and end of Revelation (1:8, 17; 21:6; 22:13) comes the fourth-century hymn: "Of the Father's Love Begotten."

> Of the Father's love begotten
> Ere the worlds began to be.
> He is alpha and omega.
> He the source, the ending He.
> Of the things that are, that have been.
> And that future years shall see.
> Evermore and evermore.

From the vision of heaven in chapter 4 comes the classic hymn by Reginald Heber (1723-1826), "Holy, Holy, Holy":

Holy, holy, holy, Lord God Almighty!
Early in the morning our song shall rise to thee.
Holy, holy, holy! Merciful and mighty,
God in three persons, blessed Trinity.

Holy, holy, holy! All the saints adore thee,
Casting down their golden crowns around the glassy sea.
Cherubim and seraphim falling down before thee,
Which wert and art and evermore shalt be.

The vision of the Lamb in chapter 5 is the basis for Edward Perronet's (1726-1792) "All Hail the Power of Jesus' Name:"

All hail the pow'r of Jesus' name!
Let angels prostrate fall;
Bring forth the royal diadem,
And crown him Lord of all.

Another verse of that song comes from the vision of the saints under the altar (6:9-11):

Crown him ye martyrs of your God,
Who from his altar call;
Extol the stem of Jesse's rod
And crown him Lord of all.

The praise of the great multitude (7:10-12) inspires the hymn of Charles Wesley (1707-88), "Ye Servants of God:"

Salvation to God, who sits on the throne!
Let all cry aloud and honor the Son.
The praises of Jesus the angels proclaim,
Fall down on their faces, and worship the Lamb.

Then let us adore and give him his right,
All glory and power, all wisdom and might
All honor and blessing, with angels above,
And thanks never ceasing, and infinite love.

The seventh trumpet (11:15) serves as the basis for Georg Friedrich Handel's (1674-48) "Hallelujah Chorus:"

Hallelujah. For the Lord God Omnipotent reigneth. Hallelujah.
The kingdoms of this world have become the kingdom of our God
and of his Christ, and he shall reign forever and ever.

Vintage and wine press passages yield imagery for the "Battle Hymn of the Republic" by Julia Ward Howe (1819-1910):

Mine eyes have seen the glory of the coming of the Lord.
He is trampling out the vintage where the grapes of wrath are stored.
He hath loosed the fateful lightening of his terrible swift sword.
His truth is marching on.

Glory, glory hallelujah! Glory, glory hallelujah! Glory, glory hallelujah!
His truth is marching on.

The vision of the New Jerusalem (chs. 21–22) inspired the hymn, "For All the Saints," by William How (1823-97):

From earth's wide bounds, from ocean's farthest coast,
Through gates of pearl streams in the countless host,
Singing to Father, Son, and Holy Ghost: Alleluia! Alleluia!

Perhaps Saint Francis of Assisi focused the purpose of music in Revelation in his answers to the following three questions: "Where are you coming from?" "From the next world." "And where are you going?" "To the next world." "And why do you sing?" "To keep from losing my way" (Kazantzakis, 1962:89).

In addition to its hymnody, Revelation's basic message of the completed work of Christ's redemption on the cross and still incomplete mission of the faithful to bear witness against sin and Satan carries considerable potential for preaching. Although the seven letters to the churches have served the church as texts for sermons and texts on the redemption of Christ and are included in the lectionary for the Easter season, Gonzalez (1999) has suggested that two passages are also homiletically appropriate for the Lenten season. Revelation 12:7-12 affirms that, because Christ has won the battle in the heavenly realm, the devil fights ferociously "because he knows his time is short." The faithful are called to a steadfast witness, knowing that the victory is theirs. Revelation 18:9-24 is more specific about that witness against the powers of this world. The Roman system of commerce is tied to providing luxuries to the wealthy. While the Christian's witness will not change the Roman system of injustice, the proclamation that the powers of the world have been defeated will be good news to those that the system oppresses. Such a relevant message is easy to preach in the twenty-first century.

Because of the rich resources in Revelation for praise and proclamation, it is not surprising that the word *worship (proskyneō)* occurs repeatedly in Revelation, where obeisance is directed eleven times to the beast or his allies (9:20; 13:4, 4, 8, 12, 15; 14:9,11; 16:2; 19:20; 20:4), but twelve times toward God and the Lamb (4:10; 5:14; 7:11; 11:1, 16; 14:7; 15:4; 19:4, 10 [twice]; 22:8, 9), indicating the greater majesty of the latter pair. Perhaps, the most impressive use of the word is in the repeated phrase "Worship God!" Piper argues that similarities between Revelation and early Christian liturgies imply that the heavenly worship of Revelation was patterned after the liturgy of the primitive church, which in turn was borrowed from contemporary Jewish temple and synagogue worship. He concludes that, although actual liturgies are not found in Revelation, "the great significance which this book has for our knowledge of the early Christian liturgy" must be recognized (1951:18-19). Conversely, Beale contends that Revelation presents a heavenly pattern for the worship of the church (1999:312).

Consistent with this early worship tradition, Swartley has provided a beautiful service taken directly from Revelation. It includes many voices—God, Christ, angels, elders, choirs. The hour-long worship service is especially appropriate for Easter or perhaps for the nation's independence day. It is available from the Mennonite Board of Congregational Ministries, 500 S. Main Street, Elkhart, IN 46515 or in his forthcoming book on "Peace in the New Testament." Swartley's liturgy gives a powerful impression that Revelation may be a pattern for a Lord's day service (1:10).

Glossary

BABYLON The city whose great empire in the sixth century B.C. destroyed the city of Jerusalem, exiled the citizens, and, most important, destroyed its temple. In Revelation, Babylon symbolizes the great evil city and empire of the first-century A.D., Rome, which also overcame Jerusalem, caused its inhabitants to flee to the mountains of Pella, and again destroyed the temple. Although some argue that Jerusalem is herself the harlot city of Revelation (Ford, 1975:285; Barker, 2000:xii, 279), it is best to assume that Rome is the "Babylon" of John's day. Yet Babylon may by extension also be any political entity that threatens God's people. It is a counter-image to the New Jerusalem, which symbolizes the kingdom of God that will eventually supplant all the "Babylons" of this world. Indeed, futurists would argue that an eschatological "Babylon" will attack the saints to bring on the end of the world.

THE BEAST The evil counterpart of Christ the Lamb, the beast from the sea in Revelation is the political power of Babylon/Rome, which becomes demonic by usurping authority that belongs only to God. In John's day, the beast was primarily the personification of the Roman Empire that, during the reign of Nero, actively persecuted Christians and, in the era of Domitian, seduced the saints to economic and material wealth by compromising with the idolatrous Roman government through eating food sacrificed to idols and practicing fornication. In addition to the forfeit of material gain, faithfulness to God also brought the threat that persecution by the Roman Empire would be renewed. Yet the image of the beast must not be limited to the empire of John's day, but can be extended to include all political governments that demand the total allegiance the faithful saint can give only to God. Indeed, futurists would insist the beast is also the eschatological antichrist who will appear as the great enemy of God's people at the end of time.

THE BRIDE The counter-image of the whore, the bride personifies the saints who remain faithful to God in the face of the seduction to compromise with the world and to participate in its sensual materialism. The bride's clothes of fine linen are the righteous deeds of the saints and symbolize their holiness.

CHURCH The word *church (ekklēsia)* means "assembly" or "congregation." In popular parlance, it is used four ways. First, it designates the group of believers that gather together for worship and disperse for service—the visible church. This is the meaning that has predominated in the Anabaptist tradition and is the only way the word is used in Revelation. It refers to local churches like those seven to which Revelation is addressed. The second usage of the word *church* is the spiritual and universal body of all believers in all parts of the world. Although this meaning is implied in the identification of the seven churches with the complete church, this is not the primary meaning of the word in Revelation. The third meaning of *church* is the place where Christians meet for worship—the church building. Because the first-century church met in houses, this usage of the word is not found in the Bible. The fourth way that *church* is used is to indicate its affiliation—the denomination. Because denominations are a relatively recent phenomenon, the word does not carry this meaning in the Bible. Therefore, when the word *church* is encountered in Revelation, it means the visible community of saints that share life together—the meaning most common in the Anabaptist tradition.

THE FALSE PROPHET The counterpart of the Holy Spirit in the evil trinity, the false prophet (16:13; 19:20; 20:10), is the religious authority of Babylon/Rome that enforces worship of the beastly empire. In John's day, priests oversaw the local worship of the emperors in the temples that had been erected throughout the province. All were required to affirm "Caesar is Lord" liturgically, and, more importantly, to witness to that affirmation by eating food sacrificed to idols and practicing immorality. Of course, faithful saints refused, even if it meant martyrdom. Yet the false prophet must not be limited to the context of emperor worship of the first century but is also that religious force that pressures the saints to give to the state the worship that should only be offered to God. The futurist would insist that such pressure will intensify as the eschatological antichrist appears at the end of time.

FOUR LIVING CREATURES The entire animate universe is represented by the four living creatures. The lion symbolizes the wild animals, the ox domesticated animals, the man humanity, and the eagle the birds of the air. They break the seals to permit the four horsemen to bring their tribulations upon the earth, and they join with the twenty-four elders to form the heavenly chorus singing praises. The meaning carried by this symbol is that even creation itself lifts its voice in praise to God and the Lamb.

GEHENNA One of two words translated "hell" in the Bible (see *Hades*), in a literal sense, it refers to the valley of Ben-hinnom, a garbage dump southwest of Jerusalem where human sacrifices were occasionally offered (2 Kings 16:1-4; 21:6; 23:10; Jer. 7:31-33; 19:6). In apocalyptic literature, it became the place of final punishment (2 Esd. 7:36; 1 Enoch 27:1-2; 48:9; 54:1-6; 56:3-4; 90:26-27; 2 Bar. 59:10; 85:13; Asc. Moses 10:10). In the New Testament, it is equivalent to the hell of fire (Matt. 5:22; 25:41; Mark 9:43-

48; cf. Matt. 8:12; 22:13; 25:30). Although not used in Revelation, it is the idea behind the lake of fire and sulfur (19:20; 20:10; 21:8; see also 14:10).

HADES   Equivalent to the Hebrew *sheol, hades* is one of the words translated "hell" in the scriptures. It is not the place of judgment *(Gehenna)* but the intermittent state between death and resurrection (Matt. 16:18; Acts 2:27; but see Luke 16:23). As in the rest of the Bible, Revelation uses *hades* in parallel construction with death, indicating that *hades* is a symbol for death (Rev. 1:18; 6:8; 20:13-14).

INHABITANTS OF THE EARTH   Revelation's most common term for the faithless (3:10; 6:10; 8:13; 11:10; 13:8, 12, 14; 17:2, 8; see also 1:7; 12:9, 12), the inhabitants of the earth are those who give in to persecution, wear the mark of the beast, and conform to the world's values rather than to those of God and the Lamb. The tribulations of Revelation fall on them for their apostasy. They are contrasted with the saints who faithfully follow the Lamb, wear the seal of the redeemed on their foreheads, and "are like pilgrims passing through this world" (Beale, 1999:175). The final destiny of the inhabitants of the earth is the lake of fire.

JERUSALEM   The city of God, which was destroyed twice by an evil counterpart—first by Babylon in 586 B.C. and then by Rome, the symbolic equivalent of Babylon in A.D. 70. Jerusalem is the holy city of the faithful, who suffer at the hands of the rulers of Babylon/Rome. To them, the promise of Revelation is the renewal of Jerusalem. The faithful saints will live eternally in the New Jerusalem, where they will rule with Christ the Lamb over their former oppressors.

LAMB   The righteous counter-image to the beast, the Lamb is Christ, who through his suffering, death, and resurrection overcame Satan and his beast to bring about deliverance from the oppression of this world. The activity of the Lamb reminds the saints that their evil seducers and persecutors have been ultimately defeated in the heavenly, spiritual realm. Yet the battle continues in the physical world between the saints and beastly Babylon/Rome. The faithful saints realize that, as they conquer their persecutors, they are reaffirming the spiritual victory already won by Christ the Lamb.

MARTYR   From the word for "witness" *(martys),* martyr has this literal meaning in most occurrences in the Bible. Yet in Revelation it seems to also carry the technical sense of one who is killed for this witness to the faith. Revelation singles out one martyr, Antipas, who died in the city of Pergamum (3:13), but expects that all Christians will witness to the faith in the face of death. The redemption spoken of in Revelation is in answer to the prayer of the martyrs under the altar (6:9-11) that divine justice will avenge their deaths. A message of Revelation is that it is through the death of Jesus Christ and the deaths of the martyrs that God brings about the plan for the salvation of the world.

SAINTS   The term "saints" is used in Revelation for those who overcome temptation and persecution for the cause of Christ. They refuse to compromise with the world by accepting its violent and materialistic values. Their destiny is to join the 144,000 and wear the seal of the redeemed on their foreheads. They are contrasted with the inhabitants of the earth, who give in to persecution and wear the mark of the beast by accepting the values of this world. The destiny of the saints is to share in the joys of the new heaven and earth.

TWENTY-FOUR ELDERS   Composed of the twelve patriarchs of the Hebrew people and the twelve apostles of the New Covenant, the twenty-four elders stand for the entire people of God (4:4, 10; 5:5-7, 14; 7:11, 13; 11:16; 14:3; 19:4). Serving somewhat like the chorus in Greek tragedy, they form a heavenly choir singing praise to God and to the Lamb. Thus, they are the representatives of the church in heaven.

THE WHORE   The evil counterpart of the bride, the whore personifies the inhabitants of the earth who seduce the faithful to compromise with the world by eating food offered to idols and practicing immorality. Her garish garments add to the image of seduction and mark her as the epitome of the wealth that lures Christians into the idolatrous worship of the materialism of Babylon/Rome.

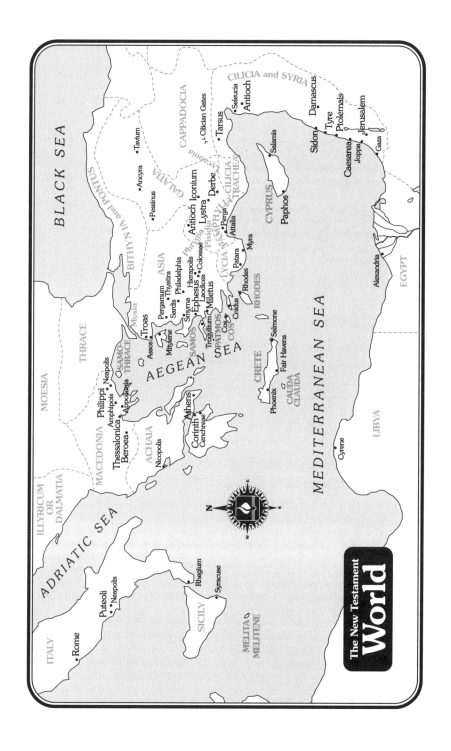

The New Testament World

Bibliography

Achtemeier, Paul J.
  1986   "Expository Articles: Revelation 5:1-14." *Interpretation* 40:283-88.
Aland, Kurt, and Barbara Aland
  1989   *The Text of the New Testament: An Introduction to the Critical Editions and the Theory and Practice of Modern Textual Criticism.* Translated by Erroll F. Rhodes. 2d ed. Grand Rapids: Eerdmans.
Alford, Henry
  1861   *The Greek New Testament: With a Critically Revised Greek Text: A Digest of Various Readings: Marginal References to Verbal and Idiomatic Usage: Prolegomena: and a Critical and Exegetical Commentary.* Vol. 4, Part 2. London: Gilbert & Rivington.
Allis, Oswald
  1945   *Prophecy and the Church.* Philadelphia: Presbyterian and Reformed Publishing Company.
Anderson, B. W.
  1962   "God, Names of." *Interpreter's Dictionary of the Bible.* Vol. 2. Nashville: Abingdon.
Arnold, Clinton E.
  1989   *Ephesians: Power and Magic; The Concept of Power in Ephesians in Light of Its Historical Setting.* Cambridge: Cambridge University Press.
Aune, David E.
  1983   *Prophecy in Early Christianity and the Ancient Mediterranean World.* Grand Rapids: Eerdmans.
  1986   "The Apocalypse of John and the Problem of Genre." *Early Christian Apocalypticism: Genre and Social Setting.* Semeia, No. 36. Edited by Adela Yarbro Collins. Decatur, Ga.: Scholars Press.

1989 "The Prophetic Circle of John of Patmos and the Exegesis of Revelation 22.16." *Journal for the Study of the New Testament* 37:103-16.

1997 *Revelation 1-5* (Word Biblical Commentary). Dallas: Word Books.

1998a *Revelation 6-16* (Word Biblical Commentary). Nashville: Thomas Nelson.

1998b *Revelation 17-22* (Word Biblical Commentary). Nashville: Word Publishing.

Bachman, E. Theodore, ed.
1960 *Luther's Works.* Vol. 55. Philadelphia: Muhlenberg Press.

Barclay, William
1960 *The Revelation of John* (The Daily Study Bible). 2 vols. Philadelphia: Westminster.

Barker, Margaret
2000 *The Revelation of Jesus Christ: Which God Gave to Him to Show to His Servants What Must Soon Take Place (Revelation 1.1).* Edinburgh: T&T Clark.

Barr, David L.
1984 "The Apocalypse as a Symbolic Transformation of the World: A Literary Analysis." *Interpretation* 38:39-50.

1986 "The Apocalypse of John as Oral Enactment." *Interpretation* 40:243-56.

1998 *Tales of the End: A Narrative Commentary on the Book of Revelation* (The Storyteller's Bible). Santa Rosa, Calif.: Polebridge Press.

Barrett, C. K.
1961 *The New Testament Background: Selected Documents.* New York: Harper & Row.

Bauckham, Richard
1993a *The Climax of Prophecy: Studies on the Book of Revelation.* Edinburgh: T&T Clark.

1993b *The Theology of the Book of Revelation* (New Testament Theology). Cambridge: Cambridge University Press.

1998 *God Crucified: Monotheism and Christology in the New Testament.* Grand Rapids: Eerdmans.

Beale, G. K.
1999 *The Book of Revelation: A Commentary on the Greek Text.* Grand Rapids: Eerdmans; Carlisle: Paternoster.

Beasley-Murray, G. R.
1974 *The Book of Revelation* (New Century Bible). Greenwood, S.C.: Attic Press.

Beasley-Murray, G. R., Herschel H. Hobbs, and Ray Frank Robbins
1977 *Revelation: Three Viewpoints.* Nashville: Broadman.

Beckwith, Isbon T.
1919 *The Apocalypse of John: Studies in Introduction with a Critical and Exegetical Commentary.* Grand Rapids: Baker, reprint 1967.

Belk, Fred Richard
1976 *The Great Trek of the Russian Mennonites to Central Asia 1880-1884.* Studies in Anabaptist and Mennonite History, No. 18. Scottdale, Pa. and Kitchener, Ont.: Herald Press.

Bender, Philip
    1985   *Revelation: New Heaven on a New Earth* (Faith & Life Bible
            Studies). Newton, Kan.: Faith & Life Press.
Boesak, Allan A.
    1987   *Comfort and Protest: The Apocalypse from a South African
            Perspective.* Philadelphia: Westminster.
Boettner, Loraine
    1958   *The Millennium.* Grand Rapids: Baker.
Boring, M. Eugene
    1986   "The Theology of Revelation: 'The Lord Our God the Almighty
            Reigns.'" *Interpretation* 40:257-69.
    1989   *Revelation* (Interpretation: A Bible Commentary for Teaching and
            Preaching). Louisville: John Knox Press.
Boyer, Paul
    1992   *When Time Shall Be No More: Prophecy Belief in Modern
            American Culture.* Cambridge: Harvard University Press.
Bredin, Mark R. J.
    1998   "The Synagogue of Satan Accusation in Revelation 2:9." *Biblical
            Theology Bulletin* 28:160-64.
Brensinger, Terry L.
    1999   *Judges* (Believers Church Bible Commentary). Scottdale: Herald
            Press.
Brewer, R. R.
    1952   "Revelation 4:6 and Translations Thereof." *Journal of Biblical
            Literature* 71:227-31.
Bromiley, David G., and Edward D. Silver
    1995   "The Davidian Tradition: From Patriarchal Clan to Prophetic
            Movement." *Armageddon in Waco.* Edited by Stuart A. Wright.
            Chicago: University of Chicago Press.
Brown, Raymond E.
    1979   *The Community of the Beloved Disciple: The Life, Loves, and
            Hates of an Individual Church in New Testament Times.* New
            York: Paulist Press.
Browning, Robert
    1934   *The Poems and Plays of Robert Browning.* New York: Modern
            Library.
Bruce, F. F.
    1969   "The Revelation to John." *A New Testament Commentary.*
            Edited by G. C. D. Howley. London: Pickering & Inglis.
Bunyan, John
    1960   *The Pilgrim's Progress from This World to That which is to
            Come.* Edited by James Blanton Wharey. 2d. ed. Revised by
            Roger Sharrock. Oxford: Clarendon Press.
Caird, G. B.
    1966   *A Commentary on the Revelation of St. John the Divine* (Harper's
            New Testament Commentaries). New York: Harper & Row.
Carey, Greg
    1999   *Elusive Apocalypse: Reading Authority in the Revelation of
            John* (Studies in American Biblical Hermeneutics 15). Macon,
            Ga.: Mercer University Press.
    2000   "Teaching and Preaching the Book of Revelation in the Church."
            Review and Expositor 98:87-100.

Carrington, Philip
 1931 *The Meaning of Revelation.* New York: Macmillan.
Carroll, John T.
 2000 "Creation and Apocalypse." In William P. Brown and S. Dean McBride Jr., eds. *God Who Creates: Essays in Honor of W. Sibley Towner.* Grand Rapids: Eerdmans.
Cary, Ernest, trans.
 1960 *Dio's Roman History.* 9 vols. The Loeb Classical Library. Cambridge: Harvard University Press.
Charles, J. Daryl
 1999 *2 Peter, Jude* (Believers Church Bible Commentary). Scottdale: Herald Press.
Charles, R. H.
 1920 *A Critical and Exegetical Commentary on the Revelation of St. John* (International Critical Commentary). 2 vols. Edinburgh: T&T Clark.
Charlesworth, James H., ed.
 1983 *The Old Testament Pseudepigrapha.* Volume 1, *Apocalyptic Literature and Testaments.* Garden City, N.Y.: Doubleday.
 1985 *The Old Testament Pseudepigrapha.* Volume 2, *Expansions of the Old Testament and Legends, Wisdom and Philosophical Literature, Psalms, and Odes, Fragments of Lost Judeo-Hellenistic Works.* Garden City, N.Y.: Doubleday.
 1987 *The New Testament Apocrypha and Pseudepigrapha: A Guide to Publications, with Excursus on Apocalypses.* (ATLA Bibliography Series, No. 17). Metuchen, N.J.: Scarecrow Press.
Clasen, Claus-Peter
 1972 *Anabaptism: A Social History, 1525-1618, Switzerland, Austria, Moravia, South and Central Germany.* Ithaca, N.Y.: Cornell University Press.
Clouse, Robert G., ed.
 1977 *The Meaning of the Millennium: Four Views.* Downers Grove, Ill.: InterVarsity.
Cohn, Norman
 1970 *The Pursuit of the Millennium: Revolutionary Millenarians and Mystical Anarchists of the Middle Ages.* Rev. and exp. New York: Oxford University Press.
 1993 *Chaos, Cosmos, and the World to Come: The Ancient Roots of Apocalyptic Faith.* New Haven: Yale University Press.
Cohoon, J. W., trans.
 1940 *Dio Chrysostom.* 5 vols. The Loeb Classical Library. Cambridge, Mass.: Harvard University Press.
Collins, John J.
 1979 "Introduction: Towards the Morphology of a Genre." In *Apocalypse: Morphology of a Genre,* 1-20. Semeia, 14. Edited by John J. Collins. Missoula, Mont.: Scholars Press.
 1983 *Between Athens and Jerusalem: Jewish Identity in the Hellenistic Diaspora.* New York: Crossroad.
 1987 *The Apocalyptic Imagination: An Introduction to the Jewish Matrix of Christianity.* New York: Crossroad.

Colson, F. H., trans.
> 1948   *Philo.* 10 vols. The Loeb Classical Library. Cambridge: Harvard University Press.

Correll, Ernst H.
> 1956   "Eschatology." *Mennonite Encyclopedia,* 2:247. Scottdale, Pa.: Mennonite Publishing House.

Court, John M.
> 1979   *Myth and History in the Book of Revelation.* Atlanta: John Knox.
>
> 2000   *The Book of Revelation and the Johannine Apocalyptic Tradition.* JSNTSS, 190. Sheffield, U.K.: Sheffield Academic Press.

Craddock, Fred B.
> 1986   "Preaching the Book of Revelation." *Interpretation* 40:270-82.

Crockett, William, ed.
> 1992   *Four Views on Hell.* Grand Rapids: Zondervan.

Crouzel, Henri
> 1989   *Origen.* Translated by A. S. Worrall. San Francisco: Harper & Row.

Culpepper, R. Alan
> 1975   *The Johannine School: An Evaluation of the Johannine-School Hypothesis Based on an Investigation of the Nature of Ancient Schools* (Society of Biblical Literature Dissertation Series, Number 26). Missoula, Mont: Scholars Press.

Culpepper, R. Alan, ed.
> 2000   *The Johannine Literature: An Introduction.* Sheffield, U.K.: Sheffield Academic Press.

Dante Alighieri
> 1995   *Dante's Inferno: The Indiana Critical Edition.* Translated and edited by Mark Musa. Bloomington: Indiana University Press.

Deissmann, G. Adolf.
> 1901   *Bible Studies: Contributions Chiefly from Papyri and Inscriptions to the History of the Language, the Literature, and the Religion of Hellenistic Judaism and Primitive Christianity.* Translated by Alexander Grieve. Peabody, Mass.: Hendrickson.
>
> 1965   *Light from the Ancient East: The New Testament Illustrated by Recently Discovered Texts of the Graeco-Roman World.* Translated by Lionel R. M. Strachan. Grand Rapids: Baker.

Dirk Philips
> 1992   *The Writings of Dirk Philips: 1504-1568.* Translated and edited by Cornelius J. Dyck, William E. Keeney, and Alvin J. Beachy. Waterloo, Ont. and Scottdale: Herald Press.

Drescher, John M.
> 1974   *Spirit Fruit.* Scottdale: Herald Press.

Duff, Paul B.
> 2001   *Who Rides the Beast? Prophetic Rivalry and the Rhetoric of Crisis in the Churches of the Apocalypse.* Oxford: Oxford University Press.

Eco, Umberto
> 1980   *The Name of the Rose.* Translated by William Weaver. San Diego: Harcourt Brace Jovanovich.

Efird, James M.
    1986   *End-times, Rapture, Antichrist, Millennium: What the Bible Says.* Nashville: Abingdon.
    1989   *Revelation for Today: An Apocalyptic Approach.* Nashville: Abingdon.
Elias, Jacob W.
    1995   *1 and 2 Thessalonians* (Believers Church Bible Commentary). Scottdale: Herald Press.
Eliot, T. S.
    1958   *The Complete Poems and Plays 1909-1950.* New York: Harcourt, Brace.
Eller, Vernard
    1974   *The Most Revealing Book in the Bible: Making Sense out of Revelation.* Grand Rapids: Eerdmans.
Ellul, Jacques
    1977   *Apocalypse: The Book of Revelation.* Translated by George W. Schreiner. New York: Seabury Press.
Emmerson, R. K., and B. McGinn, eds.
    1993   *The Apocalyse in the Middle Ages.* Ithaca: Cornell University Press.
Epiphanius of Salamis
    1990   *The* Panarion *of St. Epiphanius, Bishop of Salamis: Selected Passages.* Translated by Philip R. Amidon, S.J. Oxford: Oxford University Press.
Erdman, Charles R.
    1936   *The Revelation of John.* Philadelphia: Westminster.
Estep, William R.
    1975   *The Anabaptist Story.* Rev. edition. Nashville: Broadman.
Eusebius Pamphilus
    1955   *The Ecclesiastical History.* Translated by Christian Frederic Cruse. Grand Rapids: Baker.
Ewert, David
    1980   *And Then Comes the End.* Kitchener, Ont. and Scottdale: Herald Press.
Farrer, Austin
    1964   *The Revelation of St. John the Divine: Commentary on the English Text.* Oxford: Clarendon.
Fekkes, Jan, III
    1994   *Isaiah and Prophetic Traditions in Revelation: Visionary Antecedents and Their Development.* Journal for the Study of the New Testament: Supplement Series, 93. Sheffield, U.K.: Sheffield Academic Press.
Felix, Minucius, trans.
    1960   *Tertullian.* The Loeb Classical Library. Cambridge: Harvard University Press.
Ferre, Nels
    1951   *The Christian Understanding of God.* New York: Harper.
Ford, J. Massyngberde
    1975   *Revelation: Introduction, Translation and Commentary* (Anchor Bible). Garden City, N.Y.: Doubleday.

Forsyth, Neil
  1987   *The Old Enemy: Satan and the Combat Myth.* Princeton: Princeton University Press.
Franzmann, Martin H.
  1976   *The Revelation to John.* St. Louis: Concordia Publishing House.
Friedmann, Robert
  1973   *The Theology of Anabaptism: An Interpretation.* Studies in Anabaptist and Mennonite History, No. 15. Scottdale: Herald Press.
Friesen, Steven
  1993   "Ephesus: Key to a Vision in Revelation." *Biblical Archeology Review* 19(3):24-37.
  2001   *Imperial Cults and the Apocalypse of John: Reading Revelation in the Ruins.* Oxford: Oxford University Press.
Geddert, Tim
  2000   *Mark* (Believers Church Bible Commentary). Scottdale: Herald Press.
Gerstner, John
  1980   *Jonathan Edwards on Heaven and Hell.* Grand Rapids: Baker.
Glasson, T. F.
  1965   *The Revelation of John* (The Cambridge Bible Commentary on the New English Bible). Cambridge: Cambridge University Press.
Gloer, W. Hulitt
  2001   "Worship God! Liturgical Elements in the Apocalypse." *Review and Expositor* 98:35-57.
Goldsworthy, Graeme
  1984   *The Lion and the Lamb: The Gospel in Revelation.* Nashville: Thomas Nelson Publishers.
Goodspeed, Edgar J.
  1937   *An Introduction to the New Testament.* Chicago: University of Chicago Press.
Gonzàlez, Catherine Gunsalus
  1999   "Mission Accomplished; Mission Begun: Lent and the Book of Revelation." *Journal for Preachers* 22(2):9-13.
Gonzàlez, Catherine Gunsalus, and Justo L. Gonzàlez
  1997   *Revelation* (Westminster Bible Companion). Louisville: Westminster John Knox.
Grimsrud, Ted
  1987   *Triumph of the Lamb: A Self-Study Guide to the Book of Revelation.* Scottdale: Herald Press.
Guenther, Allen R.
  1998   *Hosea, Amos* (Believers Church Bible Commentary). Scottdale: Herald Press.
Guthrie, Donald
  1987   *The Relevance of John's Apocalypse* (The Didsbury Lectures). Grand Rapids: Eerdmans.
Gwynn, John
  1897   *The Apocalypse of St. John in a Syriac Version Hitherto Unknown.* Amsterdam: APA-Philo Press.
Harmon, A. M., trans.
  1953   *Lucian.* The Loeb Classical Library. Cambridge: Harvard University Press.

Harrington, Wilfred J.
1993   *Revelation* (Sacra Pagina Series). Collegeville, Minn.: Liturgical Press.
Hayes, Zachary J.
1992   "The Purgatorial View." *Four Views on Hell.* Edited by William Crockett. Grand Rapids: Zondervan.
Hays, David M.
1973   *Glory at the Right Hand: Psalm 110 in Early Christianity.* Nashville: Abingdon.
Hays, Richard B.
1996   "Revelation: Resisting the Beast." In *The Moral Vision of the New Testament: Community, Cross, New Creation; A Contemporary Introduction to New Testament Ethics,* 169-85. San Francisco: Harper Collins.
Hellholm, David
1986   "The Problem of the Apocalyptic Genre and the Apocalypse of John." *Early Christian Apocalypticism: Genre and Social Setting,* 13-64. Semeia, No. 36. Edited by Adela Yarbro Collins. Decatur, Ga.: Scholars Press.
Hemer, Colin J.
1986   *The Letters to the Seven Churches of Asia in Their Local Setting.* JSNTSS, 11. Sheffield, U.K.: Sheffield Academic Press.
Hendricksen, William
1982   *More than Conquerors: An Interpretation of the Book of Revelation.* Grand Rapids: Baker.
Herford, R. Travers, ed.
1945   *Pirke Aboth. The Ethics of the Talmud: Sayings of the Fathers.* New York: Schocken Books.
Herodotus
1942   "The Persian Wars." Translated by George Rawlinson. *The Greek Historians: The Complete and Unabridged Works of Herodotus, Thycydides, Xenephon, Arrian,* Vol. 1. Edited by Francis R. B. Godolphin. New York: Random House.
Hughes, Philip Edgcumbe
1990   *The Book of the Revelation: A Commentary.* Grand Rapids: Eerdmans.
Janzen, Waldemar
2000   *Exodus.* (Believers Church Bible Commentary). Scottdale: Herald Press.
Jerome, Saint
1953   *Lettres: Tome III* (Collection des Universités de France). Text established and translated into French by Jerome Labourt. Paris: Société D'Édition "Les Belles Lettres."
Jeske, Richard L.
1983   *Revelation for Today: Images of Hope.* Philadelphia: Fortress.
Jewett, Robert
1979   *Jesus Against the Rapture: Seven Unexpected Prophecies.* Philadelphia: Westminster.
Johns, Loren
1998   "The Origins and Rhetorical Force of the Lamb Christology of the Apocalypse of John." Ph.D. diss. Princeton Theological Seminary.

Jones, Thomas Robert
1998   *A Non-Violent Revelation to John.* Farwell, Mich.: Tobacco River Publishers.
Juvenal
1940   *Juvenal and Persius.* Translated by G. G. Ramsay. Cambridge: Harvard University Press.
Kazantzakis, Nikos
1962   *Saint Francis.* New York: Simon & Schuster.
Kelly, Balmer H.
1986   "Expository Articles: Revelation 7:9-17." *Interpretation* 40:288-95.
Keeney, William Echard
1968   *The Development of Dutch Anabaptist Thought and Practice from 1539-1564.* Nieuwkoop: B. de Graaf.
Kittel, Gerhard, and Gerhard Friedrich, eds.
         Theological Dictionary of the New Testament. Translated and edited by Geoffrey W. Bromiley. 9 vols. Grand Rapids: Eerdmans.
Klaassen, Walter
1981   *Anabaptism in Outline: Selected Primary Sources.* Classics of the Radical Reformation Series. Waterloo, Ont. and Scottdale: Herald Press.
1999   *Armageddon and the Peaceable Kingdom.* Waterloo, Ont. and Scottdale: Herald Press.
Klassen, William
1966   "Vengeance in the Apocalypse of John." *Catholic Biblical Quarterly* 28:300-11.
Knohl, Israel
1996   "Between Voice and Silence: The Relationship between Prayer and Temple Cult." *Journal of Biblical Literature* 115(1):17-30.
Koester, Craig R.
2001   *Revelation and the End of All Things.* Grand Rapids: Eerdmans.
Kraft, Heinrich
1974   *Die Offenbarung Des Johannes. Handbuch zum Neuen Testament 16a.* Tubingen: Mohr-Siebeck.
Krahn, Cornelius
1981   *Dutch Anabaptism: Origin, Spread, Life, and Thought.* Scottdale: Herald Press.
Kraybill, J. Nelson
1996   *Imperial Cult and Commerce in John's Apocalypse.* JSNTSS, 132. Sheffield, U.K.: Sheffield Academic Press.
Krodel, Gerhard A.
1989   *Revelation* (Augsburg Commentary on the New Testament). Minneapolis: Augsburg Publishing House.
Küng, Hans
1984   *Eternal Life, Life after Death as a Medical, Philosophical, and Theological Problem.* New York: Doubleday.
Ladd, George Eldon
1972   *A Commentary on the Revelation of John.* Grand Rapids: Eerdmans.
LaHaye, Tim
1975   *Revelation Illustrated and Made Plain.* Grand Rapids: Zondervan.

LaHaye, Tim, and Jerry B. Jenkins
  1995- *The Left Behind Series*. Carol Stream, Ill.: Tyndale House.
LaSor, William Sanford
  1982 *The Truth about Armageddon: What the Bible Says about the End Times*. San Francisco: Harper & Row.
Lawrence, David Herbert
  1982 *Apocalypse*. Edited by Mara Kalnins. New York: Viking.
Lederach, Paul. M.
  1994 *Daniel* (Believers Church Bible Commentary). Scottdale: Herald Press.
Lehn, Cornelia
  1980 *Peace Be with You*. Newton, Kan.: Faith & Life Press.
Lewis, C. S.
  1943 *The Screwtape Letters*. New York: MacMillan.
  1965 *The Problem of Pain*. New York: MacMillan.
  1967 *Mere Christianity*. New York: MacMillan.
Liechty, Daniel, trans., ed.
  1994 *Early Anabaptist Spirituality: Selected Writings*. The Classics of Western Spirituality: A Library of the Great Spiritual Masters. New York and Mahwah: Paulist Press.
Lilje, Hanns
  1957 *The Last Book of the Bible: The Meaning of the Revelation of St. John*. Translated by Olive Wyon. Philadelphia: Fortress Press.
Lind, Millard C.
  1996 *Ezekiel* (Believers Church Bible Commentary). Scottdale: Herald Press.
Lindsey, Hal, with C. C. Carlson
  1970 *The Late Great Planet Earth*. Grand Rapids: Zondervan.
  1972 *Satan Is Alive and Well on Planet Earth*. Grand Rapids: Zondervan.
  1980 *The 1980's: Countdown to Armageddon*. King of Prussia, Pa.: Westgate Press.
Littell, Franklin Hamlin
  1958 *The Anabaptist View of the Church: A Study of the Origins of Sectarian Protestantism*. 2d ed. Boston: Beacon Hill.
Lohse, Eduard
  1976 *The New Testament Environment*. Translated by John E. Steely. Nashville: Abingdon.
MacKenzie, Robert K.
  1997 *The Author of the Apocalypse: A Review of the Prevailing Hypothesis of Jewish-Christian Authorship*. Mellen Biblical Press Series 51. Lewiston, N.Y.: Mellen.
Malina, Bruce J.
  2000 *The New Jerusalem in the Revelation of John: The City as Symbol of Life with God*. Collegeville, Minn.: Liturgical Press.
Malina, Bruce J. and John J. Pilch
  2000 *Social Science Commentary on the Book of Revelation*. Minneapolis: Fortress Press.
Martens, Elmer A.
  1986 *Jeremiah* (Believers Church Bible Commentary). Scottdale: Herald Press.

Martin, Ernest D.
    1993   *Colossians, Philemon* (Believers Church Bible Commentary).
           Scottdale: Herald Press.
Mauser, Ulrich
    1992   *The Gospel of Peace: A Scriptural Message for Today's World.*
           Louisville: Westminster/John Knox.
McGinn, Bernard
    1987   "Revelation." *The Literary Guide to the Bible.* Edited by Robert
           Alter and Frank Kermode. Cambridge: Harvard University Press.
McKelvey, R. J.
    1999   *The Millennium and the Book of Revelation.* Cambridge, U.K.:
           Lutterworth.
Menno Simons
    1956   *The Complete Writings of Menno Simons c. 1496-1561.*
           Translated by Leonard Verduin. Edited by John Christian Wenger.
           Scottdale: Herald Press.
Merritt, Bruce
    1990   *The Patmos Conspiracy.* Nappanee, Ind.: Evangel Press.
Metzger, Bruce M.
    1972   "Literary Forgeries and Canonical Pseudepigrapha." *Journal of
           Biblical Literature* 91(1):3-24.
    1993   *Breaking the Code: Understanding the Book of Revelation.*
           Nashville: Abingdon.
Metzger, Bruce M., et al.
    1971   *A Textual Commentary on the Greek New Testament.* New
           York: United Bible Societies.
Michaels, J. Ramsey
    1997   *Revelation* (The IVP New Testament Commentary Series).
           Downers Grove, Ill.: InterVarsity.
Milton, John
    1991   *Paradise Lost.* Edited by Stephen Orgel and Jonathan Goldberg.
           New York: Oxford University Press.
Minear, Paul S.
    1968   *I Saw a New Earth.* Washington, D.C.: Corpus Books.
    1981   *New Testament Apocalyptic* (Interpreting Biblical Texts).
           Nashville: Abingdon.
Morris, Leon
    1969   *The Revelation of St. John* (Tyndale Commentaries). Grand
           Rapids: Eerdmans.
    1984   "Eternal Punishment." *Evangelical Dictionary of Theology.*
           Edited by Walter Elwell. Grand Rapids: Baker.
Morrish, George
    1976   *A Concordance of the Septuagint.* Grand Rapids: Zondervan.
Moulton, W. F., and A. S. Geden, eds.
    1926   *A Concordance to the Greek New Testament: According to the
           Notes of Westcott and Hort, Tischendorf and the English
           Revisers.* Edinburgh: T&T Clark.
Mounce, Robert H.
    1977   *The Book of Revelation* (The New International Commentary on
           the New Testament). Grand Rapids: Eerdmans.
    1992   *What Are We Waiting For? A Commentary on Revelation.*
           Grand Rapids: Eerdmans.

Mowinckel, Sigmund
  1954 *He That Cometh*. Translated by G. W. Anderson. Nashville: Abingdon.
Mulholland, M. Robert, Jr.
  1990 *Holy Living in an Unholy World: Revelation* (A Francis Asbury Commentary). Grand Rapids: Francis Asbury Press (Zondervan).
Murphy, Frederick J.
  1998 *Fallen Is Babylon: The Revelation to John* (The New Testament in Context). Harrisburg, Pa.: Trinity Press International.
Musurillo, H., ed.
  1972 *The Acts of the Christian Martyrs*. New York: Oxford.
New Catholic Encyclopedia
  1967 New York: McGraw-Hill.
Nicholas of Lyra
  1997 *Apocalypse Commentary*. Translated with Introduction and Notes by Philip D. W. Krey. Kalamazoo, Mich.: Medieval Institute Publications.
O'Brien, Michael
  1997 *Father Elijah: An Apocalypse*. San Francisco: Ignatius Press.
O'Connor, Flannery
  1988 *Collected Works*. New York: Library of America.
Okholm, Dennis L., and Timothy R. Phillips, eds.
  1996 *Four Views on Salvation in a Pluralistic World*. Grand Rapids: Zondervan.
Oldfather, C. H., trans.
  1960 *Diodorus of Sicily*. The Loeb Classical Library. Cambridge: Harvard University Press.
Ortlund, Raymond C., Jr.
  1996 *Whoredom: God's Unfaithful Wife in Biblical Theology* (New Studies in Biblical Theology). Grand Rapids: Eerdmans.
Pate, C. Marvin, gen. ed.
  1998 *Four Views on the Book of Revelation*. Grand Rapids: Zondervan.
Paton, Alan
  1981 *Ah, But Your Land Is Beautiful*. New York: Charles Scribner's Sons.
Pentecost, J. Dwight
  1958 *Things to Come: Study in Biblical Eschatology*. Grand Rapids: Zondervan.
Peretti, Frank
  1986 *This Present Darkness*. Westchester, Ill.: Crossway Books.
Perry, Marvin, et al.
  1985 *Western Civilization: Ideas, Politics, and Society*. 2d ed. Boston: Houghton Mifflin.
Peterson, Eugene H.
  1988 *Reversed Thunder: The Revelation of John and the Praying Imagination*. San Francisco: Harper Collins.
Philips, Dirk
  See Dirk Philips.
Pieters, Albertus
  1954 *Studies in the Revelation of St. John*. Grand Rapids: Eerdmans.

Pilgrim, Walter E.
1999 *Uneasy Neighbors: Church and State in the New Testament* (Overtures to Biblical Theology). Minneapolis: Fortress Press.

Piper, Otto
1951 "The Apocalypse of John and the Liturgy of the Ancient Church." *Church History* 20:10-22.

Pippin, Tina
1999 *Apocalyptic Bodies: The Biblical End of the World in Text and Image.* London: Routledge.

Polanyi, Michael
1964 *Personal Knowledge: Towards a Post-Critical Philosophy.* Rev. edition. New York: Harper & Row (Harper Torchbooks).

Powaski, Ronald E.
1987 *March to Armageddon: The United States and the Nuclear Arms Race, 1939 to the Present.* New York: Oxford University Press.

Raber, Rudolph W.
1986 "Expository Articles: Revelation 21:1-8." *Interpretation* 40:296-301.

Ramsay, William M.
1904 *The Letters to the Seven Churches of Asia: And Their Place in the Plan of the Apocalypse.* London: Hodder & Stoughton.

Reddish, Mitchell G., ed.
1990 *Apocalyptic Literature: A Reader.* Nashville: Abingdon.

Reeves, Margorie
1976 *Joachim of Fiore and the Prophetic Future.* New York: Harper & Row (Harper Torchbooks).

Richard, Pablo
1995 *Apocalypse: A People's Commentary on the Book of Revelation* (The Bible and Liberation Series). Maryknoll, N.Y.: Orbis Books.

Rissi, M.
1966 *Time and History: A Study on the Revelation.* Translated by Gordon C. Winsor. Richmond, Va.: John Knox Press.

Rist, Martin
1957 "The Revelation of St. John the Divine." *The Interpreter's Bible.* Nashville: Abingdon.

Roberts, Alexander, and James Donaldson, eds.
1956 *The Anti-Nicene Fathers: Translations of the Writings of the Fathers down to A.D. 325.* Revised by A. Cleveland Coxe. Grand Rapids: Eerdmans.

Robinson, John A. T.
1976 *Redating the New Testament.* Philadelphia: Westminster.

Roloff, Jürgen
1993 *The Revelation of John: A Continental Commentary.* Translated by John E. Alsup. Minneapolis: Fortress.

Rostovtzeff, M.
1938 *Dura-Europos and Its Art.* Oxford: Clarendon Press.

Rowland, Christopher C.
1982 *The Open Door: A Study of Apocalyptic in Judaism and Early Christianity.* New York: Crossroad.

1988   *Radical Christianity: A Reading of Recovery.* Maryknoll, N.Y.:
       Orbis Books.
1998   "The Book of Revelation." *The Interpreter's Bible.* Vol. 12.
       Nashville: Abingdon.
Royalty, Robert M., Jr.
1998   *The Streets of Heaven: The Ideology of Wealth in the
       Apocalypse of John.* Macon, Ga.: Mercer University Press.
Russell, D. S.
1964   *The Method and Message of Jewish Apocalyptic, 200 B.C.–
       A.D. 100* (The Old Testament Library). Philadelphia: Westminster.
Sanders, Harry A.
1918   "The Number of the Beast in Revelation." *Journal of Biblical
       Literature* 37:95-99.
Schüssler Fiorenza, Elisabeth
1985   *The Book of Revelation: Justice and Judgment.* Philadelphia:
       Fortress.
1989   "Revelation." In *The New Testament and Its Modern
       Interpreters.* Edited by Eldon J. Epp and George W. MacRae,
       407-27. Atlanta: Scholars Press.
1991   *Revelation: Vision of a Just World* (Proclamation Series).
       Minneapolis: Fortress.
Scofield, C. I.
1945   *The Scofield Reference Bible.* New York: Oxford University
       Press.
Scobie, Charles H. H.
1993   "Local References in the Letters to the Seven Churches." *New
       Testament Studies* 39:606-24.
Shaw, George Bernard
1933   *The Adventures of the Black Girl in Her Search for God.* New
       York: Capricorn Books.
Sherwin-White, A. N.
1966   *The Letters of Pliny.* Clarendon Press.
Sider, Ronald J.
1997   *Rich Christians in an Age of Hunger: Moving from Affluence
       to Generosity.* Dallas: Word Publishing.
Simons, Menno
       See Menno Simons
Slater, Thomas B.
1999   *Christ and Community: A Socio-Historical Study of the
       Christology of Revelation.* JSNTSS, 178. Sheffield, U.K.:
       Sheffield Academic Press.
Smith, Robert H.
2000   *Apocalypse: A Commentary on Revelation in Words and
       Images.* Collegeville, Minn.: Liturgical Press.
Smith, T. C.
1997   *Reading the Signs: A Sensible Approach to Revelation and
       Other Apocalyptic Writings.* Macon, Ga.: Smyth & Helwys.
Sordie, M.
1986   *The Christians in the Roman Empire.* Translated by Annabel
       Bedini. Norman: University of Oklahoma Press.

Spurgeon, Charles Haddon
  1870 *The Treasury of David: Containing an Original Exposition of the Book of Psalms; a Collection of Illustrative Extracts from the Whole Range of Literature; a Series of Homiletical Hints upon Almost Every Verse; and Lists of Writers upon Each Psalm.* 6 vols. New York: Marshall Brothers.
Stanley, John E.
  1998 "Two Futures—Jürgen Moltmann's Eschatology and Revelation's Apocalyptic." *Asbury Theological Journal* 53:39-40.
Stauffer, Ethelbert
  1955 *Christ and the Caesars.* London: S.C.M. Press.
Stringfellow, William
  1973 *An Ethic for Christians and Other Aliens in a Strange Land.* Waco, Tex.: Word, Inc.
  1977 *Conscience and Obedience: The Politics of Romans 13 and Revelation 13 in the Light of the Second Coming.* Waco, Tex.: Word, Inc.
Swartley, Willard M.
  1981 *Mark: The Way for All Nations.* Scottdale: Herald Press. Reprint: Eugene, Ore.: Wipf and Stock Publishers, 1999.
  1996 "War and Peace in the New Testament." *Aufstieg und Niedergang der römischen Welt [Rise and Decline of the Roman World].* Edited by Wolfgang Haase and Hildegard Temporini. II.26.3:2298-2408. Berlin, New York: De Gruyter.
Sweet, John
  1990 *Revelation* (TPI New Testament Commentaries). Reprint. Philadelphia: Trinity Press International.
Swete, Henry Barclay
  1908 *The Apocalypse of St. John: The Greek Text with Introduction, Notes, and Indices.* 3rd ed. Grand Rapids: Eerdmans.
Talbert, Charles H.
  1994 *The Apocalypse: A Reading of the Revelation of John.* Louisville: Westminster John Knox.
Tenney, Merrill C.
  1957 *Interpreting Revelation.* Grand Rapids: Eerdmans.
Thompson, Leonard L.
  1986 "A Sociological Analysis of Tribulation in the Apocalypse of John." *Early Christian Apocalypticism: Genre and Social Setting.* Semeia 36. Edited by Adela Yarbro Collins. Decatur, Ga.: Scholars Press.
  1990 *The Book of Revelation: Apocalypse and Empire.* New York: Oxford University Press.
  1998 *Revelation* (Abingdon New Testament Commentaries). Nashville: Abingdon.
Turner, William L.
  2000 *Making Sense of the Revelation: A Clear Message of Hope.* Macon, Ga.: Smyth & Helwys.
Van Braght, Thieleman J.
  1950 *The Bloody Theater or Martyrs Mirror of the Defenseless Christians.* Translated by Joseph F. Sohm. Scottdale: Herald Press.

Van Buren, Paul M.
 1998 *According to the Scriptures: The Origins of the Gospel and of the Church's Old Testament.* Grand Rapids: Eerdmans.
Van Impe, Jack
 1983 *11:59 and Counting.* Royal Oak, Mich.: Jack Van Impe Ministries.
Vinson, Richard B.
 2001 "The Social World of the Book of Revelation." *Review and Expositor* 98:11-33.
Wagner, Donald E.
 1995 *Anxious for Armageddon.* Waterloo, Ont. and Scottdale: Herald Press.
Wainwright, Arthur W.
 1993 *Mysterious Apocalypse: Interpreting the Book of Revelation.* Nashville: Abingdon.
Walhout, Edwin
 2000 *Revelation: Making Sense of John's Visions.* Grand Rapids: CRC Publications.
Wall, Robert W.
 1991 *Revelation* (New International Biblical Commentary). Peabody, Mass.: Hendrickson.
Walsh, Gerald G., and Daniel J. Honan, trans.
 1954 *Saint Augustine: The City of God, Books XVII-XXII.* Washington, D.C.: Catholic University of America Press.
Waltner, Erland
 1999 *1 Peter* (Believers Church Bible Commentary). Scottdale: Herald Press.
Walvoord, John F.
 1959 *The Millennial Kingdom.* Findlay, Ohio: Dunham Publishing Company.
 1966 *The Revelation of Jesus Christ.* Chicago: Moody Press.
 1988 *The Nations, Israel, and the Church in Prophecy.* Grand Rapids: Zondervan.
Weaver, J. Denny
 1994a "Christus Victor, Ecclesiology, and Christology." *Mennonite Quarterly Review* 68:277-90.
 1994b "Some Theological Implications of Christus Victor." *Mennonite Quarterly Review* 68:483-99.
 2001 *The Nonviolent Atonement.* Grand Rapids: Eerdmans.
Weber, Timothy P.
 1987 *Living in the Shadow of the Second Coming: American Premillennialism, 1875-1982.* Expanded ed. Chicago: University of Chicago Press.
Wengst, Klaus
 1987 *Pax Roman and the Peace of Jesus Christ.* Translated by John Bowden. Philadelphia: Fortress Press.
Wesley, John
 1986 *The Works of John Wesley.* 3rd ed. Grand Rapids: Baker.
Westcott, B. F., and F. J. A. Hort
 1988 *Introduction to the New Testament in the Original Greek: With Notes on Selected Readings.* Reprint. Peabody, Mass.: Hendrickson.

Wick, Peter
>1998   "There Was Silence in Heaven (Revelation 8:1): An Annotation to Israel Knohl's 'Between Voice and Silence.'" *Journal of Biblical Literature* 117(3):512-14.

Wigram, George V.
>1996   *The Englishman's Greek Concordance of the New Testament.* Peabody, Mass.: Hendrickson.

Wilcock, Michael
>1975   *The Message of Revelation: I Saw Heaven Opened.* Downers Grove, Ill.: InterVarsity.

Wilson, Dwight
>1977   *Armageddon Now! The Premillenarian Response to Russia and Israel Since 1917.* Grand Rapids: Baker.

Wilson, J. Christian
>1993   "The Problem of the Domitianic Date of the Revelation." *New Testament Studies* 39:587-605.

Wink, Walter
>1984   *Naming the Powers: The Language of Power in the New Testament.* Philadelphia: Fortress Press.
>1986   *Unmasking the Powers: The Invisible Forces That Determine Human Existence.* Philadelphia: Fortress Press.
>1992   *Engaging the Powers: Discernment and Resistance in a World of Domination.* Minneapolis: Fortress Press.
>1998   *The Powers That Be: Theology for a New Millennium.* London: Galilee-Doubleday.

Wittlinger, Carlton O.
>1978   *Quest for Piety and Obedience: The Story of the Brethren in Christ.* Nappanee, Ind.: Evangel Press.

Worth, Roland H., Jr.
>1999   *The Seven Cities of the Apocalypse and Roman Culture.* New York: Paulist Press.

Yarbro Collins, Adela
>1977   "The Political Perspective of the Revelation of John." *Journal of Biblical Literature* 96:241-56.
>1984   *Crisis and Catharsis: The Power of the Apocalypse.* Philadelphia: Westminster.
>1986a   *Early Christian Apocalypticism: Genre and Social Setting.* Semeia, No. 36. Decatur, Ga.: Scholars Press.
>1986b   "Reading the Book of Revelation in the Twentieth Century." *Interpretation* 40:229-42.
>1991   *The Apocalypse* (New Testament Message 22). Collegeville, Minn.: Liturgical Press.
>1998   "Pergamon in Early Christian Literature." In *Pergamon: Citadel of the Gods.* Edited by Helmut Koester. Harrisburg, Pa.: Trinity Press International, 163-84.

Yeatts, John R.
>1993   Review of *The Patmos Conspiracy* by Bruce Merritt. *Brethren in Christ History and Life* 16(1):133-36.
>2001   "The Fictionalizing of Fundamentalist Eschatology: The Left Behind Series" (Review Essay). *Brethren in Christ History and Life* 24(1):109-26.

Yoder Neufeld, Thomas R.
    2002 *Ephesians* (Believers Church Bible Commentary). Scottdale: Herald Press.
Yoder, John Howard
    1972 *The Politics of Jesus.* Grand Rapids: Eerdmans.

Ancient Sources

APOCRYPHAL and PSUEDEPIGRAPHAL BOOKS

Apoc. Abraham	1st -2nd C. AD	Apocalypse of Abraham
2 Bar.	2nd C. AD	Syriac Apocalypse of Baruch
3 Bar.	1st -3rd C. AD	Greek Apocalypse of Baruch
1 Enoch	2nd C. BC-1st C. AD	Ethiopic Apocalypse of Enoch
2 Enoch	1st C. AD	Slavonic Apocalypse of Enoch
Asmpt. Moses	1st C. AD	Assumption of Moses
Apoc. Peter	1st -2nd C. AD	Apocalypse of Peter
Apoc. Pseudo John		Apocalypse of PseudoJohn
Apoc. Zephaniah	1st C. BC-1st C. AD	Apocalypse of Zephaniah
Jub.	2nd C. BC	Jubilees
Odes Sol.	1st -2nd C. AD	Odes of Solomon
3 Macc.	1st C. BC	3 Maccabees
4 Macc.	1st C. AD	4 Maccabees
Asc. Isa.	2nd C. BC-4th C. AD	Martyrdom and Ascension of Isaiah
Ps. Sol.	1st C. BC	Psalms of Solomon
Sib. Or.	2nd C. BC-7th C. AD	Sibylline Oracles
Test. Dan	2nd C. BC	Testament of Dan
Test. Joseph	2nd C. BC	Testament of Joseph
Test. Judah	2nd C. BC	Testament of Judah
Test. Levi	2nd C. BC	Testament of Levi
Test. Naphtali	2nd C. B.C	Testament of Naphali
Test. Moses	1st C. AD	Testament of Moses

JEWISH HISTORY

Jos.	Josephus
Ant.	*The Antiquities of the Jews*

GREEK HISTORY

Lucian	
Syr. Dea	*The Goddesse of Surrye*
Alex.	*Alexander the False Prophet*

ROMAN HISTORY
Pliny The Elder
Nat. Hist.   *Natural History*
Tac.   Tacitus

Annals   *Annals of Imperial Rome*
Hist.   *Histories*

Strabo
Geog.   *Geography*

Suet.   Suetonius

Listed by the Caesar   *The Twelve Caesars*

DEAD SEA SCROLLS
CD   Damascus Document
DJD   Discoveries in the Judean Desert
1 QH   Thanksgiving Hymns
1 QS   Rule of the Community
1 QM   War Scroll
4 Qp Nah.   Nahum Commentary
1 Qp Hab.   Habakkuk Commentary

CHURCH WRITINGS
Did.   Didache
Herm.   Shepherd of Hermas
Sim.   *Similitudes*
Ignatius
Eph.   *Letter to the Ephesians*
Magn.   *Letter to the Magnesians*
Smyrn.   *Letter to the Smyrnaeans*
Trall.   *Letter to the Trallians*
Barn.   The Epistle of Barnabas
1 Clem.   1 Clement
2 Clem.   2 Clement
Irenaeus
Adv. Haer.   *Against All Heresies*
Eusebius
Eccl. Hist.   *Ecclesiastical History*
Hippolytus
Com. on Dan.   *Commentary on Daniel*
The Refutation   *The Refutation of All Heresies*
de Ant.   *Treatise on Christ and Antichrist*

Index of Ancient Sources

491

The Author

John R. Yeatts has served on the faculty of Messiah College in Grantham, Pennsylvania, for the past twenty-two years. Currently he teaches in psychology and religion in the School of the Humanities, and for ten years he was chair of the Department of Biblical Studies, Religion, and Philosophy. Twice, Yeatts has received the college's Excellence in Teaching Award, and he was awarded the Messiah College Scholarship Award.

Yeatts began his professional life in the pastoral and denominational ministry. While completing his schooling, he was a youth pastor. Later, he served five years as a pastor of Fairland Brethren in Christ Church near Lebanon, Pennsylvania. He served the Brethren in Christ denomination for three years as Christian education staff and was the denomination's representative on Anabaptist curriculum projects such as the *Foundation Series* youth and adult curriculum and *Jubilee: God's Good News* children's curriculum.

Born in Springfield, Ohio, John Yeatts grew up in the Brethren in Christ Church. He graduated from Messiah College with degrees in mathematics and religion, later receiving his M.Div. in Biblical Studies from Princeton Theological Seminary and the doctorate from Purdue University in educational psychology.

His scholarship has been wide-ranging, and for the past decade, he has served as book review editor for the *Brethren in Christ History and Life*. His writings have included entries in the *Baker Dictionary of Christian Education* and articles published in journals such as the *Journal for the Scientific Study of Religion*, *Review of Religious Research*, *Christian Education Journal*, *Journal of Research in Christian Education*, and *Christian Scholars Review*.

Yeatts and his wife, Amy, are members of Grantham Brethren in Christ Church and parents of two adult children, Marcus and Helena.